Basic Technical Mathematics

SECOND EDITION

Other books by the author

Essentials of Basic Mathematics

Introduction to Technical Mathematics

Basic Technical Mathematics with Calculus
Second Edition

Technical Calculus with Analytic Geometry

Allyn J. Washington

Dutchess Community College
Poughkeepsie, New York

Basic Technical Mathematics

SECOND EDITION

CUMMINGS PUBLISHING COMPANY

Menlo Park, California

Cummings Publishing Company
2727 Sand Hill Road
Menlo Park, California   94025

Preface

This book is intended primarily for students in technical or pre-engineering technology programs where a coverage of basic mathematics is required.

Chapters 1 through 19 provide the necessary background in algebra and trigonometry for analytic geometry and calculus courses, and Chapters 1 through 20 provide the background necessary for calculus courses. There is an integrated treatment of mathematical topics, primarily algebra and trigonometry, which have been found necessary for a sound mathematical background for the technician. Numerous applications from many fields of technology are included primarily to indicate where and how mathematical techniques are used.

It is assumed that students using this text will have a background including algebra and geometry. However, the material is presented in sufficient detail for use by those whose background is possibly deficient to some extent in these areas. The material presented here is sufficient for two to three semesters.

One of the primary reasons for the arrangement of topics in this text is to present material in such an order that it is possible for a student to take courses in allied technical areas, such as physics and electricity, concurrently. These allied courses normally require that a student know certain mathematical topics by certain definite times, and yet, with the traditional mathematical order of topics, it is difficult to attain this coverage without loss of continuity. However, this material can be arranged to fit any appropriate sequence of topics, if this is deemed necessary. Another feature of the material in this text is that certain topics which are traditionally included, primarily for mathematical completeness, have been omitted.

The approach used here is basically an intuitive one. It is not unduly mathematically rigorous, although all appropriate terms and concepts are introduced as needed and given an intuitive or algebraic foundation. The book's aim is to help the student develop a feeling for mathematical methods, and not simply to have a collection of formulas when he has completed his work in the text.

There is emphasis on the fact that it is essential that the student have a fluent background in algebra and trigonometry if he is to understand and succeed in any subsequent work in mathematics.

This second edition includes all of the basic features of the first edition. However, nearly all sections have been rewritten to some degree to include additional explanatory material, examples and exercises. Specifically, among the new features of the second edition are the following: (1) Chapter 15, on determinants and matrices, is new; (2) New sections are Section 2-4, devoted to solving equations graphically, Section 5-6, devoted to equations involving fractions, Section 12-7, which takes up logarithms to bases other than ten, and Appendix D, on a review of geometry. (3) Scientific notation is now included as Section 10-2 in the chapter on exponents and radicals. (4) Fitting nonlinear curves to data is a separate section, Section 21-5. (5) There are now about 700 worked examples, an increase of about 125. (6) There are now about 4500 exercises, an increase of about 1800. (7) The early chapters on basic algebra have been expanded considerably. (8) Exercises are now generally grouped such that there is an even-numbered exercise equivalent to each odd-numbered exercise.

One of the unique features of this text is that the topics of significant digits and the slide rule are covered in the Appendix. This allows these topics to be introduced whenever the instructor wishes. At Dutchess Community College, we devote a few minutes each day for the first several weeks to this material. It has been found that this policy of many brief discussions works as well as, if not better than, a concentrated coverage at the beginning.

Another feature is that this text contains many more worked examples than are ordinarily included in such a book. These examples are often used advantageously to introduce concepts, as well as to clarify and illustrate points made in the text. Also, there is extensive use of graphical methods.

Other features are (1) stated problems are included a few at a time in order to allow the student to develop techniques of solution; (2) those topics which experience has shown to be more difficult for the student have been developed in more detail, with many examples; (3) the order of coverage can be changed in several places without loss of continuity. Also, certain sections may be omitted without loss of continuity. Any omissions or changes in order will, of course, depend on the type of course and the completeness required. (4) The chapter on statistics is included in order to introduce the student to statistical and empirical methods. (5) Miscellaneous exercises are included after each chapter. These may be used either for additional problems or for review assignments. (6) The answers to nearly all the odd-numbered exercises are given at the back of the book. Included are answers to graphical problems, and other types which are often not included in textbooks.

The author wishes to acknowledge the help and suggestions given him by many of those who have used the first edition of this text. In particular, I wish to thank Harry Boyd, Gail Brittain, Stephen Lange, and Michael Mayer of

Dutchess Community College. Many others contributed to this second edition through their response to my publisher's extensive survey of opinion from technical educators and mathematicians throughout the United States and Canada. Their efforts are most appreciated, and there is space here only to thank them collectively.

In addition I wish to thank John Davenport and Mario Triola of Dutchess Community College for their help in reviewing the manuscript, reading proof, and checking answers for this second edition. The assistance and cooperation of the Cummings staff is also greatly appreciated. Finally, special mention is due my wife, who helped in many phases of the preparation of this text, including checking many of the answers.

A.J.W.

Poughkeepsie, New York
January, 1970

Contents

10   Exponents and Radicals

11   The *j*-Operator

12   Logarithms

13   Additional Types of Equations and Systems of Equations

Fundamental Concepts and Operations

1

1-1 Numbers and literal symbols

Mathematics has played a most important role in the development and understanding of the various fields of technology, in the endless chain of technological and scientific advances of our time. With the mathematics we shall develop in this text, many kinds of applied problems can and will be solved. Of course, we cannot solve the more advanced types of problems which arise, but we can form a foundation for the more advanced mathematics which is used to solve such problems. Therefore, the development of a real understanding of the mathematics presented in this text will be of great value to you in your future work.

A thorough understanding of algebra is essential to the comprehension of any of the fields of elementary mathematics. It is important for the reader to learn and understand the basic concepts and operations presented here, or he will find the development and the applications of later topics difficult to comprehend. If the reader does not know and understand algebraic operations well, he will have a weak foundation for further work in mathematics and in many of the technical areas where mathematics may be applied.

We shall begin our study of mathematics by developing some of the basic concepts and operations that deal with numbers and symbols. With these we shall be able to develop the topics in algebra which are necessary for further progress into other fields of mathematics, such as trigonometry and calculus.

The way we represent numbers today has been evolving for thousands of years. The first numbers used were those which stand for whole quantities, and these we call the *positive integers*. The positive integers are represented by the symbols 1, 2, 3, 4, and so forth.

To this point we have been dealing with numbers in their explicit form. However, it is normally more convenient to state definitions and operations on numbers in a generalized form. To do this we represent the numbers by letters, often referred to as *literal numbers.*

For example, we can say, "if a is to the right of b on the number scale, then a is greater than b, or $a > b$." This is more convenient than saying, "if a first number is to the right of a second number, then the first number is greater than the second number." The statement "the reciprocal of a number a is $1/a$" is another example of using letters to stand for numbers in general.

In an algebraic discussion, certain letters are sometimes allowed to take on any value, while other letters represent the same number throughout the discussion. Those which may vary in a given problem are called *variables,* and those which are held fixed are called *constants.*

Common usage today normally designates the letters near the end of the alphabet as variables, and letters near the beginning of the alphabet as constants. There are exceptions, but these are specifically noted. Letters in the middle of the alphabet are also used, but their meaning in any problem is specified.

Example F. The electric resistance R of a wire may be related to the temperature T by the equation $R = aT + b$. R and T may take on various values, and a and b are fixed for any particular wire. However, a and b may change if a different wire is considered. Here, R and T are the variables and a and b are constants.

Exercises

In Exercises 1 through 4 designate each of the given numbers as being an integer, rational, irrational, real, or imaginary. (More than one designation may be correct.)

1. 3, $-\pi$
2. $\dfrac{5}{4}$, $\sqrt{-4}$
3. $6j$, $\dfrac{\sqrt{7}}{3}$
4. $-\dfrac{7}{3}$, $\dfrac{\pi}{6}$

In Exercises 5 through 8 find the absolute value of each of the given numbers.

5. 3, $\dfrac{7}{2}$
6. -4, $\sqrt{2}$
7. $-\dfrac{6}{7}$, $-\sqrt{3}$
8. $-\dfrac{\pi}{2}$, $-\dfrac{19}{4}$

In Exercises 9 through 14 insert the correct sign of inequality ($>$ or $<$) between the given pairs of numbers.

9. 6   8
10. 7 -5
11. π -1
12. -4 -3
13. $-\sqrt{2}$ -9
14. 0.2   0.6

In Exercises 15 through 18 find the reciprocals of the given numbers.

15. 3, -2
16. $\dfrac{1}{6}$, $-\dfrac{7}{4}$
17. $-\dfrac{5}{\pi}$, x
18. $-\dfrac{8}{3}$, $\dfrac{y}{b}$

In Exercises 19 through 22 locate the given numbers on a number line as in Fig. 1-1.

19. $2.5, \quad -\dfrac{1}{2}$ 20. $\sqrt{3}, \quad -\dfrac{12}{5}$ 21. $-\dfrac{\sqrt{2}}{2}, \quad 2\pi$ 22. $\dfrac{123}{19}, \quad -\dfrac{\pi}{6}$

In Exercises 23 through 29 answer the given questions.

23. List the following numbers in their numerical sequence, starting with the smallest: $-1, 9, \pi, \sqrt{5}, |-8|, -|-3|, -18$.

24. If a and b represent positive integers, what kind of number is represented by (a) $a + b$, (b) a/b, (c) $a \cdot b$?

25. Describe the location of a number x on the number scale when (a) $x > 0$, (b) $x < -4$.

26. Describe the location of a number x on the number scale when (a) $|x| < 1$, (b) $|x| > 2$.

27. The pressure P and volume V of a certain body of gas are related by the equation $P = c/V$ for certain conditions. Identify the symbols as variables or constants.

28. In writing a laboratory report, a student wrote "$-20°F > -30°F$." Is this statement correct?

29. After 2 sec, the current in a certain circuit is less than 3 amp. Using t to represent time and i to represent current, this statement may be written, "for $t > 2$, $i < 3$." In this way write the statement, "less than three feet from the light source the intensity is greater than 8 lumens." (Let I represent intensity and s represent distance.)

1-2 Fundamental laws of algebra

In performing the basic operations with numbers, we know that certain basic laws are valid. These basic statements are called the fundamental laws of algebra.

For example, we know that if two numbers are to be added, it does not matter in which order they are added. Thus $5 + 3 = 8$, as well as $3 + 5 = 8$. For this case we can say that $5 + 3 = 3 + 5$. This statement, generalized and assumed correct for all possible combinations of numbers to be added, is called the *commutative law* for addition. The law states that "the sum of two numbers is the same, regardless of the order in which they are added." We make no attempt to prove this in general, but accept its validity.

In the same way we have the *associative law* for addition, which states that "the sum of three or more numbers is the same, regardless of the manner in which they are grouped for addition." For example,

$$3 + (5 + 6) = (3 + 5) + 6.$$

The laws which we have just stated for addition are also true for multiplication. Therefore, "the product of two numbers is the same, regardless of the order in which they are multiplied," and "the product of three or more numbers is the same, regardless of the manner in which they are grouped for multiplication." For example, $2 \cdot 5 = 5 \cdot 2$ and $5 \cdot (4 \cdot 2) = (5 \cdot 4) \cdot 2$.

There is one more important law, called the *distributive law*. It states that "the product of one number and the sum of two or more other numbers is equal to the sum of the products of the first number and each of the other numbers of the sum." For example, $4(3 + 5) = 4 \cdot 3 + 4 \cdot 5$.

In practice these laws are used intuitively. However, it is necessary to state them and to accept their validity, so that we may build our later results with them.

Not all operations are associative and commutative. For example, division is not commutative, since the indicated order of division of two numbers *does* matter. For example, $6/5 \neq 5/6$ ($\neq$ is read "does not equal").

Using literal symbols, the fundamental laws of algebra are as follows:

Commutative law of addition: $a + b = b + a$
Associative law of addition: $a + (b + c) = (a + b) + c$
Commutative law of multiplication: $ab = ba$
Associative law of multiplication: $a(bc) = (ab)c$
Distributive law: $a(b + c) = ab + ac$

Having identified the fundamental laws of algebra, we shall state the laws which govern the operations of addition, subtraction, multiplication, and division of signed numbers. These laws will be of primary and direct use in all of our work.

1. To add two real numbers with like signs, add their absolute values and affix their common sign to the result.

Example A. $+2 + (+6) = +(2 + 6) = +8,$
$\qquad\qquad (-2) + (-6) = -(2 + 6) = -8$

2. To add two real numbers with unlike signs, subtract the smaller absolute value from the larger and affix the sign of the number with the larger absolute value to the result.

Example B. $+2 + (-6) = -(6 - 2) = -4,$
$\qquad\qquad +6 + (-2) = +(6 - 2) = +4$

3. To subtract one real number from another, change the sign of the number to be subtracted, and then proceed as in addition.

Example C. $+2 - (+6) = +2 + (-6) = -(6 - 2) = -4,$
$\qquad\qquad -a - (-a) = -a + a = 0$

The second part of Example C shows that subtracting a negative number from itself results in zero. Subtracting the negative number is equivalent to adding a positive number of the same absolute value. This reasoning is the basis of the rule which states, "the negative of a negative number is a positive number."

4. The product (or quotient) of two real numbers of like signs is the product (or quotient) of their absolute values. The product (or quotient) of two real numbers of unlike signs is the negative of the product (or quotient) of their absolute values.

Example D. $\dfrac{+3}{+5} = +\left(\dfrac{3}{5}\right) = +\dfrac{3}{5},$

$$(-3)(+5) = -(3 \cdot 5) = -15$$

$$\dfrac{-3}{-5} = +\left(\dfrac{3}{5}\right) = +\dfrac{3}{5}$$

1-3 Operations with zero

Since the basic operations with zero tend to cause some difficulty, we shall demonstrate them separately in this section.

If a represents any real number, the various operations with zero are defined as follows:

$$a \pm 0 = a \text{ (the symbol } \pm \text{ means ''plus or minus''),}$$

$$a \cdot 0 = 0,$$

$$\dfrac{0}{a} = 0 \quad \text{if} \quad a \neq 0.$$

Note that there is no answer defined for division by zero. To understand the reason for this, consider the problem of 4/0. If there were an answer to this expression, it would mean that the answer, which we shall call b, should give 4 when multiplied by 0. That is, $0 \cdot b = 4$. However, no such number b exists, since we already know that $0 \cdot b = 0$. Also, the expression 0/0 has no meaning, since $0 \cdot b = 0$ for any value of b which may be chosen. Thus *division by zero is not defined*. All other operations with zero are the same as for any other number.

Example. $5 + 0 = 5, \quad 7 - 0 = 7, \quad 0 - 4 = -4,$

$$\dfrac{0}{6} = 0, \qquad \dfrac{0}{-3} = 0, \qquad \dfrac{5 \cdot 0}{7} = 0,$$

$$\dfrac{8}{0} \text{ is undefined,} \quad \dfrac{7 \cdot 0}{0 \cdot 6} \text{ is undefined}$$

There is no need for confusion in the operations with zero. They will not cause any difficulty if we remember that

division by zero is undefined,

and that this is the only undefined operation.

Exercises

In Exercises 1 through 24 evaluate each of the given expressions by performing the indicated operations.

1. $6 + 5$
2. $8 + (-4)$
3. $(-4) + (-7)$
4. $(-3) + (+9)$
5. $16 - 7$
6. $(+8) - (+11)$
7. $-9 - (-6)$
8. $8 - (-4)$
9. $(8)(-3)$
10. $(+9)(-3)$
11. $(-7)(-5)$
12. $(-5)(-4)(-2)$
13. $\dfrac{-9}{+3}$
14. $\dfrac{-18}{-6}$
15. $\dfrac{(+2)(-5)}{10}$
16. $\dfrac{8(-8)}{-4}$
17. $9 - 0$
18. $\dfrac{0}{-6}$
19. $\dfrac{+17}{0}$
20. $\dfrac{(+3)(0)}{0}$
21. $\dfrac{9 \cdot (0)(7 - 2)}{3}$
22. $0 - (-6)(-8)$
23. $\dfrac{(+3)(-6)(-2)}{0 - 4}$
24. $\dfrac{(+2)(-7) - (4)(-2)}{-9 - (-9)}$

In Exercises 25 through 30 determine which of the fundamental laws of algebra is demonstrated.

25. $(6)(7) = (7)(6)$
26. $6 + 8 = 8 + 6$
27. $6(3 + 1) = 6(3) + 6(1)$
28. $4(5 \cdot 7) = (4 \cdot 5)(7)$
29. $3 + (5 + 9) = (3 + 5) + 9$
30. $8(3 - 2) = 8(3) - 8(2)$

In Exercises 31 through 33 answer the given questions.

31. What is the sign of the product of an even number of negative numbers?
32. Is subtraction commutative? Illustrate.
33. A boat travels at 6 mi/hr in still water. A stream flows at 4 mi/hr. If the boat travels downstream for 2 hours, set up the expression which would be used to evaluate the distance traveled. What fundamental law is illustrated?

1-4 Exponents and radicals

We have introduced numbers and the fundamental laws which are used with them in the fundamental operations. Also, we have shown the use of literal numbers to represent numbers. In this section we shall introduce some basic terminology and notation which are important to the basic algebraic operations developed in the following sections.

In multiplication we often encounter a number which is to be multiplied by itself several times. Rather than writing this number over and over repeatedly, we use the notation a^n, where a is the number being considered and n is the number of times it appears in the product. The number a is called the *base*, the number n is called the *exponent*, and, in words, the expression is read as the "nth power of a."

Example A. $4 \cdot 4 \cdot 4 \cdot 4 \cdot 4 = 4^5$ (the fifth power of 4),

$\quad\quad\quad\quad (-2)(-2)(-2)(-2) = (-2)^4$ (the fourth power of -2),

$\quad\quad\quad\quad a \cdot a = a^2$ (the second power of a, called "a squared"),

$\quad\quad\quad\quad (\tfrac{1}{5})(\tfrac{1}{5})(\tfrac{1}{5}) = (\tfrac{1}{5})^3$ (the third power of $\tfrac{1}{5}$, called "$\tfrac{1}{5}$ cubed"),

$\quad\quad\quad\quad 8 \cdot 8 \cdot 8 \cdot 8 \cdot 8 \cdot 8 \cdot 8 \cdot 8 \cdot 8 = 8^9$

Certain important operations with exponents will now be stated symbolically. These operations are developed here for positive integers as exponents; they will be verified and illustrated by the examples which follow.

$$a^m \cdot a^n = a^{m+n} \tag{1-1}$$

$$\frac{a^m}{a^n} = a^{m-n} \quad (m > n, \quad a \neq 0) \qquad \frac{a^m}{a^n} = \frac{1}{a^{n-m}} \quad (m < n, \ a \neq 0) \tag{1-2}$$

$$(a^m)^n = a^{mn} \tag{1-3}$$

$$(ab)^n = a^n b^n, \quad \left(\frac{a}{b}\right)^n = \frac{a^n}{b^n} \ (b \neq 0) \tag{1-4}$$

In applying Eqs. (1-1) and (1-2), the base a must be the same for the exponents to be added or subtracted. When a problem involves a product of different bases, only exponents of the same base may be combined. The following three examples illustrate the use of Eqs. (1-1) to (1-4).

Example B. $a^3 \cdot a^5 = a^{3+5} = a^8$ since $a^3 \cdot a^5 = (a \cdot a \cdot a)(a \cdot a \cdot a \cdot a \cdot a) = a^8,$

$$\frac{a^5}{a^3} = a^{5-3} = a^2 \quad \text{since} \quad \frac{a^5}{a^3} = \frac{\cancel{a} \cdot \cancel{a} \cdot \cancel{a} \cdot a \cdot a}{\cancel{a} \cdot \cancel{a} \cdot \cancel{a}} = a^2,$$

$$\frac{a^3}{a^5} = \frac{1}{a^{5-3}} = \frac{1}{a^2} \quad \text{since} \quad \frac{a^3}{a^5} = \frac{\cancel{a} \cdot \cancel{a} \cdot \cancel{a}}{\cancel{a} \cdot \cancel{a} \cdot \cancel{a} \cdot a \cdot a} = \frac{1}{a^2}$$

Example C. $(a^5)^3 = a^{5(3)} = a^{15}$ since $(a^5)^3 = (a^5)(a^5)(a^5)$

$$= a^{5+5+5} = a^{15},$$

$$(ab)^3 = a^3 b^3 \quad \text{since} \quad (ab)^3 = (ab)(ab)(ab) = a^3 b^3,$$

$$\left(\frac{a}{b}\right)^3 = \frac{a^3}{b^3} \quad \text{since} \quad \left(\frac{a}{b}\right)^3 = \left(\frac{a}{b}\right)\left(\frac{a}{b}\right)\left(\frac{a}{b}\right) = \frac{a^3}{b^3}$$

Example D. $\dfrac{(3 \cdot 2)^4}{(3 \cdot 5)^3} = \dfrac{3^4 2^4}{3^3 5^3} = \dfrac{3 \cdot 2^4}{5^3},$

$$ax^2(ax)^3 = ax^2(a^3 x^3) = a^4 x^5,$$

$$\frac{(ry^3)^2}{r(y^2)^4} = \frac{r^2 y^6}{ry^8} = \frac{r}{y^2}$$

Another problem often encountered is, "what number multiplied by itself n times gives another specified number?" For example we may ask, "what number squared is 9?" The answer to this question is the *square root* of 9, which is denoted by $\sqrt{9}$.

The general notation for the nth root of a is $\sqrt[n]{a}$. (When $n = 2$, it is common practice not to put the 2 where n appears). The $\sqrt{\ }$ sign is called a *radical sign*.

Example E. $\sqrt{2}$ (the square root of two),

$\sqrt[3]{2}$ (the cube root of two),

$\sqrt[4]{2}$ (the fourth root of two),

$\sqrt[7]{6}$ (the seventh root of six),

$\sqrt[3]{8}$ (the cube root of 8, which also equals 2)

In considering the question "what number squared is 9?" we can easily see that either $+3$ or -3 gives a proper result. This would imply that both of these values equaled $\sqrt{9}$. To avoid this ambiguity, we define the *principal nth root* of a to be positive if a is positive, and the principal nth root of a to be negative if a is negative and n is odd. This means that $\sqrt{9} = 3$ and not -3, and that $-\sqrt{9} = -3$.

Example F. $\sqrt{4} = 2$ ($\sqrt{4} \neq -2$), $\sqrt{169} = 13$ ($\sqrt{169} \neq -13$),

$-\sqrt{64} = -8,$ $-\sqrt{81} = -9,$ $\sqrt[4]{256} = 4,$

$\sqrt[3]{27} = 3,$ $\sqrt[3]{-27} = -3,$ $-\sqrt[3]{27} = -(+3) = -3$

Another important property of radicals is that the square root of a product of positive numbers is the product of the square roots. That is,

$$\sqrt{ab} = \sqrt{a} \cdot \sqrt{b} \tag{1-5}$$

This property is useful in simplifying radicals. It is most useful if either a or b is a perfect square. Consider the following example.

Example G. $\sqrt{8} = \sqrt{(4)(2)} = \sqrt{4}\sqrt{2} = 2\sqrt{2},$

$\sqrt{75} = \sqrt{(25)(3)} = \sqrt{25}\sqrt{3} = 5\sqrt{3},$

$\sqrt{80} = \sqrt{(16)(5)} = \sqrt{16}\sqrt{5} = 4\sqrt{5},$

$\sqrt{-4} = \sqrt{(4)(-1)} = \sqrt{4}\sqrt{-1} = 2j,$

$\sqrt{-27} = \sqrt{(27)(-1)} = \sqrt{27}\sqrt{-1} = \sqrt{(9)(3)}\,\sqrt{-1})$

$= \sqrt{9}\sqrt{3}\sqrt{-1} = 3\sqrt{3}j$

It should be emphasized that although the square root of a negative number gives an imaginary number, the cube root of a negative number gives a negative real number. For example, $\sqrt{-64} = 8j$ and $\sqrt[3]{-64} = -4$.

Exercises

In Exercises 1 through 40 simplify the given expressions.

1. x^3x^4

2. y^2y^7

3. $2b^4b^2$

4. $3k(k^5)$

5. $\dfrac{m^5}{m^3}$

6. $\dfrac{x^8}{x}$

7. $\dfrac{n^5}{n^9}$

8. $\dfrac{s}{s^4}$

9. $(2n)^3$

10. $(ax)^5$

11. $(a^2)^4$

12. $(x^3)^3$

13. $(-t^2)^7$

14. $(-y^3)^5$

15. $\left(\dfrac{2}{b}\right)^3$

16. $\left(\dfrac{x}{y}\right)^7$

17. $(2x^2)^6$

18. $(-c^4)^4$

19. $(-8gs^3)^2$

20. $ax^2(-a^2x)^2$

21. $\dfrac{15a^2n^5}{3an^6}$

22. $\dfrac{(ab^2)^3}{a^2b^8}$

23. $\dfrac{a(a^2y^3)^2}{y^7}$

24. $\dfrac{-ax^4(-ax)^4}{(-a^4x)^4}$

25. $\sqrt{25}$

26. $-\sqrt{121}$

27. $\sqrt[3]{125}$

28. $\sqrt[3]{-216}$

29. $\sqrt[4]{16}$

30. $\sqrt[5]{-32}$

31. $(\sqrt{5})^2$

32. $(\sqrt[3]{31})^3$

33. $\sqrt{18}$

34. $\sqrt{32}$

35. $\sqrt{12}$

36. $\sqrt{50}$

37. $2\sqrt{98}$

38. $4\sqrt{108}$

39. $\dfrac{\sqrt{81}(6\cdot7)^2}{(3\cdot2)^2\sqrt{49}}$

40. $\dfrac{\sqrt[5]{243}(2\cdot3)^4}{2^43^5}$

In Exercises 41 through 43 solve the given problems.

41. In analyzing the deformation of a certain beam, it might be necessary to simplify the expression

$$\frac{wx(-2Lx^2)}{24EI}.$$

Perform this simplification.

42. In a certain electric circuit, it might be necessary to simplify the expression

$$\frac{gM}{j\omega C(\omega^2M^2)} \quad (\omega \text{ is the Greek omega}).$$

Perform this simplification.

43. Is the mathematical statement $\sqrt{a^2} = a$ always true?

1-5 Addition and subtraction of algebraic expressions

It is the basic characteristic of algebra that letters are used to represent numbers. Since we have used literal symbols to represent numbers, even if in a general sense, we may conclude that all operations valid for numbers are valid for these literal symbols. In this section we shall discuss the terminology and methods for combining literal symbols.

Addition, subtraction, multiplication, division, and taking of roots are known as *algebraic operations*. Any combination of numbers and literal symbols which results from algebraic operations is known as an *algebraic expression*.

When an algebraic expression consists of several parts connected by plus signs and minus signs, each part is known as a *term* of the expression. If a given term is made up of the product of a number of symbols, each of the quantities making up the product is called a *factor*. It is important to distinguish between these, since some operations that are valid for terms are not valid for factors, and conversely.

Example A. $4x^2 + 6y\sqrt{x} - 7x^3\sqrt{y}$ is an algebraic expression with terms $4x^2$, $6y\sqrt{x}$, and $7x^3\sqrt{y}$. The term $4x^2$ has the factors 4 and x^2. The term $6y\sqrt{x}$ has the factors 6, y, and $\sqrt{x}$.

Example B. $7x(y^2 + x) - (x + y)/4x$ is an algebraic expression with terms $7x(y^2 + x)$ and $(x + y)/4x$. The first term has factors 7, x, and $(y^2 + x)$. The last factor has two terms, y^2 and x. In the term $(x + y)/4x$ the numerator has two terms, x and y, and the denominator has two factors, 4 and x.

An algebraic expression containing only one term is called a *monomial*. An expression containing two terms is called a *binomial*. An expression containing two or more terms is called a *multinomial*. Thus any binomial expression can also be considered as a multinomial.

In any given term, the numbers and literal symbols multiplying any given factor constitute the *coefficient* of that factor. The product of all the numbers in explicit form is known as the *numerical coefficient* of the term. All terms which differ only in their numerical coefficients are known as *similar* or *like* terms.

Example C. $7x^3\sqrt{y}$ is a monomial. It has a numerical coefficient of 7. The coefficient of $\sqrt{y}$ is $7x^3$, and the coefficient of x^3 is $7\sqrt{y}$.

Example D. $4 \cdot 2b + 81b - 6ab$ is a multinomial of three terms. The first term has a numerical coefficient of 8, the second has a numerical coefficient of 81, and the third has a numerical coefficient of -6 (the sign of the term is attached to the numerical coefficient). The first and second terms are similar, since they differ only in their numerical coefficient. The third term is not similar to either of the others, for it has the factor a.

In adding and subtracting algebraic expressions, we combine similar terms. All of the similar terms may be combined into a single term, and the final simplified expression will be made up entirely of terms which are not similar.

Example E. $3x + 2x - 5y = 5x - 5y$. Since there are two similar terms in the original expression, they are added together, so the simplified result has two unlike terms.

$6a^2 - 7a + 8ax$ cannot be simplified, since none of the terms are like terms.

Similarly, $6a + 5c + 2a - c = 6a + 2a + 5c - c = 8a + 4c$. (Here we use the commutative and associative laws).

In writing algebraic expressions, it is often necessary to group certain terms together. For this purpose we use *symbols of grouping*. In this text we shall use *parentheses* ( ), *brackets* [ ], and *braces* { }. The *bar*, which is used with radicals and fractions, also groups terms. The bar attached to the radical sign groups the terms under it, and the bar separating the numerator and denominator of a fraction groups the terms above and under it.

When adding and subtracting algebraic expressions, it is often necessary to remove symbols of grouping. To do so we must *change the sign of every term within the symbols if the grouping is preceded by a minus sign.* If the symbols of grouping are preceded by a plus sign, each term within the symbols retains its original sign. This is a result of the distributive law. Normally when several symbols of grouping are to be removed, it is more convenient to remove the innermost symbols first. This is illustrated in Examples H and I.

Example F. $2a - (3a + 2b) - b = 2a - 3a - 2b - b = -a - 3b,$
$$-(2x - 3c) + (c - x) = -2x + 3c + c - x = 4c - 3x$$

Example G. $3 - 2(m^2 - 2) = 3 - 2m^2 + 4 = 7 - 2m^2,$
$$4(t - 3 - 2t^2) - (6t + t^2 - 4) = 4t - 12 - 8t^2 - 6t - t^2 + 4$$
$$= -9t^2 - 2t - 8$$

Example H. $-[(4 - 5x) - (a - 2x - 7)] = -[4 - 5x - a + 2x + 7]$
$$= -[11 - 3x - a] = -11 + 3x + a,$$
$$3ax - [ax - (5s - 2ax)] = 3ax - [ax - 5s + 2ax]$$
$$= 3ax - ax + 5s - 2ax = 5s$$

Example I. $[a^2b - ab + (ab - 2a^2b)] - \{[(3a^2b + b) - (4ab - 2a^2b)] - b\}$
$$= [a^2b - ab + ab - 2a^2b] - \{[3a^2b + b - 4ab + 2a^2b] - b\}$$
$$= a^2b - ab + ab - 2a^2b - \{3a^2b + b - 4ab + 2a^2b - b\}$$
$$= a^2b - ab + ab - 2a^2b - 3a^2b - b + 4ab - 2a^2b + b$$
$$= -6a^2b + 4ab$$

One of the most common errors made by beginning students is changing the sign of only the first term when removing symbols of grouping preceded by a minus sign. Remember, if the symbols are preceded by a minus sign, we must change the sign of *all* terms.

Exercises

In the following exercises simplify the given algebraic expressions.

1. $5x + 7x - 4x$

2. $6t - 3t - 4y$

3. $2a - 2c - e + 3c - a$

4. $a^2b - a^2b^2 - 2a^2b$

5. $-(4 - 5x + 2v)$

6. $2a - (b - a)$

7. $3xy + (x - y) + y$

8. $x^2y^2 - (x^2y + x) + 3x$

9. $2 - 3 - (4 - 5a)$

10. $\sqrt{x} + (y - 2\sqrt{x}) - 3\sqrt{x}$

11. $(a - 3) + (5 - 6a)$

12. $(4x - y) - (2x - 4y)$

13. $3(2r + s) - (5s - r)$

14. $3(a - b) - 2(a - 2b)$

15. $-7(6 - 3c) - 2(c + 4)$

16. $-(5t + a^2) - 2(3a^2 - 2st)$

17. $[4 - (t^2 - 5)]$

18. $-[(a - b) - (b - a)]$

19. $3[3 - (a - 4)]$

20. $-2[-x - 2a - (a - x)]$

21. $a\sqrt{xy} - [3 - (a\sqrt{xy} + 4)]$

22. $-2[-3(x - 2y) + 4x]$

23. $\{5 - [2 - (3 + 4c)]\}$

24. $7y - \{y - [2y - (x - y)]\}$

25. $-2\{-(4 - x^2) - [3 + (4 - x^2)]\}$

26. $-\{-[-(x - 2a) - b] - a\}$

27. When discussing gear trains, the expression $-(-R - 1)$ is found. Simplify this expression.

28. In analyzing a certain electric circuit, the expression $I_1 + I_2 - (I_2 - I_3)$ is found. Simplify this expression. (The numbers below the I's are *subscripts*. Different subscripts denote different unknowns.)

29. When determining the center of mass of a certain object, the expression $[(8x - x^2) - (x^2 - 4x)]$ is used. Simplify this expression.

30. In developing the theory for an elastic substance, we find the following expression:

$$[(B + \tfrac{4}{3}\alpha) + 2(B - \tfrac{2}{3}\alpha)] - [(B + \tfrac{4}{3}\alpha) - (B - \tfrac{2}{3}\alpha)].$$

Simplify this expression.

1-6 Multiplication of algebraic expressions

To find the product of two or more monomials, we use the laws of exponents as given in Section 1-4 and the laws for multiplying signed numbers as stated in Section 1-2. We first multiply the numerical coefficients to determine the numerical coefficient of the product. Then we multiply the literal factors, remembering that the exponents may be combined only if the base is the same. Consider the illustrations in the following example.

Example A. $3ac^3(4sa^2c) = 12a^3c^4s,$

$\qquad\qquad (-2b^2y)(-9aby^5) = 18ab^3y^6,$

$\qquad\qquad 2xy(-6cx^2)(3xcy^2) = -36c^2x^4y^3$

We find the product of a monomial and a multinomial by using the distributive law, which states that we multiply each term of the multinomial by the monomial. We must be careful to assign the correct sign to each term of the result, using the rules for multiplication of signed numbers. Also, we must properly combine literal factors in each term of the result.

Example B. $2ax(3ax^2 - 4yz) = 2ax(3ax^2) - (2ax)(4yz) = 6a^2x^3 - 8axyz,$

$\qquad\qquad 5cy^2(-7cx - ac) = (5cy^2)(-7cx) + (5cy^2)(-ac)$

$\qquad\qquad\qquad\qquad\qquad = -35c^2xy^2 - 5ac^2y^2$

In practice, it is generally not necessary to write out the middle step as it appears in the example above. We can generally write the answer directly. For example, the first part of Example B would usually appear as

$$2ax(3ax^2 - 4yz) = 6a^2x^3 - 8axyz.$$

We find the product of two or more multinomials by using the distributive law and the laws of exponents. We multiply each term of one multinomial by each term of the other, and add the results.

Example C. $(x - 2)(x + 3) = x(x) + x(3) + (-2)(x) + (-2)(3)$

$\qquad\qquad\qquad = x^2 + 3x - 2x - 6 = x^2 + x - 6,$

$\qquad (a^2 - 2ab)(xy^2 + x^2) = a^2(xy^2) + a^2(x^2) - 2ab(xy^2) - 2ab(x^2)$

$\qquad\qquad\qquad\qquad = a^2xy^2 + a^2x^2 - 2abxy^2 - 2abx^2,$

$\qquad (x - 2y)(x^2 + 2xy + 4y^2) = x^3 + 2x^2y + 4xy^2 - 2x^2y - 4xy^2 - 8y^3$

$\qquad\qquad\qquad\qquad\qquad = x^3 - 8y^3$

Finding the power of an algebraic expression is equivalent to multiplying the expression by itself the number of times indicated by the exponent. In practice, it is often convenient to write the power of an algebraic expression in this form before multiplying. Consider the following example.

Example D. $(x + 5)^2 = (x + 5)(x + 5) = x^2 + 5x + 5x + 25$

$\qquad\qquad\qquad = x^2 + 10x + 25,$

$\qquad (2a - b)^3 = (2a - b)(2a - b)(2a - b)$

$\qquad\qquad\qquad = (2a - b)(4a^2 - 4ab + b^2)$

$\qquad\qquad\qquad = 8a^3 - 8a^2b + 2ab^2 - 4a^2b + 4ab^2 - b^3$

$\qquad\qquad\qquad = 8a^3 - 12a^2b + 6ab^2 - b^3$

Exercises

In the following exercises perform the indicated multiplications.

1. $(a^2)(ax)$ 2. $(2xy)(x^2y^3)$
3. $-ac^2(acx^3)$ 4. $-2s^2(-4cs)^2$
5. $(2ax^2)^2(-2ax)$ 6. $6pq^3(3pq^2)^2$
7. $a(-a^2x)(-2a)$ 8. $-2m^2(-3mn)(m^2n)^2$
9. $a^2(x+y)$ 10. $-3b(2b^2-b)$
11. $5m(m^2n+3mn)$ 12. $a^2bc(2ac-3a^2b)$
13. $3x(x-y+2)$ 14. $b^2x^2(x^2-2x+1)$
15. $ab^2c^4(ac-bc-ab)$ 16. $-4c^2(9gc-2c+g^2)$
17. $ax(cx^2)(x+y^3)$ 18. $-2(-3st^3)(3s-4t)$
19. $(x-3)(x+5)$ 20. $(a+7)(a+1)$
21. $(x+5)(2x-1)$ 22. $(4t+s)(2t-3s)$
23. $(x^2-2x)(x+4)$ 24. $(2ab^2-5t)(-ab^2-6t)$
25. $(x+1)(x^2-3x+2)$ 26. $(2x+3)(x^2-x+5)$
27. $(4x-x^3)(2+x-x^2)$ 28. $(5a-3c)(a^2+ac-c^2)$
29. $2x(x-1)(x+4)$ 30. $ax(x+4)(7-x^2)$
31. $(2x-5)^2$ 32. $(x-3)^2$
33. $(xyz-2)^2$ 34. $(b-2x^2)^2$
35. $(2+x)(3-x)(x-1)$ 36. $(3x-c^2)^3$
37. $3x(x+2)^2(2x-1)$ 38. $[(x-2)^2(x+2)]^2$

39. Simplify the following expression, which arises in determining the final temperature of a certain mixture of objects originally at different temperatures:

$$500(0.22)(T_f-20)+120(T_f-20)-22(75-T_f).$$

40. In determining a certain chemical volume, the expression $a+b(1-X)+c(1-X)^2$ is found. Perform the indicated multiplications.

41. The analysis of the deflection of a certain concrete beam involves the expression $w(l^2-x^2)^2$. Perform the indicated multiplication.

42. In finding the maximum power in a particular electric circuit, the expression $(R+r)^2-2r(R+r)$ is used. Multiply and simplify.

43. In the study of the dispersion of light, the expression $(k+2)[(n-jK)^2-1]$ is found. Expand this expression.

1-7 Division of algebraic expressions

To find the quotient of one monomial divided by another, we use the laws of exponents as given in Section 1-4 and the laws for dividing signed numbers as stated in Section 1-2. Again, the exponents may be combined only if the base is the same.

Example A. $\dfrac{16x^3y^5}{4xy^2} = 4x^2y^3,$ $\dfrac{-6a^2xy^2}{2axy^4} = -\dfrac{3a}{y^2}$

The quotient of a multinomial divided by a monomial is found by dividing each term of the multinomial by the monomial and adding the results. This process is a result of the equivalent operation with arithmetic fractions.

Example B. $\dfrac{16r^3st^2 - 8r^2t^3}{4rt^2} = \dfrac{16r^3st^2}{4rt^2} - \dfrac{8r^2t^3}{4rt^2} = 4r^2s - 2rt,$

$\dfrac{4x^2y - 3x^3y^2 + 6xy^4}{2x^2y} = \dfrac{4x^2y}{2x^2y} - \dfrac{3x^3y^2}{2x^2y} + \dfrac{6xy^4}{2x^2y} = 2 - \dfrac{3xy}{2} + \dfrac{3y^3}{x},$

$\dfrac{a^3bc^4 - 6abc + 9a^2b^3c - 3}{3ab^2c^3} = \dfrac{a^2c}{3b} - \dfrac{2}{bc^2} + \dfrac{3ab}{c^2} - \dfrac{1}{ab^2c^3}$

Usually in practice we would not write the middle step as shown in the first two illustrations of Example B. The divisions are done by inspection, and the expression would appear as shown in the third illustration. However, we must remember that each term in the numerator is divided by the monomial in the denominator.

If each term of an algebraic sum is a number or is of the form ax^n, where n is a positive integer, we call the expression a *polynomial* in x. The distinction between a multinomial and a polynomial is that a polynomial does not contain terms like $\sqrt{x}$ or $1/x^2$, whereas a multinomial may contain such terms. Also, a polynomial may consist of only one term, whereas a multinomial must have at least two terms. In a polynomial, the greatest value of n which appears is the *degree* of the polynomial.

Example C. $3 + 2x^2 - x^3$ is a polynomial of degree 3,
  $x^4 - 3x^2 - \sqrt{x}$ is not a polynomial,
  $4x^5$ is a polynomial of degree 5;
the first two expressions are multinomials.

The problem often arises of dividing one polynomial by another. To solve this problem, we first arrange the dividend (the polynomial to be divided) and the divisor in descending powers of x. Then we divide the first term of the dividend by the first term of the divisor. The result gives the first term of the quotient. Next, we multiply the entire divisor by the first term of the quotient and subtract the product from the dividend. We divide the first term of this difference by the first term of the divisor. This gives the second term of the quotient. We multiply this term by each of the terms of the divisor and subtract this result from the first difference. We repeat this process until the remainder is either zero or a term which is of lower degree than the divisor.

Example D.   Divide $4x^3 + 6x^2 + 1$ by $2x - 1$. Since there is no x-term in the dividend, it is advisable to leave space for any x-terms which might arise.

$$
\begin{array}{r}
2x^2 + 4x \qquad\ + 2 \qquad \text{(quotient)} \\
(\text{divisor}) \quad 2x - 1\overline{\smash{)}4x^3 + 6x^2 \qquad\ + 1} \qquad \text{(dividend)} \\
\underline{4x^3 - 2x^2} \qquad\qquad\qquad \\
8x^2 \qquad\ + 1 \\
\underline{8x^2 - 4x} \qquad\ \\
4x + 1 \\
\underline{4x - 2} \\
3 \qquad \text{(remainder)}
\end{array}
$$

Exercises

In the following exercises perform the indicated divisions.

1. $\dfrac{8x^3y^2}{-2xy}$ 2. $\dfrac{-18b^7c^3}{bc^2}$ 3. $\dfrac{-16r^3t^5}{-5r^5t}$

4. $\dfrac{51mn^5}{17m^2n^2}$ 5. $\dfrac{(15x^2)(4bx)(2y)}{30bxy}$ 6. $\dfrac{6(ax)^2}{-ax^2}$

7. $\dfrac{a^2x + 4xy}{x}$ 8. $\dfrac{3rst - 6r^2st^2}{3rs}$ 9. $\dfrac{(an)^2 - 5a^2n - 10an^2}{5an}$

10. $\dfrac{xy^2 + ax^3 - 4ax^2}{ax}$ 11. $\dfrac{2\pi fL - \pi fR^2}{\pi fR}$ 12. $\dfrac{3ab^2 - 6ab^3 + 9a^3b}{9a^2b^2}$

13. $\dfrac{2(ab)^4 - a^3b^4}{3(ab)^3}$ 14. $\dfrac{4x^2y^3 + 8xy - 12x^2y^3}{2x^2y^2}$ 15. $\dfrac{x^{n+2} + ax^n}{x^n}$

16. $\dfrac{3a(x + y)b^2 - (x + y)}{a(x + y)}$ 17. $\dfrac{x^2 - 3x + 2}{x - 2}$ 18. $\dfrac{2x^2 - 5x + 4}{x + 1}$

19. $\dfrac{x - 14x^2 + 8x^3}{2x - 3}$ 20. $\dfrac{x^3 + 3x^2 - 4x - 12}{x + 2}$ 21. $\dfrac{6x^2 + 6 + 7x}{2x + 1}$

22. $\dfrac{2x^3 - 3x^2 + 8x - 2}{x^2 - x + 2}$ 23. $\dfrac{3x^3 + 19x^2 + 16x - 20}{3x - 2}$ 24. $\dfrac{x^3 - 1}{x - 1}$

25. $\dfrac{x^2 - 2xy + y^2}{x - y}$ 26. $\dfrac{3a^2 - 5ab + 2b^2}{a - 3b}$

27. In determining the volume of a certain gas, the following expression is used:

$$\frac{RTV^2 - aV + ab}{RT}.$$

Perform the indicated division.

28. In hydrodynamics the following expression is found:

$$\frac{2p + v^2d + 2ydg}{2dg}.$$

Perform the indicated division.

29. The expression for the total resistance of three resistances in parallel in an electric circuit is

$$\frac{R_1R_2R_3}{R_2R_3 + R_1R_3 + R_1R_2}.$$

Find the reciprocal of this expression, and then perform the indicated division.

30. The following expression is found when analyzing the motion of a certain object:

$$\frac{s + 6}{s^2 + 8s + 25}.$$

Find the reciprocal of this expression and perform the indicated division.

1-8 Equations and formulas

The basic operations for algebraic expressions that we have developed are used in the important process of solving equations.

An *equation* is an algebraic statement that two algebraic expressions are equal. It is possible that many values of the letter representing the *unknown* will satisfy the equation; that is, many values may produce equality when *substituted* in the equation. It is also possible that only one value for the unknown will satisfy the equation (and this will be true of the equations we solve in this section). Or possibly there may be no values which satisfy the equation, although the statement is still an equation.

Example A. The equation $x^2 - 4 = (x - 2)(x + 2)$ is true for all values of x. For example, if we substitute $x = 3$ we have $9 - 4 = (3 - 2)(3 + 2)$ or $5 = 5$. If we let $x = -1$, we have $-3 = -3$. An equation that is true for all values of the unknown is termed an *identity*.

The equation $x^2 - 2 = x$ is true if $x = 2$ or if $x = -1$, but it is not true for any other values of x. If $x = 2$ we obtain $2 = 2$, and if $x = -1$ we obtain $-1 = -1$. However, if we let $x = 4$, we obtain $14 = 4$, which of course is not correct. An equation valid only for certain values of the unknown is termed a *conditional equation*. These equations are those which are generally encountered.

Example B. The equation $3x - 5 = x + 1$ is true only for $x = 3$. When $x = 3$ we obtain $4 = 4$; if we let $x = 2$, we obtain $1 = 3$, which is not correct.

The equation $x + 5 = x + 1$ is not true for any value of x. For any value of x we try, we will find that the left side is 4 greater than the right side. However, it is still an equation.

To *solve* an equation we find the values of the unknown which satisfy it. There is one basic rule to follow when solving an equation: *Perform the same operation on both sides of the equation.* We do this to isolate the unknown and thus to find its values.

Performing the same operation on both sides of an equation means that we may add the same quantity to both sides, we may subtract the same quantity from both sides ("transposing" is a term frequently used to denote these operations), and we may multiply or divide both sides by the same quantity (provided it is not zero). These operations are illustrated in the following examples.

Example C.   Solve the equation $2x - 7 = 9$.

We are to perform basic operations to both sides of the equation to finally isolate x on one side. The steps to be followed are suggested by the form of the equation, and in this case are as follows.

$$2x - 7 = 9$$
$$2x = 16$$
$$x = 8$$

add 7 to both sides

divide both sides by 2

Therefore we conclude that $x = 8$. Checking in the original equation, we see that we have $2(8) - 7 = 9$, $16 - 7 = 9$, or $9 = 9$. Therefore the solution checks.

Example D.   Solve the equation $3x + 4 = x - 6$.

$$2x + 4 = -6 \qquad \text{x subtracted from both sides}$$
$$2x = -10 \qquad \text{4 subtracted from both sides}$$
$$x = -5 \qquad \text{both sides divided by 2}$$

Example E.   Solve the equation $x - 7 = 3x - (6x - 8)$.

$$x - 7 = 3x - 6x + 8 \qquad \text{parentheses removed}$$
$$x - 7 = -3x + 8 \qquad \text{x's combined on right}$$
$$4x - 7 = 8 \qquad \text{$3x$ added to both sides}$$
$$4x = 15 \qquad \text{7 added to both sides}$$
$$x = \tfrac{15}{4} \qquad \text{both sides divided by 4}$$

Equations are used in many ways. One of the most important applications occurs in mathematics, physics, and engineering formulas. A *formula* is an algebraic statement that two expressions stand for the same number. For example, the formula for the area of a circle is $A = \pi r^2$. The symbol A stands for the area, as does the expression πr^2, but πr^2 expresses the area in terms of another quantity, the radius.

Often it is necessary to solve a formula for a particular letter or symbol which appears in it. We do this in the same manner as we solve any equation: we isolate the letter or symbol desired.

Example F.   Solve $A = \pi r^2$ for π.

$$\frac{A}{r^2} = \pi \qquad \text{both sides divided by } r^2$$

$$\pi = \frac{A}{r^2} \qquad \text{since each side equals the other, it makes no difference which expression appears on the left}$$

Example G.   A formula relating acceleration a, velocity v, initial velocity v_0, and time t, is $v = v_0 + at$. Solve for t.

$$v - v_0 = at \qquad v_0 \text{ subtracted from both sides}$$

$$t = \frac{v - v_0}{a} \qquad \text{both sides divided by } a \text{ and then sides are switched}$$

In practice it is often necessary to set up equations to be solved by using known formulas and given conditions. To solve such stated problems, it is very important to read the problem very carefully, understanding all terms and phrases, so that the information which leads to the necessary equation is recognized. The following examples illustrate typical problems in which we must first set up an equation from given statements in order to find the solution.

Example H.   Two machine parts together weigh 17 lb. If one weighs 3 lb more than the other, what is the weight of each?

Since the weight of each part is required, we write

$$\text{let } w = \text{the weight of the lighter part,}$$

as a way of establishing the unknown for the equation. Any appropriate letter could be used, and we could have let it represent the heavier part.

Also, since "one weighs 3 lb more than the other," we can write

$$\text{let } w + 3 = \text{the weight of the heavier part.}$$

Since the two parts together weigh 17 lb, we have the equation

$$w + (w + 3) = 17.$$

This can now be solved.

$$2w + 3 = 17$$
$$2w = 14$$
$$w = 7$$

Thus the lighter part weighs 7 lb and the heavier part weighs 10 lb. This checks with the original statement of the problem.

Example I.   A man rowing x mi/hr covers 8 mi in one hour when going downstream. By rowing twice as fast while going upstream, he is able to cover only 7 mi in one hour. Find the original rate of speed of his rowing, x, and the rate of flow of the stream.

In this problem we have let x equal the man's original rate of rowing. From the fact that the man was able to cover 8 mi in one hour while going downstream, we conclude that his rate plus the rate of the stream equals 8 mi/hr. Thus $8 - x$ is the rate of the stream. When he is going upstream, the stream retards his progress, which means that the rate at which he actually proceeds upstream is $2x - (8 - x)$. He goes at this rate for one hour, traveling 7 mi. Using the formula $d = rt$ (distance equals rate times time), we have

$$7 = [2x - (8 - x)](1).$$

Solving for x, we obtain $x = 5$. The original rate of rowing was 5 mi/hr, and the stream flows at the rate of 3 mi/hr.

Example J. A solution of alcohol and water contains 2 qt of alcohol and 6 qt of water. How much pure alcohol must be added to this solution so that the resulting solution will be $\frac{2}{5}$ alcohol?

First we let x equal the number of quarts of alcohol to be added. The statement of the problem tells us that we want the volume of alcohol compared to the total volume of the final mixture to be $\frac{2}{5}$. The final total volume of alcohol will be $2 + x$, and the final total volume of the mixture of water and alcohol will be $8 + x$. This means that

$$\frac{2 + x}{8 + x} = \frac{2}{5}.$$

Multiplying each side by $5(8 + x)$, we have $5(2 + x) = 2(8 + x)$, or $10 + 5x = 16 + 2x$, or $x = 2$ qt. Note that this result checks, since there would be 4 qt of alcohol of a total volume of 10 qt when 2 qt of pure alcohol are added to the original solution.

Exercises

In exercises 1 through 10 solve for the unknown which is present.

1. $x + 4 = 7$
2. $x - 5 = 2$
3. $3t + 5 = -4$
4. $5x - 2 = 13$
5. $3x + 7 = x$
6. $6 + 8y = 5 - y$
7. $6 - (r - 4) = 2r$
8. $3(n - 2) = -n$
9. $7 - 3(1 - 2p) = 4 + 2p$
10. $5x - 2(x - 5) = 4x$

In Exercises 11 through 20 solve each of the equations for either x, y, s, or t.

11. $ax + 6 = 2ax$
12. $by - b^2 = -by$
13. $\frac{1}{2}x + a = 2a$
14. $s - 6n^2 = 3s + 4$
15. $x(x + 5) = x^2 - 7$
16. $at = 5ac - a^2c^2$
17. $6abc = 3ax - 9ac$
18. $\frac{6}{5}ax - a = a^2 - 9$
19. $b^2x + b^3 - b^2 = 3b^2 - 2b^2x + 4b^3$
20. $(a - 2)x = a^3 - 8$

Each of the formulas in Exercises 21 through 32 arises in the technical or scientific area of study listed. Solve for the indicated letter.

21. $E = IR$, for R (electricity)

22. $V = \frac{4}{3}\pi r^3$, for π (geometry)

23. $v = v_0 - gt$, for g (physics: motion)

24. $PV = RT$, for T (chemistry: gas law)

25. $A = \dfrac{M}{fjd}$, for d (mechanical design)

26. $s = s_0 + v_0 t - 16t^2$, for v_0 (physics: motion)

27. $l = a + (n - 1)d$, for n (mathematics: progressions)

28. $h = \dfrac{1}{r_e + r_c\,(1 - a)}$, for r_e (electricity: transistors)

29. $F = \dfrac{9C}{5} + 32$, for C   (science: temperature)

30. $L = \pi(r_1 + r_2) + 2d$, for r_1 (physics: pulleys)

31. $R = \dfrac{2(E - E_p)}{m_0 g}$, for E (modern physics)

32. $PV^2 = RT(1 - e)(V + b) - A$, for T (thermodynamics)

In Exercises 33 through 38 solve the given stated problems by first setting up an appropriate equation.

33. Together, two computers cost \$7800 per month to rent. If one costs twice as much as the other, what is the monthly cost of each?

34. The sum of three electric currents is 12 amp. If the smallest is 2 amp less than the next, which in turn is 2 amp less than the largest, what are the values of the three currents?

35. The length of a spring increases $\frac{1}{4}$ foot for each pound it supports. If the spring is 8 ft long when 6 lb are hung from it, what was the original length of the spring?

36. A temperature measured in fahrenheit degrees is 32 more than $\frac{9}{5}$ the corresponding reading in centigrade degrees. If the centigrade reading of a certain room is $25°$, what is the fahrenheit reading?

37. A car traveling at 30 mi/hr leaves a certain point 2 hr before a second car. If the second car travels 40 mi/hr, when will it overtake the first car?

38. An alloy weighing 20 lb is 30% copper. How many pounds of another alloy which is 80% copper must be added in order for the final alloy to be 50% copper?

1-9 Miscellaneous Exercises

In Exercises 1 through 12 simplify the given expressions.

1. $(-2) + (-5) - (+3)$ 2. $(+6) - (+8) - (-4)$

3. $\dfrac{(-5)(+6)(-4)}{(-2)(+3)}$ 4. $\dfrac{(-9)(-12)(-4)}{24}$

5. $\dfrac{(-6) - (+4)(-4)}{-5}$ 6. $\dfrac{(-3) - (-4) - (+6)}{(-3)(-4)(+6)}$

7. $\sqrt{16} - \sqrt{64}$ 8. $\sqrt{144} + 2\sqrt{169}$

9. $x(x^5) - \dfrac{2x^8}{x^2}$ 10. $(ax^2)^3 + ax^4(a^2x^2)$

11. $\dfrac{18m^3n^4t}{3mn^5t^3}$ 12. $\dfrac{(-rt)^2(2rst)}{(st^2)^2}$

In Exercises 13 through 32 perform the indicated operations.

13. $6 - (xy - 3)$ 14. $-(2x - b) - 3(x - 5b)$

15. $(2x - 1)(x + 5)$ 16. $(x - 4y)(2x + y)$

17. $4a - [2b - (3a - 4b)]$ 18. $3b - [2b + 3a - (2a - 3b)] + 4a$

19. $\dfrac{2h^3k^2 - 6h^4k^5}{2h^2k}$ 20. $\dfrac{4a^2x^3 - 8ax^4}{2ax^2}$

21. $2xy - \{3z - [5xy - (7z - 6xy)]\}$ 22. $x^2 + 3b + [(b - y) - 3(2b - y + z)]$

23. $3p[(q - p) - 2p(1 - 3q)]$ 24. $3x[2y - r - 4(s - 2r)]$

25. $\dfrac{12p^3q^2 - 4p^4q + 6pq^5}{2p^4q}$ 26. $\dfrac{x^3 - 4x^2 + 7x - 12}{x - 3}$

27. $-3y(x - 4y)^2$ 28. $(4s - 3t)^2(t + s)$

29. $-3\{(r + s - t) - 2[(3r - 2s) - (t - 2s)]\}$

30. $(1 - 2x)(x - 3) - (x + 4)(4 - 3x)$

31. $\dfrac{2y^3 + 9y^2 - 7y + 5}{2y - 1}$ 32. $\dfrac{6x^2 + 5xy - 4y^2}{2x - y}$

In Exercises 33 through 36 solve the given equations.

33. $6x - 5 = 3(x - 4)$ 34. $-2(4 - y) = 3y$

35. $2s + 4(3 - s) = 6$ 36. $-(4 - v) = 2(2v - 5)$

In Exercises 37 and 38 solve for the indicated letter.

37. $4bt = b^2 - (2bt + 3b^2)$, for t 38. $x(x^2 - 3) = -2(x - 1)(2 - a)$, for a

Each of the formulas in Exercises 39 through 48 arises in the technical or scientific area of study listed. Solve for the indicated letter.

39. $B = \dfrac{\phi}{A}$, for A (ϕ is Greek phi)   (electricity: magnetism)

40. $v^2 = v_0^2 + 2gh$, for h (physics: motion)

41. $E_k = \dfrac{me^4}{4\epsilon_0^2n^2h^2}$, for m (ϵ is Greek epsilon)   (atomic physics)

42. $R(R_1 + R_2) = R_1R_2$, for R (electricity)

43. $D_p = \dfrac{ND_0}{N + 2}$, for D_0 (mechanics: gears)

44. $L = L_0[1 + \alpha(t_2 - t_1)]$, for α (the Greek alpha)   (physics: heat)

45. $Y_{n+1} = \dfrac{R_D X_n + X_0}{R_D + 1}$, for X_n (chemistry: distillation)

46. $P_a - P_b = \dfrac{32LV\mu}{g_c D^2}$, for μ (the Greek mu)   (fluid dynamics)

47. $S = \frac{1}{2}n[2a + (n - 1)d]$, for a (mathematics: progressions)
48. $M = Rx - P(x - a)$, for a (mechanics: beams)

In Exercises 49 through 52 solve the stated problems by first setting up an appropriate equation.

49. The combustion of carbon usually results in the production of both carbon monoxide and carbon dioxide. If 500 lb of oxygen are available for combustion and it is desired that 9 times as much oxygen be converted to carbon dioxide as is converted to carbon monoxide, how much oxygen would be converted to each of the compounds?

50. The electric current in one transistor is three times that in another transistor. If the sum of the currents is 0.012 amp, what is the current in each?

51. One engine has 2 hp more than a second engine. A third engine has a power equal to the first two. If the three engines together have 12 hp, what is the horsepower of each?

52. Fifty pounds of a cement-sand mixture is 40% sand. How many pounds of sand must be added for the resulting mixture to be 60% sand?

Functions and Graphs

2

2-1 Functions

In Chapter 1 we established many of the basic algebraic operations. At the end of the chapter we discussed the solution of equations, with applications to formulas. In most of the formulas, one quantity was given in terms of one or more other quantities. It is obvious, then, that the various quantities are related by means of the formula. We see that in the study of natural phenomena, a relationship can be found to exist between certain quantities.

If we were to perform an experiment to determine whether or not a relationship exists between the distance an object drops and the time it falls, observation of the results would indicate (approximately, at least) that $s = 16t^2$, where s is the distance in feet and t is the time in seconds. We would therefore see that distance and time for a falling object are related.

A similar study of the pressure and the volume of a gas at constant temperature would show that as pressure increases, volume decreases according to the formula $PV = k$, where k is a constant. Electrical measurements of current and voltage with respect to a particular resistor would show that $V = kI$, where V is the voltage, I is the current, and k is a constant.

Considerations such as these lead us to the mathematical concept of a *function*, which is one of the most important and basic concepts in mathematics. The concept of a function is important because *whenever a relationship exists between two sets* * *of numbers, this relationship defines a function.*

---

* In the "modern" development of mathematics, the word *set* is used formally to designate a *collection of objects*. The usage here is consistent with this meaning, although none of the topics in this text will be presented formally by means of sets and set notation. Also, a definite distinction is made between the words *function* and *relation*. The usage here is consistent with the modern definition of a function, which restricts this term to single-valued functions. The word *relation* is used to designate a case in which one or more values of y may exist for a given value of x.

There are many ways to express functions. Every formula, such as those we have discussed, defines a function. Other ways to express functions are by means of tables, charts, and graphs.

In the formula for the area of a circle, $A = \pi r^2$, we say that A is a function of r, since for each value of r there is only one value of A. Whenever such a relationship exists between two variables (that is, for every value of a variable x there is only one value of a corresponding variable y), we say that *y is a function of x*. Here we call the variable x the *independent variable* (since x may be chosen arbitrarily so long as the value chosen produces a real number for y), and y the *dependent variable* (since, once the value of x is chosen, the value of y is determined—y depends on x).

Example A. The volume of a cube of edge e is given by $V = e^3$. Here V is a function of e, since for each value of e there is one value of V. The dependent variable is V and the independent variable is e.

Example B. If the equation given in Example A was written as $e = \sqrt[3]{V}$, that is, if the edge of a cube was expressed in terms of its volume, we would say that e is a function of V. In this case e would be the dependent variable and V the independent variable.

Example C. The power P developed in a certain resistor by a current I is given by $P = 4I^2$. Here P is a function of I. The dependent variable is P, and the independent variable is I.

Example D. If the formula in Example C is written as $I = \sqrt{P}/2$, then I is a function of P. The independent variable is P, and the dependent variable is I. Even though P is the independent variable, it is restricted to values which are positive or zero. (This is written as $P \geq 0$.) Otherwise the values of I would be imaginary. Except when specified, we shall restrict ourselves to real numbers.

Example E. For the equation $y = 2x^2 - 6x$ we say that y is a function of x. The dependent variable is y, and the independent variable is x. Some of the values of y corresponding to chosen values of x are given in the following table.

x	-2	-1	0	$\frac{1}{2}$	1	2	3	π	10
y	20	8	0	$-\frac{5}{2}$	-4	-4	0	$2\pi^2 - 6\pi$	140

For convenience of notation, the phrase "function of x" is written as $f(x)$. This, in turn, is a simplification of the statement that "y is a function of x," so we may now write $y = f(x)$. [Notice that $f(x)$ does *not* mean f times x. The symbols must be written in this form, and not separated, to indicate a function.]

One of the most important uses of this notation is to designate the value of a function for a particular value of the independent variable. That is, for the expression "the value of the function $f(x)$ when $x = a$" we may write $f(a)$.

In certain instances we need to define more than one function of x. Then we use different symbols to denote the functions. For example, $f(x)$ and $g(x)$ may represent different functions of x, such as $f(x) = 5x^2 - 3$ and $g(x) = 6x - 7$. Special functions are represented by particular symbols. For example, in trigonometry we shall come across the "sine of the angle ϕ," where the sine is a function of ϕ. This is designated by sin ϕ.

Example F.   If $y = 6x^3 - 5x$ we may say that y is a function of x, where this function $f(x)$ is $6x^3 - 5x$. We may also write $f(x) = 6x^3 - 5x$. It is common to write functions in this manner, rather than in the form $y = 6x^3 - 5x$. However, y and $f(x)$ represent the same expression.

Example G.   If $f(x) = 3x^2 - 5$, and we wish to find $f(2)$, it is necessary to substitute 2 for x in the equation. Therefore, $f(2) = 3(2)^2 - 5 = 7$. Also, $f(-1) = 3(-1)^2 - 5 = -2$ and $f(c^2) = 3(c^2)^2 - 5 = 3c^4 - 5$.

Example H.   If $f(x) = \sqrt{4x} + x$ and $g(x) = ax^4 - 5x$, then $f(4) = 8$ and $g(4) = 256a - 20$.

Example I.   If $g(t) = 4t^3 - 5t$, $h(t) = 6t + \sqrt{t}$, and $F(t) = 6t$, then $g(2) = 22$, $h(2) = 12 + \sqrt{2}$ and $F(2) = 12$.

A function may be looked upon as a set of instructions. These instructions tell us how to obtain the value of the dependent variable for a particular value of the independent variable, even if the set of instructions is expressed in literal symbols.

Example J.   The function $f(x) = x^2 - 3x$ tells us to "square the value of the independent variable, multiply the value of the independent variable by 3, and subtract the second result from the first." An analogy would be a machine which was so made that when a number was fed into the machine, it would square the number and then subtract 3 times the value of the number. This is represented in diagram form in Fig. 2-1.

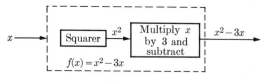

Figure 2-1

The functions $f(t) = t^2 - 3t$ and $f(n) = n^2 - 3n$ are the same as the function $f(x) = x^2 - 3x$, since the operations performed on the independent variable are the same. Although different literal symbols appear, this does not change the function.

Example K.   The resistance of a particular resistor as a function of temperature is $R = 10 + 0.1T + 0.001T^2$. If a given temperature T is increased by 10 degrees, what is the value of R for the increased temperature as a function of the temperature T?

We are to determine R for a temperature of $T + 10$. Since $f(T) = 10 + 0.1T + 0.001T^2$, we know that

$$f(T + 10) = 10 + 0.1(T + 10) + 0.001(T + 10)^2$$
$$= 10 + 0.1T + 1 + 0.001T^2 + 0.02T + 0.1$$
$$= 11.1 + 0.12T + 0.001T^2.$$

As we mentioned earlier, we must be certain that the function is defined for any value of x that may be chosen. Values of x which lead to division by zero or to imaginary values of y may not be chosen. Example D and the following example illustrate this point.

Example L.   If $f(u) = u/(u - 4)$, this function is not defined if $u = 4$, since this would require division by zero. Therefore the values of u are restricted to values other than 4.

Exercises

In Exercises 1 through 10 determine the appropriate function.

1. Find the area of a square as a function of its side s.
2. Find the circumference of a circle as a function of its radius.
3. Find the circumference of a circle as a function of its diameter.
4. Find the area of a circle as a function of its diameter.
5. Find the area of a rectangle of width 5 as a function of its length.
6. Find the volume of a right circular cone of height 8 as a function of the radius of the base.
7. Find the perimeter of a square as a function of its area.
8. A taxi fare is 35¢ plus 10¢ for every $\frac{1}{5}$ mile traveled. Express the fare F as a function of the distance s traveled.
9. Express the simple interest I on \$200 at 4% per year as a function of the number of years t.
10. A total of x ft are cut from a 24 ft board. Express the remaining length y as a function of x.

In Exercises 11 through 20 evaluate the given functions.

11. Given $f(x) = 2x + 1$, find $f(1)$, $f(-1)$, and $f(4)$.
12. Given $f(x) = 5x - 9$, find $f(2)$, $f(-2)$, and $f(0)$.
13 Given $f(x) = x^2 - 9x$, find $f(3)$, $f(-5)$, and $f(4)$.
14. Given $f(x) = 2x^3 - 7x$, find $f(1)$ and $f(\frac{1}{2})$.
15. Given $f(x) = ax^2 - a^2x$, find $f(a)$ and $f(2a)$.

16. Given $g(x) = 6\sqrt{x} - 3$, find $g(9)$ and $g(a^2)$.
17. Given $\phi(x) = 6x - x^2 + 2x^3$, find $\phi(1)$ and $\phi(-a)$.
18. Given $H(t) = t^4 - t + 3$, find $H(0)$ and $H(-2)$.
19. Given $K(s) = 3s^2 - s + 6$, find $K(2s)$ and $K(s - 1)$.
20. Given $T(t) = 5t + 7$, find $T(-t)$ and $T(T(t))$.

In Exercises 21 through 24 state the instructions of the function in words as in Example J.

21. $f(x) = x^2 + 2$ 22. $f(x) = 2x - 6$

23. $g(y) = 6y - y^3$ 24. $\phi(s) = 8 - 5s + s^5$

In Exercises 25 through 28 state any restrictions that might exist on the values of the independent variable.

25. $Y(y) = \dfrac{y + 1}{y - 1}$ 26. $F(y) = \sqrt{y - 1}$

27. $G(z) = \dfrac{1}{(z - 1)(z + 2)}$ 28. $X(x) = \dfrac{2}{\sqrt{1 - x}}$

In Exercises 29 through 33 answer the given questions.

29. If the temperature within a certain refrigerator is maintained at 273 degrees absolute (32°F), its *coefficient of performance* p as a function of the external temperature T (in degrees absolute) is

$$p = \frac{273}{T - 273}.$$

What is its coefficient of performance at 308 degrees absolute (95°F)?

30. The vertical distance of a point on a suspension cable from its lowest point as a function of the horizontal distance from the lowest point is given by

$$f(x) = \frac{x^4 + 600x^2}{2,000,000},$$

where x is measured in feet. How far above the lowest point is a point on the cable at a horizontal distance of 50 ft from the lowest point?

31. A piece of wire 60 in. long is cut into two pieces, one of which is bent into a circle and the other into a square. Express the total area of the two figures as a function of the perimeter of the square.

32. The electrical resistance of a certain ammeter as a function of the resistance of the coil of the meter is

$$R = \frac{10R_c}{10 + R_c}.$$

Find the function which represents the resistance of the meter if the resistance of the coil is doubled.

33. The voltage of a certain thermocouple as a function of the temperature is given by $E = 2.8T + 0.006T^2$. Find the voltage when the temperature is $T + h$.

2-2 Rectangular coordinates

One of the most valuable ways of representing functions is by graphical representation. By using graphs we are able to obtain a "picture" of the function, and by using this picture we can learn a great deal about the function.

To make a graphical representation, we recall that numbers can be represented by points on a line. Since a function represents two connected sets of numbers, it is necessary to use a line to represent each of these sets. We do this most conveniently by placing the lines perpendicular to each other.

We place one line horizontally and label it the *x-axis*. The numbers of the set for the independent variable are normally placed on this axis. The other line we place vertically, and label the *y-axis*. Normally the *y*-axis is used for values of the dependent variable. The point of intersection is called the *origin*. This is the *rectangular coordinate system*.

On the *x*-axis, positive values are to the right of the origin, and negative values are to the left of the origin. On the *y*-axis, positive values are above the origin, and negative values are below it. The four parts into which the plane is divided are called *quadrants*, which are numbered as in Fig. 2-2.

A point P in the plane is designated by the pair of numbers (x, y), where x is the value of the independent variable and y is the corresponding value of the dependent variable. The *x*-value (called the *abscissa*) is the perpendicular distance of P from the *y*-axis. The *y*-value (called the *ordinate*) is the perpendicular distance of P from the *x*-axis. The values x and y together, written as (x, y), are the *coordinates* of the point P.

Example A. The positions of points $P(4, 5)$, $Q(-2, 3)$, $R(-1, -5)$, $S(4, -2)$, and $T(0, 3)$ are shown in Fig. 2-2. Note that this representation allows for *one point for any pair of values* (x, y).

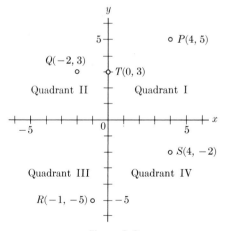

Figure 2-2

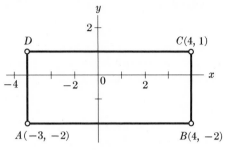

Figure 2-3

Example B. Three of the vertices of the rectangle in Fig. 2-3 are $A(-3, -2)$, $B(4, -2)$ and $C(4, 1)$. What is the fourth vertex?

We use the fact that opposite sides of a rectangle are equal and parallel to find the solution. Since both vertices of the base AB of the rectangle have a y-coordinate of -2, the base is parallel to the x-axis. Therefore, the top of the rectangle must also be parallel to the x-axis. Thus the vertices of the top must both have a y-coordinate of 1, since one of them has a y-coordinate of 1. In the same way the x-coordinates of the left side must both be -3. Therefore, the fourth vertex is $D(-3, 1)$.

Example C. Where are all the points whose ordinates are 2?

All such points are 2 units above the x-axis; thus the answer can be stated as "on a line 2 units above the x-axis."

Exercises

In Exercises 1 and 2 determine (at least approximately) the coordinates of the points specified in Fig. 2-4.

1. A, B, C
2. D, E, F

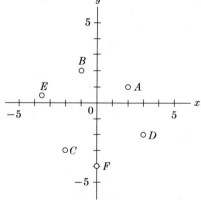

Figure 2-4

In Exercises 3 and 4 plot (at least approximately) the given points.

3. $A(2, 7)$, $B(-1, -2)$, $C(-4, 2)$ 4. $A(3, \frac{1}{2})$, $B(-6, 0)$, $C(-\frac{5}{2}, -5)$

In Exercises 5 and 6 plot the given points and then join these points, in the order given by straight-line segments. Name the geometric figure formed.

5. $A(-1, 4)$, $B(3, 4)$, $C(1, -2)$ 6. $A(-5, -2)$, $B(4, -2)$, $C(6, 3)$, $D(-3, 3)$

In Exercises 7 through 18 answer the given questions.

7. Plot the points $A(1, 3)$, $B(-1, -1)$, $C(6, 13)$. Join these points by straight-line segments. What conclusion can you reach?

8. Three vertices of a rectangle are $(5, 2)$, $(-1, 2)$, and $(-1, 4)$. What are the co-ordinates of the fourth vertex?

9. Two vertices of an equilateral triangle are $(7, 1)$ and $(2, 1)$. What is the abscissa of the third vertex?

10. Where are all the points whose abscissas are 1?

11. Where are all the points whose ordinates are -3?

12. Where are all the points whose abscissas equal their ordinates?

13. What is the abscissa of all points on the y-axis?

14. What is the ordinate of all points on the x-axis?

15. Where are all the points for which $x > 0$?

16. Where are all points (x, y) for which $x > 0$ and $y < 0$?

17. Where are all points (x, y) for which $x < 0$ and $y > 1$?

18. In which quadrants is the ratio y/x positive?

2-3 The graph of a function

Now that we have introduced the concepts of a function and the rectangular coordinate system, we are in a position to determine the graph of a function. In this way we shall obtain a visual representation of a function.

The graph of a function is the set of all points whose coordinates (x, y) satisfy the functional relationship $y = f(x)$. Since $y = f(x)$, we can write the coordinates of the points on the graph as $[x, f(x)]$. Writing the coordinates in this manner tells us exactly how to find them. We assume a certain value for x and then find the value of the function of x. These two numbers are the coordinates of the point.

Since there is no limit to the possible number of points which can be chosen, we normally select a few values of x, obtain the corresponding values of the function, and plot these points. These points are then connected by a *smooth* curve (not short straight lines from one point to the next), and are normally connected from left to right.

Example A. Graph the function $(3x - 5)$.

For purposes of graphing, we let y [or $f(x)$] $= 3x - 5$. We then let x take on various values and determine the corresponding values of y. If $x = 0$ we find

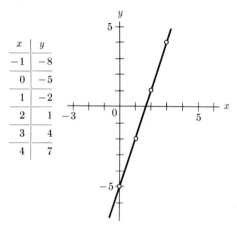

x	y
-1	-8
0	-5
1	-2
2	1
3	4
4	7

Figure 2-5

that $y = -5$. This means that the point $(0, -5)$ is on the graph of the function $3x - 5$. Choosing another value of x, for example, 1, we find that $y = -2$. This means that the point $(1, -2)$ is on the graph of the function $3x - 5$. Continuing to choose a few other values of x, we tabulate the results, as shown in Fig. 2-5. It is best to arrange the table so that the values of x increase; then there is no doubt how they are to be connected, for they are then connected in the order shown. Finally, we connect the points as shown in Fig. 2-5, and see that the graph of the function $3x - 5$ is a straight line.

Example B. Graph the function $(2x^2 - 4)$.

First we let $y = 2x^2 - 4$ and tabulate the values as shown in Fig. 2-6. Then we plot and connect the points with a smooth curve, as shown in Fig. 2-6.

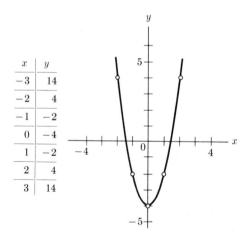

x	y
-3	14
-2	4
-1	-2
0	-4
1	-2
2	4
3	14

Figure 2-6

Be careful to obtain the correct values of y for negative values of x. Mistakes are relatively common when dealing with negative numbers. We must carefully use the laws for signed numbers. For example, considering the function $2x^2 - 4$, if $x = -2$, $y = 2(-2)^2 - 4 = 2(4) = 8 - 4 = 4$.

There are some special points which should be noted. Since most common functions are smooth, any irregularities or sudden changes in the graph should be carefully checked. In these cases it usually helps to take values of x between those values where the question arises. Also, if the function is not defined for some value of x (remember, division by zero is not defined, and only real values of the variables are permissible), the function does not exist for that value of x. Finally, in applications, we must be careful to plot values that are meaningful; often negative values for quantities such as time are not physically meaningful. The following examples illustrate these points.

Example C.   Graph the function $y = x - x^2$.

First we determine the values in the table as shown with Fig. 2-7. In plotting these points we note that $y = 0$ for both $x = 0$ and $x = 1$. The question arises—what happens between these values? Trying $x = \frac{1}{2}$, we find that $y = \frac{1}{4}$. Using this point completes the necessary information. Note that in plotting these graphs we do not stop the graph with the last point determined, but indicate that the curve continues.

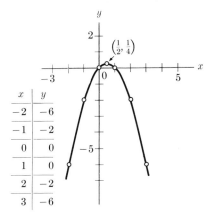

x	y
-2	-6
-1	-2
0	0
1	0
2	-2
3	-6

Figure 2-7

Example D.   Graph the function $y = 1 + \dfrac{1}{x}$.

In finding the points on this graph as shown in Fig. 2-8, we note that y is not defined if we try $x = 0$. Thus we must be careful not to have any part of the curve cross the y-axis ($x = 0$). We choose points between $x = -1$ and $x = 1$, to choose values near $x = 0$, since we cannot let $x = 0$.

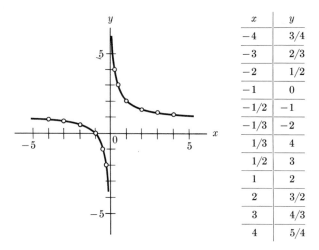

x	y
-4	$3/4$
-3	$2/3$
-2	$1/2$
-1	0
$-1/2$	-1
$-1/3$	-2
$1/3$	4
$1/2$	3
1	2
2	$3/2$
3	$4/3$
4	$5/4$

Figure 2-8

Example E. Graph the function $y = \sqrt{x + 1}$.

When finding the points for the graph, we may not let x equal any negative value less than -1, for all such values of x lead to imaginary values for y. Also, since we have the positive square root indicated, all values of y are positive. See Fig. 2-9. Note that the graph stops at the point $(-1, 0)$.

x	y
-1	0
0	1
1	1.4
2	1.7
3	2
4	2.2
5	2.4
6	2.6
7	2.8
8	3

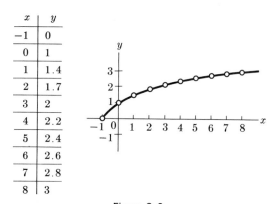

Figure 2-9

Example F. The power of a certain voltage source as a function of the load resistance is given by

$$P = \frac{100R}{(0.5 + R)^2},$$

where P is measured in watts and R in ohms. Plot the power as a function of the resistance.

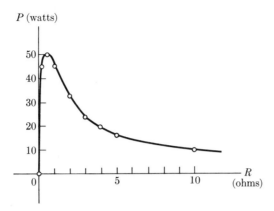

Figure 2-10

Since a negative value for the resistance has no physical significance, we need to plot P for positive values of R only. The following table of values is obtained.

R(ohms)	0	0.25	0.50	1.0	2.0	3.0	4.0	5.0	10.0
P(watts)	0.0	44.4	50.0	44.4	32.0	24.5	19.8	16.5	9.1

The values 0.25 and 0.50 are used for R when it is found that P is less for $R = 2$ than for $R = 1$. In this way a smoother curve is obtained (see Fig. 2-10).

Empirical data may also be plotted in graphical form, although there may not be a formula connecting the values. When there is no possible formula which relates the sets of numbers, it is customary to connect the points with straight-line segments, merely to make them stand out better. The maximum temperature recorded weekly at a particular location would be an example of this. However, if it is reasonable that a functional relationship may exist, although it is unknown, the points may be connected by a smooth curve. Data from a physics experiment would be an example of this case. Illustrations of such cases are found in the exercises.

Exercises

In Exercises 1 through 26 graph the given functions.

1. $y = 2x - 4$
2. $y = 5 - 3x$
3. $y = \frac{1}{2}x - 2$
4. $y = 3x + 5$
5. $y = 7 - 2x$
6. $y = 4x + 1$
7. $y = x^2$
8. $y = x^2 - 3$
9. $y = 3 - x^2$
10. $y = 2x^2 + 1$
11. $y = x^2 + 2x$
12. $y = 2x - x^2$
13. $y = x^2 - 3x + 1$
14. $y = 2 + 3x + x^2$
15. $y = x^3$
16. $y = 3x - x^3$
17. $y = x^4 - 4x^2$
18. $y = x^3 - x^4$

19. $y = \dfrac{1}{x}$

20. $y = x + \dfrac{1}{x}$

21. $y = \dfrac{1}{x^2}$

22. $y = \dfrac{1}{x^2 + 1}$

23. $y = \sqrt{x}$

24. $y = \sqrt{4 - x}$

25. $y = \dfrac{1}{x + 2}$

26. $y = \sqrt{x^2 - 16}$

In Exercises 27 through 32 represent the data graphically.

27. The rainfall, in inches, in a certain city was recorded as follows.

Year	1960	1961	1962	1963	1964	1965	1966	1967	1968
Rainfall (in.)	35.4	36.7	40.4	40.2	38.2	32.8	33.4	41.2	40.4

28. The hourly temperatures on a certain day were recorded as follows.

Hour	6 AM	7	8	9	10	11	12	1 PM	2	3	4
Temp. (°F)	16	18	20	25	32	36	39	41	39	42	36

29. The density (in grams per cubic centimeter) of water from 0° to 10°C is given in the following table.

Density	0.99985	0.99990	0.99994	0.99996	0.99997	0.99996
Temperature	0	1	2	3	4	5
Density	0.99994	0.99990	0.99985	0.99978	0.99969	
Temperature	6	7	8	9	10	

30. The voltage (in volts) and current (in milliamps) for a certain electrical experiment were measured as follows.

Voltage	10	20	30	40	50	60	70	80
Current	145	188	220	255	285	315	335	370

31. An experiment measuring the load (in pounds) on a spring and the scale reading of the spring (in centimeters) produced the following results.

Load	0	1	2	3	4	5	6
Reading	7.0	7.6	8.2	8.8	9.4	10.1	12.8

32. The vapor pressure (in atmospheres) of ethane gas as a function of temperature (in °C) is given by the following table.

Pressure	2.6	3.8	5.6	7.8	10.5	14.1	18.2	23.6	32.3
Temperature	−70	−60	−50	−40	−30	−20	−10	0	15

In each of Exercises 33 through 38, graph the given functions. When you are instructed to plot a first variable A as a function of a second variable B, plot A as the ordinate and B as the abscissa.

33. The surface area of a cube is given by $A = 6e^2$, where e is the side of the cube. Plot A as a function of e.

34. The velocity (in feet per second) of an object under the influence of gravity is given by $v = v_0 - at$. Plot v as a function of t (sec), if $v_0 = 100$ and $a = 32$.

35. The intensity (in lumens) of a certain source of light as a function of the distance (in centimeters) from the source is given by $I = 400/r^2$. Plot I as a function of r.

36. The heat capacity (in calories per gram) of an organic liquid is related to the temperature (in °C) by the equation $c_p = 0.555 + 0.00113T$ for the temperature range of $-40°C$ to $120°C$. Graphically show that this equation does not satisfy experimental data above $120°C$. Plot the graph of the equation and the following data points.

c_p	0.725	0.770	0.800
T	140	160	200

37. The energy in the electric field around an inductor is given by $E = \frac{1}{2}LI^2$, where I is the current in the inductor and L is the inductance. Plot E as a function of I (a) if $L = 1$ unit, (b) if $L = 0.1$ unit and (c) if the E-axis is marked off in units of L.

38. The deflection y of a beam at a horizontal distance x from one end is given by $y = -k(x^4 - 30x^2 + 1000x)$, where k is a constant. Plot the deflection (in terms of k) as a function of x (in feet) if there are 10 ft between the end supports of the beam.

2-4 Solving equations graphically

It is possible to solve equations by the use of graphs. This is particularly useful when algebraic methods cannot be applied conveniently to the equation. Before taking up graphical solutions, however, we shall briefly introduce the related concept of the zero of a function.

Those values of the independent variable for which the function equals zero are known as the *zeros* of the function. To find the zeros of a given function, we must set the function equal to zero and solve the resulting equation. Using functional notation, we may write this as $f(x) = 0$.

Example A.   Find any zeros of the function $(3x - 9)$.

We write $f(x) = 3x - 9$ and then let $f(x) = 0$, which means that $3x - 9 = 0$. Thus we obtain the solution $x = 3$, which means that 3 is a zero of the function $(3x - 9)$.

Graphically, the zeros of a function may be found where the curve crosses the x-axis. This is true since the x-axis represents all points for which y is zero, or $f(x) = 0$.

Example B.   Graphically determine any zeros of the function $x^2 - 2x - 1$.

First we set $y = x^2 - 2x - 1$ and then find the points for the graph. From the graph in Fig. 2-11 we see that the curve crosses the x-axis at approximately $x = -0.4$ and $x = 2.4$ (estimating to the nearest tenth). Thus the zeros of this function are -0.4 and 2.4.

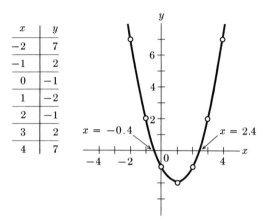

x	y
-2	7
-1	2
0	-1
1	-2
2	-1
3	2
4	7

Figure 2-11

Example C.   Graphically determine any zeros of the function $x^2 + 1$.

Graphing the function $y = x^2 + 1$ in Fig. 2-12, we see that it does not cross the x-axis anywhere. Therefore, this function does not have any real zeros. We therefore can see that not all functions have real zeros.

We can now see how to solve equations graphically and how this is related to the zeros of a function. To solve an equation, we collect all terms on one side of the equals sign, giving the equation $f(x) = 0$. This equation is solved graphically by first setting $y = f(x)$ and graphing this function. We then find those values of x for which $y = 0$. This means that we are finding the zeros of this function. The following examples illustrate the method.

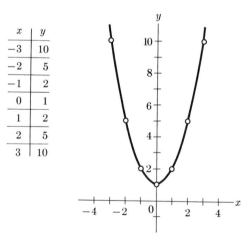

x	y
-3	10
-2	5
-1	2
0	1
1	2
2	5
3	10

Figure 2-12

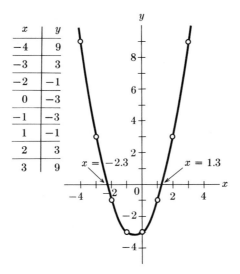

x	y
-4	9
-3	3
-2	-1
0	-3
-1	-3
1	-1
2	3
3	9

Figure 2-13

Example D.   Solve the equation $3x = x(2 - x) + 3$ graphically.

We first collect algebraically all terms on the left side of the equals sign. This leads to the equation $x^2 + x - 3 = 0$. We then let $y = x^2 + x - 3$ and graph this function, as shown in Fig. 2-13. From the graph we see that $y = 0$ ($x^2 + x - 3$ is zero) for $x = -2.3$ and $x = 1.3$. Therefore, the solutions to the original equation are $x = -2.3$ and $x = 1.3$.

Example E.   A box, whose volume is 30 cu in., is made with a square base and a height which is 2 in. less than the length of a side of the base. To find the dimensions of the box we must solve the equation $x^2(x - 2) = 30$, where x is the length of a side of the base. (Verify the equation.) What are the dimensions of the box?

We are to solve the equation

$$x^2(x - 2) = 30$$

graphically. First we write the equation as $x^3 - 2x^2 - 30 = 0$. Now we set $y = x^3 - 2x^2 - 30$ and graph this equation as shown in Fig. 2-14. Only positive values of x are used since negative values of x have no meaning to the problem. From the graph we see that $x = 3.9$ is the solution. Therefore the dimensions are 3.9 in., 3.9 in. and 1.9 in.

x	y
0	-30
1	-31
2	-30
3	-21
4	2
5	45

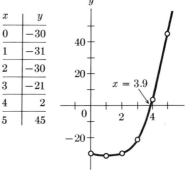

Figure 2-14

Exercises

In Exercises 1 through 4 find the zeros of the given functions algebraically as in Example A.

1. $5x - 10$ 2. $7x - 4$ 3. $4x + 9$ 4. $2 - 3(x - 5)$

In Exercises 5 through 12 find the zeros of the given functions graphically. Check the solutions in 5 through 8 algebraically.

5. $2x - 7$ 6. $3x - 2$ 7. $5x - (3 - x)$ 8. $3 - 2(2x - 7)$

9. $x^2 + x$ 10. $2x^2 - x$ 11. $x^2 - x + 3$ 12. $x^2 + 3x - 5$

In Exercises 13 through 24 solve the given equations graphically.

13. $7x - 5 = 0$ 14. $8x + 3 = 0$ 15. $6x = 15$ 16. $7x = -18$

17. $x^2 + x - 5 = 0$ 18. $2x^2 - x - 7 = 0$

19. $x(x - 4) = 9$ 20. $x = 1 + (x + 2)^2$

21. $x^3 - 4x = 0$ 22. $x^3 - 3x - 3 = 0$

23. $x^4 - 2x = 0$ 24. $x - 2 = \dfrac{1}{x}$

In Exercises 25 through 28 solve the given problems graphically.

25. Under certain conditions the velocity (in feet per second) of an object as a function of the time (in seconds) is given by the equation $v = 60 - 32t$. When is the velocity zero?

26. In the study of the velocities of nuclear fission fragments, it is found that under certain conditions the velocity would be zero if the expression $(1 + b)^2 - 3b$ were zero. For what values of b ($b > 0$), if any, is the velocity zero?

27. In order to find the distance x (in feet) from one end of a certain beam to the point where the deflection is zero, it is necessary to solve the equation $x^3 + x^2 - 5x = 0$. Determine where the deflection is zero.

28. If two electrical resistors, one of which is 1 ohm greater than the other, are placed in parallel, their combined resistance R_T as a function of the smaller resistance R is

$$R_T = \frac{R(R + 1)}{2R + 1}.$$

What are the values of the resistors if $R_T = 10$ ohms?

2-5 Miscellaneous Exercises

In Exercises 1 through 4 determine the appropriate functions.

1. Find the volume of a right circular cylinder of height 8 ft as a function of the radius of the base.

2. Find the surface area of a cube as a function of one of the edges.

3. Find the temperature in degrees fahrenheit as a function of degrees centigrade ($32°F = 0°C$ and $212°F = 100°C$).

4. Fencing 1000 ft long is to be used to enclose three sides of a rectangular field. Express the area of the field as a function of its length (parallel to the fourth side).

In Exercises 5 through 10 evaluate the given functions.

5. Given $f(x) = 7x - 5$, find $f(3)$ and $f(-6)$.

6. Given $g(y) = \dfrac{4y^2 - y}{2}$, find $g(-1)$ and $g(2a)$.

7. Given $F(u) = u - 3u^3$, find $F(2u) - F(u)$.

8. Given $\phi(v) = \dfrac{3v - 2}{v + 1}$, find $\phi(-2)$ and $\phi(v + 1)$.

9. Given $f(x) = 3x^2 - 2x + 4$, find $f(x + h) - f(x)$.

10. Given $F(x) = x^3 + 2x^2 - 3x$, find $F(3 + h) - F(3)$.

In Exercises 11 through 20 graph the given functions.

11. $y = 4x + 2$

12. $y = 5x - 10$

13. $y = 4x - x^2$

14. $y = x^2 - 8x - 5$

15. $y = 3 - x - 2x^2$

16. $y = 6 + 4x + x^2$

17. $y = x^3 - 6x$

18. $y = x^4 - 4x$

19. $y = \dfrac{x}{x + 1}$

20. $y = \sqrt{16 - x^2}$

In Exercises 21 through 30 find any real zeros of the functions of Exercises 11 through 20 by examining their graphs. Estimate the answer to the nearest tenth if this is necessary.

In Exercises 31 through 38 solve the given equations graphically.

31. $7x - 3 = 0$

32. $2x + 11 = 0$

33. $x^2 + 1 = 6x$

34. $3x - 2 = x^2$

35. $x^3 - x^2 = 2 - x$

36. $5 - x^3 = 2x^2$

37. $\dfrac{1}{x} = 2x$

38. $\sqrt{x} = 2x - 1$

In Exercises 39 through 42 answer the given questions.

39. Where are all the points (x, y) whose abscissas are 1 and for which $y > 0$?

40. Three vertices of a rectangle are $(6, 5)$, $(-4, 5)$, and $(-4, 2)$. What are the coordinates of the fourth vertex?

41. An equation which is found in electronics is

$$h = \frac{\alpha}{1 - \alpha}.$$

Find h when $\alpha = 0.95$. That is, since $h = f(\alpha)$, find $f(0.95)$.

42. Under certain conditions, the distance s that an object is above the ground is given by $s = 96t - 16t^2$, where t is the time in seconds. When is the object 100 ft above the ground? Solve graphically.

In Exercises 43 through 50 plot the indicated functions.

43. The sales (in millions of dollars) of a certain corporation from 1960 through 1968 are shown in the following table.

Year	1960	1961	1962	1963	1964	1965	1966	1967	1968
Sales	12	14	17	18	20	24	32	35	39

44. The amplitude (in inches) of a certain pendulum, measured after each swing, as a function of time (in seconds), is given by the following table. Plot the graph of amplitude as a function of time.

Amplitude	5.0	2.8	1.6	0.9	0.5
Time	0.0	1.2	2.4	3.6	4.8

45. The length (in inches) of a brass rod is measured as a function of the temperature (in °C). From the following table, plot the length as a function of temperature (make your scale meaningful).

Length	100.0	100.2	100.4	100.7	101.0	101.2
Temperature	0	100	200	300	400	500

46. The solubility (in grams of solute per 100 grams of water) of potassium nitrate as a function of temperature is given in the following table. Plot solubility as a function of temperature (in °C).

Solubility	13.3	20.9	31.6	45.8	63.9	85.5	110	169
Temperature	0	10	20	30	40	50	60	80

47. A computer-leasing firm charges $150 plus $100 for every hour the computer is used during the month. What is the function relating the monthly charge C and the number of hours h that the computer is used? Plot a graph of the function for use up to 50 hours.

48. A surveyor measuring the elevation of a point must consider the effect of the curvature of the earth. An approximate relation between the effect H (in feet) of this curvature, and the distance D (in miles) between the surveyor and the point of which he is measuring the elevation is given by $H = 0.65D^2$. Plot H as a function of D.

49. The resonant frequency f (in cycles per second) of a certain electric circuit is given by $f = 10,000/\sqrt{L}$, where L is the inductance (in henrys) in the circuit. Plot f as a function of L. (Take values of $L = 0.25, 0.49, 0.64, 1.00, 2.25$ and 4.00.)

50. The pneumatic resistance, in lb-sec/ft^5, of a certain type of tubing is given by $R = 0.05/A^2$, where A is the cross-sectional area in square feet. Plot R as a function of A. (Take values of A in the range of 0.001 to 0.01.)

The Trigonometric Functions

3

3-1 Introduction; angles

The solution to a great many kinds of applied problems involves the use of triangles, especially right triangles. Problems which can be solved by the use of triangles include the determination of distances which cannot readily be determined directly, such as the widths of rivers and distances between various points in the universe. Also, problems involving forces and velocities lend themselves readily to triangle solution. Even certain types of electric circuits are analyzed by the use of triangles.

The basic properties of triangles will allow us to set up some very basic and useful functions involving their sides and angles. These functions are very important to the development of mathematics and to its applications in most fields of technology.

Thus we come to the study of *trigonometry*, the literal meaning of which is "triangle measurement." In this chapter we shall introduce the basic trigonometric functions and some of their elementary applications. Later chapters will consider additional topics in trigonometry. We shall begin our study by considering the concept of an angle.

An *angle* is defined as being *generated* by rotating a *half*-line about its endpoint from an initial position to a terminal position. A half-line is that portion of a line to one side of a fixed point on the line. We call the initial position of the half-line the *initial side,* and the terminal position of the half-line the *terminal* side. The fixed point is the *vertex.* The angle itself is the amount of rotation from the initial side to the terminal side.

If the rotation of the terminal side from the initial side is counterclockwise, the angle is said to be *positive*. If the rotation is clockwise the angle is *negative*. In Fig. 3-1, Angle 1 is positive and Angle 2 is negative.

There are many symbols used to designate angles. Probably the most widely used are certain Greek letters such as θ (theta), ϕ (phi), α (alpha), and β (beta).

Two measurements of angles are widely used. These are the *degree* and the radian. A degree is defined as $\frac{1}{360}$ of a complete rotation. The radian will be discussed in Chapter 7. The degree is divided into 60 equal parts called *minutes*, and each minute is divided into 60 equal parts called *seconds*. The symbols °, ′ and ″ are used to designate degrees, minutes, and seconds, respectively. Decimal parts of angles are also commonly used.

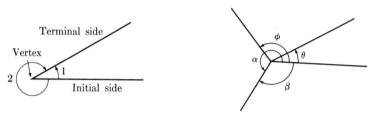

Figure 3-1   Figure 3-2

Example A. The angles $\theta = 30°$, $\phi = 140°$, $\alpha = 240°$ and $\beta = -120°$ are shown in Fig. 3-2. Note that angles α and β have the same initial and terminal sides. Such angles are called *coterminal*.

Example B. To change the angle 43°24′ to decimal form we use the fact that $1' = (\frac{1}{60})°$. Therefore, $24' = (\frac{24}{60})° = 0.4°$. Therefore,

$$43°24' = 43.4°.$$

To change 154.36° to an angle measured to the nearest minute, we use the fact that $0.01° = 0.6'$. Therefore, $0.36° = 36(0.6)' = 21.6'$, which is 22′ to the nearest minute. Therefore,

$$154.36° = 154°22'.$$

Example C. Determine the values of two angles which are coterminal with an angle of 145°32′.

Since there are 360° in a complete rotation, we can find one coterminal angle by considering the angle which is 360° larger than the given angle. This gives us an angle of 505°32′. Another method of finding a coterminal angle is to subtract 145°32′ from 360°, and then consider the resulting angle to be negative. This means that the original angle and the derived angle would make up one complete rotation, when put together. This method leads us to the angle of −214°28′ (see Fig. 3-3). These methods could be employed repeatedly to find other coterminal angles.

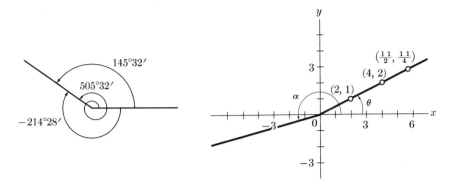

Figure 3-3   Figure 3-4

If the initial side of the angle is the positive x-axis and the vertex is at the origin, the angle is said to be in *standard position*. The angle is then determined by the position of the terminal side. If the terminal side is in the first quadrant, the angle is called a "first-quadrant angle." Similar terms are used when the terminal side is in the other quadrants. If the terminal side coincides with one of the axes, the angle is a *quadrantal* angle. When an angle is in standard position, the terminal side can be determined if we know any point, other than the origin, on the terminal side.

Example D.   To draw a third-quadrant angle of 205°, we simply measure 205° from the positive x-axis and draw the terminal side. See angle α in Fig. 3-4.

Also in Fig. 3-4, θ is in standard position and the terminal side is uniquely determined by knowing that it passes through the point $(2, 1)$. The same terminal side passes through $(4, 2)$ and $(\frac{11}{2}, \frac{11}{4})$, among other points. Knowing that the terminal side passes through any one of these points makes it possible to determine the terminal side.

3-2 Defining the trigonometric functions

Let us place an angle θ in standard position and drop perpendicular lines from points on the terminal side to the x-axis as shown in Fig. 3-5. In doing this we set up similar triangles, each with one vertex at the origin. Using the basic fact from geometry that corresponding sides of similar triangles are proportional, we may set up equal ratios of corresponding sides.

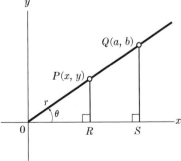

Figure 3-5

Example A. In Fig. 3-5 triangles *OPR* and *OQS* are similar. Therefore, the ratio of the abscissa (*x*-value) to the ordinate (*y*-value) of points *P* and *Q* is the same in each triangle. We can state this as

$$\frac{x}{y} = \frac{a}{b}.$$

For any other point on the terminal side of θ that we might choose, the ratio of its abscissa to ordinate would still be the same as those already given.

The length of the line from the origin to a point on the terminal side is called the *radius vector* and is denoted r.

For any angle θ in standard position, there are six ratios which may be set up. It can be seen that these ratios depend on the position of the terminal side of the angle. Therefore, the ratios depend on the angle and are functions of it. These functions are called the *trigonometric functions*, and are defined as follows:

$$\text{sine } \theta = \frac{\text{ordinate of } P}{\text{radius vector of } P} = \frac{y}{r} \qquad \text{cosine } \theta = \frac{\text{abscissa of } P}{\text{radius vector of } P} = \frac{x}{r},$$

$$\text{tangent } \theta = \frac{\text{ordinate of } P}{\text{abscissa of } P} = \frac{y}{x} \qquad \text{cotangent } \theta = \frac{\text{abscissa of } P}{\text{ordinate of } P} = \frac{x}{y}, \qquad (3\text{-}1)$$

$$\text{secant } \theta = \frac{\text{radius vector of } P}{\text{abscissa of } P} = \frac{r}{x} \qquad \text{cosecant } \theta = \frac{\text{radius vector of } P}{\text{ordinate of } P} = \frac{r}{y}.$$

For convenience, the names of the various functions are usually abbreviated to sin θ, cos θ, tan θ, cot θ, sec θ, and csc θ. Note that a given function is not defined if the denominator is zero. The denominator is zero in tan θ and sec θ for $x = 0$, and in the cot θ and csc θ for $y = 0$. In all cases we will assume that $r > 0$. If $r = 0$ there would be no terminal side and therefore no angle.

There are many other important properties of the trigonometric functions, which we shall discuss in Chapters 7 and 19. For the moment, we shall restrict our use of the functions to first-quadrant angles.

Example B. Determine the trigonometric functions of the angle with a terminal side passing through the point $(3, 4)$.

By placing the angle in standard position, as shown in Fig. 3-6, and drawing the terminal side through $(3, 4)$, we find that $r = 5$ (by use of the Pythagorean theorem). Using the values $x = 3, y = 4$, and $r = 5$, we find that

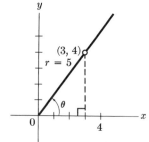

$$\sin \theta = \tfrac{4}{5}, \qquad \cos \theta = \tfrac{3}{5},$$
$$\tan \theta = \tfrac{4}{3}, \qquad \cot \theta = \tfrac{3}{4},$$
$$\sec \theta = \tfrac{5}{3}, \qquad \csc \theta = \tfrac{5}{4}.$$

Figure 3-6

If one of the trigonometric functions is known, we can determine the other functions of the angle, using the Pythagorean theorem and the definitions of the functions. The following example illustrates the method.

Example C. If we know that $\sin \theta = \frac{3}{7}$ and that θ is a first quadrant angle, we know that the ratio of the ordinate to the radius vector (of y to r) is 3 to 7. Therefore, the point on the terminal side for which y is 3 can be determined by use of the Pythagorean theorem. The x-value for this point is

$$x = \sqrt{7^2 - 3^2} = \sqrt{49 - 9} = \sqrt{40} = 2\sqrt{10}.$$

Therefore, the point $(2\sqrt{10}, 3)$ is on the terminal side as shown in Fig. 3-7.

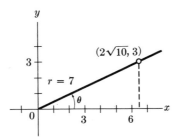

Figure 3-7

Therefore, using the values $x = 2\sqrt{10}$, $y = 3$, and $r = 7$ we have the other trigonometric functions of θ. They are

$$\cos \theta = \frac{2\sqrt{10}}{7}, \quad \tan \theta = \frac{3}{2\sqrt{10}}, \quad \cot \theta = \frac{2\sqrt{10}}{3},$$

$$\sec \theta = \frac{7}{2\sqrt{10}}, \quad \csc \theta = \frac{7}{3}.$$

Exercises

In Exercises 1 through 4 draw the given angles.

1. $60°$, $120°$, $-90°$
2. $330°$, $-150°$, $450°$
3. $50°$, $-360°$, $-30°$
4. $45°$, $225°$, $-250°$

In Exercises 5 through 8 determine a negative coterminal angle for each of the angles given.

5. $45°$
6. $150°$
7. $70°30'$
8. $153°47'$

In Exercises 9 through 12 change the given angles to equal angles expressed in decimal form.

9. $15°12'$
10. $246°48'$
11. $86°3'$
12. $157°39'$

In Exercises 13 through 16 change the given angles to equal angles expressed to the nearest minute.

13. 47.5°   14. 315.8°   15. 5.62°   16. 238.21°

In Exercises 17 through 24 determine the trigonometric functions of the angles whose terminal sides pass through the given points.

17. (4, 3)   18. (5, 12)   19. (15, 8)   20. (7, 24)
21. $(1, \sqrt{15})$ 22. (1, 1)   23. (2, 5)   24. $(1, \frac{1}{2})$

In Exercises 25 through 30 use the given trigonometric functions to find the indicated trigonometric functions.

25. $\tan \theta = 1$, find $\sin \theta$ and $\sec \theta$ 26. $\sin \theta = \frac{1}{2}$, find $\cos \theta$ and $\csc \theta$

27. $\cos \theta = \frac{2}{3}$, find $\tan \theta$ and $\cot \theta$ 28. $\sec \theta = 3$, find $\tan \theta$ and $\sin \theta$

29. $\sin \theta = 0.7$, find $\cot \theta$ and $\csc \theta$ 30. $\cos \theta = \frac{5}{12}$, find $\sec \theta$ and $\tan \theta$

In Exercises 31 and 32 each of the listed points is on the terminal side of an angle. Show that each of the indicated functions is the same for each of the points.

31. (3, 4), (6, 8), (4.5, 6), $\sin \theta$ and $\tan \theta$

32. (5, 12), (15, 36), (7.5, 18), $\cos \theta$ and $\cot \theta$

In Exercises 33 and 34 answer the given questions.

33. From the definitions of the trigonometric functions, it can be seen that the csc θ is the reciprocal of sin θ. What function is the reciprocal of $\cos \theta$? of $\cot \theta$?

34. Divide the expression for $\sin \theta$ by that for $\cos \theta$. Is the result the expression for any of the other functions?

3-3 Values of the trigonometric functions

We have been able to calculate the trigonometric functions if we knew one point on the terminal side of the angle. However, in practice it is more common to know the angle in degrees, for example, and to be required to find the functions of this angle. Therefore, we must be able to determine the trigonometric functions of angles in degrees.

One way to determine the functions of a given angle is to make a scale drawing. That is, we draw the angle in standard position using a protractor, and then measure the lengths of the values of x, y, and r for some point on the terminal side. By using the proper ratios we may determine the functions of this angle.

We may also use certain geometric facts to determine the functions of some particular angles. The following two examples illustrate this procedure.

Example A.   From geometry we know that the side opposite a 30° angle in a right triangle is one-half the hypotenuse. By using this fact and letting $y = 1$ and $r = 2$ (see Fig. 3-8), we determine that $\sin 30° = \frac{1}{2}$. Also, by use of the Pythagorean theorem we determine that $x = \sqrt{3}$. Thus, $\cos 30° = \sqrt{3}/2$ and $\tan 30° = 1/\sqrt{3}$. In a similar way we may determine the values of the functions of 60° to be as follows: $\sin 60° = \sqrt{3}/2$, $\cos 60° = \frac{1}{2}$ and $\tan 60° = \sqrt{3}$.

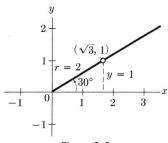

Figure 3-8

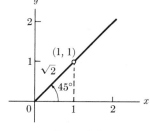

Figure 3-9

Example B. Determine the sin 45°, cos 45°, and tan 45°.

From geometry we know that in an isosceles right triangle the angles are 45°, 45°, and 90°. We know that the sides are in proportion 1, 1, $\sqrt{2}$, respectively. Putting the 45° angle in standard position, we find $x = 1$, $y = 1$, and $r = \sqrt{2}$ (see Fig. 3-9). From this we determine

$$\sin 45^\circ = \frac{1}{\sqrt{2}}, \qquad \cos 45^\circ = \frac{1}{\sqrt{2}}, \qquad \text{and} \qquad \tan 45^\circ = 1.$$

Summarizing the results for 30°, 45°, and 60°, we have the following table.

				(decimal approximations).		
θ	30°	45°	60°	30°	45°	60°
sin θ	1/2	$1/\sqrt{2}$	$\sqrt{3}/2$	0.500	0.707	0.866
cos θ	$\sqrt{3}/2$	$1/\sqrt{2}$	1/2	0.866	0.707	0.500
tan θ	$1/\sqrt{3}$	1	$\sqrt{3}$	0.577	1.000	1.732

Of course, more complete tables are necessary, and we present them in Appendix E. Since the scale-drawing method is only approximate, and the geometric methods work only for certain angles, the values in the tables are determined by using calculus and what are known as power series.

To obtain the value of a function, we note that the angles from 0° to 45° are listed in the left-hand column and are read down. The angles from 45° to 90° are listed on the right-hand side and are read *up*. The functions for angles from 0° to 45° are listed along the top, and those for the angles from 45° to 90° are listed along the bottom.

Example C. Sin 34° is found under sin θ (at top) and to the right of 34° (at left). Sin 34° = 0.5592.

Cos 72° is found over cos θ (at bottom) and to the left of 72° (at right). Cos 72° = 0.3090.

Example D. Tan 42°20′ is found under tan θ (at top) and to the right of 20′ (which appears under 42°). Tan 42°20′ = 0.9110.

Sin 64°40′ is found over sin θ (at bottom) and to the left of 40′ (which appears *over* 64°). Sin 64°40′ = 0.9038.

Using these tables, we can obtain values for the trigonometric functions to the nearst minute. Greater accuracy requires tables which give five or more figures for the values of the functions. Since the tables are given only to the nearest 10′, it is necessary to use linear *interpolation* for angles which cannot be found directly. Interpolation assumes that if a particular angle lies between two of those listed in the table, then the functions of that angle are at the same proportional distance between the functions listed. This assumption is not strictly correct, although it is a very good approximation.

Example E.   To find the sin 23°27′ we must interpolate between the sin 23°20′ and 23°30′. Since 27′ is $\frac{7}{10}$ of the way between 20′ and 30′, we shall assume that the sin 23°27′ is $\frac{7}{10}$ of the way between sin 23°20′ and the sin 23°30′. These values are 0.3961 and 0.3987. The *tabular difference* between them is 26, and $\frac{7}{10}$ of this is 18. Adding .0018 to 0.3961, we obtain sin 23°27′ = 0.3979. Another method of indicating the interpolation is shown in Fig. 3-10. From the figure we see that $\frac{7}{10} = x/26$, which means that $x = 18$ (to the nearest unit).

$$10 \left[7 \left[\begin{array}{l} \sin 23°20′ = 0.3961 \\ \sin 23°27′ = \ \cdots \\ \sin 23°30′ = 0.3987 \end{array} \right] x \right] 26$$

Figure 3-10

Example F.   To find the cos 76°14′, we first determine that we want the value $\frac{4}{10}$ of the way from cos 76°10′ to cos 76°20′. These values are 0.2391 and 0.2363, and their tabular difference is 28. Four-tenths of this is 11 (to the nearest unit). Thus, subtracting this (the value of cos 76°10′ is greater than cos 76°20′—the values of the cos θ get *smaller* as θ gets larger) from 0.2391, we get cos 76°14′ = 0.2380. Again we can indicate the interpolation, as in Fig. 3-11. From the figure we see that $\frac{4}{10} = x/28$, or $x = 11$.

$$10 \left[4 \left[\begin{array}{l} \cos 76°10′ = 0.2391 \\ \cos 76°14′ = \ \cdots \\ \cos 76°20′ = 0.2363 \end{array} \right] x \right] 28$$

Figure 3-11

Not only are we able to find values of the functions if we know the angle, but also we can find the angle if we know the function. This requires that we reverse the procedures mentioned above.

Example G.   Given that sin θ = 0.2616, find θ.

We look for 0.2616, or the nearest number to it, in the columns for sin θ. Since this number appears exactly, we conclude that θ = 15°10′.

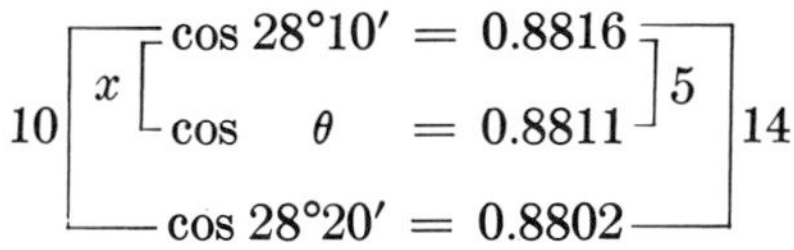

$$10 \begin{bmatrix} x \begin{bmatrix} \cos 28°10' = 0.8816 \\ \cos \quad \theta \quad = 0.8811 \end{bmatrix} 5 \\ \cos 28°20' = 0.8802 \end{bmatrix} 14$$

Figure 3-12

Example H.   Given that $\cos \theta = 0.8811$, find θ.

We find that this number lies between $\cos 28°10'$ and $\cos 28°20'$. These values are 0.8816 and 0.8802. The tabular difference between $\cos \theta$ and $\cos 28°10'$ is 5, and the tabular difference between the two values given in the table is 14. Thus $\cos \theta$ is assumed to be $\frac{5}{14}$ of the way from the first to the second. To the nearest tenth, this is $\frac{4}{10}$. Hence $\theta = 28°14'$ (to the nearest '). The solution of this type of problem can also be indicated by means of a figure such as Fig. 3-12, from which we see that $\frac{5}{14} = x/10$, or $x = 4$.

Exercises

In Exercises 1 through 4 use a protractor to draw the given angle. Measure off 10 units (centimeters are convenient) along the radius vector. Then measure the corresponding values of x and y. From these values determine the trigonometric functions of the angle.

1. 40°	2. 75°	3. 15°	4. 53°

In Exercises 5 through 24 find the value of each of the trigonometric functions from the table in the Appendix.

5. sin 19°	6. cos 43°	7. tan 67°	8. cot 76°
9. cos 22°20'	10. tan 34°50'	11. sin 56°30'	12. cot 80°10'
13. sec 13°40'	14. csc 52°20'	15. sin 63°15'	16. tan 28°56'
17. cos 48°44'	18. cot 7°8'	19. sin 17°52'	20. cos 88°39'
21. tan 44°1'	22. tan 64°26'	23. csc 12°14'	24. sec 71°47'

In Exercises 25 through 36 find θ for each of the given trigonometric functions.

25. $\sin \theta = 0.0958$	26. $\cos \theta = 0.1593$	27. $\tan \theta = 3.108$
28. $\sin \theta = 0.9520$	29. $\tan \theta = 0.6539$	30. $\cot \theta = 0.8070$
31. $\sec \theta = 1.289$	32. $\csc \theta = 1.168$	33. $\cos \theta = 0.7044$
34. $\sin \theta = 0.8605$	35. $\tan \theta = 5.284$	36. $\cot \theta = 0.0708$

In Exercises 37 through 40 solve the given problems.

37. When a projectile is fired into the air, its horizontal velocity v_x is related to the velocity v with which it is fired by the relation $v_x = v(\cos \theta)$, where θ is the angle between the horizontal and the direction in which it is fired. What is the horizontal velocity of a projectile fired with a velocity of 200 ft/sec at an angle of 36° with respect to the horizontal?

38. The coefficient of friction between an object moving down an inclined plane with constant speed and the plane equals the tangent of the angle that the plane makes with the horizontal. If the coefficient of friction between a metal block and a wooden plane is 0.150, at what angle (to the nearest degree) is the plane inclined?

39. The voltage at any instance in a coil of wire which is turning in a magnetic field is given by $E = E_{max} (\cos \alpha)$, where E_{max} is the maximum voltage and α is the angle the coil makes with the field. If the maximum voltage produced by a certain coil is 120 volts, what voltage is generated when the coil makes an angle of 55°35′ with the field?

40. When a light ray enters glass from the air it bends somewhat toward a line perpendicular to the surface. The *index of refraction* of the glass is defined as

$$n = \frac{\sin i}{\sin r},$$

where i is the angle between the perpendicular and the ray in the air and r is the angle between the perpendicular and the ray in the glass. A typical case for glass is $i = 59°$ and $r = 34°$. Find the index of refraction for this case.

3-4 The right triangle with applications

From geometry we know that a triangle, by definition, consists of three sides and has three angles. If one side and any other two of these six parts of the triangle are known, it is possible to determine the other three parts. One of the three known parts must be a side, for if we know only the three angles, we can conclude only that an entire set of similar triangles has those particular angles.

Example A. Assume that one side and two angles are known. Then we may determine the third angle by the fact that the sum of the angles of a triangle is always 180°. Of all the possible similar triangles having these three angles, we have the one with the particular side which is known. Only one triangle with these parts is possible.

To *solve* a triangle means that, when we are given three parts of a triangle (at least one a side), we are to find the other three parts. In this section we are going to demonstrate the method of solving a right triangle. Since one angle of the triangle will be 90°, it is necessary to know one side and one other part. Also, we know that the sum of the three angles of a triangle is 180°, and this in turn tells us that the sum of the other two angles, both acute, is 90°. Any two acute angles whose sum is 90° are said to be *complementary*.

For consistency, when we are labeling the parts of the right triangle we shall use the letters A and B to denote the acute angles, and C to denote the right angle. The letters a, b, and c will denote the sides opposite these angles, respectively. Thus, side c is the hypotenuse of the right triangle.

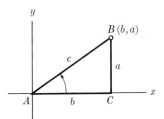

Figure 3-13

We shall find it convenient in solving right triangles to define the trigonometric functions of the acute angles in terms of the sides (see Fig. 3-13). Placing the vertex of angle A at the origin and the vertex of angle C on the positive x-axis, we obtain the following definitions.

$$\sin A = \frac{y}{r} = \frac{a}{c}, \qquad \cos A = \frac{x}{r} = \frac{b}{c}, \qquad \tan A = \frac{y}{x} = \frac{a}{b},$$

$$\cot A = \frac{x}{y} = \frac{b}{a}, \qquad \sec A = \frac{r}{x} = \frac{c}{b}, \qquad \csc A = \frac{r}{y} = \frac{c}{a}. \tag{3-2}$$

If we should place the vertex of angle B at the origin, instead of the vertex of angle A, we would obtain the following definitions for the functions of angle B.

$$\sin B = \frac{b}{c}, \qquad \cos B = \frac{a}{c}, \qquad \tan B = \frac{b}{a},$$

$$\cot B = \frac{a}{b}, \qquad \sec B = \frac{c}{a}, \qquad \csc B = \frac{c}{b}. \tag{3-3}$$

Inspecting these results, we may generalize our definitions of the trigonometric functions of acute angles of a right triangle to be as follows:

$$\sin \alpha = \frac{\text{opposite side}}{\text{hypotenuse}}, \quad \cos \alpha = \frac{\text{adjacent side}}{\text{hypotenuse}}, \quad \tan \alpha = \frac{\text{opposite side}}{\text{adjacent side}},$$

$$\cot \alpha = \frac{\text{adjacent side}}{\text{opposite side}}, \quad \sec \alpha = \frac{\text{hypotenuse}}{\text{adjacent side}}, \quad \csc \alpha = \frac{\text{hypotenuse}}{\text{opposite side}}. \tag{3-4}$$

Using the definitions in this form, we can solve right triangles without placing the angle in standard position. The angle need only be a part of any right triangle.

We note from the above discussion that $\sin A = \cos B$, $\tan A = \cot B$, and $\sec A = \csc B$. From this we conclude that *cofunctions of acute complementary angles are equal*. The sine function and *co*sine function are cofunctions, and so forth. From this we can see how the tables of trigonometric functions are constructed. Since $\sin A = \cos (90° - A)$, the number representing either of these need appear only once in the tables.

Example B.   Given $a = 4$, $b = 7$, and $c = \sqrt{65}$ ($C = 90°$), find $\sin A$, $\cos A$, and $\tan A$. (See Fig. 3-14.)

$$\sin A = \frac{\text{side opposite angle } A}{\text{hypotenuse}} = \frac{4}{\sqrt{65}} = 0.50,$$

$$\cos A = \frac{\text{side adjacent angle } A}{\text{hypotenuse}} = \frac{7}{\sqrt{65}} = 0.87,$$

$$\tan A = \frac{\text{side opposite angle } A}{\text{side adjacent angle } A} = \frac{4}{7} = 0.57.$$

Example C.   In Fig. 3-14, we have

$$\sin B = \frac{\text{side opposite angle } B}{\text{hypotenuse}} = \frac{7}{\sqrt{65}} = 0.87,$$

$$\cos B = \frac{\text{side adjacent angle } B}{\text{hypotenuse}} = \frac{4}{\sqrt{65}} = 0.50,$$

$$\tan B = \frac{\text{side opposite angle } B}{\text{side adjacent angle } B} = \frac{7}{4} = 1.75.$$

We also note that $\sin A = \cos B$ and $\cos A = \sin B$.

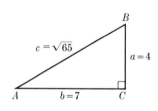

Figure 3-14

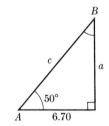

Figure 3-15

We are now ready to solve right triangles. We do this by expressing the un-known parts in terms of the known parts, as the following examples illustrate. (For consistency, all answers and numbers used are "rounded off" to three significant digits. This allows for slide-rule solutions, if the reader is familiar with its use at this time. Discussions of "rounding off," significant digits, and the slide rule are given in the appendices.)

Example D.   Given $A = 50°$ and $b = 6.70$, solve the right triangle of which these are parts (see Fig. 3-15).

Since $a/b = \tan A$, we have $a = b \tan A$. Thus

$$a = 6.70 \, (\tan 50°)$$
$$= 6.70 \, (1.19) = 7.97.$$

Since $A = 50°$, $B = 40°$. Since $b/c = \cos A$, we have

$$c = \frac{b}{\cos A} = \frac{6.70}{0.643} = 10.4.$$

We have found that $a = 7.97$, $c = 10.4$, and $B = 40°$.

Example E.   Assuming that A and a are known, express the unknown parts of the right triangle in terms of a and A (see Fig. 3-16).

Since $a/b = \tan A$, we have $b = a/\tan A$. Since A is known, $B = 90° - A$. Since $a/c = \sin A$, we have $c = a/\sin A$.

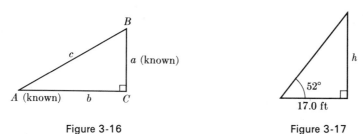

Figure 3-16   Figure 3-17

Many applied problems can be solved by setting up the solutions in terms of right triangles. These applications are essentially the same as solving right triangles, although it is usually one specific part of the triangle that we wish to determine. The following examples illustrate some of the basic applications of right triangles.

Example F.   A tree has a shadow 17.0 ft long. From the point on the ground at the end of the shadow, the *angle of elevation* (the angle between the horizontal and the line of sight, when the object is above the horizontal) of the top of the tree is measured to be 52°. How tall is the tree?

By drawing an appropriate figure, as shown in Fig. 3-17, we note the information given and that which is required. Here we have let h be the height of the tree. Thus we see that

$$\frac{h}{17.0} = \tan 52°,$$

or

$$h = 17.0(\tan 52°)$$
$$= 17.0(1.28)$$
$$= 21.8 \text{ ft.}$$

Example G.   From the roof of a building 46.0 ft high, the *angle of depression* (the angle between the horizontal and the line of sight, when the object is below horizontal) of an object in the street is 74°. What is the distance of the observer from the object?

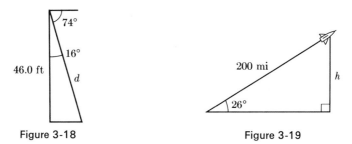

Figure 3-18   Figure 3-19

Again we draw an appropriate figure (Fig. 3-18). Here we let d represent the required distance. From the figure we see that

$$\frac{46.0}{d} = \cos 16°,$$

$$d = \frac{46.0}{\cos 16°} = \frac{46.0}{0.961}$$

$$= 47.9 \text{ ft.}$$

Example H.   A missile is launched at an angle of 26° with respect to the horizontal. If it travels in a straight line over level terrain for 2 minutes, and its average speed is 6000 mi/hr, what is its altitude at this time?

In Fig. 3-19 we have let h represent the altitude of the missile after 2 minutes (altitude is measured on a perpendicular). Also, we determine that the missile has flown 200 mi in a direct line from the launching site. This is found from the fact that it travels at 6000 mi/hr for $\frac{1}{30}$ hr (2 min) and from the fact that $(6000 \text{ mi/hr})(\frac{1}{30} \text{ hr}) = 200$ mi. Therefore

$$\frac{h}{200} = \sin 26°,$$

$$h = 200(\sin 26°) = 200(0.438)$$

$$= 87.6 \text{ mi.}$$

Exercises

In Exercises 1 and 2 verify by observation that only one triangle may contain the indicated parts.

1. Draw a 30° angle included between sides of 3 in. and 6 in.
2. Draw a side of 4 in. included between angles of 40° and 70°.

In Exercises 3 through 14 solve the right triangles which have the given parts. Refer to Fig. 3-20.

3. $a = 56.7, b = 44.0$ 4. $B = 12°, c = 18.0$
5. $B = 37°, a = 0.886$ 6. $A = 77°48', a = 6700$

7. $a = 9.98, c = 12.6$

8. $A = 32°, c = 56.8$

9. $B = 9°, b = 0.0762$

10. $A = 18°, c = 8.97$

11. $A = 42.5°, b = 8.40$

12. $b = 86.7, c = 167$

13. $B = 14.2°, c = 345$

14. $A = 83.6°, b = 0.504$

In Exercises 15 through 18 the parts listed refer to those in Fig. 3-20 and are assumed to be known. Express the other parts in terms of these known parts.

15. A, c

16. a, b

17. B, a

18. b, c

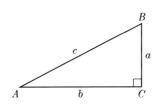

Figure 3-20

In Exercises 19 through 33 solve the given applied problems.

19. The angle of elevation of the sun is 48° at the time a television tower casts a shadow 346 ft long on level ground. Find the height of the tower.

20. A rope is stretched from the top of a vertical pole to a point 17.5 ft from the foot of the pole. The rope makes an angle of 20° with the pole. How tall is the pole?

21. The length of a kite string (assumed straight) is 560 ft. The angle of elevation of the kite is 64°. How high is the kite?

22. A 20-ft ladder leans against the side of a house. The angle between the ground and ladder is 70°. How far from the house is the foot of the ladder?

23. From the top of a cliff 200 ft high the angle of depression to a boat is 23°. How far is the boat from the foot of the cliff?

24. A roadway rises 120 ft for every 2200 ft along the road. Find the angle of inclination of the roadway.

25. A jet crusing at 590 mi/hr climbs at an angle of 15°. What is its gain in altitude in 2 min?

26. Ten rivets are equally spaced on the circumference of a circular plate. If the center-to-center distance between two rivets is 6.25 in, what is the radius of the circle?

27. A way of representing the impedance and resistance in an alternating-current circuit is equivalent to letting the impedance be the hypotenuse of a right triangle and the resistance be the side adjacent to the phase angle. If the resistance in a given circuit is 25.4 ohms and the phase angle is 24.5°, what is the impedance?

28. A flagpole is atop a building. From a point on the ground 700 ft from the building, the angles of elevation of the top and bottom of the flagpole are 33° and 31°, respectively. How tall is the flagpole?

29. If a light ray strikes a reflecting surface (Fig. 3-21), the angle of reflection r equals the angle of incidence i. If a light ray has an angle of incidence of 42°, what is the distance y from the plane of the surface of a point on the reflected ray, if the horizontal distance x from the point of incidence is 7.42 cm?

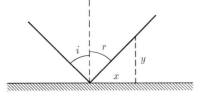

Figure 3-21

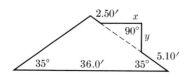

Figure 3-22

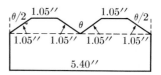

Figure 3-23

30. A man considers building a dormer on his house. What are the dimensions x and y of the dormer in his plans (see Fig. 3-22)?

31. A machine part is indicated in Fig. 3-23. What is the angle θ?

32. A surveyor wishes to determine the width of a river. He sights a point B on the opposite side of the river from point C. He then measures off 400 ft from C to A such that C is a right angle. He then determines that $\angle A = 56°$. How wide is the river?

33. An astronaut circling the moon at an altitude of 100 mi notes that the angle of depression of the horizon is 23.8°. What is the radius of the moon?

3-5 Miscellaneous Exercises

In Exercises 1 and 2 find the smallest positive angle and the smallest negative angle (numerically) coterminal with, but not equal to, the given angles.

1. 17°; −217°

2. 248°; −17°40″

In Exercises 3 and 4 change the given angles to equal angles expressed in decimal form.

3. 31°54′; 174°45′

4. 38°6′; 321°27′

In Exercises 5 and 6 change the given angles to equal angles expressed to the nearest minute.

5. 17.5°; 65.4°

6. 49.7°; 126.25°

In Exercises 7 through 10 determine the trigonometric functions of the angles whose terminal side passes through the given points.

7. (24, 7)   8. (5, 4)   9. (4, 4)   10. (1.2, 0.5)

In Exercises 11 through 14 using the given trigonometric functions, find the indicated trigonometric functions.

11. Given $\sin \theta = \frac{5}{13}$, find $\cos \theta$ and $\cot \theta$.

12. Given $\cos \theta = \frac{3}{8}$, find $\sin \theta$ and $\tan \theta$.

13. Given $\tan \theta = 2$, find $\cos \theta$ and $\csc \theta$.

14. Given $\cot \theta = 4$, find $\sin \theta$ and $\sec \theta$.

In Exercises 15 through 22 find the value of each of the given trigonometric functions.

15. sin 72°   16. cos 40°10′   17. tan 61°20′   18. csc 19°30′

19. tan 81°15′   20. cot 37°17′   21. cos 55°53′   22. sec 58°54′

In Exercises 23 through 30 find θ for each of the functions given.

23. $\sin \theta = 0.5324$ 24. $\tan \theta = 1.265$

25. $\cos \theta = 0.4669$ 26. $\sec \theta = 2.107$

27. $\cot \theta = 1.132$ 28. $\cos \theta = 0.7365$

29. $\sin \theta = 0.8666$ 30. $\csc \theta = 1.533$

In Exercises 31 through 36 solve the right triangles with the given parts.

31. $A = 17°,\ b = 6.50$ 32. $a = 81.4,\ b = 64.5$ 33. $B = 68°,\ a = 1076$

34. $A = 49°30',\ c = 0.806$ 35. $a = 1.06,\ c = 9.45$ 36. $B = 4°30',\ b = 0.0560$

In Exercises 37 through 50 solve the given applied problems.

37. An approximate equation found in the diffraction of light through a narrow opening is

$$\sin \theta = \frac{\lambda}{d},$$

where λ (the greek lambda) is the wavelength of the light and d is the width of the opening. If $\theta = 1°10'$ and $d = 0.00300$ cm, what is the wavelength of the light?

38. A formula used with a certain type of gear is

$$D = \frac{N \sec \theta}{4},$$

where D is the pitch diameter of the gear, N is the number of teeth on the gear, and θ is called the spiral angle. If $D = 6.75$ in. and $N = 20$ find θ (to the nearest $10'$).

39. A ship's captain, desiring to travel due south, discovers that, due to an improperly functioning instrument, he has gone 22.6 mi in a direction 4° east of south. How far from his course (to the east) is he?

40. A helicopter pilot notes that he is 150 ft above a certain rooftop. If the angle of depression to the rooftop is 18°, how far on a direct line from the rooftop is the helicopter?

41. An observer 3500 ft from the launch pad of a rocket measures the angle of inclination to the rocket soon after liftoff to be 54°. How high is the rocket, assuming it has moved vertically?

42. A hemispherical bowl is standing level. Its inside radius is 6.50 in. and it is filled with water to a depth of 3.10 in. Through what angle may it be tilted before the water will spill?

43. A railroad embankment has a level top 22.0 ft wide, equal sloping sides of 14.5 ft and a height of 7.2 ft. What is the width of the base of the embankment?

44. The horizontal distance between the extreme positions of a certain pendulum is 6.50 in. If the length of the pendulum is 18.0 in., through what angle does it swing?

45. The span of a roof is 32 ft. Its rise is 7.5 ft at the center of the span. What angle does the roof make with the horizontal?

46. If the impedance in a certain alternating-current circuit is 56.5 ohms and the resistance in the circuit is 17.0 ohms, what is the phase angle? (See Exercise 27 of Section 3-4.)

47. A bridge is 32 ft above the surrounding area. If the angle of elevation of the approach to the bridge is 5°, how long is the approach?

48. The windshield on an automobile is inclined 42.5° with respect to the horizontal. Assuming that the windshield is flat and rectangular, what is its area if it is 4.80 ft wide and the bottom is 1.50 ft in front of the top?

49. A person in a tall building observes an object drop from a window 20 ft away and directly opposite him. If the distance the object drops as a function of time is $s = 16t^2$, how far is the object from the observer (on a direct line) after 2 sec?

50. The distance from ground level to the underside of a cloud is called the *ceiling*. One observer 1000 ft from a searchlight aimed vertically notes that the angle of elevation of the spot of light on a cloud is 76°. What is the ceiling?

Systems of Linear Equations; Determinants

4

4-1 Linear equations

In Chapter 1 we introduced the topic of solving equations and showed some of the types of technical problems which could be solved. Many of the equations we encountered at that time were examples of a very important type of equation, the *linear equation*. In general, an equation is termed linear in a given set of variables if each term contains only one variable, to the first power, or is a constant.

Example A. $5x - t + 6 = 0$ is linear in x and t, but $5x^2 - t + 6 = 0$ is not, due to the presence of x^2.

The equation $4x + y = 8$ is linear in x and y, but $4xy + y = 8$ is not, due to the presence of xy.

The equation $x - 6y + z - 4w = 7$ is linear in x, y, z, and w, but $x - 6/y + z - 4w = 7$ is not, due to the presence of $6/y$ where y appears in the denominator.

An equation which can be written in the form

$$ax + b = 0 \tag{4-1}$$

is known as a *linear equation in one unknown*. We have already discussed the solution to this type of equation in Section 1-8. In general, the solution, or *root*, of the equation is $x = -b/a$. Also, it will be noted that finding the solution is equivalent to finding the zero of the *linear function* $ax + b$.

There are a great many applied problems which involve more than one unknown. When forces are analyzed in physics, equations with two unknowns (the forces) often result. In electricity, equations relating several unknown currents arise. Numerous kinds of stated problems from various technical areas involve equations with more than one unknown. The use of equations involving more than one unknown is well established in technical applications.

Example B.   A very basic law of direct current electricity, known as Kirchhoff's first law, may be stated as "The algebraic sum of the currents entering any junction in a circuit is zero." If three wires are joined at a junction, this law leads to the equation

$$i_1 + i_2 + i_3 = 0,$$

where i_1, i_2 and i_3 are the currents in each of the wires.

When determining two forces F_1 and F_2 acting on a beam, we might encounter an equation such as

$$2F_1 + 4F_2 = 200.$$

An equation which can be written in the form

$$ax + by = c \tag{4-2}$$

is known as a *linear equation in two unknowns*. In Chapter 2, when we were discussing functions we considered many functions of this type. We found that for each value of x there is a corresponding value of y. Each of these pairs of numbers is a *solution* to the equation, although we did not call it that at the time. A solution is any set of numbers, one for each variable, which satisfies the equation. When we represent the solutions in the form of a graph, we see that the graph of any linear equation in two unknowns is a straight line. Also, graphs of linear equations in one unknown, those for which $a = 0$ or $b = 0$, are also straight lines. Thus we see the significance of the name "linear."

Example C.   The equation $4x + 8 = 0$ is a linear equation in one unknown, x. We find its solution by subtracting 8 from both sides and then dividing both sides by 4. This results in the root $x = -2$. Solving this equation is equivalent to finding the zero of the function $4x + 8$.

Example D.   The equation $2x - y - 6 = 0$ is a linear equation in two unknowns, x and y. To sketch the graph of this equation, we write it in the more convenient form $y = 2x - 6$. The coordinates of each point on the graph, which is a straight line, are solutions of this equation. For example, the point $(1, -4)$ is a point on the line. This means that $x = 1$, $y = -4$ is a solution of the equation. In the same way, $x = 0$, $y = -6$ is a solution (see Fig. 4-1).

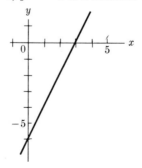

Figure 4-1

Two linear equations, each containing the same two unknowns,

$$a_1x + b_1y = c_1, \qquad a_2x + b_2y = c_2, \qquad (4\text{-}3)$$

are said to form a *system of simultaneous linear equations*. A *solution of the system* is any pair of values (x, y) which satisfies both equations. Methods of finding the solutions to such systems are the principal concern of this chapter.

Example E.   The two linear equations

$$2x - y = 5,$$
$$3x + 2y = 4,$$

form a system of simultaneous linear equations. The solution of this system is $x = 2$, $y = -1$. These values satisfy both equations, since $2(2) - (-1) = 4 + 1 = 5$ and $3(2) + 2(-1) = 6 - 2 = 4$. This is the only pair of values which satisfies *both* equations. Methods for finding such solutions are taken up in the following sections.

Exercises

In Exercises 1 through 4 determine whether or not the given pairs of values are solutions of the given linear equations in two unknowns.

1. $2x + 3y = 9$; $(3, 1)$, $(5, \frac{1}{3})$

2. $5x + 2y = 1$; $(2, -4)$, $(1, -2)$

3. $-3x + 5y = 13$; $(-1, 2)$, $(4, 5)$

4. $x - 4y = 10$; $(2, -2)$, $(2, 2)$

In Exercises 5 through 8, for each given value of x, determine the value of y which gives a solution to the given linear equations in two unknowns.

5. $5x - y = 6$; $x = 1$, $x = -2$

6. $2x + 7y = 8$; $x = -3$, $x = 2$

7. $x - 5y = 12$; $x = 3$, $x = -4$

8. $3x - 2y = 9$; $x = \frac{2}{3}$, $x = -3$

In Exercises 9 through 14 determine whether or not the given pair of values is a solution of the given system of simultaneous linear equations.

9. $x - y = 5$ $x = 4, y = -1$
   $2x + y = 7$

10. $2x + y = 8$ $x = -1, y = 10$
    $3x - y = -13$

11. $3x - 4y = -10$ $x = -2, y = 1$
    $x + 5y = -7$

12. $-3x + y = 1$ $x = \frac{1}{3}, y = 2$
    $6x - 3y = -4$

13. $2x - 5y = 0$ $x = \frac{1}{2}, y = -\frac{1}{5}$
    $4x + 10y = 4$

14. $3x - 4y = -1$ $x = 1, y = -1$
    $6x - y = 5$

In Exercises 15 through 17 answer the given questions.

15. If a board 84 in. long is cut into two pieces such that one piece is 6 in. longer than the other, the lengths x and y of the two pieces are found by solving the system of equations

$$x + y = 84, \quad x - y = 6.$$

Are the resulting lengths 45 in. and 39 in.?

16. If two forces F_1 and F_2 support a 98 lb weight, the forces can be found by solving the system of equations $0.7F_1 - 0.6F_2 = 0$, $0.7F_1 + 0.8F_2 = 98$. Are the forces 60 lb and 70 lb?

17. Under certain conditions two electric currents i_1 and i_2 can be found by solving the system of equations $3i_1 + 4i_2 = 3$, $3i_1 - 5i_2 = -6$. Are the currents $-\frac{1}{3}$ amp and 1 amp?

4-2 Solving systems of two linear equations in two unknowns graphically

We shall now take up the problem of solving for the unknowns when we have a system of two simultaneous linear equations in two unknowns. In this section we shall show how the solution may be found graphically. The sections which follow will discuss other basic methods of solution.

Since a solution of a system of simultaneous linear equations in two unknowns is any pair of values (x, y) which satisfies both equations, graphically, the solution would be the coordinates of the point of intersection of the two lines. This must be the case, for the coordinates of this point constitute the only pair of values to satisfy *both* equations. (In some special cases there may be no solution, in others there may be many solutions. See Examples D and E.)

Therefore, when we solve two simultaneous linear equations in two unknowns graphically, we must plot the graph of each line and determine the point of intersection. This may, of course, lead to approximate results if the lines cross at values between those chosen to determine the graph.

We may use the knowledge that each equation represents a straight line to advantage. By finding two points on the line, we can draw the line. Two points which are easily determined are those where the curve crosses the y-axis and the x-axis. These points are known as the *intercepts* of the line. These points are easily found because in each case one of the coordinates is zero. By setting $x = 0$ and $y = 0$, in turn, and determining the corresponding value of the other unknown, we obtain the coordinates of the intercepts. A third point should be found as a check. This method is sufficient unless the line passes through the origin. Then both intercepts are at the origin and one more point must be determined. Example A illustrates how a line is plotted by finding its intercepts.

Example A. Plot the graph of $2x - 3y = 6$ by finding its intercepts and one check point (see Fig. 4-2).

First let $x = 0$. This gives $-3y = 6$, or $y = -2$. Thus the point $(0, -2)$ is on the graph. Next we let $y = 0$, and this gives $2x = 6$, or $x = 3$. Thus the point $(3, 0)$ is on the graph. The point $(0, -2)$ is the y-intercept, and $(3, 0)$ is the x-intercept. These two points are sufficient to plot the line, but we should find another point as a check. Choosing $x = 1$, we find $y = -\frac{4}{3}$. Thus the point $(1, -\frac{4}{3})$ should be on the line. From Fig. 4-2 we see that it is on the line.

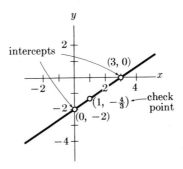

Figure 4-2

Now that we have discussed the meaning of a graphical solution of a system of simultaneous equations and the method of plotting a line, we are in a position to find graphical solutions of systems of linear equations. The following examples illustrate the method.

Example B.   Solve the system of equations

$$2x + 5y = 10,$$
$$3x - y = 6.$$

We find that the intercepts of the first line are the points $(5, 0)$ and $(0, 2)$. A third point is $(-5, 4)$. The intercepts of the second line are $(2, 0)$ and $(0, -6)$. A third point is $(1, -3)$. Plotting these points and drawing the proper straight lines, we see that the lines cross at about $(2.3, 1.1)$. [The actual values are $(\frac{40}{17}, \frac{18}{17})$.] The solution of the system of equations is approximately $x = 2.3$, $y = 1.1$ (see Fig. 4-3).

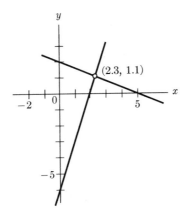

Figure 4-3

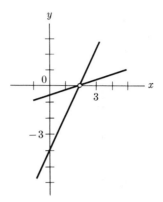

Figure 4-4

Example C.   Solve the system of equations

$$x - 4y = 2,$$
$$-2x + y = -4.$$

The intercepts and a third point for the first line are $(2, 0)$, $(0, -0.5)$ and $(6, 1)$. For the second line they are $(2, 0)$, $(0, -4)$ and $(1, -2)$. Since they have one point in common, the point $(2, 0)$, we conclude that the exact solution to the system is $x = 2$, $y = 0$ (see Fig. 4-4).

Example D.   Solve the system of equations

$$x - 2y = 6,$$
$$3x - 6y = 6.$$

The intercepts and a third point for the first line are $(6, 0)$, $(0, -3)$ and $(2, -2)$. For the second line they are $(2, 0)$, $(0, -1)$ and $(4, 1)$. The graphs of these two equations do not intersect (see Fig. 4-5). Therefore there are no solutions. Such a system is called *inconsistent*.

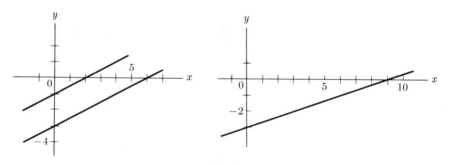

Figure 4-5   Figure 4-6

Example E. Solve the system of equations

$$x - 3y = 9,$$
$$-2x + 6y = -18.$$

The intercepts and a third point for the first line are $(9, 0)$, $(0, -3)$ and $(3, -2)$. In determining the intercepts for the second line, we find that they are $(9, 0)$ and $(0, -3)$, which are also the intercepts of the first line (see Fig. 4-6). As a check we note that $(3, -2)$ also satisfies the equation of the second line. This means the two lines are really the same line, and the coordinates of any point on this common line constitute a solution of the system. Such a system is called *dependent*.

Exercises

In the following exercises solve each system of equations graphically. Estimate the answer to the nearest tenth of a unit if necessary.

1. $x + y = 4$
   $x - y = 2$

2. $x - 2y = 2$
   $x + y = 8$

3. $2x - y = 6$
   $x + 3y = 3$

4. $-x + 2y = -8$
   $2x - y = -2$

5. $3x + 2y = 6$
   $x - 3y = 3$

6. $4x - 3y = -8$
   $6x + y = 6$

7. $2x - 5y = 10$
   $3x + 4y = -12$

8. $-5x + 3y = 15$
   $2x + 7y = 14$

9. $x - 5y = 10$
   $2x - 10y = 20$

10. $4x - y = 6$
    $2x - y = -4$

11. $y = -x + 3$
    $4x = 6 - 2y$

12. $x - 6 = 6y$
    $y = 3 - 3x$

13. $x - 4y = 6$
    $-x + 2y = 4$

14. $x + y = 3$
    $3x - 2y = 14$

15. $-2x + 2y = 7$
    $4x - 2y = 1$

16. $2x - 3y = -5$
    $3x + 2y = 12$

17. $x - 4y = 2$
    $-2x + 3y = 3$

18. $x - 2y = 4$
    $3x + 2y = 7$

19. $8x - 7y = 3$
    $7y + x = 7$

20. $5x - 2y = 7$
    $3x + 4y = 8$

21. $3x = 8y + 12$
    $-6x + 16y = 6$

22. $18x - 3y = 7$
    $2y = 1 + 12x$

23. $y = 3x$
    $x - 2y = 6$

24. $4x - y = 3$
    $2x + 3y = 0$

25. The perimeter of a rectangular area is 24 mi, and the length is 6 mi longer than the width. The dimensions l and w can be found by solving the equations

$$2l + 2w = 24, \quad l - w = 6.$$

(Notice that the first equation represents the perimeter of this rectangle and the second equation represents the relationship of the length to the width.)

26. To assemble a particular piece of machinery, 18 bolts are used. There are two kinds of bolts, and 4 more of one kind are used than the other. The numbers of each kind, a and b, can be found by solving the equations

$$a + b = 18, \quad a - b = 4.$$

27. In electricity, applying Ohm's law to a particular circuit gives the equations needed to find a specified voltage E and current I (in amps) as

$$E - 4I = 0, \quad E + 6I = 9.$$

28. A computer requires 12 seconds to do two series of calculations. The first series of calculations requires twice as much time as the second series. The times t_1 and t_2 can be found by solving the equations

$$t_1 + t_2 = 12, \quad t_1 = 2t_2.$$

4-3 Solving systems of two linear equations in two unknowns algebraically

We have just seen how a system of two linear equations can be solved graphically. This technique is good for obtaining a "picture" of the solution. Finding the solution of systems of equations by graphical methods has one difficulty: the results are usually approximate. If exact solutions are required, we must turn to other methods. In this section we shall present two algebraic methods of solution.

The first method involves elimination by *substitution*. To follow this method, we first solve one of the equations for one of the unknowns. This solution is then substituted into the other equation, resulting in one linear equation in one unknown. This equation can then be solved for the unknown it contains. By substituting this value into one of the original equations, we can find the corresponding value of the other unknown. The following two examples illustrate the method.

Example A.   Use the method of elimination by substitution to solve the system of equations

$$x - 3y = 6,$$
$$2x + 3y = 3.$$

The first step is to solve one of the equations for one of the unknowns. The choice of which equation and which unknown depends on ease of manipulation. In this system, it is somewhat easier to solve the first equation for x. Therefore, performing this operation we have

$$x = 3y + 6.$$

We then substitute this expression into the second equation in place of x, giving

$$2(3y + 6) + 3y = 3.$$

Solving this equation for y we obtain

$$6y + 12 + 3y = 3,$$
$$9y = -9,$$
$$y = -1.$$

We now put the value $y = -1$ into the first of the original equations. Since we have already solved this equation for x in terms of y, we obtain

$$x = 3(-1) + 6 = 3.$$

Therefore, the solution of the system is $x = 3$, $y = -1$.

Example B.   Use the method of elimination by substitution to solve the system of equations

$$-5x + 2y = -4$$
$$10x + 6y = \quad 3.$$

It makes little difference which equation or which unknown is chosen. Therefore, choosing to solve the first equation for y, we obtain

$$2y = 5x - 4,$$
$$y = \frac{5x - 4}{2}.$$

Substituting this expression into the second equation, we have

$$10x + 6 \left(\frac{5x - 4}{2} \right) = 3.$$

We now proceed to solve this equation for x.

$$10x + 3(5x - 4) = 3$$
$$10x + 15x - 12 = 3$$
$$25x = 15$$
$$x = \tfrac{3}{5}$$

Substituting this value into the expression for y, we obtain

$$y = \frac{5(3/5) - 4}{2} = \frac{3 - 4}{2} = -\frac{1}{2}.$$

Therefore, the solution of this system is $x = \tfrac{3}{5}$, $y = -\tfrac{1}{2}$.

The method of elimination by substitution is useful if one equation can easily be solved for one of the unknowns. However, the numerical coefficients often make this method somewhat cumbersome. So we use another method, that of elimination by *addition or subtraction*. To use this method we multiply each equation by a number chosen so that the coefficients for one of the unknowns will be numerically the same in both equations. If these numerically equal coefficients are opposite in sign, we *add* the two equations. If the numerically equal coefficients have the same signs, we subtract one equation from the other. That is, we subtract the left side of one equation from the left side of the other equation, and also do the same to the right sides. After adding or subtracting, we have a simple linear equation in one unknown, which we then solve for the unknown. We substitute this value into one of the original equations to obtain the value of the other unknown.

Example C. Use the method of elimination by addition or subtraction to solve the system of equations

$$x - 3y = 6,$$
$$2x + 3y = 3,$$

We look at the coefficients to determine the best way to eliminate one of the unknowns. In this case, since the coefficients of the y-terms are numerically the same and are opposite in sign, we may immediately add the two equations to eliminate y. Adding the left sides together and the right sides together, we obtain

$$x + 2x - 3y + 3y = 6 + 3,$$
$$3x = 9,$$
$$x = 3.$$

Substituting this value into the first equation, we obtain

$$3 - 3y = 6,$$
$$-3y = 3,$$
$$y = -1.$$

The solution $x = 3$, $y = -1$ agrees with the results obtained for the same problem illustrated in Example A of this section.

Example D. Use the method of elimination by addition or subtraction to solve the system of equations

$$3x - 2y = 4,$$
$$x + 3y = 2.$$

Probably the most convenient method is to multiply the second equation by 3. Then subtract the second equation from the first and solve for y. Substitute this value of y into the second equation and solve for x.

$$
\begin{aligned}
3x - 2y &= 4 \\
\underline{3x + 9y} &= \underline{6} \\
-11y &= -2 \\
y &= \tfrac{2}{11} \\
x + 3(\tfrac{2}{11}) &= 2 \\
11x + 6 &= 22 \\
x &= \tfrac{16}{11}
\end{aligned}
$$

We arrive at the solution $x = \tfrac{16}{11}$, $y = \tfrac{2}{11}$.

Example E. The system of Example D can also be solved by multiplying the first equation by 3 and the second by 2.

$$9x - 6y = 12$$
$$\underline{2x + 6y = 4}$$
$$11x = 16 \qquad \text{Adding the equations}$$
$$x = \tfrac{16}{11}$$
$$3(\tfrac{16}{11}) - 2y = 4 \qquad \text{Substituting into the first of original equations}$$
$$48 - 22y = 44 \qquad \text{Multiplying each term by 11}$$
$$-22y = -4$$
$$y = \tfrac{2}{11}$$

Therefore, the solution is $x = \tfrac{16}{11}$, $y = \tfrac{2}{11}$, as we obtained in Example D.

Example F.   Use the method of elimination by addition or subtraction to solve the system of equations

$$4x - 2y = 3,$$
$$2x - y = 2.$$

When we multiply the second equation by 2 and subtract, we obtain

$$4x - 2y = 3,$$
$$\underline{4x - 2y = 4,}$$
$$0 = -1.$$

Since we know that 0 does not equal -1, we must conclude that there is no solution. When we obtain a result of $0 = a$ $(a \neq 0)$, the system of equations is inconsistent. If we obtain the result $0 = 0$, the system is dependent.

After solving systems of equations by these methods, it is always a good policy to check the results by substituting the values of the two unknowns into the other original equation to see that the values satisfy the equation. Remember, we are finding the one pair of values which satisfies both equations.

Linear equations in two unknowns are often useful in solving stated problems. In such problems we must read the statement carefully in order to identify the unknowns and the method of setting up the proper equations. Exercises 25, 26, and 28 of Section 4-2 give statements and the resulting equations, which the reader should be able to derive. The following example gives a complete illustration of the method.

Example G.   By weight, one alloy is 70% copper and 30% zinc. Another alloy is 40% copper and 60% zinc. How many grams of each of these would be required to make 300 gm of an alloy which is 60% copper and 40% zinc?

Let A = required number of grams of first alloy, and B = required number of grams of second alloy. We know that the total weight of the final alloy is 300 gm, which leads us to the equation $A + B = 300$. We also know that the final alloy will contain 180 gm of copper (60% of 300). The weight of copper from the first alloy is $0.70A$ and that from the second is $0.40B$. This leads to the equation $0.70A + 0.40B = 180$. These two equations can now be solved simultaneously.

$$A + B = 300$$
$$0.70A + 0.40B = 180$$

$$
\begin{array}{ll}
4A + 4B = 1200 & \text{Multiplying the first equation by 4} \\
\underline{7A + 4B = 1800} & \text{Multiplying the second equation by 10} \\
3A = 600 & \text{Subtracting the first equation from the second} \\
A = 200 \text{ gm} & \\
B = 100 \text{ gm} & \text{By substituting into the first equation}
\end{array}
$$

Substitution shows that this solution checks with the given information.

Exercises

In Exercises 1 through 12 solve the given systems of equations by the method of elimination by substitution.

1. $x = y + 3$
   $x - 2y = 5$

2. $x = 2y + 1$
   $2x - 3y = 4$

3. $y = x - 4$
   $x + y = 10$

4. $y = 2x + 10$
   $2x + y = -2$

5. $x + y = -5$
   $2x - y = 2$

6. $3x + y = 1$
   $3x - 2y = 16$

7. $2x + 3y = 7$
   $6x - y = 1$

8. $2x + 2y = 1$
   $4x - 2y = 17$

9. $3x + 2y = 7$
   $-9x + 2y = 11$

10. $3x + 3y = -1$
    $-5x - 6y = 1$

11. $4x - 3y = 6$
    $2x + 4y = -5$

12. $5x + 4y = -7$
    $3x - 5y = -6$

In Exercises 13 through 24 solve the given systems of equations by the method of elimination by addition or subtraction.

13. $x + 2y = 5$
    $x - 2y = 1$

14. $x + 3y = 7$
    $2x + 3y = 5$

15. $2x - 3y = 4$
    $2x + y = -4$

16. $x - 4y = 17$
    $3x + 4y = 3$

17. $2x + 3y = 8$
    $x - 2y = -3$

18. $3x - y = 3$
    $4x - 3y = 14$

19. $x + 2y = 7$
    $2x + 4y = 9$

20. $3x - y = 5$
    $-9x + 3y = -15$

21. $2x - 3y = 4$
    $3x - 2y = -2$

22. $3x + 4y = -5$
    $5x - 3y = 2$

23. $3x - 7y = 4$
    $2x + 5y = 7$

24. $5x + 2y = -4$
    $3x - 5y = 6$

In Exercises 25 through 30 solve the given systems of equations by either method of this section.

25. $2x - y = 5$
    $6x + 2y = -5$

26. $3x + 2y = 4$
    $6x - 6y = 13$

27. $6x + 3y = -4$
    $9x + 5y = -6$

28. $5x - 6y = 1$
    $3x - 4y = 7$

29. $3x - 6y = 15$
    $4x - 8y = 20$

30. $2x + 6y = -3$
    $-6x - 18y = 5$

In Exercises 31 and 32 solve the given systems of equations by an appropriate algebraic method.

31. An electrical experiment results in the following equations for currents (in amps) i_1 and i_2 of a certain circuit:

$$i_1 = 3i_2, \quad 4i_1 - 2i_2 = 5.$$

Find i_1 and i_2.

32. In finding moments M_1 and M_2 (in foot-pounds) of certain forces acting on a given beam, the following equations are used:

$$10M_1 + 3M_2 = -140, \quad 4M_1 + 14M_2 = -564.$$

Find M_1 and M_2.

In Exercises 33 through 38 set up appropriate systems of two linear equations in two unknowns, and solve the systems algebraically.

33. A piece of wire is 18 ft long. Where must it be cut for one piece to be 3 ft longer than the other piece?

34. The voltage across an electric resistor equals the current times the resistance. The sum of two resistances is 16 ohms. When a current of 4 amp passes through the smaller resistance and 3 amp through the larger resistance, the sum of the voltages is 52 volts. What is the value of each resistance?

35. One electronic data-processing card sorter can sort a cards per minute, and a second card sorter can sort b cards per minute. If the first sorts for 3 minutes and the second for 2 minutes, 12,200 cards can be sorted. If the times are reversed, 11,300 cards can be sorted. Find the sorting rates a and b.

36. An airplane travels 1860 mi in 2 hr with the wind and then returns in 2.5 hr traveling against the wind. Find the speed of the airplane with respect to the air and the velocity of the wind.

37. A chemist has a 20% solution and an 8% solution of sulfuric acid. How many cubic centimeters of each solution should he mix in order to obtain 180 cm^3 of a 15% solution?

38. Analyze the following statement from a student's laboratory report. "The sum of the currents was 10 amps, and twice the first current was 3 amps less twice the second current."

4-4 Solving systems of two linear equations in two unknowns by determinants

Consider two linear equations in two unknowns,

$$a_1x + b_1y = c_1,$$
$$a_2x + b_2y = c_2. \tag{4-3}$$

If we multiply the first of these equations by b_2 and the second by b_1, we obtain

$$a_1b_2x + b_1b_2y = c_1b_2,$$
$$a_2b_1x + b_2b_1y = c_2b_1. \tag{4-4}$$

If we now subtract the second equation of (4-4) from the first, we obtain

$$a_1b_2x - a_2b_1x = c_1b_2 - c_2b_1,$$

which by use of the distributive law may be written as

$$(a_1b_2 - a_2b_1)x = c_1b_2 - c_2b_1. \tag{4-5}$$

Solving Eq. (4-5) for x, we obtain

$$x = \frac{c_1b_2 - c_2b_1}{a_1b_2 - a_2b_1}. \tag{4-6}$$

In the same manner, we may show that

$$y = \frac{a_1c_2 - a_2c_1}{a_1b_2 - a_2b_1}. \tag{4-7}$$

If the denominator $a_1b_2 - a_2b_1 = 0$, there is no solution for Eqs. (4-6) and (4-7), since division by zero is not defined.

The expression $a_1b_2 - a_2b_1$, which appears in each of the denominators of Eqs. (4-6) and (4-7), is an example of a special kind of expression called a *determinant of the second order*. The determinant $a_1b_2 - a_2b_1$ is denoted by the symbol

$$\begin{vmatrix} a_1 & b_1 \\ a_2 & b_2 \end{vmatrix}.$$

Thus, by definition, a determinant of the second order is given by

$$\begin{vmatrix} a_1 & b_1 \\ a_2 & b_2 \end{vmatrix} = a_1b_2 - a_2b_1. \tag{4-8}$$

The numbers a_1 and b_1 are called the *elements* of the first *row* of the determinant. The numbers a_1 and a_2 are the elements of the first *column* of the determinant. In the same manner, the numbers a_2 and b_2 are the elements of the second row, and the numbers b_1 and b_2 are the elements of the second column. The numbers a_1 and b_2 are the elements of the *principal diagonal*, and the numbers a_2 and b_1 are the elements of the *secondary diagonal*. Thus one way of stating the definition indicated in Eq. (4-8) is that *the value of a determinant of the second order is found by taking the product of the elements of the principal diagonal and subtracting the product of the elements of the secondary diagonal.*

A diagram which is often helpful for remembering the expansion of a second-order determinant is shown in Fig. 4-7. The examples on the following page illustrate how we carry out the evaluation of determinants.

Figure 4-7

Example A. $\begin{vmatrix} 1 & 4 \\ 3 & 2 \end{vmatrix} = 1(2) - 3(4) = 2 - 12 = -10$

Example B. $\begin{vmatrix} -5 & 8 \\ 3 & 7 \end{vmatrix} = (-5)(7) - 3(8) = -35 - 24 = -59$

Example C. $\begin{vmatrix} 4 & 6 \\ -3 & 17 \end{vmatrix} = 4(17) - (-3)(6) = 68 + 18 = 86$

We note that the numerators of Eqs. (4-6) and (4-7) may also be written as determinants. The numerators of Eqs. (4-6) and (4-7) are

$$\begin{vmatrix} c_1 & b_1 \\ c_2 & b_2 \end{vmatrix} \quad \text{and} \quad \begin{vmatrix} a_1 & c_1 \\ a_2 & c_2 \end{vmatrix}. \tag{4-9}$$

Therefore the solutions for x and y of the system of equations (4-3) may be written directly in terms of determinants, without any algebraic operations, as

$$x = \frac{\begin{vmatrix} c_1 & b_1 \\ c_2 & b_2 \end{vmatrix}}{\begin{vmatrix} a_1 & b_1 \\ a_2 & b_2 \end{vmatrix}} \quad \text{and} \quad y = \frac{\begin{vmatrix} a_1 & c_1 \\ a_2 & c_2 \end{vmatrix}}{\begin{vmatrix} a_1 & b_1 \\ a_2 & b_2 \end{vmatrix}}. \tag{4-10}$$

For this reason determinants provide a very quick and easy method of solution of systems of equations. Here again the denominator of each of Eqs. (4-10) is the same. *The determinant of the denominator is made up of the coefficients of x and y.* Also, we can see that *the determinant of the numerator of the solution for x may be obtained by replacing the column of a's by the column of c's. The numerator of the solution for y may be obtained from the determinant of the denominator by replacing the column of b's by the column of c's.* This result is often referred to as *Cramer's rule*.

The following examples illustrate the method of solving systems of equations by determinants.

Example D.   Solve the following system of equations by determinants:

$$2x + y = 1,$$
$$5x - 2y = -11.$$

First we set up the determinant for the denominator. This consists of the four coefficients in the system written as shown. Therefore, the determinant of the denominator is

$$\begin{vmatrix} 2 & 1 \\ 5 & -2 \end{vmatrix}.$$

For finding x, the determinant in the numerator is obtained from this determinant by replacing the first column by the constants which appear on the right sides of the equations. Thus the numerator for the solution for x is

$$\begin{vmatrix} 1 & 1 \\ -11 & -2 \end{vmatrix}.$$

For finding y, the determinant in the numerator is obtained from the determinant of the denominator by replacing the second column by the constants which appear on the right sides of the equations. Thus the determinant for the numerator for finding y is

$$\begin{vmatrix} 2 & 1 \\ 5 & -11 \end{vmatrix}.$$

Now we set up the solutions for x and y using the determinants above.

$$x = \frac{\begin{vmatrix} 1 & 1 \\ -11 & -2 \end{vmatrix}}{\begin{vmatrix} 2 & 1 \\ 5 & -2 \end{vmatrix}} = \frac{1(-2) - (1)(-11)}{2(-2) - (1)(5)} = \frac{-2 + 11}{-4 - 5} = \frac{9}{-9} = -1$$

$$y = \frac{\begin{vmatrix} 2 & 1 \\ 5 & -11 \end{vmatrix}}{\begin{vmatrix} 2 & 1 \\ 5 & -2 \end{vmatrix}} = \frac{2(-11) - (5)(1)}{-9} = \frac{-22 - 5}{-9} = 3$$

Therefore, the solution to the system of equations is $x = -1$, $y = 3$.

Since the determinant in the denominators is the same, it needs to be evaluated only once. This means that three determinants are to be evaluated in order to solve the system.

Example E.   Solve the following system of equations by determinants:

$$x - y = 4,$$
$$2x + y = 11.$$

$$x = \frac{\begin{vmatrix} 4 & -1 \\ 11 & 1 \end{vmatrix}}{\begin{vmatrix} 1 & -1 \\ 2 & 1 \end{vmatrix}} = \frac{4 - (-11)}{1 - (-2)} = 5 \qquad y = \frac{\begin{vmatrix} 1 & 4 \\ 2 & 11 \end{vmatrix}}{\begin{vmatrix} 1 & -1 \\ 2 & 1 \end{vmatrix}} = \frac{11 - 8}{3} = 1$$

Therefore, the solution is $x = 5$, $y = 1$.

Example F. Solve the following system of equations by determinants:

$$5x + 7y = 4,$$
$$3x - 6y = 5.$$

$$x = \frac{\begin{vmatrix} 4 & 7 \\ 5 & -6 \end{vmatrix}}{\begin{vmatrix} 5 & 7 \\ 3 & -6 \end{vmatrix}} = \frac{-24 - 35}{-30 - 21} = \frac{59}{51} \qquad y = \frac{\begin{vmatrix} 5 & 4 \\ 3 & 5 \end{vmatrix}}{\begin{vmatrix} 5 & 7 \\ 3 & -6 \end{vmatrix}} = \frac{25 - 12}{-51} = -\frac{13}{51}$$

Therefore, the solution is $x = \frac{59}{51}$, $y = -\frac{13}{51}$.

Example G. Two investments totaling \$18,000 yield an annual income of \$700. If the first investment has an interest rate of 5.5% and the second a rate of 3.0%, what is the value of each of the investments?

Let x = the value of the first investment, and y = the value of the second investment. We know that the total of the two investments is \$18,000. This leads to the equation $x + y = 18,000$. The first investment yields $0.055x$ dollars annually, and the second yields $0.03y$ dollars annually. This leads to the equation $0.055x + 0.03y = 700$. These two equations are then solved simultaneously.

$$x + y = 18,000$$
$$0.055x + 0.030y = 700$$

$$x = \frac{\begin{vmatrix} 18,000 & 1 \\ 700 & 0.03 \end{vmatrix}}{\begin{vmatrix} 1 & 1 \\ 0.055 & 0.03 \end{vmatrix}} = \frac{540 - 700}{0.03 - 0.055} = \frac{160}{0.025} = 6400$$

The value of y can be found most easily by substituting this value of x into the first equation.

$$y = 18,000 - x = 18,000 - 6400 = 11,600$$

Therefore, the values invested are \$6400 and \$11,600, respectively.

Some other points should be made here. The equations must be in the form of Eqs. (4-3) before the determinants are set up. This is because the equations for the solutions in terms of determinants are based on that form of writing the system. Also, if either of the unknowns is missing from either equation, its coefficient is taken as zero, and zero is put in the appropriate position in the determinant. Finally, if the determinant of the denominator is zero, and that of the numerator is not zero, the system is inconsistent. If determinants of both numerator and denominator are zero, the system is dependent.

Exercises

In Exercises 1 through 12 evaluate the given determinants.

1. $\begin{vmatrix} 2 & 4 \\ 3 & 1 \end{vmatrix}$

2. $\begin{vmatrix} -1 & 3 \\ 2 & 6 \end{vmatrix}$

3. $\begin{vmatrix} 3 & -5 \\ 7 & -2 \end{vmatrix}$

4. $\begin{vmatrix} -4 & 7 \\ 1 & -3 \end{vmatrix}$

5. $\begin{vmatrix} 8 & -10 \\ 0 & 4 \end{vmatrix}$

6. $\begin{vmatrix} -4 & -3 \\ 9 & -2 \end{vmatrix}$

7. $\begin{vmatrix} -2 & 11 \\ -7 & -8 \end{vmatrix}$

8. $\begin{vmatrix} -6 & 12 \\ -15 & 3 \end{vmatrix}$

9. $\begin{vmatrix} 7 & -13 \\ 1 & 10 \end{vmatrix}$

10. $\begin{vmatrix} 20 & -5 \\ 28 & 9 \end{vmatrix}$

11. $\begin{vmatrix} 16 & -8 \\ 42 & -15 \end{vmatrix}$

12. $\begin{vmatrix} 43 & -7 \\ -81 & 16 \end{vmatrix}$

For Exercises 13 through 30 use problems of Exercises 13 through 30 of Section 4-3, and solve the systems of equations by use of determinants.

In Exercises 31 and 32 solve the given systems of equations by use of determinants.

31. An object traveling at a constant velocity v (in feet per second) is 25 ft from a certain reference point after one second, and 35 ft from it after two seconds. Its initial distance s_0 from the reference point and its velocity can be found by solving the equations

$$s_0 + v = 25,$$
$$s_0 + 2v = 35.$$

Find s_0 and v.

32. When determining two forces F_1 and F_2 acting on a certain object, the following equations are obtained.

$$0.500F_1 + 0.600F_2 = 10,$$
$$0.866F_1 - 0.800F_2 = 20.$$

Find F_1 and F_2 (in pounds).

In Exercises 33 through 38 set up appropriate systems of two linear equations in two unknowns and then solve the system by use of determinants.

33. Two meshing gears together have 89 teeth. One of the gears has 4 less than twice the number of teeth of the other gear. How many teeth does each gear have?

34. A rocket is launched so that it averages 3000 mi/hr. An hour later, another rocket is launched along the same path at an average speed of 4500 mi/hr. Find the times of flight, t_1 and t_2, of the rockets when the second rocket overtakes the first.

35. A total of $8000 is invested, part at 3% and the remainder at 5%. Find the amount invested at each rate if the total annual income is $388.

36. A roof truss is in the shape of an isosceles triangle. The perimeter of the truss is 108 ft, and the base is 18 ft shorter than a rafter (neglecting overhang). Find the length of the base and the length of a rafter.

37. The resistance of a certain wire as a function of temperature can be found from the following equation: $R = \alpha T + \beta$. If the resistance is 0.4 ohm at 20°C and 0.5 ohm at 80°C, find α and β, and then the resistance as a function of temperature.

38. The velocity of sound in steel is 15,900 ft/sec faster than the velocity of sound in air. One end of a long steel bar is struck and an observer at the other end measures the time it takes for the sound to reach him. He finds that the sound through the bar takes 0.012 sec to reach him and that the sound through the air takes 0.180 sec. What are the velocities of sound in air and in steel?

4-5 Solving systems of three linear equations in three unknowns algebraically

Many problems involve the solution of systems of linear equations which involve three, four, and occasionally even more unknowns. Solving such systems algebraically or by determinants is essentially the same as solving systems of two linear equations in two unknowns. Graphical solutions are not used, since a linear equation in three unknowns represents a plane in space. In this section we shall discuss the algebraic method of solving a system of three linear equations in three unknowns.

A system of three linear equations in three unknowns written in the form

$$a_1x + b_1y + c_1z = d_1,$$
$$a_2x + b_2y + c_2z = d_2, \qquad\qquad (4\text{-}11)$$
$$a_3x + b_3y + c_3z = d_3,$$

has as its solution the set of values x, y, and z which satisfy all three equations simultaneously. The method of solution involves multiplying *two* of the equations by the proper numbers to eliminate *one* of the unknowns between these equations. We then repeat this process, using a *different pair* of the original equations, being sure that we eliminate the same unknown as we did between the first pair of equations. At this point we have two linear equations in two unknowns which can be solved by any of the methods previously discussed. The unknown originally eliminated may then be found by substitution into one of the original equations. It is wise to check these three values in one of the other original equations.

Example A.   Solve the following system of equations:

(1) $$x + 2y - z = -5,$$
(2) $$2x - y + 2z = 8,$$
(3) $$3x + 3y + 4z = 5.$$

(4) $\quad 2x + 4y - 2z = -10 \qquad$ (1) multiplied by 2

$\qquad\quad 2x - y + 2z = 8 \qquad$ (2)

(5) $\quad \overline{4x + 3y = -2} \qquad$ Adding (4) and (2)

(6)	$4x - 2y + 4z = 16$	(2) multiplied by 2
	$3x + 3y + 4z = 5$	(3)
(7)	$x - 5y = 11$	Subtracting

	$4x + 3y = -2$	(5)
(8)	$4x - 20y = 44$	(7) multiplied by 4
(9)	$23y = -46$	Subtracting
(10)	$y = -2$	

(11)	$x - 5(-2) = 11$	Substituting (10) in (7)
(12)	$x = 1$	

(13)	$1 + 2(-2) - z = -5$	Substituting (12) and (10) in (1)
(14)	$z = 2$	

To check, we substitute the solution $x = 1$, $y = -2$, $z = 2$ in (2).

$$2(1) - (-2) + 2(2) \overset{?}{=} 8$$
$$8 = 8 \quad \text{(It checks.)}$$

It should be noted that Eqs. (1), (2), and (3) could be solved just as well by eliminating y between (1) and (2), and then again between (1) and (3). We would then have two equations to solve in x and z. Also, z could have been eliminated between Eq. (1) and (3) to obtain the second equation in x and y.

Example B. Solve the following system of equations:

(1)	$4x + y + 3z = 1,$	
(2)	$2x - 2y + 6z = 11,$	
(3)	$-6x + 3y + 12z = -4.$	

(4)	$8x + 2y + 6z = 2$	(1) multiplied by 2
	$2x - 2y + 6z = 11$	(2)
(5)	$10x + 12z = 13$	Adding
(6)	$12x + 3y + 9z = 3$	(1) multiplied by 3
	$-6x + 3y + 12z = -4$	(3)
(7)	$18x - 3z = 7$	Subtracting
	$10x + 12z = 13$	(5)
(8)	$72x - 12z = 28$	(7) multiplied by 4
(9)	$82x = 41$	Adding
(10)	$x = \frac{1}{2}$	

(11) $\qquad 18(\tfrac{1}{2}) - 3z = \quad 7 \qquad$ Substituting (10) in (7)

(12) $\qquad\qquad\quad -3z = -2$

(13) $\qquad\qquad\qquad z = \quad \tfrac{2}{3}$

(14) $\qquad 4(\tfrac{1}{2}) + y + 3(\tfrac{2}{3}) = \quad 1 \qquad$ Substituting (13) and (10) in (1)

(15) $\qquad\quad 2 + y + 2 \quad = \quad 1$

(16) $\qquad\qquad\qquad y = -3$

Therefore, the solution is $x = \tfrac{1}{2}$, $y = -3$, $z = \tfrac{2}{3}$. Checking the solution in (2) we have $2(\tfrac{1}{2}) - 2(-3) + 6(\tfrac{2}{3}) = 1 + 6 + 4 = 11$.

Example C. Three forces F_1, F_2, and F_3 are acting on a beam. Find the forces (in pounds). The forces are determined by solving the following equations:

(1) $\qquad\qquad\qquad F_1 + \quad F_2 + \quad F_3 = 25,$

(2) $\qquad\qquad\qquad F_1 + 2F_2 + 3F_3 = 59,$

(3) $\qquad\qquad\qquad 2F_1 + 2F_2 - \quad F_3 = \quad 5.$

(4) $\qquad 3F_1 + 3F_2 + 3F_3 = 75 \qquad$ (1) multiplied by 3

$\qquad\qquad F_1 + 2F_2 + 3F_3 = 59 \qquad$ (2)

(5) $\qquad 2F_1 + \quad F_2 \qquad\quad = 16 \qquad$ Subtracting

(6) $\qquad 3F_1 + 3F_2 \qquad\quad = 30 \qquad$ (1) added to (3)

$\qquad 2F_1 + \quad F_2 \qquad\quad = 16 \qquad$ (5)

(7) $\qquad\quad F_1 + \quad F_2 \qquad\quad = 10 \qquad$ (6) divided by 3

(8) $\qquad\quad F_1 \qquad\qquad\quad = \quad 6 \qquad$ Subtracting

(9) $\qquad\qquad\qquad 6 + F_2 = 10 \qquad$ (8) substituted in (7)

(10) $\qquad\qquad\qquad\quad F_2 = \quad 4$

(11) $\qquad\qquad 6 + 4 + F_3 = 25 \qquad$ Substituting (8) and (10) in (1)

(12) $\qquad\qquad\qquad\quad F_3 = 15$

Therefore, the three forces are 6 lb, 4 lb, and 15 lb, respectively. This solution can be checked by substituting in Eq. (2) or Eq. (3).

Example D. A triangle has a perimeter of 37 in. The longest side is 3 in. longer than the next longest, which in turn is 8 in. longer than the shortest side. Find the length of each side.

Let a = length of the longest side, b = length of the next-longest side, and c = length of the shortest side. Since the perimeter is 37 in. we have $a + b + c = 37$. The statement of the problem also leads to the equations $a = b + 3$

and $b = c + 8$. These equations are then put into standard form and solved simultaneously.

(1)	$a + b + c = 37$	
(2)	$a - b = 3$	Rewriting the second equation
(3)	$ b - c = 8$	Rewriting the third equation
(4)	$a + 2b = 45$	Adding (1) and (3)
	$a - b = 3$	(2)
(5)	$3b = 42$	Subtracting
(6)	$b = 14$	
(7)	$a - 14 = 3$	Substituting (6) in (2)
(8)	$a = 17$	
(9)	$14 - c = 8$	Substituting (6) in (3)
(10)	$c = 6$	

Therefore the three sides of the triangle are 17 in., 14 in., and 6 in.

Checking the solution, the sum of the lengths of the three sides is 17 in. + 14 in. + 6 in. = 37 in., and the perimeter was given to be 37 in.

For systems of equations with more than three unknowns, the solution is found in a manner similar to that used with three unknowns. For example, with four unknowns one of the unknowns is eliminated between three different pairs of equations. The result is three equations in the remaining three unknowns. The solution then follows the procedure used with three unknowns.

Exercises

In Exercises 1 through 14 solve the given systems of equations.

1. $x + y + z = 2$
   $x - z = 1$
   $x + y = 1$

2. $x + y - z = -3$
   $x + z = 2$
   $2x - y + 2z = 3$

3. $2x + 3y + z = 2$
   $-x + 2y + 3z = -1$
   $-3x - 3y + z = 0$

4. $2x + y - z = 4$
   $4x - 3y - 2z = -2$
   $8x - 2y - 3z = 3$

5. $5x + 6y - 3z = 6$
   $4x - 7y - 2z = -3$
   $3x + y - 7z = 1$

6. $3r + s - t = 2$
   $r - 2s + t = 0$
   $4r - s + t = 3$

7. $2x - 2y + 3z = 5$
   $2x + y - 2z = -1$
   $4x - y - 3z = 0$

8. $2u + 2v + 3w = 0$
   $3u + v + 4w = 21$
   $-u - 3v + 7w = 15$

9. $3x - 7y + 3z = 6$
   $3x + 3y + 6z = 1$
   $5x - 5y + 2z = 5$

10. $8x + y + z = 1$
    $7x - 2y + 9z = -3$
    $4x - 6y + 8z = -5$

11. $r - s - 3t - u = 1$
    $2r + 4s - 2u = 2$
    $3r + 4s - 2t = 0$
    $r + 2t - 3u = 3$

12. $3x + 2y - 4z + 2t = 3$
    $5x - 3y - 5z + 6t = 8$
    $2x - y + 3z - 2t = 1$
    $-2x + 3y + 2z - 3t = -2$

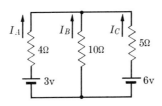

Figure 4-8

13. In applying Kirchhoff's laws (e.g., see Angus, *Electrical Engineering Fundamentals*, p. 117) to the electric circuit shown in Fig. 4-8, the following equations are found. Determine the indicated currents. (In Fig. 4-8, Ω signifies ohms, v signifies volts, and I signifies current, in amperes).

$$I_A + I_B + I_C = 0,$$
$$4I_A - 10I_B \quad\quad = 3,$$
$$\quad\quad - 10I_B + 5I_C = 6.$$

14. In a laboratory experiment to measure the acceleration of an object, the distances traveled by the object were recorded for three time intervals. These data led to the following equations:

$$s_0 + 2v_0 + 2a = 20,$$
$$s_0 + 4v_0 + 8a = 54,$$
$$s_0 + 6v_0 + 18a = 104.$$

Here s_0 is the initial displacement (in feet), v_0 is the initial velocity (in feet per second) and a is the acceleration (in ft/sec²). Find s_0, v_0, and a.

In Exercises 15 through 17 set up systems of three linear equations and solve for the indicated quantities.

15. Three machines together produce 64 parts each hour. Three times the production of the first machine equals the production of the other two machines together. Five times the production of the second is 12 parts per hour more than twice the rate of the other two together. Find the production rates of the three machines.

16. Angle A of a triangle equals 20° less than the sum of angles B and C. (The triangle is not a right triangle.) Angle B is one-fifth the sum of angles A and C. Find the angles.

17. By weight, one alloy is 60% copper, 30% zinc and 10% nickel. A second alloy has percentages 50, 30, and 20, respectively, of the three metals. A third alloy is 30% copper and 70% nickel. How much of each must be mixed so that the resulting alloy has percentages of 40, 15, and 45, respectively?

4-6 Solving systems of three linear equations in three unknowns by determinants

Just as systems of two linear equations in two unknowns can be solved by the use of determinants, so can systems of three linear equations in three unknowns. The system as given in Eqs. (4-11) can be solved in general terms by the method of elimination by addition or subtraction. This leads to the following solutions for x, y, and z.

$$x = \frac{d_1b_2c_3 + d_3b_1c_2 + d_2b_3c_1 - d_3b_2c_1 - d_1b_3c_2 - d_2b_1c_3}{a_1b_2c_3 + a_3b_1c_2 + a_2b_3c_1 - a_3b_2c_1 - a_1b_3c_2 - a_2b_1c_3},$$

$$y = \frac{a_1d_2c_3 + a_3d_1c_2 + a_2d_3c_1 - a_3d_2c_1 - a_1d_3c_2 - a_2d_1c_3}{a_1b_2c_3 + a_3b_1c_2 + a_2b_3c_1 - a_3b_2c_1 - a_1b_3c_2 - a_2b_1c_3}, \qquad (4\text{-}12)$$

$$z = \frac{a_1b_2d_3 + a_3b_1d_2 + a_2b_3d_1 - a_3b_2d_1 - a_1b_3d_2 - a_2b_1d_3}{a_1b_2c_3 + a_3b_1c_2 + a_2b_3c_1 - a_3b_2c_1 - a_1b_3c_2 - a_2b_1c_3}.$$

The expression that appears in each of the denominators of Eqs. (4-12) is an example of a *determinant of the third order*. This determinant is denoted by the symbol

$$\begin{vmatrix} a_1 & b_1 & c_1 \\ a_2 & b_2 & c_2 \\ a_3 & b_3 & c_3 \end{vmatrix}.$$

Therefore, a determinant of the third order is defined by the equation

$$\begin{vmatrix} a_1 & b_1 & c_1 \\ a_2 & b_2 & c_2 \\ a_3 & b_3 & c_3 \end{vmatrix} = a_1b_2c_3 + a_3b_1c_2 + a_2b_3c_1 - a_3b_2c_1 - a_1b_3c_2 - a_2b_1c_3. \qquad (4\text{-}13)$$

The elements, rows, columns, and diagonals of a third-order determinant are defined just as are those of a second-order determinant. For example, the principal diagonal is made up of the elements a_1, b_2, and c_3.

Probably the easiest way of remembering the method of determining the value of a third-order determinant is as follows (this method does *not* work for determinants of order higher than three): *Rewrite the first and second columns to the right of the determinant.* The products of the elements of the principal diagonal and the two parallel diagonals to the right of it are then added. The products of the elements of the secondary diagonal and the two parallel diagonals to the right of it are subtracted from the first sum. The algebraic sum of these six products gives the value of the determinant (see Fig. 4-9). Examples A through C illustrate the evaluation of third-order determinants.

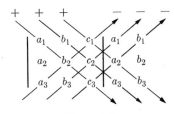

Figure 4-9

Example A.

$$\begin{vmatrix} 1 & 5 & 4 \\ -2 & 3 & -1 \\ 2 & -1 & 5 \end{vmatrix}\begin{matrix} 1 & 5 \\ -2 & 3 \\ 2 & -1 \end{matrix} = 15 + (-10) + (+8) - (24) - (1) - (-50) = 38$$

Example B.

$$\begin{vmatrix} -1 & 4 & -5 \\ 6 & 1 & 0 \\ 9 & -7 & 3 \end{vmatrix}\begin{matrix} -1 & 4 \\ 6 & 1 \\ 9 & -7 \end{matrix} = (-3) + 0 + 210 - (-45) - 0 - 72 = 180$$

Example C.

$$\begin{vmatrix} 3 & -2 & 8 \\ -5 & 5 & -2 \\ 4 & 9 & -6 \end{vmatrix}\begin{matrix} 3 & -2 \\ -5 & 5 \\ 4 & 9 \end{matrix} = \begin{aligned} &+(-90) + 16 + (-360) - 160 - (-54) \\ &\qquad\qquad\qquad\qquad - (-60) = -480 \end{aligned}$$

Inspection of Eqs. (4-12) reveals that the numerators of these solutions may also be written in terms of determinants. Thus we may write the general solution to a system of three equations in three unknowns as

$$x = \frac{\begin{vmatrix} d_1 & b_1 & c_1 \\ d_2 & b_2 & c_2 \\ d_3 & b_3 & c_3 \end{vmatrix}}{\begin{vmatrix} a_1 & b_1 & c_1 \\ a_2 & b_2 & c_2 \\ a_3 & b_3 & c_3 \end{vmatrix}}, \quad y = \frac{\begin{vmatrix} a_1 & d_1 & c_1 \\ a_2 & d_2 & c_2 \\ a_3 & d_3 & c_3 \end{vmatrix}}{\begin{vmatrix} a_1 & b_1 & c_1 \\ a_2 & b_2 & c_2 \\ a_3 & b_3 & c_3 \end{vmatrix}}, \quad z = \frac{\begin{vmatrix} a_1 & b_1 & d_1 \\ a_2 & b_2 & d_2 \\ a_3 & b_3 & d_3 \end{vmatrix}}{\begin{vmatrix} a_1 & b_1 & c_1 \\ a_2 & b_2 & c_2 \\ a_3 & b_3 & c_3 \end{vmatrix}}. \quad (4\text{-}14)$$

If the determinant of the denominator is zero and the determinant of the numerator is not zero, the system is *inconsistent*. If the determinant of the denominator is not equal to zero, then there is a unique solution to the system of equations.

An analysis of Eqs. (4-14) shows that the situation is precisely the same as it was when we were using determinants to solve systems of two linear equations. That is, the determinants in the denominators in the expressions for x, y, and z are the same. They consist of elements which are the coefficients of the unknowns. The determinant of the numerator of the solution for x is the same as that of the denominator, except that the column of d's replaces the column of a's. The determinant in the numerator of the solution for y is the same as that of the denominator, except that the column of d's replaces the column of b's. The determinant of the numerator of the solution for z is the same as the determinant of the denominator, except that the column of d's replaces the column of c's. To summarize, we can state that *the determinants in the numerators are the same as those in the denominators, except that the column of d's replaces the column of coefficients of the unknown for which we are solving.* This again is Cramer's rule. Remember that the equations must be written in the standard form shown in Eqs. (4-11) before the determinants are formed.

Example D. Solve the following system of equations by determinants.

$$x + 2y + 2z = 1,$$
$$2x - y + z = 3,$$
$$4x + y + 2z = 0.$$

$$x = \frac{\begin{vmatrix} 1 & 2 & 2 \\ 3 & -1 & 1 \\ 0 & 1 & 2 \end{vmatrix} \begin{matrix} 1 & 2 \\ 3 & -1 \\ 0 & 1 \end{matrix}}{\begin{vmatrix} 1 & 2 & 2 \\ 2 & -1 & 1 \\ 4 & 1 & 2 \end{vmatrix} \begin{matrix} 1 & 2 \\ 2 & -1 \\ 4 & 1 \end{matrix}} = \frac{-2 + 0 + 6 - 0 - 1 - 12}{-2 + 8 + 4 - (-8) - 1 - 8} = \frac{-9}{+9} = -1$$

Since the value of the denominator is already determined, there is no need to write the denominator in determinant form when solving for y and z.

$$y = \frac{\begin{vmatrix} 1 & 1 & 2 \\ 2 & 3 & 1 \\ 4 & 0 & 2 \end{vmatrix} \begin{matrix} 1 & 1 \\ 2 & 3 \\ 4 & 0 \end{matrix}}{9} = \frac{6 + 4 + 0 - 24 - 0 - 4}{9} = \frac{-18}{9} = -2$$

$$z = \frac{\begin{vmatrix} 1 & 2 & 1 \\ 2 & -1 & 3 \\ 4 & 1 & 0 \end{vmatrix} \begin{matrix} 1 & 2 \\ 2 & -1 \\ 4 & 1 \end{matrix}}{9} = \frac{0 + 24 + 2 - (-4) - 3 - 0}{9} = \frac{27}{9} = 3$$

As a check, we substitute these values into the first equation.

$$-1 + 2(-2) + 2(3) \overset{?}{=} 1, \qquad 1 = 1. \text{ Thus it checks.}$$

Example E.   Solve the following system by determinants.

$$3x + 2y - 5z = -1,$$
$$2x - 3y - z = 11,$$
$$5x - 2y + 7z = 9.$$

$$x = \frac{\begin{vmatrix} -1 & 2 & -5 \\ 11 & -3 & -1 \\ 9 & -2 & 7 \end{vmatrix} \begin{matrix} -1 & 2 \\ 11 & -3 \\ 9 & -2 \end{matrix}}{\begin{vmatrix} 3 & 2 & -5 \\ 2 & -3 & -1 \\ 5 & -2 & 7 \end{vmatrix} \begin{matrix} 3 & 2 \\ 2 & -3 \\ 5 & -2 \end{matrix}} = \frac{21 - 18 + 110 - 135 + 2 - 154}{-63 - 10 + 20 - 75 - 6 - 28}$$

$$= \frac{-174}{-162} = \frac{29}{27}$$

$$y = \frac{\begin{vmatrix} 3 & -1 & -5 \\ 2 & 11 & -1 \\ 5 & 9 & 7 \end{vmatrix} \begin{matrix} 3 & -1 \\ 2 & 11 \\ 5 & 9 \end{matrix}}{-162} = \frac{231 + 5 - 90 + 275 + 27 + 14}{-162} = \frac{462}{-162}$$

$$= -\frac{77}{27}$$

$$z = \frac{\begin{vmatrix} 3 & 2 & -1 \\ 2 & -3 & 11 \\ 5 & -2 & 9 \end{vmatrix} \begin{matrix} 3 & 2 \\ 2 & -3 \\ 5 & -2 \end{matrix}}{-162} = \frac{-81 + 110 + 4 - 15 + 66 - 36}{-162} = \frac{48}{-162}$$

$$= -\frac{8}{27}$$

Substituting into the second equation, we have

$$2\left(\frac{29}{27}\right) - 3\left(-\frac{77}{27}\right) - \left(-\frac{8}{27}\right) = \frac{58 + 231 + 8}{27} = \frac{297}{27}$$
$$= 11,$$

which shows that the solution checks.

Example F.   An 8% solution, a 10% solution, and a 20% solution of nitric acid are to be mixed in order to get 100 cm³ of a 12% solution. If the volume of acid from the 8% solution equals half the volume of acid from the other two solutions, how much of each is needed?

Let x = volume of 8% solution needed, y = volume of 10% solution needed, and z = volume of 20% solution needed.

We first use the fact that the sum of the volumes of the three solutions is 100 cm³. This leads to the equation $x + y + z = 100$. Next we note that there is $0.08x$ cm³ of pure nitric acid from the first solution, $0.10y$ cm³ from the second, $0.20z$ cm³ from the third solution, and $0.12(100)$ cm³ in the final solution. This leads to the equation $0.08x + 0.10y + 0.20z = 12$. Finally, using the last stated condition, we have $0.08x = \frac{1}{2}(0.10y + 0.20z)$. These equations are then re-written in standard form, simplified, and solved.

$$
\begin{aligned}
x + \quad y + \quad z &= 100 \\
0.08x + 0.10y + 0.20z &= \quad 12 \\
0.08x \qquad\qquad &= 0.05y + 0.10z
\end{aligned}
$$

$$
\begin{aligned}
x + \quad y + \quad z &= 100 \\
4x + \quad 5y + \quad 10z &= 600 \\
8x - \quad 5y - \quad 10z &= \quad 0
\end{aligned}
$$

$$
x = \frac{\begin{vmatrix} 100 & 1 & 1 \\ 600 & 5 & 10 \\ 0 & -5 & -10 \end{vmatrix} \begin{matrix} 100 & 1 \\ 600 & 5 \\ 0 & -5 \end{matrix}}{\begin{vmatrix} 1 & 1 & 1 \\ 4 & 5 & 10 \\ 8 & -5 & -10 \end{vmatrix} \begin{matrix} 1 & 1 \\ 4 & 5 \\ 8 & -5 \end{matrix}} = \frac{-5000 + 0 - 3000 - 0 + 5000 + 6000}{-50 + 80 - 20 - 40 + 50 + 40}
$$

$$
= \frac{3000}{60} = 50
$$

$$
y = \frac{\begin{vmatrix} 1 & 100 & 1 \\ 4 & 600 & 10 \\ 8 & 0 & -10 \end{vmatrix} \begin{matrix} 1 & 100 \\ 4 & 600 \\ 8 & 0 \end{matrix}}{60} = \frac{-6000 + 8000 + 0 - 4800 - 0 + 4000}{60}
$$

$$
= \frac{1200}{60} = 20
$$

$$
z = \frac{\begin{vmatrix} 1 & 1 & 100 \\ 4 & 5 & 600 \\ 8 & -5 & 0 \end{vmatrix} \begin{matrix} 1 & 1 \\ 4 & 5 \\ 8 & -5 \end{matrix}}{60} = \frac{0 + 4800 - 2000 - 4000 + 3000 - 0}{60}
$$

$$
= \frac{1800}{60} = 30
$$

Therefore, 50 cm³ of the 8% solution, 20 cm³ of the 10% solution and 30 cm³ of the 20% solution are required to make the 12% solution. Substitution into the first equation shows that this answer is correct.

Additional techniques which are useful in solving systems of equations are taken up in Chapter 15. Also, methods of evaluating determinants which are particularly useful for higher order determinants are also discussed.

Exercises

In Exercises 1 through 8 evaluate the given third-order determinants.

1. $\begin{vmatrix} 5 & 4 & -1 \\ -2 & -6 & 8 \\ 7 & 1 & 1 \end{vmatrix}$

2. $\begin{vmatrix} -7 & 0 & 0 \\ 2 & 4 & 5 \\ 1 & 4 & 2 \end{vmatrix}$

3. $\begin{vmatrix} 8 & 9 & -6 \\ -3 & 7 & 2 \\ 4 & -2 & 5 \end{vmatrix}$

4. $\begin{vmatrix} -2 & 6 & -2 \\ 5 & -1 & 4 \\ 8 & -3 & -2 \end{vmatrix}$

5. $\begin{vmatrix} -3 & -4 & -8 \\ 5 & -1 & 0 \\ 2 & 10 & -1 \end{vmatrix}$

6. $\begin{vmatrix} 10 & 2 & -7 \\ -2 & -3 & 6 \\ 6 & 5 & -2 \end{vmatrix}$

7. $\begin{vmatrix} 4 & -3 & -11 \\ -9 & 2 & -2 \\ 0 & 1 & -5 \end{vmatrix}$

8. $\begin{vmatrix} 9 & -2 & 0 \\ -1 & 3 & -6 \\ -4 & -6 & -2 \end{vmatrix}$

In Exercises 9 through 22 solve the indicated systems of equations by use of determinants.

9. $2x + 3y + z = 4$
   $3x - z = -3$
   $x - 2y + 2z = -6$

10. $4x + y + z = 2$
    $2x - y - z = 4$
    $3y + z = 2$

11-20. Use Exercises 1 through 10 of Section 4-5.

21. Use Exercise 13 of Section 4-5.

22. Use Exercise 14 of Section 4-5.

In Exercises 23 and 24 set up appropriate systems of three equations in three unknowns, and solve by the use of determinants.

23. Twenty thousand dollars is invested part at 5.5%, part at 4.5% and part at 4.0% (all of the amount is invested), yielding an annual interest of $1015. The income from the 5.5% investment yields $305 more annually than the other two investments combined. How much money is invested at each percentage?

24. A person traveled a total of 1870 mi from the time he left home until he reached his destination. He averaged 40 mi/hr while driving to the airport. The plane averaged 600 mi/hr, and he spent twice as long in the plane as in his car. The taxi averaged 30 mi/hr between the airport and the destination. Assuming 40 min were used in making connections, what were the times he spent in his car, in the plane, and in the taxi, if the trip took 5.5 hr?

4-7 Miscellaneous Exercises

In Exercises 1 through 4 evaluate the given determinants.

1. $\begin{vmatrix} -2 & 5 \\ 3 & 1 \end{vmatrix}$
2. $\begin{vmatrix} 4 & 0 \\ -2 & -6 \end{vmatrix}$
3. $\begin{vmatrix} -8 & -3 \\ -1 & 4 \end{vmatrix}$
4. $\begin{vmatrix} 9 & -1 \\ 7 & -5 \end{vmatrix}$

In Exercises 5 through 10 solve the given systems of equations graphically.

5. $2x - y = 4$
   $3x + 2y = 6$
6. $3x + y = 3$
   $2x - y = 6$
7. $4x - y = 6$
   $3x + 2y = 12$
8. $2x - 5y = 10$
   $3x + y = 6$
9. $3x + 4y = 6$
   $2x - 3y = 2$
10. $5x + 2y = 5$
    $2x - 4y = 3$

In Exercises 11 through 20 solve the given systems of equations algebraically.

11. $x + 2y = 5$
    $x + 3y = 7$
12. $2x - y = 7$
    $x + y = 2$
13. $4x + 3y = -4$
    $2x - y = 3$
14. $x + 3y = -2$
    $-2x - 9y = 2$
15. $3x + 4y = 6$
    $9x + 8y = 11$
16. $3x - 6y = 5$
    $7x + 2y = 4$
17. $2x - 5y = 8$
    $5x - 3y = 7$
18. $3x + 4y = 8$
    $2x - 3y = 9$
19. $7x - 2y = -6$
    $4x + 7y = 12$
20. $5x + 3y = 8$
    $6x - 8y = 11$

For Exercises 21 through 30 solve the systems of equations given in Exercises 11 through 20 by use of determinants.

In Exercises 31 through 34 evaluate the given determinants.

31. $\begin{vmatrix} 4 & -1 & 8 \\ -1 & 6 & -2 \\ 2 & 1 & -1 \end{vmatrix}$
32. $\begin{vmatrix} -5 & 0 & -5 \\ 2 & 3 & -1 \\ -3 & 2 & 2 \end{vmatrix}$

33. $\begin{vmatrix} -2 & -4 & 7 \\ 1 & 6 & -3 \\ -7 & 2 & -1 \end{vmatrix}$
34. $\begin{vmatrix} 3 & 2 & -1 \\ 0 & -3 & 4 \\ 3 & -4 & -2 \end{vmatrix}$

In Exercises 35 through 40 solve the given systems of equations algebraically.

35. $2x + y + z = 4$
    $x - 2y - z = 3$
    $3x + 3y - 2z = 1$
36. $x + 2y + z = 2$
    $3x - 6y + 2z = 2$
    $2x - z = 8$
37. $3x + 2y + z = 1$
    $9x - 4y + 2z = 8$
    $12x - 18y = 17$
38. $2x + 2y - z = 2$
    $3x + 4y + z = -4$
    $5x - 2y - 3z = 5$
39. $2r + s + 2t = 8$
    $3r - 2s - 4t = 5$
    $-2r + 3s + 6t = 0$
40. $2u + 2v - w = -2$
    $4u - 3v + 2w = -2$
    $8u - 4v - 3w = 13$

For Exercises 41 through 46 solve the systems of equations given in Exercises 35 through 40 by use of determinants.

In Exercises 47 through 50, let $1/x = u$ and $1/y = v$. Solve for u and v, and then solve for x and y. In this way we will see how to solve systems of equations involving reciprocals.

47. $\dfrac{1}{x} - \dfrac{1}{y} = \dfrac{1}{2}$

$\dfrac{1}{x} + \dfrac{1}{y} = \dfrac{1}{4}$

48. $\dfrac{1}{x} + \dfrac{1}{y} = 3$

$\dfrac{2}{x} + \dfrac{1}{y} = 1$

49. $\dfrac{2}{x} + \dfrac{3}{y} = 3$

$\dfrac{5}{x} - \dfrac{6}{y} = 3$

50. $\dfrac{3}{x} - \dfrac{2}{y} = 4$

$\dfrac{2}{x} + \dfrac{4}{y} = 1$

In Exercise 51 determine the value of a which makes the system dependent. In Exercise 52 determine the value of a which makes the system inconsistent.

51. $3x - ay = 6$

$x + 2y = 2$

52. $ax - 2y = 5$

$4x + 6y = 1$

Solve the systems of equations in Exercises 53 through 56 by any appropriate method.

53. In an experiment to determine the values of two electrical resistors, the following equations were determined:

$$2R_1 + 3R_2 = 16, \quad 3R_1 + 2R_2 = 19.$$

Determine the resistances R_1 and R_2 (in ohms).

54. The production of nitric acid makes use of air and nitrogen compounds. In order to determine requirements as to size of equipment, a relationship between the air flow rate m (in moles/hour) and exhaust nitrogen rate n is often used. One particular operation produces the following equations.

$$1.58m + 41.5 = 38.0 + 2.00n$$
$$0.424m + 36.4 = 189 + 0.0728n$$

Solve for m and n.

55. In a certain machine there are three important types of parts. Considering the total number of parts used, their cost, and the time used in their manufacture, the number of each type used can be determined by solving the system of equations

$$a + b + c = 37,$$
$$2a + 3b + 5c = 131,$$
$$3a + 4b + 6c = 168,$$

where a, b, and c are the numbers of each part used, respectively. Find a, b, and c.

56. In applying Kirchhoff's laws (see Exercise 13 of Section 4-5) to the given electric circuit, these equations result.

$I_A + I_B + I_C = 0$

$6I_A \quad\quad - 10I_C = 8$

$6I_A - 2I_B \quad\quad = 5$

Determine the indicated currents (See Fig. 4-10).

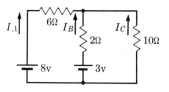

Figure 4-10

In Exercises 57 through 62 set up systems of equations and solve by any appropriate method.

57. A plane traveled 2000 mi, with the wind, in 4 hr and made the return trip in 5 hr. Determine the speed of the plane and that of the wind.

58. The relation between fahrenheit temperature F and centigrade temperature C can be indicated by $F = aC + b$. If 0°C is equivalent to 32°F and 100°C is equivalent to 212°F, find a and b.

59. If a lever is balanced by placing a single support (fulcrum) under a certain point, then the product of a weight on one side of the fulcrum and its distance from the fulcrum equals the product of a weight on the other side of the fulcrum times its distance from the fulcrum. A certain lever is balanced if a weight of 80 lb is put at one end and a weight of 30 lb at the other end. If the 80-lb weight is moved 1 ft closer to the fulcrum, it requires 20 lb at the other end to maintain the balance. How long is the lever? (Neglect the weight of the lever itself.)

60. The specific gravity of an object may be defined as its weight in air divided by the difference of its weight in air and its weight when submerged in water. If the sum of the weights in water and in air of an object of specific gravity equal to 10 is 30 lb, what is its weight in air?

61. An alloy important in the manufacture of electric transformers contains nickel, iron and molybdenum. The percentage of nickel is 1% less than five times the percentage of iron. The percentage of iron is 1% more than three times the percentage of molybdenum. Find the percentage of each metal in the alloy.

62. A businessman is interested in a building site for a new factory. He determines that at least 30 acres of land are necessary and that over 40 acres would be too expensive. He learns of a 160-acre tract of land which has been subdivided according to terrain such that one portion is 16 acres less than the sum of the other two and that twice the area of the second portion is 8 acres more than the area of the third portion. Would any of the portions be of interest to him?

Factoring and Fractions

5

5-1 Special products

In Chapter 1 we introduced certain fundamental algebraic operations. These have been sufficient for our purposes to this point. However, material we shall encounter later requires additional algebraic techniques. In this chapter we shall develop certain basic algebraic topics, which in turn will allow us to develop other topics having technical and scientific applications.

In working with algebraic expressions, we encounter certain types of products so frequently that we should become extremely familiar with them. These products are stated here in general form.

$$a(x + y) = ax + ay \tag{5-1}$$
$$(x + y)(x - y) = x^2 - y^2 \tag{5-2}$$
$$(x + y)^2 = x^2 + 2xy + y^2 \tag{5-3}$$
$$(x - y)^2 = x^2 - 2xy + y^2 \tag{5-4}$$
$$(x + a)(x + b) = x^2 + (a + b)x + ab \tag{5-5}$$
$$(ax + b)(cx + d) = acx^2 + (bc + ad)x + bd \tag{5-6}$$

Knowing and recognizing these *special products* allows us to perform many multiplications quickly and easily, often by inspection. We must also realize that they are written in their most concise form. Any of the literal numbers appearing in these products may represent an expression which in turn represents a number.

Example A.   Using Eq. (5-1) in the following product, we have

$$6(3r + 2s) = 6(3r) + 6(2s) = 18r + 12s.$$

Using Eq. (5-2), we have

$$(3r + 2s)(3r - 2s) = (3r)^2 - (2s)^2 = 9r^2 - 4s^2.$$

When we use Eq. (5-1) in the first illustration, we see that $a = 6$. In both illustrations $3r = x$ and $2s = y$.

Example B.   Using Eqs. (5-3) and (5-4) in the following products, we have

$$(5a + 2)^2 = (5a)^2 + 2(5a)(2) + 2^2 = 25a^2 + 20a + 4,$$
$$(5a - 2)^2 = (5a)^2 - 2(5a)(2) + 2^2 = 25a^2 - 20a + 4.$$

In these illustrations, we have let $x = 5a$ and $y = 2$.

Example C.   Using Eqs. (5-5) and (5-6) in the following products, we have

$$(x + 5)(x - 3) = x^2 + [(5 + (-3)]x + (5)(-3) = x^2 + 2x - 15,$$
$$(4x + 5)(2x - 3) = (4x)(2x) + [5(2) + 4(-3)]x + (5)(-3) = 8x^2 - 2x - 15.$$

Generally, when we use these special products, we do the middle step as shown in each of the examples above mentally and write down the result directly. This is indicated in the following example.

Example D. $2(x - 6) = 2x - 12$
$(y - 5)(y + 5) = y^2 - 25$
$(3x - 2)^2 = 9x^2 - 12x + 4$
$(x - 4)(x + 7) = x^2 + 3x - 28$

At times these special products may appear in combinations. When this happens it may be necessary to indicate an intermediate step.

Example E.   In expanding $7(a + 2)(a - 2)$, we use Eqs. (5-2) and (5-1), preferably in that order. Performing this operation, we have

$$7(a + 2)(a - 2) = 7(a^2 - 4) = 7a^2 - 28.$$

Example F.   In determining the product $(x + y - 2)^2$, we may group the quantity $(x + y)$ in an intermediate step. This leads to

$$(x + y - 2)^2 = [(x + y) - 2]^2 = (x + y)^2 - 2(x + y)(2) + 2^2$$
$$= x^2 + 2xy + y^2 - 4x - 4y + 4.$$

In this example we used Eqs. (5-3) and (5-4).

There are four other special products which occur less frequently. However, they are sufficiently important that they should be readily recognized. They are shown in Eqs. (5-7) through (5-10).

$$(x + y)^3 = x^3 + 3x^2y + 3xy^2 + y^3 \qquad (5\text{-}7)$$
$$(x - y)^3 = x^3 - 3x^2y + 3xy^2 - y^3 \qquad (5\text{-}8)$$
$$(x + y)(x^2 - xy + y^2) = x^3 + y^3 \qquad (5\text{-}9)$$
$$(x - y)(x^2 + xy + y^2) = x^3 - y^3 \qquad (5\text{-}10)$$

The following examples illustrate the use of Eqs. (5-7) through (5-10).

Example G. $(x + 4)^3 = x^3 + 3(x^2)(4) + 3(x)(4^2) + 4^3$
$$= x^3 + 12x^2 + 48x + 64$$
$$(2x - 5)^3 = (2x)^3 - 3(2x)^2(5) + 3(2x)(5^2) - 5^3$$
$$= 8x^3 - 60x^2 + 150x - 125$$

Example H. $(x + 3)(x^2 - 3x + 9) = x^3 + 3^3 = x^3 + 27$
$$(x - 2)(x^2 + 2x + 4) = x^3 - 2^3 = x^3 - 8$$

Exercises

In Exercises 1 through 24 find the indicated products directly *by inspection*. It should not be necessary to write down intermediate steps.

1. $40(x - y)$
2. $2x(a - 3)$
3. $2x^2(x - 4)$
4. $3a^2(2a + 7)$
5. $(y + 6)(y - 6)$
6. $(s + 2t)(s - 2t)$
7. $(3v - 2)(3v + 2)$
8. $(ab - c)(ab + c)$
9. $(5f + 4)^2$
10. $(i_1 + 3)^2$
11. $(2x + 7)^2$
12. $(5a + 2b)^2$
13. $(x - 2y)^2$
14. $(a - 5p)^2$
15. $(6s - t)^2$
16. $(3p - 4q)^2$
17. $(x + 1)(x + 5)$
18. $(y - 8)(y + 5)$
19. $(3 + c)(6 + c)$
20. $(t - 1)(t - 7)$
21. $(3x - 1)(2x + 5)$
22. $(2x - 7)(2x + 1)$
23. $(4x - 5)(5x + 1)$
24. $(2y - t)(3y - t)$

Use the special products of this section to determine the products of Exercises 25 through 40. You may need to write down one or two intermediate steps.

25. $6a(x + 2b)^2$
26. $4y^2(y - 6)^2$
27. $4a(2a - 3)^2$
28. $6t^2(5t - 3s)^2$
29. $(x + y + 1)^2$
30. $(x + 2 + 3y)^2$
31. $(3 - x - y)^2$
32. $2(x - y + 1)^2$
33. $(5 - t)^3$
34. $(2s + 3)^3$
35. $(2x + 5t)^3$
36. $(x - 5y)^3$
37. $(x + 2)(x^2 - 2x + 4)$
38. $(a - 3)(a^2 + 3a + 9)$
39. $(4 - 3x)(16 + 12x + 9x^2)$
40. $(2x + 3a)(4x^2 - 6ax + 9a^2)$

Use the special products of this section to determine the products in Exercises 41 through 44. Each comes from the technical area indicated.

41. $R(i_1 + i_2)^2$ (electricity)
42. $Fa(L - a)(L + a)$ (mechanics: force on a beam)
43. $16(4 + t)(3 - t)$ (physics: motion)
44. $V^2(V - b)^2$ (thermodynamics)

5-2 Factoring

We often find that we want to determine what expressions can be multiplied together to equal a given algebraic expression. We know from Section 1-5 that when an algebraic expression is the product of two or more quantities, each of these quantities is called a *factor* of the expression. Therefore, determining these factors, which is essentially reversing the process of finding a product, is called *factoring*.

In our work on factoring we shall consider only the factoring of polynomials (see Section 1-7) which have integers as coefficients for all terms. Also, all factors will have integral coefficients. A polynomial or a factor is called *prime* if it contains no factors other than $+1$ or -1 and plus or minus itself. We say that an expression is *factored completely* if it is expressed as a product of its prime factors.

Example A.   When we factor the expression $12x + 6x^2$ as

$$12x + 6x^2 = 2(6x + 3x^2),$$

we see that it has not been factored completely. The factor $6x + 3x^2$ is not prime, for it may be factored as

$$6x + 3x^2 = 3x(2 + x).$$

Therefore, the expression $12x + 6x^2$ is factored completely as

$$12x + 6x^2 = 6x(2 + x).$$

Here the factors x and $2 + x$ are prime. The numerical coefficient, 6, could be factored into $(2)(3)$, but it is normal practice not to factor numerical coefficients.

To factor expressions easily, we must be familiar with algebraic multiplication, particularly the special products of the preceding section. The solution of factoring problems is heavily dependent on the recognition of special products. The special products also provide methods of checking answers and deciding whether or not a given factor is prime.

Often an algebraic expression contains a monomial that is common to each term of the expression. Therefore, in accordance with Eq. (5-1), the first step in factoring any expression should be to factor out any *common monomial factor* that may exist.

Example B.   In factoring the expression $6x - 2y$, we note that each term contains the factor 2. Therefore,

$$6x - 2y = 2(3x - y).$$

In a similar manner, we have

$$2ax^2 + 4ax - 8ax^4 = 2ax(x + 2 - 4x^3).$$

Here, the common monomial factor is $2ax$.

Another important form for factoring is based on the special product of Eq. (5-2). In Eq. (5-2) we see that the product of the sum and the difference of two numbers results in the difference between the squares of the numbers. Therefore, factoring the difference between squares gives factors which are the sum and the difference of the numbers.

Example C.   Since $4x^2$ is the square of $2x$ and 9 is the square of 3, we may factor $4x^2 - 9$ as

$$4x^2 - 9 = (2x + 3)(2x - 3).$$

In the same way,

$$16x^4 - 25y^2 = (4x^2 + 5y)(4x^2 - 5y).$$

It is also important to note perfect squares in factoring expressions based on the special products of Eqs. (5-3) and (5-4). However, expressions of this type which are to be factored will contain three terms. The first and last terms, when written in the proper order, will be perfect squares. We must then check to determine if the middle term is correct for these forms.

Example D.   In factoring $9x^2 - 6x + 1$, we note that $9x^2$ is the square of $3x$ and 1 is the square of 1. Therefore, we tentatively factor this expression as

$$9x^2 - 6x + 1 = (3x - 1)^2.$$

However, before we can be certain that this factorization is correct, we must check to see if the middle term of the expansion of $(3x - 1)^2$ is $-6x$. Since $-6x$ properly fits the form of Eq. (5-4), the factorization is correct.

In the same way, we have

$$36x^2 + 84xy + 49y^2 = (6x + 7y)^2.$$

Factoring expressions based on the special product of Eq. (5-5) will result in factors of the form $x + a$ and $x + b$. The numbers a and b are found by analyzing the constant and the coefficient of x in the expression to be factored.

Example E. In factoring $x^2 + 3x + 2$, the constant term, 2, suggests that the only possibilities for a and b are 2 and 1. The plus sign before the 2 indicates that the sign before the 1 and the 2 in the factors must be the same, either both plus or both minus. Since the coefficient of the middle term is the sum of a and b, the plus sign before the 3 tells us that the sign before the 2 and 1 must be plus. Therefore,

$$x^2 + 3x + 2 = (x + 2)(x + 1).$$

For an expression containing x^2 and 2 to be factored, the middle term must be $3x$. No other combination of a and b gives the proper middle term. Therefore, the expression

$$x^2 + 4x + 2$$

cannot be factored. The a and b would have to be 2 and 1, but the middle term would not be $4x$.

Example F. Other examples of factoring based upon the special product of Eq. (5-5) are as follows:

$$x^2 - x - 12 = (x - 4)(x + 3),$$
$$x^2 - 5x + 6 = (x - 3)(x - 2),$$
$$x^2 + 7x - 8 = (x + 8)(x - 1).$$

Factoring expressions based upon the special product of Eq. (5-6) often requires some trial and error. The coefficient of x^2 gives the possibilities for the coefficients a and c in the factors. The constant gives the possibilities for the numbers b and d in the factors. It is then necessary to try possible combinations to determine which combination provides the middle term of the given expression.

Example G. When factoring the expression $2x^2 + 11x + 5$, the coefficient 2 indicates that the only possibilities for the x-terms in the factors are $2x$ and x. The 5 indicates that only 5 and 1 may be the constants. Therefore, possible combinations are $2x + 1$, and $x + 5$ or $2x + 5$ and $x + 1$. The combination which gives the coefficient of the middle term, 11, is

$$2x^2 + 11x + 5 = (2x + 1)(x + 5).$$

According to this analysis, the expression $2x^2 + 10x + 5$ is not factorable, but the following expression is:

$$2x^2 + 7x + 5 = (2x + 5)(x + 1).$$

Example H.   Other examples of factoring based upon the special product of Eq. (5-6) are as follows:

$$4x^2 + 4x - 3 = (2x - 1)(2x + 3),$$
$$3x^2 - 13x + 12 = (3x - 4)(x - 3),$$
$$6s^2 + 19s - 20 = (6s - 5)(s + 4).$$

In the first illustration, possible factors with x terms of $4x$ and x can be shown to be incorrect if tried. In the second illustration, other possible factorizations of 12, such as 6×2 and 12×1, can be shown to give improper middle terms. In the third illustration, there are numerous possibilities for the combination of 6 and 20. We must remember to check carefully that the the middle term of the expression is the proper result of the factors we have chosen.

Finally, we must be careful when we have factored an expression to see that it has been factored completely. We look for common monomial factors first and check to make sure our factors are correct every time we complete a step in factoring.

Example I.   When factoring $2x^2 + 6x - 8$, we first note the common monomial factor of 2. This leads to

$$2x^2 + 6x - 8 = 2(x^2 + 3x - 4).$$

We now notice that $x^2 + 3x - 4$ is also factorable. Therefore,

$$2x^2 + 6x - 8 = 2(x + 4)(x - 1).$$

Now each factor is prime.

Example J.   When factoring $x^4 - y^4$, we note that this expression is the difference between squares. Thus

$$x^4 - y^4 = (x^2 + y^2)(x^2 - y^2).$$

However, the second factor is itself the difference of squares. Therefore we have

$$x^4 - y^4 = (x^2 + y^2)(x + y)(x - y).$$

Now each term in the factorization is prime.

Exercises

In Exercises 1 through 40 factor the given expressions completely.

1. $6x + 6y$
2. $2x^2 + 2$
3. $3x^2 - 9x$
4. $5a^2 - 20ax$
5. $3ab^2 - 6ab + 12ab^3$
6. $4pq - 14q^2 - 16pq^2$
7. $a(x + y) - b(x + y)$
8. $3(a - c)^2 + 6(a - c)$

9. $4 - x^2$	10. $25 - r^2$	11. $81s^2 - 25t^2$	12. $36a^2b^2 - 121c^2$
13. $x^2 + 2x + 1$	14. $y^2 + 8y + 16$	15. $4m^2 + 20m + 25$	16. $16q^2 + 24q + 9$
17. $x^2 - 4x + 4$	18. $b^2 - 12b + 36$	19. $4x^2 - 12x + 9$	20. $a^2c^2 - 2ac + 1$
21. $x^2 + 5x + 4$	22. $x^2 - 5x - 6$	23. $s^2 - s - 42$	24. $a^2 + 14a - 32$
25. $3x^2 - 5x - 2$	26. $4x^2 + 11x - 3$	27. $3y^2 + y - 3$	28. $7p^2 - 16p + 2$
29. $9t^2 - 15t + 4$	30. $3x^2 + x - 14$	31. $8b^2 + 31b - 4$	32. $12n^2 + 8n - 15$
33. $2x^2 - 8$	34. $4x^2 - 100y^2$	35. $4x^2 + 14x - 8$	36. $12x^2 + 22x - 4$
37. $x^4 - 16$	38. $x^8 - 1$	39. $2x^4 - 8y^4$	40. $12a^2 - 36a + 27$

In Exercises 41 through 44 factor the given expressions by referring directly to the special products in Eqs. (5-7) through (5-10), respectively.

41. $x^3 + 3x^2 + 3x + 1$ 42. $x^3 - 6x^2 + 12x - 8$ 43. $8x^3 + 1$ 44. $x^3 - 27$

In Exercises 45 through 48 the expressions are to be factored by a method known as *factoring by grouping*. An illustration of this method is

$$2x - 2y + ax - ay = (2x - 2y) + (ax - ay)$$
$$= 2(x - y) + a(x - y) = (2 + a)(x - y).$$

The terms are put into groups, a common factor is factored from each group, and then the factoring is continued.

45. $3x - 3y + bx - by$ 46. $am + an + cn + cm$
47. $a^2 + ax - ab - bx$ 48. $2y - y^2 - 6y^4 + 12y^3$

Factor the expressions given in Exercises 49 through 55. Each comes from the technical area indicated.

49. $iR_1 + iR_2 + ir$ (electricity)
50. $kD^2 - 4kr^2$ (hydrodynamics)
51. $16t^2 - 32t - 128$ (physics: motion)
52. $(R_1 + r)^2 - 2r(R_1 + r)$ (electricity)
53. $x^2 - 3Lx + 2L^2$ (mechanics: beams)
54. $V^2 - 2nBV + n^2B^2$ (chemistry)
55. $pa^2 + (1 - p)b^2 - [pa + (1 - p)b]^2$ (nuclear physics)
    (Expand the third term and then use factoring by grouping.)

5-3 Equivalent fractions

When we deal with algebraic expressions, we must be able to work effectively with fractions. Since algebraic expressions are representations of numbers, the basic operations on fractions from arithmetic will form the basis of our algebraic operations. In this section we shall demonstrate a very important property of fractions, and in the following two sections we shall establish the basic algebraic operations with fractions.

This important property of fractions, often referred to as the *fundamental principle of fractions*, is that the *value of a fraction is unchanged if both numerator and denominator are multiplied or divided by the same number, provided this number is not zero*. Two fractions are said to be *equivalent* if one can be obtained from the other by use of the fundamental theorem.

Example A. If we multiply the numerator and denominator of the fraction $\frac{6}{8}$ by 2, we obtain the equivalent fraction $\frac{12}{16}$. If we divide the numerator and denominator of $\frac{6}{8}$ by 2, we obtain the equivalent fraction $\frac{3}{4}$. Therefore, the fractions $\frac{6}{8}$, $\frac{3}{4}$, and $\frac{12}{16}$ are equivalent.

Example B. We may write

$$\frac{xa}{2} = \frac{3a^2x}{6a},$$

since the right fraction is obtained from the left fraction by multiplying the numerator and the denominator by $3a$. Therefore, the fractions are equivalent.

One of the most important operations to be performed on a fraction is that of reducing it to its *simplest form*, or *lowest terms*. A fraction is said to be in its simplest form if the numerator and the denominator have no common factors other than $+1$ or -1. In reducing a fraction to its simplest form, we use the fundamental theorem by dividing both the numerator and the denominator by all factors which are common to each. (It will be assumed throughout this text that if any of the literal symbols were to be evaluated, numerical values would be restricted so that none of the denominators would be zero. Thereby, we avoid the undefined operation of division by zero.)

Example C. In order to reduce the fraction

$$\frac{16ab^3c^2}{24ab^2c^5}$$

to its lowest terms, we note that both the numerator and the denominator contain the factor $8ab^2c^2$. Therefore, we may write

$$\frac{16ab^3c^2}{24ab^2c^5} = \frac{2b(8ab^2c^2)}{3c^3(8ab^2c^2)} = \frac{2b}{3c^3}.$$

Here we have divided out the common factor. The resulting fraction is in lowest terms since there are no common factors in the numerator and the denominator other than $+1$ or -1.

We must note very carefully that in simplifying fractions, we *divide* both the numerator and the denominator by the common *factor*. This process is called *cancellation*. However, many students are tempted to try to remove any expression which appears in both the numerator and the denominator. If a *term* is removed in this way, it is an incorrect application of the cancellation process. The following example illustrates this common error in the simplification of fractions.

Example D.   When simplifying the expression

$$\frac{x^2(x-2)}{x^2-4},$$

many students would "cancel" the x^2 from the numerator and the denominator. This is *incorrect*, since x^2 is only a term of the denominator.

In order to simplify the fraction above properly, we should factor the denominator. We obtain

$$\frac{x^2(x-2)}{(x-2)(x+2)} = \frac{x^2}{x+2}.$$

Here, the common *factor* $x-2$ has been divided out.

The following examples illustrate the proper simplification of fractions.

Example E. $\dfrac{4a}{2a^2x} = \dfrac{2}{ax}$

We divide out the common factor of $2a$.

$$\frac{4a}{2a^2+x}$$

This cannot be reduced, since there are no common *factors* in the numerator and the denominator.

Example F. $\dfrac{x^2-4x+4}{x^2-4} = \dfrac{(x-2)(x-2)}{(x+2)(x-2)} = \dfrac{x-2}{x+2}$

In this simplification, the numerator and the denominator have each been factored first and then the common factor $x-2$ has been divided out. In the final form, neither the x's or 2's may be cancelled, since they are not common *factors.*

Example G. $\dfrac{4x^2+14x-30}{8x-12} = \dfrac{2(2x^2+7x-15)}{4(2x-3)} = \dfrac{2(2x-3)(x+5)}{4(2x-3)} = \dfrac{x+5}{2}$

Here, the factors common to the numerator and the denominator are 2 and $(2x-3)$.

In simplifying fractions we must be able to distinguish between factors which differ only in *sign*. Since $-(y - x) = -y + x = x - y$, we have

$$x - y = -(y - x). \tag{5-11}$$

Here we see that factors $x - y$ and $y - x$ differ only in sign. The following examples illustrate the simplification of fractions where a change of signs is necessary.

Example H. $\dfrac{x^2 - 1}{1 - x} = \dfrac{(x - 1)(x + 1)}{-(x - 1)} = \dfrac{x + 1}{-1} = -(x + 1)$

In the second fraction, we replaced $1 - x$ with the equal expression $-(x - 1)$. In the third fraction the common factor $x - 1$ was divided out. Finally, we expressed the result in the more convenient form by dividing $x + 1$ by -1, which makes the quantity $x + 1$ negative.

Example I. $\dfrac{2x^3 - 32x}{20 + 7x - 3x^2} = \dfrac{2x(x^2 - 16)}{(4 - x)(5 + 3x)} = \dfrac{2x(x - 4)(x + 4)}{-(x - 4)(3x + 5)}$

$$= -\frac{2x(x + 4)}{3x + 5}$$

Again, the factor $4 - x$ has been replaced by the equal expression $-(x - 4)$. This allows us to recognize the common factor of $x - 4$. Notice also that the order of the terms of the factor $5 + 3x$ has been changed to $3x + 5$. This is merely an application of the commutative law of addition.

Exercises

In Exercises 1 through 6 multiply the numerator and the denominator of each of the given fractions by the given factor and obtain an equivalent fraction.

1. $\dfrac{2}{3}$ (by 7)

2. $\dfrac{7}{5}$ (by 9)

3. $\dfrac{ax}{y}$ (by $2x$)

4. $\dfrac{2x^2y}{3n}$ (by $2xn^2$)

5. $\dfrac{a(x - y)}{x - 2y}$ (by $x + y$)

6. $\dfrac{x - 1}{x + 1}$ (by $x - 1$)

In Exercises 7 through 12 divide the numerator and the denominator of each of the given fractions by the given factor and obtain an equivalent fraction.

7. $\dfrac{28}{44}$ (by 4)

8. $\dfrac{25}{65}$ (by 5)

9. $\dfrac{4x^2y}{8xy^2}$ (by $2x$)

10. $\dfrac{6a^3b^2}{9a^5b^4}$ (by $3a^2b^2$)

11. $\dfrac{x^2 - 3x - 10}{2x^2 + 3x - 2}$ (by $x + 2$)

12. $\dfrac{6x^2 + 13x - 5}{6x^3 - 2x^2}$ (by $3x - 1$)

In Exercises 13 through 34 reduce each fraction to its simplest form.

13. $\dfrac{2a}{8a}$

14. $\dfrac{6x}{15x}$

15. $\dfrac{18x^2y}{24xy}$

16. $\dfrac{2a^2xy}{6axyz^2}$

17. $\dfrac{a+b}{5a^2+5ab}$

18. $\dfrac{t-a}{t^2-a^2}$

19. $\dfrac{6a-4b}{4a-2b}$

20. $\dfrac{x^2-y^2}{x^2+y^2}$

21. $\dfrac{x^2-8x+16}{x^2-16}$

22. $\dfrac{4a^2+12ab+9b^2}{4a^2+6ab}$

23. $\dfrac{2x^2+5x-3}{x^2+11x+24}$

24. $\dfrac{4r^2-8rs-5s^2}{6r^2-17rs+5s^2}$

25. $\dfrac{x^4-16}{x+2}$

26. $\dfrac{2x^2-8}{4x+8}$

27. $\dfrac{x^2y^4-x^4y^2}{y^2-2xy+x^2}$

28. $\dfrac{8x^3+8x^2+2x}{4x+2}$

29. $\dfrac{(x-1)(3+x)}{(3-x)(1-x)}$

30. $\dfrac{(2x-1)(x+6)}{(x-3)(1-2x)}$

31. $\dfrac{y-x}{2x-2y}$

32. $\dfrac{x^2-y^2}{y-x}$

33. $\dfrac{(x+5)(x-2)(x+2)(3-x)}{(2-x)(5-x)(3+x)(2+x)}$

34. $\dfrac{(2x-3)(3-x)(x-7)(3x+1)}{(3x+2)(3-2x)(x-3)(7+x)}$

In Exercises 35 through 38 reduce each fraction to its simplest form. This will require the use of Eqs. (5-7) through (5-10).

35. $\dfrac{x^3-y^3}{x^2-y^2}$

36. $\dfrac{x^3-8}{x^2+2x+4}$

37. $\dfrac{x^3+3x^2+3x+1}{x^3+1}$

38. $\dfrac{a^3-6a^2+12a-8}{a^2-4a+4}$

In Exercises 39 and 40 determine which fractions are in simplest form.

39. (a) $\dfrac{x^2(x+2)}{x^2+4}$ (b) $\dfrac{x^4+4x^2}{x^4-16}$

40. (a) $\dfrac{2x+3}{2x+6}$ (b) $\dfrac{x^2-x-2}{x^2-x}$

5-4 Multiplication and division of fractions

From arithmetic we recall that the product of two fractions is a fraction whose numerator is the product of the numerators and whose denominator is the product of the denominators of the given fractions. Also, we recall that we can find the quotient of two fractions by inverting the divisor and proceeding as in multiplication. Symbolically, multiplication of fractions is indicated by

$$\frac{a}{b}\cdot\frac{c}{d}=\frac{ac}{bd},$$

and division is indicated by

$$\frac{a/b}{c/d}=\frac{a}{b}\cdot\frac{d}{c}=\frac{ad}{bc}.$$

The rule for division may be verified by use of the fundamental principle of fractions. By multiplying the numerator and denominator of the fraction

$$\frac{\dfrac{a}{b}}{\dfrac{c}{d}} \quad \text{by} \quad \frac{d}{c}, \qquad \text{we obtain} \qquad \frac{\dfrac{a}{b} \cdot \dfrac{d}{c}}{\dfrac{c}{d} \cdot \dfrac{d}{c}}.$$

In the resulting denominator $\dfrac{c}{d} \cdot \dfrac{d}{c}$ becomes 1, and therefore the fraction is written as ad/bc.

Example A. $\dfrac{3}{5} \cdot \dfrac{2}{7} = \dfrac{(3)(2)}{(5)(7)} = \dfrac{6}{35}$

$$\frac{3a}{5b} \cdot \frac{15b^2}{a} = \frac{(3a)(15b^2)}{(5b)(a)} = \frac{45ab^2}{5ab} = \frac{9b}{1} = 9b$$

In the second illustration, we have divided out the common factor of $5ab$ to reduce the resulting fraction to its simplest form.

We shall usually want to express the result in its simplest form. Since all factors in the numerators and all factors in the denominators are to be multiplied, we should first only *indicate* the multiplication and then factor the numerator and the denominator. In this way we can easily identify any factors common to both. If we were to multiply out the numerator and the denominator before factoring, it is very possible that we would be unable to factor the result to simplify it. The following example illustrates this point.

Example B.   In performing the multiplication

$$\frac{3(x - y)}{(x - y)^2} \cdot \frac{(x^2 - y^2)}{6x + 9y},$$

if we multiply out the numerators and the denominators before performing any factoring, we would have to simplify the fraction

$$\frac{3x^3 - 3x^2y - 3xy^2 + 3y^3}{6x^3 - 3x^2y - 12xy^2 + 9y^3}.$$

It is possible to factor the numerator and the denominator, but finding any common factors this way is very difficult. If we first indicate the multiplications and then factor completely, we have

$$\frac{3(x - y)}{(x - y)^2} \cdot \frac{(x^2 - y^2)}{6x + 9y} = \frac{3(x - y)(x^2 - y^2)}{(x - y)^2(6x + 9y)} = \frac{3(x - y)(x + y)(x - y)}{(x - y)^2(3)(2x + 3y)}$$

$$= \frac{3(x - y)^2(x + y)}{3(x - y)^2(2x + 3y)}$$

$$= \frac{x + y}{2x + 3y}.$$

The common factor of $3(x - y)^2$ is readily recognized using this procedure.

Example C. $\dfrac{2x-4}{4x+12} \cdot \dfrac{2x^2+x-15}{3x-1} = \dfrac{2(x-2)(2x-5)(x+3)}{4(x+3)(3x-1)}$

$$= \dfrac{(x-2)(2x-5)}{2(3x-1)}$$

Here the common factor is $2(x+3)$. It is permissible to multiply out the final form of the numerator and the denominator, but it is often preferable to leave the numerator and denominator in factored form, as indicated.

The following examples illustrate the division of fractions.

Example D. $\dfrac{6x}{7} \div \dfrac{5}{3} = \dfrac{6x}{7} \cdot \dfrac{3}{5} = \dfrac{18x}{35}$

$$\dfrac{\dfrac{3a^2}{5c}}{\dfrac{2c^2}{a}} = \dfrac{3a^2}{5c} \cdot \dfrac{a}{2c^2} = \dfrac{3a^3}{10c^3}$$

Example E. $\dfrac{x+y}{3} \div \dfrac{2x+2y}{6x+15y} = \dfrac{x+y}{3} \cdot \dfrac{6x+15y}{2x+2y} = \dfrac{(x+y)(3)(2x+5y)}{3(2)(x+y)}$

$$= \dfrac{2x+5y}{2}$$

Example F.

$$\dfrac{\dfrac{4-x^2}{x^2-3x+2}}{\dfrac{x+2}{x^2-9}} = \dfrac{4-x^2}{x^2-3x+2} \cdot \dfrac{x^2-9}{x+2} = \dfrac{(2-x)(2+x)(x-3)(x+3)}{(x-2)(x-1)(x+2)}$$

$$= \dfrac{-(x-2)(x+2)(x-3)(x+3)}{(x-2)(x-1)(x+2)}$$

$$= -\dfrac{(x-3)(x+3)}{x-1} \quad \text{or} \quad \dfrac{(x-3)(x+3)}{1-x}$$

Note the use of Eq. (5-11) in the simplification and in expressing an alternate form of the result. The factor $2-x$ was replaced by its equivalent $-(x-2)$, and then $x-1$ was replaced by $-(1-x)$.

Exercises

In Exercises 1 through 26 perform the indicated operations and simplify.

1. $\dfrac{3}{8} \cdot \dfrac{2}{7}$

2. $\dfrac{11}{5} \cdot \dfrac{13}{33}$

3. $\dfrac{4x}{3y} \cdot \dfrac{9y^2}{2}$

4. $\dfrac{18sy^3}{ax^2} \cdot \dfrac{(ax)^2}{3s}$

5. $\dfrac{2}{9} \div \dfrac{4}{7}$

6. $\dfrac{5}{16} \div \dfrac{25}{13}$

7. $\dfrac{xy}{az} \div \dfrac{bz}{ay}$

8. $\dfrac{sr^2}{2t} \div \dfrac{st}{4}$

9. $\dfrac{4x + 12}{5} \cdot \dfrac{15t}{3x + 9}$

10. $\dfrac{y^2 + 2y}{6z} \cdot \dfrac{z^3}{y^2 - 4}$

11. $\dfrac{u^2 - v^2}{u + 2v} \cdot \dfrac{3u + 6v}{u - v}$

12. $(x - y) \cdot \dfrac{x + 2y}{x^2 - y^2}$

13. $\dfrac{2a + 8}{15} \div \dfrac{a^2 + 8a + 16}{25}$

14. $\dfrac{a^2 - a}{3a + 9} \div \dfrac{a^2 - 2a + 1}{a^2 - 9}$

15. $\dfrac{x^2 - 9}{x} \div (x + 3)^2$

16. $\dfrac{9x^2 - 16}{x + 1} \div (4 - 3x)$

17. $\dfrac{3ax^2 - 9ax}{10x^2 + 5x} \cdot \dfrac{2x^2 + x}{a^2x - 3a^2}$

18. $\dfrac{2x^2 - 18}{x^3 - 25x} \cdot \dfrac{3x - 15}{2x^2 + 6x}$

19. $\dfrac{x^4 - 1}{8x + 16} \cdot \dfrac{2x^2 - 8x}{x^3 + x}$

20. $\dfrac{2x^2 - 4x - 6}{x^2 - 3x} \cdot \dfrac{x^3 - 4x^2}{4x^2 - 4x - 8}$

21. $\dfrac{ax + x^2}{2b - cx} \div \dfrac{a^2 + 2ax + x^2}{2bx - cx^2}$

22. $\dfrac{x^2 - 11x + 28}{x + 3} \div \dfrac{x - 4}{x + 3}$

23. $\dfrac{35a + 25}{12a + 33} \div \dfrac{28a + 20}{36a + 99}$

24. $\dfrac{2a^3 + a^2}{2b^3 + b^2} \div \dfrac{2ab + a}{2ab + b}$

25. $\dfrac{7x^2}{3a} \div \left(\dfrac{a}{x} \cdot \dfrac{a^2x}{x^2} \right)$

26. $\dfrac{2x^2 - 5x - 3}{x - 4} \div \left(\dfrac{x - 3}{x^2 - 16} \cdot \dfrac{1}{3 - x} \right)$

In Exercises 27 through 30 perform the indicated operations and simplify. Exercises 27 and 28 require the use of Eqs. (5-7) through (5-10), and Exercises 29 and 30 require the use of factoring by grouping.

27. $\dfrac{x^3 - y^3}{2x^2 - 2y^2} \cdot \dfrac{x^2 + 2xy + y^2}{x^2 + xy + y^2}$

28. $\dfrac{x^3 + 3x^2 + 3x + 1}{6x - 6} \div \dfrac{5x + 5}{x^2 - 1}$

29. $\dfrac{ax + bx + ay + by}{p - q} \cdot \dfrac{3p^2 + 4pq - 7q^2}{a + b}$

30. $\dfrac{x^4 + x^5 - 1 - x}{x - 1} \div \dfrac{x + 1}{x}$

In Exercises 31 and 32 solve the given problems.

31. A rectangular metal plate expands when heated. For small values of centigrade temperature, the length and width of a certain plate, as functions of the temperature, are

$$\frac{20,000 + 300T + T^2}{1600 - T^2} \quad \text{and} \quad \frac{16,000 + 360T - T^2}{400 + 2T},$$

respectively. Find the resulting expression for the area of the plate as a function of the temperature.

32. The current in a simple electric circuit is the voltage in the circuit divided by the resistance. Given that the voltage and resistance in a certain circuit are expressed as functions of time

$$V = \frac{5t + 10}{2t + 1} \quad \text{and} \quad R = \frac{t^2 + 4t + 4}{2t},$$

find the formula for the current as a function of time.

5-5 Addition and subtraction of fractions

From arithmetic we recall that the sum of a set of fractions that all have the same denominator is the sum of the numerators divided by the common denominator. Since algebraic expressions represent numbers, this fact is also true in algebra. Addition and subtraction of such fractions are illustrated in the following example.

Example A. $\dfrac{5}{9} + \dfrac{2}{9} - \dfrac{4}{9} = \dfrac{5 + 2 - 4}{9} = \dfrac{3}{9} = \dfrac{1}{3}$

$$\frac{b}{ax} - \frac{1}{ax} + \frac{2b - 1}{ax} = \frac{b - 1 + (2b - 1)}{ax} = \frac{b - 1 + 2b - 1}{ax}$$

$$= \frac{3b - 2}{ax}$$

If the fractions to be combined do not all have the same denominator, we must first change each to an equivalent fraction so that the resulting fractions do have the same denominator. Normally the denominator which is most convenient and useful is the *lowest common denominator*. This is the product of all of the prime factors which appear in the denominators, with each factor raised to the highest power to which it appears in any one of the denominators. Thus the lowest common denominator is the simplest algebraic expression into which all the given denominators will divide evenly. The following two examples illustrate the method used in finding the lowest common denominator of a set of fractions.

Example B.   Find the lowest common denominator of the fractions

$$\frac{3}{4a^2b}, \qquad \frac{5}{6ab^3}, \qquad \text{and} \qquad \frac{1}{4ab^2}.$$

Expressing each of the denominators in terms of powers of the prime factors, we have

$$4a^2b = 2^2a^2b, \qquad 6ab^3 = 2 \cdot 3 \cdot ab^3, \qquad \text{and} \qquad 4ab^2 = 2^2ab^2.$$

The prime factors to be considered are 2, 3, a and b. The largest exponent of 2 which appears is 2. This means that 2^2 is a factor of the lowest common denominator. The largest exponent of 3 which appears is 1 (understood in the second denominator). Therefore 3 is a factor of the lowest common denominator. The largest power of a which appears is 2, and the largest power of b which appears is 3. Thus a^2 and b^3 are factors of the lowest common denominator. Therefore, the lowest common denominator of the fractions is $2^2 \cdot 3 \cdot a^2b^3 = 12a^2b^3$. This is the simplest expression into which *each* of the denominators above will divide evenly.

Example C. Find the lowest common denominator of the following fractions:

$$\frac{x-4}{x^2-2x+1}, \qquad \frac{1}{x^2-1}, \qquad \frac{x+3}{x^2-x}.$$

Factoring each of the denominators, we find that the fractions are

$$\frac{x-4}{(x-1)^2}, \qquad \frac{1}{(x-1)(x+1)}, \qquad \text{and} \qquad \frac{x+3}{x(x-1)}.$$

The factor $(x - 1)$ appears in all of the denominators. It is squared in the denominator of the first fraction and appears to the first power only in the other two fractions. Thus we must have $(x - 1)^2$ as a factor of the common denominator. We do not need a higher power of $x - 1$ since, as far as this factor is concerned, each denominator will divide into it evenly. Next, the second denominator contains a factor of $(x + 1)$. Therefore the common denominator must also contain a factor of $(x + 1)$, otherwise the second denominator would not divide into it evenly. Finally, the third denominator indicates that a factor of x is also required in the common denominator. The lowest common denominator is, therefore, $x(x + 1)(x - 1)^2$. All three denominators will divide evenly into this expression, and there is no simpler expression for which this is true.

Once we have found the lowest common denominator for the fractions, we multiply the numerator and denominator of each fraction by the proper quantity to make the resulting denominator in each case the common denominator. After this step, it is necessary only to add the numerators, place this result over the common denominator, and simplify.

Example D. Combine $\dfrac{2}{3r^2} + \dfrac{4}{rs^3} - \dfrac{5}{3s}$.

By looking at the denominators, we see that the factors necessary in the lowest common denominator are 3, r, and s. The 3 appears only to the first power, the highest power of r is 2, and the highest power of s is 3. Therefore, the lowest common denominator is $3r^2s^3$. We now wish to write each fraction with this quantity as the denominator. Since the denominator of the first fraction already contains factors of 3 and r^2, it is necessary to introduce the factor of s^3. In other words, we must multiply the numerator and denominator of this fraction by s^3. For similar reasons, we must multiply the numerators and the denominators of the second and third fractions by $3r$ and r^2s^2, respectively. This leads to

$$\frac{2}{3r^2} + \frac{4}{rs^3} - \frac{5}{3s} = \frac{2(s^3)}{(3r^2)(s^3)} + \frac{4(3r)}{(rs^3)(3r)} - \frac{5(r^2s^2)}{(3s)(r^2s^2)}$$

$$= \frac{2s^3}{3r^2s^3} + \frac{12r}{3r^2s^3} - \frac{5r^2s^2}{3r^2s^3}$$

$$= \frac{2s^3 + 12r - 5r^2s^2}{3r^2s^3}.$$

Example E. $\dfrac{a}{x-1} + \dfrac{a}{x+1} = \dfrac{a(x+1)}{(x-1)(x+1)} + \dfrac{a(x-1)}{(x+1)(x-1)}$

$$= \dfrac{ax+a+ax-a}{(x+1)(x-1)} = \dfrac{2ax}{(x+1)(x-1)}$$

When we multiply each fraction by the quantity required to obtain the proper denominator, we do not actually have to write the common denominator under each numerator. Placing all the products which appear in the numerators over the common denominator is sufficient. Hence the illustration in this example would appear as

$$\dfrac{a}{x-1} + \dfrac{a}{x+1} = \dfrac{a(x+1)+a(x-1)}{(x-1)(x+1)} = \dfrac{ax+a+ax-a}{(x-1)(x+1)}$$

$$= \dfrac{2ax}{(x-1)(x+1)}.$$

Example F. $\dfrac{x-1}{x^2-25} - \dfrac{2}{x-5} = \dfrac{(x-1)-2(x+5)}{(x-5)(x+5)} = \dfrac{x-1-2x-10}{(x-5)(x+5)}$

$$= \dfrac{-(x+11)}{(x-5)(x+5)}$$

Example G. $\dfrac{3x}{x^2-x-12} - \dfrac{x-1}{x^2-8x+16} - \dfrac{6-x}{2x-8}$

$$= \dfrac{3x}{(x-4)(x+3)} - \dfrac{x-1}{(x-4)^2} - \dfrac{6-x}{2(x-4)}$$

$$= \dfrac{3x(2)(x-4) - (x-1)(2)(x+3) - (6-x)(x-4)(x+3)}{2(x-4)^2(x+3)}$$

$$= \dfrac{6x^2 - 24x - 2x^2 - 4x + 6 + x^3 - 7x^2 - 6x + 72}{2(x-4)^2(x+3)}$$

$$= \dfrac{x^3 - 3x^2 - 34x + 78}{2(x-4)^2(x+3)}$$

One note of caution must be sounded here. In doing this kind of problem, many errors may arise in the use of the minus sign. Remember, if a minus sign precedes a given expression, the signs of *all* terms in that expression must be changed before they can be combined with the other terms.

Example H. Simplify the fraction

$$\dfrac{1 + \dfrac{2}{x-1}}{\dfrac{x^2+x}{x^2+x-2}}.$$

Before performing the indicated division, we must first perform the indicated addition in the numerator. The numerator becomes

$$\frac{(x-1)+2}{x-1} \quad \text{or} \quad \frac{x+1}{x-1}.$$

This expression now replaces the numerator of the original fraction. Making this substitution and inverting the divisor, we then proceed with the simplification:

$$\frac{x+1}{x-1} \cdot \frac{x^2+x-2}{x^2+x} = \frac{(x+1)(x+2)(x-1)}{(x-1)(x)(x+1)} = \frac{x+2}{x}.$$

This is an example of what is known as a *complex fraction*. In a complex fraction the numerator, the denominator, or both numerator and denominator contain fractions.

Exercises

In Exercises 1 through 28 perform the indicated operations and simplify.

1. $\dfrac{3}{5} + \dfrac{6}{5}$

2. $\dfrac{2}{13} + \dfrac{6}{13}$

3. $\dfrac{1}{x} + \dfrac{7}{x}$

4. $\dfrac{2}{a} + \dfrac{3}{a}$

5. $\dfrac{1}{2} + \dfrac{3}{4}$

6. $\dfrac{5}{9} - \dfrac{1}{3}$

7. $\dfrac{a}{x} - \dfrac{b}{x^2}$

8. $\dfrac{t-3}{a} - \dfrac{t}{2a}$

9. $\dfrac{2}{5a} + \dfrac{1}{a} - \dfrac{a}{10}$

10. $\dfrac{2}{a} - \dfrac{6}{b} - \dfrac{9}{c}$

11. $\dfrac{x+1}{x} - \dfrac{x-3}{y} - \dfrac{2-x}{xy}$

12. $5 + \dfrac{1-x}{2} - \dfrac{3+x}{4}$

13. $\dfrac{4}{x(x+1)} - \dfrac{3}{2x}$

14. $\dfrac{3}{ax+ay} - \dfrac{1}{a^2}$

15. $\dfrac{s}{2s-6} + \dfrac{1}{4} - \dfrac{3s}{4s-12}$

16. $\dfrac{2}{x+2} - \dfrac{3-x}{x^2+2x} + \dfrac{1}{x}$

17. $\dfrac{3x}{x^2-9} - \dfrac{2}{x+3}$

18. $\dfrac{1}{a^2-1} - \dfrac{2}{1-a}$

19. $\dfrac{3}{x^2-11x+30} - \dfrac{2}{x^2-25}$

20. $\dfrac{x-1}{2x^3-4x^2} + \dfrac{5}{x-2}$

21. $\dfrac{x-1}{3x^2-13x+4} - \dfrac{3x+1}{4-x}$

22. $\dfrac{x}{4x^2-12x+5} + \dfrac{2x-1}{4x^2-4x-15}$

23. $\dfrac{t}{t^2-t-6} - \dfrac{2t}{t^2+6t+9} + \dfrac{t}{t^2-9}$

24. $\dfrac{5}{2x^3-3x^2+x} - \dfrac{x}{x^4-x^2} + \dfrac{2-x}{2x^2+x-1}$

25. $\dfrac{1 + \dfrac{1}{x}}{1 - \dfrac{1}{x}}$ 26. $\dfrac{x - \dfrac{1}{x}}{1 - \dfrac{1}{x}}$

27. $\dfrac{x - \dfrac{1}{x} - \dfrac{2}{x+1}}{\dfrac{1}{x^2 + 2x + 1} - 1}$ 28. $\dfrac{\dfrac{2}{a} - \dfrac{1}{4} - \dfrac{3}{4a - 4b}}{\dfrac{1}{4a^2 - 4b^2} - \dfrac{2}{b}}$

The expression $f(x + h) - f(x)$ is frequently used in the study of calculus. In Exercises 29 and 30 determine and then simplify this expression for the given functions.

29. $f(x) = \dfrac{x}{x + 1}$ 30. $f(x) = \dfrac{2}{x^2 + 4}$

In Exercises 31 through 36 simplify the given expressions.

31. Using the definitions of the trigonometric functions given in Section 3-2, find an expression equivalent to $(\tan \theta)(\cot \theta) + (\sin \theta)^2 - \cos \theta$, in terms of x, y, and r.

32. If $f(x) = x^2 + x$, find $f(a + 1/a)$.

33. The analysis of the forces acting on a certain type of concrete slab gives the expression

$$1 - \frac{4c}{\pi l} + \frac{c^3}{3l^3}.$$

Combine and simplify.

34. Experimentation to determine the velocity of light may use the expression

$$1 + \frac{v^2}{2c^2} + \frac{3v^4}{4c^4}.$$

Combine and simplify.

35. In finding an expression to describe a magnetic field, the following expression is found.

$$\frac{b}{x^2 + y^2} - \frac{2bx^2}{(x^2 + y^2)^2}$$

Perform the indicated subtraction.

36. The expression for the volumetric expansion of liquids in terms of density ρ and temperature T is

$$\frac{1/\rho_2 - 1/\rho_1}{[(T_2 - T_1)(1/\rho_1 + 1/\rho_2)]/2}.$$

Simplify this expression.

5-6 Equations involving fractions

Many important equations in science and technology have fractions in them. Although the solution of these equations will still involve the use of the basic operations stated in Section 1-8, an additional procedure can be used to eliminate the fractions and thereby help lead to the solution. The method is to *multiply each term of the equation by the lowest common denominator*. The resulting equation will not involve fractions and can be solved by methods previously discussed. The following examples illustrate how to solve equations involving fractions.

Example A.   Solve for x: $\dfrac{x}{12} - \dfrac{1}{8} = \dfrac{x+2}{6}$.

We first note that the lowest common denominator of the terms of the equation is 24. Therefore, we multiply each term by 24. This gives

$$\frac{24(x)}{12} - \frac{24(1)}{8} = \frac{24(x+2)}{6}.$$

We reduce each term to its lowest terms, and solve the resulting equation.

$$2x - 3 = 4(x+2),$$
$$2x - 3 = 4x + 8,$$
$$-2x = 11,$$
$$x = -11/2.$$

When we check this solution in the original equation, we obtain $-7/12$ on each side of the equals sign. Therefore, the solution is correct.

Example B.   Solve for x: $\dfrac{x}{2} - \dfrac{1}{b^2} = \dfrac{x}{2b}$.

We first determine that the lowest common denominator of the terms of the equation is $2b^2$. We then multiply each term by $2b^2$ and continue with the solution.

$$\frac{2b^2(x)}{2} - \frac{2b^2(1)}{b^2} = \frac{2b^2(x)}{2b}$$

$$b^2x - 2 = bx$$

$$b^2x - bx = 2$$

To complete the solution for x, we must factor x from the terms on the left. Therefore, we have

$$x(b^2 - b) = 2,$$

$$x = \frac{2}{b^2 - b}$$

Checking shows that each side of the original equation is $1/b^2(b-1)$.

Example C.   When developing the equations which describe the motion of the planets, the equation

$$\frac{1}{2}v^2 - \frac{GM}{r} = -\frac{GM}{2a}$$

is found. Solve for M.

We first determine that the lowest common denominator of the terms of the equation is $2ar$. Multiplying each term by $2ar$ and proceeding with the solution, we have

$$\frac{2ar(v^2)}{2} - \frac{2ar(GM)}{r} = -\frac{2ar(GM)}{2a},$$

$$arv^2 - 2aGM = -rGM,$$

$$rGM - 2aGM = -arv^2,$$

$$M(rG - 2aG) = -arv^2,$$

$$M = -\frac{arv^2}{rG - 2aG} \quad \text{or} \quad \frac{arv^2}{2aG - rG}.$$

The second form of the result is obtained by using Eq. (5-11). Again, note the use of factoring to arrive at the final result.

Example D. Solve for x: $\dfrac{2}{x+1} - \dfrac{1}{x} = -\dfrac{2}{x^2 + x}$.

Multiplying each term by the lowest common denominator $x(x + 1)$, and continuing with the solution, we have

$$\frac{2(x)(x+1)}{x+1} - \frac{x(x+1)}{x} = -\frac{2x(x+1)}{x(x+1)},$$

$$2x - (x + 1) = -2,$$

$$2x - x - 1 = -2,$$

$$x = -1.$$

Checking this solution *in the original equation,* we see that we have zero in the denominators of the first and third terms of the equation. Since division by zero is undefined (see Section 1-3), $x = -1$ cannot be a solution. Thus there is no solution to this equation. This example points out clearly why it is necessary to check solutions in the original equation. It also shows that whenever we multiply each term by a lowest common denominator which *contains the unknown,* it is possible to obtain a solution which is not a solution of the original equation. Such a solution is termed *extraneous.* Only certain equations will lead to extraneous solutions, but we must be careful to identify them when they occur.

Example E. One pipe can fill a certain oil storage tank in 4 hours, while a second pipe can fill it in 6 hours. How long will it take to fill the tank if both pipes operate together?

First, we let $x =$ the number of hours required to fill the tank with both pipes operating.

We know that it takes the first pipe 4 hours to fill the tank. Therefore it fills $\frac{1}{4}$ of the tank each hour it operates. This means that it fills $\frac{1}{4}x$ of the tank in x hours. In the same way, the second pipe fills $\frac{1}{6}x$ of the tank in x hours. When x hours have passed, the two pipes will have filled the whole tank (1 represents *one* tank).

$$\frac{x}{4} + \frac{x}{6} = 1$$

Multiplying each term by 12, we have

$$\frac{12x}{4} + \frac{12x}{6} = 12(1),$$

$$3x + 2x = 12,$$

$$5x = 12,$$

$$x = \tfrac{12}{5} = 2.4 \text{ hr.}$$

Therefore, it takes the two pipes 2.4 hr to fill the tank when operating together.

Exercises

In Exercises 1 through 20 solve the given equations and check the results.

1. $\dfrac{x}{2} + 6 = 2x$

2. $\dfrac{x}{5} + 2 = \dfrac{15 + x}{10}$

3. $\dfrac{x}{6} - \dfrac{1}{2} = \dfrac{x}{3}$

4. $\dfrac{3x}{8} - \dfrac{3}{4} = \dfrac{x - 4}{2}$

5. $\dfrac{1}{2} - \dfrac{t - 5}{6} = \dfrac{3}{4}$

6. $\dfrac{2x - 7}{3} + 5 = \dfrac{1}{5}$

7. $\dfrac{3}{x} + 2 = \dfrac{5}{3}$

8. $\dfrac{1}{2y} - \dfrac{1}{2} = 4$

9. $3 - \dfrac{x - 2}{x} = \dfrac{1}{3}$

10. $\dfrac{1}{2x} - \dfrac{1}{3} = \dfrac{2}{x}$

11. $\dfrac{2}{s} = \dfrac{3}{s - 1}$

12. $\dfrac{x}{2x - 3} = 4$

13. $\dfrac{5}{2x + 4} + \dfrac{3}{x + 2} = 2$

14. $\dfrac{3}{4x - 6} + \dfrac{1}{4} = \dfrac{5}{2x - 3}$

15. $\dfrac{4}{4 - x} + 2 - \dfrac{2}{12 - 3x} = \dfrac{1}{3}$

16. $\dfrac{2}{z - 5} - \dfrac{3}{10 - 2z} = 3$

17. $\dfrac{1}{x^2 - x} - \dfrac{1}{x} = \dfrac{1}{x - 1}$

18. $\dfrac{2}{x^2 - 1} - \dfrac{2}{x + 1} = \dfrac{1}{x - 1}$

19. $\dfrac{2}{x^2 - 4} - \dfrac{1}{x - 2} = \dfrac{1}{2x + 4}$

20. $\dfrac{2}{2x^2 + 5x - 3} - \dfrac{1}{4x - 2} + \dfrac{3}{2x + 6} = 0$

In Exercises 21 through 28 solve for the indicated letter.

21. $2 - \dfrac{1}{b} + \dfrac{3}{c} = 0$, for c

22. $\dfrac{2}{3} - \dfrac{h}{x} = \dfrac{1}{2x}$, for x

23. $\dfrac{t-3}{b} - \dfrac{t}{2b-1} = \dfrac{1}{2}$, for t **24.** $\dfrac{1}{a^2+2a} - \dfrac{y}{2a} = \dfrac{2y}{a+2}$, for y

25. An equation used in nuclear physics is

$$E = V_0 + \frac{(m+M)V^2}{2} + \frac{p^2}{2I}.$$

Solve for M.

26. An equation obtained in analyzing a certain electric circuit is

$$\frac{V-6}{5} + \frac{V-8}{15} + \frac{V}{10} = 0.$$

Solve for V.

27. Under specified conditions, the combined resistance R of resistances R_1, R_2 and r is given by the equation

$$\frac{1}{R} = \frac{1}{R_1+r} + \frac{1}{R_2}.$$

Solve for R_1.

28. An equation used in hydrodynamics is

$$F = PA + \frac{dQ^2}{gA_1} - \frac{dQ^2}{gA_2}.$$

Solve for A.

In Exercises 29 through 32 set up appropriate equations and solve the given stated problems.

29. One data-processing card sorter can sort a certain number of cards in 6 min, and a second sorter can sort the same number in 9 min. How long would it take the two sorters together to sort this number of cards?

30. One steamshovel can excavate a certain site in 5 days, while it takes a second steamshovel 8 days. How long would it take the two working together?

31. The width of a particular rectangular land area is $\frac{3}{5}$ that of the length. If the perimeter is 192 yd, find the dimensions.

32. The current in a certain stream flows at 3 mi/hr. A motorboat can travel downstream 23 mi in the same time it can travel 11 mi upstream. What is the boat's rate in still water?

5-7 Miscellaneous Exercises

In Exercises 1 through 12 find the products *by inspection*. No intermediate steps should be necessary.

1. $3a(4x+5a)$	**2.** $-7xy(4x^2-7y)$	**3.** $(2a+7b)(2a-7b)$
4. $(x-4z)(x+4z)$	**5.** $(2a+1)^2$	**6.** $(4x-3y)^2$
7. $(b-4)(b+7)$	**8.** $(y-5)(y-7)$	**9.** $(2x+5)(x-9)$
10. $(4ax-3)(5ax+7)$	**11.** $(2c+d)(8c-d)$	**12.** $(3s-2t)(8s+3t)$

In Exercises 13 through 30 factor the given expressions completely. Exercises 27 and 28 illustrate Eqs. (5-7) through (5-10), and Exercises 29 and 30 illustrate factoring by grouping.

13. $a^2x^2 + a^2$

14. $3ax - 6ax^4 - 9a$

15. $x^2 - 144$

16. $25s^4 - 36t^2$

17. $9t^2 - 6t + 1$

18. $4x^2 - 12x + 9$

19. $x^2 + x - 56$

20. $x^2 - 4x - 45$

21. $2x^2 - x - 36$

22. $9x^2 + 7x - 16$

23. $10b^2 + 23b - 5$

24. $12x^2 - 7xy - 12y^2$

25. $4x^2 - 64$

26. $4a^2x^2 + 26a^2x + 36a^2$

27. $x^3 - 3x^2 + 3x - 1$

28. $8x^3 + 27$

29. $ab^2 - 3b^2 + a - 3$

30. $axy - ay + ax - a$

In Exercises 31 through 46 perform the indicated operations and express results in simplest form.

31. $\dfrac{48ax^3y^6}{9a^3xy^6}$

32. $\dfrac{-39r^2s^4t^8}{52rs^5t}$

33. $\dfrac{6x^2 - 7x - 3}{4x^2 - 8x + 3}$

34. $\dfrac{x^2 - 3x - 4}{x^2 - x - 12}$

35. $\dfrac{4x + 4y}{35x^2} \cdot \dfrac{28x}{x^2 - y^2}$

36. $\dfrac{6x - 3}{x^2} \cdot \dfrac{4x^2 - 12x}{12x - 6}$

37. $\dfrac{18 - 6x}{x^2 - 6x + 9} \div \dfrac{x^2 - 2x - 15}{x^2 - 9}$

38. $\dfrac{6x^2 - xy - y^2}{2x^2 + xy - y^2} \div \dfrac{4x^2 - 16y^2}{x^2 + 3xy + 2y^2}$

39. $\dfrac{x + \dfrac{1}{x} + 1}{x^2 - \dfrac{1}{x}}$

40. $\dfrac{\dfrac{3x - 3y}{2x^2 + 3xy - 2y^2}}{\dfrac{3x^2 - 3y^2}{x^2 + 4xy + 4y^2}}$

41. $\dfrac{6}{x} - \dfrac{7}{2x} + \dfrac{3}{xy}$

42. $\dfrac{4}{a^2b} - \dfrac{5}{2ab} + \dfrac{1}{2b}$

43. $\dfrac{a + 1}{a + 2} - \dfrac{a + 3}{a}$

44. $\dfrac{2x - 1}{4 - x} + \dfrac{x + 2}{5x - 20}$

45. $\dfrac{3x}{x^2 + 2x - 3} - \dfrac{2}{x^2 + 3x} + \dfrac{x}{x - 1}$

46. $\dfrac{3}{y^4 - 2y^3 - 8y^2} + \dfrac{y - 1}{y^2 + 2y} - \dfrac{y + 3}{y^2 - 4y}$

In Exercises 47 through 54 solve the given equations.

47. $\dfrac{x}{2} - 3 = \dfrac{x - 10}{4}$

48. $\dfrac{x}{6} - \dfrac{1}{2} = \dfrac{3 - x}{12}$

49. $\dfrac{2x}{c} - \dfrac{1}{2c} = \dfrac{3}{c} - x$, for x

50. $\dfrac{x}{a} - b + \dfrac{x}{c} = \dfrac{a}{b} - c$, for x

51. $\dfrac{2}{t} - \dfrac{1}{at} = 2 + \dfrac{a}{t}$, for t

52. $\dfrac{3}{a^2y} - \dfrac{1}{ay} = \dfrac{9}{a}$, for y

53. $\dfrac{2x}{x^2 - 3x} - \dfrac{3}{x} = \dfrac{1}{2x - 6}$

54. $\dfrac{3}{x^2 + 3x} - \dfrac{1}{x} = \dfrac{1}{x + 3}$

In Exercises 55 through 64 perform the indicated operations.

55. In finding the velocity of an object subject to specified conditions, it is necessary to simplify the expression

$$\frac{(t+1)^2 - 2t(t+1)}{(t+1)^4}.$$

Simplify this expression.

56. An expression found in solving a problem related to alternating current power is

$$\frac{\dfrac{s+10}{10}}{\left(\dfrac{s+20}{20}\right)\left(\dfrac{s+60}{60}\right)}.$$

Simplify this expression.

57. An expression found in determining the tension in a certain cable is

$$1 + \frac{w^2 x^2}{6T^2} - \frac{w^4 x^4}{40T^4}.$$

Combine and simplify.

58. An expression found in the analysis of the dynamics of missile firing is

$$\frac{1}{s} - \frac{1}{s+4} + \frac{8}{(s+4)^2}.$$

Perform the indicated operations.

59. An expression found in the study of electronic amplifiers is

$$\frac{\left(\dfrac{\mu}{\mu+1}\right)R}{\dfrac{r}{\mu+1} + R}.$$

Simplify this expression. (μ is the Greek letter mu.)

60. An expression which arises when finding the path between two points requiring the least time is

$$\frac{\dfrac{u^2}{2g} - x}{\dfrac{1}{2gc^2} - \dfrac{u^2}{2g} + x}.$$

Simplify this expression.

61. The focal length f of a lens, in terms of its image distance q and object distance p is given by

$$\frac{1}{f} = \frac{1}{p} + \frac{1}{q}.$$

Solve for q.

62. The combined capacitance C of three capacitors connected in series is

$$\frac{1}{C} = \frac{1}{C_1} + \frac{1}{C_2} + \frac{1}{C_3}.$$

Solve for C_1.

63. An equation used in studying the deflection of a beam is

$$\theta = \frac{wL^3}{24EI} - \frac{ML}{6EI}.$$

Solve for M.

64. An equation determined during the study of the characteristics of a certain chemical solution is

$$X = \frac{H}{RT_1} - \frac{H}{RT}.$$

Solve for T.

In Exercises 65 and 66 set up appropriate equations and solve the given stated problems.

65. If one riveter can do a certain job in 12 days, and a second riveter can do it in 16 days, how long will it take them to do it together?

66. A person travels from city A to city B on a train which averages 40 mi/hr. He spends 4 hr in city B and then returns to city A on a jet which averages 600 mi/hr. If the total trip takes 20 hr, how far is it from city A to city B?

Quadratic Equations

6

6-1 Quadratic equations; solution by factoring

The solution of simple equations was first introduced in Chapter 1. Then, in Chapter 4, we extended the solution of equations to systems of linear equations. With the development of the algebraic operations in Chapter 5, we are now in a position to solve another important type of equation, the *quadratic equation*.

Given that a, b, and c are constants, the equation

$$ax^2 + bx + c = 0 \tag{6-1}$$

is called the *general quadratic equation in x*. From Eq. (6-1) we can see that the left side of the equation is a polynomial function of degree 2. This function, $ax^2 + bx + c$, is known as the *quadratic function*.

Quadratic equations and quadratic functions are found in applied problems of many technical fields of study. For example, in describing projectile motion, the equation $s_0 + v_0 t - 16t^2 = 0$ is found; in analyzing electric power, the function $EI - RI^2$ is found; and in determining the forces on beams, the function $ax^2 + bLx + cL^2$ is used.

Since it is the x^2 term that distinguishes the quadratic equation from other types of equations, the equation is not quadratic if $a = 0$. However, b, or c, or both may be zero, and the equation is quadratic. We should recognize a quadratic equation even when it does not initially appear in the form of Eq. (6-1). The following examples illustrate the recognition of quadratic equations.

Example A. The following are quadratic equations.

$x^2 - 4x - 5 = 0$ $\qquad$ ($a = 1$, $b = -4$, and $c = -5$)

$3x^2 - 6 = 0$ $\qquad$ ($a = 3$, $b = 0$, and $c = -6$)

$2x^2 + 7x = 0$ $\qquad$ ($a = 2$, $b = 7$, and $c = 0$)

$(a - 3)x^2 - ax + 7 = 0$ (The constants in Eq. (6-1) may include literal expressions. In this case, $a - 3$ takes the place of a, $-a$ takes the place of b, and $c = 7$.)

$4x^2 - 2x = x^2$ (After all terms are collected on the left, the equation becomes $3x^2 - 2x = 0$.)

$(x + 1)^2 = 4$ (Expanding the left side, and collecting all terms on the left, we have $x^2 + 2x - 3 = 0$.)

Example B.   The following are not quadratic equations.

$bx - 6 = 0$ (There is no x^2-term.)

$x^3 - x - 5 = 0$ (There should be no term of degree higher than 2. Thus there can be no x^3-term in a quadratic equation.)

$x^2 + x - 7 = x^2$ (When terms are collected on the left, there will be no x^2-term.)

From our previous work, we recall that the solution of an equation consists of all numbers which, when substituted in the equation, produce equality. Normally there are two such numbers for a quadratic equation, although occasionally there is only one number. In any case, there cannot be more than two roots of a quadratic equation. Also, due to the presence of the x^2-term, the roots may be imaginary numbers.

Example C.   The quadratic equation

$$3x^2 - 7x + 2 = 0$$

has the roots $x = \frac{1}{3}$ and $x = 2$. This can be seen by substituting these values into the equation.

$$3\left(\frac{1}{3}\right)^2 - 7\left(\frac{1}{3}\right) + 2 = 3\left(\frac{1}{9}\right) - \frac{7}{3} + 2 = \frac{1}{3} - \frac{7}{3} + 2 = \frac{0}{3} = 0$$

$$3(2)^2 - 7(2) + 2 = 3(4) - 14 + 2 = 12 - 14 + 2 = 0$$

The quadratic equation

$$4x^2 - 4x + 1 = 0$$

has the double root (both roots the same) of $x = \frac{1}{2}$. This can be seen to be a solution by substitution.

$$4(\tfrac{1}{2})^2 - 4(\tfrac{1}{2}) + 1 = 4(\tfrac{1}{4}) - 2 + 1 = 1 - 2 + 1 = 0$$

The quadratic equation

$$x^2 + 9 = 0$$

has roots of $x = 3j$ and $x = -3j$. Remembering that $j = \sqrt{-1}$, which means that $j^2 = -1$, we have

$$(3j)^2 + 9 = 9j^2 + 9 = 9(-1) + 9 = -9 + 9 = 0,$$
$$(-3j)^2 + 9 = (-3)^2 j^2 + 9 = 9j^2 + 9 = 9(-1) + 9 = 0.$$

In this section we shall deal only with those quadratic equations whose quadratic expression is factorable. Therefore all roots will be real. To solve a quadratic equation by factoring, we collect all terms on the left so that the equation will be in the general form of Eq. (6-1). Then we factor the left side and set each factor, individually, equal to zero. The resulting numbers constitute the solution of the quadratic equation.

Example D.

$$x^2 - x - 12 = 0$$
$$(x - 4)(x + 3) = 0$$
$$x - 4 = 0 \quad \text{or} \quad x = 4$$
$$x + 3 = 0 \quad \text{or} \quad x = -3$$

The solutions are $x = 4$ and $x = -3$. We can check them in the original equation by substitution. For the solution $x = 4$, we have

$$(4)^2 - (4) - 12 \overset{?}{=} 0$$
$$0 = 0.$$

For the solution $x = -3$, we have

$$(-3)^2 - (-3) - 12 \overset{?}{=} 0$$
$$0 = 0.$$

Both solutions satisfy the original equation.

Example E.

$$2x^2 + 7x - 4 = 0$$
$$(2x - 1)(x + 4) = 0$$
$$2x - 1 = 0 \quad \text{or} \quad x = \tfrac{1}{2}$$
$$x + 4 = 0 \quad \text{or} \quad x = -4$$

Therefore, the roots are $x = \tfrac{1}{2}$ and $x = -4$. These roots can be checked by the same procedure used in Example D.

Example F.

$$x^2 + 4 = 4x$$
$$x^2 - 4x + 4 = 0$$
$$(x - 2)(x - 2) = 0$$
$$x - 2 = 0 \quad \text{or} \quad x = 2$$

Since both factors are the same, there is a double root of $x = 2$.

It is essential for the expression on the left to be equal to zero, because of the fact that $0 \cdot a = 0$. Thus for every solution one factor must equal zero. Even though the other factor may not be zero, the product will be zero. (If another number appeared on the right side of the equation, it would be essential that the product of the factors equal that number, when a "solution" is checked.) Of course, it is always wise to check our solutions.

Example G. A car travels to and from a city 180 mi distant in 8.5 hr. If the average speed on the return trip is 5 mi/hr less than on the trip to the city, what was the average speed of the car when it was going toward the city?

Let x = average speed of car going to the city, and t = time to travel to the city. By our choice of unknowns we may state that xt = 180 (speed times time equals distance). Also, we know that the speed on the return trip was $x - 5$ and that the required time for the return trip was $8.5 - t$. Since the distance traveled returning was also 180 mi, we may state that $(x - 5)(8.5 - t)$ = 180. Because we wish to find x, we can eliminate t between the equations by substitution.

$$(x - 5) \left(8.5 - \frac{180}{x} \right) = 180$$

$(x - 5)(17x - 360) = 360x$	Each side multiplied by $2x$
$17x^2 - 360x - 85x + 1800 = 360x$	Remove parentheses
$17x^2 - 805x + 1800 = 0$	Collect all terms to one side
$(17x - 40)(x - 45) = 0$	Factor the quadratic expression

$$17x - 40 = 0 \quad \text{or} \quad x = \tfrac{40}{17}$$
$$x - 45 = 0 \quad \text{or} \quad x = 45$$

The factors lead to two possible solutions, but only one of them has meaning for this problem. The solution $x = \frac{40}{17}$ cannot be the solution, since the return rate of 5 mi/hr less would then be negative. Therefore the solution is $x = 45$ mi/hr. By substitution it is found that this solution satisfies the given conditions.

Exercises

In Exercises 1 through 8 determine whether or not the given equations are quadratic by performing algebraic operations which could put each in the form of Eq. (6-1). If the resulting form is quadratic, identify a, b, and c, with $a > 0$.

1. $x^2 + 5 = 8x$ 2. $5x^2 = 9 - x$ 3. $x(x - 2) = 4$

4. $(3x - 2)^2 = 2$ 5. $x^2 = (x + 2)^2$ 6. $x(2x + 5) = 7 + 2x^2$

7. $x(x^2 + x - 1) = x^3$ 8. $(x - 7)^2 = (2x + 3)^2$

In Exercises 9 through 38 solve the given quadratic equations by factoring.

9. $x^2 - 4 = 0$ 10. $s^2 + s - 6 = 0$ 11. $x^2 - 7x + 12 = 0$

12. $x^2 - 11x + 30 = 0$ 13. $x^2 = -2x$ 14. $x^2 = 7x$

15. $4y^2 - 9 = 0$ 16. $5p^2 - 80 = 0$ 17. $3x^2 - 13x + 4 = 0$

18. $7x^2 + 3x - 4 = 0$ 19. $x^2 + 8x + 16 = 0$ 20. $4x^2 - 20x + 25 = 0$

21. $6x^2 = 13x - 6$ 22. $6z^2 = 6 + 5z$ 23. $4x^2 - 3 = -4x$

24. $10t^2 = 9 - 43t$ 25. $x^2 - x - 1 = 1$ 26. $2x^2 - 7x + 6 = 3$

27. $x^2 - 4b^2 = 0$ 28. $a^2x^2 - 1 = 0$ 29. $40x - 16x^2 = 0$

30. $18t^2 - 48t + 32 = 0$ 31. $(x + 2)^3 = x^3 + 8$ 32. $x(x^2 - 4) = x^2(x - 1)$

33. $(x + a)^2 - b^2 = 0$ 34. $x^2(a^2 + 2ab + b^2) - x(a + b) = 0$

35. A projectile is fired vertically into the air. The distance (in feet) above the ground, as a function of the time (in seconds), is given by $s = 160t - 16t^2$. How long will it take the projectile to hit the ground?

36. In a certain electric circuit there is a resistance R of 2 ohms and a voltage E of 60 volts. The relationship between current i (in amperes), E and R is $i^2R + iE = 8000$. What current i ($i > 0$) flows in the circuit?

37. Under certain conditions, the motion of an object suspended by a helical spring requires the solution of the equation

$$D^2 + 8D + 15 = 0.$$

Solve for D.

38. In electricity the equivalent resistance of two resistances connected in parallel is given by

$$\frac{1}{R} = \frac{1}{R_1} + \frac{1}{R_2}.$$

Two resistances connected in series have an equivalent resistance given by $R = R_1 + R_2$. If two resistances connected in parallel have an equivalent resistance of 3 ohms and the same two resistances have an equivalent resistance of 16 ohms when connected in series, what are the resistances? (This equation is not quadratic. However, after the proper substitution is made, a fractional equation will exist. After fractions have been cleared, a quadratic equation will exist.)

In Exercises 39 and 40 set up appropriate equations and solve.

39. A certain rectangular machine part has a length which is 4 mm longer than its width. If the area of the part is 96 mm², what are its dimensions?

40. A jet, by increasing its speed by 200 mi/hr, could decrease the time needed to cover 4000 mi by one hour. What is its speed?

6-2 Completing the square

Many quadratic equations cannot be factored by inspection. Therefore we must look for another method of solution. The following example illustrates the method known as *completing the square*.

Example A. We wish to find the roots of the quadratic equation

$$x^2 - 6x - 8 = 0.$$

First we note that this equation is not factorable. However, we do recognize that $x^2 - 6x$ is part of one of the special products. If 9 were added to this expression, we would have $x^2 - 6x + 9$, which is $(x - 3)^2$. We can solve this expression for x by taking a square root, which would leave us with $x - 3$. This expression can then be solved for x by any proper method of solving a linear equation. Thus, by creating an expression which is a perfect square and then taking the square root, we may solve the problem as an ordinary linear equation.

We may write the original equation as

$$x^2 - 6x = 8,$$

and then add 9 to both sides of the equation. The result is

$$x^2 - 6x + 9 = 17.$$

The left side of this equation may be rewritten, giving

$$(x - 3)^2 = 17.$$

Taking square roots of both sides of the equation, we arrive at

$$x - 3 = \pm \sqrt{17}.$$

The $\pm$ sign is necessary, since by the definition of a square root, $(-\sqrt{17})^2 = 17$ and $(+\sqrt{17})^2 = 17$. Now, adding 3 to both sides, we obtain

$$x = 3 \pm \sqrt{17},$$

which means that $x = 3 + \sqrt{17}$ and $x = 3 - \sqrt{17}$ are the two roots of the equation.

How do we determine the number which must be added to complete the square? The answer to this question is based on the special products in Eqs. (5-3) and (5-4). We rewrite these in the form

$$(x + a)^2 = x^2 + 2ax + a^2 \tag{6-2}$$

and

$$(x - a)^2 = x^2 - 2ax + a^2. \tag{6-3}$$

The coefficient of x in each case is numerically $2a$, and the number added to complete the square is a^2. Thus if we take half the coefficient of the x-term and square this result, we have the number which completes the square. In our example, the numerical coefficient of the x-term was 6, and 9 was added to complete the square. We must be certain that the coefficient of the x^2 term is 1 before we start to complete the square. The following example outlines the steps necessary to complete the square.

Example B. Solve the following quadratic equation by the method of completing the square:

$$2x^2 + 16x - 9 = 0.$$

First we divide each term by 2 so that the coefficient of the x^2 term becomes 1.

$$x^2 + 8x - \tfrac{9}{2} = 0$$

Now we put the constant term on the right-hand side by adding 9/2 to both sides of the equation.

$$x^2 + 8x = \tfrac{9}{2}$$

Next we divide the coefficient of the x-term, 8, by 2, which gives us 4. We square 4 and obtain 16, which is the number to be added to both sides of the equation.

$$x^2 + 8x + 16 = \tfrac{9}{2} + 16 = \tfrac{41}{2}$$

We write the left side as the square of $(x + 4)$.

$$(x + 4)^2 = \tfrac{41}{2}$$

Taking the square root of both sides of the equation, we obtain

$$x + 4 = \pm \sqrt{\tfrac{41}{2}}$$

Solving for x, we have

$$x = -4 \pm \sqrt{\tfrac{41}{2}}.$$

Since $\sqrt{\tfrac{41}{2}} = \sqrt{\tfrac{82}{4}} = \tfrac{1}{2}\sqrt{82}$, we may write the solution without a radical in the denominator as

$$x = \frac{-8 \pm \sqrt{82}}{2}.$$

Therefore, the roots are $\tfrac{1}{2}(-8 + \sqrt{82})$ and $\tfrac{1}{2}(-8 - \sqrt{82})$. If we approximate $\sqrt{82}$ with 9.055 (see the Table of Square Roots in the Appendix), the approximate values of the roots are 0.528 and -8.528.

Example C.   Solve $4x^2 - 12x + 5 = 0$ by completing the square.

$$4x^2 - 12x + 5 = 0$$
$$x^2 - 3x + \tfrac{5}{4} = 0$$
$$x^2 - 3x \quad\;\; = -\tfrac{5}{4}$$
$$x^2 - 3x + \tfrac{9}{4} = -\tfrac{5}{4} + \tfrac{9}{4}$$
$$(x - \tfrac{3}{2})^2 = \tfrac{4}{4} = 1$$
$$x - \tfrac{3}{2} = \pm 1$$
$$x = \tfrac{3}{2} \pm 1$$
$$x = \tfrac{5}{2},\, x = \tfrac{1}{2}$$

This equation could have been solved by factoring. However, at this point, we want to illustrate the method of completing the square.

Exercises

Solve the following quadratic equations by completing the square. Exercises 1 through 4 and 7 and 8 may be checked by factoring.

1. $x^2 + 2x - 8 = 0$ 2. $x^2 - x - 6 = 0$ 3. $x^2 + 3x + 2 = 0$

4. $t^2 + 5t - 6 = 0$ 5. $x^2 - 4x + 2 = 0$ 6. $x^2 + 10x - 4 = 0$

7. $2s^2 + 5s - 3 = 0$ 8. $4x^2 + x - 3 = 0$ 9. $2y^2 - y - 2 = 0$

10. $9v^2 - 6v - 2 = 0$ 11. $x^2 + 2bx + c = 0$ 12. $px^2 + qx + r = 0$

6-3 The quadratic formula

We shall now use the method of completing the square to derive a general formula which may be used for the solution of *any* quadratic equation.

Consider Eq. (6-1), the general quadratic equation

$$ax^2 + bx + c = 0,$$

with $a > 0$. When we divide through by a, we obtain

$$x^2 + \frac{b}{a}x + \frac{c}{a} = 0.$$

Subtracting c/a from each side, we have

$$x^2 + \frac{b}{a}x = -\frac{c}{a}.$$

Half of b/a is $b/2a$, which squared is $b^2/4a^2$. Adding $b^2/4a^2$ to each side gives us

$$x^2 + \frac{b}{a}x + \frac{b^2}{4a^2} = -\frac{c}{a} + \frac{b^2}{4a^2}.$$

Writing the left side as a perfect square, and combining fractions on the right side, we have

$$\left(x + \frac{b}{2a}\right)^2 = \frac{b^2 - 4ac}{4a^2}.$$

Taking the square root of each side results in

$$x + \frac{b}{2a} = \frac{\pm\sqrt{b^2 - 4ac}}{2a}.$$

When we subtract $b/2a$ from each side and simplify the resulting expression, we obtain the *quadratic formula*:

$$x = \frac{-b \pm \sqrt{b^2 - 4ac}}{2a}. \tag{6-4}$$

To solve a quadratic equation by using the quadratic formula we need only to write the equation in standard form (see Eq. 6-1), identify a, b, and c, and substitute these numbers directly into the formula. We shall use the quadratic formula to solve the quadratic equations in the following examples.

Example A. $x^2 - 5x + 6 = 0$

In this equation $a = 1$, $b = -5$, and $c = 6$. Thus we have

$$x = \frac{-(-5) \pm \sqrt{25 - 4(1)(6)}}{2} = \frac{5 \pm 1}{2} = 3, 2.$$

The solutions are $x = 3$ and $x = 2$. (This particular equation could have been solved by the method of factoring.)

Example B. $2x^2 - 7x + 5 = 0$

In this equation $a = 2$, $b = -7$, and $c = 5$. Hence

$$x = \frac{7 \pm \sqrt{49 - 4(2)(5)}}{4} = \frac{7 \pm 3}{4} = \frac{5}{2}, 1.$$

Thus the roots are $x = \frac{5}{2}$ and $x = 1$.

Example C. $9x^2 + 24x + 16 = 0$

In this example, $a = 9$, $b = 24$, and $c = 16$. Thus

$$x = \frac{-24 \pm \sqrt{576 - 4(9)(16)}}{18} = \frac{-24 \pm 0}{18} = -\frac{4}{3}.$$

Here both roots are $-\frac{4}{3}$, and the answer should be written as $x = -\frac{4}{3}$ and $x = -\frac{4}{3}$.

Example D. $3x^2 - 5x + 4 = 0$

In this example, $a = 3$, $b = -5$, and $c = 4$. Therefore

$$x = \frac{5 \pm \sqrt{25 - 4(3)(4)}}{6} = \frac{5 \pm \sqrt{-23}}{6}.$$

Here we note that the roots contain imaginary numbers. This happens if $b^2 < 4ac$.

Example E. $2x^2 = 4x + 3$

First we must put the equation in the proper form. This is

$$2x^2 - 4x - 3 = 0.$$

Now we can identify $a = 2$, $b = -4$, and $c = -3$. This leads to the solution

$$x = \frac{-(-4) \pm \sqrt{(-4)^2 - 4(2)(-3)}}{2(2)} = \frac{4 \pm \sqrt{16 + 24}}{4}$$

$$= \frac{4 \pm \sqrt{40}}{4} = \frac{4 \pm 2\sqrt{10}}{4} = \frac{2(2 \pm \sqrt{10})}{4}$$

$$= \frac{2 \pm \sqrt{10}}{2}.$$

Here we used the method of simplifying radicals as introduced in Section 1-4.

Example F. $dx^2 - (3 + d)x + 4 = 0$

In this example, $a = d$, $b = -(3 + d)$, and $c = 4$. We can use the quadratic formula to solve quadratic equations which have literal coefficients. Thus

$$x = \frac{3 + d \pm \sqrt{[-(3+d)]^2 - 4(d)(4)}}{2d} = \frac{3 + d \pm \sqrt{9 - 10d + d^2}}{2d}.$$

Example G.   A square field has a diagonal which is 10 ft longer than one of the sides. What is the length of a side?

Let $x =$ the length of a side of the field, and $y =$ the length of the diagonal. Using the Pythagorean theorem, we know that $y^2 = x^2 + x^2$. From the given information we know that $y = x + 10$. Thus we have

$$(x + 10)^2 = x^2 + x^2.$$

We can now simplify and solve this equation as follows.

$$x^2 + 20x + 100 = 2x^2$$
$$x^2 - 20x - 100 = 0$$
$$x = \frac{20 \pm \sqrt{400 + 400}}{2} = 10 \pm 10\sqrt{2}$$

The negative solution has no meaning in this problem. This means that the solution is $10 + 10\sqrt{2} = 24.1$ ft.

The quadratic formula provides a quick general method for solving quadratic equations. Proper recognition and substitution of the coefficients a, b, and c is all that is required to complete the solution, regardless of the nature of the roots.

Exercises

In Exercises 1 through 28 solve the given quadratic equations using the quadratic formula. For Exercises 1 through 10 use Exercises 1 through 10 of Section 6-2.

11. $2x^2 - 7x + 4 = 0$

12. $3x^2 - 5x - 4 = 0$

13. $2t^2 + 10t = -15$

14. $2d^2 + 7 = 4d$

15. $3s^2 = s + 9$

16. $6r^2 - 6r - 1 = 0$

17. $4x^2 - 9 = 0$

18. $x^2 - 6x = 0$

19. $15 + 4z - 32z^2 = 0$

20. $4x^2 - 12x = 7$

21. $x^2 + 2cx - 1 = 0$

22. $x^2 - 7x + (6 + a) = 0$

23. $b^2x^2 - (b + 1)x + (1 - a) = 0$

24. $c^2x^2 - x - 1 = x^2$

25. Under certain conditions, the partial pressure P of a certain gas (in atmospheres) is found by solving the equation $P^2 - 3P + 1 = 0$. Solve for P such that $P < 1$ atm.

26. A projectile is fired vertically into the air. The distance (in feet) above the ground as a function of time (in seconds) is given by $s = 300 - 100t - 16t^2$. When will the projectile hit the ground?

27. The formula for the total surface area of a right circular cylinder is $A = 2\pi r^2 + 2\pi rh$. If the height of the cylinder is 4 in., how much is the radius if the area is 9π in²?

28. In calculating the current in an electric circuit with an inductance L (in henrys), a resistance R (in ohms) and capacitance C (in farads), it is necessary to solve the equation $Lx^2 + Rx + 1/C = 0$. Find x in terms of L, R, and C.

In Exercises 29 through 32 set up appropriate equations and solve the given stated problems.

29. A metal cube expands when heated. If the volume changes by 6.00 mm³ and each edge is 0.20 mm longer after being heated, what was the original length of an edge of the cube?

30. After a laboratory experiment, a student reported that two particular resistances had a combined resistance of 4 ohms when connected in parallel, and a combined resistance of 7 ohms when connected in series. What values would he obtain for the resistances? (See Exercise 38 of Section 6-1.)

31. To cover a given floor with square tiles of a certain size, it is found that 648 tiles are needed. If the tiles were 1 in. larger in both dimensions, only 512 tiles would be required. What is the length of a side of one of the smaller tiles?

32. A jet pilot flies 2400 mi at a given speed. If the speed were increased by 300 mi/hr, the trip would take one hour less. What is the speed of the jet?

6-4 Miscellaneous Exercises

In Exercises 1 through 10 solve the given quadratic equations by factoring.

1. $x^2 + 3x - 4 = 0$
2. $x^2 + 3x - 10 = 0$
3. $x^2 - 10x + 16 = 0$
4. $x^2 - 6x - 27 = 0$
5. $3x^2 + 11x = 4$
6. $6y^2 = 11y - 3$
7. $6t^2 = 13t - 5$
8. $3x^2 + 5x + 2 = 0$
9. $6s^2 = 25s$
10. $6n^2 - 23n - 35 = 0$

In Exercises 11 through 20 solve the equations of Exercises 1 through 10 above using the quadratic formula.

In Exercises 21 through 30 solve the given quadratic equations by any appropriate method.

21. $x^2 + 4x - 4 = 0$
22. $x^2 + 3x + 1 = 0$
23. $3x^2 + 8x + 2 = 0$
24. $3p^2 = 28 - 5p$
25. $4v^2 = v + 5$
26. $6x^2 - x + 2 = 0$
27. $2x^2 + 3x + 7 = 0$
28. $4y^2 - 5y = 8$
29. $a^2x^2 + 2ax + 2 = 0$
30. $16r^2 - 8r + 1 = 0$

In Exercises 31 through 34 solve the given quadratic equations by completing the square.

31. $x^2 - x - 30 = 0$
32. $x^2 - 2x - 5 = 0$
33. $2x^2 - x - 4 = 0$
34. $4x^2 - 8x - 3 = 0$

In Exercises 35 through 38 solve the equations involving fractions. After multiplying through by the lowest common denominator, quadratic equations should result.

35. $\dfrac{x-4}{x+1} = \dfrac{2}{x}$

36. $\dfrac{x-1}{3} = \dfrac{5}{x} + 1$

37. $\dfrac{x^2 - 3x}{x - 3} = \dfrac{x^2}{x + 2}$

38. $\dfrac{x - 2}{x - 5} = \dfrac{15}{x^2 - 5x}$

In Exercises 39 through 42 solve the given quadratic equations by any appropriate method.

39. To determine the electric current in a certain alternating-current circuit, it is necessary to solve the equation $m^2 + 10m + 2000 = 0$. Solve for m.

40. Under specified conditions, the deflection of a beam requires the solution of the equation $40x - x^2 - 400 = 0$, where x is the distance in feet from one end of the beam. Solve for x.

41. A general formula for the distance s traveled by an object, given an initial velocity v and acceleration a in time t is $s = vt + \frac{1}{2}at^2$. Solve for t.

42. For laminar flow of fluids, the coefficient K_e, used to calculate energy loss due to sudden enlargements, is given by

$$K_e = 1.00 - 2.67\frac{S_a}{S_b} + \left(\frac{S_a}{S_b}\right)^2,$$

where S_a/S_b is the ratio of cross-sectional areas. If $K_e = -0.500$, what is the value of S_a/S_b?

In Exercises 43 through 46 set up appropriate equations and solve the given stated problems.

43. The sum of two electric voltages is 20 volts, and their product is 96 volts². What are the voltages?

44. The length of one field is 400 yd more than the side of a square field. The width is 100 yd more than the side of the square field. If the rectangular field has twice the area of the square field, what are the dimensions of each field?

45. The manufacturer of a disk-shaped machine part of radius 1.00 in. discovered that he could prevent taking a loss in its production if the amount of material used in each was reduced by 20%. If the thickness remains the same, by how much must the radius be reduced in order to prevent a loss?

46. A roof truss is in the shape of a right triangle with the hypotenuse along the base. If one rafter (neglect overhang) is 4 ft longer than the other, and the base is 36 ft, what are the lengths of the rafters?

Trigonometric Functions of Any Angle or Number

7

7-1 Signs of the trigonometric functions

When we were dealing with trigonometric functions in Chapter 3, we restricted ourselves primarily to the functions of acute angles measured in degrees. Since we did define the functions in general, we can use these same definitions for finding the functions of any possible angle. We shall not only find the trigonometric functions of angles measured in degrees, but we shall introduce radian measure as well. From there we shall show how the trigonometric functions can be defined for numbers. In this section we shall determine the signs of the trigonometric functions in each of the four quadrants.

We recall the definitions of the trigonometric functions which were given in Section 3-2:

$$\sin \theta = \frac{y}{r}, \qquad \cos \theta = \frac{x}{r}, \qquad \tan \theta = \frac{y}{x},$$

$$\cot \theta = \frac{x}{y}, \qquad \sec \theta = \frac{r}{x}, \qquad \csc \theta = \frac{r}{y}. \tag{7-1}$$

We see that the functions are defined so long as we know the abscissa, ordinate, and radius vector of the terminal side of θ. Remembering that r is always considered positive, we can see that the various functions will vary in sign, depending on the signs of x and y.

If the terminal side of the angle is in the first or second quadrant, the value of $\sin \theta$ will be positive, but if the terminal side is in the third or fourth quadrant, $\sin \theta$ is negative. This is because y is positive if the point defining the terminal side is above the x-axis, and y is negative if this point is below the x-axis.

Example A.   The value of sin 20° is positive, since the terminal side of 20° is in the first quadrant. The value of sin 160° is positive, since the terminal side of 160° is in the second quadrant. The values of sin 200° and sin 340° are negative, since the terminal sides of these angles are in the third and fourth quadrants, respectively.

The sign of tan θ depends upon the ratio of y to x. In the first quadrant both x and y are positive, and therefore the ratio y/x is positive. In the third quadrant both x and y are negative, and therefore the ratio y/x is positive. In the second and fourth quadrants either x or y is positive and the other is negative, and so the ratio of y/x is negative.

Example B.   The values of tan 20° and tan 200° are positive, since the terminal sides of these angles are in the first and third quadrants, respectively. The values of tan 160° and tan 340° are negative, since the terminal sides of these angles are in the second and fourth quadrants, respectively.

The sign of cos θ depends upon the sign of x. Since x is positive in the first and fourth quadrants, cos θ is positive in these quadrants. In the same way, cos θ is negative in the second and third quadrants.

Example C.   The values of cos 20° and cos 340° are positive, since these angles are first and fourth quadrants angles, respectively. The values of cos 160° and cos 200° are negative, since these angles are second- and third-quadrant angles, respectively.

Since csc θ is defined in terms of r and y, as is sin θ, the sign of csc θ is the same as that of sin θ. For the same reason, cot θ has the same sign as tan θ, and sec θ has the same sign as cos θ. A method for remembering the signs of the functions in the four quadrants is as follows:

All functions of first-quadrant angles are positive. The sin θ and csc θ are positive for second-quadrant angles. The tan θ and cot θ are positive for third-quadrant angles. The cos θ and sec θ are positive for fourth-quadrant angles. All others are negative.

This discussion does not include the quadrantal angles, those angles with terminal sides on one of the axes. They will be discussed later.

Example D.   sin 50°, sin 150°, sin (-200°), cos 300°, cos (-40°), tan 220°, tan (-100°), cot 260°, cot (-310°), sec 280°, sec (-37°), csc 140°, and csc (-190°) are all positive.

Example E.   sin 190°, sin 325°, cos 100°, cos (-95°), tan 172°, tan 295°, cot 105°, cot (-6°), sec 135°, sec (-135°), csc 240°, and csc 355° are all negative.

Example F. Determine the trigonometric functions of θ if the terminal side of θ passes through $(-1, \sqrt{3})$.

We know that $x = -1$, $y = +\sqrt{3}$, and from the Pythagorean theorem we find that $r = 2$. Therefore, the trigonometric functions of θ are:

$$\sin \theta = +\frac{\sqrt{3}}{2}, \qquad \cos \theta = -\frac{1}{2}, \qquad \tan \theta = -\sqrt{3},$$

$$\cot \theta = -\frac{1}{\sqrt{3}}, \qquad \sec \theta = -2, \qquad \csc \theta = +\frac{2}{\sqrt{3}}.$$

We note that the point $(-1, \sqrt{3})$ is on the terminal side of a second-quadrant angle, and that the signs of the functions of θ are those of a second-quadrant angle.

Exercises

In Exercises 1 through 8 determine the algebraic sign of the given trigonometric functions.

1. $\sin 60°$, $\cos 120°$, $\tan 320°$
2. $\tan 185°$, $\sec 115°$, $\sin (-36°)$
3. $\cos 300°$, $\csc 97°$, $\cot (-35°)$
4. $\sin 100°$, $\sec (-15°)$, $\cos 188°$
5. $\cot 186°$, $\sec 280°$, $\sin 470°$
6. $\tan (-91°)$, $\csc 87°$, $\cot 103°$
7. $\cos 700°$, $\tan (-560°)$, $\csc 530°$
8. $\sin 256°$, $\tan 321°$, $\cos (-370°)$

In Exercises 9 through 16 find the trigonometric functions of θ, where the terminal side of θ passes through the given point.

9. $(2, 1)$ 10. $(-1, 1)$ 11. $(-2, -3)$ 12. $(4, -3)$
13. $(-5, 12)$ 14. $(-3, -4)$ 15. $(5, -2)$ 16. $(3, 5)$

In Exercises 17 through 20 determine the quadrant in which the terminal side of θ lies, subject to the given conditions.

17. $\sin \theta$ is positive, $\cos \theta$ is negative.
18. $\tan \theta$ is positive, $\cos \theta$ is negative.
19. $\sec \theta$ is negative, $\cot \theta$ is negative.
20. $\cos \theta$ is positive, $\csc \theta$ is negative.

7-2 Trigonometric functions of any angle

The trigonometric functions of acute angles were determined in Section 3-3, and in the last section we determined the signs of the trigonometric functions in each of the four quadrants. In this section we shall show how we can find the trigonometric functions of an angle of any magnitude. This information will be very important in Chapter 8 when we discuss oblique triangles, and in Chapter 9 when we graph the trigonometric functions.

Any angle in standard position is coterminal with some positive angle less than 360°. Since the terminal sides of coterminal angles are the same, the trigonometric functions of coterminal angles are the same. Therefore, we need consider only the problem of finding the values of the trigonometric functions of positive angles less than 360°.

Example A.   The following pairs of angles are coterminal.

$$390° \text{ and } 30°, \qquad -60° \text{ and } 300°,$$
$$900° \text{ and } 180°, \qquad -150° \text{ and } 210°$$

From this we conclude that the trigonometric functions of both angles in these pairs are equal. That is, for example, $\sin 390° = \sin 30°$ and $\tan (-150°) = \tan 210°$.

Considering the definitions of the functions, we see that the values of the functions depend only on the values of x, y, and r. The values of the functions of second-quadrant angles are numerically equal to the functions of corresponding first-quadrant angles. For example, considering the angles shown in Fig. 7-1, for angle θ_2 with terminal side passing through $(-3, 4)$, $\tan \theta_2 = -\frac{4}{3}$, and for angle θ_1 with terminal side passing through $(3, 4)$, $\tan \theta_1 = \frac{4}{3}$. In Fig. 7-1, we see that the triangles containing angles θ_1 and α (the *reference angle*) are congruent, which means that θ_1 and α are equal. We know that the trigonometric functions of θ_1 and θ_2 are numerically equal. This means that

$$|F(\theta_2)| = |F(\theta_1)| = |F(\alpha)|, \tag{7-2}$$

where F represents any of the trigonometric functions.

Using Eq. (7-2) and the fact that $\alpha = 180° - \theta_2$, we may conclude that the value of any trigonometric function of any second-quadrant angle is found from

$$F(\theta_2) = \pm F(180° - \theta_2). \tag{7-3}$$

The sign to be used depends on whether the *function* is positive or negative in the second quadrant.

Example B.   In Fig. 7-1, the trigonometric functions of θ_2 are as follows.

$$\sin \theta_2 = +\sin (180° - \theta_2)$$
$$= +\sin \alpha = +\sin \theta_1 = \tfrac{4}{5},$$
$$\cos \theta_2 = -\cos \theta_1 = -\tfrac{3}{5},$$
$$\tan \theta_2 = -\tfrac{4}{3}, \qquad \cot \theta_2 = -\tfrac{3}{4},$$
$$\sec \theta_2 = -\tfrac{5}{3}, \qquad \csc \theta_2 = +\tfrac{5}{4}.$$

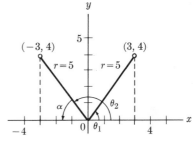

Figure 7-1

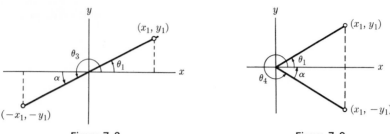

Figure 7-2   Figure 7-3

In the same way we may derive the formulas for finding the trigonometric functions of any third- or fourth-quadrant angle. Considering the angles shown in Fig. 7-2, we see that the reference angle α is found by subtracting 180° from θ_3 and that functions of α and θ_1 are numerically equal. Considering the angles shown in Fig. 7-3, we see that the reference angle α is found by subtracting θ_4 from 360°. Therefore, we have

$$F(\theta_3) = \pm F(\theta_3 - 180°), \tag{7-4}$$

and

$$F(\theta_4) = \pm F(360° - \theta_4). \tag{7-5}$$

Example C. In Fig. 7-2, if $\theta_3 = 210°$, the trigonometric functions of θ_3 are found by using Eq. (7-4) as follows.

$$\sin 210° = -\sin (210° - 180°) = -\sin 30° = -\tfrac{1}{2}$$
$$\cos 210° = -\cos 30° = -0.8660$$
$$\tan 210° = +0.5774 \qquad \cot 210° = +1.732$$
$$\sec 210° = -1.155 \qquad \csc 210° = -2$$

Example D. In Fig. 7-3, if $\theta_4 = 315°$, the trigonometric functions of θ_4 are found by using Eq. (7-5) as follows.

$$\sin 315° = -\sin (360° - 315°) = -\sin 45° = -0.7071$$
$$\cos 315° = +\cos 45° = +0.7071$$
$$\tan 315° = -1 \qquad \cot 315° = -1$$
$$\sec 315° = +1.414 \qquad \csc 315° = -1.414$$

Example E. Other illustrations of the use of Eqs. (7-3), (7-4) and (7-5) are as follows.

$$\sin 160° = +\sin (180° - 160°) = \sin 20° = 0.3420$$
$$\tan 110° = -\tan (180° - 110°) = -\tan 70° = -2.747$$
$$\cos 225° = -\cos (225° - 180°) = -\cos 45° = -0.7071$$
$$\cot 260° = +\cot (260° - 180°) = \cot 80° = 0.1763$$
$$\sec 304° = +\sec (360° - 304°) = \sec 56° = 1.788$$
$$\sin 357° = -\sin (360° - 357°) = -\sin 3° = -0.0523$$

The following examples illustrate how Eqs. (7-3) through (7-5) are used to determine θ when a function of θ is given.

Example F. Given that $\sin \theta = 0.2250$, find θ for $0° < \theta < 360°$.

Here we are to find any angles between $0°$ and $360°$ for which $\sin \theta = 0.2250$. Since $\sin \theta$ is positive for first- and second-quadrant angles, there will be two such angles.

From the tables we find $\theta = 13°$. We also know that $\theta = 180° - 13° = 167°$. These are the two required answers.

Example G. Given that $\tan \theta = 2.050$ and that $\cos \theta < 0$, find θ when $0° < \theta < 360°$.

Since $\tan \theta$ is positive and $\cos \theta$ is negative, θ must be in the third quadrant. We note from the tables that $2.050 = \tan 64°$. Thus $\theta = 180° + 64° = 244°$. Since the required angle is to be between $0°$ and $360°$, this is the only possible answer.

With the use of Eqs. (7-3) through (7-5) we may find the value of any function, as long as the terminal side of the angle lies *in* one of the quadrants. This problem reduces to finding the function of an acute angle. We are left with the case of the terminal side being along one of the axes, a *quadrantal angle*. Using the definitions of the functions, and remembering that $r > 0$, we arrive at the values in the following table.

θ	$\sin \theta$	$\cos \theta$	$\tan \theta$	$\cot \theta$	$\sec \theta$	$\csc \theta$
$0°$	0.000	1.000	0.000	Undef.	1.000	Undef.
$90°$	1.000	0.000	Undef.	0.000	Undef.	1.000
$180°$	0.000	-1.000	0.000	Undef.	-1.000	Undef.
$270°$	-1.000	0.000	Undef.	0.000	Undef.	-1.000
$360°$	Same as the functions of $0°$ (same terminal side)					

The values in the table may be verified by referring to the figures in Fig. 7-4.

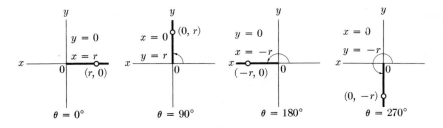

Figure 7-4

Example H.   Since $\sin \theta = y/r$, from Fig. 7-4 (a) we see that $\sin 0° = 0/r = 0$.
Since $\tan \theta = y/x$, from Fig. 7-4 (b) we see that $\tan 90° = r/0$, which is undefined due to the division by zero.
Since $\cos \theta = x/r$, from Fig. 7-4 (c) we see that $\cos 180° = -r/r = -1$.

Exercises

In Exercises 1 through 8 express the given trigonometric functions in terms of the same function of a positive acute angle.

1. $\sin 160°$, $\cos 220°$

2. $\tan 91°$, $\sec 345°$

3. $\tan 105°$, $\csc 302°$

4. $\cos 190°$, $\cot 290°$

5. $\sin (-123°)$, $\cot 174°$

6. $\sin 98°$, $\sec (-315°)$

7. $\cos 400°$, $\tan (-400°)$

8. $\tan 920°$, $\csc (-550°)$

In Exercises 9 through 20 determine the values of the given trigonometric functions by use of tables.

9. $\sin 195°$

10. $\tan 311°$

11. $\cos 106°$

12. $\sin 254°$

13. $\cot 136°$

14. $\cos 297°$

15. $\sec (-115°)$

16. $\csc (-193°)$

17. $\sin 322°52'$

18. $\cot 254°17'$

19. $\tan 118°33'$

20. $\cos (-67°5')$

In Exercises 21 through 28 find θ when $0° < \theta < 360°$.

21. $\tan \theta = 0.5317$

22. $\cos \theta = 0.6428$

23. $\sin \theta = -0.8480$

24. $\cot \theta = -0.2126$

25. $\sin \theta = -0.9527$

26. $\sec \theta = 2.281$

27. $\cot \theta = -0.7144$

28. $\tan \theta = -2.664$

In Exercises 29 through 32 determine the function which satisfies the given conditions.

29. Find $\tan \theta$ when $\sin \theta = -0.5736$ and $\cos \theta > 0$.

30. Find $\sin \theta$ when $\cos \theta = 0.4226$ and $\tan \theta < 0$.

31. Find $\cos \theta$ when $\tan \theta = -0.8098$ and $\csc \theta > 0$.

32. Find $\cot \theta$ when $\sec \theta = 1.122$ and $\sin \theta < 0$.

In Exercises 33 through 36 insert the proper sign, $>$ or $<$ or $=$, between the given expressions.

33. $\sin 90°$ $2 \sin 45°$

34. $\cos 360°$ $2 \cos 180°$

35. $\tan 180°$ $\tan 0°$

36. $\sin 270°$ $3 \sin 90°$

In Exercises 37 and 38 evaluate the given expressions.

37. Under specified conditions, a force F (in pounds) is determined by solving the following equation for F:

$$\frac{F}{\sin 115°} = \frac{46.0}{\sin 35°}.$$

Find the magnitude of the force.

38. A certain a-c voltage can be found from the equation $V = 100 \sin 565°$. Find the voltage V.

In Exercises 39 and 40 the trigonometric functions of negative angles are considered.

39. From Fig. 7-5 we see that $\sin \theta = y/r$ and $\sin (-\theta) = -y/r$. From this we conclude that $\sin (-\theta) = -\sin \theta$. In the same way, verify the remaining Equations (7-6):

$$\sin (-\theta) = -\sin \theta, \qquad \cos (-\theta) = \cos \theta, \qquad \tan (-\theta) = -\tan \theta,$$
$$\cot (-\theta) = -\cot \theta, \qquad \sec (-\theta) = \sec \theta, \qquad \csc (-\theta) = -\csc \theta. \tag{7-6}$$

40. By using the results of Exercise 39, find the values of

(a) $\sin (-60°)$ (b) $\cos (-76°)$ (c) $\tan (-100°)$.

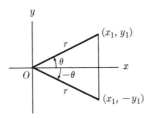

Figure 7-5

7-3 Radians

For many problems in which trigonometric functions are used, particularly those involving the solution of triangles, the degree measurement of angles is quite sufficient. However, in numerous other types of applications and in more theoretical discussions, another way of expressing the measure of angle is more meaningful and convenient. This unit of measurement is the *radian*. A radian is the measure of an angle with its vertex at the center of a circle and with an intercepted arc on the circle equal in length to the radius of the circle. See Fig. 7-6.

Since the circumference of any circle in terms of its radius is given by $c = 2\pi r$, the ratio of the circumference to the radius is 2π. This means that the radius may be laid off 2π (about 6.28) times along the circumference, regardless of the length of the radius. Therefore we see that radian measure is independent of the radius of the circle. In Fig. 7-7 the numbers on each of the radii indicates the number of radians in the angle measured in standard position. The circular arrow shows an angle of 6 radians.

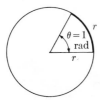

Figure 7-6

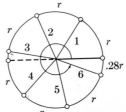

Figure 7-7

Since the radius may be laid off 2π times along the circumference, it follows that there are 2π radians in one complete rotation. Also, there are $360°$ in one complete rotation. Therefore $360°$ is *equivalent* to 2π radians. It then follows that the relation between degrees and radians is 2π rad $= 360°$, or

$$\pi \text{ rad} = 180°. \tag{7-7}$$

From this relation we find that

$$1° = \frac{\pi}{180} \text{ rad} = 0.01745 \text{ rad}, \tag{7-8}$$

and that

$$1 \text{ rad} = \frac{180°}{\pi} = 57.3°. \tag{7-9}$$

We see from Eqs. (7-7) through (7-9) that (1) to convert an angle measured in degrees to the same angle measured in radians, we *multiply the number of degrees by* $\pi/180$, and (2) to convert an angle measured in radians to the same angle measured in degrees, we *multiply the number of radians by* $180/\pi$.

Example A.
$$18° = \left(\frac{\pi}{180}\right)(18) = \frac{\pi}{10} = \frac{3.14}{10} = 0.314 \text{ rad}$$

$$120° = \left(\frac{\pi}{180}\right)(120) = \frac{2\pi}{3} = \frac{6.28}{3} = 2.09 \text{ rad}$$

$$0.4 \text{ rad} = \left(\frac{180°}{\pi}\right)(0.4) = \frac{72°}{3.14} = 22.9°$$

$$2 \text{ rad} = \left(\frac{180°}{\pi}\right)(2) = \frac{360°}{3.14} = 114.6°$$

Due to the nature of the definition of the radian, it is very common to express radians in terms of π. Expressing angles in terms of π is illustrated in the following example.

Example B.
$$30° = \left(\frac{\pi}{180}\right)(30) = \frac{\pi}{6} \text{ rad}$$

$$45° = \left(\frac{\pi}{180}\right)(45) = \frac{\pi}{4} \text{ rad}$$

$$\frac{\pi}{2} \text{ rad} = \left(\frac{180°}{\pi}\right)\left(\frac{\pi}{2}\right) = 90°$$

$$\frac{3\pi}{4} \text{ rad} = \left(\frac{180°}{\pi}\right)\left(\frac{3\pi}{4}\right) = 135°$$

We wish now to make a very important point. Since π is a special way of writing the number (slightly greater than 3) that is the ratio of the circumference of a circle to its diameter, it is the ratio of one distance to another. Thus radians really have no units and *radian measure amounts to measuring angles in terms of numbers.* It is this property of radians that makes them useful in many situations. Therefore, when radians are being used, it is customary that no units are indicated for the angle. When no units are indicated, the radian is understood to be the unit of angle measurement.

Example C. $60° = \left(\dfrac{\pi}{180}\right)(60) = \dfrac{\pi}{3} = 1.05$

$2.50 = \left(\dfrac{180°}{\pi}\right)(2.50) = \dfrac{450°}{3.14} = 143°$

Since no units are indicated for 1.05 or 2.50 in this example, they are known to be radian measure.

Often when one first encounters radian measure, expressions such as sin 1 and sin $\theta = 1$ are confused. The first is equivalent to sin 57.3°, since 57.3° = 1 (radian). The second means that θ is the angle for which the sine is 1. Since sin 90° = 1, we can say that $\theta = 90°$ or that $\theta = \pi/2$. The following examples give additional illustrations of evaluating expressions involving radians.

Example D. $\sin \dfrac{\pi}{3} = \dfrac{\sqrt{3}}{2}$, since $\dfrac{\pi}{3} = 60°$

$\quad\quad\quad$ sin 0.6 = 0.5646, since 0.6 = 34°23′

$\quad\quad\quad$ tan θ = 1.709 means that θ = 59°40′ (smallest positive θ).

Since 59°40′ = 1.04, we can state that tan 1.04 = 1.709.

Example E.   Express θ in radians, such that cos θ = 0.8829 and $0 < \theta < 2\pi$.

We are to find θ in radians for the given value of the cos θ. Also, since θ is restricted to values between 0 and 2π, we must find a first-quadrant angle and a fourth-quadrant angle (cos θ is positive in the first and the fourth quadrants). From the table we see that

$$\cos 28° = 0.8829.$$

Therefore, for the fourth-quadrant angle, cos (360° − 28°) = cos 332° = 0.8829. Converting 28° and 332° to radians, we have

$$\theta = 0.489 \quad \text{or} \quad \theta = 5.79.$$

Exercises

In Exercises 1 through 6 express the given angle measurements in terms of π.

1. 15°,   150°
2. 12°,   225°
3. 75°,   330°
4. 36°,   315°
5. 210°,   270°
6. 240°,   300°

In Exercises 7 through 12 the given numbers express angle measure. Express the measure of each angle in terms of degrees.

7. $\dfrac{2\pi}{5}, \dfrac{3\pi}{2}$

8. $\dfrac{3\pi}{10}, \dfrac{5\pi}{6}$

9. $\dfrac{\pi}{18}, \dfrac{7\pi}{4}$

10. $\dfrac{7\pi}{15}, \dfrac{4\pi}{3}$

11. $\dfrac{17\pi}{18}, \dfrac{5\pi}{3}$

12. $\dfrac{11\pi}{36}, \dfrac{5\pi}{4}$

In Exercises 13 through 18 express the given angles in radian measure. (Use 3.14 as an *approximation* for π.)

13. 23°

14. 54.6°

15. 252°

16. 104.4°

17. 333°30′

18. 168°40′

In Exercises 19 through 24 the given numbers express angle measure. Express the measure of each angle in terms of degrees.

19. 0.75

20. 0.24

21. 3.0

22. 1.7

23. 2.45

24. 34.4

In Exercises 25 through 32 evaluate the given trigonometric functions.

25. $\sin \dfrac{\pi}{4}$

26. $\cos \dfrac{\pi}{6}$

27. $\tan \dfrac{5\pi}{12}$

28. $\sin \dfrac{7\pi}{18}$

29. $\cot \dfrac{5\pi}{6}$

30. $\tan \dfrac{4\pi}{3}$

31. $\cos 4.59$

32. $\sec 3.27$

In Exercises 33 through 40 find θ for $0 < \theta < 2\pi$.

33. $\sin \theta = 0.3090$

34. $\cos \theta = -0.9135$

35. $\tan \theta = -0.2126$

36. $\sin \theta = -0.0436$

37. $\cos \theta = 0.6742$

38. $\tan \theta = 1.860$

39. $\sec \theta = -1.307$

40. $\csc \theta = 3.940$

In Exercises 41 through 43 evaluate the given expressions.

41. In optics, when determining the positions of maximum light intensity under specified conditions, the equation $\tan \alpha = \alpha$ is found. Show that a solution to this equation is $\alpha = 1.43\pi$.

42. The instantaneous voltage in a "120 volt," 60 cycle/sec power line is given approximately by the equation $V = 170 \sin 377t$, where t is the time (measured in seconds) after the generator started. Calculate the instantaneous voltage (a) after 0.001 sec and (b) after 0.01 sec.

43. The velocity v of an object undergoing simple harmonic motion at the end of a spring is given by

$$v = A\sqrt{\dfrac{m}{k}} \; \cos \sqrt{\dfrac{m}{k}} \, t \, .$$

Here m is the mass of the object in grams, k is a constant depending on the spring, A is the maximum distance the object moves, and t is the time in seconds. Find the velocity (in centimeters per second) after 0.1 sec of a 36-gm object at the end of a spring for which $k = 400$ dynes/cm, if $A = 5.00$ cm.

7-4 Applications of the use of radian measure

Radian measure has numerous applications in mathematics and technology, some of which were indicated in the last three exercises of the previous section. In this section we shall illustrate the usefulness of radian measure in three specific geometric and physical applications.

From geometry we know that the length of an arc on a circle is proportional to the central angle, and that the length of the arc of a complete circle is the circumference. Letting s stand for the length of arc, we may state that $s = 2\pi r$ for a complete circle. Since 2π is the central angle (in radians) of the complete circle, we have

$$s = \theta r \tag{7-10}$$

for any circular arc with central angle θ. If we know the central angle in radians and the radius of a circle, we can find the length of a circular arc directly by using Eq. (7-10). (See Fig. 7-8.)

Example A.   If $\theta = \pi/6$ and $r = 3$ in.,

$$s = \left(\frac{\pi}{6}\right)(3) = \frac{\pi}{2} = 1.57 \text{ in.}$$

If the arc length is 7.20 ft for a central angle of 150° on a certain circle, we may find the radius of the circle by

$$7.20 = (150)\left(\frac{\pi}{180}\right)r = \frac{5\pi}{6}r, \quad \text{or} \quad r = \frac{6(7.20)}{5(3.14)} = 2.75 \text{ ft.}$$

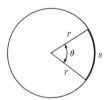

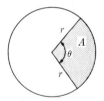

Figure 7-8   Figure 7-9

Another geometric application of radians is in finding the area of a sector of a circle. (See Fig. 7-9.) We recall from geometry that areas of sectors of circles are proportional to their central angles. The area of a circle is given by $A = \pi r^2$. This can be written as $A = \frac{1}{2}(2\pi)r^2$. We now note that the angle for a complete circle is 2π, and therefore the area of any sector of a circle in terms of the radius and the central angle is

$$A = \tfrac{1}{2}\theta r^2. \tag{7-11}$$

Example B.   The area of a sector of a circle with central angle 18° and radius 5.00 in. is

$$A = \frac{1}{2}(18)\left(\frac{\pi}{180}\right)(5.00)^2 = \frac{1}{2}\left(\frac{\pi}{10}\right)(25.0) = 3.93 \text{ in}^2.$$

Given that the area of a sector is 75.5 ft² and the radius is 12.2 ft, we can find the central angle by

$$75.5 = \frac{1}{2}\theta(12.2)^2, \qquad \theta = \frac{2(75.5)}{(12.2)^2} = \frac{151}{149} = 1.01.$$

This means that the central angle is 1.01 radians, or 57.9°.

The next illustration deals with velocity. We know that average velocity is defined by the equation $v = s/t$, where v is the average velocity, s is the distance traveled, and t is the elapsed time. If an object is moving around a circular path with constant speed, the actual distance traveled is the length of arc traversed. Therefore, if we divide both sides of Eq. (7-10) by t, we obtain

$$\frac{s}{t} = \frac{\theta}{t}r \qquad \text{or} \qquad v = \omega r. \qquad (7\text{-}12)$$

Equation (7-12) expresses the relationship between the *linear velocity* v and the *angular velocity* ω of an object moving around a circle of radius r. The most convenient units for ω are radians per unit of time. In this way the formula can be used directly. However, in practice, ω is often given in revolutions per minute, or in some similar unit. In cases like these, it is necessary to convert the units of ω to radians per unit of time before substituting in Eq. (7-12).

Example C.   An object is moving about a circle of radius 6.00 in. with an angular velocity of 4.00 rad/sec. The linear velocity is

$$v = (6.00)(4.00) = 24.0 \text{ in./sec.}$$

(Remember that radians are numbers and are not included in the final set of units.) This means that the object is moving along the circumference of the circle at 24.0 in./sec.

Example D.   A flywheel rotates with an angular velocity of 20 rev/min. If its radius is 18.0 in., find the linear velocity of a point on the rim.

Since there are 2π radians in each revolution,

$$20 \text{ rev/min} = 40\pi \text{ rad/min.}$$

Therefore,

$$v = (40.0)(3.14)(18.0) = 2260 \text{ in./min.}$$

This means that the linear velocity is 2260 in./min, which is equivalent to 188 ft/min, or 3.13 ft/sec.

Example E.   A pulley belt 10.0 ft long takes 2.00 sec to make one complete revolution. The radius of the pulley is 6.00 in. What is the angular velocity (in rev/min) of a point on the rim of the pulley?

Since the linear velocity of a point on the rim of the pulley is the same as the velocity of the belt, $v = 10.0/2.00 = 5.00$ ft/sec. The radius of the pulley is $r = 6.00$ in. $= 0.50$ ft, and we can find ω by substuting into Eq. (7-12). This gives us

$$5.00 = \omega(0.50),$$

or

$$\omega = 10.0 \text{ rad/sec}$$
$$= 600 \text{ rad/min}$$
$$= 95.5 \text{ rev/min.}$$

As it is shown in Appendix B, the change of units can be handled algebraically as

$$10.0 \frac{\text{rad}}{\cancel{\text{sec}}} \times 60 \frac{\cancel{\text{sec}}}{\text{min}} = 600 \frac{\text{rad}}{\text{min}}, \qquad \frac{600 \text{ rad/min}}{2\pi \text{ rad/rev}} = 600 \frac{\cancel{\text{rad}}}{\text{min}} \times \frac{1}{2\pi} \frac{\text{rev}}{\cancel{\text{rad}}}.$$

Exercises

1. In a circle of radius 10.0 in., find the length of arc subtended on the circumference by a central angle of 60°.
2. In a circle of diameter 4.50 ft, find the length of arc subtended on the circumference by a central angle of 42°.
3. Find the area of the circular sector indicated in Exercise 1.
4. Find the area of a sector of a circle, given that the central angle is 120° and the diameter is 56.0 cm.
5. Find the radian measure of an angle at the center of a circle of radius 5.00 in. which intercepts an arc length of 60.0 in.
6. Find the central angle of a circle which intercepts an arc length of 780 mm when the radius of the circle is 520 mm.
7. Two concentric (same center) circles have radii of 5.00 and 6.00 in. Find the portion of the area of the sector of the larger circle which is outside the smaller circle when the central angle is 30°.
8. In a circle of radius 6.00 in., the length of arc of a sector is 10.0 in. What is the area of the sector?
9. A pendulum 3.00 ft long oscillates through an angle of 5°. Find the distance through which the end of the pendulum swings in going from one extreme position to the other.
10. The radius of the earth is about 3960 mi. What is the length, in miles, of an arc of the earth's equator for a central angle of 1°?
11. In turning, an airplane traveling at 540 mi/hr moves through a circular arc for 2 min. What is the radius of the circle, given that the central angle is 8°?

12. An ammeter needle is deflected 52° by a current of 0.20 amp. The needle is 3.0 in. long and a circular scale is used. How long is the scale for a maximum current of 1.00 amp?

13. A flywheel rotates at 300 rev/min. If the radius is 6.00 in., through what total distance does a point on the rim travel in 30.0 sec?

14. For the flywheel in Exercise 13, how far does a point halfway out along a radius, move in one second?

15. An automobile is traveling at 60.0 mi/hr (88.0 ft/sec). The tires are 28.0 in. in diameter. What is the angular velocity of the tires in rad/sec?

16. Find the velocity, due to the rotation of the earth, of a point on the surface of the earth at the equator (see Exercise 10).

17. An astronaut in a spacecraft circles the moon once each 1.95 hr. If his altitude is constant at 70 mi, what is his velocity? The radius of the moon is 1080 mi.

18. What is the linear velocity of the point in Exercise 13?

19. The armature of a dynamo is 1.38 ft in diameter and is rotating at 1200 rev/min. What is the linear velocity of a point on the rim of the armature?

20. A pulley belt 9.50 ft long takes 2.50 sec to make one complete revolution. The diameter of the pulley is 11.0 in. What is the angular velocity, in rev/min, of the pulley?

21. The moon is about 240,000 mi from the earth. It takes the moon about 28 days to make one revolution. What is its angular velocity about the earth, in radians per second?

22. A phonograph record 6.90 in. in diameter rotates 45.0 times per minute. What is the linear velocity of a point on the rim in feet/second?

23. A circular sector whose central angle is 210° is cut from a circular piece of sheet metal of diameter 12.0 in. A cone is then formed by bringing the two radii of the sector together. What is the lateral surface area of the cone?

24. The propeller of an airplane is 8.00 ft in diameter and rotates at 2200 rev/min. What is the linear velocity of a point on the tip of the propeller?

7-5 Miscellaneous Exercises

In Exercises 1 through 4 express the given angle measurements in terms of π.

1. 40°, 153°   2. 22.5°, 324°   3. 48°, 202.5°   4. 27°, 162°

In Exercises 5 through 12 the given numbers represent angle measure. Express the measure of each angle in terms of degrees.

5. $\dfrac{7\pi}{5}, \dfrac{13\pi}{18}$ 6. $\dfrac{3\pi}{8}, \dfrac{7\pi}{20}$ 7. $\dfrac{\pi}{15}, \dfrac{11\pi}{6}$ 8. $\dfrac{17\pi}{10}, \dfrac{5\pi}{4_1}$

9. 0.560   10. 1.35   11. 3.60   12. 14.5

In Exercises 13 through 16 express the given angles in radians. (Do not answer in terms of π.)

13. 100°   14. 305°   15. 20°30′   16. 148°20′

In Exercises 17 through 20 express the given trigonometric functions in terms of the same function of a positive acute angle.

17. cos 132°,   tan 194°

18. sin 243°,   cot 318°

19. sin 289°,   sec (−15°)

20. cos 103°,   csc (−100°)

In Exercises 21 through 28 determine the values of the given trigonometric functions.

21. cos 245°

22. sin 141°

23. tan 256°42′

24. cos 162°32′

25. $\sin \dfrac{9\pi}{5}$

26. $\sec \dfrac{5\pi}{8}$

27. csc 2.15

28. tan 0.8

In Exercises 29 through 32 find θ, when $0° < \theta < 360°$.

29. sin θ = 0.2924

30. cot θ = −2.560

31. cos θ = 0.3297

32. tan θ = −0.7730

In Exercises 33 through 36 find θ, when $0 < \theta < 2\pi$.

33. cos θ = 0.8387

34. sin θ = 0.1045

35. sin θ = −0.8650

36. tan θ = 2.840

In Exercises 37 through 45 solve the given problems.

37. The voltage in a certain alternating current circuit is given by $v = V \cos 25t$, where V is the maximum possible voltage and t is the time in seconds. Find v for $t = 0.1$ sec and $V = 150$ volts.

38. The displacement (distance from equilibrium position) of a particle moving with simple harmonic motion is given by $d = A \sin 5t$, where A is the maximum displacement and t is the time. Find d, given that $A = 16.0$ cm and $t = 0.46$ sec.

39. A pendulum 5.00 ft long swings through an angle of 4.50°. Through what distance does the bob swing in going from one extreme position to the other?

40. Two pulleys have radii of 10.0 in. and 6.00 in., and their centers are 40.0 in. apart. If the pulley belt is uncrossed, what must be the length of the belt?

41. If the apparatus shown in Fig. 7-10 is rotating at 2.00 rev/sec, what is the linear velocity of the ball?

42. A lathe is to cut material at the rate of 350 ft/min. Calculate the radius of a cylindrical piece that is turned at the rate of 120 rev/min.

43. A thermometer needle passes through 55° for a temperature change of 40°. If the needle is 5.0 in. long and the scale is circular, how long must the scale be for a maximum temperature change of 150°?

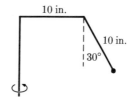

Figure 7-10

44. Under certain conditions an electron will travel in a circular path when in a magnetic field. If an electron is moving with a linear velocity of 20,000 m/sec in a circular path of radius 0.50 m, how far does it travel in 0.10 sec?

45. A horizontal water pipe has a radius of 6.00 ft. If the depth of water in the pipe is 3.00 ft, what percentage of the volume of the pipe is filled?

Vectors and
Oblique Triangles

8

8-1 Vectors

A great many quantities with which we deal may be described by specifying their magnitudes. Generally, one can describe lengths of objects, areas, time intervals, monetary amounts, temperatures, and numerous other quantities by specifying a number: the magnitude of the quantity. Such quantities are known as *scalar* quantities.

Many other quantities are fully described only when both their magnitude and direction are specified. Such quantities are known as *vectors*. Examples of vectors are velocity, force, and momentum. Vectors are of utmost importance in many fields of science and technology. The following example illustrates a vector quantity and the distinction between scalars and vectors.

Example A. A jet flies over a certain point traveling at 600 mi/hr. From this statement alone we know only the *speed* of the jet. Speed is a scalar quantity, and it designates only the magnitude of the rate.

If we were to add the phrase "in a direction 10° south of west" to the sentence above about the jet, we would be specifying the direction of travel as well as the speed. We then know the *velocity* of the jet; that is, we know the *direction* of travel as well as the *magnitude* of the rate at which the jet is traveling. Velocity is a vector quantity.

Let us analyze an example of the action of two vectors: Consider a boat moving in a stream. For purposes of this example, we shall assume that the boat is driven by a motor which can move it at 4 mi/hr in still water. We shall assume that the current is moving downstream at 3 mi/hr. We immediately see that the motion of the boat depends on the direction in which it is headed. If the boat heads downstream, it can travel at 7 mi/hr, for the current is going 3 mi/hr and the boat moves at 4 mi/hr with respect to the water. If the boat heads upstream, however, it progresses at the rate of only 1 mi/hr, since the action of the boat and that of the stream are counter to each other. If the boat heads across the stream, the point which it reaches on the other side will not be directly opposite the point from which it started. We can see that this is so because we know that as the boat heads across the stream, the stream is moving the boat downstream *at the same time.*

This last case should be investigated further. Let us assume that the stream is $\frac{1}{2}$ mi wide where the boat is crossing. It will then take the boat $\frac{1}{8}$ hr to cross. In $\frac{1}{8}$ hr the stream will carry the boat $\frac{3}{8}$ mi downstream. Therefore, when the boat reaches the other side it will be $\frac{3}{8}$ mi downstream. From the Pythagorean theorem, we find that the boat traveled $\frac{5}{8}$ mi from its starting point to its finishing point.

$$d^2 = \left(\frac{4}{8}\right)^2 + \left(\frac{3}{8}\right)^2 = \frac{16 + 9}{64} = \frac{25}{64}; \qquad d = \frac{5}{8} \text{ mi}$$

Since this $\frac{5}{8}$ mi was traveled in $\frac{1}{8}$ hr, the magnitude of the velocity of the boat was actually

$$v = \frac{d}{t} = \frac{5/8}{1/8} = \frac{5}{8} \cdot \frac{8}{1} = 5 \text{ mi/hr.}$$

Also, we see that the direction of this velocity can be represented along a line making an angle θ with the line directed across the stream (see Fig. 8-1).

We have just seen two velocity vectors being *added.* Note that these vectors are not added the way numbers are added. We have to take into account their direction as well as their magnitude. Reasoning along these lines, let us now define the sum of two vectors. [*Note:* a vector quantity is represented by a letter printed in boldface type. (In writing, one usually places an arrow over the letter.) The same letter in italic (lightface) type represents the magnitude only.]

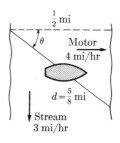

Figure 8-1

Let **A** and **B** represent vectors directed from O to P and from P to Q, respectively (see Fig. 8-2). The resultant vector **R** from the *initial point O* to the *terminal point Q* represents the sum of vectors **A** and **B**. This is equivalent to letting the two vectors that are added be the sides of a parallelogram. The resultant is then the diagonal of the parallelogram, as shown in Fig. 8-3. (When a parallelogram is used to find the resultant of two vectors, the vectors are generally placed with their endpoints together.)

Three or more vectors may be added by placing the initial point of the second at the terminal point of the first, the initial point of the third at the terminal point of the second, and so forth (Fig. 8-4). The resultant is the vector from the initial point of the first to the terminal point of the last. In general, a *resultant* is a single vector which can replace any number of other vectors and still produce the same physical effect.

Vectors may be subtracted by reversing the direction of the vector being subtracted, and then proceeding as in adding vectors.

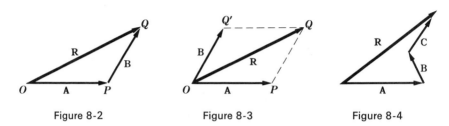

Figure 8-2   Figure 8-3   Figure 8-4

Note that in Figs. 8-2, 8-3, and 8-4 no attempt was made to place the vectors in particular positions, except with respect to direction and magnitude. Any vector may be moved for purposes of adding and subtracting, so long as its magnitude and direction remain unchanged.

Example B.   Given vectors **A** and **B**, as shown in Fig. 8-5(a), we move them for purposes of addition as shown in Fig. 8-5(b). The parallelogram method of adding is indicated in Fig. 8-5(c). The vector difference **A** − **B** is shown in Fig. 8-5(d). Note that the direction of vector **B** is reversed for the subtraction, but the magnitude is the same.

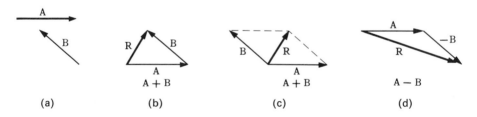

(a)   (b)   (c)   (d)

Figure 8-5

In addition to being able to add and subtract vectors, we often need to consider a given vector as the sum of two other vectors. Two vectors which when added together give the original vector are called the *components* of the original vector. In the example of the boat, the velocities of 4 mi/hr crossstream and 3 mi/hr downstream are components of the 5 mi/hr vector directed at the angle θ.

In practice, there are certain components of a vector which are of particular importance. If a vector is so placed that its initial point is at the origin of a rectangular coordinate system, and its direction is indicated by an angle in standard position, we may find its x- and y- components. These components are vectors directed along the coordinate axes which, when added together, result in the given vector. Finding these component vectors is called *resolving* the vector into its components.

Example C. Resolve a vector 10 units long and directed at an angle of 120° into its x- and y-components (see Fig. 8-6).

Placing the initial point of the vector at the origin, and putting the angle in standard position, we see that the vector directed along the x-axis $\mathbf{V}_x$, is related to the vector $\mathbf{V}$, of magnitude V by

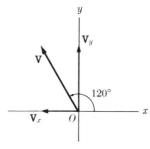

Figure 8-6

$$V_x = V \cos 120° = -V \cos 60°.$$

(The minus sign indicates that the x-component is directed in the negative direction; that is, to the left.) The vector directed along the y-axis, $\mathbf{V}_y$, is related to the vector $\mathbf{V}$ by

$$V_y = V \sin 120° = V \sin 60°.$$

Thus the vectors $\mathbf{V}_x$ and $\mathbf{V}_y$ have the magnitudes

$$V_x = -10(0.500) = -5.00, \qquad V_y = 10(0.866) = 8.66.$$

Therefore, we have resolved the given vector into two components, one directed along the negative x-axis of magnitude 5.00, and the other directed along the positive y-axis of magnitude 8.66.

Adding vectors by diagrams gives only approximate results. By use of the trigonometric functions and the Pythagorean theorem it is possible to obtain accurate numerical results for the sum of vectors. In the following example we shall illustrate how this is done in the case when the two given vectors are at right angles.

Example D. Add vectors **A** and **B**, with $A = 14.5$ and $B = 9.10$. The vectors are at right angles as shown in Fig. 8-7.

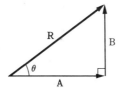

Figure 8-7

We can find the magnitude R of the resultant vector **R** by use of the Pythagorean theorem. This leads to

$$R = \sqrt{A^2 + B^2} = \sqrt{(14.5)^2 + (9.10)^2}$$
$$= \sqrt{210 + 82.8} = \sqrt{293} = 17.1.$$

(Notice that the numbers have been rounded off to three significant digits.) We shall now determine the direction of **R** by specifying its direction as the angle θ, that is, the angle **R** makes with **A**. Therefore,

$$\tan \theta = \frac{B}{A} = \frac{9.10}{14.5} = 0.628.$$

To the nearest 10′, $\theta = 32°10′$ (a slide rule solution would be $\theta = 32.1°$). Thus **R** is a vector with magnitude $R = 17.1$ and in a direction $32°10′$ from vector **A**.

The following two examples show how vectors which are not at right angles are added. The basic procedure is to resolve each into its x- and y-components. These x-components and y-components are added, thus giving the x- and y-components of the resultant. Then, by using the Pythagorean theorem and the tangent, as in Example D, we find the magnitude and direction of the resultant.

Example E.   Find the resultant **R** of the two vectors given in Fig. 8-8(a), **A** of magnitude 8.00 and direction 57° and **B** of magnitude 5.00 and direction 322°.

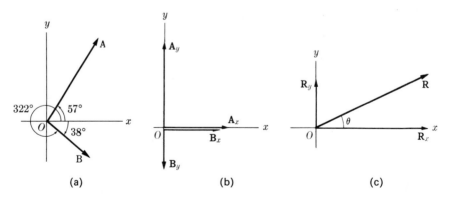

(a)   (b)   (c)

Figure 8-8

$$A_x = (8.00)(\cos 57°) = (8.00)(0.5446) = 4.36$$
$$A_y = (8.00)(\sin 57°) = (8.00)(0.8387) = 6.71$$
$$B_x = (5.00)(\cos 38°) = (5.00)(0.7880) = 3.94$$
$$B_y = -(5.00)(\sin 38°) = -(5.00)(0.6157) = -3.08$$

$$R_x = A_x + B_x = 4.36 + 3.94 = 8.30$$
$$R_y = A_y + B_y = 6.71 - 3.08 = 3.63$$
$$R = \sqrt{(8.30)^2 + (3.63)^2} = \sqrt{68.9 + 13.2} = \sqrt{82.1} = 9.06$$
$$\tan \theta = \frac{R_y}{R_x} = \frac{3.63}{8.30} = 0.437, \qquad \theta = 23.6°$$

The resultant vector is 9.06 units long and is directed at an angle of 23.6°, as shown in Fig. 8-8(c).

Some general formulas can be derived from the previous examples. For a given vector **A**, directed at an angle θ, and of magnitude A, with components A_x and A_y, we have the following relations:

$$A_x = A \cos \theta, \qquad A_y = A \sin \theta, \tag{8-1}$$
$$A = \sqrt{A_x{}^2 + A_y{}^2}, \tag{8-2}$$
$$\tan \theta = A_y/A_x. \tag{8-3}$$

Example F. Find the resultant of the three given vectors with $A = 422$, $B = 405$, and $C = 210$, as shown in Fig. 8-9.

We can find the x- and y-components of the vectors by using Eq. (8-1). The following table is helpful for determining the necessary values.

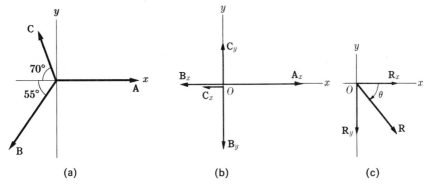

Figure 8-9

Vector	x-component		y-component	
A		$= +422$		$= 0$
B	$-405 \cos 55°$	$= -232$	$-405 \sin 55°$	$= -332$
C	$-210 \cos 70°$	$= -72$	$+210 \sin 70°$	$= +197$
R		$+118$		-135

From this table it is possible to compute R and θ:

$$R = \sqrt{(118)^2 + (-135)^2} = 179, \qquad \tan \theta = \frac{-135}{118} = -1.14, \ \theta = -48.7°.$$

Exercises

In Exercises 1 through 12, with the vectors indicated in Fig. 8-10, find the vector sums by means of diagrams.

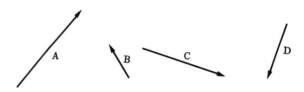

Figure 8-10

1. **A + B**
2. **A + C**
3. **B + C**
4. **B + D**
5. **A + B + D**
6. **B − C**
7. **A + D − C**
8. **C − A**
9. **2A + B**   (2A = A + A)
10. **B − 2C + 3D**
11. **A + 2B + 3C − 4D**
12. **½A − C + 2B**

In Exercises 13 through 20 find the x- and y-components of the given vectors by use of the trigonometric functions.

13. Magnitude 8.6, $\theta = 68°$
14. Magnitude 9750, $\theta = 243°$
15. Magnitude 76.8, $\theta = 145°$
16. Magnitude 0.0998, $\theta = 476°$
17. Magnitude 9.04, $\theta = 283°44'$
18. Magnitude 16,000, $\theta = 156.5°$
19. Magnitude 1, $\theta = 1$
20. Magnitude 67.8, $\theta = 15\pi/8$

In Exercises 21 through 28 with the given sets of components, find R and θ.

21. $R_x = 5.18$, $R_y = 8.56$
22. $R_x = 89.6$, $R_y = -52.0$
23. $R_x = -0.982$, $R_y = 2.56$
24. $R_x = -729$, $R_y = -209$
25. $R_x = -646$, $R_y = 2030$
26. $R_x = -31.2$, $R_y = -41.2$
27. $R_x = 0.694$, $R_y = -1.24$
28. $R_x = 7.62$, $R_y = -6.35$

In Exercises 29 through 36 add the given vectors by using the trigonometric functions and the Pythagorean theorem.

29. $A = 18.0$, $\theta_A = 0°$
    $B = 12.0$, $\theta_B = 27°$
30. $A = 150$, $\theta_A = 90°$
    $B = 128$, $\theta_B = 43°$
31. $A = 56$, $\theta_A = 76°$
    $B = 24$, $\theta_B = 200°$
32. $A = 6.89$, $\theta_A = 123°$
    $B = 29.0$, $\theta_B = 260°$
33. $A = 9.82$, $\theta_A = 34°$
    $B = 17.4$, $\theta_B = 752°$
34. $A = 1.65$, $\theta_A = 36°$
    $B = 0.980$, $\theta_B = 253°$
35. $A = 21.9$, $\theta_A = 236.2°$
    $B = 96.7$, $\theta_B = 11.5°$
    $C = 62.9$, $\theta_C = 143.4°$
36. $A = 6300$, $\theta_A = 189°$
    $B = 1760$, $\theta_B = 320°$
    $C = 3240$, $\theta_C = 75°$

In Exercises 37 and 38 add the given vectors.

37. The forces shown in Fig. 8-11.
38. The vectors shown in Fig. 8-12.

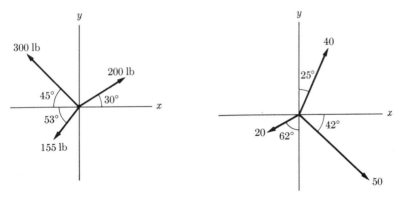

Figure 8-11   Figure 8-12

8-2 Application of vectors

The following examples show how vectors are used in certain situations.

Example A. An object on a horizontal table is acted on by two horizontal forces. The two forces have magnitudes of 6.0 and 8.0 lb, and the angle between their lines of action is 90°. What is the resultant of these forces?

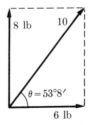

Figure 8-13

By means of an appropriate diagram (Fig. 8-13) we may better visualize the actual situation. We then note that a good choice of axes (unless specified, it is often convenient to choose the x- and y-axes to fit the problem) is to have the x-axis in the direction of the 6.0-lb force and the y-axis in the direction of the 8.0-lb force. (This is possible since the angle between them is 90°.) With this choice we note that the two given forces will be the x- and y-components of the resultant. Therefore, we arrive at the following results:

$$F_x = 6.0 \text{ lb}, \qquad F_y = 8.0 \text{ lb}, \qquad F = \sqrt{36 + 64} = 10 \text{ lb};$$

$$\tan \theta = \frac{F_y}{F_x} = \frac{8.0}{6.0} = 1.33, \qquad \theta = 53°.$$

We would state that the resultant has a magnitude of 10 lb and acts at an angle of 53° from the 6.0-lb force.

Example B. A ship sails 32 mi due east and then turns 40° N of E. After sailing an additional 16 mi, where is it with reference to the starting point?

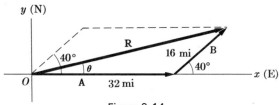

Figure 8-14

The distance an object moves and the direction in which it moves give the *displacement* of an object. Therefore, in this problem we are to determine the resultant displacement of the ship from the two given displacements. The problem is diagramed in Fig. 8-14, where the first displacement has been labeled vector **A** and the second as vector **B**.

Since east corresponds to the positive x-direction, we see that the x-component of the resultant is $A + B_x$, and the y-component of the resultant is B_y. Therefore. we have the following results.

$$R_x = A + B_x = 32 + 16 \cos 40°$$
$$= 32 + 16(0.766) = 32 + 12$$
$$= 44 \text{ mi}$$
$$R_y = 16 \sin 40° = 16(0.643)$$
$$= 10 \text{ mi}$$
$$R = \sqrt{(44)^2 + (10)^2} = \sqrt{2040} = 45 \text{ mi}$$
$$\tan \theta = \frac{10}{44} = 0.227$$
$$\theta = 13°$$

Therefore, the ship is 45 mi (to the nearest mile) from the starting point, in a direction 13° (to the nearest degree) N of E. (Here we have rounded off to two significant digits.)

Example C. An airplane headed due east is in a wind which is blowing from the southeast. What is the resultant velocity of the plane with respect to the surface of the earth, if the plane's velocity with respect to the air is 600 mi/hr, and that of the wind is 100 mi/hr (see Fig. 8-15).

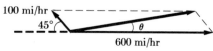

Figure 8-15

Let v_{px} be the velocity of the plane in the x-direction (east), v_{py} the velocity of the plane in the y-direction, v_{wx} the x-component of the velocity of the wind,

v_{wy} the y-component of the velocity of the wind, and v_{pa} the velocity of the plane with respect to the air. Therefore

$$v_{px} = v_{pa} - v_{wx} = 600 - 100 \, (\cos 45°) = 600 - 71 = 529 \text{ mi/hr,}$$

$$v_{py} = v_{wy} = 100 \, (\sin 45°) = 71 \text{ mi/hr;}$$

$$v = \sqrt{(529)^2 + (71)^2} = \sqrt{280{,}000 + 5000} = 534 \text{ mi/hr,}$$

$$\tan \theta = \frac{v_{py}}{v_{px}} = \frac{71}{529} = 0.134, \qquad \theta = 7.6°.$$

We have determined that the plane is traveling 534 mi/hr and is flying in a direction 7.6° north of east. From this we observe that a plane does not necessarily head in the direction of its desired destination.

Example D. A block is resting on an inclined plane which makes an angle of 30° with the horizontal. If the block weighs 100 lb, what is the force of friction between the block and the plane?

The weight of the block is the force exerted on the block due to gravity. Therefore, the weight is directed vertically downward. The frictional force tends to oppose the motion of the block and is directed upward along the plane. The frictional force must be sufficient to counterbalance that component of the weight of the block which is directed down the plane for the block to be at rest. The plane itself "holds up" that component of the weight which is perpendicular to the plane. A convenient set of coordinates (Fig. 8-16) would be one with the x-axis directed up the plane and the y-axis perpendicular to the plane. The magnitude of the frictional force $\mathbf{F}_f$ is given by

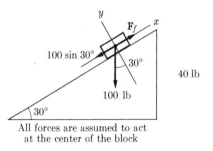

Figure 8-16

$$F_f = 100 \sin 30° = 100(0.500) = 50.0 \text{ lb.}$$

(Since the component of the weight down the plane is 100 sin 30° and is equal to the frictional force, this relation is true.)

Example E. A 60-lb object hangs from a hook on a wall. If a horizontal force of 40 lb pulls the object away from the wall so that the object is in equilibrium (no resultant force in any direction), what is the tension T in the rope attached to the wall?

For the object to be in equilibrium, the tension in the rope must be equal and opposite to the resultant of the 40-lb force and the 60-lb force which is

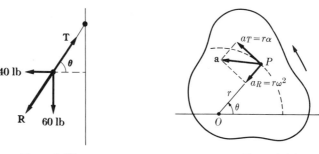

Figure 8-17   Figure 8-18

the weight of the object (see Fig. 8-17). Thus the magnitude of the x-component of the tension is 40 lb and the magnitude of the y-component is 60 lb.

$$T = \sqrt{(40)^2 + (60)^2} = \sqrt{5200} = 72 \text{ lb}, \qquad \tan \theta = \frac{60}{40} = 1.5, \qquad \theta = 56°.$$

Example F.   If an object rotates about a point O, the tangential component of the acceleration $\mathbf{a}_T$ and the centripetal component of the acceleration $\mathbf{a}_R$ of a point P are given by the expressions shown in Fig. 8-18. The radius of the circle through which P is moving is r, the angular velocity at any instant is ω, and α is the rate at which the angular velocity ω is changing. Given that $r = 2.0$ ft, $\omega = 6.0$ rad/sec and $\alpha = 4.0$ rad/sec^2, calculate the magnitude of the resultant acceleration and the angle it makes with the tangential component.

$$(\mathbf{a}_R \perp \mathbf{a}_T), \qquad a_R = r\omega^2 = 2.0(6.0)^2 = 72 \text{ ft/sec}^2,$$

$$a_T = r\alpha = 2.0(4.0) = 8.0 \text{ ft/sec}^2,$$

$$a = \sqrt{a_R{}^2 + a_T{}^2} = \sqrt{72^2 + 8.0^2} = 72.5 \text{ ft/sec}^2.$$

The angle ϕ between $\mathbf{a}$ and $\mathbf{a}_T$ is found from the relation $\cos \phi = a_T/a$. Hence

$$\cos \phi = \frac{8.0}{72.5} = 0.110, \qquad \text{or} \qquad \phi = 83.7°.$$

Exercises

1. Two forces, one of 45.0 lb and the other of 68.0 lb, act on the same object and at right angles to each other. Find the resultant of these forces.

2. Two forces, one of 150 lb and the other of 220 lb, pull on an object. The angle between these forces is 45°. What is the resultant of these forces?

3. A jet travels 450 mi due west from a city. It then turns and travels 240 mi south. What is its displacement from the city?

4. Town B is 52.0 mi southeast of town A. Town C is 45.0 mi due west of town B. What is the displacement of town C from town A?

5. What are the horizontal and vertical components of the velocity of a stone thrown into the air with a velocity of 120 ft/sec at an angle of 48° with respect to the horizontal?

6. A rocket is traveling at an angle of 74° with respect to the horizontal at a speed of 3500 mi/hr. What are the horizontal and vertical components of the velocity?

7. A boy weighing 60 lb sits in a swing and is pulled sideways by a horizontal force of 20 lb. What is the tension in each of the supporting ropes? What is the angle between the horizontal and the ropes?

8. A rope 10 ft long is fastened to supports which are 8 ft apart and at the same level. A 100-lb weight is then hung from its center. How much is the tension in the supporting rope?

9. A stone is thrown horizontally from a plane traveling at 300 ft/sec. If the stone is thrown at 140 ft/sec in a direction perpendicular to the direction of the plane, what is the velocity of the stone just after it is released?

10. A plane is headed due north at a velocity of 500 mi/hr with respect to the air. If the wind is from the southwest at 80 mi/hr, what is the resultant speed of the plane, and in what direction is it traveling?

11. A 70-lb force is applied to a 40-lb box by a rigid metal rod at an angle of 45° above the horizontal (see Fig. 8-19). Will the box be lifted from the ground?

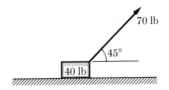

Figure 8-19

12. Assume that the plane in Fig. 8-16 is frictionless. If the acceleration due to gravity is 32 ft/sec², what is the component of the acceleration of the object down the plane? (This is the acceleration the object will have, since it is restricted to moving down the plane.)

13. In Fig. 8-16, if the plane is inclined at 20°, what is the force exerted on the 100-lb object by the plane itself?

14. In Fig. 8-16, if a horizontal 10-lb force is exerted to the right on the 100-lb object, what would the force of friction have to be so that the object did not move down the plane?

15. An object is dropped from a plane moving at 400 ft/sec. If the vertical velocity, as a function of time, is given by $v_y = 32t$, what is the velocity of the object after 4 sec? In what direction is it moving?

16. The magnitude of the horizontal and vertical components of displacement of a certain projectile are given by $d_H = 120t$ and $d_V = 160t - 16t^2$, where t is the time in seconds. Find the displacement (in ft) of the object after 3.00 sec.

17. In Fig. 8-18, given that $a = 56.4$ ft/sec², $a_R = 37.9$ ft/sec², and $r = 6.00$ ft, find α, the rate of change of angular velocity.

18. A boat travels across a river, reaching the opposite bank at a point directly opposite that from which it left. If the boat travels 6.00 mi/hr in still water, and the current of river flows at 3.00 mi/hr, what was the velocity of the boat in the water?

19. In Fig. 8-20, a long straight conductor
perpendicular to the plane of the paper
carries an electric current i. A bar magnet having poles of strength m lies in the
plane of the paper. The vectors $\mathbf{H}_i$, $\mathbf{H}_N$,
and $\mathbf{H}_S$ represent the components of the
magnetic intensity $\mathbf{H}$ due, respectively,
to the current and to the N and S poles
of the magnet. The magnitude of the
components of $\mathbf{H}$ are given by

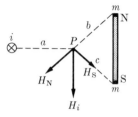

Figure 8-20

$$H_i = \frac{1}{2\pi}\frac{i}{a}, \qquad H_N = \frac{1}{4\pi}\frac{m}{b^2}, \qquad \text{and} \qquad H_S = \frac{1}{4\pi}\frac{m}{c^2}.$$

Given that $a = 0.3$ meter, $b = 0.4$ meter, $c = 0.3$ meter, the length of the magnet
is 0.5 meter, $i = 4$ amp, and $m = 2$ amp-m, calculate the resultant magnetic intensity $\mathbf{H}$. The component $\mathbf{H}_i$ is parallel to the magnet.

20. Solve the problem of Exercise 19 if $\mathbf{H}_i$ is directed away from the magnet, making
an angle of 10° with the direction of the magnet.

8-3 Oblique triangles, the Law of Sines

To this point we have limited our study of triangle solution to right triangles.
However, many triangles which require solution do not contain a right angle.
Such a triangle is termed an *oblique triangle*. Let us now discuss the solutions of
oblique triangles.

In Section 3-4 we stated that we need three parts, at least one of them a side,
in order to solve any triangle. With this in mind we may determine that there
are four possible combinations of parts from which we may solve a triangle.
These combinations are:

Case 1. Two angles and one side
Case 2. Two sides and the angle opposite one of them
Case 3. Two sides and the included angle
Case 4. Three sides

There are several ways in which oblique triangles may be solved, but we shall
restrict our attention to the two most useful methods, the *Law of Sines* and the
Law of Cosines. In this section we shall discuss the Law of Sines, and show that
it may be used to solve Case 1 and Case 2.

Let ABC be an oblique trangle with sides a, b, and c opposite angles A, B,
and C, respectively. By drawing a perpendicular h from B to side b, or its extension, we see from Fig. 8-21(a) that

$$h = c \sin A \qquad \text{or} \qquad h = a \sin C, \tag{8-4}$$

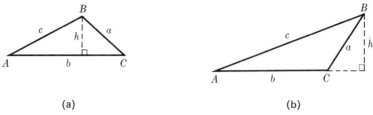

Figure 8-21

and from Fig. 8-21(b),

$$h = c \sin A \qquad \text{or} \qquad h = a \sin (180° - C) = a \sin C. \qquad (8\text{-}5)$$

We note that the results are precisely the same in Eqs. (8-4) and (8-5). Setting the results for h equal to each other, we have

$$c \sin A = a \sin C \qquad \text{or} \qquad \frac{a}{\sin A} = \frac{c}{\sin C}. \qquad (8\text{-}6)$$

By dropping a perpendicular from A to a we also derive the result

$$c \sin B = b \sin C \qquad \text{or} \qquad \frac{b}{\sin B} = \frac{c}{\sin C}. \qquad (8\text{-}7)$$

Combining Eqs. (8-6) and (8-7) we have the *Law of Sines*:

$$\frac{a}{\sin A} = \frac{b}{\sin B} = \frac{c}{\sin C}. \qquad (8\text{-}8)$$

The Law of Sines is a statement of proportionality between the sides of a triangle and the sines of the angles opposite them.

Now we may see how the Law of Sines is applied to the solution of a triangle in which two angles and one side are known (Case 1). If two angles are known, the third may be found from the fact that the sum of the angles in a triangle is 180°. At this point we must be able to determine the ratio between the given side and the sine of the angle opposite it. Then, by use of the Law of Sines, we may find the other sides.

Example A.   Given that $c = 6$, $A = 60°$, and $B = 40°$, find a, b and C.
First we can see that

$$C = 180° - (60° + 40°) = 80°.$$

Thus

$$\frac{a}{\sin 60°} = \frac{6}{\sin 80°} \qquad \text{or} \qquad a = \frac{6(0.8660)}{0.9848} = 5.28,$$

$$\frac{b}{\sin 40°} = \frac{6}{\sin 80°} \qquad \text{or} \qquad b = \frac{6(0.6428)}{0.9848} = 3.92.$$

The Law of Sines makes it possible for us to solve triangles by using a slide rule. With one setting we may solve a triangle completely, after the angles are determined. Thus the first step is to find the third angle. Next put the hairline over the given side on the D-scale. Place the angle, opposite that side, on the S-scale under the hairline. The other two sides will be found on the D-scale opposite the corresponding angles of the S-scale.

Example B.   Using a slide rule, solve the triangle with the following given parts: $a = 63.7$, $A = 56°$, and $B = 77°$.

We immediately determine that $C = 47°$. Opposite 63.7 of the D-scale, we place 56° of the S-scale. The sides b and c are then read on the D-scale opposite 77° and 47° of the S-scale. Thus $b = 74.9$ and $c = 56.2$ (see Fig. 8-22).

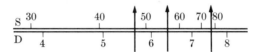

Figure 8-22

Example C.   Using a slide rule, solve the triangle with the following given parts: $b = 5.06$, $A = 42°$, and $C = 29°$.

We determine that $B = 109°$. To solve this triangle, we use the fact that $\sin 109° = \sin 71°$. Place 71° on the S-scale opposite 5.06 of the D-scale. We read $a = 3.58$ on the D-scale opposite 42° of the S-scale. We find that $c = 2.60$ on the D-scale opposite 29° of the S-scale (see Fig. 8-23).

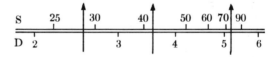

Figure 8-23

If the given information is appropriate, the Law of Sines may be used to solve applied problems. The following example illustrates the use of the Law of Sines in such a problem.

Example D.   A plane traveling at 650 mi/hr with respect to the air is headed 30° east of north. The wind is blowing from the south, which causes the actual course to be 27° east of north. Find the velocity of the wind and the velocity of the plane with respect to the ground.

From the given information the angles are determined, as shown in Fig. 8-24. Then applying the Law of Sines, we have the relations

$$\frac{v_w}{\sin 3°} = \frac{v_{pg}}{\sin 150°} = \frac{650}{\sin 27°},$$

where v_w is the magnitude of the velocity of the wind and v_{pg} is the magnitude of the velocity of the plane with respect to the ground. The slide rule may be used by setting 650 on the D-scale opposite 27° on the S-scale. The value of v_{pg} may be found on the D-scale opposite 30° (since sin 150° = sin 30°) of the S-scale. The value of v_w is found on the D-scale opposite 3° of the ST-scale. Thus $v_w =$ 75.0 mi/hr and $v_{pg} = 716$ mi/hr.

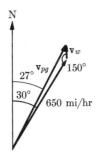

Figure 8-24

If we have information equivalent to Case 2 (two sides and the angle opposite one of them), we may find that there are *two* triangles which satisfy the given information. The following example illustrates this point.

Example E.   Solve the triangle with the following given parts: $a = 60$, $b = 40$ and $B = 30°$.

By making a good scale drawing (Fig. 8-25) we note that the angle opposite a may be either at position A or A'. Both positions of this angle satisfy the given parts. Therefore, there are two triangles which result. When we use a slide rule, we can easily solve them. We place 30° on the S-scale opposite 40 on the

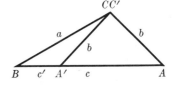

Figure 8-25

D-scale. Opposite 60 on the D-scale we find 48.5 (approximately) on the S-scale. Thus $A = 48.5°$, and therefore we find that $C = 101.5°$. We also find $c = 78.4$ opposite 78.5° (sin 101.5° = sin 78.5°). Therefore, one solution is $A = 48.5°$, $C = 101.5°$ and $c = 78.4$.

The other solution is found by interpreting the 48.5° reading as being $A' = 131.5°$. For this case we have C' (the angle opposite c when $A' = 131.5°$) as 18.5°. Therefore, c' is found opposite 18.5° and is 25.4. This means that the second solution is $A' = 131.5°$, $C' = 18.5°$ and $c' = 25.4$.

Example F.   In Example E, if $b > 60$, only one solution would result. In this case, side b would intercept side c at A. It also intercepts the extension of side c, but whis would require that angle B not be included in the triangle (see Fig. 8-26). Thus only one solution may result if $b > a$.

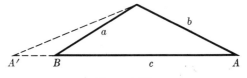

Figure 8-26

In Example E, there would be no solution if side b were not at least 30. For if this were the case, side b would not be sufficiently long to even touch side c. It can be seen that b must at least equal $a \sin B$. If it is just equal to $a \sin B$, there is one solution, a right triangle (Fig. 8-27).

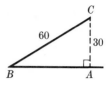

Figure 8-27

Summarizing the results for Case 2 as illustrated in Examples E and F, we make the following conclusions. Given sides a and b, and angle A (assuming here that a and A ($A < 90°$) are the given corresponding parts), we have:

(1) no solution if $a < b \sin A$,

(2) a right triangle solution if $a = b \sin A$,

(3) two solutions if $b \sin A < a < b$,

(4) one solution if $a > b$.

For the reason that two solutions may result from it, Case 2 is often referred to as the "ambiguous case."

If we attempt to use the Law of Sines for the solution of Case 3 or Case 4, we find that we do not have sufficient information to complete one of the ratios. These cases can, however, be solved by the Law of Cosines, which we shall consider in the next section.

Example G.   Given the 3 sides, $a = 5$, $b = 6$, $c = 7$, we would set up the ratios

$$\frac{5}{\sin A} = \frac{6}{\sin B} = \frac{7}{\sin C}.$$

However, since there is no way to determine a complete ratio from these equations, we cannot find the solution of the triangle in this manner.

Exercises

In Exercises 1 through 16 solve the triangles with the given parts.

1. $a = 45.7$, $A = 65°$, $B = 49°$

2. $b = 3.07$, $A = 26°$, $C = 120°$

3. $c = 4380$, $A = 37°$, $B = 34°$

4. $a = 93.2$, $B = 17.9°$, $C = 82.6°$

5. $a = 4.60$, $b = 3.10$, $A = 18°$

6. $b = 3.62$, $c = 2.94$, $B = 69.3°$

7. $b = 0.0742$, $B = 51°$, $C = 3°$

8. $c = 729$, $B = 121°$, $C = 44°$

9. $a = 63.8$, $B = 58.4°$, $C = 22.2°$

10. $a = 13.0$, $A = 55.2°$, $B = 67.5°$

11. $b = 438$, $B = 47.4°$, $C = 64.5°$

12. $b = 283$, $B = 13.7°$, $C = 76.3°$

13. $a = 5.24$, $b = 4.44$, $B = 48.1°$

14. $a = 89.4$, $c = 37.3$, $C = 15.6°$

15. $a = 45.0$, $b = 126$, $A = 64°$

16. $a = 10$, $c = 5$, $C = 30°$

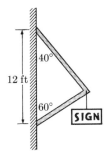

Figure 8-28

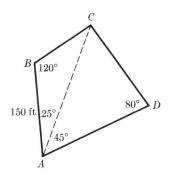

Figure 8-29

In Exercises 17 through 23 use the Law of Sines to solve the given problems.

17. Determine the lengths of the two steel supports of the sign shown in Fig. 8-28.

18. Determine the unknown sides of the four-sided piece of land shown in Fig. 8-29.

19. The angles of elevation of an airplane, measured from points A and B, 7540 ft apart on the same side of the airplane (the airplane and points A and B are in the same vertical plane), are 32° and 44°. How far is point A from the airplane?

20. Resolve vector **A** ($A = 160$) into two components in the directions u and v, as shown in Fig. 8-30.

21. A ship leaves a port and travels due west. At a certain point it turns 30°N of W and travels an additional 42.0 mi to a point 63.0 mi from the port. How far from the port is the point where the ship turned?

22. City B is 40° south of east of city A. A pilot wishes to know what direction he should head the plane in flying from A to B if the wind is from the west at 40 mi/hr and his velocity with respect to the air is 300 mi/hr. What should his heading be?

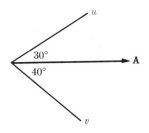

Figure 8-30

23. A person measures a triangular piece of land and reports the following information: "One side is 58.4 ft long and another side is 21.1 ft long. The angle opposite the shorter side is 24°." Could this information be correct?

8-4 The Law of Cosines

As we noted at the end of the preceding section, the Law of Sines cannot be used if the only information given is that of Case 3 or Case 4. Therefore it is necessary to develop a method of finding at least one more part of the triangle. Here we can use the Law of Cosines. After obtaining another part by the Law of Cosines, we can then use the Law of Sines to complete the solution. We do this because the Law of Sines generally provides a simpler method of solution than the Law of Cosines.

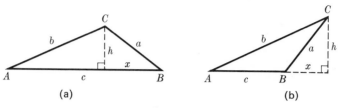

Figure 8-31

Consider any oblique triangle, for example either of the ones in Fig. 8-31. For each we obtain $h = b \sin A$. By using the Pythagorean theorem we obtain $a^2 = h^2 + x^2$ for each. Thus

$$a^2 = b^2 \sin^2 A + x^2. \tag{8-9}$$

In Fig. 8-31(a), we have $c - x = b \cos A$, or $x = c - b \cos A$. In Fig. 8-31(b), we have $c + x = b \cos A$, or $x = b \cos A - c$. Substituting these relations into Eq. (8-9), we obtain

$$a^2 = b^2 \sin^2 A + (c - b \cos A)^2$$

and

$$a^2 = b^2 \sin^2 A + (b \cos A - c)^2, \tag{8-10}$$

respectively. Each of these, when expanded, gives

$$a^2 = b^2 \sin^2 A + b^2 \cos^2 A + c^2 - 2bc \cos A,$$

or

$$a^2 = b^2 (\sin^2 A + \cos^2 A) + c^2 - 2bc \cos A. \tag{8-11}$$

Recalling the definitions of the trigonometric functions, we know that $\sin \theta = y/r$ and $\cos \theta = x/r$. Therefore $\sin^2 \theta + \cos^2 \theta = (y^2 + x^2)/r^2$. However, $x^2 + y^2 = r^2$, which means that

$$\sin^2 \theta + \cos^2 \theta = 1. \tag{8-12}$$

This equation holds for any angle θ, since we made no assumptions as to the properties of θ. By substituting Eq. (8-12) into Eq. (8-11), we arrive at the Law of Cosines:

$$a^2 = b^2 + c^2 - 2bc \cos A. \tag{8-13}$$

Using the method above, we may also show that

$$b^2 = a^2 + c^2 - 2ac \cos B$$

and

$$c^2 = a^2 + b^2 - 2ab \cos C.$$

Therefore, if we know two sides and the included angle (Case 3) we may directly solve for the side opposite the given angle. Then, by using the Law of Sines, we may complete the solution. If we are given all three sides (Case 4) we may solve for the angle opposite one of these sides by use of the Law of Cosines. Again we use the Law of Sines to complete the solution.

Example A.   Solve the triangle with $a = 45$, $b = 67$, and $C = 35°$.

$$c^2 = (45)^2 + (67)^2 - 2(45)(67)(0.819)$$
$$= 2020 + 4490 - 4940 = 1570$$
$$c = 39.6 \text{ (Slide-rule solution)}$$

By using the Law of Sines, we find that to the nearest degree

$$A = 41° \quad \text{and} \quad B = 104°.$$

Example B.   If, in Example A, $C = 145°$, we have

$$c^2 = 45^2 + 67^2 - 2(45)(67)(-0.819)$$
$$= 2020 + 4490 + 4940 = 11{,}450,$$
$$c = 107.$$

The Law of Sines then gives $A = 14°$ and $B = 21°$.

Example C.   Solve the triangle for which $a = 49.3$, $b = 21.6$ and $c = 42.6$.

$$\cos A = \frac{b^2 + c^2 - a^2}{2bc} = \frac{(21.6)^2 + (42.6)^2 - (49.3)^2}{2(21.6)(42.6)}$$

$$= \frac{467 + 1810 - 2430}{1840} = -0.0818,$$

$$A = 180° - 85.3° = 94.7°.$$

We then find $B = 25.9°$ and $C = 59.4°$.

Example D.   Find the resultant of two vectors having magnitudes of 78 and 45, and directed toward the east and 15° east of north, respectively (see Fig. 8-32).

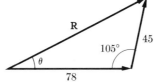

Figure 8-32

The magnitude of the resultant is given by

$$R = \sqrt{(78)^2 + (45)^2 - 2(78)(45)\,(\cos 105°)}$$
$$= \sqrt{6080 + 2020 + 1820} = 99.6.$$

Also, $\theta = 25.9°$.

Example E.   A vertical radio antenna is to be built on a hill which makes an angle of 6° with the horizontal. If guy wires are to be attached at a point 150 ft up on the antenna and at points 100 ft from the base of the antenna, what will be the lengths of guy wires which are positioned directly up and directly down the hill?

Making an appropriate figure such as Fig. 8-33, we are able to establish the equations necessary for the solution:

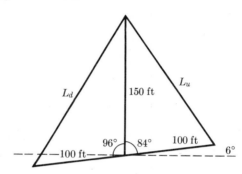

Figure 8-33

$$L_u{}^2 = (100)^2 + (150)^2 - 2(100)(150) \cos 84°,$$
$$L_d{}^2 = (100)^2 + (150)^2 - 2(100)(150) \cos 96°,$$
$$L_u{}^2 = 10{,}000 + 22{,}500 - 30{,}000(0.1045)$$
$$= 32{,}500 - 3140 = 29{,}360,$$
$$L_u = 171 \text{ ft};$$
$$L_d{}^2 = 32{,}500 + 3140 = 35{,}640,$$
$$L_d = 189 \text{ ft}.$$

Exercises

In Exercises 1 through 16 solve the triangles with the given parts.

1. $a = 6.00$, $b = 7.56$, $C = 54°$
2. $b = 87.3$, $c = 34.0$, $A = 130°$
3. $a = 4530$, $b = 924$, $C = 98°$
4. $a = 0.0845$, $c = 0.116$, $B = 85°$
5. $a = 39.5$, $b = 45.2$, $c = 67.1$
6. $a = 23.3$, $b = 27.2$, $c = 29.1$
7. $a = 385$, $b = 467$, $c = 800$
8. $a = 0.243$, $b = 0.263$, $c = 0.153$
9. $a = 320$, $b = 847$, $C = 158°$
10. $b = 18.3$, $c = 27.1$, $A = 58.7°$
11. $a = 21.4$, $c = 4.28$, $B = 86.3°$
12. $a = 11.3$, $b = 5.10$, $C = 77.6°$
13. $a = 103$, $c = 159$, $C = 104.6°$
14. $a = 49.3$, $b = 54.5$, $B = 114°$
15. $a = 0.493$, $b = 0.595$, $c = 0.639$
16. $a = 69.7$, $b = 49.3$, $c = 56.2$

In Exercises 17 through 23 use the Law of Cosines to solve the given problems.

17. To measure the distance AC, a man walks 500 ft from A to B, then turns 30° to face C, and walks 680 ft to C. What is the distance AC?

18. An airplane traveling at 700 mi/hr leaves the airport at noon going due east. At 2 P.M. the pilot turns 10° north of east. How far is the plane from the airport at 3 P.M.?

19. Two forces, one of 56 lb and the other of 67 lb, are applied to the same object. The resultant force is 82 lb. What is the angle between the two forces?

20. A triangular metal frame has sides of 8.00 ft, 12.0 ft and 16.0 ft. What is the largest angle between parts of the frame?

21. A boat, which can travel 6 mi/hr in still water, heads downstream at an angle of 20° with the bank. If the stream is flowing at the rate of 3 mi/hr, how fast is the boat traveling, and in what direction?

22. An airplane's velocity with respect to the air is 520 mi/hr, and it is headed 24° north of west. The wind is from due southwest and has a velocity of 55 mi/hr. What is the true direction of the plane and what is its velocity with respect to the ground?

23. One end of a 13.1-ft pole is 15.7 ft from an observer's eyes and the other end is 19.3 ft from his eyes. Through what angle does the observer see the pole?

8-5 Miscellaneous Exercises

In Exercises 1 through 4 find the x- and y- components of the given vectors by use of the trigonometric functions.

1. $A = 65.0,\ \theta_A = 28.0°$ 2. $A = 8.05,\ \theta_A = 149°$
3. $A = 0.920,\ \theta_A = 215°$ 4. $A = 657,\ \theta_A = 343°$

In Exercises 5 through 10 add the given vectors by use of the trigonometric functions and the Pythagorean theorem.

5. $A = 780,\ \theta_A = 28°$ 6. $A = 0.0120,\ \theta_A = 10.5°$
   $B = 346,\ \theta_B = 320°$ $B = 0.0078,\ \theta_B = 260°$
7. $A = 22.5,\ \theta_A = 130°$ 8. $A = 18{,}700,\ \theta_A = 110°$
   $B = 7.60,\ \theta_B = 200°$ $B = 4830,\ \theta_B = 350°$
9. $A = 75.0,\ \theta_A = 15.0°$ 10. $A = 8100,\ \theta_A = 141°$
   $B = 26.5,\ \theta_B = 192°$ $B = 1540,\ \theta_B = 165°$
   $C = 54.8,\ \theta_C = 344°$ $C = 3470,\ \theta_C = 296°$

In Exercises 11 through 26 solve the triangles with the given parts.

11. $A = 48°,\ B = 68°,\ a = 14.5$ 12. $A = 132°,\ b = 7.50,\ C = 32°$
13. $a = 22.8,\ B = 33.5°,\ C = 125.3°$ 14. $A = 71.0°,\ B = 48.5°,\ c = 8.42$
15. $b = 76.0,\ c = 40.5,\ B = 110°$ 16. $A = 77°,\ a = 12,\ c = 5.0$
17. $b = 14.5,\ c = 13.0,\ C = 56.6°$ 18. $B = 40°,\ b = 7.0,\ c = 18$
19. $a = 186,\ B = 130°,\ c = 106$ 20. $b = 750,\ c = 1100,\ A = 56.0°$
21. $a = 7.86,\ b = 2.45,\ C = 22.0°$ 22. $a = 0.208,\ c = 0.697,\ B = 105°$
23. $a = 17,\ b = 12,\ c = 25$ 24. $a = 900,\ b = 995,\ c = 1100$
25. $a = 5.30,\ b = 8.75,\ c = 12.5$ 26. $a = 47.4,\ b = 40.0,\ c = 45.5$

In Exercises 27 through 38 solve the given problems.

27. A jet climbs at an angle 35° while traveling 600 mi/hr. How long will it take to climb to an altitude of 10,000 ft?

28. A bullet is fired into the air at 2000 mi/hr at an angle of 25° with the horizontal. What is the vertical component of the velocity?

29. A balloon is rising at the rate of 15.0 ft/sec and at the same time is being blown horizontally by the wind at the rate of 22.5 ft/sec. Find the resultant velocity.

30. A motorboat which travels at 8.0 mi/hr in still water heads directly across a stream which flows at 3.0 mi/hr. What is the resultant velocity of the boat?

31. A velocity vector is the resultant of two other vectors. If the given velocity is 450 mi/hr and makes angles of 34° and 76° with the two components, find the magnitudes of the components.

32. A person on a hill in the middle of a plain relates that the angles of depression of two objects on the plain below (on directly opposite sides of the hill) are 30° and 40°. He knows that the objects are 15,800 ft apart. How far is he from the closest object?

33. In order to find the distance between points A and B on opposite sides of a river, a distance AC is measured off as 1000 ft, where point C is on the same side of the river as A. Angle BAC is measured to be 102° and angle ACB is 33°. What is the distance between A and B?

34. A 22.0-ft ladder leans against a wall, making an angle of 29° with the wall. If the foot of the ladder is 10.7 ft from the foot of the wall, find the angle of inclination of the wall to the ground.

35. Two points on opposite sides of an obstruction are respectively 117 ft and 88 ft from a third point. The lines joining the first two points and the third point intersect at an angle of 115° at the third point. How far apart are the original two points?

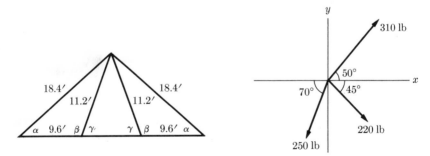

Figure 8-34   Figure 8-35

36. Determine the angles of the structure indicated in Fig. 8-34.

37. Find the resultant of the forces indicated in Fig. 8-35.

38. A jet plane is traveling horizontally at 1200 ft/sec. A missile is fired horizontally from it 30° from the direction in which the plane is traveling. If the missile leaves the plane at 2000 ft/sec, what is its velocity 10 sec later if the vertical component is given by $v_V = 32t$ (in ft/sec)?

Graphs of the Trigonometric Functions

9

9-1 Graphs of $y = a \sin x$ and $y = a \cos x$

One of the clearest ways to demonstrate the variation of the trigonometric functions is by means of their graphs. The graphs are useful for analyzing properties of the trigonometric functions, and in themselves are valuable in many applications. Several of these applications are indicated in the exercises, particularly in the last two sections of this chapter.

The graphs are constructed on the rectangular coordinate system. In plotting the trigonometric functions, it is normal to express the angle in radians. In this way x and the function of x are expressed as *numbers*, and these numbers may have any desired unit of measurement. Therefore, in order to determine the graphs, it is necessary to be able to readily use angles expressed in radians. If necessary, Section 7-3 should be reviewed for this purpose.

In this section the graphs of the sine and cosine functions are demonstrated. We begin by constructing a table of values of x and y, for the function $y = \sin x$:

x	0	$\dfrac{\pi}{6}$	$\dfrac{\pi}{3}$	$\dfrac{\pi}{2}$	$\dfrac{2\pi}{3}$	$\dfrac{5\pi}{6}$	π	$\dfrac{7\pi}{6}$	$\dfrac{4\pi}{3}$	$\dfrac{3\pi}{2}$	$\dfrac{5\pi}{3}$	$\dfrac{11\pi}{6}$	2π
y	0	0.5	0.87	1	0.87	0.5	0	-0.5	-0.87	-1	-0.87	-0.5	0

Plotting these values, we obtain the graph shown in Fig. 9-1.

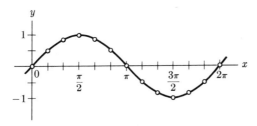

Figure 9-1

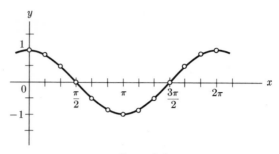

Figure 9-2

The graph of $y = \cos x$ may be constructed in the same manner. The table below gives the proper values for the graph of $y = \cos x$. The graph is shown in Fig. 9-2.

x	0	$\dfrac{\pi}{6}$	$\dfrac{\pi}{3}$	$\dfrac{\pi}{2}$	$\dfrac{2\pi}{3}$	$\dfrac{5\pi}{6}$	π	$\dfrac{7\pi}{6}$	$\dfrac{4\pi}{3}$	$\dfrac{3\pi}{2}$	$\dfrac{5\pi}{3}$	$\dfrac{11\pi}{6}$	2π
y	1	0.87	0.5	0	-0.5	-0.87	-1	-0.87	-0.5	0	0.5	0.87	1

The graphs are continued beyond the values shown in the table to indicate that they continue on indefinitely in each direction. From the values and the graphs, it can be seen that the two graphs are of exactly the same shape, with the cosine curve displaced $\pi/2$ units to the left of the sine curve. The shape of these curves should be recognized readily, with special note as to the points at which they cross the axes. This information will be especially valuable in "sketching" similar curves, since the basic shape always remains the same. We shall find it unnecessary to plot numerous points every time we wish to sketch such a curve.

To obtain the graph of $y = a \sin x$, we note that all of the y-values obtained for the graph of $y = \sin x$ are to be multiplied by the number a. In this case the greatest value of the sine function is a, instead of 1. The number a is called the *amplitude* of the curve and represents the greatest y-value of the curve. This is also true for $y = a \cos x$.

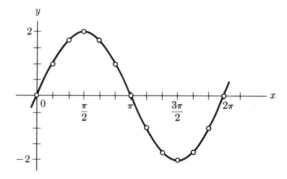

Figure 9-3

Example A.   Plot the curve of $y = 2 \sin x$.
The table of values to be used is as follows; Fig. 9-3 shows the graph.

x	0	$\dfrac{\pi}{6}$	$\dfrac{\pi}{3}$	$\dfrac{\pi}{2}$	$\dfrac{2\pi}{3}$	$\dfrac{5\pi}{6}$	π	$\dfrac{7\pi}{6}$	$\dfrac{4\pi}{3}$	$\dfrac{3\pi}{2}$	$\dfrac{5\pi}{3}$	$\dfrac{11\pi}{6}$
y	0	1	1.73	2	1.73	1	0	-1	-1.73	-2	-1.73	-1

Example B.   Plot the curve of $y = -3 \cos x$.
The table of values to be used is as follows; Fig. 9-4 shows the graph.

x	0	$\dfrac{\pi}{6}$	$\dfrac{\pi}{3}$	$\dfrac{\pi}{2}$	$\dfrac{2\pi}{3}$	$\dfrac{5\pi}{6}$	π	$\dfrac{7\pi}{6}$	$\dfrac{4\pi}{3}$	$\dfrac{3\pi}{2}$	$\dfrac{5\pi}{3}$	$\dfrac{11\pi}{6}$
y	-3	-2.6	-1.5	0	1.5	2.6	3	2.6	1.5	0	-1.5	-2.6

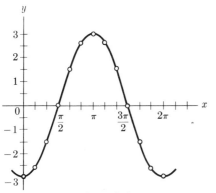

Figure 9-4

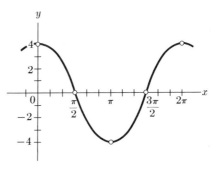

Figure 9-5

Note from Example B that the effect of the minus sign before the number a is to invert the curve. The effect of the number a can also be seen readily from these examples.

By knowing the general shape of the sine curve, where it crosses the axes, and the amplitude, we can rapidly *sketch* curves of the form $y = a \sin x$ and $y = a \cos x$. There is generally no need to plot any more points than those corresponding to the values of the amplitude and those where the curve crosses the axes.

Example C.   Sketch the graph of $y = 4 \cos x$.
First we set up a table of values for the points where the curve crosses the x-axis and for the highest and lowest points on the curve.

x	0	$\dfrac{\pi}{2}$	π	$\dfrac{3\pi}{2}$	2π
y	4	0	-4	0	4

Now, we plot the above points and join them, knowing the basic shape of the curve. See Fig. 9-5.

Example D. Sketch the curve of $y = -2 \sin x$.

We list here the important values associated with this curve.

x	0	$\dfrac{\pi}{2}$	π	$\dfrac{3\pi}{2}$	2π
y	0	-2	0	2	0

Since we know the general shape of the sine curve, we can now sketch the graph as shown in Fig. 9-6. Note the inversion of the curve due to the minus sign.

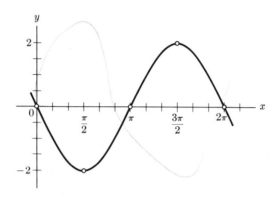

Figure 9-6

Exercises

In Exercises 1 and 2 complete the following table for the given functions, and then plot the resulting graph.

x	$-\pi$	$-\dfrac{3\pi}{4}$	$-\dfrac{\pi}{2}$	$-\dfrac{\pi}{4}$	0	$\dfrac{\pi}{4}$	$\dfrac{\pi}{2}$	$\dfrac{3\pi}{4}$	π	$\dfrac{5\pi}{4}$	$\dfrac{3\pi}{2}$	$\dfrac{7\pi}{4}$	2π	$\dfrac{9\pi}{4}$	$\dfrac{5\pi}{2}$	$\dfrac{11\pi}{4}$	3π
y																	

1. $y = \sin x$ 2. $y = \cos x$

In Exercises 3 through 14 sketch the curves of the indicated functions.

3. $y = 3 \sin x$ 4. $y = 5 \sin x$ 5. $y = \frac{5}{2} \sin x$ 6. $y = 0.5 \sin x$

7. $y = 2 \cos x$ 8. $y = 3 \cos x$ 9. $y = 0.8 \cos x$ 10. $y = \frac{3}{2} \cos x$

11. $y = -\sin x$ 12. $y = -3 \sin x$ 13. $y = -\cos x$ 14. $y = -8 \cos x$

Although units of π are often convenient, we must remember that π is really only a number. Numbers which are not multiples of π may be used as well. In Exercises 15 through 18 plot the indicated graphs by finding the values of y corresponding to the values of 0, 1, 2, 3, 4, 5, 6, and 7 for x. (Remember, the numbers 0, 1, 2, and so forth represent radian measure.)

15. $y = \sin x$ 16. $y = 3 \sin x$ 17. $y = \cos x$ 18. $y = 2 \cos x$

9-2 Graphs of $y = a \sin bx$ and $y = a \cos bx$

In graphing the curve of $y = \sin x$ we note that the values of y start repeating every 2π units of x. This is because $\sin x = \sin (x + 2\pi) = \sin (x + 4\pi)$, and so forth. For any trigonometric function F, we say that it has a *period P*, if $F(x) = F(x + P)$. For functions which are periodic, such as the sine and cosine, the period refers to the x-distance between any point and the next corresponding point for which the values of y start repeating.

Let us now plot the curve $y = \sin 2x$. This means that we choose a value for x, multiply this value by two, and find the sine of the result. This leads to the following table of values for this function.

x	0	$\dfrac{\pi}{8}$	$\dfrac{\pi}{4}$	$\dfrac{3\pi}{8}$	$\dfrac{\pi}{2}$	$\dfrac{5\pi}{8}$	$\dfrac{3\pi}{4}$	$\dfrac{7\pi}{8}$	π	$\dfrac{9\pi}{8}$	$\dfrac{5\pi}{4}$
$2x$	0	$\dfrac{\pi}{4}$	$\dfrac{\pi}{2}$	$\dfrac{3\pi}{4}$	π	$\dfrac{5\pi}{4}$	$\dfrac{3\pi}{2}$	$\dfrac{7\pi}{4}$	2π	$\dfrac{9\pi}{4}$	$\dfrac{5\pi}{2}$
y	0	0.7	1	0.7	0	−0.7	−1	−0.7	0	0.7	1

Plotting these values, we have the curve shown in Fig. 9-7.

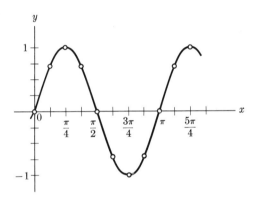

Figure 9-7

From the table and Fig. 9-7, we note that the function $y = \sin 2x$ starts repeating after π units of x. The effect of the 2 before the x has been to make the period of this curve half the period of the curve of $\sin x$. This leads us to the following conclusion: If the period of the trigonometric function $F(x)$ is P, then the period of $F(bx)$ is P/b. Since each of the functions $\sin x$ and $\cos x$ has a period of 2π, each of the functions $\sin bx$ and $\cos bx$ has a period of $2\pi/b$.

Example A.   The period of $\sin 3x$ is $2\pi/3$. That is, the curve of the function $y = \sin 3x$ will repeat every $2\pi/3$ (approximately 2.09) units of x.

The period of $\cos 4x$ is $2\pi/4 = \pi/2$. The period of $\sin \frac{1}{2}x$ is $2\pi/\frac{1}{2} = 4\pi$.

Example B.   The period of sin πx is $2\pi/\pi = 2$. That is, the curve of the function sin πx will repeat every 2 units. It will be noted that the periods of sin $3x$ and sin πx are nearly equal. This is to be expected since π is only slightly greater than 3.

The period of cos $3\pi x$ is $2\pi/3\pi = 2/3$.

Combining the result for the period with the results of Section 9-1, we conclude that *each of the functions $y = a$ sin bx and $y = a$ cos bx has an amplitude of $|a|$ and a period of $2\pi/b$*. These properties are very useful in sketching these functions, as it is shown in the following examples.

Example C.   Sketch the graph of $y = 3$ sin $4x$ for $0 \leq x \leq \pi$.

We immediately conclude that the amplitude is 3 and the period is $2\pi/4 = \pi/2$. Therefore, we know that $y = 0$ when $x = 0$ and $y = 0$ when $x = \pi/2$. Also we recall that the sine function is zero halfway between these values, which means that $y = 0$ when $x = \pi/4$. The function reaches its amplitude values halfway between the zeros. Therefore, $y = 3$ for $x = \pi/8$ and $y = -3$ for $x = 3\pi/8$. A table for these important values of the function $y = 3$ sin $4x$ is as follows.

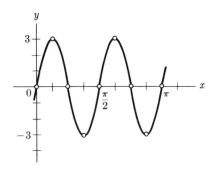

Figure 9-8

x	0	$\dfrac{\pi}{8}$	$\dfrac{\pi}{4}$	$\dfrac{3\pi}{8}$	$\dfrac{\pi}{2}$	$\dfrac{5\pi}{8}$	$\dfrac{3\pi}{4}$	$\dfrac{7\pi}{8}$	π
y	0	3	0	-3	0	3	0	-3	0

Using this table and the knowledge of the form of the sine curve, we sketch the function (Fig. 9-8).

Example D.   Sketch the graph of $y = -2$ cos $3x$ for $0 \leq x \leq 2\pi$.

We note that the amplitude is 2 and that the period is $2\pi/3$. Since the cosine curve is at its amplitude value for $x = 0$, we have $y = -2$ for $x = 0$ (the negative value is due to the minus sign before the function) and $y = -2$ for $x = 2\pi/3$. The cosine function also reaches its amplitude value halfway between these values, or $y = 2$ for $x = \pi/3$. The cosine function is zero halfway between the x-values listed for the amplitude; that is, $y = 0$ for $x = \pi/6$ and for $x = \pi/2$. A table of the important values is as follows.

x	0	$\dfrac{\pi}{6}$	$\dfrac{\pi}{3}$	$\dfrac{\pi}{2}$	$\dfrac{2\pi}{3}$	$\dfrac{5\pi}{6}$	π	$\dfrac{7\pi}{6}$	$\dfrac{4\pi}{3}$	$\dfrac{3\pi}{2}$	$\dfrac{5\pi}{3}$	$\dfrac{11\pi}{6}$	2π
y	-2	0	2	0	-2	0	2	0	-2	0	2	0	-2

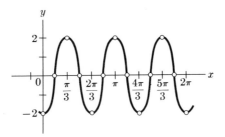

Figure 9-9

Using this table and the knowledge of the form of the cosine curve, we sketch the function as shown in Fig. 9-9.

Example E. Sketch the function $y = \cos \pi x$ for $0 \le x \le \pi$.

For this function the amplitude is 1; the period is $2\pi/\pi = 2$. Since the value of the period is not in terms of π, it is more convenient to use regular decimal units for x when sketching than to use units in terms of π as in the previous graphs. Therefore, we have the following table.

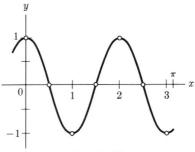

Figure 9-10

x	0	0.5	1	1.5	2	2.5	3
y	1	0	-1	0	1	0	-1

The graph of this function is shown in Fig. 9-10.

Exercises

In Exercises 1 through 20 find the period of each of the given functions.

1. $y = 2 \sin 6x$
2. $y = 4 \sin 2x$
3. $y = 3 \cos 8x$
4. $y = \cos 10x$
5. $y = -2 \sin 12x$
6. $y = -\sin 5x$
7. $y = -\cos 16x$
8. $y = -4 \cos 2x$
9. $y = 5 \sin 2\pi x$
10. $y = 2 \sin 3\pi x$
11. $y = 3 \cos 4\pi x$
12. $y = 4 \cos 10\pi x$
13. $y = 3 \sin \frac{1}{3}x$
14. $y = -2 \sin \frac{2}{5}x$
15. $y = -\frac{1}{2} \cos \frac{2}{3}x$
16. $y = \frac{1}{3} \cos \frac{1}{4}x$
17. $y = 0.4 \sin \frac{2\pi x}{3}$
18. $y = 1.5 \cos \frac{\pi x}{10}$
19. $y = 3.3 \cos \pi^2 x$
20. $y = 2.5 \sin \frac{2x}{\pi}$

In Exercises 21 through 40 sketch the graphs of the given functions. For this, use the functions given for Exercises 1 through 20.

In Exercises 41 and 42 sketch the indicated graphs.

41. The electric current in a certain "60 cycle" alternating current circuit is given by $i = 10 \sin 120\pi t$, where i is the current in amperes and t is the time in seconds. Sketch the graph of i vs. t for $0 \le t \le 0.1$ sec.

42. The vertical displacement x of a certain object oscillating at the end of a spring is given by $x = 6 \cos 4\pi t$, where x is measured in inches and t in seconds. Sketch the graph of x vs. t for $0 \le t \le 1$ sec.

9-3 Graphs of $y = a \sin (bx + c)$ and $y = a \cos (bx + c)$

There is one more important quantity to be discussed in relation to graphing the sine and cosine functions. This quantity is the *phase angle* of the function. In the function $y = a \sin (bx + c)$, c represents this phase angle. Its meaning is illustrated in the following example.

Example A.   Sketch the graph of $y = \sin (2x + \pi/4)$.

Note that $c = \pi/4$. This means that in order to obtain the values for the table we must assume a value of x, multiply it by two, add $\pi/4$ to this value and then find the sine of this result. In this manner we arrive at the following table:

x	$-\dfrac{\pi}{8}$	0	$\dfrac{\pi}{8}$	$\dfrac{\pi}{4}$	$\dfrac{3\pi}{8}$	$\dfrac{\pi}{2}$	$\dfrac{5\pi}{8}$	$\dfrac{3\pi}{4}$	$\dfrac{7\pi}{8}$	π
y	0	0.7	1	0.7	0	-0.7	-1	-0.7	0	0.7

We use the value of $x = -\pi/8$ in the table, for we note that it corresponds to finding $\sin 0$. Now using the values listed in the table, we plot the graph of $y = \sin (2x + \pi/4)$. See Fig. 9-11.

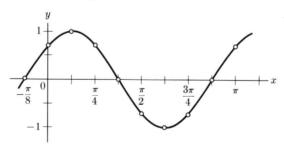

Figure 9-11

We can see from the table and from the graph that the curve of

$$y = \sin (2x + \pi/4)$$

is precisely the same as that of $y = \sin 2x$, except that it is shifted $\pi/8$ units to the left. The effect of c in the equation of $y = a \sin (bx + c)$ is to shift the curve of $y = a \sin bx$ to the left if $c > 0$, and to shift the curve to the right if $c < 0$. The amount of this shift is given by c/b. Due to its importance in sketching curves, the quantity c/b is called the *displacement*.

Therefore the results above combined with the results of Section 9-2 may be used to sketch curves of the functions $y = a \sin (bx + c)$ and $y = a \cos (bx + c)$. These are the important quantities to determine:

(1) the amplitude (equal to $|a|$)

(2) the period (equal to $2\pi/b$)

(3) the displacement (equal to c/b)

By use of these quantities, the curves of these sine and cosine functions can be readily sketched.

Example B.   Sketch the graph of $y = 2 \sin (3x - \pi)$ for $0 \le x \le \pi$.

First we note that $a = 2$, $b = 3$ and $c = -\pi$. Therefore, the amplitude is 2, the period is $2\pi/3$, and the displacement is $\pi/3$ to the right.

With this information we can tell that the curve "starts" at $x = \pi/3$ and "starts repeating" $2\pi/3$ units to the right of this point. (Be sure to grasp this point well. The period tells how many units there are along the x-axis *between* such corresponding points.) The value of y is zero when $x = \pi/3$ and when $x = \pi$. It is also zero halfway between these values of x, or when $x = 2\pi/3$. The curve reaches the amplitude value of 2 midway between $x = \pi/3$ and $x = 2\pi/3$, or when $x = \pi/2$. Extending the curve to the left to $x = 0$, we note that, since the period is $2\pi/3$, the curve passes through $(0, 0)$. Therefore, we have the following table of important values:

x	0	$\dfrac{\pi}{6}$	$\dfrac{\pi}{3}$	$\dfrac{\pi}{2}$	$\dfrac{2\pi}{3}$	$\dfrac{5\pi}{6}$	π
y	0	-2	0	2	0	-2	0

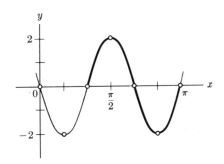

Figure 9-12

From these values we sketch the graph shown in Fig. 9-12.

Example C.   Sketch the graph of the function $y = -\cos (2x + \pi/6)$.

First we determine that the amplitude is 1, the period is $2\pi/2 = \pi$, and that the displacement is $(\pi/6) \div 2 = \pi/12$ to the left ($c > 0$). From these values we construct the following table, remembering that the curve starts repeating π units to the right of $-\pi/12$.

x	$-\dfrac{\pi}{12}$	$\dfrac{\pi}{6}$	$\dfrac{5\pi}{12}$	$\dfrac{2\pi}{3}$	$\dfrac{11\pi}{12}$
y	-1	0	1	0	-1

From this table we sketch the graph as shown in Fig. 9-13.

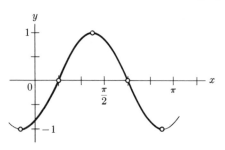

Figure 9-13   Figure 9-14

Example D. Sketch the graph of the function $y = 2 \cos (x/2 - \pi/6)$.

From the values $a = 2$, $b = 1/2$, and $c = -\pi/6$, we determine that the amplitude is 2, the period is $2\pi/\frac{1}{2} = 4\pi$, and the displacement is $(\pi/6) \div \frac{1}{2} = \pi/3$ to the right. From these values we construct the table of values.

x	$\dfrac{\pi}{3}$	$\dfrac{4\pi}{3}$	$\dfrac{7\pi}{3}$	$\dfrac{10\pi}{3}$	$\dfrac{13\pi}{3}$
y	2	0	-2	0	2

The graph is shown in Fig. 9-14. We note that when the coefficient of x is less than 1, the period is greater than 2π.

Example E. Sketch the graph of the function $y = 0.7 \sin (\pi x + \pi/4)$.

From the values $a = 0.7$, $b = \pi$, and $c = \pi/4$, we determine that the amplitude is 0.7, the period is $2\pi/\pi = 2$, and the displacement is $(\pi/4) \div \pi = 1/4$ to the left. From these values we construct the following table of values.

x	$-\dfrac{1}{4}$	$\dfrac{1}{4}$	$\dfrac{3}{4}$	$\dfrac{5}{4}$	$\dfrac{7}{4}$
y	0	0.7	0	-0.7	0

Since π is not used in the values of x, it is more convenient to use decimal number units for the graph (Fig. 9-15).

The heavy portions of the graphs in Figs. 9-12, 9-13, 9-14, and 9-15 are known as *cycles* of the curves.

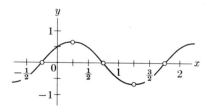

Figure 9-15

Exercises

In Exercises 1 through 22 determine the amplitude, period, and displacement for each of the functions. Then sketch the graphs of the functions.

1. $y = \sin\left(x - \dfrac{\pi}{6}\right)$

2. $y = 3 \sin\left(x + \dfrac{\pi}{4}\right)$

3. $y = \cos\left(x + \dfrac{\pi}{6}\right)$

4. $y = 2 \cos\left(x - \dfrac{\pi}{8}\right)$

5. $y = 2 \sin\left(2x + \dfrac{\pi}{2}\right)$

6. $y = -\sin\left(3x - \dfrac{\pi}{2}\right)$

7. $y = -\cos(2x - \pi)$

8. $y = 4 \cos\left(3x + \dfrac{\pi}{3}\right)$

9. $y = \dfrac{1}{2} \sin\left(\dfrac{1}{2}x - \dfrac{\pi}{4}\right)$

10. $y = 2 \sin\left(\dfrac{1}{4}x + \dfrac{\pi}{2}\right)$

11. $y = 3 \cos\left(\dfrac{1}{3}x + \dfrac{\pi}{3}\right)$

12. $y = \dfrac{1}{3} \cos\left(\dfrac{1}{2}x - \dfrac{\pi}{8}\right)$

13. $y = \sin\left(\pi x + \dfrac{\pi}{8}\right)$

14. $y = -2 \sin(2\pi x - \pi)$

15. $y = \dfrac{3}{4} \cos\left(4\pi x - \dfrac{\pi}{5}\right)$

16. $y = 6 \cos\left(3\pi x + \dfrac{\pi}{2}\right)$

17. $y = -0.6 \sin(2\pi x - 1)$

18. $y = 1.8 \sin\left(\pi x + \dfrac{1}{3}\right)$

19. $y = 4 \cos(3\pi x + 2)$

20. $y = 3 \cos(6\pi x - 1)$

21. $y = \sin(\pi^2 x - \pi)$

22. $y = \pi \cos\left(\dfrac{1}{\pi}x + \dfrac{1}{3}\right)$

In Exercises 23 and 24 sketch the indicated curves.

23. A wave traveling in a string may be represented by the equation

$$y = A \sin\left(\dfrac{t}{T} - \dfrac{x}{\lambda}\right).$$

Here A is the amplitude, t is the time the wave has traveled, x is the distance from the origin, T is the time required for the wave to travel one *wavelength* λ (the Greek lambda). Sketch three cycles of the wave for which $A = 2$ cm, $T = 0.1$ sec, $\lambda = 20$ cm, and $x = 5$ cm.

24. The voltage in a certain alternating current circuit is given by

$$y = 120 \cos\left(120\pi t + \dfrac{\pi}{6}\right),$$

where t represents the time in seconds. Sketch three cycles of the curve.

9-4 Graphs of y = tan x, y = cot x, y = sec x, y = csc x

In this section we shall briefly consider the graphs of the other trigonometric functions. We shall establish the basic form of each curve, and from these we shall be able to sketch other curves for these functions.

Considering the values and signs of the trigonometric functions as established in Chapter 7, we set up the following table for the function $y = \tan x$. The graph is shown in Fig. 9-16.

x	0	$\dfrac{\pi}{6}$	$\dfrac{\pi}{3}$	$\dfrac{\pi}{2}$	$\dfrac{2\pi}{3}$	$\dfrac{5\pi}{6}$	π	$\dfrac{7\pi}{6}$	$\dfrac{4\pi}{3}$	$\dfrac{3\pi}{2}$	$\dfrac{5\pi}{3}$	$\dfrac{11\pi}{6}$	2π
y	0	0.6	1.7	*	-1.7	-0.6	0	0.6	1.7	*	-1.7	-0.6	0

*Undefined.

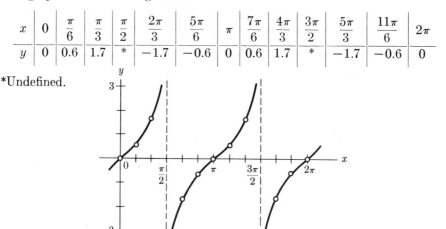

Figure 9-16

Since the curve is not defined for $x = \pi/2$, $x = 3\pi/2$, and so forth, we look at the table and note that the value of tan x becomes very large when x approaches the value $\pi/2$. We must keep in mind, however, that there is no point on the curve corresponding to $x = \pi/2$. We note that the period of the tangent curve is π. This differs from the period of the sine and cosine functions.

By following the same procedure, we can set up tables for the graphs of the other functions. We present in Figures 9-17 through 9-20 the graphs of $y = \tan x$, $y = \cot x$, $y = \sec x$, and $y = \csc x$ (the graph of $y = \tan x$ is shown again to illustrate it more completely). The dashed lines in these figures are called *asymptotes* (see Section 20-6).

To sketch functions such as $y = a \sec x$, we first sketch $y = \sec x$, and then then multiply each y-value by a. Here a is not an amplitude, since these functions are not limited in the values they take on, as are the sine and cosine functions.

Example A. Sketch the graph of $y = 2 \sec x$.

First we sketch in $y = \sec x$, shown as the light curve in Fig. 9-21. Now we multiply the y-values of the secant function by 2 (approximately, of course). In this way we obtain the desired curve, shown as the heavy curve in Fig. 9-21.

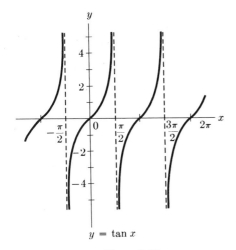

$y = \tan x$

Figure 9-17

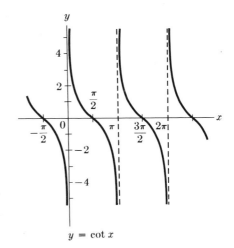

$y = \cot x$

Figure 9-18

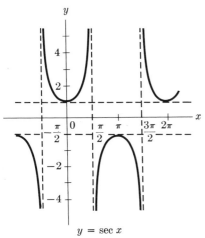

$y = \sec x$

Figure 9-19

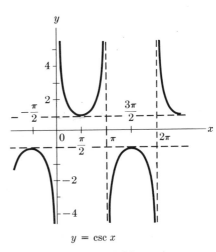

$y = \csc x$

Figure 9-20

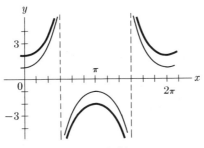

Figure 9-21

Example B.   Sketch the graph of $y = -\frac{1}{2} \cot x$.

We sketch in $y = \cot x$, shown as the light curve in Fig. 9-22. Now we multiply each y-value by $-\frac{1}{2}$. The effect of the negative sign is to invert the curve. The resulting curve is shown as the heavy curve in Fig. 9-22.

By knowing the graphs of the sine, cosine, and tangent functions, it is possible to graph the other three functions. Remembering the definitions of the trigonometric functions (Eqs. 7-1), we see that sin x and csc x are reciprocals, cos x and sec x are reciprocals, and tan x and cot x are reciprocals. That is

$$\csc x = \frac{1}{\sin x}, \qquad \sec x = \frac{1}{\cos x}, \qquad \cot x = \frac{1}{\tan x}. \qquad (9\text{-}1)$$

Thus, to sketch $y = \cot x$, $y = \sec x$, or $y = \csc x$, we sketch the corresponding reciprocal function, and from this graph determine the necessary values.

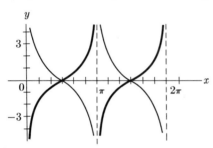

Figure 9-22

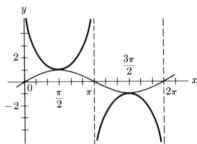

Figure 9-23

Example C.   Sketch the graph of $y = \csc x$.

We first sketch in the graph of $y = \sin x$ (light curve). Where sin x is 1, csc x will also be 1, since $1/1 = 1$. Where sin x is 0, csc x is undefined, since $1/0$ is undefined. Where sin x is 0.5, csc x is 2, since $1/0.5 = 2$. Thus, as sin x becomes larger, csc x becomes smaller, and as sin x becomes smaller, csc x becomes larger. The two functions always have the same sign. We sketch the graph of $y = \csc x$ from this information, as shown in Fig. 9-23.

Exercises

In Exercises 1 through 4 fill in the following table for each function and then plot the curve from these points.

x	$-\dfrac{\pi}{2}$	$-\dfrac{\pi}{3}$	$-\dfrac{\pi}{4}$	$-\dfrac{\pi}{6}$	0	$\dfrac{\pi}{6}$	$\dfrac{\pi}{4}$	$\dfrac{\pi}{3}$	$\dfrac{\pi}{2}$	$\dfrac{2\pi}{3}$	$\dfrac{3\pi}{4}$	$\dfrac{5\pi}{6}$	π
y													

1. $y = \tan x$ 2. $y = \cot x$ 3. $y = \sec x$ 4. $y = \csc x$

In Exercises 5 through 12 sketch the curves of the given functions by use of the basic curve forms (Figs. 9-17, 9-18, 9-19, 9-20). See Examples A and B.

5. $y = 2 \tan x$

6. $y = 3 \cot x$

7. $y = \frac{1}{2}\sec x$

8. $y = \frac{3}{2}\csc x$

9. $y = -2 \cot x$

10. $y = -\tan x$

11. $y = -3 \csc x$

12. $y = -\frac{1}{2} \sec x$

In Exercises 13 through 20 plot the graphs by first making an appropriate table for $0 \le x \le \pi$.

13. $y = \tan 2x$

14. $y = 2 \cot 3x$

15. $y = \frac{1}{2} \sec 3 x$

16. $y = \csc 2x$

17. $y = 2 \cot \left(2x + \dfrac{\pi}{6} \right)$

18. $y = \tan \left(3x - \dfrac{\pi}{2} \right)$

19. $y = \csc \left(3x - \dfrac{\pi}{3} \right)$

20. $y = 3 \sec \left(2x + \dfrac{\pi}{4} \right)$

In Exercises 21 through 24 sketch the given curves by first sketching the appropriate reciprocal function. See Example C.

21. $y = \sec x$

22. $y = \cot x$

23. $y = \csc 2x$

24. $y = \sec \pi x$

In Exercises 25 and 26 construct the appropriate graphs.

25. For an object sliding down an inclined plane at constant speed, the coefficient of friction μ (the Greek mu) between the object and the plane is given by $\mu = \tan \theta$, where θ is the angle between the plane and the horizontal. Sketch a graph of the coefficient of friction vs. the angle of inclination of the plane for $0 \le \theta \le 60°$.

26. The tension T at any point in a cable supporting a distributed load is given by $T = T_0 \sec \theta$, where T_0 is the tension where the cable is horizontal, and θ is the angle between the cable and the horizontal at any point. Sketch a graph of T vs. θ for a cable for which $T_0 = 200$ lb.

9-5 Applications of the trigonometric graphs

There are a great many applications of the trigonometric functions and their graphs, a few of which have been indicated in the exercises of the previous sections. In this section we shall introduce an important physical concept and indicate some of the technical applications.

In Section 7-4, we discussed the velocity of an object moving in a circular path. The movement of the *projection* on a diameter of a particle revolving about a circle with constant velocity is known as *simple harmonic motion*. For example, this could be the motion of the shadow of an object which is moving around a circle. Another example would be the vertical (or horizontal) position of the end of a spoke of a wheel in motion.

Example A. When we consider Fig. 9-24, let us assume that motion starts with the end of the radius at $(R, 0)$ and that it is moving with constant angular velocity ω. This means that the length of the projection of the radius along the y-axis is given by $d = R \sin \theta$. The length of this projection is shown for a few different positions of the end of the radius. Since $\theta/t = \omega$, or $\theta = \omega t$, we have

$$d = R \sin \omega t \qquad\qquad (9\text{-}2)$$

as the equation for the length of the projection, with time as the independent variable. Normally, the position as a function of time is the important relationship.

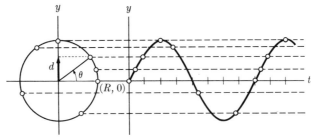

Figure 9-24

For the case where $R = 10$ in., and $\omega = 4.0$ rad/sec, we have

$$d = 10 \sin 4.0t.$$

By sketching the graph of this function, we can readily determine the length of the projection d for a given time t. The graph is shown in Fig. 9-25.

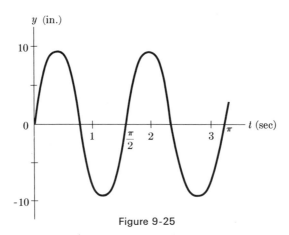

Figure 9-25

Example B. If the end of the radius is at $(R/\sqrt{2}, R/\sqrt{2})$, where $\theta = \pi/4$, when $t = 0$, we can express the projection d as a function of the time as

$$d = R \sin \left(\omega t + \frac{\pi}{4}\right).$$

If the end of the radius is at $(0, R)$, where $\theta = \pi/2$, when $t = 0$, we can express the projection d as a function of the time as $d = R \sin (\omega t + \pi/2)$, or

$$d = R \cos \omega t.$$

This can be seen from Fig. 9-24. If the motion started at the first maximum of the indicated curve, the resulting curve would be that of the cosine function.

Other examples of simple harmonic motion are (1) the movement of a pendulum bob through its arc (a very close approximation to simple harmonic motion), (2) the motion of an object on the end of a spring, (3) the motion of an object "bobbing" in the water, and (4) the movement of the end of a vibrating rod (which we hear as sound). Other phenomena which give rise to equations just like those for simple harmonic motion are found in the fields of optics, sound, and electricity. Such phenomena have the same mathematical form because they result from vibratory motion or motion in a circle.

Example C. A very important use of the trigonometric curves arises in the study of alternating current, which is caused by the motion of a wire passing through a magnetic field. If this wire is moving in a circular path, with angular velocity ω, the current i in the wire at time t is given by an equation of the form

$$i = I_m \sin (\omega t + \alpha), \tag{9-3}$$

where I_m is the maximum current attainable, and α is the phase angle. The current may be represented by a sine wave, as in the following example.

Example D.   In Example C, given that $I_m = 6.0$ amp, $\omega = 120\pi$ rad/sec (60 cycles/sec), and $\alpha = \pi/6$, we have the equation

$$i = 6.0 \sin \left(120\pi t + \frac{\pi}{6}\right).$$

From this equation we see that the amplitude is 6.0, the period is $\frac{1}{60}$ sec, and the displacement is $\frac{1}{720}$ sec to the left. From these values we draw the graph as shown in Fig. 9-26. Since the current takes on both positive and negative values, we conclude that it moves in opposite directions.

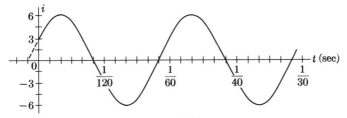

Figure 9-26

Exercises

In Exercises 1 and 2 draw two cycles of the curve of the projection of Example A as a function of time for the given values.

1. $R = 4.0$ in., $\omega = 1$ rad/sec   2. $R = 8.0$ cm, $\omega = 0.5$ cycle/sec

In Exercises 3 and 4, for the projection described in Example A, assume that the end of the radius starts at $(0, R)$. Draw two cycles of the projection as a function of time for the given values. (See Example B.)

3. $R = 2.0$ ft, $\omega = 1$ cycle/sec   4. $R = 2.5$ in., $\omega = 0.3$ rad/sec

In Exercises 5 and 6, for the projection described in Example A, assume that the end of the radius starts at the indicated point. Draw two cycles of the projection as a function of time for the given values. (See Example B.)

5. $R = 6.0$ cm, $\omega = 2$ cycles/sec, starting point $(\sqrt{3}R/2), R/2)$

6. $R = 3.2$ ft, $\omega = 0.2$ rad/sec, starting point $(R/2, \sqrt{3}R/2)$

In Exercises 7 and 8, for the alternating-current discussed in Example C, draw two cycles of the current as a function of time for the given values.

7. $I_m = 2.0$ amps, $\omega = 60$ cycles/sec, $\alpha = 0$
8. $I_m = 0.6$ amp, $\omega = 100$ rad/sec, $\alpha = \pi/4$

In Exercises 9 and 10, for an alternating-current circuit, in which the voltage is given by

$$e = E \cos (\omega t + \alpha),$$

draw two cycles of the voltage as a function of time for the given values.

9. $E = 170$ volts, $\omega = 50$ rad/sec, $\alpha = 0$
10. $E = 110$ volts, $\omega = 60$ cycles/sec, $\alpha = -\pi/3$

In Exercises 11 through 14 draw the required curves.

11. The angular displacement θ of a pendulum bob is given in terms of its initial ($t = 0$) displacement θ_0 by the equation $\theta = \theta_0 \cos \omega t$. If $\omega = 2$ rad/sec and $\theta_0 = \pi/30$ rad, draw two cycles for the resulting equation.

12. The displacement, as a function of time, from the position of equilibrium, of an object on the end of a spring is given by $x = A \cos (\omega t + \alpha)$. Draw two cycles of the curve for displacement as a function of time for $A = 2$ in., $\omega = 0.5$ cycle/sec, and $\alpha = \pi/6$.

13. An object of weight w and cross-sectional area A is depressed a distance x_0 from its equilibrium position when in a liquid of density d and then released; its displacement as a function of time is given by

$$x = x_0 \cos \sqrt{\frac{dgA}{w}}\, t,$$

where g (= 32 ft/sec²) is the acceleration due to gravity. If a 4.0-lb object with a cross-sectional area of 2.0 ft² is depressed 3.0 ft in water (let $d = 62.4$ lb/ft³), find the equation which expresses the displacement as a function of time. Draw two cycles of the curve.

14. A wave is traveling in a string. The displacement, as a function of time, from its equilibrium position, is given by $y = A \cos (2\pi/T)t$. T is the period (measured in seconds) of the motion. If $A = 0.2$ in., and $T = 0.1$ sec, draw two cycles of the displacement as a function of time.

9-6 Composite trigonometric curves

Many applications of trigonometric functions involve the combination of two or more functions. In this section we shall discuss two important methods in which trigonometric curves can be combined.

If we wish to find the curve of a function which itself is the sum of two other functions, we may find the resulting graph by first sketching the two individual functions, and then adding the y-values graphically. This method is called *addition of ordinates*, and is illustrated in the following examples.

Example A.   Sketch the graph of $y = 2 \cos x + \sin 2x$.

On the same set of coordinate axes we sketch the curves $y = 2 \cos x$ and $y = \sin 2x$. These are shown as dashed curves in Fig. 9-27. We then graphically add the y-values of these two curves for various values of x to obtain the points on the resulting curve shown as a heavy curve in Fig. 9-27. We add the y-values for a sufficient number of x-values to obtain the proper representation. Some points are easily found. Where one curve crosses the x-axis, its y-value is zero, and therefore the resulting curve has its point on the other curve for this value of x. In this example, $\sin 2x$ is zero at $x = 0$, $\pi/2$, π, and so forth. We see that points on the resulting curve lie on the curve of $2 \cos x$. We should also add the values where each curve is at its amplitude values. In this case, $\sin 2x$ equals 1 at $\pi/4$, and the two y-values should be added together here to get a point on the resulting curve. At $x = 5\pi/4$, we must take care in adding the values, since $\sin 2x$ is positive and $2 \cos x$ is negative. Reasonable care and accuracy are necessary to obtain a proper resulting curve.

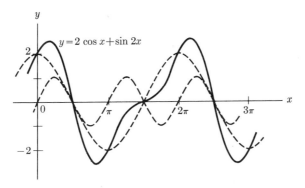

Figure 9-27

Example B.   Sketch the graph of $y = (x/2) - \cos x$.

The method of addition of ordinates is applicable regardless of the kinds of functions being added. Here we note that $y = x/2$ is a straight line, and that it is to be combined with a trigonometric curve.

We could graph the functions $y = x/2$ and $y = \cos x$ and then subtract the ordinates of $y = \cos x$ from the ordinates of $y = x/2$. But it is easier, and far less confusing, to add values, so we shall sketch $y = x/2$ and $y = -\cos x$ and add the ordinates to obtain points on the resulting curve. These graphs are shown as dashed curves in Fig. 9-28. The important points on the resulting curve are obtained by using the values of x corresponding to the zeros and amplitude values of $y = -\cos x$.

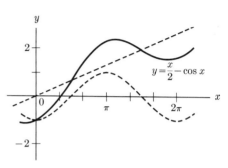

Figure 9-28

Example C.   Sketch the graph of $y = \cos \pi x - 2 \sin 2x$.

The curves of $y = \cos \pi x$ and $y = -2 \sin 2x$ are shown as dashed curves in Fig. 9-29. Points for the resulting curve are found primarily at the x-values where each of the curves has its zero or amplitude values. Again, special care should be taken where one of the curves is negative and the other is positive.

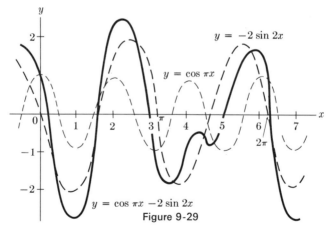

Figure 9-29

Another important application of trigonometric curves is made when they are added at *right angles*. This can be accomplished in practice by applying different voltages to an oscilloscope. Let us consider the following examples.

Example D.   Plot the graph for which the values of x and y are given by the equations $y = \sin 2\pi t$ and $x = 2 \cos \pi t$. (Equations given in this form, x and y in terms of a third variable, are called *parametric equations*.)

Since both x and y are given in terms of t, by assuming values for t we may find corresponding values of x and y, and use these values to plot the resulting points (see Fig. 9-30).

t	0	$\frac{1}{4}$	$\frac{1}{2}$	$\frac{3}{4}$	1	$\frac{5}{4}$	$\frac{3}{2}$	$\frac{7}{4}$	2	$\frac{9}{4}$
x	2	1.4	0	-1.4	-2	-1.4	0	1.4	2	1.4
y	0	1	0	-1	0	1	0	-1	0	1
Point Number	1	2	3	4	5	6	7	8	9	10

Since x and y are trigonometric functions of a third variable t, and since the x- and y-axes are at right angles, values of x and y obtained in this manner result in a combination of two trigonometric curves at right angles. Figures obtained in this manner are called *Lissajous figures*.

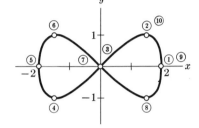

Figure 9-30

Example E.   If we place a circle on the x-axis and another on the y-axis, we may represent the coordinates (x, y) for the curve of Example D by the lengths of the projections (see Example A of Section 9-5) of a point moving around each circle. A careful study of Fig. 9-31 will clarify this. We note that the radius of the circle giving the x-values is 2, whereas the radius of the other is 1. This is due to the manner in which x and y are defined. Also due to the definitions, the point revolves around the y-circle twice as fast as the corresponding point revolves around the x-circle.

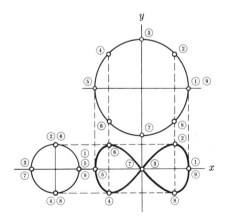

Figure 9-31

Example F. Plot the Lissajous figure for which the *x*- and *y*-values are given by $x = 2 \sin 3t$ and $y = 3 \sin (t + \pi/3)$.

Since values of *t* which are multiples of π give convenient values of *x* and *y*, the table is constructed with these values of *t*. Figure 9-32 shows the graph.

t	x	y	Point number
0	0	2.6	1
$\pi/6$	2	3	2
$\pi/3$	0	2.6	3
$\pi/2$	-2	1.5	4
$2\pi/3$	0	0	5
$5\pi/6$	2	-1.5	6
π	0	-2.6	7
$7\pi/6$	-2	-3	8
$4\pi/3$	0	-2.6	9
$3\pi/2$	2	-1.5	10
$5\pi/3$	0	0	11
$11\pi/6$	-2	1.5	12
2π	0	2.6	13

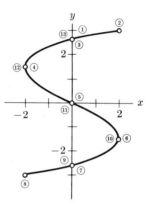

Figure 9-32

Exercises

In Exercises 1 through 16, use the method of addition of ordinates to sketch the given curves.

1. $y = x + \sin x$

2. $y = x + 2 \cos x$

3. $y = \frac{1}{10}x^2 + \sin 2x$

4. $y = \frac{1}{5}x^3 - \cos \pi x$

5. $y = \sin x + \cos x$

6. $y = \sin x + \sin 2x$

7. $y = \sin x - \sin 2x$

8. $y = \cos 3x - \sin x$

9. $y = 2 \cos 2x + 3 \sin x$

10. $y = \frac{1}{2} \sin 4x + \cos 2x$

11. $y = 2 \sin x - \cos x$

12. $y = \sin \dfrac{x}{2} - \sin x$

13. $y = 2 \cos 4x - \cos \left(x - \dfrac{\pi}{4} \right)$

14. $y = \sin \pi x - \cos 2x$

15. $y = 2 \sin \left(2x - \dfrac{\pi}{6} \right) + \cos \left(2x + \dfrac{\pi}{3} \right)$

16. $y = 3 \cos 2\pi x + \sin \dfrac{\pi}{2}x$

In Exercises 17 through 24 plot the Lissajous figures.

17. $y = \sin t,\ x = \sin t$

18. $y = 2 \cos t,\ x = \cos t$

19. $y = \sin \pi t,\ x = \cos \pi t$

20. $y = \sin 2t,\ x = \cos \left(t + \dfrac{\pi}{4} \right)$

21. $y = 2 \sin \pi t,\ x = \cos \pi \left(t + \dfrac{1}{6} \right)$

22. $y = \sin^2 \pi t,\ x = \cos 2\pi t$

23. $y = \cos 2t,\ x = 2 \cos 3t$

24. $y = 3 \sin 3\pi t,\ x = 2 \sin \pi t$

In Exercises 25 through 30 sketch the appropriate figures.

25. The current in a certain electric circuit is given by $i = 4 \sin 60\pi t + 2 \cos 120\pi t$. Sketch the curve representing the current in amps as a function of time in seconds.

26. In optics, two waves are said to interfere destructively if, when they pass through the same medium, the amplitude of the resulting wave is zero. Sketch the curve of $y = \sin x + \cos (x + \pi/2)$, and determine whether or not it would represent destructive interference of two waves.

27. An object oscillating on a spring, under specific conditions, has a displacement given by $y = 0.4 \sin 4t + 0.3 \cos 4t$. Plot y (in feet) versus t (in seconds).

28. The resultant voltage in a certain electric circuit is given by $e = 50 \sin 50\pi t + 80 \sin 60\pi t$. Sketch the curve representing voltage as a function of time.

29. Two signals are being sent to an oscilloscope, and are seen on the oscilloscope as being at right angles. The equations governing the displacement of these signals are $x = 2 \cos 120\pi t$ and $y = 3 \cos 120\pi t$, respectively. Sketch the figure which would appear on the oscilloscope.

30. In the study of optics, light is said to be elliptically polarized if certain optic vibrations are out of phase. These may be represented by Lissajous figures. Determine the Lissajous figure for two waves of light given by $w_1 = \sin \omega t$, $w_2 = \sin (\omega t + \pi/4)$.

9-7 Miscellaneous Exercises

In Exercises 1 through 24 sketch the curves of the given trigonometric functions.

1. $y = \frac{2}{3} \sin x$
2. $y = -4 \sin x$
3. $y = -2 \cos x$
4. $y = 2.3 \cos x$

5. $y = 2 \sin 3x$
6. $y = 3 \sin \frac{1}{2}x$
7. $y = 2 \cos 2x$
8. $y = 4 \cos 6x$

9. $y = \sin \pi x$
10. $y = 3 \sin 4\pi x$
11. $y = 5 \cos 2\pi x$
12. $y = -\cos 3\pi x$

13. $y = 2 \sin \left(3x - \frac{\pi}{2} \right)$
14. $y = 3 \sin \left(\frac{x}{2} + \frac{\pi}{2} \right)$

15. $y = -2 \cos (4x + \pi)$
16. $y = 0.8 \cos \left(\frac{x}{6} - \frac{\pi}{2} \right)$

17. $y = -\sin \left(\pi x + \frac{\pi}{6} \right)$
18. $y = 2 \sin (3\pi x - \pi)$

19. $y = 8 \cos \left(4\pi x - \frac{\pi}{2} \right)$
20. $y = 3 \cos (2\pi x + \pi)$

21. $y = 3 \tan x$
22. $y = \frac{1}{4} \sec x$

23. $y = -\frac{1}{3}\csc x$
24. $y = -5 \cot x$

In Exercises 25 through 28 sketch the given curves by the method of addition of ordinates.

25. $y = \frac{1}{2} \sin 2x - x$
26. $y = \sin 3x + 2 \cos 2x$

27. $y = \cos \left(x + \frac{\pi}{4} \right) - 2 \sin 2x$
28. $y = 2 \cos \pi x + \cos (2\pi x - \pi)$

In Exercises 29 and 30 plot the Lissajous figures.

29. $y = 2 \sin \pi t$, $x = -\cos 2\pi t$ 30. $y = \cos \left(2t + \dfrac{\pi}{3} \right)$, $x = \cos \left(t - \dfrac{\pi}{6} \right)$

In Exercises 31 through 40 sketch the appropriate figures.

31. A simple pendulum is started by giving it a velocity from its equilibrium position. The angle θ between the vertical and the pendulum is given by $\theta = a \sin (\sqrt{g/l}\ t)$, where a is the amplitude in radians, g ($= 32$ ft/sec^2) is the acceleration due to gravity, l is the length of the pendulum in feet, and t is the length of time of the motion. Sketch two cycles of θ as a function of t for the pendulum whose length is 2.0 ft and $a = 0.1$ rad.

32. The electric current in a certain circuit is given by $i = i_0 \sin (t/\sqrt{LC})$, where i_0 is the initial current in the circuit, L is an inductance, and C is a capacitance. Sketch two cycles of i as a function of t (in seconds) for the case where $i_0 = 0.50$ amp, $L = 1$ henry, and $C = 0.0001$ farad.

33. A certain object is oscillating at the end of a spring. The displacement as a function of time is given by the relation $y = 0.5 \cos (8t + \pi/3)$, where y is measured in feet and t in seconds. Plot the graph of y versus t.

34. A circular disk suspended by a thin wire attached to the center at one of its flat faces is twisted through an angle θ. Torsion in the wire tends to turn the disk back in the opposite direction (thus the name "torsion pendulum" is given to this device). The angular displacement as a function of time is given by $\theta = \theta_0 \cos (\omega t + \alpha)$, where θ_0 is the maximum angular displacement, ω is a constant which depends on the properties of the disk and wire, and α is the phase angle. Plot the graph of θ versus t if $\theta_0 = 0.1$ rad, $\omega = 2.5$ rad/sec and $\alpha = \pi/4$.

35. The charge q on a certain capacitor as a function of time is given by $q = 0.001(1 - \cos 100t)$. Sketch two cycles of q as a function of t. Capacitance is measured in farads, and t is measured in seconds.

36. If the upper end of a spring is not fixed and is being moved with a sinusoidal motion, the motion of the bob at the end of the spring is affected. Plot the curve of the motion of the upper end of a spring which is being moved by an external force according to the equation $y = 4 \sin 2t - 2 \cos 2t$.

37. Under certain conditions, the path of a certain moving particle is given by $x = 2 \cos 3\pi t$ and $y = \sin 3\pi t$. Plot the path of the object.

38. Two signals are applied to an oscilloscope. The equations governing the displacement of these signals are $x = 2 \cos 40\pi t$ and $y = \sin 120\pi t$. Sketch the figure which appears on the oscilloscope.

39. An object is h ft high and d ft from an observer. The relationship giving d as a function of h is $d = h \cot \theta$, where θ is the angle of elevation of the top of the object. Sketch d as a function of θ for an object 100 ft high.

40. The instantaneous power in an electric circuit is defined as the product of the instantaneous voltage e and the instantaneous current i. If $e = 100 \cos 200t$ and $i = 2 \cos (200t + \pi/4)$, plot the graph of the voltage and the graph of the current (in amperes), on the same coordinate system, versus the time (in seconds). Then sketch the power (in watts) versus time by multiplying appropriate values of e and i.

Exponents and Radicals

10

10-1 Integral exponents

Much of our future work will involve a more detailed understanding of the use of exponents and radicals. In certain areas we shall use these tools extensively. Therefore in this chapter we shall develop the necessary operations.

The laws of exponents were given in Section 1-4. We now write them again for reference.

$$a^m \cdot a^n = a^{m+n} \tag{10-1}$$

$$\frac{a^m}{a^n} = a^{m-n} \text{ if } m > n, \quad a \neq 0, \quad \frac{a^m}{a^n} = \frac{1}{a^{n-m}} \text{ if } m < n, \quad a \neq 0 \tag{10-2}$$

$$(a^m)^n = a^{mn} \tag{10-3}$$

$$(ab)^n = a^n b^n, \quad \left(\frac{a}{b}\right)^n = \frac{a^n}{b^n} \text{ if } b \neq 0 \tag{10-4}$$

As we pointed out in Section 1-4, these equations are valid for positive integers as exponents. In this section we shall extend their use so that zero and the negative integers may be used as exponents. Later in the chapter we shall show how fractions may also be used as exponents. Since the equations above are very important to the development of this chapter, they should be learned well, or there may be difficulty in working with them.

In Eq. (10-2), if $n = m$, we would have $a^m/a^m = a^{m-m} = a^0$. Also, $a^m/a^m = 1$, since any nonzero quantity divided by itself equals 1. Therefore, for Eq. (10-2) to hold when $m = n$, we have

$$a^0 = 1, \quad (a \neq 0). \tag{10-5}$$

Equation (10-5) shows the definition of zero as an exponent. Since a has not been specified, this equation states that any nonzero algebraic expression raised to the zero power is 1. Also, the other laws of exponents are valid for this definition.

Example A.   Equation (10-1) states that $a^m \cdot a^n = a^{m+n}$. If $n = 0$, we have $a^m \cdot a^0 = a^{m+0} = a^m$. Since $a^0 = 1$, this equation could be written as $a^m(1) = a^m$. This provides further verification for the validity of Eq. (10-5).

Example B. $5^0 = 1$, $(2x)^0 = 1$, $(ax + b)^0 = 1$,
$\qquad\qquad (a^2xb^4)^0 = 1$, $(a^2b^0c)^2 = a^4b^0c^2 = a^4c^2$.

If we apply the first form of Eq. (10-2) to the case where $n > m$, the resulting exponent is negative. This leads us to the definition of a negative exponent.

Example C.   Applying the first form of Eq. (10-2) to a^2/a^7, we have

$$\frac{a^2}{a^7} = a^{2-7} = a^{-5}.$$

Applying the second form of Eq. (10-2) to the same fraction leads to

$$\frac{a^2}{a^7} = \frac{1}{a^{7-2}} = \frac{1}{a^5}.$$

In order that these results can be consistent, it must be true that

$$a^{-5} = \frac{1}{a^5}.$$

Following the reasoning in Example C, if we define

$$a^{-n} = \frac{1}{a^n} \qquad (a \neq 0), \tag{10-6}$$

then all of the laws of exponents will hold for negative integers.

Example D. $3^{-1} = \dfrac{1}{3}$, $4^{-2} = \dfrac{1}{16}$, $\dfrac{1}{a^{-3}} = a^3$, $a^4 = \dfrac{1}{a^{-4}}$

Example E. $(a^0b^2c)^{-2} = \dfrac{1}{(b^2c)^2} = \dfrac{1}{b^4c^2}$,

$$\left(\frac{a^3t}{b^2x}\right)^{-2} = \frac{(a^3t)^{-2}}{(b^2x)^{-2}} = \frac{(b^2x)^2}{(a^3t)^2} = \frac{b^4x^2}{a^6t^2}$$

From Eq. (10-6) and Examples D and E, we see that when a factor is moved from the denominator to the numerator of a fraction, or conversely, the *sign* of the *exponent* is changed. We should heed the word "factor"; this rule does not apply to moving terms in the numerator or denominator.

Example F.
$$\frac{1}{x^{-1}}\left(\frac{x^{-1}-y^{-1}}{x^2-y^2}\right) = \frac{x}{1}\left(\frac{\dfrac{1}{x}-\dfrac{1}{y}}{x^2-y^2}\right) = x\left(\frac{\dfrac{y-x}{xy}}{x^2-y^2}\right)$$

$$= \frac{\dfrac{x(y-x)}{xy}}{(x-y)(x+y)} = \frac{x(y-x)}{xy}\cdot\frac{1}{(x-y)(x+y)}$$

$$= \frac{x(y-x)}{xy(x-y)(x+y)} = \frac{-(x-y)}{y(x-y)(x+y)}$$

$$= -\frac{1}{y(x+y)}$$

Note that in this example the x^{-1} and y^{-1} in the numerator could not be moved directly to the denominator with positive exponents because they are only terms of the original numerator.

Example G. $3(x+4)^2(x-3)^{-2} - 2(x-3)^{-3}(x+4)^3$

$$= \frac{3(x+4)^2}{(x-3)^2} - \frac{2(x+4)^3}{(x-3)^3} = \frac{3(x-3)(x+4)^2 - 2(x+4)^3}{(x-3)^3}$$

$$= \frac{(x+4)^2[3(x-3)-2(x+4)]}{(x-3)^3} = \frac{(x+4)^2(x-17)}{(x-3)^3}$$

Expressions such as the one in this example are commonly found in problems in the calculus.

Exercises

In Exercises 1 through 36 express each of the given expressions in the simplest form which contains only positive exponents.

1. $(8a)^0$
2. $(3x^2)^0$
3. $2a^{-2}$
4. $(2a)^{-2}$

5. $3x^0c^{-2}$
6. $5^0x^{-2}z$
7. $(a+b)^{-1}$
8. $a^{-1}+b^{-1}$

9. $(4xa^{-2})^0$
10. $3(a+b)^0$
11. b^5b^{-3}
12. $2c^4c^{-7}$

13. $\dfrac{a^2b^5}{a^{-4}b}$
14. $\dfrac{3a^{-1}y^3}{a^5y^{-1}}$
15. $(5^0x^2a^{-1})^{-1}$
16. $(3m^{-2}n^4)^{-2}$

17. $\left(\dfrac{4a}{x}\right)^{-3}$
18. $\left(\dfrac{2b^2}{y^5}\right)^{-2}$
19. $\left(\dfrac{4x^{-1}}{y^3}\right)^{-2}$
20. $\left(\dfrac{2b^{-1}}{c^{-5}}\right)^{-3}$

21. $(3x^2)^{-4}(2c)^0$
22. $3x^{-4}(6y)^2$

23. $(5t^{-6})(4t^{-7})$
24. $(5x^0b)^07^{-2}$

25. $\left(\dfrac{3a^2}{4b}\right)^{-3}\left(\dfrac{4}{a}\right)^{-5}$

26. $\left(\dfrac{a^{-2}}{b^2}\right)^{-3}\left(\dfrac{a^{-3}}{b^5}\right)^{2}$

27. $(x^2y^{-1})^2 - x^{-4}$

28. $3(a^{-1}z^2)^{-3} + c^{-2}z^{-1}$

29. $(a^{-1} + b^{-1})^{-1}$

30. $(2^{-3} - 4^{-1})^2$

31. $\dfrac{x - y^{-1}}{x^{-1} - y}$

32. $\dfrac{x^{-2} - y^{-2}}{x^{-1} - y^{-1}}$

33. $\dfrac{ax^{-2} + a^{-2}x}{a^{-1} + x^{-1}}$

34. $\dfrac{2x^{-2} - 2y^{-2}}{(xy)^{-3}}$

35. $(x - 1)^{-1} + (x + 1)^{-1}$

36. $4(2x - 1)(x + 2)^{-1} - (2x - 1)^2(x + 2)^{-2}$

In Exercises 37 through 39 perform the indicated operations.

37. When discussing electronic amplifiers, the expression $(1/r + 1/R)^{-1}$ is found. Simplify this expression.

38. Physical units associated with numbers are often expressed in terms of negative exponents (see Appendix B). If the units of a certain quantity are $(\text{ft} \cdot \text{sec}^{-1})^2$, express these units without the use of negative exponents.

39. An expression for the focal length of a certain lens is $[(\mu - 1)(r_1^{-1} - r_2^{-1})]^{-1}$. Rewrite this expression without the use of negative exponents.

10-2 Scientific notation

In technical and scientific work we often encounter numbers which are either very large or very small in magnitude. Illustrations of such numbers are given in the following example.

Example A.   Television signals travel at about 30,000,000,000 cm/sec. The weight of the earth is about 6,600,000,000,000,000,000,000 tons. A typical protective coating used on aluminum is about 0.0005 in. thick. The wavelength of some x-rays is about 0.000000095 cm.

Writing numbers such as these is inconvenient in ordinary notation, as shown in Example A, particularly when the numbers of zeros needed for the proper location of the decimal point is excessive. Therefore, a convenient notation, known as *scientific notation*, is normally used to represent such numbers.

A number written in scientific notation is expressed as the product of a number between 1 and 10 and a power of ten. Symbolically this can be written as

$$P \times 10^k$$

where $1 \leq P < 10$, and k can take on any integral value. The following example illustrates how numbers are written in scientific notation.

Example B. $340,000 = 3.4(100,000) = 3.4 \times 10^5$,

$$0.017 = \frac{1.7}{100} = 1.7 \times 10^{-2},$$

$$0.000503 = \frac{5.03}{10000} = 5.03 \times 10^{-4},$$

$$6.82 = 6.82(1) = 6.82 \times 10^0$$

From Example B we can establish a method for changing numbers from ordinary notation to scientific notation. The decimal point is moved so that only one nonzero digit is to its left. The number of places moved is the value of k. It is positive if the decimal point is moved to the left, and it is negative if it moved to the right. Consider the illustrations in the following example.

Example C. $\underset{\text{5 places}}{\underline{3{.}40000}} = 3.4 \times 10^5$, $\qquad \underset{\text{2 places}}{0.0\overset{\frown}{17}} = 1.7 \times 10^{-2}$,

$\qquad\qquad \underset{\text{4 places}}{0.0005\overset{\frown}{03}} = 5.03 \times 10^{-4}$, $\qquad \underset{\text{0 places}}{6.82} = 6.82 \times 10^0$

To change a number from scientific notation to ordinary notation, the procedure above is reversed. The following example illustrates the procedure.

Example D. To change 5.83×10^6 to ordinary notation, we must move the decimal point 6 places to the right. Therefore, additional zeros must be included for the proper location of the decimal point. Thus, $5.83 \times 10^6 = 5,830,000$.

To change 8.06×10^{-3} to ordinary notation, we must move the decimal point 3 places to the left. Again, additional zeros must be included. Thus, $8.06 \times 10^{-3} = 0.00806$.

Scientific notation provides a practical way to handle calculations involving numbers of very large or very small magnitude. This includes calculations made on the slide rule, particularly in the determination of the decimal point of the result. If all numbers are expressed in scientific notation, the laws of exponents are used to find the decimal point in the result. It is proper to leave the result in scientific notation.

Example E. In determining the result of $95,600,000,000/0.0286$, we may estimate the result as

$$\frac{9 \times 10^{10}}{3 \times 10^{-2}} = 3 \times 10^{12}.$$

The slide rule indicates the digits 334 for the result. Therefore, the result is 3.34×10^{12}. The power of ten here is sufficiently large that we would generally leave the result in this form.

Exercises

In Exercises 1 through 8 change the numbers from scientific notation to ordinary notation.

1. 4.5×10^4 　　　 2. 6.8×10^7 　　　 3. 2.01×10^{-3} 　　　 4. 9.61×10^{-5}

5. 3.23×10^0 　　　 6. 8.40×10^0 　　　 7. 1.86×10 　　　 8. 5.44×10^{-1}

In Exercises 9 through 16 change the given numbers from ordinary notation to scientific notation.

9. 40000 　　　 10. 5600000 　　　 11. 0.0087 　　　 12. 0.702

13. 6.89 　　　 14. 1.09 　　　 15. 0.063 　　　 16. 0.0000908

In Exercises 17 through 24 perform the indicated calculations on a slide rule, making any necessary estimations by the use of scientific notation.

17. $(67000)(3040)$ 　　　　　　　　　　 18. $(56200)(0.00632)$

19. $(1280)(86500)(43.8)$ 　　　　　　 20. $(0.0000659)(0.00486)(31900)$

21. $\dfrac{87400}{0.00895}$ 　　 22. $\dfrac{0.00728}{670000}$ 　　 23. $\dfrac{(0.0732)(6700)}{0.00134}$ 　　 24. $\dfrac{(2430)(97000)}{0.00452}$

In Exercises 25 through 34 change any numbers in ordinary notation to scientific notation or change any numbers in scientific notation to ordinary notation.

25. The stress on a certain structure is 22,500 lb/in².

26. The half-life of uranium 235 is 710,000,000 years.

27. The pressure of a certain gas is 6.1×10^{-4} atm.

28. Some computers can perform an addition in 1.5×10^{-6} sec.

29. A certain electrical resistor has a resistance of 4.5×10^3 ohms.

30. The diameter of the sun is 8.64×10^5 mi.

31. One foot of steel pipe will increase about 0.000011 ft for a one–degree centigrade rise in temperature.

32. The wave length of yellow light is about 0.00000059 meter.

33. The mass of a proton is 1.67×10^{-24} gm.

34. The average distance from the earth to the sun is 9.29×10^7 mi.

In Exercises 35 and 36 perform the indicated calculations on the slide rule.

35. The resistance R, in ohms, of a wire of length l cm and cross-sectional area A cm² is given by $R = \rho l/A$, where ρ (the Greek rho) is known as the resistivity. Find R for a wire for which $\rho = 1.75 \times 10^{-6}$ ohm-cm, $l = 150$ cm and $A = 0.00435$ cm².

36. For a certain gas, the product of the volume and pressure is 165 atm-cm³. If the pressure is 1.08×10^{-2} atm, what is the volume?

10-3 Fractional exponents

We originally defined the laws of exponents as being valid for the positive integers. Then we extended their use to include negative integers and zero. In this section we shall show how these definitions can be further extended to include the rational numbers as well.

Equation (10-3) states that $(a^m)^n = a^{mn}$. If we were to let $m = \frac{1}{2}$ and $n = 2$, we would have $(a^{1/2})^2 = a^1$. However, we already have a way of writing a quantity which when squared equals a. This is written as $\sqrt{a}$. To be consistent with previous definitions and to allow the laws of exponents to hold, we define

$$a^{1/n} = \sqrt[n]{a}.\tag{10-7}$$

In order that Eqs. (10-3) and (10-7) may hold at the same time, we define

$$a^{m/n} = \sqrt[n]{a^m}.\tag{10-8}$$

It can be shown that these definitions are valid for all the laws of exponents.

Example A.   We shall verify here that Eq. (10-1) holds for the above definitions:

$$a^{1/4}a^{1/4}a^{1/4}a^{1/4} = a^{(1/4)+(1/4)+(1/4)+(1/4)} = a^1.$$

Now $a^{1/4} = \sqrt[4]{a}$, by definition. Also, by definition $\sqrt[4]{a}\,\sqrt[4]{a}\,\sqrt[4]{a}\,\sqrt[4]{a} = a$. Equation (10-1) is thereby verified for $n = 4$. Equation (10-3) is verified by the following:

$$a^{1/4}a^{1/4}a^{1/4}a^{1/4} = a^{4(1/4)} = a = \sqrt[4]{a^4}.$$

We may interpret Eq. (10-8) as "the mth power of the nth root of a," as well as the way in which it is written, which is "the nth root of the mth power of a." This is illustrated in the following example.

Example B. $(\sqrt[3]{a})^2 = \sqrt[3]{a^2} = a^{2/3}$,

$$8^{2/3} = (\sqrt[3]{8})^2 = (2)^2 = 4, \qquad \text{or} \qquad 8^{2/3} = \sqrt[3]{8^2} = \sqrt[3]{64} = 4$$

Although both interpretations of Eq. (10-8) are possible as indicated in Example B, in evaluating numerical expressions involving fractional exponents, it is almost always best to find the root first, as indicated by the denominator of the fractional exponent. This will allow us to find the root of the smaller number, which is normally easier to find.

Example C.   To evaluate $(64)^{5/2}$, we should proceed as follows:

$$(64)^{5/2} = [(64)^{1/2}]^5 = 8^5 = 32{,}768.$$

If we raised 64 to the fifth power first we would have

$$(64)^{5/2} = (64^5)^{1/2} = (1{,}073{,}741{,}824)^{1/2}.$$

We would now have to evaluate the indicated square root. This demonstrates why it is preferable to find the indicated root first.

Example D. $(16)^{3/4} = (16^{1/4})^3 = 2^3 = 8$,

$$4^{-1/2} = \frac{1}{4^{1/2}} = \frac{1}{2}, \qquad\qquad 9^{3/2} = (9^{1/2})^3 = 3^3 = 27$$

The question may arise as to why we use fractional exponents, since we have already defined expressions which are equivalent to their meanings. The answer is that fractional exponents are often easier to handle in more complex expressions involving roots, and therefore any expression involving radicals can be solved by use of fractional exponents.

Example E. $(8a^2b^4)^{1/3} = [(8^{1/3})(a^2)^{1/3}(b^4)^{1/3}] = 2a^{2/3}b^{4/3}$,

$$a^{3/4}a^{4/5} = a^{3/4+4/5} = a^{31/20},$$

$$(25a^{-2}c^4)^{3/2} = \left(\frac{(25)^{1/2}(c^4)^{1/2}}{(a^2)^{1/2}}\right)^3 = \left(\frac{5c^2}{a}\right)^3 = \frac{125c^6}{a^3}$$

Example F. $\left(\dfrac{4^{-3/2}x^{2/3}y^{-7/4}}{2^{3/2}x^{-1/3}y^{3/4}}\right)^{2/3} = \left(\dfrac{x^{2/3+1/3}}{2^{3/2}4^{3/2}y^{3/4+7/4}}\right)^{2/3}$

$$= \frac{x^{(1)(2/3)}}{2^{(3/2)(2/3)}4^{(3/2)(2/3)}y^{(10/4)(2/3)}} = \frac{x^{2/3}}{8y^{5/3}}$$

Example G. $(2x+1)^{1/2} + (x+3)(2x+1)^{-1/2}$

$$= (2x+1)^{1/2} + \frac{x+3}{(2x+1)^{1/2}}$$

$$= \frac{(2x+1)^{1/2}(2x+1)^{1/2} + (x+3)}{(2x+1)^{1/2}}$$

$$= \frac{(2x+1) + (x+3)}{(2x+1)^{1/2}} = \frac{3x+4}{(2x+1)^{1/2}}$$

Exercises

In Exercises 1 through 20 evaluate the given expressions.

1. $(25)^{1/2}$
2. $(49)^{1/2}$
3. $(27)^{1/3}$
4. $(81)^{1/4}$

5. $8^{4/3}$
6. $(125)^{2/3}$
7. $(100)^{25/2}$
8. $(16)^{5/4}$

9. $8^{-1/3}$
10. $16^{-1/4}$
11. $(64)^{-2/3}$
12. $(32)^{-4/5}$

13. $5^{1/2}5^{3/2}$
14. $8^{1/3}4^{1/2}$
15. $(4^4)^{3/2}$
16. $(3^6)^{2/3}$

17. $\dfrac{(-27)^{1/3}}{6}$
18. $\dfrac{(-8)^{2/3}}{-2}$

19. $(125)^{-2/3} - (100)^{-3/2}$
20. $\dfrac{4^{-1}}{(36)^{-1/2}} - \dfrac{5^{-1/2}}{5^{1/2}}$

In Exercises 21 through 36 use the laws of exponents to simplify the given expressions. Express all answers with positive exponents.

21. $a^{2/3}a^{1/2}$
22. $x^{5/6}x^{-1/3}$
23. $\dfrac{y^{-1/2}}{y^{2/5}}$
24. $\dfrac{2r^{4/5}}{r^{-1}}$

25. $\dfrac{s^{1/4}s^{2/3}}{s^{-1}}$ 26. $\dfrac{x^{3/10}}{x^{-1/5}x^2}$ 27. $(8a^3b^6)^{1/3}$ 28. $(8b^{-4}c^2)^{2/3}$

29. $\left(\dfrac{9t^{-2}}{16}\right)^{3/2}$ 30. $\left(\dfrac{a^{5/7}}{a^{2/3}}\right)^{7/4}$ 31. $\left(\dfrac{4a^{5/6}b^{-1/5}}{a^{2/3}b^2}\right)^{-1/2}$ 32. $\left(\dfrac{a^0b^8c^{-1/8}}{ab^{63/64}}\right)^{32/3}$

33. $\dfrac{6x^{-1/2}y^{2/3}}{18x^{-1}}\cdot\dfrac{2y^{1/4}}{x^{1/3}}$ 34. $\dfrac{3^{-1}a^{1/2}}{4^{-1/2}b}\div\dfrac{9^{1/2}a^{-1/3}}{2b^{-1/4}}$

35. $(x^{-1}+2x^{-2})^{-1/2}$ 36. $(a^{-2}-a^{-4})^{-1/4}$

37. $(a^3)^{-4/3}+a^{-2}$ 38. $(4x^6)^{-1/2}-2x^{-1}$

39. $[(a^{1/2}-a^{-1/2})^2+4]^{1/2}$ 40. $(3x-1)^{-2/3}(1-x)-(3x-1)^{1/3}$

In Exercises 41 and 42 perform the indicated operations.

41. An approximate expression for the efficiency of an engine is $E = 100(1 - R^{-2/5})$, where R is the compression ratio. What is the efficiency (in percent) of an engine for which $R = 243/32$.

42. An estimate of gas diffusivity may be made by the equation

$$D_m = 0.01\frac{T^{1/2}}{(v_a{}^{1/3}+v_b{}^{1/3})^2}\left(\frac{1}{m_a}+\frac{1}{m_b}\right)^{1/2},$$

where T is the temperature (°F) and the other symbols are constants which depend on the gases under consideration. Calculate the diffusivity of a gas in air at 484°F if $v_a = 27$, $v_b = 125$, $m_a = 25$, and $m_b = 144$. (The units of diffusivity are in lb-mole/ft-hr.)

10-4 Simplest radical form

Radicals were first introduced in Section 1-4, and we used them again in developing the concept of a fractional exponent. As we mentioned in the preceding section, it is possible to use fractional exponents for any operation required with radicals. For operations involving multiplication and division, this method has certain advantages. But for adding and subtracting radicals, there is normally little advantage in changing form.

We shall now define the operations with radicals so that these definitions are consistent with the laws of exponents. This will enable us from now on to use either fractional exponents or radicals, whichever is more convenient.

$$\sqrt[n]{a^n} = (\sqrt[n]{a})^n = a \tag{10-9}$$

$$\sqrt[n]{a}\,\sqrt[n]{b} = \sqrt[n]{ab}, \tag{10-10}$$

$$\sqrt[m]{\sqrt[n]{a}} = \sqrt[mn]{a}, \tag{10-11}$$

$$\frac{\sqrt[n]{a}}{\sqrt[n]{b}} = \sqrt[n]{\frac{a}{b}}, \qquad b \neq 0 \tag{10-12}$$

The number under the radical is called the *radicand,* and the number indicating the root being taken is called the *order* of the radical. To avoid difficulties with imaginary numbers (which are considered in the next chapter), we shall assume that all letters represent positive numbers.

Example A. $\sqrt[3]{2}\,\sqrt[3]{3} = \sqrt[3]{6},\qquad \sqrt[3]{\sqrt{5}} = \sqrt[6]{5},\qquad \dfrac{\sqrt{7}}{\sqrt{3}} = \sqrt{\dfrac{7}{3}}$

There are certain operations which should be performed on radicals to put them in their simplest form. The following examples will illustrate these operations.

Example B.   To simplify $\sqrt{75}$, we recall that $75 = (25)(3)$ and that $\sqrt{25} = 5$. Using Eq. (10-10), we write $\sqrt{75} = \sqrt{25}\,\sqrt{3} = 5\sqrt{3}$. This illustrates one step which should always be carried out in simplifying radicals. *Always remove all perfect nth-power factors from the radicand of a radical of order n.*

Example C. $\sqrt[3]{40} = \sqrt[3]{8}\,\sqrt[3]{5} = 2\sqrt[3]{5},$

$\qquad\qquad \sqrt{a^3b^2} = \sqrt{a^2}\,\sqrt{a}\,\sqrt{b^2} = ab\,\sqrt{a},$

$\qquad\qquad \sqrt{72} = \sqrt{(36)(2)} = \sqrt{36}\,\sqrt{2} = 6\sqrt{2},$

$\qquad\qquad \sqrt[5]{64x^8y^{12}} = \sqrt[5]{(32)(2)(x^5)(x^3)(y^{10})(y^2)} = \sqrt[5]{(32)(x^5)(y^{10})}\,\sqrt[5]{2x^3y^2}$

$\qquad\qquad\qquad = 2xy^2\,\sqrt[5]{2x^3y^2}$

Example D. $\sqrt{\tfrac{2}{5}}$ may appear to be in simplest form, but if we wanted a numerical approximation to this, we would find both the square root of 2 and the square root of 5 and then perform the indicated division. This process can be greatly simplified if we first multiply the numerator and denominator of the radicand by 5. This leads to $\sqrt{\tfrac{10}{25}}$. The denominator is a perfect square, so that we may write $\sqrt{\tfrac{2}{5}} = \sqrt{10}/5$. In order to evaluate this last expression, we need only find the square root of 10 and divide this by 5. This process is called *rationalizing the denominator,* and illustrates another step to be followed in simplifying radicals. *Always rationalize the denominators.*

Example E. $\sqrt{\dfrac{5}{7}} = \sqrt{\dfrac{5\cdot 7}{7\cdot 7}} = \dfrac{\sqrt{35}}{\sqrt{49}} = \dfrac{\sqrt{35}}{7},\qquad \dfrac{3}{\sqrt{8}} = \dfrac{3\sqrt{2}}{\sqrt{8\cdot 2}} = \dfrac{3\sqrt{2}}{\sqrt{16}} = \dfrac{3\sqrt{2}}{4},$

$\qquad\qquad \sqrt[3]{\dfrac{2}{3}} = \sqrt[3]{\dfrac{2\cdot 9}{3\cdot 9}} = \sqrt[3]{\dfrac{18}{27}} = \dfrac{\sqrt[3]{18}}{\sqrt[3]{27}} = \dfrac{\sqrt[3]{18}}{3}$

Example F. $\sqrt[6]{8} = \sqrt[6]{2^3} = 2^{3/6} = \sqrt{2}$

In this example we started with a sixth root and ended with a square root. This illustrates another operation which simplifies radicals. If possible, *reduce the order of the radical.* Often when we perform this step, fractional exponents are helpful.

Example G. $\sqrt[8]{16} = \sqrt[8]{2^4} = 2^{4/8} = 2^{1/2} = \sqrt{2},$

$$\frac{\sqrt[4]{9}}{\sqrt{3}} = \frac{3^{2/4}}{3^{1/2}} = 1,$$

$$\frac{\sqrt[6]{8}}{\sqrt{7}} = \frac{2^{1/2}}{7^{1/2}} = \sqrt{\frac{2}{7}} = \frac{\sqrt{14}}{7},$$

$$\sqrt[9]{27x^6y^{12}} = \sqrt[9]{3^3x^6y^9y^3} = 3^{3/9}x^{6/9}y^{9/9}y^{3/9} = 3^{1/3}x^{2/3}y\, y^{1/3}$$

$$= y\sqrt[3]{3x^2y}$$

A radical is said to be simplified if the above steps are completed. That is, (1) always remove all perfect *n*th-power factors from the radicand of a radical of order *n*, (2) rationalize all denominators, and (3) if possible, reduce the order of the radical.

Example H. Simplify the radical $\sqrt{\dfrac{3a}{4b} - 2 + \dfrac{4b}{3a}}$, for $3a > 4b$.

$$\sqrt{\frac{3a}{4b} - 2 + \frac{4b}{3a}} = \sqrt{\frac{(3a)(3a) - 2(3a)(4b) + (4b)(4b)}{(3a)(4b)}}$$

$$= \sqrt{\frac{(3a-4b)^2}{4(3ab)}} = \frac{3a-4b}{2}\sqrt{\frac{1}{3ab}}$$

$$= \frac{3a-4b}{6ab}\sqrt{3ab} \qquad \text{(valid if } 3a \geq 4b\text{)}$$

Exercises

In Exercises 1 through 46 write each expression in simplest radical form.

1. $\sqrt{24}$ 2. $\sqrt{150}$ 3. $\sqrt{45}$ 4. $\sqrt{98}$

5. $\sqrt{5x^2}$ 6. $\sqrt{12ab^2}$ 7. $\sqrt{18a^3bc^4}$ 8. $\sqrt{54m^5n^3}$

9. $\sqrt[3]{16}$ 10. $\sqrt[3]{48}$ 11. $\sqrt[5]{96}$ 12. $\sqrt[3]{-16}$

13. $\sqrt[3]{8a^2}$ 14. $\sqrt[3]{5a^4b^2}$ 15. $\sqrt[4]{64r^3s^4t^5}$ 16. $\sqrt[5]{16x^5y^3z^{11}}$

17. $\sqrt[5]{8}\sqrt[5]{4}$ 18. $\sqrt[7]{4}\sqrt[7]{64}$ 19. $\sqrt[3]{ab^4}\sqrt[3]{a^2b}$ 20. $\sqrt[3]{3m^4n^5}\sqrt[6]{9m^2n^8}$

21. $\sqrt{3/2}$ 22. $\sqrt{6/5}$ 23. $\sqrt{a/b}$ 24. $\sqrt{a/b^3}$

25. $\sqrt[3]{3/4}$ 26. $\sqrt[3]{2/5}$ 27. $\sqrt[4]{400}$ 28. $\sqrt[8]{81}$

29. $\sqrt{4 \times 10^4}$ 30. $\sqrt{4 \times 10^5}$ 31. $\sqrt{4 \times 10^6}$ 32. $\sqrt{16 \times 10^5}$

33. $\sqrt[4]{4a^2}$ 34. $\sqrt[6]{b^2c^4}$ 35. $\sqrt[6]{1/4}$ 36. $\sqrt[4]{80}/\sqrt[4]{5}$

37. $\sqrt[4]{\sqrt[3]{16}}$ 38. $\sqrt[5]{\sqrt[4]{9}}$ 39. $\sqrt{\sqrt{\sqrt{2}}}$ 40. $\sqrt{b^4 \sqrt{a}}$

41. $\sqrt{1/2 - 1/3}$ 42. $\sqrt{5/4 - 1/8}$ 43. $\sqrt{a^2 + 2ab + b^2}$ 44. $\sqrt{a^2 + b^2}$

45. $\sqrt{1/a^2 + 1/b}$ 46. $\sqrt{1/2 + 2r + 2r^2}$

In Exercises 47 through 49 perform the required operation.

47. The period (in seconds) for one cycle of a simple pendulum is given by $T = 2\pi\sqrt{L/g}$, where L is the length of the pendulum and g is the acceleration due to gravity ($g = 32$ ft/sec²). If L is 3 ft, what is the period of the pendulum?

48. Under certain circumstances, the frequency in an electric circuit containing an inductance L and capacitance C is given by $f = 1/(2\pi\sqrt{LC})$. If $L = 0.1$ henry and $C = 250 \times 10^{-6}$ farad, find f.

49. The distance between ion layers in a crystalline solid such as table salt is given by the expression $\sqrt[3]{M/2N\rho}$, where M is the molecular weight, N is called Avagodro's number, and ρ is the density. Express this in simplest form.

10-5 Addition and subtraction of radicals

When we first introduced the concept of adding algebraic expressions, we found that it was possible to combine similar terms, that is, those which differed only in numerical coefficients. The same is true in adding radicals. We must have similar radicals in order to perform the addition, rather than simply to be able to indicate addition. By similar radicals we mean radicals which differ only in their numerical coefficients, and which must therefore be of the same order and have the same radicand.

In order to add radicals, we first express each radical in its simplest form, and then add those which are similar. For those which are not similar, we can only indicate the addition.

Example A. $2\sqrt{7} - 5\sqrt{7} + \sqrt{7} = -2\sqrt{7}$,
$\sqrt[5]{6} + 4\sqrt[5]{6} - 2\sqrt[5]{6} = 3\sqrt[5]{6}$,
$\sqrt{5} + 2\sqrt{3} - 5\sqrt{5} = 2\sqrt{3} - 4\sqrt{5}$

We note that in that last illustration that we are able only to indicate the final subtraction.

Example B. $\sqrt{2} + \sqrt{8} = \sqrt{2} + 2\sqrt{2} = 3\sqrt{2}$,
$\sqrt[3]{24} + \sqrt[3]{81} = 2\sqrt[3]{3} + 3\sqrt[3]{3} = 5\sqrt[3]{3}$

Notice that $\sqrt{8}$, $\sqrt[3]{24}$, and $\sqrt[3]{81}$ were simplified before performing the addition.

Example C.

$$6\sqrt{7} - \sqrt{28} + 3\sqrt{63} = 6\sqrt{7} - 2\sqrt{7} + 3(3\sqrt{7}) = 6\sqrt{7} - 2\sqrt{7} + 9\sqrt{7}$$
$$= 13\sqrt{7},$$
$$3\sqrt{125} - \sqrt{20} + \sqrt{27} = 3(5\sqrt{5}) - 2\sqrt{5} + 3\sqrt{3}$$
$$= 13\sqrt{5} + 3\sqrt{3}$$

Example D. $\sqrt{24} + \sqrt{\dfrac{3}{2}} = 2\sqrt{6} + \dfrac{\sqrt{6}}{2} = \dfrac{5}{2}\sqrt{6}$

One radical was simplified by removing the perfect square factor and the other by rationalizing the denominator.

Example E. $\sqrt{\dfrac{2}{3a}} - 2\sqrt{\dfrac{3}{2a}} = \dfrac{1}{3a}\sqrt{6a} - \dfrac{2}{2a}\sqrt{6a} = -\dfrac{2}{3a}\sqrt{6a}$

Example F. $\sqrt{\dfrac{4}{a} - 4 + a} + \sqrt{\dfrac{1}{a}} - \sqrt{16a^3} = \sqrt{\dfrac{4 - 4a + a^2}{a}} + \sqrt{\dfrac{1}{a}} - 4a\sqrt{a}$

$$= \sqrt{\dfrac{(2-a)^2 \cdot a}{a \cdot a}} + \sqrt{\dfrac{1 \cdot a}{a \cdot a}} - 4a\sqrt{a}$$

$$= \dfrac{2-a}{a}\sqrt{a} + \dfrac{1}{a}\sqrt{a} - 4a\sqrt{a}$$

$$= \sqrt{a}\left(\dfrac{2-a}{a} + \dfrac{1}{a} - 4a\right) = \sqrt{a}\left(\dfrac{2-a+1-4a^2}{a}\right)$$

$$= \dfrac{(3-a-4a^2)\sqrt{a}}{a}$$

This simplification is valid for $a < 2$, since we let $\sqrt{(2-a)^2} = 2 - a$.

Exercises

In the following exercises perform the indicated operations and express the answer in simplest form.

1. $2\sqrt{3} + 5\sqrt{3}$

2. $8\sqrt{11} - 3\sqrt{11}$

3. $\sqrt{8} - \sqrt{32}$

4. $\sqrt{27} + 2\sqrt{18}$

5. $\sqrt[3]{81} + \sqrt[3]{3000}$

6. $\sqrt[3]{-16} + \sqrt[3]{54}$

7. $2\sqrt{20} - \sqrt{125} - \sqrt{45}$

8. $2\sqrt{44} - \sqrt{99} + \sqrt{176}$

9. $3\sqrt{75} + 2\sqrt{48} - 2\sqrt{18}$

10. $2\sqrt{28} - \sqrt{108} - 2\sqrt{175}$

11. $\sqrt[4]{32} - \sqrt[8]{4}$

12. $\sqrt[6]{\sqrt{2}} - \sqrt[12]{2^{13}}$

13. $\sqrt{60} + \sqrt{5/3}$

14. $\sqrt{84} - \sqrt{3/7}$

15. $\sqrt{\frac{1}{2}} + \sqrt{\frac{25}{2}} - \sqrt{18}$

16. $\sqrt[4]{36} - \sqrt{\frac{2}{3}} - \sqrt{18}$

17. $\sqrt{a^3b} - \sqrt{4ab^5}$

18. $\sqrt{2x^2y} + \sqrt{8y^3}$

19. $\sqrt{6}\sqrt{5}\sqrt{3} - \sqrt{40a^2}$

20. $\sqrt{60n} + 2\sqrt{15b^2n} - b\sqrt{135n}$

21. $\sqrt[3]{24a^2b^4} - \sqrt[3]{3a^5b}$

22. $\sqrt[3]{32a^6b^4} + 3a\sqrt[3]{243ab^9}$

23. $\sqrt{\dfrac{a}{c^5}} - \sqrt{\dfrac{c}{a^3}}$

24. $\sqrt{\dfrac{2x}{3y}} + \sqrt{\dfrac{27y}{8x}}$

25. $\sqrt[3]{\dfrac{a}{b}} - \sqrt[3]{\dfrac{8b^2}{a^2}}$

26. $\sqrt[4]{\dfrac{c}{b}} - \sqrt[4]{bc}$

27. $\sqrt{\dfrac{a-b}{a+b}} - \sqrt{\dfrac{a+b}{a-b}}$

28. $\sqrt{\dfrac{16}{x} + 8 + x} - \sqrt{1 - \dfrac{1}{x}}$

29. $\sqrt{\dfrac{a-1}{a+1}} - \sqrt{1 - \dfrac{1}{a^2}} + \sqrt{a^3 - a}$

30. Find the sum of the two roots of the quadratic equation $ax^2 + bx + c = 0$.

10-6 Multiplication of radicals

When multiplying expressions containing radicals, we use Eq. (10-10) along with the normal procedures of algebraic multiplication. The following examples illustrate the method.

Example A. $\quad \sqrt{5}\sqrt{2} = \sqrt{10}, \qquad \sqrt[3]{6}\sqrt[3]{4} = \sqrt[3]{24} = \sqrt[3]{8}\sqrt[3]{3} = 2\sqrt[3]{3},$

$\qquad \sqrt[5]{8a^3b^4}\sqrt[5]{8a^2b^3} = \sqrt[5]{64a^5b^7} = \sqrt[5]{32a^5b^5}\sqrt[5]{2b^2} = 2ab\sqrt[5]{2b^2}$

Example B. $\quad \sqrt{2}(3\sqrt{5} - 4\sqrt{2}) = 3\sqrt{2}\sqrt{5} - 4\sqrt{2}\sqrt{2} = 3\sqrt{10} - 4\sqrt{4}$

$\qquad\qquad\qquad = 3\sqrt{10} - 4(2) = 3\sqrt{10} - 8$

Example C. $\quad (\sqrt{a} - \sqrt{b})^2 = (\sqrt{a})^2 - 2\sqrt{a}\sqrt{b} + (\sqrt{b})^2 = a + b - 2\sqrt{ab}$

Example D. $\quad (\sqrt{6} - \sqrt{2} - \sqrt{3})(\sqrt{6} + \sqrt{2})$

$\qquad\qquad = (\sqrt{6} - \sqrt{2})(\sqrt{6} + \sqrt{2}) - \sqrt{3}(\sqrt{6} + \sqrt{2})$

$\qquad\qquad = (6 - 2) - \sqrt{18} - \sqrt{6} = 4 - 3\sqrt{2} - \sqrt{6}$

Example E. $\quad \left(3\sqrt{\dfrac{a}{b}} - \sqrt{ab}\right)\left(2\sqrt{\dfrac{a}{b}} - \sqrt{ab}\right) = 6\dfrac{a}{b} - 5\sqrt{\dfrac{a^2b}{b}} + ab$

$\qquad\qquad\qquad = \dfrac{6a}{b} - 5a + ab = \dfrac{6a - 5ab + ab^2}{b} = \dfrac{a(6 - 5b + b^2)}{b}$

We must note one thing carefully; *to combine radicals under one radical sign, it is necessary that the order of the radicals be the same.* If necessary we can make the order of each radical the same by appropriate operations on each radical separately. Fractional exponents are frequently useful for this purpose.

Example F. $\sqrt[3]{2}\sqrt{5} = 2^{1/3}5^{1/2} = 2^{2/6}5^{3/6} = (2^2 5^3)^{1/6} = \sqrt[6]{500}$,

$$\sqrt[3]{4a^2b}\,\sqrt[4]{8a^3b^2} = (2^2a^2b)^{1/3}(2^3a^3b^2)^{1/4} = (2^2a^2b)^{4/12}(2^3a^3b^2)^{3/12}$$

$$= (2^8a^8b^4)^{1/12}(2^9a^9b^6)^{1/12} = (2^{17}a^{17}b^{10})^{1/12}$$

$$= 2a(2^5a^5b^{10})^{1/12}$$

$$= 2a\sqrt[12]{32a^5b^{10}}$$

Exercises

In Exercises 1 through 32 perform the indicated multiplications, expressing answers in simplest form.

1. $\sqrt{6}\sqrt{2}$

2. $\sqrt{2}\sqrt{51}$

3. $\sqrt[3]{4}\sqrt[3]{2}$

4. $\sqrt[3]{25}\sqrt[3]{50}$

5. $(5\sqrt{2})^2$

6. $(3\sqrt{3})^2$

7. $\sqrt{\tfrac{2}{3}}\sqrt{5}$

8. $\sqrt{\tfrac{6}{7}}\sqrt{\tfrac{2}{3}}$

9. $\sqrt{3}(\sqrt{2}-\sqrt{5})$

10. $\sqrt{5}(\sqrt{7}+\sqrt{2})$

11. $2\sqrt{2}(\sqrt{8}-3\sqrt{6})$

12. $3\sqrt{5}(\sqrt{15}-2\sqrt{5})$

13. $(2-\sqrt{5})(2+\sqrt{5})$

14. $(2-\sqrt{5})^2$

15. $(3\sqrt{5}-2\sqrt{3})(6\sqrt{5}+7\sqrt{3})$

16. $(3\sqrt{7}-\sqrt{8})(\sqrt{7}+\sqrt{2})$

17. $\sqrt{a}(\sqrt{ab}+\sqrt{c})$

18. $\sqrt{2x}(\sqrt{8xy}-3\sqrt{y})$

19. $(\sqrt{2a}-\sqrt{b})(\sqrt{2a}+3\sqrt{b})$

20. $(2\sqrt{mn}-3\sqrt{n})(3\sqrt{mn}+2\sqrt{n})$

21. $(\sqrt{2}+\sqrt{3}+\sqrt{5})(\sqrt{3}-\sqrt{5})$

22. $(2\sqrt{7}-\sqrt{5})(\sqrt{14}-2\sqrt{5}+\sqrt{7})$

23. $(\sqrt[5]{\sqrt{6}}-\sqrt{5})\,(\sqrt[5]{\sqrt{6}}+\sqrt{5})$

24. $(\sqrt{a}-\sqrt[3]{b})(2\sqrt{a}-\sqrt[3]{b})$

25. $\sqrt{2}\sqrt[3]{3}$

26. $\sqrt[5]{16}\sqrt[3]{8}$

27. $\sqrt[4]{ab}\sqrt[3]{bc}$

28. $\sqrt{2x}\sqrt[5]{16x}$

29. $(\sqrt{2/a}+\sqrt{a/2})\,(\sqrt{2/a}-2\sqrt{a/2})$

30. $(\sqrt{x/y}-\sqrt{xy})(\sqrt{y/x}+\sqrt{xy}-1)$

31. $(2x-\sqrt{x-2y})^2$

32. $(3+\sqrt{6-2a})(2-\sqrt{6-2a})$

In Exercises 33 and 34 perform the indicated operations.

33. Find the product of the two roots of the quadratic equation $ax^2 + bx + c = 0$.

34. Relationships involving mass transfer of liquid involve the expression

$$\sqrt{\frac{dG}{u}}\;\sqrt[3]{\frac{MD}{u}}\,.$$

Express this in simplest radical form.

10-7 Division of radicals

The process of division of radicals is defined by Eq. (10-12). We have already dealt with some cases of division in the previous sections. In the process of division, the rationalization of denominators, as we did in Section 10-4, is the principal step to be carried out.

Example A.
$$\frac{\sqrt{3}}{\sqrt{5}} = \frac{\sqrt{3}\sqrt{5}}{\sqrt{5}\sqrt{5}} = \frac{\sqrt{15}}{5}, \qquad \frac{\sqrt{a}}{\sqrt[3]{b}} = \frac{\sqrt{a}}{\sqrt[3]{b}} \cdot \frac{\sqrt[3]{b^2}}{\sqrt[3]{b^2}} = \frac{\sqrt{a}\sqrt[3]{b^2}}{b}$$

$$= \frac{a^{3/6}b^{4/6}}{b} = \frac{\sqrt[6]{a^3b^4}}{b}$$

Notice that the denominator was rationalized and that the factors of the numerator were written in terms of fractional exponents so they could be combined under one radical.

If the denominator is the sum (or difference) of two terms, at least one of which is a radical, the fraction can be rationalized by multiplying both the numerator and the denominator by the difference (or sum) of the same two terms.

Example B.   The fraction $1/(\sqrt{3} - \sqrt{2})$ can be rationalized by multiplying the numerator and the denominator by $\sqrt{3} + \sqrt{2}$. In this way the radicals will be removed from the denominator.

$$\frac{1}{\sqrt{3} - \sqrt{2}} \cdot \frac{\sqrt{3} + \sqrt{2}}{\sqrt{3} + \sqrt{2}} = \frac{\sqrt{3} + \sqrt{2}}{(\sqrt{3})^2 - (\sqrt{2})^2} = \frac{\sqrt{3} + \sqrt{2}}{3 - 2} = \sqrt{3} + \sqrt{2}$$

The reason this technique works is that an expression of the form $a^2 - b^2$ is created in the denominator, where a or b (or both) is a radical. We see that the result is a denominator free of radicals.

Example C.

$$\frac{\sqrt{2}}{2\sqrt{5} + \sqrt{3}} = \frac{\sqrt{2}}{2\sqrt{5} + \sqrt{3}} \cdot \frac{2\sqrt{5} - \sqrt{3}}{2\sqrt{5} - \sqrt{3}} = \frac{2\sqrt{2}\sqrt{5} - \sqrt{2}\sqrt{3}}{(2\sqrt{5})^2 - (\sqrt{3})^2}$$

$$= \frac{2\sqrt{10} - \sqrt{6}}{2^2(\sqrt{5})^2 - (\sqrt{3})^2} = \frac{2\sqrt{10} - \sqrt{6}}{20 - 3} = \frac{2\sqrt{10} - \sqrt{6}}{17}$$

Example D.
$$\frac{\sqrt{x - y}}{1 - \sqrt{x - y}} = \frac{\sqrt{x - y}\,(1 + \sqrt{x - y})}{(1 - \sqrt{x - y})(1 + \sqrt{x - y})}$$

$$= \frac{\sqrt{x - y} + x - y}{1 - x + y}$$

Example E. $\dfrac{1+\sqrt{3}/2}{1-\sqrt{3}/2} = \dfrac{(2+\sqrt{3})/2}{(2-\sqrt{3})/2} = \dfrac{2+\sqrt{3}}{2} \cdot \dfrac{2}{2-\sqrt{3}} = \dfrac{2+\sqrt{3}}{2-\sqrt{3}}$

$$= \dfrac{(2+\sqrt{3})(2+\sqrt{3})}{(2-\sqrt{3})(2+\sqrt{3})} = \dfrac{4+4\sqrt{3}+3}{4-3} = 7+4\sqrt{3}$$

Exercises

In Exercises 1 through 24 perform the indicated operations and express answers in simplest form.

1. $\dfrac{\sqrt{21}}{\sqrt{3}}$

2. $\dfrac{\sqrt{105}}{\sqrt{5}}$

3. $\dfrac{\sqrt{7}}{\sqrt{2}}$

4. $3\sqrt{2} \div 2\sqrt{3}$

5. $\sqrt[3]{x^2} \div \sqrt[3]{24}$

6. $\dfrac{\sqrt{6}}{\sqrt[3]{2}}$

7. $\dfrac{\sqrt[4]{a}}{\sqrt[3]{4}}$

8. $\dfrac{\sqrt[4]{32}}{\sqrt[5]{b^3}}$

9. $\dfrac{\sqrt{2a-b}}{\sqrt{a}}$

10. $\dfrac{\sqrt{8x}+\sqrt{2}}{\sqrt{2}}$

11. $\dfrac{1}{\sqrt{7}+\sqrt{3}}$

12. $\dfrac{4}{\sqrt{6}+\sqrt{2}}$

13. $\dfrac{\sqrt{7}}{\sqrt{5}-\sqrt{2}}$

14. $\dfrac{\sqrt{8}}{2\sqrt{3}-\sqrt{5}}$

15. $\dfrac{3}{2\sqrt{5}-6}$

16. $\dfrac{\sqrt{7}}{4-2\sqrt{7}}$

17. $\dfrac{\sqrt{2}-1}{\sqrt{7}-3\sqrt{2}}$

18. $\dfrac{2\sqrt{6}+\sqrt{11}}{\sqrt{6}-3\sqrt{11}}$

19. $\dfrac{2-\sqrt{3}}{5-2\sqrt{3}}$

20. $\dfrac{2\sqrt{15}-3}{\sqrt{15}+4}$

21. $\dfrac{8}{3\sqrt{a}-2\sqrt{b}}$

22. $\dfrac{6}{1+2\sqrt{x}}$

23. $\dfrac{\sqrt{x+y}}{\sqrt{x-y}-\sqrt{x}}$

24. $\dfrac{\sqrt{1+a}}{a-\sqrt{1-a}}$

In Exercises 25 through 28 find the numerical value of each expression, to three significant digits, before and after rationalizing. Use Table 1.

25. $\dfrac{1}{\sqrt{11}-\sqrt{7}}$

26. $\dfrac{1-\sqrt{2}}{5+\sqrt{2}}$

27. $\dfrac{\sqrt{5}}{\sqrt[3]{4}}$

28. $\dfrac{\sqrt[3]{15}}{\sqrt{3}}$

In Exercises 29 and 30 perform the indicated operations.

29. When dealing with the voltage within an electronic tube, the expression $V(x/d)^{4/3}$ arises. Write this expression in rationalized radical form.

30. In the theory of waves in wires, the following expression is found:

$$\dfrac{\sqrt{d_1}-\sqrt{d_2}}{\sqrt{d_1}+\sqrt{d_2}}.$$

Evaluate this expression if $d_1 = 10$ and $d_2 = 3$.

10-8 Miscellaneous Exercises

In Exercises 1 through 4 change the numbers from scientific notation to ordinary notation.

1. 4.93×10^4 2. 7.03×10^0 3. 9.1×10^{-1} 4. 1.07×10^{-4}

In Exercises 5 through 8 change the numbers from ordinary notation to scientific notation.

5. $95{,}000$ 6. 0.0152 7. 0.000667 8. 3.01

In Exercises 9 through 22 express each of the given expressions in the simplest form which contains only positive exponents.

9. $(2a^2n^3)(3an^0)$ 10. $\dfrac{5x^2y}{30xy^4}$ 11. $2a^{-2}b^0$ 12. $(2c)^{-1}z^{-2}$

13. $3(25)^{3/2}$ 14. $(32)^{2/5}$ 15. $(2a^{1/3}b^{5/6})^6$ 16. $(27x^{-6}y^9)^{2/3}$

17. $\dfrac{2x^{-1}}{x^{-1}+y^{-1}}$ 18. $a^{-1}+b^{-2}$

19. $(8a^3)^{2/3}(4a^{-2}+1)^{1/2}$ 20. $\left[\dfrac{(9a)^0(4x^2)^{1/3}(3b^{1/2})}{(2b^0)^2}\right]^{-6}$

21. $2x(x-1)^{-2}-2(x^2+1)(x-1)^{-3}$ 22. $4(1-x^2)^{1/2}-(1-x^2)^{-1/2}$

In Exercises 23 through 48 perform the indicated operations and express the answer in simplest radical form.

23. $\sqrt{68}$ 24. $\sqrt{96}$ 25. $\sqrt{9a^3b^4}$ 26. $\sqrt{8x^5y^2}$

27. $\sqrt[4]{8m^6n^9}$ 28. $\sqrt[3]{9a^7b^{-3}}$ 29. $\sqrt[4]{\sqrt[3]{64}}$ 30. $\sqrt{a^{-3}\sqrt[5]{b^{12}}}$

31. $\dfrac{5}{\sqrt{2s}}$ 32. $\sqrt{\frac{7}{8}}$ 33. $\sqrt{200}+\sqrt{32}$

34. $2\sqrt{20}-\sqrt{80}-2\sqrt{125}$ 35. $a\sqrt{2x^3}+\sqrt{8a^2x^3}$ 36. $\sqrt{a/b}-\sqrt{b/a}+\sqrt{a^2b}$

37. $\sqrt{5}(2\sqrt{5}-\sqrt{11})$ 38. $2\sqrt{8}(5\sqrt{2}-\sqrt{6})$

39. $(2\sqrt{7}-3\sqrt{3})(3\sqrt{7}+\sqrt{3})$ 40. $(3\sqrt{2}-\sqrt{13})(5\sqrt{2}+3\sqrt{13})$

41. $\dfrac{\sqrt{2}}{\sqrt{3}-4\sqrt{2}}$ 42. $\dfrac{4}{3-2\sqrt{7}}$

43. $\dfrac{\sqrt{7}-\sqrt{5}}{\sqrt{5}+3\sqrt{7}}$ 44. $\dfrac{4-2\sqrt{6}}{3+2\sqrt{6}}$

45. $\sqrt{a^{-1}+b^2}$ 46. $\sqrt{a^{-2}+1/b^2}$

47. $\left(\dfrac{2-\sqrt{15}}{2}\right)^2-\left(\dfrac{2-\sqrt{15}}{2}\right)$ 48. $\sqrt{2+b/a+a/b}+\sqrt{a^4b^2+2a^3b^2+a^2b^2}$

In Exercises 49 through 56 change any numbers in ordinary notation to scientific notation or change any numbers in scientific notation to ordinary notation.

49. The escape velocity (the velocity required to leave the earth's gravitational field) of a rocket is in excess of 25,000 mi/hr.

50. There are about 185,000 cm in one mile.

51. The ratio of the charge to the mass of an electron is 1.76×10^{11} coul/kg.

52. Atmospheric pressure is about 1.013×10^6 dynes/cm^2.

53. An oil film on water is about 0.0000002 in. thick.

54. A typical capacitor has a capacitance of 0.00005 farad.

55. The specific heat of aluminum is about 2.2×10^{-1} cal/kg·°C.

56. The electric field intensity in a certain electromagnetic wave is 2.5×10^{-3} volt/m.

In Exercises 57 through 61, perform the indicated operations.

57. In the study of electricity, the expression $e^{-i(\omega t - \alpha t)}$ is found. Rewrite this expression so that it contains no minus signs in the exponent.

58. An expression found when convection of heat is discussed is $k^{-1}x + h^{-1}$. Write this expression without the use of negative exponents.

59. The root-mean-square velocity of a gas molecule is given by $v = \sqrt{3RT/M}$, where R is called the "gas constant," T is the absolute temperature, and M is the molecular weight. Express the velocity (in cm/sec) of an oxygen molecule in simplest radical form if $T = 300°$K, $R = 8.31 \times 10^7$ ergs/°K-mole, and $M = 32$ gm/mole. Then calculate the value to slide-rule accuracy.

60. A surveyor measuring distances with a steel tape must be careful to correct for the tension which is applied to the tape and for the sag in the tape. If he applies what is known as "normal tension," these two effects will cancel each other. An expression involving the normal tension T_n which is found for a certain tape is

$$\frac{0.2W\sqrt{2.7 \times 10^5}}{\sqrt{T_n - 20}}.$$

Express this in simplest radical form.

61. The frequency of a certain electric circuit is given by

$$\frac{1}{2\pi\sqrt{LC_1C_2/(C_1 + C_2)}}.$$

Express this in simplest radical form.

The *j*-Operator

11

11-1 Imaginary and complex numbers

In Chapter 1, when we were introducing the topic of numbers, imaginary numbers were mentioned. Again, when we considered quadratic equations and their solutions in Chapter 6, we briefly came across this type of number. However, until now we have purposely avoided any extended discussion of imaginary numbers. In this chapter we shall discuss the properties of these numbers and show some of the ways in which they may be applied.

When we defined radicals we were able to define square roots of positive numbers easily, since any positive or negative number squared equals a positive number. For this reason we can see that it is impossible to square any real number and have the product equal a negative number. We must define a new number system if we wish to include square roots of negative numbers. With the proper definitions, we shall find that these numbers can be used to great advantage in certain applications.

If the radicand in a square root is negative, we can express the indicated root as the product of $\sqrt{-1}$ and the square root of a positive number. The symbol $\sqrt{-1}$ is defined as the *imaginary unit*, and is denoted by the symbol j. (The symbol i is also often used for this purpose, but in electrical work i usually represents current. Therefore, we shall use j for the imaginary unit to avoid confusion.) In keeping with the definition of j, we have

$$j^2 = -1. \tag{11-1}$$

Example A. $\quad \sqrt{-9} = \sqrt{(9)(-1)} = \sqrt{9}\sqrt{-1} = 3j,$

$\qquad\qquad \sqrt{-16} = \sqrt{16}\sqrt{-1} = 4j$

Example B. $\quad (\sqrt{-4})^2 = (\sqrt{4}\,j)^2 = 4j^2 = -4$

We note from this Example B that imaginary numbers—those which are simply multiples of j—do not follow Eq. (10–10). If Example B did follow this equation, we would have $(\sqrt{-4})^2 = \sqrt{(-4)(-4)} = \sqrt{16} = 4$. But $4 \neq -4$. This is one reason why imaginary numbers are given special consideration.

From Example B we see that when we are dealing with the square roots of negative numbers, *each should be expressed in terms of j before proceeding.* To do this, for any positive real number a we write

$$\sqrt{-a} = \sqrt{a}\,j, \qquad (a > 0). \tag{11-2}$$

Example C. $\sqrt{-6} = \sqrt{(6)(-1)} = \sqrt{6}\sqrt{-1} = \sqrt{6}\,j,$

$\sqrt{-18} = \sqrt{(18)(-1)} = \sqrt{(9)(2)}\sqrt{-1} = 3\sqrt{2}\,j$

In working with imaginary numbers, we often need to be able to raise these numbers to some power. Therefore, using the definitions of exponents and of j, we have the following results:

$$j = j, \qquad\qquad j^4 = j^2 j^2 = (-1)(-1) = 1,$$
$$j^2 = -1, \qquad\qquad j^5 = j^4 j = j,$$
$$j^3 = j^2 j = -j, \qquad j^6 = j^4 j^2 = (1)(-1) = -1.$$

The powers of j go through the cycle of j, -1, $-j$, 1, j, -1, $-j$, 1, and so forth. Remembering this fact, it is possible to raise j to any integral power almost on sight.

Example D. $j^{10} = j^8 j^2 = (1)(-1) = -1,$

$j^{45} = j^{44} j = (1)(j) = j,$

$j^{531} = j^{528} j^3 = (1)(-j) = -j$

Using real numbers and the imaginary unit j, we define a new kind of number. A *complex number* is any number which can be written in the form $a + bj$, where a and b are real numbers. If $a = 0$, we have a number of the form bj, which is a *pure imaginary number.* If $b = 0$, then $a + bj$ is a real number. The form $a + bj$ is known as the *rectangular form* of a complex number, where a is known as the *real part* and bj is known as the *imaginary part.* We can see that complex numbers include all the real numbers and all of the imaginary numbers.

For complex numbers written in terms of j to follow all the operations defined in algebra, we define equality of two complex numbers in a special way. Complex numbers are not positive or negative in the ordinary sense of these terms, but the real and imaginary parts of complex numbers *are* positive or negative. We define two complex numbers to be equal if the real parts are equal and the imaginary parts are equal. That is, two imaginary numbers, $a + bj$ and $x + yj$, are equal if $a = x$ and $b = y$.

Example E. $a + bj = 3 + 4j$, if $a = 3$ and $b = 4$,

$x + yj = 5 - 3j$, if $x = 5$ and $y = -3$

Example F.   What values of x and y satisfy the equation $4 - 6j - x = j + jy$?

One way to solve this is to rearrange the terms so that all the known terms are on the right and all the terms containing the unknowns x and y are on the left. This leads to $-x - jy = -4 + 7j$. From the definition of equality of complex numbers, $-x = -4$ and $-y = 7$, or $x = 4$ and $y = -7$.

Example G.   What values of x and y satisfy the equation

$$x + 3(xj + y) = 5 - j - jy?$$

Rearranging the terms so that the known terms are on the right and the terms containing x and y are on the left, we have

$$x + 3y + 3jx + jy = 5 - j.$$

Next, factoring j from the two terms on the left will put the expression on the left into proper form. This leads to

$$(x + 3y) + j(3x + y) = 5 - j.$$

Using the definition of equality, we have

$$x + 3y = 5 \quad \text{and} \quad 3x + y = -1.$$

We now solve this system of equations. The solution is $x = -1$ and $y = 2$. Actually, the solution can be obtained at any point by writing each side of the equation in the form $a + bj$ and then equating first the real parts and then the imaginary parts.

The *conjugate* of the complex number $a + bj$ is the complex number $a - bj$. We see that the sign of the imaginary part of a complex number is changed to obtain its conjugate.

Example H. $3 - 2j$ is the conjugate of $3 + 2j$. We may also say that $3 + 2j$ is the conjugate of $3 - 2j$. Thus each is the conjugate of the other.

Exercises

In Exercises 1 through 8 express each number in terms of j.

1. $\sqrt{-81}$ 2. $\sqrt{-121}$ 3. $-\sqrt{-4}$ 4. $-\sqrt{-0.01}$

5. $\sqrt{-8}$ 6. $\sqrt{-48}$ 7. $\sqrt{-\frac{7}{4}}$ 8. $\sqrt{-\frac{5}{3}}$

In Exercises 9 through 16 simplify the given expressions.

9. j^7 10. j^{49} 11. $-j^{22}$ 12. j^{408}

13. $j^2 - j^6$ 14. $2j^5 - j^7$ 15. $j^{15} - j^{13}$ 16. $3j^{48} + j^{200}$

In Exercises 17 through 24 perform the indicated operations and simplify each complex number to its rectangular form $a + bj$.

17. $2 + \sqrt{-9}$ 18. $-6 + \sqrt{-64}$ 19. $2j^2 + 3j$ 20. $j^3 - 6$

21. $\sqrt{18} - \sqrt{-8}$ 22. $\sqrt{-27} + \sqrt{12}$

23. $(\sqrt{-2})^2 + j^4$ 24. $(2\sqrt{2})^2 - (\sqrt{-1})^2$

In Exercises 25 through 28 find the conjugate of each complex number.

25. $6 - 7j$ 26. $-3 + 2j$ 27. $2j$ 28. 6

In Exercises 29 through 36 find the values of x and y which satisfy the given equations.

29. $7x - 2yj = 14 + 4j$ 30. $2x + 3jy = -6 + 12j$

31. $6j - 7 = 3 - x - yj$ 32. $9 - j = xj + 1 - y$

33. $x - y = 1 - xj - yj - j$ 34. $2x - 2j = 4 - 2xj - yj$

35. $x + 2 + 7j = yj - 2xj$ 36. $2x + 6xj + 3 = yj - y + 7j$

In Exercises 37 and 38 answer the given questions.

37. What condition must be satisfied if a complex number and its conjugate are to be equal?

38. What type of number is a complex number if it is equal to the negative of its conjugate?

11-2 Basic operations with complex numbers

The basic operations of addition, subtraction, multiplication, and division are defined in the same way for complex numbers in rectangular form as they are for real numbers. These operations are performed without regard for the fact that j has a special meaning. We must *be careful to express all complex numbers in terms of j before performing these operations*, but once this is done, we may proceed as with real numbers. We have the following definitions for these operations on complex numbers.

Addition (and subtraction): $(a + bj) + (c + dj) = (a + c) + (b + d)j$ (11-3)

Multiplication: $(a + bj)(c + dj) = (ac - bd) + (ad + bc)j$ (11-4)

Division: $\dfrac{a + bj}{c + dj} = \dfrac{(a + bj)(c - dj)}{(c + dj)(c - dj)} = \dfrac{(ac + bd) + (bc - ad)j}{c^2 + d^2}$ (11-5)

We note that our procedure in dividing two complex numbers is the same procedure that we used for rationalizing the denominator of a fraction with a radical in the denominator. We use this procedure so that we can express any answer in the form of a complex number. We need merely to multiply numerator and denominator by the conjugate of the denominator in order to perform this operation.

If we recall Example B of Section 11-1, we see the reason for expressing all complex numbers in terms of j before proceeding with any indicated operations.

Example A. $(3 - 2j) + (-5 + 7j) = (3 - 5) + (-2 + 7)j = -2 + 5j$

Example B. $(7 + 9j) - (6 - 4j) = 7 + 9j - 6 + 4j = 1 + 13j$

Example C. $(6 - \sqrt{-4})(\sqrt{-9}) = (6 - 2j)(3j) = 18j - 6j^2$
$$= 18j - 6(-1) = 6 + 18j$$

Example D. $(-9 - 6j)(2 + j) = -18 - 9j - 12j - 6j^2$
$$= -18 - 21j - 6(-1) = -12 - 21j$$

Example E. $\dfrac{7 - 2j}{3 + 4j} = \dfrac{7 - 2j}{3 + 4j} \cdot \dfrac{3 - 4j}{3 - 4j} = \dfrac{21 - 28j - 6j + 8j^2}{9 - 16j^2}$

$$= \frac{21 - 34j + 8(-1)}{9 - 16(-1)} = \frac{13 - 34j}{25}$$

This could be written in the form $a + bi$ as $\frac{13}{25} - \frac{34}{25}j$, but is generally left as a single fraction.

Example F. $\dfrac{6 + j}{2j} = \dfrac{6 + j}{2j} \cdot \dfrac{-2j}{-2j} = \dfrac{-12j - 2j^2}{4} = \dfrac{2 - 12j}{4} = \dfrac{1 - 6j}{2}$

Example G. $\dfrac{j^3 + 2j}{1 - j^5} = \dfrac{-j + 2j}{1 - j} = \dfrac{j}{1 - j} \cdot \dfrac{1 + j}{1 + j} = \dfrac{-1 + j}{2}$

Exercises

In Exercises 1 through 38 perform the indicated operations, expressing all answers in the form $a + bj$.

1. $(3 - 7j) + (2 - j)$

2. $(-4 - j) + (-7 - 4j)$

3. $(7j - 6) - (3 + j)$

4. $(2 - 3j) - (2 + 3j)$

5. $(4 + \sqrt{-16}) + (3 - \sqrt{-81})$

6. $(-1 + 3\sqrt{-4}) + (8 - 4\sqrt{-49})$

7. $(5 - \sqrt{-9}) - (\sqrt{-4} + 5)$

8. $(\sqrt{-25} - 1) - \sqrt{-9}$

9. $j - (j - 7) - 8$

10. $(7 - j) - (4 - 4j) + (6 - j)$

11. $(7 - j)(7j)$

12. $(-2j)(j - 5)$

13. $\sqrt{-16}(2\sqrt{-1} - 5)$

14. $(\sqrt{-4} - 1)(\sqrt{-9})$

15. $(4 - j)(5 + 2j)$

16. $(3 - 5j)(6 + 7j)$

17. $(2\sqrt{-9} - 3)(3\sqrt{-4} + 2)$

18. $(5\sqrt{-64} - 5)(7 + \sqrt{-16})$

19. $\sqrt{-18}\sqrt{-4}\sqrt{-9}$

20. $(\sqrt{-36})^4$

21. $\sqrt{-108} - \sqrt{-27}$

22. $2\sqrt{-54} + \sqrt{-24}$

23. $7j^3 - 7\sqrt{-9}$

24. $j^2\sqrt{-7} - \sqrt{-28} + 8$

25. $(3 - 7j)^2$

26. $(4j + 5)^2$

27. $(1 - j)^3$

28. $(1 + j)(1 - j)^2$

29. $\dfrac{6j}{2 - 5j}$

30. $\dfrac{4}{3 + 7j}$

31. $\dfrac{2}{6 - \sqrt{-1}}$

32. $\dfrac{\sqrt{-4}}{2 + \sqrt{-9}}$

33. $\dfrac{1 - j}{1 + j}$

34. $\dfrac{9 - 8j}{j - 1}$

35. $\dfrac{\sqrt{-2} - 5}{\sqrt{-2} + 3}$

36. $\dfrac{1 - \sqrt{-4}}{2 + 9j}$

37. $\dfrac{j^2 - j}{2j - j^8}$

38. $\dfrac{j^5 - j^3}{3 + j}$

In Exercises 39 through 41 demonstrate the indicated properties.

39. Show that the sum of a complex number and its conjugate is a real number.

40. Show that the product of a complex number and its conjugate is a real number.

41. Show that the difference between a complex number and its conjugate is an imaginary number.

11-3 Graphical representation of complex numbers

We showed in Section 1-1 how we could represent real numbers as points on a line. Because complex numbers include all real numbers as well as imaginary numbers, it is necessary to represent them graphically in a different way. Since there are two numbers associated with each complex number (the real part and the imaginary part), we find that we can represent complex numbers by representing the real parts by the x-values of the rectangular coordinate system, and the imaginary parts by the y-values. In this way each complex number is represented as a point in the plane, the point being designated as $a + bj$. When the rectangular coordinate system is used in this manner it is called the *complex plane*.

Example A.   In Fig. 11-1, the point A represents the complex number $3 - 2j$. Point B represents $-1 + j$. Point C represents $-2 - 3j$. We note that these are equivalent to the points $(3, -2)$, $(-1, 1)$, and $(-2, -3)$. However, we must keep in mind that the meaning is different. Complex numbers were not included when we first learned to graph functions.

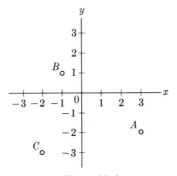

Figure 11-1

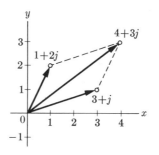

Figure 11-2

Let us represent two complex numbers and their sum in the complex plane. Consider, for example, the two complex numbers $1 + 2j$ and $3 + j$. By algebraic addition the sum is $4 + 3j$. When we draw lines from the origin to these points (see Fig. 11-2), we note that if we think of the complex numbers as being vectors, their sum is the vector sum. Because complex numbers can be used to represent vectors, these numbers are particularly important. Any complex number can be thought of as representing a vector from the origin to its point in the complex plane. To add two complex numbers graphically, we find the point corresponding to one of them and draw a line from the origin to this point. We repeat this process for the second point. Next we complete a parallelogram with the lines drawn as adjacent sides. The resulting fourth vertex is the point representing the sum of the two complex numbers. Note that this is equivalent to adding vectors by graphical means.

Example B.　Add the complex numbers $5 - 2j$ and $-2 - j$ graphically.

The solution is indicated in Fig. 11-3. We can see that the fourth vertex of the parallelogram is very near $3 - 3j$, which is, of course, the algebraic sum.

Example C.　Subtract $4 - 2j$ from $2 - 3j$ graphically.

Subtracting $4 - 2j$ is equivalent to adding $-4 + 2j$. Thus we complete the solution by adding $-4 + 2j$ and $2 - 3j$ (see Fig. 11-4). The result is $-2 - j$.

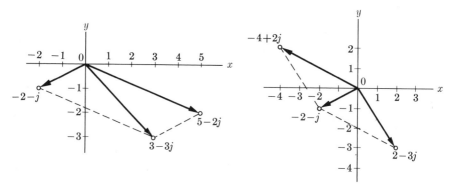

Figure 11-3　　　　　　　　　　　　Figure 11-4

Example D. Show graphically that the sum of a complex number and its conjugate is a real number.

If we choose the complex number $a + bj$, we know that its conjugate is $a - bj$. The y-coordinate for the conjugate is as far below the x-axis as the y-coordinate of $a + bj$ is above it. Therefore the sum of the imaginary parts must be zero and the sum of the two numbers must therefore lie on the x-axis, as shown in Fig. 11-5. Since any point on the x-axis is real, we have shown that the sum of $a + bj$ and $a - bj$ is real.

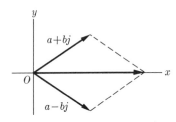

Figure 11-5

Exercises

In Exercises 1 through 12 perform the indicated operations graphically; check them algebraically.

1. $(5 - j) + (3 + 2j)$
2. $(3 - 2j) + (-1 - j)$
3. $(2 - 4j) + (-2 + j)$
4. $(-1 - 2j) + (6 - j)$
5. $(3 - 2j) - (4 - 6j)$
6. $(2 - j) - j$
7. $(1 + 4j) - (3 + j)$
8. $(-j - 2) - (-1 - 3j)$
9. $(4 - j) + (3 + 2j)$
10. $(5 + 2j) - (-4 - 2j)$
11. $(j - 6) - j + (j - 7)$
12. $j - (1 - j) + (3 + 2j)$

In Exercises 13 through 16 on the same coordinate system plot the given number, its negative, and its conjugate.

13. $3 + 2j$
14. $-2 + 4j$
15. $-3 - 5j$
16. $5 - j$

11-4 Polar form of a complex number

We have just seen the relationship between complex numbers and vectors. Since one can be used to represent the other, we shall use this fact to write complex numbers in another way. The new form has certain advantages when basic operations are performed on complex numbers.

By drawing a vector from the origin to the point in the complex plane which represents the number $x + yj$, we see the relation between vectors and complex numbers. Further observation indicates an angle in standard position has been formed. Also, the point $x + yj$ is r units from the origin. In fact, we can find any point in the complex plane by knowing this angle θ and the value of r. We have already developed the relations between x, y, r, and θ, in Eqs. (8-1) to (8-3).

Let us rewrite these equations in a slightly different form. By referring to Eqs. (8-1) through (8-3) and to Fig. 11-6, we see that

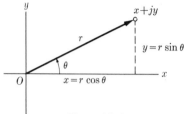

Figure 11-6

$$x = r \cos \theta, \qquad y = r \sin \theta, \qquad (11\text{-}6)$$

$$r^2 = x^2 + y^2, \qquad \tan \theta = \frac{y}{x}. \qquad (11\text{-}7)$$

Substituting Eqs. (11-6) into the rectangular form $x + yj$ of a complex number, we have

$$x + yj = r \cos \theta + j(r \sin \theta)$$

or

$$x + yj = r(\cos \theta + j \sin \theta). \qquad (11\text{-}8)$$

The right side of Eq. (11-8) is called the *polar form* of a complex number. Sometimes it is referred to as the trigonometric form. Other notations which are used to represent the polar form are $r \underline{/\theta}$ and r cis θ. The length r is called the *absolute value* or the *modulus*, and the angle θ is called the *argument* of the complex number. Therefore, Eq. (11-8), along with Eqs. (11-7), define the polar form of a complex number.

Example A.   Represent the complex number $3 + 4j$ graphically, and give its polar form.

From the rectangular form $3 + 4j$ we see that $x = 3$ and $y = 4$. Using Eqs. (11-7), we have $r = \sqrt{3^2 + 4^2} = 5$, and $\tan \theta = \frac{4}{3} = 1.333$, which means that $\theta = 53.1°$. Thus the polar form is $5(\cos 53.1° + j \sin 53.1°)$. The graphical representation is shown in Fig. 11-7.

Example B.   Represent the complex number $2 - 3j$ graphically, and give its polar form.

From Eqs. (11-7), we have $r = \sqrt{2^2 + (-3)^2} = \sqrt{13} = 3.61$, and $\tan \theta = -\frac{3}{2} = -1.500$. In Fig. 11-8 we see that θ is a fourth-quadrant angle. Therefore, since $\tan 56.3° = 1.500$, we have $\theta = 303.7°$. The polar form is

$$3.61 \, (\cos 303.7° + j \sin 303.7°).$$

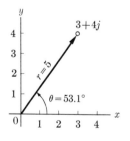

Figure 11-7

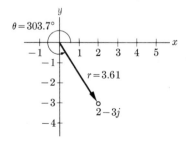

Figure 11-8

Example C.   Express the complex number $3(\cos 120° + j \sin 120°)$ in rectangular form.

From the given polar form, we know that $r = 3$ and $\theta = 120°$. Using Eqs. (11-6), we have

$$x = 3 \cos 120° = 3(-0.500) = -1.50,$$
$$y = 3 \sin 120° = 3(0.866) = 2.60.$$

Therefore, the rectangular form is $-1.50 + 2.60j$ (see Fig. 11-9).

Example D.   Represent the numbers 5, -5, $7j$, and $-7j$ in polar form.

Since any positive real number lies on the positive x-axis in the complex plane, real numbers are expressed in polar form by

$$a = a(\cos 0° + j \sin 0°).$$

Negative real numbers, being on the negative x-axis, are written as

$$a = |a|(\cos 180° + j \sin 180°).$$

Thus, $5 = 5(\cos 0° + j \sin 0°)$ and $-5 = 5(\cos 180° + j \sin 180°)$.

Positive pure imaginary numbers lie on the positive y-axis and are expressed in polar form by

$$jb = b(\cos 90° + j \sin 90°).$$

Similarly, negative pure imaginary numbers, being on the negative y-axis, are written as

$$jb = |b|(\cos 270° + j \sin 270°).$$

This means that $7j = 7(\cos 90° + j \sin 90°)$ and $-7j = 7(\cos 270° + j \sin 270°)$. The graphical representations of the *complex numbers* 5 and 7j are in Fig. 11-10.

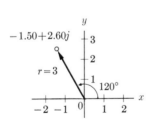

Figure 11-9

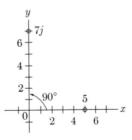

Figure 11-10

Exercises

In Exercises 1 through 12 represent each of the complex numbers graphically, and give the polar form of each number.

1. $8 + 6j$	2. $3 + 5j$	3. $3 - 4j$	4. $-5 + 12j$
5. $-2 + 3j$	6. $7 - 5j$	7. $-5 - 2j$	8. $-4 - 4j$
9. $1 + \sqrt{3}j$	10. $\sqrt{2} - \sqrt{2}j$	11. -3	12. $-2j$

In Exercises 13 through 24 represent each of the complex numbers graphically, and give the rectangular form of each number.

13. $5(\cos 54° + j \sin 54°)$

14. $3(\cos 232° + j \sin 232°)$

15. $1.6(\cos 150° + j \sin 150°)$

16. $2.5(\cos 315° + j \sin 315°)$

17. $10(\cos 345° + j \sin 345°)$

18. $2(\cos 155° + j \sin 155°)$

19. $6(\cos 180° + j \sin 180°)$

20. $7(\cos 270° + j \sin 270°)$

21. $4(\cos 200° + j \sin 200°)$

22. $1.5(\cos 62° + j \sin 62°)$

23. $\cos 240° + j \sin 240°$

24. $\cos 99° + j \sin 99°$

11-5 Exponential form of a complex number

Another important form of a complex number is known as the *exponential form*, which is written $re^{i\theta}$. In this expression r and θ have the same meaning as given in the last section and e represents a special irrational number equal to about 2.718. (In the calculus involved with exponential functions, the meaning of e is clarified.) We now define

$$re^{i\theta} = r(\cos \theta + j \sin \theta). \qquad (11\text{-}9)$$

When θ is expressed in radians, the expression $j\theta$ is an actual exponent, and it can be shown to obey all the laws of exponents. For this reason and because it is more meaningful in applications, we shall always express θ in radians when using the exponential form. The following examples show how complex numbers can be changed to and from exponential form.

Example A.   Express the number $3 + 4j$ in exponential form.

From Example A of Section 11-4, we know that this complex number may be written in polar form as $5(\cos 53.1° + j \sin 53.1°)$. Therefore, we know that $r = 5$. We now express $53.1°$ in terms of radians as

$$\frac{53.1\pi}{180} = \frac{53.1(3.14)}{180} = 0.927 \text{ radians.}$$

Thus the exponential form is $5e^{0.927j}$. This means that

$$3 + 4j = 5(\cos 53.1° + j \sin 53.1°) = 5e^{0.927j}.$$

Example B.   Express the number $3 - 7j$ in exponential form.

From the rectangular form of the number, we have $x = 3$ and $y = -7$. Therefore, $r = \sqrt{3^2 + (-7)^2} = \sqrt{58} = 7.62$. Also, $\tan \theta = -\frac{7}{3} = -2.333$. Since x is positive and y is negative, θ is a fourth-quadrant angle. From the tables we see that $2.333 = \tan 66.8°$. Therefore, $\theta = 360° - 66.8° = 293.2°$. Converting $293.2°$ to radians we have $293.2° = 5.12$ rad. Therefore, the exponential form is $7.62\, e^{5.12j}$. This means that

$$3 - 7j = 7.62e^{5.12j}.$$

Example C.   Express the complex number $2e^{4.80j}$ in polar and rectangular forms.

We first express 4.80 radians in degrees; 4.80 rad = 275°. From the exponential form we know that $r = 2$. This leads to the polar form of $2(\cos 275° + j \sin 275°)$. By finding cos 275° and sin 275°, we find the rectangular form to be $2(0.0872 - 0.9962j) = 0.1744 - 1.9924j$. This means that

$$2e^{4.80j} = 2(\cos 275° + j \sin 275°) = 0.1744 - 1.9924j.$$

Example D.   Express the complex number $3.40e^{2.46j}$ in polar and rectangular forms.

We first express 2.46 radians as 141°. From the exponential form we know that $r = 3.40$. Therefore, the polar form is $3.40(\cos 141° + j \sin 141°)$. Next we find that cos 141° = -0.777 and sin 141° = 0.629. The rectangular form is $3.40(-0.777 +0.629\,j) = -2.64 + 2.14\,j$. This means that

$$3.40e^{2.46j} = 3.40(\cos 141° + j \sin 141°) = -2.64 + 2.14\,j.$$

An important application of the use of complex numbers is in alternating current. When an alternating current flows through a given circuit, usually the current and voltage have different phases. That is, they do not reach their peak values at the same time. Therefore, one way of accounting for the magnitude as well as the phase of an electric current or voltage is to write it as a complex number. Here the modulus is the actual value of the current or voltage, and the argument is a measure of the phase.

Example E.   A current of $2 - 4j$ amp flows through a given circuit. Write this current in exponential form and determine the value of current in the circuit.

From the rectangular form, we have $x = 2$ and $y = -4$. Therefore, $r = \sqrt{2^2 + (-4)^2} = \sqrt{20} = 4.5$. Also, tan $\theta = -\frac{4}{2} = -2.0$. Since tan 63.5° = 2.0, $\theta = -63.5°$ (it is normal to express the phase in terms of negative angles). Changing 63.5° to radians, we have 63.5° = 1.11 rad. Therefore, the exponential form of the current is $4.5e^{-1.11j}$. The modulus is 4.5, which means the current is 4.5 amps.

At this point we shall summarize the three important forms of a complex number.

Rectangular:	$x + yj$
Polar:	$r(\cos \theta + j \sin \theta)$
Exponential:	$re^{j\theta}$

It follows that

$$x + yj = r(\cos \theta + j \sin \theta) = re^{j\theta}, \qquad (11\text{-}10)$$

where

$$r^2 = x^2 + y^2, \qquad \tan \theta = \frac{y}{x}. \qquad (11\text{-}7)$$

Exercises

In Exercises 1 through 12 express the given complex numbers in exponential form.

1. $3(\cos 60° + j \sin 60°)$
    2. $5(\cos 135° + j \sin 135°)$

3. $4.5(\cos 282° + j \sin 282°)$
    4. $2.1(\cos 228° + j \sin 228°)$

5. $3 - 4j$
    6. $-1 - 5j$

7. $-3 + 2j$
    8. $6 + j$

9. $5 + 2j$
    10. $4 - j$

11. $-6 - 5j$
    12. $-8 + 5j$

In Exercises 13 through 20 express the given complex numbers in polar and rectangular forms.

13. $3e^{0.5j}$
    14. $2e^{j}$

15. $4e^{1.85j}$
    16. $2.5e^{3.84j}$

17. $3.2e^{5.41j}$
    18. $0.8e^{3.00j}$

19. $0.1e^{2.39j}$
    20. $8.2e^{3.49j}$

In Exercises 21 and 22 perform the indicated operations.

21. The electric current in a certain alternating-current circuit is $0.50 + 0.22j$ amp. Write this current in exponential form and determine the magnitude of the current in the circuit.

22. The voltage in a certain alternating-current circuit is $125e^{1.31j}$. Determine the magnitude of the voltage in the circuit and the in-phase component (the real part) of the voltage.

11-6 Products, quotients, powers, and roots of complex numbers

We may find the product of two complex numbers by using the exponential form and the laws of exponents. Multiplying $r_1e^{j\theta_1}$ by $r_2e^{j\theta_2}$, we have

$$r_1e^{j\theta_1} \cdot r_2e^{j\theta_2} = r_1r_2e^{j\theta_1 + j\theta_2} = r_1r_2e^{j(\theta_1 + \theta_2)}. \tag{11-11}$$

We use Eq. (11-11) to express the product of two complex numbers in polar form:

$$r_1e^{j\theta_1} \cdot r_2e^{j\theta_2} = r_1(\cos \theta_1 + j \sin \theta_1) \cdot r_2(\cos \theta_2 + j \sin \theta_2),$$

and

$$r_1r_2e^{j(\theta_1 + \theta_2)} = r_1r_2[\cos(\theta_1 + \theta_2) + j \sin(\theta_1 + \theta_2)].$$

Therefore the polar expressions are equal:

$$r_1(\cos \theta_1 + j \sin \theta_1)r_2(\cos \theta_2 + j \sin \theta_2)$$
$$= r_1r_2[\cos(\theta_1 + \theta_2) + j \sin(\theta_1 + \theta_2)]. \tag{11-12}$$

Example A.   Multiply the complex numbers $(2 + 3j)$ and $(1 - j)$ by using the polar form of each.

$$r_1 = \sqrt{4 + 9} = 3.61, \qquad \tan \theta_1 = 1.50, \qquad \theta_1 = 56.3°;$$
$$r_2 = \sqrt{1 + 1} = 1.41, \qquad \tan \theta_2 = -1, \qquad \theta_2 = 315°;$$

$$3.61 \, (\cos 56.3° + j \sin 56.3°)(1.41)(\cos 315° + j \sin 315°)$$
$$= (3.61)(1.41)(\cos 371.3° + j \sin 371.3°)$$
$$= 5.09 \, (\cos 11.3° + j \sin 11.3°).$$

Example B.   When we use the exponential form to multiply the two complex numbers in Example A, we have:

$$r_1 = 3.61, \qquad \theta_1 = 56.3° = 0.983 \text{ rad};$$
$$r_2 = 1.41, \qquad \theta_2 = 315° = 5.50 \text{ rad};$$
$$3.61 e^{0.983j} 1.41 e^{5.50j} = 5.09 e^{6.48j} = 5.09 e^{0.20j}.$$

If we wish to *divide* one complex number in exponential form by another, we arrive at the following result:

$$r_1 e^{j\theta_1} \div r_2 e^{j\theta_2} = \frac{r_1}{r_2} e^{j(\theta_1 - \theta_2)}. \tag{11-13}$$

Therefore the result of dividing one number in polar form by another is given by:

$$\frac{r_1(\cos \theta_1 + j \sin \theta_1)}{r_2(\cos \theta_2 + j \sin \theta_2)} = \frac{r_1}{r_2} [\cos (\theta_1 - \theta_2) + j \sin (\theta_1 - \theta_2)]. \tag{11-14}$$

Example C.   Divide the first complex number of Example A by the second. Using polar form, we have the following:

$$\frac{3.61 \, (\cos 56.3° + j \sin 56.3°)}{1.41 \, (\cos 315° + j \sin 315°)} = 2.56 \, [\cos (-258.7°) + j \sin (-258.7°)]$$
$$= 2.56 \, (\cos 101.3° + j \sin 101.3°).$$

Example D.   Repeating Example C, using exponential forms, we obtain

$$\frac{3.61 e^{0.983j}}{1.41 e^{5.50j}} = 2.56 e^{-4.52j} = 2.56 e^{1.76j}.$$

To raise a complex number to a power, we simply multiply one complex number by itself the required number of times. For example, in Eq. (11-11), if the two numbers being multiplied are equal, we have (letting $r_1 = r_2 = r$ and $\theta_1 = \theta_2 = \theta$)

$$(r e^{j\theta})^2 = r^2 e^{j2\theta}. \tag{11-15}$$

Multiplying the expression in Eq. (11-15) by $r e^{j\theta}$ gives $r^3 e^{j3\theta}$. This leads to the general expression for raising a complex number to the nth power,

$$(r e^{j\theta})^n = r^n e^{jn\theta}. \tag{11-16}$$

Extending this to polar form, we have

$$[r \, (\cos \theta + j \sin \theta)]^n = r^n \, (\cos n\theta + j \sin n\theta). \tag{11-17}$$

Equation (11-17) is known as *DeMoivre's theorem.* It is valid for all real values of n, and may also be used for finding the roots of complex numbers if n is a fractional exponent.

Example E.   Using DeMoivre's theorem, find $(2 + 3j)^3$.

From Example A of this section, we know that $r = 3.61$ and $\theta = 56.3°$. Thus we have

$$[3.61\,(\cos 56.3° + j \sin 56.3°)]^3 = 46.9\,(\cos 168.9° + j \sin 168.9°).$$

From Example B we know that $\theta = 0.983$ rad. Thus, in exponential form,

$$(3.61e^{0.983j})^3 = 46.9e^{2.95j}.$$

Example F.   Find $\sqrt[3]{-1}$.

Since we know that -1 is a real number, we can find its cube root by means of the definition. That is $(-1)^3 = -1$. We shall check this by DeMoivre's theorem. Writing -1 in polar form, we have $-1 = 1\,(\cos 180° + j \sin 180°)$. Applying DeMoivre's theorem, with $n = \frac{1}{3}$, we obtain

$$(-1)^{1/3} = 1^{1/3}\,(\cos \tfrac{1}{3}180° + j \sin \tfrac{1}{3}180°) = \cos 60° + j \sin 60°$$
$$= 0.5 + 0.866j.$$

We note that we did not obtain -1 as an answer. If we check the answer which was obtained, in the form $\frac{1}{2}(1 + \sqrt{3}j)$, by actually cubing it, we obtain -1! Thus it is a correct answer.

We should note that it is possible to take $\frac{1}{3}$ of any angle up to $1080°$ and still have an angle less than $360°$. Since $180°$ and $540°$ have the same terminal side, let us try writing -1 as $1\,(\cos 540° + j \sin 540°)$. Using DeMoivre's theorem, we have

$$(-1)^{1/3} = 1^{1/3}\,(\cos \tfrac{1}{3}540° + j \sin \tfrac{1}{3}540°) = \cos 180° + j \sin 180° = -1.$$

We have found the answer we originally anticipated.

Angles of $180°$ and $900°$ also have the same terminal side, so we try

$$(-1)^{1/3} = 1^{1/3}\,(\cos \tfrac{1}{3}900° + j \sin \tfrac{1}{3}900°) = \cos 300° + j \sin 300°$$
$$= 0.5 - 0.866j.$$

Checking this, we find that it is also a correct root. We may try $1260°$, but $\frac{1}{3}(1260°) = 420°$, which has the same functional values as $60°$, and would give us the answer $0.5 + 0.866j$ again.

We have found, therefore, three cube roots of -1. They are $-1, 0.5 + 0.866j$, and $0.5 - 0.866j$. When this is generalized, it can be proved that there are n nth roots of any complex number. The method for finding the n roots is to use θ to find one root, and then add $360°$ to θ, $n - 1$ times, in order to find the other roots.

Example G.   Find the square roots of j.

We must first properly write j in polar form so that we may use DeMoivre's theorem to find the roots. In polar form, j is

$$j = 1\,(\cos 90° + j \sin 90°).$$

To find the square roots, we apply DeMoivre's theorem with $n = \frac{1}{2}$.

$$j^{1/2} = 1^{1/2}\left(\cos\frac{90°}{2} + j\sin\frac{90°}{2}\right) = \cos 45° + j\sin 45° = 0.7 + 0.7j.$$

To find the other square root, we must write j in polar form as

$$j = 1[\cos(90° + 360°) + j\sin(90° + 360°)] = 1(\cos 450° + j\sin 450°).$$

Applying DeMoivre's theorem to j in this form, we have

$$j^{1/2} = 1^{1/2}\left(\cos\frac{450°}{2} + j\sin\frac{450°}{2}\right) = \cos 225° + j\sin 225° = -0.7 - 0.7j.$$

Thus the two square roots of j are $0.7 + 0.7j$ and $-0.7 - 0.7j$.

Example H. Find the six 6th roots of 1.
   Here we shall use directly the method for finding the roots of a number, as outlined at the end of Example F:

$$1 = 1(\cos 0° + j\sin 0°).$$

First root: $1^{1/6} = 1^{1/6}\left(\cos\dfrac{0°}{6} + j\sin\dfrac{0°}{6}\right) = \cos 0° + j\sin 0° = 1$

Second root: $1^{1/6} = 1^{1/6}\left(\cos\dfrac{0° + 360°}{6} + j\sin\dfrac{0° + 360°}{6}\right)$

$$= \cos 60° + j\sin 60° = \frac{1}{2} + j\frac{\sqrt{3}}{2}$$

Third root: $1^{1/6} = 1^{1/6}\left(\cos\dfrac{0° + 720°}{6} + j\sin\dfrac{0° + 720°}{6}\right)$

$$= \cos 120° + j\sin 120° = -\frac{1}{2} + j\frac{\sqrt{3}}{2}$$

Fourth root: $1^{1/6} = 1^{1/6}\left(\cos\dfrac{0° + 1080°}{6} + j\sin\dfrac{0° + 1080°}{6}\right)$

$$= \cos 180° + j\sin 180° = -1$$

Fifth root: $1^{1/6} = 1^{1/6}\left(\cos\dfrac{0° + 1440°}{6} + j\sin\dfrac{0° + 1440°}{6}\right)$

$$= \cos 240° + j\sin 240° = -\frac{1}{2} - j\frac{\sqrt{3}}{2}$$

Sixth root: $1^{1/6} = 1^{1/6}\left(\cos\dfrac{0° + 1800°}{6} + j\sin\dfrac{0° + 1800°}{6}\right)$

$$= \cos 300° + j\sin 300° = \frac{1}{2} - j\frac{\sqrt{3}}{2}$$

At this point we can see advantages for the various forms of writing complex numbers. Rectangular form lends itself best to addition and subtraction. Polar form is generally used for multiplying, dividing, raising to powers, and finding roots. Exponential form is used for theoretical purposes (e.g., deriving DeMoivre's theorem).

Exercises

In Exercises 1 through 12 perform the indicated operations. Leave the result in polar form.

1. $[4 (\cos 60° + j \sin 60°)][2 (\cos 20° + j \sin 20°)]$

2. $[3 (\cos 120° + j \sin 120°)][5 (\cos 45° + j \sin 45°)]$

3. $[0.5 (\cos 140° + j \sin 140°)][6 (\cos 110° + j \sin 110°)]$

4. $[0.4 (\cos 320° + j \sin 320°)][5.5 (\cos 150° + j \sin 150°)]$

5. $\dfrac{8 (\cos 100° + j \sin 100°)}{4 (\cos 65° + j \sin 65°)}$

6. $\dfrac{9 (\cos 230° + j \sin 230°)}{3 (\cos 80° + j \sin 80°)}$

7. $\dfrac{12 (\cos 320° + j \sin 320°)}{5 (\cos 210° + j \sin 210°)}$

8. $\dfrac{2 (\cos 90° + j \sin 90°)}{4 (\cos 75° + j \sin 75°)}$

9. $[2 (\cos 35° + j \sin 35°)]^3$

10. $[3 (\cos 120° + j \sin 120°)]^4$

11. $[2 (\cos 135° + j \sin 135°)]^8$

12. $(\cos 142° + j \sin 142°)^{10}$

In Exercises 13 through 18 change each number to polar form and then perform the indicated operations. Express the final result in rectangular and polar forms. Check by performing the same operation in rectangular form.

13. $(3 + 4j)(5 - 12j)$

14. $(-2 + 5j)(-1 - j)$

15. $\dfrac{3 + 4j}{5 - 12j}$

16. $\dfrac{-2 + 5j}{-1 - j}$

17. $(3 + 4j)^4$

18. $(-1 - j)^8$

In Exercises 19 through 26 use DeMoivre's theorem to find the indicated roots. Be sure to find all roots.

19. $\sqrt{4 (\cos 60° + j \sin 60°)}$

20. $\sqrt[3]{27 (\cos 120° + j \sin 120°)}$

21. $\sqrt[3]{3 - 4j}$

22. $\sqrt{-5 + 12j}$

23. $\sqrt[4]{1}$

24. $\sqrt[3]{8}$

25. $\sqrt[3]{-j}$

26. $\sqrt[4]{j}$

11-7 An application to alternating-current (a-c) circuits

We shall complete our study of the *j*-operator by showing its use in one aspect of alternating-current circuit theory. This application will be made to measuring voltage between any two points in a simple a-c circuit, similar to the application mentioned in Section 11-5. We shall consider a circuit containing a resistance, a capacitance, and an inductance.

Briefly, a resistance is any part of a circuit which tends to obstruct the flow of electric current through the circuit. It is denoted by R (units of ohms) and in diagrams by ‑ᴧᴧ‑. In essence, a capacitance is two nonconnected plates in a circuit; no current actually flows across the gap between them. In an a-c circuit, an electric charge is continually going to and from each plate and, therefore, the current in the circuit is not effectively stopped. It is denoted by C (units in farads) and in diagrams by ‑ᐁ‑ (Fig. 11-11). An inductance, basically, is a coil of wire in which current is induced because the current is continuously changing in the circuit. It is denoted by L (units in henrys) and in diagrams by ‑ᴑᴑᴑ‑. All these elements affect the voltage in an alternating-current circuit. We shall state here the relation each has to the voltage and current in the circuit.

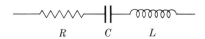

$$R \qquad C \qquad L$$

Figure 11-11

In Chapter 9, when we were discussing the graphs of the trigonometric functions, we noted that the current and voltage in an a-c circuit could be represented by a sine or cosine curve. Therefore, each reaches peak values periodically. If they reach their respective peak values at the same time, we say they are *in phase*. If the voltage reaches its peak before the current, we say that the voltage *leads* the current. If the voltage reaches its peak after the current, we say that the voltage *lags* the current. In the study of electricity it is shown that the voltage across a resistance is in phase with the current. The voltage across a capacitor lags the current by 90°, and the voltage across an inductance leads the current by 90°.

Each element in an a-c circuit tends to offer a type of resistance to the flow of current. The effective resistance of any part of the circuit is called the *reactance*, and it is denoted by X. The voltage across any part of the circuit whose reactance is X is given by $V = IX$, where I is the current (in amperes) and V is the voltage (in volts). Therefore, the voltage across a resistor, capacitor, and inductor, are, respectively

$$V_R = IX_R, \qquad V_C = IX_C, \qquad V_L = IX_L. \tag{11-18}$$

To determine the voltage across a combination of these elements of a circuit, we must account for the reactance as well as the phase of the voltage across the individual elements. Since the voltage across a resistor is in phase with the current, we shall represent X_R along the x-axis as a real number R (the actual value of the resistance). Since the voltage across an inductance *leads* the current by 90°, we shall represent this voltage as a positive, pure imaginary number. In the same way, by representing the voltage across a capacitor as a negative, pure imaginary number, we show that the voltage lags the current by 90°. These representations are meaningful since the positive *y*-axis (positive, pure imaginary numbers) is $+90°$ from the positive *x*-axis, and the negative *y*-axis (negative, pure imaginary numbers) is $-90°$ from the positive *x*-axis.

The total voltage across a combination of all three elements is $V_R + V_L + V_C$, which we shall represent by V_{RLC}. Therefore,

$$V_{RLC} = IR + IX_Lj - IX_Cj = I[R + j(X_L - X_C)].$$

This expression is also written as

$$V_{RLC} = IZ, \qquad\qquad (11\text{-}19)$$

where the symbol Z is called the *impedance* of the circuit. It is the total effective resistance to the flow of current by a combination of the elements in the circuit, taking into account the phase of the voltage in each element. From its definition, we see that Z is a complex number,

$$Z = R + j(X_L - X_C), \qquad\qquad (11\text{-}20)$$

with a magnitude

$$|Z| = \sqrt{R^2 + (X_L - X_C)^2}. \qquad\qquad (11\text{-}21)$$

Also, as a complex number, it makes an angle θ with the *x*-axis given by

$$\tan \theta = \frac{X_L - X_C}{R}. \qquad\qquad (11\text{-}22)$$

All these equations are based on phase relations of voltages with respect to the current. Therefore, the angle θ represents the phase angle between the current and the voltage (see Fig. 11-12).

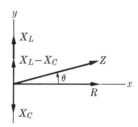

Figure 11-12

Example A.   In the series circuit shown in Fig. 11-13(a), $R = 12$ ohms and $X_L = 5.0$ ohms. A current of 2.0 amps is in the circuit. Find the voltage across each element, the impedance, the voltage across the combination, and the phase angle between the current and voltage.

Since the voltage across any element is the product of the current and reactance, we have the voltage across the resistor (between points *a* and *b*) as $V_R = (2.0)(12) = 24$ volts. The voltage across the inductor (between points *b*

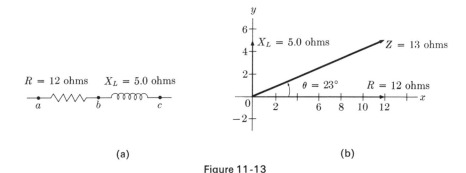

$R = 12$ ohms $X_L = 5.0$ ohms

(a)

(b)

Figure 11-13

and c) is $V_L = (2.0)(5.0) = 10$ volts. To find the voltage across the combination, between points a and c, we must first find the magnitude of the impedance. The voltage is *not* the arithmetic sum of V_R and V_L; we must account for the phase. By Eq. (11-20), the impedance is $Z = 12 + 5.0j$, with magnitude

$$|Z| = \sqrt{R^2 + X_L^2} = \sqrt{(12)^2 + (5.0)^2} = \sqrt{169} = 13 \text{ ohms.}$$

Therefore, the voltage across the combination is

$$V_{RL} = (2.0)(13) = 26 \text{ volts.}$$

The phase angle between the voltage and current is found by Eq. (11-22). This gives $\tan \theta = 5.0/12 = 0.42$, which means that $\theta = 23°$. The voltage leads the current by 23°, as shown in Fig. 11-13(b).

Example B.   For a circuit in which $R = 8.0$ ohms, $X_L = 7.0$ ohms, and $X_C = 13$ ohms, find the impedance and the phase angle between the current and the voltage.

By the definition of impedance, Eq. (11-20), we have

$$Z = 8.0 + (7.0 - 13)j = 8.0 - 6.0j,$$

where the magnitude of the impedance is

$$|Z| = \sqrt{(8.0)^2 + (-6.0)^2}$$

$$= \sqrt{64 + 36} = 10 \text{ ohms.}$$

The phase angle is found by

$$\tan \theta = \frac{-6.0}{8.0} = -0.75.$$

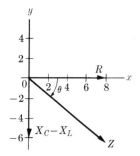

Figure 11-14

Therefore, $\theta = -37°$ (negative angles are used, having a useful purpose in this type of problem). This means that the voltage lags the current by 37° (see Fig. 11-14).

Example C. Let $R = 6.0$ ohms, $X_L = 8.0$ ohms, and $X_C = 4.0$ ohms. Find the impedance and the phase angle between the current and voltage.

$$Z = 6.0 + (8.0 - 4.0)j = 6.0 + 4.0j,$$

$$|Z| = \sqrt{(6.0)^2 + (4.0)^2} = \sqrt{36 + 16} = 7.2 \text{ ohms},$$

$$\tan \theta = \frac{4.0}{6.0} = 0.67, \qquad \theta = 34^\circ$$

The voltage leads the current by 34° (see Fig. 11-15).

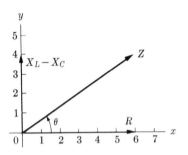

Figure 11-15

Note that the resistance is represented in the same way as a vector along the positive x-axis. Actually resistance is not a vector quantity, but is represented in this manner in order to assign an angle as the phase of the current. The important concept in this analysis is that the phase *difference* between the current and voltage is constant, and therefore any direction may be chosen arbitrarily for one of them. Once this choice is made, other phase angles are measured with respect to this direction. A common choice, as above, is to make the phase angle of the current zero. If an arbitrary angle is chosen, it is necessary to treat the current, voltage, and impedance as complex numbers.

Example D. In a particular circuit, the current is $2 - 3j$ amps and the impedance is $6 + 2j$ ohms. The voltage across this part of the circuit is

$$V = (2 - 3j)(6 + 2j) = 12 - 14j - 6j^2 = 12 - 14j + 6 = 18 - 14j \text{ volts}.$$

The magnitude of the voltage is

$$|V| = \sqrt{(18)^2 + (-14)^2} = \sqrt{324 + 196} = \sqrt{520} = 23 \text{ volts}.$$

Since the voltage across a resistor is in phase with the current, this voltage can be represented as having a phase difference of zero with respect to the current. Therefore, the resistance is indicated as an arrow in the positive x-direction, denoting the fact that the current and voltage are in phase. Such a representation is called a *phasor*. The arrow denoted by R is actually the phasor representing the voltage across the resistor. Remember, the positive x-axis is arbitrarily chosen as the direction of the phase of the current.

To show properly that the voltage across an inductance leads the current by 90°, its reactance (effective resistance) is multiplied by j. We know that there is a positive 90° angle between a real number and a positive imaginary number. In the same way, by multiplying the capacitive reactance by $-j$, we show the 90° difference in phase between the voltage and current in a capacitor, with the current leading. Therefore, jX_L represents the phasor for the voltage across an inductor and $-jX_C$ is the phasor for the voltage across the capacitor. The phasor for the voltage across the combination of the resistance, inductance, and capacitance is Z, where the phase difference between the voltage and current for the combination is the angle θ.

This also points out well the significance of the word "operator" in the term "j-operator." Multiplying a phasor by j means to perform the operation of rotating it through 90°. We have seen that this is the same result obtained when a real number is multiplied by j.

An alternating current is produced by a coil of wire rotating through a magnetic field. If the angular velocity of this wire is ω, the capacitive and inductive reactances are given by the relations

$$X_C = \frac{1}{\omega C} \quad \text{and} \quad X_L = \omega L. \tag{11-23}$$

Therefore if ω, C, and L are known, the reactance of the circuit may be determined.

Example E. Given that $R = 12$ ohms, $L = 0.30$ henry, $C = 250 \times 10^{-6}$ farad, and $\omega = 80$ rad/sec, determine the impedance and the phase difference between the current and voltage.

$$X_C = \frac{1}{(80)(250 \times 10^{-6})} = 50 \text{ ohms};$$

$$X_L = (0.30)(80) = 24 \text{ ohms};$$

$$Z = 12 + (24 - 50)j = 12 - 26j,$$

$$|Z| = \sqrt{(12)^2 + (-26)^2} = 29 \text{ ohms};$$

$$\tan \theta = \frac{-26}{12} = -2.2, \quad \theta = -65°.$$

Figure 11-16

The voltage lags the current (see Fig. 11-16).

An important concept in the application of this theory is that of *resonance*. For resonance, the impedance of any circuit is a minimum, or the total impedance is R. Thus $X_L - X_C = 0$. Also, it can be seen that the current and voltage are in phase under these conditions. Resonance is required for the tuning of radio and television receivers.

Exercises

For Exercises 1 through 4 use the circuit shown in Fig. 11-17. A current of 3.0 amps flows through the circuit. Determine the indicated quantities.

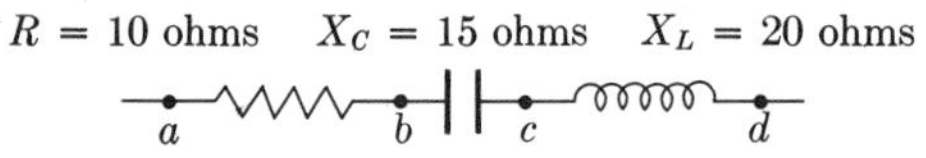

$$R = 10 \text{ ohms} \quad X_C = 15 \text{ ohms} \quad X_L = 20 \text{ ohms}$$

Figure 11-17

1. Find the voltage across the resistor (between points a and b).
2. Find the voltage across the capacitor (between points b and c).
3. (a) Find the magnitude of the impedance across the resistor and the capacitor (between points a and c).
   (b) Find the phase angle between the current and voltage for this combination.
   (c) Find the voltage across this combination.
4. (a) Find the magnitude of the impedance across the resistor, capacitor, and inductor (between points a and d).
   (b) Find the phase angle between the current and voltage for this combination.
   (c) Find the voltage across this combination.

In Exercises 5 through 8 use the following information to find the required quantities. In a given circuit $R = 6.0$ ohms, $X_C = 10$ ohms, and $X_L = 7.0$ ohms. Find (a) the magnitude of the impedance and (b) the phase angle between the current and voltage, under the specified conditions.

5. With the resistor removed (an LC circuit)
6. With the capacitor removed (an RL circuit)
7. With the inductor removed (an RC circuit)
8. With all elements present (an RLC circuit)

In Exercises 9 through 18 find the required quantities.

9. Given that the current in a given circuit is $8 - 2j$ amps and the impedance is $2 + 5j$ ohms, find the magnitude of the voltage.
10. Given that the voltage in a given circuit is $8 - 3j$ volts and the impedance is $2 - j$ ohms, find the magnitude of the current.
11. Given that $\omega = 1000$ rad/sec, $C = 0.5 \times 10^{-6}$ farad, and $L = 3$ henrys, find the capacitive and inductive reactances.
12. A coil of wire is rotating through a magnetic field at 60 cycles/sec. Determine the capacitive reactance for a capacitor of 2×10^{-6} farad which is in the circuit.
13. If the capacitor and inductor in Exercise 11 are put in a series circuit with a resistance of 4000 ohms, what is the impedance of this combination? Find the phase angle.
14. Rework Exercise 13, assuming that the capacitor is removed.
15. If $\omega = 100$ rad/sec and $L = 0.5$ henry, what must be the value of C to produce resonance?
16. What is the frequency ω (in cycles per second) for resonance in a circuit for which $L = 2.0$ henrys and $C = 25 \times 10^{-6}$ farad?

17. The average power supplied to any combination of components in an a-c circuit is given by the relation $P = VI \cos \theta$, where P is the power (in watts), V is the effective voltage, I is the effective current, and θ is the phase angle between the current and voltage. Assuming that the effective voltage across the resistor, capacitor, and inductor combination in Exercise 13 is 200 volts, determine the power supplied to these elements.

18. Find the power supplied to a resistor of 120 ohms and a capacitor of 0.7×10^{-6} farad if $\omega = 1000$ rad/sec and the effective voltage is 110 volts.

11-8 Miscellaneous Exercises

In Exercises 1 through 10 perform the indicated operations, expressing all answers in the simplest rectangular form.

1. $(6 - 2j) + (4 + j)$

2. $(12 + 7j) + (-8 + 6j)$

3. $(18 - 3j) - (12 - 5j)$

4. $(-4 - 2j) - (-6 - 7j)$

5. $(2 + j)(4 - j)$

6. $(-5 + 3j)(8 - 4j)$

7. $(2j)(6 - 3j)(4 + 3j)$

8. $j(3 - 2j) - (j^3)(5 + j)$

9. $\dfrac{j(6 - 4j)}{7 - 2j}$

10. $\dfrac{(7 - j)(8 - j)}{6 + j}$

In Exercises 11 and 12 find the values of x and y for which the equations are true.

11. $3x - 2j = yj - 2$

12. $2xj - 2y = (y + 3)j - 3$

In Exercises 13 through 16 perform the indicated operations graphically; check them algebraically.

13. $(-1 + 5j) + (4 + 6j)$

14. $(7 - 2j) + (5 + 4j)$

15. $(9 + 2j) - (5 - 6j)$

16. $(1 + 4j) - (-3 - 3j)$

In Exercises 17 through 20 give the polar and exponential forms of each of the complex numbers.

17. $1 - j$ 18. $4 + 3j$ 19. $-2 - 7j$ 20. $-4j$

In Exercises 21 through 28 give the rectangular form of each of the complex numbers.

21. $2 (\cos 225° + j \sin 225°)$

22. $4 (\cos 60° + j \sin 60°)$

23. $5 (\cos 123° + j \sin 123°)$

24. $2 (\cos 296° + j \sin 296°)$

25. $2e^{0.25j}$

26. $e^{3.62j}$

27. $5e^{1.90j}$

28. $4e^{6.04j}$

In Exercises 29 through 34 perform the indicated operations. Leave the result in polar form.

29. $[3 (\cos 32° + j \sin 32°)][5 (\cos 52° + j \sin 52°)]$

30. $[2.5 (\cos 162° + j \sin 162°)][8 (\cos 115° + j \sin 115°)]$

31. $\dfrac{24 (\cos 165° + j \sin 165°)}{3 (\cos 106° + j \sin 106°)}$

32. $\dfrac{18 (\cos 403° + j \sin 403°)}{4 (\cos 192° + j \sin 192°)}$

33. $[2 (\cos 16° + j \sin 16°)]^{10}$

34. $[3 (\cos 36° + j \sin 36°)]^6$

In Exercises 35 through 38 change each number to polar form and then perform the indicated operations. Express the final result in rectangular and polar forms. Check by performing the same operation in rectangular form.

35. $(1 - j)^{10}$

36. $(\sqrt{3} + j)^8(1 + j)^5$

37. $\dfrac{(5 + 5j)^4}{(-1 - j)^6}$

38. $(\sqrt{3} - j)^{-8}$

In Exercises 39 through 42 use DeMoivre's theorem to find the indicated roots. Be sure to find all roots.

39. $\sqrt[3]{-8}$ 40. $\sqrt[3]{1}$ 41. $\sqrt[4]{-j}$ 42. $\sqrt[5]{-32}$

In Exercises 43 through 48 find the required quantities.

43. In a given circuit $R = 7.5$ ohms and $X_C = 10$ ohms. Find the magnitude of the impedance and the phase angle between the current and voltage.

44. In a given circuit $R = 15$ ohms, $X_C = 27$ ohms and $X_L = 35$ ohms. Find the magnitude of the impedance and the phase angle between the current and voltage.

45. A coil of wire is going around a circle at 60 rev/sec. If this coil generates a current in a circuit containing a resistance of 10 ohms, an inductance of 0.01 henry, and a capacitance of 5×10^{-4} farad, what is the magnitude of the impedance of the circuit? What is the angle between the current and voltage?

46. A coil of wire rotates at 120 rev/sec. If the coil generates a current in a circuit containing a resistance of 12 ohms, an inductance of 0.04 henry and an impedance of 22 ohms, what must be the value of a capacitor (in farads) in the circuit?

47. In a given circuit, the current is $5 - 2j$ amps and the impedance is $6 + 3j$ ohms. Find the magnitude of the voltage.

48. In the theory of light reflection on metals, the expression

$$\frac{\mu(1 - kj) - 1}{\mu(1 - kj) + 1}$$

is encountered. Simplify this expression.

Logarithms

12

12-1 Definition of a logarithm

In Chapter 10, we dealt in some detail with exponents. There is a special use of exponents which is important in computational work and for theoretical purposes. Exponents used in this manner are given the name *logarithms*. Today, with the increased use of electronic computers, logarithms are used somewhat less for computation, but their usefulness in advanced mathematics and in applications in technical fields remains of great importance.

Chapter 10 dealt with exponents in expressions of the form x^n, where we showed that n could be any rational number. Here we shall deal with expressions of the form b^x, where x is any real number. When we look at these expressions, we note the primary difference is that in the second expression *the exponent is variable*. We have not previously dealt with variable exponents. Thus let us define the *exponential function* to be

$$y = b^x. \tag{12-1}$$

In Eq. (12-1), x is called the *logarithm of the number y to the base b*. In our work with logarithms we shall restrict all numbers to the real number system. This leads us to choose the base as a positive number other than 1. We know that 1 raised to any power will result in 1, which would make y a constant regardless of the value of x. Negative numbers for b would result in imaginary values for y if x were any fractional exponent with an even integer for its denominator.

Example A. $y = 2^x$ is an exponential function, where x is the logarithm of y to the base 2. This means that 2 raised to a given power gives us the corresponding value of y.

If $x = 2$, $y = 2^2 = 4$; this means that 2 is the logarithm of 4 to the base 2.
If $x = 4$, $y = 2^4 = 16$; this means that 4 is the logarithm of 16 to the base 2.
If $x = \frac{1}{2}$, $y = 2^{1/2} = 1.41$; this means that $\frac{1}{2}$ is the logarithm of 1.41 to the base 2.

Using the definition of a logarithm, Eq. (12-1) may be solved for x, and is written in the form

$$x = \log_b y. \tag{12-2}$$

This equation is read in accordance with the definition of x in Eq. (12-1): *x equals the logarithm of y to the base b*. This means that x is the power to which the base b must be raised in order to equal the number y; that is, x is a logarithm, and a logarithm is an exponent. Note that Eqs. (12-1) and (12-2) state the same relationship, but in a different manner. Equation (12-1) is the *exponential form*, and Eq. (12-2) is the *logarithmic form*.

Example B.   The equation $y = 2^x$ would be written as $x = \log_2 y$ if we put it in logarithmic form. When we choose values of y to find the corresponding values of x from this equation, we ask ourselves, "2 raised to what power gives y?" Hence if $y = 4$, we know that 2^2 is 4, and x would be 2. If $y = 8$, $2^3 = 8$, or $x = 3$.

Example C. $3^2 = 9$ in logarithmic form is $2 = \log_3 9$; $4^{-1} = \frac{1}{4}$ in logarithmic form is $-1 = \log_4 \left(\frac{1}{4}\right)$. Remember, the exponent may be negative. The base must be positive.

Example D. $(64)^{1/3} = 4$ in logarithmic form is $\frac{1}{3} = \log_{64} 4$,
$(32)^{3/5} = 8$ in logarithmic form is $\frac{3}{5} = \log_{32} 8$

Example E. $\log_2 32 = 5$ in exponential form is $32 = 2^5$,
$\log_6 \left(\frac{1}{36}\right) = -2$ in exponential form is $\frac{1}{36} = 6^{-2}$

Example F.   Find b, given that $-4 = \log_b \left(\frac{1}{81}\right)$.
Writing this in exponential form, we have $\frac{1}{81} = b^{-4}$. Thus $b = 3$, since $3^4 = 81$.

Example G.   Find y, given that $\log_4 y = \frac{1}{2}$.
In exponential form we have $y = 4^{1/2}$ or $y = 2$.

We see that exponential form is very useful for determining values written in logarithmic form. For this reason it is important that you learn to transform readily from one form to the other.

Exercises

In Exercises 1 through 12 express the given equations in logarithmic form.

1. $3^3 = 27$ 2. $5^2 = 25$ 3. $4^4 = 256$ 4. $8^2 = 64$
5. $4^{-2} = \frac{1}{16}$ 6. $3^{-2} = \frac{1}{9}$ 7. $2^{-6} = \frac{1}{64}$ 8. $(12)^0 = 1$
9. $8^{1/3} = 2$ 10. $(81)^{3/4} = 27$ 11. $\left(\frac{1}{4}\right)^2 = \frac{1}{16}$ 12. $\left(\frac{1}{2}\right)^{-2} = 4$

In Exercises 13 through 24 express the given equations in exponential form.

13. $\log_3 81 = 4$ 14. $\log_{11} 121 = 2$ 15. $\log_9 9 = 1$ 16. $\log_{15} 1 = 0$

17. $\log_{25} 5 = \frac{1}{2}$ 18. $\log_8 16 = \frac{4}{3}$ 19. $\log_{243} 3 = \frac{1}{5}$ 20. $\log_{1/32} \left(\frac{1}{8}\right) = \frac{3}{5}$

21. $\log_{10} (0.01) = -2$ 22. $\log_7 \left(\frac{1}{49}\right) = -2$ 23. $\log_{0.5} 16 = -4$ 24. $\log_{1/3} 3 = -1$

In Exercises 25 through 40 determine the value of the unknown.

25. $\log_4 16 = x$ 26. $\log_5 125 = x$ 27. $\log_{10} 0.01 = x$ 28. $\log_{16} \left(\frac{1}{4}\right) = x$

29. $\log_7 y = 3$ 30. $\log_8 N = 3$ 31. $\log_8 y = -\frac{2}{3}$ 32. $\log_7 y = -2$

33. $\log_b 81 = 2$ 34. $\log_b 625 = 4$ 35. $\log_b 4 = -\frac{1}{3}$ 36. $\log_b 4 = \frac{2}{3}$

37. $\log_{10} 10^{0.2} = x$ 38. $\log_5 5^{1.3} = x$ 39. $\log_3 27^{-1} = x$ 40. $\log_b \left(\frac{1}{4}\right) = -\frac{1}{2}$

In Exercises 41 and 42 perform the indicated operations.

41. Under specified conditions, the instantaneous voltage E in a given circuit can be expressed as
$$E = E_m e^{-Rt/L}.$$
By rewriting this equation in logarithmic form, solve for t.

42. An equation relating the number N of atoms of radium at any time t in terms of the number of atoms at $t = 0$, N_0, is $\log_e (N/N_0) = -kt$, where k is a constant. By expressing this equation in exponential form, solve for N.

12-2 Graphs of $y = b^x$ and $y = \log_b x$

When we are working with functions, we must keep in mind that a function is defined by the operation being performed on the independent variable, and not by the letter chosen to represent it. However, for consistency, it is normal practice to let y represent the dependent variable, and x represent the independent variable. Therefore, the logarithmic function is

$$y = \log_b x. \tag{12-3}$$

Equations (12-2) and (12-3) express the same *function*, the logarithmic function. They do not represent different functions, due to the difference in location of the variables, since they represent the same operation on the independent variable. Equation (12-3) simply expresses the function with the usual choice of variables.

Graphical representation of functions is often valuable when we wish to demonstrate their properties. We shall now show the graphs of the exponential function [Eq. (12-1)], and the logarithmic function [Eq. (12-3)].

Example A. Plot the graph of $y = 2^x$.

Assuming values for x and then finding the corresponding values for y, we obtain the table shown on the following page.

x	-3	-2	-1	0	1	2	3	4
y	$\frac{1}{8}$	$\frac{1}{4}$	$\frac{1}{2}$	1	2	4	8	16

From these values we plot the curve, as shown in Fig. 12-1.

Example B. Plot the graph of $y = \log_3 x$.

We can find the points for this graph more easily if we first put the equation in exponential form: $x = 3^y$. By assuming values for y, we can find the corresponding values for x.

x	$\frac{1}{9}$	$\frac{1}{3}$	1	3	9	27
y	-2	-1	0	1	2	3

Using these values, we construct the graph seen in Fig. 12-2.

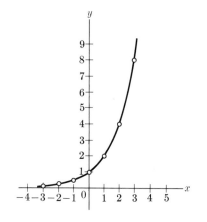

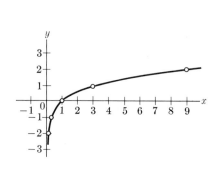

Figure 12-1   Figure 12-2

Any exponential or logarithmic curve, where $b > 1$, will be similar in shape to those of Examples A and B. From these curves we can draw certain conclusions:

(1) If $0 < x < 1$, $\log_b x < 0$; if $x = 1$, $\log_b 1 = 0$; if $x > 1$, $\log_b x > 0$.

(2) If $x > 1$, x increases more rapidly than $\log_b x$.

(3) For all values of x, $b^x > 0$.

(4) If $x > 1$, b^x increases more rapidly than x.

Although the bases important to applications are greater than 1, to understand how the curve of the exponential function differs somewhat if $b < 1$, let us consider the following example.

Example C. Plot the graph of $y = (\frac{1}{2})^x$.

The values are found for the following table; the graph is plotted in Fig. 12-3.

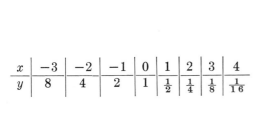

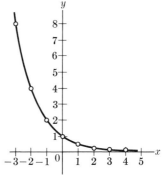

Figure 12-3

Exercises

In Exercises 1 through 6 plot graphs of the given functions for $-3 \leq x \leq 3$.

1. $y = 3^x$
2. $y = 4^x$
3. $y = \left(\frac{3}{2}\right)^x$
4. $y = \left(\frac{5}{2}\right)^x$
5. $y = \left(\frac{1}{3}\right)^x$
6. $y = \left(\frac{1}{4}\right)^x$

In Exercises 7 through 12 plot graphs of the given functions for $-3 \leq y \leq 3$.

7. $y = \log_2 x$
8. $y = \log_4 x$
9. $y = \log_{3/2} x$
10. $y = \log_{4/3} x$
11. $y = 2 \log_3 x$
12. $y = 3 \log_2 (2x)$

In Exercises 13 and 14 plot the indicated graphs.

13. The electric current in a certain type of circuit is given by $i = I_0 e^{-Rt/L}$, where I_0 is the initial current, R is a resistance, and L is an inductance (see Section 11-7). Plot the graph for i vs. t for a circuit in which $I_0 = 5.0$ amps, $R = 10$ ohms, and $L = 5$ henrys. Use $e = 2.7$, and $0 \leq t < 4$ sec.

14. In the theory dealing with the optical brightness of objects, the equation $D = \log_{10} (I_0/I)$ is found. Plot the graph of D vs. I, if $I_0 = 2$ ft-candles. Use the values $I = 0.2, 2, 20,$ and 200 ft-candles.

12-3 Properties of logarithms

Since a logarithm is an exponent, it must follow the laws of exponents. Those laws which are of the greatest importance at this time are listed here for reference.

$$b^u \cdot b^v = b^{u+v} \tag{12-4}$$

$$b^u/b^v = b^{u-v} \tag{12-5}$$

$$(b^u)^n = b^{nu} \tag{12-6}$$

We shall now show how these laws for exponents give certain useful properties to logarithms.

If we let $u = \log_b x$ and $v = \log_b y$ and write these equations in exponential form, we have $x = b^u$ and $y = b^v$. Therefore, forming the product of x and y, we obtain

$$xy = b^u b^v = b^{u+v} \qquad \text{or} \qquad xy = b^{u+v}.$$

Writing this last equation in logarthmic form yields

$$u + v = \log_b xy$$

or

$$\log_b x + \log_b y = \log_b xy. \tag{12-7}$$

Equation (12-7) states the property that *the logarithm of the product of two numbers is equal to the sum of the logarithms of the numbers.*

Using the same definitions of u and v to form the quotient of x and y, we then have

$$\frac{x}{y} = \frac{b^u}{b^v} = b^{u-v} \qquad \text{or} \qquad \frac{x}{y} = b^{u-v}.$$

Writing this last equation in logarithmic form, we have

$$u - v = \log_b \left(\frac{x}{y}\right)$$

or

$$\log_b x - \log_b y = \log_b \left(\frac{x}{y}\right). \tag{12-8}$$

Equation (12-8) states the property that *the logarithm of the quotient of two numbers is equal to the logarithm of the numerator minus the logarithm of the denominator.*

If we again let $u = \log_b x$ and write this in exponential form, we have $x = b^u$. To find the nth power of x, we write

$$x^n = (b^u)^n = b^{nu}.$$

Expressing this equation in logarithmic form yields

$$nu = \log_b (x^n)$$

or

$$n \log_b x = \log_b (x^n). \tag{12-9}$$

This last equation states that *the logarithm of the nth power of a number is equal to n times the logarithm of the number.* The exponent n may be integral or fractional and, therefore, we may use Eq. (12-9) for finding powers and roots of numbers.

Example A. $\log_4 15 = \log_4 (3 \cdot 5) = \log_4 3 + \log_4 5,$
$\qquad\qquad \log_4 \left(\frac{5}{3}\right) = \log_4 5 - \log_4 3,$
$\qquad\qquad \log_4 9 = \log_4 (3^2) = 2 \log_4 3$

Example B. $\log_2 6 = \log_2 (2 \cdot 3) = \log_2 2 + \log_2 3.$

This may be simplified further if we use the definition of a logarithm.

$$\text{Log}_b b = 1$$

is a very important property of logarithms. When written in exponential form, it is nothing more than a statement of $b = b^1$. Thus $\log_2 2 = 1$, and we have

$$\log_2 6 = 1 + \log_2 3.$$

Example C. $\log_3 \left(\frac{2}{9}\right) = \log_3 2 - \log_3 9 = \log_3 2 - \log_3 (3^2)$
$$= \log_3 2 - 2 \log_3 3 = \log_3 2 - 2(1)$$
$$= \log_3 2 - 2$$

Example D. $\log_2 16 = \log_2 (2^4) = 4 \log_2 2 = 4(1) = 4$
This particular expression could have been evaluated directly from the definition of a logarithm. However, by use of Eq. (12-9), we see that the same result is obtained. Therefore, any proper method can be followed to obtain the result.

Example E. $\log_{10} \sqrt{7} = \log_{10} (7^{1/2}) = \frac{1}{2} \log_{10} 7$
This demonstrates the property which is especially useful for finding roots of numbers. We see that we need merely to multiply the logarithm of the number by the fractional exponent representing the root to obtain the logarithm of the root. Similarly,

$$\log_{10} \sqrt[5]{6} = \log_{10} (6^{1/5}) = \frac{1}{5} \log_{10} 6.$$

Example F.   Use the basic properties of logarithms to solve for y in terms of x: $\log_b y = 2 \log_b x + \log_b a$.
Using Eq. (12-9) and then Eq. (12-7), we have

$$\log_b y = \log_b (x^2) + \log_b a = \log_b (ax^2).$$

Now, since we have the logarithm to the base b of different expressions on each side of the resulting equation, the expressions must be equal. Therefore, $y = ax^2$.

Exercises

In Exercises 1 through 16 express each as a sum, difference, or multiple of logarithms. Wherever possible, evaluate logarithms of the result.

1. $\log_5 xy$

2. $\log_6 abc$

3. $\log_3 \left(\frac{r}{s}\right)$

4. $\log_2 \left(\frac{xy}{z}\right)$

5. $\log_2 (a^3)$

6. $\log_8 (n^5)$

7. $\log_3 18$

8. $\log_5 75$

9. $\log_2 \left(\frac{1}{8}\right)$

10. $\log_{10} (0.05)$

11. $\log_3 \sqrt{6}$

12. $\log_2 \sqrt[3]{24}$

13. $\log_2 (4^2 \cdot 3^3)$

14. $\log_5 \left(\frac{4}{125}\right)$

15. $\log_{10} 3000$

16. $\log_{10} (40)^2$

In Exercises 17 through 24, express each as the logarithm of a single quantity.

17. $\log_b a + \log_b c$

18. $\log_2 3 + \log_2 x$

19. $\log_5 9 - \log_5 3$

20. $\log_8 6 - \log_8 a$

21. $\log_b x^2 - \log_b \sqrt{x}$ 22. $\log_4 3^3 + \log_4 9$

23. $2 \log_e 2 + 3 \log_e n$ 24. $\frac{1}{2} \log_b a - 2 \log_b 5$

In Exercises 25 through 28 solve for y in terms of x.

25. $\log_e y = \log_e 2 + \log_e x$ 26. $\log_b y = \log_b 6 + \log_b x - \log_b \sqrt{x}$

27. $\log_{10} y = 2 \log_{10} 7 - 3 \log_{10} x$ 28. $4 \log_2 x - 2 \log_2 y = \log_2 9$

In Exercises 29 through 32 using $\log_{10} 2 = 0.301$, evaluate each of the given expressions.

29. $\log_{10} 4$ 30. $\log_{10} 20$ 31. $\log_{10} (0.5)$ 32. $\log_{10} 8000$

In Exercises 33 and 34 perform the indicated operations.

33. An equation encountered in thermodynamics is $S = C \log_e T - nR \log_e P$. Express this equation with a single logarithm on the right side.

34. An equation used for a certain electric circuit is $\log_e i - \log_e I = -t/RC$. Solve for i.

12-4 Logarithms to the base 10

In Section 10-2, we showed that any number may be expressed in scientific notation as the product of a number between 1 and 10 and a power of 10. Writing this as $N = P \times 10^k$, and taking logarithms of both sides of this equation, we have

$$\log_b N = \log_b (P \times 10^k) = \log_b P + \log_b 10^k = \log_b P + k \log_b 10.$$

If we let $b = 10$, then $k \log_{10} 10 = k$, and this equation becomes

$$\log_{10} N = k + \log_{10} P. \tag{12-10}$$

Equation (12-10) shows us that if we have a method for finding logarithms to the base 10 of numbers between 1 and 10, then we can find the logarithm of *any* number to base 10. The value of k can be found by writing the number N in scientific notation, and P is a number between 1 and 10. Logarthms to the base 10 have been tabulated, and tables of these *common logarithms* may be found in the Appendix. Logarithms may be calculated for any base, but for purposes of computation, logarithms to the base 10 are the most convenient. From now on we shall not write the number 10 to indicate the base, and log N will be assumed to be to the base 10. Thus

$$\log N = k + \log P. \tag{12-11}$$

In Eq. (12-11), k is called the *characteristic*, and log P is known as the *mantissa*. Remember, k is the power of 10 of the number, when it is written in scientific notation, and the term log P is the logarithm of the number between 1 and 10.

Example A.   For $N = 3600 = 3.6 \times 10^3$, we see that the characteristic $k = 3$, and the mantissa log $P = \log 3.6$. Therefore, log $3600 = 3 + \log 3.6$.

For $N = 80.9 = 8.09 \times 10^1$, we see that $k = 1$ and log $P = \log 8.09$. Therefore, log $80.9 = 1 + \log 8.09$.

Example B. For $N = 0.00543 = 5.43 \times 10^{-3}$, we see that $k = -3$ and log $P =$ log 5.43. Therefore, log $0.00543 = -3 + $ log 5.43.

For $N = 0.741 = 7.41 \times 10^{-1}$, we see that $k = -1$ and log $P =$ log 7.41. Therefore, log $0.741 = -1 + $ log 7.41.

To find log P we use Table 2 in the Appendix. The following examples illustrate how to use this table.

Example C. Find log 572.

We first write the number in scientific notation as 5.72×10^2. The characteristic is 2, and we must now find log 5.72. We look in the column headed N and find 57 (the first two significant digits). Then, to the right of this, we look under the column headed 2 (the third significant digit) and we find 7574. All numbers between 1 and 10 will have common logarithms between 0 and 1 (log $1 = 0$ and log $10 = 1$). Therefore log $5.72 = 0.7574$, and the logarithm of $572 = 2 + 0.7574$. We then write this in the usual form of 2.7574.

Example D. Find log 0.00485.

When we write this number in scientific notation, we have 4.85×10^{-3}, and we see that $k = -3$. From the tables we find that log $4.85 = 0.6857$. Thus log $0.00485 = -3 + 0.6857$. We do *not* write this as -3.6857, for this would say that the mantissa was also negative, which it is not. To avoid this possible confusion, we shall write it in the form $7.6857 - 10$. We shall follow this policy whenever the characteristic is negative. That is, we shall write a negative characteristic as the appropriate positive number with 10 subtracted. For example, for a characteristic of -6, we write 4 before the mantissa and -10 after it.

Example E. Other examples of logarithms are as follows.
$89,000 = 8.9 \times 10^4$: $k = 4$, log $8.9 = 0.9494$; log $89000 = 4.9494$.
$0.307 = 3.07 \times 10^{-1}$: $k = -1$, log $3.07 = 0.4871$; log $0.307 = 9.4871 - 10$.
$0.00629 = 6.29 \times 10^{-3}$: $k = -3$, log $6.29 = 0.7987$; log $0.00629 = 7.7987 - 10$.

Table 2 is a four-place table, which means that we can obtain accuracy to four significant digits. However, only three digits may be read directly, and the fourth place is found by interpolation. We discussed this in Section 3-3, in reference to finding values from trigonometric tables. The method for finding values from logarithmic tables is the same. It is illustrated in the following examples.

Example F. Find log 686300.

In scientific notation, $686300 = 6.863 \times 10^5$. This means that the characteristic is 5. To find the mantissa from the table, we must interpolate, finding the value $\frac{3}{10}$ (since the fourth digit is 3) of the way between the log 6.86 and log 6.87. These latter two values are 0.8363 and 0.8370. The tabular difference is 7, and $(\frac{3}{10})(7) = 2$ (to one significant digit). Adding this to the mantissa 0.8363 gives 0.8365. Hence log $686300 = 5.8365$.

Example G.   Find log 0.02178.

In scientific notation, $0.02178 = 2.178 \times 10^{-2}$. Therefore, the characteristic is -2. To find the mantissa, we must interpolate, finding the value $\frac{8}{10}$ of the way between log 2.17 and log 2.18. These two values are 0.3365 and 0.3385. The tabular difference is 20, and $(\frac{8}{10})(20) = 16$. Adding this to 0.3365, we find the mantissa to be 0.3381. Therefore, log $0.02178 = 8.3381 - 10$.

We may also use Table 2 to find N if we know log N. In this case we may refer to N as the *antilogarithm* of log N. The following examples illustrate the determination of antilogarithms.

Example H.   Given log $N = 1.5263$, find N.

Direct observation of the given logarithm tells us that the characteristic is 1, and that $N = P \times 10^1$. In Table 2 we find 5263 opposite 33 and under 6. Thus $P = 3.360$. This means that $N = 3.360 \times 10^1$, or in ordinary notation, $N = 33.60$.

Example I.   Given log $N = 8.2611 - 10$, find N.

Using the method described in Example D, we determine that the characteristic is $8 - 10 = -2$. We look for 0.2611 in the tables, and find that it is between 2601 (log 1.82) and 2625 (log 1.83). These latter two values have a tabular difference of 24, and the difference between 2611 and 2601 is 10. Thus the number we want is $\frac{10}{24}$, or 0.4 of the way between 1.82 and 1.83. Hence

$$N = 1.824 \times 10^{-2} = 0.01824.$$

The basic properties of logarithms allow us to find the logarithms of products, quotients, and roots. The following example illustrates the method.

Example J.   Find log $\sqrt{0.846}$.

From the properties of logarithms we write log $\sqrt{0.846} = \frac{1}{2}$ log 0.846. From the tables we find that log $8.46 = 0.9274$. Therefore log $0.846 = 9.9274 - 10$. To obtain the desired logarithm we must divide this by 2. This will result in a 5 to be subtracted. To assure our answer being in the usual form of a negative characteristic, we shall write log 0.846 as $19.9274 - 20$. Thus log $\sqrt{0.846} = 9.9637 - 10$, when we divide through by 2. In this type of problem we choose that part of the characteristic which is to be subtracted so that 10 will result after division. This is done by *adding* the proper multiple of 10 to each part of the characteristic.

Exercises

In Exercises 1 through 16 find the common logarithm of each of the given numbers.

1. 567	2. 60.5	3. 0.0640	4. 0.000566
5. 9.24×10^6	6. 3.19×10^{15}	7. 1.17×10^{-4}	8. 8.04×10^{-8}
9. 1.053	10. 73.27	11. 0.2384	12. 0.004309
13. 7.331×10^8	14. 1.656×10^{-5}	15. $\sqrt{0.002006}$	16. $\sqrt[3]{38310000}$

In Exercises 17 through 32 find the antilogarithm N from the given logarithms.

17. 4.4378   18. 0.9294   19. 8.6955 − 10   20. 3.0212 − 10
21. 3.3010   22. 8.8241   23. 9.8597 − 10   24. 7.4409 − 10
25. 1.9495   26. 2.4367   27. 6.6090 − 10   28. 9.3755 − 10
29. 0.1543   30. 10.2750   31. 17.7625 − 20   32. 35.6641 − 40

In Exercises 33 through 36 find the logarithms of the given numbers.

33. A certain radar signal has a frequency of 1.15×10^9 cycles/sec.

34. The earth travels about 595,000,000 miles in one year.

35. A certain bank charges 7.5% interest on loans that it makes.

36. The coefficient of thermal expansion of steel is about 1.2×10^{-5} per °C.

12-5 Computations using logarithms

· For many calculations the slide rule gives an adequate answer. However, if we need more than three-place accuracy, we cannot rely on the slide rule. If the fourth significant digit is desired, we can use the logarithms as given in the tables in this text. If five significant digits are desired, tables of five-place logarithms are available in many references and are used in the same manner as the four-place tables. One use for tables of logarithms, therefore, is in computations requiring more accuracy than the slide rule can provide. Also, less complicated slide rules cannot determine the answer to such problems as $\sqrt[5]{7.6}$ or $(89)^{0.3}$. The following examples illustrate the use of logarithms in computations.

Example A.   By the use of logarithms, calculate the value of $(5.670)(21.50)$.

Equation (12-7) tells us that $\log xy = \log x + \log y$. If we find log 5.670 and log 21.50 and add them, we shall have the logarithm of the product. Using this result, we look up the antilogarithm, which is the desired product.

$$\begin{aligned}
\log\ 5.670 &= 0.7536 \\
\log 21.50\ &= 1.3324 \\
\log (5.670)(21.50) &= 2.0860 \\
\log 121.9\quad &= 2.0860
\end{aligned}$$

Thus $(5.670)(21.50) = 121.9$.

Example B.   By the use of logarithms, calculate the value of $\dfrac{8.640}{45.55}$.

From Eq. (12-8), we know that $\log x/y = \log x - \log y$. Therefore, by subtracting log 45.55 from log 8.640, we shall have the logarithm of the quotient. The antilogarithm gives the desired result.

$$\begin{aligned}
\log\ 8.640 &= 10.9365 - 10 \\
\log 45.55\ &= \underline{\ 1.6585} \\
\log (8.640/45.55) &= \ 9.2780 - 10.
\end{aligned}$$

We wrote the characteristic of log 8.640 as $10 - 10$, so that when we subtracted, the part of the result containing the mantissa would be positive although the characteristic was negative. The antilogarithm of $9.2780 - 10$ is 0.1897. Therefore,

$$\frac{8.640}{45.55} = 0.1897.$$

Example C.   By the use of logarithms, calculate the value of $\sqrt[5]{0.03760}$.

From Eq. (12-9), we know that log $x^n = n$ log x. Therefore, by writing $\sqrt[5]{0.03760} = (0.03760)^{1/5}$, we know that we can find the logarithm of the result by multiplying log 0.03760 by $\frac{1}{5}$. Now, log $0.03760 = 8.5752 - 10$. Since we wish to multiply this by $\frac{1}{5}$, we shall write this logarithm as

$$\log 0.03760 = 48.5752 - 50$$

by adding and subtracting 40. Multiplying by $\frac{1}{5}$, we have

$$\tfrac{1}{5} \log 0.03760 = \tfrac{1}{5}(48.5752 - 50) = 9.7150 - 10.$$

The antilogarithm of $9.7150 - 10$ is 0.5188. Therefore, $\sqrt[5]{0.03760} = 0.5188$.

The following examples illustrate calculations which involve the use of a combination of the basic properties of logarithms.

Example D.   Calculate the value of

$$N = \frac{6.875 \sqrt{98.66}}{7.880}.$$

$$\log N = \log 6.875 + \tfrac{1}{2} \log 98.66 \ - \log 7.880,$$
$$\log 6.875 = 0.8373, \qquad \log 98.66 = 1.9941,$$
$$\tfrac{1}{2} \log 98.66 = 0.9970$$
$$\overline{1.8343}$$
$$\log 7.880 = 0.8965$$
$$\log N \quad\;\, = 0.9378, \qquad N = 8.666.$$

Example E.   Calculate the value of

$$N = \left[\frac{(0.05325) \sqrt{0.8884}}{\sqrt[3]{895.3}} \right]^{0.3}.$$

$$\log N = 0.3 \,(\log 0.05325 + \tfrac{1}{2} \log 0.8884 - \tfrac{1}{3} \log 895.3),$$
$$\log 0.05325 = \; 8.7263 - 10, \qquad \log 0.8884 = 19.9486 - 20,$$
$$\tfrac{1}{2} \log 0.8884 = \; 9.9743 - 10$$
$$\overline{18.7006 - 20}$$
$$\tfrac{1}{3} \log 895.3 \;\; = \; 0.9840 \qquad\qquad \log 895.3 \;\; = 2.9520,$$
$$\overline{17.7166 - 20}$$
$$0.3(97.7166 - 100) = 29.3150 - 30, \qquad N = 0.2065.$$

Example F.   The velocity of an object moving with constant acceleration can be found from the equation $v = \sqrt{v_0^2 + 2as}$, where v_0 is the initial velocity, a is the acceleration, and s is the distance traveled. Determine the velocity of an object if $v_0 = 86.46$ ft/sec, $a = 17.92$ ft/sec^2, and $s = 136.7$ ft.

Before we can compute the square root, we must square v_0 and determine the product $2as$, and add these results. Another calculation is then necessary to determine the square root:

$$\log v_0^2 = 2 \log 86.46 = 2(1.9368) = 3.8736, \qquad v_0^2 = 7475,$$
$$\log 2as = \log 2 + \log 17.92 + \log 136.7,$$
$$\log 2 \quad = 0.3010$$
$$\log 17.92 = 1.2534$$
$$\log 136.7 = 2.1357$$
$$\log 2as \quad = 3.6901 \qquad\qquad 2as = \underline{\ \ 4899}$$
$$v_0^2 + 2as = 12374$$
$$\log v \quad = \tfrac{1}{2} \log 12370 = \tfrac{1}{2}(4.0924) = 2.0462,$$
$$v \quad = 111.2 \text{ ft/sec.}$$

Note that 12374 was rounded off to 12370 for purposes of calculation, since only four significant digits can be used.

Exercises

In the following exercises use logarithms to perform the indicated calculations.

1. $(5.980)(10.80)$

2. $(0.7640)(200.0)$

3. $(0.8256)(0.04532)$

4. $(0.0008080)(2623)$

5. $\dfrac{790.0}{8.000}$

6. $\dfrac{31.60}{0.4500}$

7. $\dfrac{76.98}{43.82}$

8. $\dfrac{0.008670}{0.6521}$

9. $(6.760)^3$

10. $(0.04030)^{0.6}$

11. $(0.9042)^5$

12. $(9065)^8$

13. $\sqrt[7]{7.090}$

14. $\sqrt[3]{95.40}$

15. $\sqrt{641.6}$

16. $\sqrt[8]{308.7}$

17. $\dfrac{(4510)(0.6120)}{738.0}$

18. $\dfrac{87.42}{(11.54)(0.9316)}$

19. $\dfrac{\sqrt{0.07530}}{86.02}$

20. $(\sqrt{5.270})(\sqrt[3]{42.19})$

21. $\dfrac{89.42\sqrt[3]{0.1142}}{0.04290}$

22. $\left(\dfrac{75.19}{900.5\sqrt{15.00}}\right)^{0.1}$

23. $(8.723)^{9.742}$ (Find log log 8.723.)

24. $(4.072)^{-10}$ (Be careful, especially if your method of solution leads to a negative "mantissa.")

25. The ratio of the rates of diffusion of two gases is given by the equation $r_1/r_2 = \sqrt{m_2}/\sqrt{m_1}$, where m_1 and m_2 are the masses of the molecules of the gases. Given that $m_1 = 31.44$ units of mass and $m_2 = 74.92$ units of mass, calculate the ratio of r_1 to r_2.

26. The molecular weight M of a gas may be calculated by the formula $PV = wRT/M$, where P is the pressure, V is the volume, w is the mass, R is a constant for all gases, and T is the absolute temperature. Determine M, given that $P = 1.067$ atm, $V = 0.2485$ liter, $R = 0.08208$ liter-atm/mole-°K, $T = 373.6$°K and $w = 1.267$ gm.

27. The velocity of sound in air is given by $v = \sqrt{1.410p/d}$, where p is the pressure and d is the density. Given that $p = 1.013 \times 10^6$ dynes/cm² and $d = 1.293 \times 10^{-3}$ gm/cm³, find v.

28. In undergoing an adiabatic (no *heat* gained or lost) expansion, the relation between the initial and final temperatures and volumes is given by $T_f = T_i(V_i/V_f)^{0.4}$, where the temperatures are the absolute temperatures. Given that $V_i = 1.506$ in³, $V_f = 0.1290$ in³ and $T_i = 373.2$°K, find T_f.

29. Given the density of iron as 491.0 lb/ft³, find the radius of a spherical iron ball which weighs 25.65 lb.

30. When a light ray is incident on glass, the percentage of light reflected is given by

$$I_r = 100\left(1 - \frac{4n_a n_g}{(n_a + n_g)^2}\right),$$

where n_a and n_g are the indices of refraction of air and glass, respectively. What percentage of light is reflected if $n_g = 1.532$ and $n_a = 1.000$?

12-6 Logarithms of trigonometric functions

When we are working with trigonometric functions, we sometimes require accuracy greater than that available on the slide rule. In such cases, if we wish to use logarithms, we could look up the function of the desired angle and then find the logarithm of this number to perform some operation on it.

Example A.   Find log sin 23°20′. (Use Tables 2 and 3.)

$$\sin 23°20′ = 0.3961, \qquad \log 0.3961 = 9.5978 - 10.$$

To facilitate work when using trigonometric functions, we can use tables of logarithms of the trigonometric functions, which allow us to find these logarithms in one step.

Example B.   Find log sin 23°20′. (Use Table 4.)
By direct reading we find log sin 23°20′ = 9.5978 − 10.

Like other similar tables, these tables enable us to find by interpolation values not directly listed. We may also find an angle directly, if we know the logarithm of some function of that angle.

Example C.   Find log tan 57°34′.
We find that log tan 57°30′ = 0.1958 and that log tan 57°40′ = 0.1986. The tabular difference is 28, and 0.4(28) = 11 (to 2 digits). Thus

$$\log \tan 57°34′ = 0.1969.$$

Example D.   Given that log cos θ = 9.9049 − 10, find θ.
   From Table 4 we find that

$$\log \cos 36°30' = 9.9052 - 10$$

and

$$\log \cos 36°40' = 9.9042 - 10.$$

We find that the tabular difference between listed values is 10, and the tabular difference between 9.9049 and 9.9052 is 3. Therefore

$$\theta = 36°33'.$$

(Be careful—the values of the cosine and its logarithm *decrease* as θ increases.)

Example E.   Solve the following oblique triangle, using logarithms for your calculations: $a = 34.12$, $A = 31°20'$, $B = 52°43'$.
   We first determine that the solution may be completed by the law of sines. Next we find $C = 95°57'$, and then we can find sides b and c. From the law of sines we have

$$b = \frac{a \sin B}{\sin A} \quad \text{and} \quad c = \frac{a \sin C}{\sin A}.$$

By using a and sin A in both calculations, we reduce the amount of information required from the tables.

$$\log b = \log 34.12 + \log \sin 52°43' - \log \sin 31°20',$$

$$
\begin{array}{ll}
\log 34.12 & = \quad 1.5330 \\
\log \sin 52°43' & = \quad 9.9007 - 10 \\
& \quad \overline{11.4337 - 10} \\
\log \sin 31°20' & = \quad 9.7160 - 10 \\
& \quad \overline{1.7177}
\end{array}
$$

$$b = 52.20$$

$$\log c = \log 34.12 + \log \sin 95°57' - \log \sin 31°20'$$

$$
\begin{array}{ll}
\log 34.12 & = \quad 1.5330 \\
\log \sin 95°57' & = \quad 9.9976 - 10 \;\; (\log \sin 84°3') \\
& \quad \overline{11.5306 - 10} \\
\log \sin 31°20' & = \quad 9.7160 - 10 \\
& \quad \overline{1.8146}
\end{array}
$$

$$c = 65.26$$

Example F.   A ship passes a certain point at noon going north at 12.35 mi/hr. A second ship passes the same point at 1 PM going east at 16.42 mi/hr. How far apart are the ships at 3 PM?

At 3 PM the first ship is 37.05 mi from the point and the second ship is 32.84 mi from it (Fig. 12-4). Since the angle between their directions is 90°, the distance d between them can be found from the Pythagorean theorem. Also, by finding the angle α from tan α = 37.05/32.84, we can then solve for d by using d = 32.84/cos α. This second method has the advantage that once we determine α, we can find log cos α immediately from the table by shifting from the log tan column to the log cos column:

log tan α = log 37.05 − log 32.84,

$$\log 37.05 = 1.5688$$
$$\underline{\log 32.84 = 1.5164}$$
$$\log \tan \alpha = 0.0524$$
$$\alpha = 48°27'$$

$$\log d = \log 32.84 - \log \cos \alpha,$$
$$\log 32.84 = 11.5164 - 10$$
$$\underline{\log \cos \alpha = \ \ 9.8217 - 10}$$
$$\log d = \ \ 1.6947$$
$$d = 49.51 \text{ mi.}$$

Figure 12-4

Exercises

In Exercises 1 through 12 use Table 4 to find the values of the indicated logarithms.

1. log sin 22°10′
2. log cos 31°40′
3. log sec 52°
4. log csc 61°50′
5. log sin 38°14′
6. log cos 12°7′
7. log tan 56°45′
8. log sin 75°42′
9. log cos 322°17′
10. log cot 228°12′
11. log cos 79°6′
12. log tan 85°52′

In Exercises 13 through 20 use Table 4 to find the smallest positive θ.

13. log sin θ = 9.6740 − 10
14. log sec θ = 0.0748
15. log cos θ = 9.8056 − 10
16. log tan θ = 9.9140 − 10
17. log tan θ = 0.0599
18. log sin θ = 8.9150 − 10
19. log cos θ = 9.9998 − 10
20. log csc θ = 0.0075

In Exercises 21 through 28 solve the given triangles by logarithms.

21. $A = 82°5', C = 90°, c = 86.17$
22. $B = 54°10', C = 90°, b = 15.70$
23. $A = 65°40', B = 72°10', a = 9100$
24. $A = 63°14', C = 18°16', c = 0.5320$
25. $A = 67°10', B = 44°42', b = 9.328$
26. $A = 47°36', a = 17.45, b = 10.29$
27. $a = 298.5, b = 382.6, C = 90°$
28. $a = 7392, b = 4218, c = 4005$

In Exercises 29 through 33 solve the given problems by logarithms.

29. A 56.62-lb block is on an inclined plane which makes an angle of 22°42′ with respect to the horizontal. What are the components of the weight parallel to and perpendicular to the plane?

30. A surveyor finds one side of a rectangular piece of land to be 137.8 ft, and the angle between this side and the diagonal to be 36°17′. What is the area of the piece of land?

31. Two spring balances support an object as shown in Fig. 12-5. What is the weight of the object? We can find T_2 by using the fact that there is no net force acting horizontally. This means that

$$T_1 \sin \alpha = T_2 \sin \beta.$$

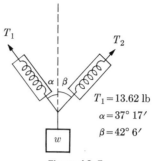

$T_1 = 13.62$ lb

$\alpha = 37° \; 17'$

$\beta = 42° \; 6'$

Figure 12-5

32. An airplane headed south has a speed with respect to the air of 418.5 mi/hr. The speed with respect to the ground is 425.0 mi/hr in a direction of 3°16′ east of south. Find the direction and speed of the wind.

33. For a given electrical circuit, $R = 21.35$ ohms and $X_C = 13.37$ ohms. Find the phase angle between the current and voltage (see Section 11-7).

12-7 Logarithms to bases other than 10

Another number which is important as a base of logarithms is the number e. We previously encountered e when we discussed the exponential form of a complex number. From that discussion, we recall that e is an irrational number equal to about 2.718.

Logarithms to the base e are called *natural logarithms*. Just as the notation $\log x$ refers to logarithms to the base 10, the notation $\ln x$ is used to denote logarithms to the base e.

Since more than one base is important, there are times when it is useful to be able to change a logarithm in one base to another base. If $u = \log_b x$, then $b^u = x$. Taking logarithms of both sides of this last expression to the base a, we have

$$\log_a b^u = \log_a x,$$
$$u \log_a b = \log_a x.$$

Solving this last equation for u, we have

$$u = \frac{\log_a x}{\log_a b}.$$

However, $u = \log_b x$, which means that

$$\log_b x = \frac{\log_a x}{\log_a b}. \tag{12-12}$$

Equation (12-12) allows us to change a logarithm in one base to a logarithm in another base. The following examples illustrate the method of performing this operation.

Example A.   Change log 20 = 1.3010 to a logarithm with base e; that is, find ln 20 .

In Eq. (12-12), if we let $b = e$ and $a = 10$, we have

$$\log_e x = \frac{\log_{10} x}{\log_{10} e},$$

or

$$\ln x = \frac{\log x}{\log e}.$$

In this example, $x = 20$. Therefore,

$$\ln 20 = \frac{\log 20}{\log e} = \frac{\log 20}{\log 2.718} = \frac{1.3010}{0.4343}.$$

This indicated division can itself be found by logarithms. Therefore,

$$\log 1.301 \ = 10.1143 - 10$$
$$\log 0.4343 = \ \underline{9.6378 - 10}$$
$$0.4765$$

The antilogarithm of 0.4765 is 2.996. Therefore, ln 20 = 2.996.

Example B.   Find $\log_5 560$.

In Eq. (12-12), if we let $b = 5$, and $a = 10$, we have

$$\log_5 x = \frac{\log x}{\log 5}.$$

In this example, $x = 560$. Therefore, we have

$$\log_5 560 = \frac{\log 560}{\log 5} = \frac{2.7482}{0.6990}.$$

Performing this division by logarithms, we have

$$\log 2.748 \ = 10.4390 - 10$$
$$\log 0.6990 = \ \underline{9.8445 - 10}$$
$$0.5945$$

(Note that 2.7482 was rounded off to four digits and written as 2.748, because we are using our four-place table.) The antilogarithm of 0.5945 is 3.931. Therefore, $\log_5 560 = 3.931$.

Example C.   Given that ln 80 = 4.382 and ln 10 = 2.303, find log 80.

In Eq. (12-12), if we choose $b = 10$, and $a = e$, we have

$$\log x = \frac{\ln x}{\ln 10}.$$

In this example, $x = 80$. Therefore,

$$\log 80 = \frac{\ln 80}{\ln 10} = \frac{4.382}{2.303}.$$

Performing this division by logarithms, we have

$$\log 4.382 = 0.6417$$

$$\log 2.303 = \frac{0.3623}{0.2794}.$$

The antilogarithm of $0.2794 = 1.903$. Therefore, from this calculation, $\log 80 = 1.903$. From the table we find that $\log 80 = 1.9031$. It can be seen that these two values agree to three decimal places.

Example D. Find $\ln 0.811$.

Following the procedure used in Example A, we have

$$\ln x = \frac{\log x}{\log e}.$$

In this case $x = 0.811$. Here we shall not express the characteristic of $\log 0.811$ as $9 - 10$. We are not using this logarithm for calculation, but as part of a calculation, and we need its value in its explicit form. Therefore, $\log 0.811 = 9.9090 - 10 = -0.0910$. Therefore,

$$\ln 0.811 = \frac{\log 0.811}{\log 2.718}$$

$$= \frac{-0.0910}{0.4343} = -0.2095.$$

The numerical value of this quotient also can be determined by using logarithms.

Exercises

In Exercises 1 through 12 use logarithms to the base 10 to find the natural logarithms of the given numbers.

1. 26.0	2. 51.4	3. 631	4. 293
5. 1.56	6. 1.39	7. 45.7	8. 65.6
9. 0.501	10. 0.991	11. 0.052	12. 0.0020

In Exercises 13 through 16 use logarithms to the base 10 to find the indicated logarithms.

13. $\log_7 42$ 14. $\log_{12} 122$ 15. $\log_2 86$ 16. $\log_{20} 86$

In Exercises 17 through 20 use $\ln 10 = 2.303$ and the indicated natural logarithm to find the indicated logarithms.

17. $\log 40$ ($\ln 40 = 3.689$)   18. $\log 150$ ($\ln 150 = 5.011$)
19. $\log 2.02$ ($\ln 2.02 = 0.7031$)   20. $\log 4.95$ ($\ln 4.95 = 1.5994$)

In Exercises 21 through 23 find the indicated values.

21. If 100 mg of radium radioactively decays, an equation relating the amount Q which remains, and the time t is

$$\ln Q - \ln 100 = kt,$$

where k is a constant. If $Q = 90$ mg, and $k = -0.00041$ per yr, find t.

22. Under specific conditions, an equation relating the pressure P and volume V of a gas is $\ln P = C - \gamma \ln V$, where C and γ (the Greek gamma) are constants. Find P (in atmospheres) if $C = 3.000$, $\gamma = 1.50$ and $V = 2.20$ ft³.

23. For a certain electric circuit, the voltage v is given by $v = e^{-0.1t}$. What is $\ln v$ after 2 sec?

12-8 Graphs on logarithmic paper

If, when we are graphing, the range of values of one variable is much greater than the corresponding range of values of the other variable, it is often convenient to use what is known as semilogarithmic paper. On this paper the y-axis (usually) is marked off in distances proportional to the logarithms of numbers. This means that the distances between numbers on this axis are not even, but this system does allow for a much greater range of values. There is another advantage to this paper: Many equations which would exhibit more complex curves on ordinary graph paper will work out as straight lines on semilogarithmic paper. In many instances this makes the analysis of the curve easier.

If we wish to indicate a large range of values for each of the variables, we use what is known as logarithmic paper. Both axes are marked off with logarithmic scales. Again, the more complicated equations give simple curves or straight lines on this paper.

Logarithmic scales are also used in the construction of the slide rule. When we multiply on the slide rule we are adding logarithmic distances, and therefore we are using the properties of logarithms. There are two equal portions of the A-scale for each corresponding length of the D-scale. This is due to the fact that $\log N^2 = 2 \log N$. The other scales are constructed in a similar manner.

The following examples will illustrate the use of semilogarithmic and logarithmic paper.

Example A.   Construct a graph of $y = 4(3)^x$ on semilogarithmic paper.
First we construct a table of values.

x	-1	0	1	2	3	4	5
y	1.3	4	12	36	108	324	972

The resulting graph is a straight line, as we see in Fig. 12-6. Taking logarithms of both sides of the equation, we have

$$\log y = \log 4 + x \log 3.$$

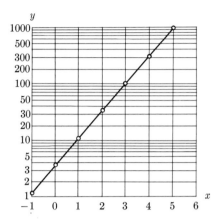

Figure 12-6

However, since log y was plotted automatically (because we used semilogarithmic paper), the graph really represents

$$u = \log 4 + x \log 3,$$

where $u = \log y$; log 3 and log 4 are constants, and therefore this equation is of the form $u = ax + b$, which is a straight line (see Section 4-2). If we had sketched this graph on regular coordinate paper, the scale would be so reduced that the values of 0.5, 1.3, 4, 12, and 36 would appear at practically the same level.

Example B. Construct the graph of $x^4y^2 = 1$ on logarithmic paper.

First we construct a table of values.

x	0.5	1	2	8	20
y	4	1	0.25	0.0156	0.0025

We again note that we have a straight line. Taking logarithms of both sides of the equation, we have

$$4 \log x + 2 \log y = 0.$$

If we let $u = \log y$ and $v = \log x$, we then have

$$4v + 2u = 0 \qquad \text{or} \qquad u = -2v,$$

which is the equation of a straight line as shown in Fig. 12-7. It should be pointed out that not all graphs on logarithmic paper are straight lines.

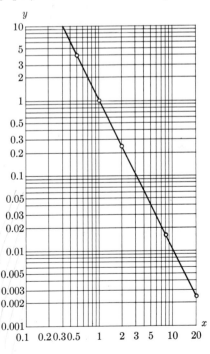

Figure 12-7

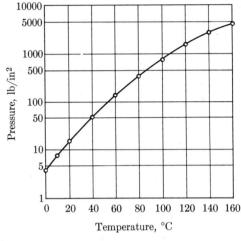

Figure 12-8

Logarithmic and semilogarithmic paper is often useful for plotting data derived from experimentation. Often the data cover too large a range of values to be plotted on ordinary graph paper. The following example illustrates how we use semilogarithmic paper to plot data.

Example C. The vapor pressure of water depends on the temperature. The following table gives the vapor pressure (in lb/in²) for corresponding values of temperature (in °C).

Pressure	4.58	8.94	17.5	55.1	149	355	760	1490	2710	4630
Temp.	0	10	20	40	60	80	100	120	140	160

These data are then plotted on semilogarithmic paper, as shown in Fig. 12-8. Intermediate values of temperature and pressure can then be read directly from the graph.

Exercises

In Exercises 1 through 6 plot the graphs of the given functions on semilogarithmic paper.

1. $y = 2^x$ 2. $y = 2(4^x)$
3. $y = 5(10^x)$ 4. $y = 2^{-x}$
5. $y = x^3$ 6. $y = 2x^4$

In Exercises 7 through 12 plot the graphs of the given functions on logarithmic paper.

7. $xy = 4$ 8. $xy^2 = 10$
9. $y^2x = 1$ 10. $x^2y^3 = 1$
11. $x^2y^2 = 25$ 12. $x^3y = 8$

In Exercises 13 through 16 plot the indicated graphs.

13. The atmospheric pressure p at a given height h is given by the equation $p = p_0 e^{-kh}$, where p_0 and k are constants. On semilogarithmic paper plot p in atmospheres vs. h in feet for $0 \leq h \leq 10^5$. Use $e = 2.7$, $p_0 = 1$ atm, and $k = 10^{-5}$ per ft.

14. At constant temperature, the relation between the volume V and pressure P of a gas is $PV = c$, where c is a constant. On logarithmic paper, plot the graph of P (in atm) vs V (in ft³) for $c = 4$ atm-ft³. Use values of $0.1 \leq P \leq 10$.

15. One end of a very hot steel bar is sprayed with a stream of cool water. The rate of cooling as a function of the distance from the end of the bar is then measured. The following results are obtained.

Cooling rate, °F/sec	600	190	100	72	46	29	17	10	6
Distance, in.	0.0625	0.125	0.1875	0.25	0.375	0.50	0.75	1.0	1.5

Plot the data on logarithmic paper. Such experiments are made to determine the hardenability of steel.

16. The magnetic intensity H (in amp-turns/m) and flux density B (in webers/m²) of annealed iron are given in the following table.

H	10	50	100	150	200	500	1000	10000	100000
B	0.0042	0.043	0.67	1.01	1.18	1.44	1.58	1.72	2.26

Plot these data (H versus B) on logarithmic paper.

12-9 Miscellaneous Exercises

In Exercises 1 through 12 determine the value of x.

1. $\log_{10} x = 4$
2. $\log_9 x = 3$
3. $\log_5 x = -1$
4. $\log_4 x = -\frac{1}{2}$
5. $\log_2 64 = x$
6. $\log_{12} 144 = x$
7. $\log_8 32 = x$
8. $\log_9 27 = x$
9. $\log_x 36 = 2$
10. $\log_x 243 = 5$
11. $\log_x 10 = \frac{1}{2}$
12. $\log_x 8 = \frac{3}{4}$

In Exercises 13 through 16 express each as a sum, difference or multiple of logarithms. Wherever possible, evaluate logarithms of the result.

13. $\log_2 28$
14. $\log_6 \left(\frac{5}{36}\right)$
15. $\log_4 \sqrt{48}$
16. $\log_3 (9^2 \cdot 6^3)$

In Exercises 17 through 20, solve for y in terms of x.

17. $\log_6 y = \log_6 4 - \log_6 x$
18. $\log_3 y = \frac{1}{2} \log_3 7 + \frac{1}{2} \log_3 x$
19. $\log_2 y + \log_2 x = 3$
20. $6 \log_4 y = 8 \log_4 4 - 3 \log_4 x$

In Exercises 21 through 32 use logarithms to perform the indicated calculations.

21. $(13.60)(0.6930)$

22. $(0.07255)(4320)$

23. $\dfrac{9.826}{0.08004}$

24. $\dfrac{87.64}{108.2}$

25. $(5.670)^{20}$

26. $(0.9823)^{10}$

27. $\sqrt[4]{17.22}$

28. $(0.006247)^{0.2}$

29. $\dfrac{\sqrt{8645}}{19.49}$

30. $[(9.060)(13.45)]^{1/3}$

31. $\dfrac{\sqrt[5]{22.46}\,(14.98)}{\sqrt[3]{0.8664}}$

32. $(12.66)^{1.096}$

In Exercises 33 and 34, use logarithms to solve the given triangles.

33. $A = 45°00'$, $B = 67°10'$, $a = 76.50$ 34. $B = 123°00'$, $C = 15°43'$, $a = 0.9122$

In Exercises 35 through 38, by using logarithms to the base 10, find the natural logarithms of the given numbers.

35. 8.86   36. 33.0   37. 2.07   38. 0.542

In Exercises 39 through 46, use logarithms to make any indicated calculations.

39. The vapor pressure P over a liquid may be related to temperature by $\log P = a/T + b$, where a and b are constants. Solve for P.

40. The Beer-Lambert law of light absorption may be expressed as

$$\log \frac{I}{I_0} = -\alpha x,$$

where I/I_0 is that fraction of the incident light beam which is transmitted, α is a constant, and x is the distance the light travels through the medium. Solve for I.

41. Under certain circumstances the efficiency of an internal combustion engine is given by

$$\text{eff (in percent)} = 100 \left(1 - \frac{1}{(V_1/V_2)^{0.4}} \right),$$

where V_1 and V_2 are, respectively, the maximum and minimum volumes of air in a cylinder. The ratio V_1/V_2 is called the compression ratio. Compute the efficiency of an engine with a compression ratio of 6.550.

42. If P dollars are invested at an interest rate r which is compounded n times a year, the value A of the investment t years later is given by the formula

$$A = P(1 + r/n)^{nt}.$$

What is the value after 5 years of \$5636 invested at $4\frac{1}{2}\%$ and compounded quarterly?

43. Points A and B are on opposite sides of a lake. A third point C is found such that $AC = 402.5$ ft and $BC = 317.9$ ft. What is the distance AB if the angle BAC is 41°18'?

44. The Nernst equation,

$$E = E_0 - \frac{0.05910}{n} \log Q,$$

is used for oxidation-reduction reactions. In the equation, E and E_0 are voltages, n is the number of electrons involved in the reaction, and Q is a measure of the activity of reaction. Given that $E_0 = 1.1000$ volts, $E = 1.1300$ volts, and $n = 2$, what is the value of Q?

45. Under certain conditions, the potential (in volts) due to a magnet is given by $V = -k \ln (1 + l/b)$, with l the length of the magnet and b the distance from the point where the potential is measured. Find V, if $k = 2$ units, $l = 5.00$ cm, and $b = 2.00$ cm.

46. The luminous efficiency (measured in lumens/watt) of a tungsten lamp as a function of its input power (in watts) is given by the following table. On semilogarithmic paper, plot efficiency versus power.

Efficiency	7.8	10.4	11.7	13.9	16.3	18.3	19.9	21.5
Power	10	25	40	60	100	200	500	1000

Additional Types of Equations and Systems of Equations

13

13-1 Graphical solution of systems of equations

In Chapter 2 we learned how to graph a function as well as how to solve equations graphically. Since then we have dealt with methods for solving quadratic equations and systems of linear equations. Also, we have graphed the trigonometric, logarithmic, and exponential functions. In this section we shall introduce one more general type of equation: the general quadratic equation. We shall then discuss graphical solutions of systems of equations involving quadratic equations as well as other types of equations. Here again, as in solving systems of linear equations, we shall obtain the desired solution by finding the values of x and y which satisfy both equations in a system at the same time. From the standpoint of graphs, this means that we wish to find all points which the graphs of the given functions have in common.

An equation of the form

$$ax^2 + bxy + cy^2 + dx + ey + f = 0 \qquad (13\text{-}1)$$

is called a *general quadratic equation in x and y.* We shall be interested primarily in some special cases of this equation. The graphs of the various possible forms of this equation result in curves known as *conic sections.* These curves are the circle, parabola, ellipse, and hyperbola. The following examples will illustrate these curves. A more complete discussion will be found in Chapter 20.

Example A. Plot the graph of the equation $x^2 + y^2 = 25$.

We first solve this equation for y, obtaining $y = \pm\sqrt{25 - x^2}$. We now assume values for x and find the corresponding values for y.

x	0	± 1	± 2	± 3	± 4	± 5
y	± 5	± 4.9	± 4.6	± 4	± 3	0

If we try values greater than 5, we have imaginary numbers. These cannot be plotted, for we assume that both x and y are real. (The complex plane is only for *numbers* of the form $a + bj$ and does not represent pairs of numbers representing two variables.) When we give the value $x = \pm 4$ when $y = \pm 3$, this is simply a short way of representing 4 points. These points are $(4, 3)$, $(4, -3)$, $(-4, 3)$, $(-4, -3)$. We note in Fig. 13-1 that the resulting curve is a circle. A circle always results from an equation of the form $x^2 + y^2 = r^2$, and r is the radius of the circle.

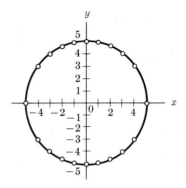

Figure 13-1

Example B. Plot the graph of the equation $y = 3x^2 - 6x$.

We plotted curves of this form in Section 2-3, and we follow the same method here.

x	-1	0	1	2	3
y	9	0	-3	0	9

This curve (Fig. 13-2) is called a *parabola*. A parabola always results if the equation is of the form $y = ax^2 + dx + f$.

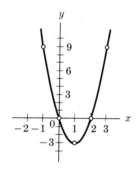

Figure 13-2

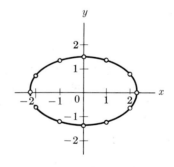

Figure 13-3

Example C. Plot the graph of the equation $2x^2 + 5y^2 = 10$.

We first solve for y, then we construct the table of values.

$$y = \pm \sqrt{\frac{10 - 2x^2}{5}}.$$

x	0	± 1	± 2	$\pm \sqrt{5} \, (= \pm 2.2)$
y	± 1.4	± 1.3	± 0.6	0

Values of x greater than $\sqrt{5}$ result in imaginary values of y. The curve (Fig. 13-3) is an *ellipse*. An ellipse results from an equation of the form $ax^2 + cy^2 = k$.

Example D.   Plot the graph of the equation $xy = 4$.

Solving for y, we obtain $y = 4/x$. Now, constructing the table of values, we have the following points.

x	-8	-4	-2	-1	$-\frac{1}{2}$	$\frac{1}{2}$	1	2	4	8
y	$-\frac{1}{2}$	-1	-2	-4	-8	8	4	2	1	$\frac{1}{2}$

Plotting these points, we obtain the curve in Fig. 13-4. This curve is called a *hyperbola*. A hyperbola always results if the equation is of the form $xy = k$. We also obtain a hyperbola if the equation is of the form $ax^2 - cy^2 = k$.

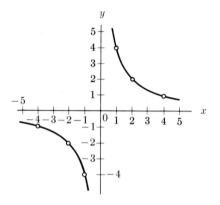

Figure 13-4

To solve any systems of equations graphically, we need only graph the equations and then find the points of intersection. If the curves do not intersect, the system has no real solution.

Example E.   Graphically solve the system of equations

$$2x^2 - y^2 = 4,$$
$$x - 3y = 6.$$

We should recognize the second equation as that of a straight line. Now constructing the tables, we solve $2x^2 - y^2 = 4$ for y and get $y = \pm \sqrt{2x^2 - 4}$. Therefore we obtain the following table.

x	± 1.4	± 2	± 4	± 6
y	0	± 2	± 5.3	± 8.2

For the straight line we have the points

x	0	6	3
y	-2	0	-1

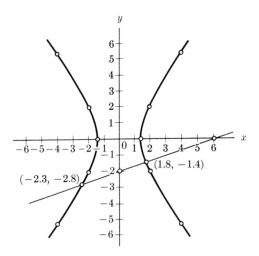

Figure 13-5

The solutions, as indicated on the graph in Fig. 13-5, are approximately $x = 1.8$, $y = -1.4$, and $x = -2.3$, $y = -2.8$.

The following example illustrates the graphical solution of a system of equations in which one of the equations is not algebraic.

Example F.   Graphically solve the system of equations

$$9x^2 + 4y^2 = 36,$$
$$y = 3^x.$$

The first equation is of the form represented by an ellipse, as indicated in Example C. The second equation is an exponential function, as discussed in Chapter 12. Solving the first equation for y, we have $y = \pm \frac{1}{2}\sqrt{36 - 9x^2}$. Substituting values for x, we obtain the following table.

x	0	± 1	± 2
y	± 3	± 2.6	0

For the exponential function, we obtain the following table.

x	-3	-2	-1	0	1	2
y	$\frac{1}{27}$	$\frac{1}{9}$	$\frac{1}{3}$	1	3	9

We plot these curves as shown in Fig. 13-6. The points of intersection are approximately $x = -1.9$, $y = 0.1$, and $x = 0.9$, $y = 2.7$.

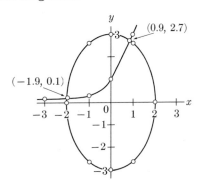

Figure 13-6

Example G.   Graphically solve the system of equations

$$x^2 = 2y,$$
$$3x - y = 5.$$

We note that the two curves in this system are a parabola and a straight line. Solving the equation of the parabola for y, we obtain $y = \frac{1}{2}x^2$. We construct the following table.

x	0	± 1	± 2	± 3	± 4
y	0	$\frac{1}{2}$	2	$\frac{9}{2}$	8

For the straight line we have the following points:

x	0	$\frac{5}{3}$	3
y	-5	0	4

We plot these curves and see in Fig. 13-7 that they do not intersect, so we conclude that there are no real solutions to the system.

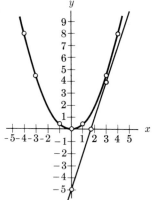

Figure 13-7

Exercises

In the following exercises solve the given systems of equations graphically.

1. $y = 2x$
   $x^2 + y^2 = 16$

2. $3x - y = 4$
   $y = 6 - 2x^2$

3. $x^2 + 2y^2 = 8$
   $x - 2y = 4$

4. $y = 3x - 6$
   $xy = 6$

5. $y = x^2 - 2$
   $4y = 12x - 17$

6. $x^2 + 4y^2 = 4$
   $2y = 12 - x$

7. $y = -x^2 + 4$
   $x^2 + y^2 = 9$

8. $y = 2x^2 - 1$
   $x^2 + 2y^2 = 16$

9. $x^2 - 4y^2 = 16$
   $x^2 + y^2 = 1$

10. $y = 2x^2 - 4x$
    $xy = -4$

11. $2x^2 + 3y^2 = 19$
    $x^2 + y^2 = 9$

12. $x^2 - y^2 = 4$
    $2x^2 + y^2 = 16$

13. $x^2 + y^2 = 1$
    $xy = \frac{1}{2}$

14. $x^2 + y^2 = 25$
    $x^2 - y^2 = 7$

15. $y = x^2$
    $y = \sin x$

16. $y = 2^x$
    $x^2 + y^2 = 4$

17. $x^2 - y^2 = 1$
    $y = \log_2 x$

18. $y = \cos x$
    $y = \log_3 x$

19. A rectangular field has a perimeter of 1140 yd and an area of 75,600 yd². Show that the equations necessary to find the dimensions l and w are $l + w = 570$, $lw = 75600$. Graphically solve for l and w.

20. The diagonal of a rectangular metal plate is 10 in. and the area is 50 in². Show that the equations necessary to find the dimensions l and w are $l^2 + w^2 = 100$, $lw = 50$. Graphically solve for l and w.

13-2 Algebraic solution of systems of equations

Often the graphical method is the easiest way to solve a system of equations. However, this method does not usually give an exact answer. Using algebraic methods to find exact solutions for some systems of equations is either not possible or quite involved. There are some systems, however, which do lend themselves to relatively simple solutions by algebraic means. In this section we shall consider two useful methods, both of which we discussed before when we were studying systems of linear equations.

The first method is substitution. If we can solve one equation for one of its variables, we can substitute this solution into the other equation. We then have only one unknown in the resulting equation, and we can solve this equation by methods discussed in earlier chapters.

Example A.   Solve by substitution the system of equations

$$2x - y = 4,$$
$$x^2 - y^2 = 4.$$

We solve the first equation for y, obtaining $y = 2x - 4$. We now substitute this into the second equation, getting $x^2 - (2x - 4)^2 = 4$. When simplified, this gives a quadratic equation.

$$x^2 - (4x^2 - 16x + 16) = 4,$$
$$-3x^2 + 16x - 20 = 0;$$

$$x = \frac{-16 \pm \sqrt{256 - 4(-3)(-20)}}{-6} = \frac{-16 \pm \sqrt{16}}{-6} = \frac{-16 \pm 4}{-6} = \frac{10}{3}, \quad 2.$$

We now find the corresponding values of y by substituting into $y = 2x - 4$. Thus we have the solutions $x = \frac{10}{3}$, $y = \frac{8}{3}$, and $x = 2$, $y = 0$. By substitution, these values also satisfy the equation $x^2 - y^2 = 4$. (We do this as a check.)

Example B.   Solve by substitution the system of equations

$$xy = -2,$$
$$2x + y = 2.$$

From the first equation we have $y = -2/x$. Substituting this into the second equation, we have

$$2x - \left(\frac{2}{x}\right) = 2,$$

$$2x^2 - 2 = 2x,$$

$$x^2 - x - 1 = 0,$$

$$x = \frac{1 \pm \sqrt{1 + 4}}{2} = \frac{1 \pm \sqrt{5}}{2}.$$

We find the corresponding values of y, and we have the solutions

$$x = \frac{1 + \sqrt{5}}{2}, \quad y = 1 - \sqrt{5} \quad \text{and} \quad x = \frac{1 - \sqrt{5}}{2}, \quad y = 1 + \sqrt{5}.$$

Now let us use the other algebraic method of solution, that of addition or subtraction. This method can be used to great advantage if both equations have only squared terms and constants.

Example C.   Solve, by addition or subtraction, the system of equations

$$2x^2 + y^2 = 9,$$
$$x^2 - y^2 = 3.$$

We note that if we add the two equations we get $3x^2 = 12$. Thus $x = \pm 2$. The corresponding y-values are ± 1 for both $x = +2$ and $x = -2$. Thus we have four solutions: $x = 2$, $y = 1$; $x = 2$, $y = -1$; $x = -2$, $y = 1$; and $x = -2$, $y = -1$.

Example D.   Solve, by addition or subtraction, the system of equations

$$3x^2 - 2y^2 = 5,$$
$$x^2 + y^2 = 5.$$

If we multiply the second equation by 2 and then add the two resulting equations, we get $5x^2 = 15$. Thus $x = \pm\sqrt{3}$. The corresponding values of y for each value of x are $\pm\sqrt{2}$. Again we have four solutions: $x = \sqrt{3}$, $y = \sqrt{2}$; $x = \sqrt{3}$, $y = -\sqrt{2}$; $x = -\sqrt{3}$, $y = \sqrt{2}$; and $x = -\sqrt{3}$, $y = -\sqrt{2}$.

Example E.   A certain number of machine parts cost $1000. If they cost $5 less per part, ten additional parts could be purchased for the same amount of money. What is the cost of each?

Since the cost of each part is required, we let $c = $ the cost per part. Also, we let $n = $ the number of parts. From the first statement of the problem, we see that $cn = 1000$. Also, from the second statement, we have $(c - 5)(n + 10) = 1000$. Therefore, we are to solve the system of equations

$$cn = 1000,$$
$$(c - 5)(n + 10) = 1000.$$

Solving the first equation for n, and multiplying out the second equation, we have

$$n = \frac{1000}{c},$$
$$cn + 10c - 5n - 50 = 1000.$$

Now, substituting the expression for n into the second equation, we solve for c.

$$c\left(\frac{1000}{c}\right) + 10c - 5\left(\frac{1000}{c}\right) - 50 = 1000$$

$$1000 + 10c - \frac{5000}{c} - 50 = 1000$$

$$10c - \frac{5000}{c} - 50 = 0$$

$$10c^2 - 50c - 5000 = 0$$

$$c^2 - 5c - 500 = 0$$

$$(c + 20)(c - 25) = 0$$

$$c = -20, \quad 25$$

Since a negative answer has no significance in this particular situation, we see that the solution is $c = \$25$ per part. Checking with the original statement of the problem, we see that this is correct.

Exercises

In Exercises 1 through 20 solve the given systems of equations algebraically.

1. $y = x + 1$
   $y = x^2 + 1$

2. $y = 2x - 1$
   $y = 2x^2 + 2x - 3$

3. $x + 2y = 3$
   $x^2 + y^2 = 26$

4. $y = x + 1$
   $x^2 + y^2 = 25$

5. $2x - y = 2$
   $2x^2 + 3y^2 = 4$

6. $6y - x = 6$
   $x^2 + 3y^2 = 36$

7. $xy = 3$
   $3x - 2y = -7$

8. $xy = -4$
   $2x + y = -2$

9. $x^2 - y = -1$
   $x^2 + y^2 = 5$

10. $x^2 + y = 5$
    $x^2 + y^2 = 25$

11. $x^2 - 1 = y$
    $x^2 - 2y^2 = 1$

12. $2y^2 - 4x = 7$
    $y^2 + 2x^2 = 3$

13. $x^2 + y^2 = 25$
    $x^2 - 2y^2 = 7$

14. $3x^2 - y^2 = 4$
    $x^2 + 4y^2 = 10$

15. $y^2 - 2x^2 = 6$
    $5x^2 + 3y^2 = 20$

16. $y^2 - 2x^2 = 17$
    $2y^2 + x^2 = 54$

17. $x^2 + 3y^2 = 37$
    $2x^2 - 9y^2 = 14$

18. $5x^2 - 4y^2 = 15$
    $3y^2 + 4x^2 = 12$

19. The horizontal and vertical distances which a certain projectile travels from its starting point are given by $x = 80t$, $y = 60t - 16t^2$. Find how long it takes for x to equal $2y$. The time is in seconds.

20. A 300-gm block and a 200-gm block collide. Using the physical laws of conservation of energy and conservation of momentum, along with certain given conditions, we can establish the following equations involving velocities of each block after collision:

$$150v_1^2 + 100v_2^2 = 1375000,$$
$$300v_1 + 200v_2 = -5000.$$

Find these velocities (in cm/sec).

In Exercises 21 through 24 set up a system of equations and solve it algebraically.

21. Find two positive numbers such that the sum of their squares is 233 and the difference between their squares is 105.

22. To enclose a rectangular field of 11,200 ft² in area, 440 ft of fence are required. What are the dimensions of the field?

23. The radii of two spheres differ by 4 in., and the difference between the spherical surfaces is 320π in². Find the radii. (The surface area of a sphere is $4\pi r^2$.)

24. Two cities are 2000 mi apart. If an airplane increases its usual speed between these two cities by 100 mi/hr, the trip would take 1 hr less. Find the normal speed of the plane and the normal time of the flight.

13-3 Equations in quadratic form

Often we encounter equations which can be solved by methods applicable to quadratic equations, even though these equations are not actually quadratic. They do have the property, however, that with a proper substitution they may be written in the form of a quadratic equation. All that is necessary is that the equation have terms including some quantity, its square, and perhaps a constant term. The following example illustrates these types of equations.

Example A.   The equation $x - 2\sqrt{x} - 5 = 0$ is an equation in quadratic form, because if we let $y = \sqrt{x}$, we have the equivalent equation $y^2 - 2y - 5 = 0$.

Other examples of equations in quadratic form are as follows:

$t^{-4} - 5t^{-2} + 3 = 0$;   by letting $y = t^{-2}$ we have $y^2 - 5y + 3 = 0$,

$t^3 - 3t^{3/2} - 7 = 0$;   by letting $y = t^{3/2}$ we have $y^2 - 3y - 7 = 0$,

$(x + 1)^4 - (x + 1)^2 - 1 = 0$;   by letting $y = (x + 1)^2$ we have $y^2 - y - 1 = 0$,

$x^{10} - 2x^5 + 1 = 0$;   by letting $y = x^5$ we have $y^2 - 2y + 1 = 0$,

$(x - 3) + \sqrt{x - 3} - 6 = 0$;   by letting $y = \sqrt{x - 3}$ we have $y^2 + y - 6 = 0$.

The following examples illustrate the method of solving equations in quadratic form.

Example B.   Solve the equation $x^4 - 5x^2 + 4 = 0$.

We first let $y = x^2$, and obtain the equivalent equation $y^2 - 5y + 4 = 0$. This equation may be factored into $(y - 4)(y - 1) = 0$. Thus we have the solutions $y = 4$ and $y = 1$. Therefore $x^2 = 4$ and $x^2 = 1$, which means that we have $x = \pm 2$ and $x = \pm 1$. Substitution into the original equation verifies that each of these is a solution.

Example C.   Solve the equation $x - \sqrt{x} - 2 = 0$.

By letting $y = \sqrt{x}$, we obtain the equivalent equation $y^2 - y - 2 = 0$. This is factorable into $(y - 2)(y + 1) = 0$. Thus we have $y = 2$ and $y = -1$. Since

$y = \sqrt{x}$, $x = y^2$, which means that $x = 4$ or $x = 1$. When we check these solutions in the original equation, we find that $x = 4$ checks, but $x = 1$ does not check. (To obtain $x = 1$, we squared -1.) Thus, the only solution is $x = 4$.

Example C illustrates a very important point. *Whenever any operation involving the unknown is performed on an equation, this operation may introduce roots into a subsequent equation which are not roots of the original equation. Therefore we must check all answers in the original equation.* Only operations involving constants—that is, adding, subtracting, multiplying by, or dividing by constants—are certain not to introduce these *extraneous* roots. Squaring both sides of an equation is a common way of introducing extraneous roots. We first encountered the concept of an extraneous root in Section 5-6, when we were discussing equations involving fractions.

Example D. Solve the equation $x^{-2} + 3x^{-1} + 1 = 0$.

By substituting $y = x^{-1}$, we have $y^2 + 3y + 1 = 0$. To solve this equation we may use the quadratic formula:

$$y = \frac{-3 \pm \sqrt{9 - 4}}{2} = \frac{-3 \pm \sqrt{5}}{2}.$$

Thus

$$x = \frac{2}{-3 + \sqrt{5}}, \quad \frac{2}{-3 - \sqrt{5}}.$$

Rationalizing the denominators of the values of x, we have

$$x = \frac{-6 - 2\sqrt{5}}{4} = \frac{-3 - \sqrt{5}}{2} \quad \text{and} \quad x = \frac{-3 + \sqrt{5}}{2}.$$

Checking these solutions, we have

$$\left(\frac{-3 - \sqrt{5}}{2}\right)^{-2} + 3\left(\frac{-3 - \sqrt{5}}{2}\right)^{-1} + 1 \overset{?}{=} 0 \quad \text{or} \quad 0 = 0,$$

and

$$\left(\frac{-3 + \sqrt{5}}{2}\right)^{-2} + 3\left(\frac{-3 + \sqrt{5}}{2}\right)^{-1} + 1 \overset{?}{=} 0 \quad \text{or} \quad 0 = 0.$$

Thus these solutions check.

Example E. Solve the equation $(x^2 - x)^2 - 8(x^2 - x) + 12 = 0$.

By substituting $y = x^2 - x$, we have $y^2 - 8y + 12 = 0$. This is solved by factoring, giving us the solutions $y = 2$ and $y = 6$. Thus $x^2 - x = 2$ and $x^2 - x = 6$. Solving these, we find that $x = 2, -1, 3, -2$. Substituting these in the original equation, we find that all are solutions.

Example F illustrates a stated problem which leads to an equation in quadratic form.

Example F.   A rectangular plate has an area of 60 cm². The diagonal of the plate is 13 cm. Find the length and width of the plate.

Since the required quantities are the length and width, let l = the length of the plate, and w = the width of the plate. Now, since the area is 60 cm², $lw = 60$. Also, using the Pythagorean theorem and the fact that the diagonal is 13 cm, we have $l^2 + w^2 = 169$. Therefore, we are to solve the system of equations

$$lw = 60, \quad l^2 + w^2 = 169.$$

Solving the first equation for l, we have $l = 60/w$. Substituting this expression into the second equation we have

$$\left(\frac{60}{w}\right)^2 + w^2 = 169.$$

We now solve for w as follows.

$$\frac{3600}{w^2} + w^2 = 169,$$

$$3600 + w^4 = 169w^2,$$

$$w^4 - 169w^2 + 3600 = 0.$$

Let $x = w^2$.

$$x^2 - 169x + 3600 = 0,$$

$$(x - 144)(x - 25) = 0,$$

$$x = 25, \quad 144.$$

Therefore,

$$w^2 = 25, \quad 144.$$

Solving for w, we obtain $w = \pm 5$ or $w = \pm 12$. Only the positive values of w are meaningful in this problem. Therefore, if $w = 5$ cm, then $l = 12$ cm. Normally, we designate the length as the longer dimension. Checking in the original equation, we find that this solution is correct.

Exercises

In Exercises 1 through 16 solve the given equations.

1. $x^4 - 13x^2 + 36 = 0$
2. $x^4 - 20x^2 + 64 = 0$
3. $x^{-2} - 2x^{-1} - 8 = 0$
4. $10x^{-2} + 3x^{-1} - 1 = 0$
5. $x - 4\sqrt{x} + 3 = 0$
6. $\sqrt{x} + 3\sqrt[4]{x} = 28$
7. $x^6 + 7x^3 - 8 = 0$
8. $x^6 - 19x^3 - 216 = 0$
9. $x^{2/3} - 2x^{1/3} - 15 = 0$
10. $x^{5/2} + 2x^{3/2} - 24x^{1/2} = 0$
11. $(x - 1) - \sqrt{x - 1} - 2 = 0$
12. $(x + 1)^{-2/3} + 5(x + 1)^{-1/3} - 6 = 0$
13. $(x^2 - 2x)^2 - 11(x^2 - 2x) + 24 = 0$
14. $3(x^2 + 3x)^2 - 2(x^2 + 3x) - 5 = 0$
15. $x - 3\sqrt{x - 2} = 6$ (Let $y = \sqrt{x - 2}$.)
16. $(x^2 - 1)^2 + (x^2 - 1)^{-2} = 2$

In Exercises 17 and 18 set up equations in quadratic form and solve.

17. Find the dimensions of a rectangular area having a diagonal of 40 ft and an area of 768 ft².

18. A metal plate is in the shape of an isosceles triangle. The length of the base equals the square root of one of the equal sides. Determine the lengths of the sides if the perimeter of the plate is 55 in.

13-4 Equations with radicals

Equations with radicals in them are normally solved by squaring both sides of the equation, or by a similar operation. However, when we do this, we often introduce extraneous roots. Thus it is very important that all solutions be checked in the original equation.

Example A. Solve the equation $\sqrt{x-4} = 2$.

By squaring both sides of the equation, we have

$$(\sqrt{x-4})^2 = 2^2 \quad \text{or} \quad x - 4 = 4 \quad \text{or} \quad x = 8.$$

This solution checks when put into the original equation.

Example B. Solve the equation $\sqrt{x-1} = x - 3$.

Squaring both sides of the equation, we have

$$(\sqrt{x-1})^2 = (x-3)^2.$$

(Remember, we are squaring each *side* of the equation, not just the terms separately on each side.) Hence

$$x - 1 = x^2 - 6x + 9,$$
$$x^2 - 7x + 10 = 0,$$
$$(x-5)(x-2) = 0,$$
$$x = 5 \quad \text{or} \quad x = 2.$$

The solution $x = 5$ checks, but the solution $x = 2$ gives $1 = -1$. Thus the solution is $x = 5$, and $x = 2$ is an extraneous root.

Example C. Solve the equation $\sqrt[3]{x-8} = 2$.

Cubing both sides of the equation, we have $x - 8 = 8$. Thus $x = 16$, which checks.

Example D. Solve the equation $\sqrt{x+1} + \sqrt{x-4} = 5$.

This is most easily solved by first placing one of the radicals on the right side and then squaring both sides of the equation:

$$\sqrt{x+1} = 5 - \sqrt{x-4},$$
$$(\sqrt{x+1})^2 = (5 - \sqrt{x-4})^2,$$
$$x + 1 = 25 - 10\sqrt{x-4} + (x-4).$$

Now, isolating the radical on one side of the equation and squaring again, we have

$$10\sqrt{x-4} = 20,$$
$$\sqrt{x-4} = 2,$$
$$x - 4 = 4,$$
$$x = 8.$$

This solution checks.

Example E. Solve the equation $\sqrt{x} - \sqrt[4]{x} = 2$.
We can solve this most easily by handling it as an equation in quadratic form. By letting $y = \sqrt[4]{x}$, we have

$$y^2 - y - 2 = 0,$$
$$(y - 2)(y + 1) = 0,$$
$$y = 2 \qquad \text{or} \qquad y = -1,$$
$$x = 16 \qquad \text{or} \qquad x = 1.$$

The solution $x = 16$ checks, but the solution $x = 1$ does not. Thus the only solution is $x = 16$.

Example F. The perimeter of a right triangle is 60 ft, and its area is 120 ft². Find the lengths of the three sides (see Fig. 13-8).
If we let the two legs of the triangle be x and y, the perimeter can be expressed as $p = x + y + \sqrt{x^2 + y^2}$. Also, the area is $A = \frac{1}{2}xy$. In this way we arrive at the equations $x + y + \sqrt{x^2 + y^2} = 60$ and $xy = 240$. Solving the first of these for the radical, we have $\sqrt{x^2 + y^2}$
$= 60 - x - y$. Squaring both sides and combining terms, we have

$$0 = 3600 - 120x - 120y + 2xy.$$

Solving the second of the original equations for y, we have $y = 240/x$. Substituting, we have

$$0 = 3600 - 120x - 120\left(\frac{240}{x}\right) + 480.$$

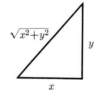

Figure 13-8

Multiplying each side by x, dividing through by 120, and rearranging the terms, we have $x^2 - 34x + 240 = 0$, which factors into $(x - 10)(x - 24) = 0$. This means that x can be either 10 or 24. From the equation $xy = 240$, if $x = 10$, then $y = 24$. This means that the two legs are 10 ft and 24 ft, and the hypotenuse is 26 ft. The same solution is found by using the value of 24 ft for x.

Exercises

In Exercises 1 through 22 solve the given equations.

1. $\sqrt{x - 8} = 2$ 2. $\sqrt{x + 4} = 3$

3. $\sqrt{8 - 2x} = x$ 4. $\sqrt{3x + 4} = x$

5. $\sqrt{x - 2} = x - 2$ 6. $\sqrt{5x - 1} = x - 3$

7. $\sqrt[3]{y - 5} = 3$ 8. $\sqrt[4]{5 - x} = 2$

9. $\sqrt{x + 12} = x$ 10. $4\sqrt{x} = x + 3$

11. $2\sqrt{x + 2} - \sqrt{3x + 4} = 1$ 12. $\sqrt{x - 1} + \sqrt{x + 2} = 3$

13. $\sqrt{5x + 1} - 1 = 3\sqrt{x}$ 14. $\sqrt{2x + 1} + \sqrt{3x} = 11$

15. $\sqrt{2x - 1} - \sqrt{x + 11} = -1$ 16. $\sqrt{5x - 4} - \sqrt{x} = 2$

17. $\sqrt[3]{2x - 1} = \sqrt[3]{x + 5}$ 18. $\sqrt[4]{x + 10} = \sqrt{x - 2}$

19. $\sqrt{x - 2} = \sqrt[4]{x - 2} + 12$ 20. $\sqrt{3x + \sqrt{3x + 4}} = 4$

21. The velocity of an object falling under the influence of gravity in terms of its initial velocity v_0, the acceleration due to gravity g, and the height fallen, is given by $v = \sqrt{v_0^2 - 2gh}$. Solve this equation for h.

22. The theory of relativity states that the mass m of an object increases with its velocity v according to the relation

$$m = \frac{m_0}{\sqrt{1 - v^2/c^2}},$$

where m_0 is the "rest mass" and c is the velocity of light. Solve for v in terms of m.

In Exercises 23 and 24 set up the proper equations and solve them.

23. Find the dimensions of the rectangle for which the diagonal is 3 in. more than the longer side, which in turn is 3 in. longer than the shorter side.

24. The sides of a certain triangle are $\sqrt{x - 1}, \sqrt{5x - 1}$, and $x - 1$. Find x when the perimeter of the triangle is 19.

13-5 Exponential and logarithmic equations

In solving equations in which there is an unknown exponent, it is often advantageous to take logarithms of both sides of the equation and then proceed. In solving logarithmic equations, one should keep in mind the basic properties of logarithms, since these can often help transform the equation into a solvable form. There is, however, no general method for solving such equations, and here we shall solve only some special cases.

Example A.   Solve the equation $2^x = 8$.

By writing this in logarithmic form, we have

$$x = \log_2 8 = 3.$$

We could also solve this equation by taking logarithms (to the base 10) of both sides. This would yield

$$\log 2^x = \log 8,$$
$$x \log 2 = \log 8,$$
$$x = \frac{\log 8}{\log 2} = \frac{0.9031}{0.3010} = 3.00.$$

This last method is more generally applicable, since the first method is good only if we can directly evaluate the logarithm which results.

Example B.   Solve the equation $3^{x-2} = 5$.

Taking logarithms of both sides, we have

$$\log 3^{x-2} = \log 5 \quad\text{or}\quad (x - 2) \log 3 = \log 5.$$

Solving this last equation for x, we have

$$x = 2 + \frac{\log 5}{\log 3} = 2 + \frac{0.6990}{0.4771}.$$

If three-place accuracy is sufficient, we may use a slide rule to find this quotient. If four-place accuracy is desired, we can use logarithms to calculate the quotient. (These logarithms are used only for the calculation, and have no other bearing on the solution.) And so

$$\log 0.6990 = 9.8445 - 10$$
$$\log 0.4771 = 9.6786 - 10$$
$$\overline{\log 1.465 = 0.1659}$$

Thus $x = 2 + 1.465 = 3.465$.

Example C.   Solve the equation $2(4^{x-1}) = 17^x$.

By taking logarithms of both sides, we have the following:

$$\log 2 + (x - 1) \log 4 = x \log 17,$$
$$x \log 4 - x \log 17 = \log 4 - \log 2,$$
$$x (\log 4 - \log 17) = \log 4 - \log 2,$$
$$x = \frac{\log 4 - \log 2}{\log 4 - \log 17} = \frac{\log (4/2)}{\log 4 - \log 17};$$

$$x = \frac{\log 2}{\log 4 - \log 17} = \frac{0.3010}{0.6021 - 1.2304}$$

$$= \frac{0.3010}{-0.6283} = -0.479 \quad\text{(to 3 digits).}$$

Example D.   Solve the equation $\log_2 7 - \log_2 14 = x$.
Using the basic properties of logarithms, we arrive at the following result:

$$\log_2 \left(\tfrac{7}{14}\right) = x,$$

$$\log_2 \left(\tfrac{1}{2}\right) = x \quad \text{or} \quad \tfrac{1}{2} = 2^x.$$

Thus $x = -1$.

Example E.   Solve the equation $2 \log x - 1 = \log (1 - 2x)$.

$$\log x^2 - \log (1 - 2x) = 1,$$

$$\log \frac{x^2}{1 - 2x} = 1,$$

$$\frac{x^2}{1 - 2x} = 10^1,$$

$$x^2 = 10 - 20x,$$

$$x^2 + 20x - 10 = 0,$$

$$x = \frac{-20 \pm \sqrt{400 + 40}}{2} = -10 \pm \sqrt{110}.$$

Since logarithms of negative numbers are not defined, we have the result that $x = \sqrt{110} - 10$.

Exercises

In Exercises 1 through 20 solve the given equations.

1. $2^x = 16$

2. $3^x = \frac{1}{81}$

3. $5^x = 4$

4. $6^x = 15$

5. $6^{x+1} = 10$

6. $5^{x-1} = 2$

7. $4(3^x) = 5$

8. $14^x = 40$

9. $0.8^x = 0.4$

10. $0.6^x = 100$

11. $(15.6)^{x+2} = 23^x$

12. $5^{x+2} = 3^{2x}$

13. $2 \log_2 x = 4$

14. $3 \log_8 x = 1$

15. $\log_5 (x - 3) + \log_5 x = \log_5 4$

16. $\log_7 x + \log_7 (2x - 5) = \log_7 3$

17. $2 \log (3 - x) = 1$

18. $\frac{1}{2} \log (x - 1) - \log x = 0$

19. $\log (2x - 1) + \log (x + 4) = 1$

20. $\log_2 x + \log_2 (x + 2) = 3$

In Exercises 21 through 24 determine the required quantities.

21. For a certain electric circuit, the current i is given by $i = 1.50e^{-200t}$. For what value of t (in seconds) is $i = 1.00$ amp? (Use 2.718 to approximate e.)

22. The amount q of a certain radioactive substance remaining after t years is given by $q = 100(0.90)^t$. After how many years are there 50 mg of the substance remaining?

23. In acoustics, the decibel b is defined by the equation $b = 10 \log (I/I_0)$, where I is the intensity of the sound and I_0 is the "threshold" intensity. If I_0 is assumed to be one unit, how many units of intensity is I for a 50-decibel sound?

24. In chemistry, the pH-value of a solution is a measure of its acidity. The pH-value is defined by the relation pH $= -\log (H^+)$, where H^+ is the hydrogen ion concentration. If the pH of a certain solution is 6.4065, find the hydrogen ion concentration. (If the pH-value is less than 7, the solution is acid. If the pH-value is above 7, the solution is basic.)

To solve more complicated problems, we may use graphical methods. For example, if we wish to solve the equation $2^x + 3^x = 50$, we can set up the function $y = 2^x + 3^x - 50$ and then determine its zeros graphically. Note that the given equation can be written as $2^x + 3^x - 50 = 0$, and therefore the zeros of the function which has been set up will give the desired solution. In Exercises 25 and 26 solve the given equations in this way.

25. $2^x + 3^x = 50$ 　　　　　　　　　　　26. $3^{x+1} - 4^x = 1$

13-6 Miscellaneous Exercises

In Exercises 1 through 6 solve the given systems of equations graphically.

1. $x + 2y = 6$
   $y = 4x^2$

2. $x + y = 3$
   $x^2 + y^2 = 25$

3. $3x + 2y = 6$
   $x^2 + 4y^2 = 4$

4. $x^2 - 2y = 0$
   $y = 3x - 5$

5. $y = x^2 + 1$
   $2x^2 + y^2 = 4$

6. $\dfrac{x^2}{4} + y^2 = 1$
   $x^2 - y^2 = 1$

In Exercises 7 through 12 solve the given systems of equations algebraically.

7. $y = 4x^2$
   $y = 8x$

8. $x + y = 2$
   $xy = 1$

9. $4x^2 - 7y^2 = 21$
   $x^2 + 2y^2 = 99$

10. $3x^2 + 2y^2 = 11$
    $2x^2 - y^2 = 30$

11. $4x^2 + 3xy = 4$
    $x + 3y = 4$

12. $\dfrac{6}{x} + \dfrac{3}{y} = 4$
    $\dfrac{36}{x^2} + \dfrac{36}{y^2} = 13$

In Exercises 13 through 26 solve the given equations.

13. $x^4 - 20x^2 + 64 = 0$

14. $x^{1/2} + 3x^{1/4} - 28 = 0$

15. $x^{-2} + 4x^{-1} - 21 = 0$

16. $(x^2 + 5x)^2 - 5(x^2 + 5x) = 6$

17. $\sqrt{x + 5} = 4$

18. $\sqrt[3]{x - 2} = 3$

19. $x - 1 = \sqrt{5x + 9}$

20. $x + 2 = \sqrt{11x - 2}$

21. $\sqrt{x + 1} + \sqrt{x} = 2$

22. $\sqrt{3 + x} + \sqrt{3x - 2} = 1$

23. $3^{x+2} = 5^x$

24. $5^x = 10$

25. $2^x + 16(2^{-x}) = 8$

26. $\log (x + 2) + \log x = 0.4771$

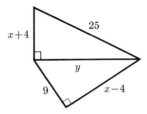

Figure 13-9

In Exercises 27 through 30 find the required quantities.

27. Find the values of x and y in Fig. 13-9.

28. Under certain conditions, the frequency ω of an RLC circuit is given by

$$\omega = \frac{\sqrt{R^2 + 4(L/C)} + R}{2L}.$$

Solve for C.

29. For first-order chemical reactions, concentration of a reacting chemical species is related to time by the expression

$$\log \frac{x_0}{x} = kt,$$

where x_0 is the initial concentration and x is the concentration after time t. Determine the quantity of sucrose remaining after 3 hr, if the initial concentration is 9.00 gm-mole/liter and $k = 0.00158$ min^{-1}.

30. If two objects collide and the kinetic energy remains constant, the collision is termed perfectly elastic. Under these conditions, if an object of mass m_1 and initial velocity u_1 strikes a second object (initially at rest) of mass m_2, such that the velocities after collision are v_1 and v_2, the following equations are found:

$$m_1 u_1 = m_1 v_1 + m_2 v_2,$$
$$\tfrac{1}{2} m_1 u_1^2 = \tfrac{1}{2} m_1 v_1^2 + \tfrac{1}{2} m_2 v_2^2.$$

Solve these equations for m_2 in terms of u_1, v_1, and m_1.

In Exercises 31 and 32 set up the appropriate equations and solve.

31. An object is dropped from the top of a building. Six seconds later it is heard to hit the street below. How high is the building? (The velocity of sound is 1100 ft/sec and the distance the object falls as a function of time is $s = 16t^2$.)

32. Two trains are approaching the same crossing on tracks which are at right angles to each other. Each is traveling at 60 mi/hr. If one is 6 mi from the crossing when the other is 3 mi from it, how much later will they be 4 mi apart?

Equations of Higher Degree

14

14-1 The remainder theorem and the factor theorem

In previous chapters we have discussed methods of solving many kinds of equations. Except for special cases, however, we have not solved polynomial equations of degree higher than two (a polynomial equation of the first degree is a linear equation, and a polynomial equation of the second degree is a quadratic equation.) In this chapter we shall develop certain methods for solving polynomial equations, especially the higher-degree equations. Since we shall be discussing equations involving only polynomials, in this chapter $f(x)$ will be assumed to be a polynomial.

Any polynomial is a function of the form

$$f(x) = a_0 x^n + a_1 x^{n-1} + \cdots + a_n. \tag{14-1}$$

If we divide a polynomial by $x - r$, we find a result of the following form:

$$f(x) = (x - r)q(x) + R, \tag{14-2}$$

where $q(x)$ is the quotient and R is the remainder.

Example A. Divide $f(x) = 3x^2 + 5x - 8$ by $x - 2$.

$$
\begin{array}{r}
3x + 11 \\
x - 2 \enclose{longdiv}{3x^2 + 5x - 8} \\
\underline{3x^2 - 6x} \\
11x - 8 \\
\underline{11x - 22} \\
14
\end{array}
$$

Thus

$$3x^2 + 5x - 8 = (x - 2)(3x + 11) + 14.$$

If we now set $x = r$ in Eq. (14-2), we have

$$f(r) = q(r)(r - r) + R = R. \qquad (14\text{-}3)$$

The equation above states that the remainder equals the function of r. This leads us to the *remainder theorem*, which states that *if a polynomial $f(x)$ is divided by $x - r$ until a constant remainder (R) is obtained, then $f(r) = R$.*

Example B.   In Example A, $f(x) = 3x^2 + 5x - 8$, $R = 14$, $r = 2$.
We find by the definition of a function that

$$f(2) = 3(4) + 5(2) - 8 = 14.$$

Thus $f(2) = 14$ verifies that $f(r) = R$.

The remainder theorem leads immediately to another important theorem known as the *factor theorem*. The factor theorem states that *if $f(r) = R = 0$, then $x - r$ is a factor of $f(x)$.* Inspection of Eq. (14-2) justifies this theorem. It is also true that if $x - r$ is a factor of $f(x)$, then r is a zero of $f(x)$.

Example C.   Is $x + 1$ a factor of $f(x) = x^3 + 2x^2 - 5x - 6$?
Here $r = -1$, and thus

$$f(-1) = -1 + 2 + 5 - 6 = 0.$$

Therefore $x + 1$ is a factor of $f(x)$.

Example D.   The expression $x + 2$ is not a factor of the function in Example C, since

$$f(-2) = -8 + 8 + 10 - 6 = 4.$$

But $x - 2$ is a factor, since $f(2) = 8 + 8 - 10 - 6 = 0$.

We now have one way of determining whether or not a given expression is a factor of a function. If we find $f(r)$ readily, we can determine whether or not $x - r$ is a factor, and whether or not r is a zero of the function.

Example E.   Determine whether or not $2x - 3$ is a factor of

$$2x^3 - 3x^2 + 8x - 12.$$

We first note that the coefficient of x in the possible factor is not 1. Thus we cannot use $f(3)$ to determine whether or not $2x - 3$ is a factor, since the factor is not of the assumed form $x - r$. However, $2x - 3 = 2(x - \frac{3}{2})$, which means that if $x - \frac{3}{2}$ is zero, then $2x - 3$ must be zero. Thus, if we evaluate $f(\frac{3}{2})$ and find that it is zero, then $2x - 3$ is a factor of $2x^3 - 3x^2 + 8x - 12$.

$$f(\tfrac{3}{2}) = 2(\tfrac{3}{2})^3 - 3(\tfrac{3}{2})^2 + 8(\tfrac{3}{2}) - 12 = \tfrac{27}{4} - \tfrac{27}{4} + 12 - 12 = 0.$$

Therefore $2x - 3$ is a factor.

Exercises

In Exercises 1 through 6 find the remainder R by long division and by the remainder theorem.

1. $(x^3 + 2x^2 - x - 2) \div (x - 1)$

2. $(x^3 - 3x^2 - x + 2) \div (x - 2)$

3. $(x^3 + 2x + 3) \div (x + 1)$

4. $(x^4 - 4x^3 - x^2 + x - 100) \div (x + 3)$

5. $(2x^5 - x^2 + 8x + 44) \div (x + 2)$

6. $(x^3 + 4x^2 - 25x - 98) \div (x - 5)$

In Exercises 7 through 12 find the remainder using the remainder theorem.

7. $(x^3 + 2x^2 - 3x + 4) \div (x + 1)$

8. $(2x^3 - 4x^2 + x - 1) \div (x + 2)$

9. $(x^4 + x^3 - 2x^2 - 5x + 3) \div (x + 4)$

10. $(2x^4 - x^2 + 5x - 7) \div (x - 3)$

11. $(2x^4 - 7x^3 - x^2 + 8) \div (x - 3)$

12. $(x^4 - 5x^3 + x^2 - 2x + 6) \div (x + 4)$

In Exercises 13 through 22 use the factor theorem to determine whether or not the second expression is a factor of the first.

13. $x^2 - 2x - 3,\ x - 3$

14. $3x^3 + 2x^2 - 3x - 2,\ x + 2$

15. $4x^3 + x^2 - 16x - 4,\ x - 2$

16. $3x^3 + 14x^2 + 7x - 4,\ x + 4$

17. $5x^3 - 3x^2 + 4,\ x - 2$

18. $x^5 - 2x^4 + 3x^3 - 6x^2 - 4x + 8,\ x - 2$

19. $x^6 + 1,\ x + 1$

20. $x^7 - 128,\ x + 2$

21. $x^4 - 2x^2 + 4x - 2,\ 2x - 1$

22. $3x^3 + 4x^2 + 6x + 8,\ 3x + 4$

In Exercises 23 and 24 determine whether or not the given numbers are zeros of the given functions.

23. $f(x) = x^3 - 2x^2 - 9x + 18;\quad 2$

24. $f(x) = 2x^3 + 3x^2 - 8x - 12;\quad -\tfrac{3}{2}$

14-2 Synthetic division

We shall now develop a method which greatly simplifies the procedure for dividing a polynomial by an expression of the form $x - r$. Using *synthetic division*, which is an abbreviated form of long division, we can determine the coefficients of the quotient as well as the remainder. Of course, for some values of r, we can easily calculate $f(r)$ directly. However, if the degree of the equation is high, this requires finding and combining high powers of r. Synthetic division therefore allows us to find $f(r)$ easily by finding the remainder. The method is developed in the following example.

Example A.   Divide $x^4 + 4x^3 - x^2 - 16x - 14$ by $x - 2$.

We shall first perform this division in the usual manner.

$$\begin{array}{r} x^3 + 6x^2 + 11x + 6 \\ \hline x - 2 \overline{\smash{\big)}\, x^4 + 4x^3 - x^2 - 16x - 14} \\ \underline{x^4 - 2x^3} \\ 6x^3 - x^2 \\ \underline{6x^3 - 12x^2} \\ 11x^2 - 16x \\ \underline{11x^2 - 22x} \\ 6x - 14 \\ \underline{6x - 12} \\ -2 \end{array}$$

We now note that, when we performed this division, we repeated many terms. Also, the only quantities of importance in the function being divided are the coefficients. There is no real need to put in the powers of x all the time. Therefore we shall now write the above example without any x's and also eliminate the writing of identical terms:

$$\begin{array}{r} 1 \quad\ \ 6 \quad\ 11 \quad\ \ 6 \\ \hline -2 \,\big)\, 1 \quad\ \ 4 \quad -1 \ -16 \ -14 \\ \underline{-2} \\ 6 \\ \underline{-12} \\ 11 \\ \underline{-22} \\ 6 \\ \underline{-12} \\ -2 \end{array}$$

All but the first of the numbers which represent coefficients of the quotient are repeated below. Also, all the numbers below the dividend may be written in two lines. Thus we have the following form.

$$\begin{array}{r} -2 \,\big)\, 1 \quad\ \ \ 4 \quad -1 \ -16 \ -14 \\ \underline{-2 \ -12 \ -22 \ -12} \\ 6 \quad\ \ 11 \quad\ \ 6 \quad\ -2 \end{array}$$

All the coefficients of the actual quotient appear except the first, so we shall now repeat the 1 in the bottom line. Also, we shall change -2 to 2, which is the actual value of r. Then, to conform to the normal practice of writing r to the right, we have the following form:

$$\begin{array}{r} 1 \quad\ \ 4 \quad -1 \ -16 \ -14 \quad\ \big|\,2 \\ \underline{-2 \ -12 \ -22 \ -12} \\ 1 \quad\ \ 6 \quad\ \ 11 \quad\ \ 6 \quad\ -2 \end{array}$$

In this form the 1, 6, 11, and 6 represent the coefficients of the x^3, x^2, x, and constant terms of the quotient. The -2 is the remainder. Finally, we find it easier to use addition rather than subtraction in the process, so we change the signs of the numbers in the middle row. Remember that originally the bottom line was found by subtraction. Thus we have

$$
\begin{array}{rrrrr|r}
1 & 4 & -1 & -16 & -14 & 2 \\
  & 2 & 12 & 22 & 12 & \\
\hline
1 & 6 & 11 & 6 & -2 &
\end{array}
$$

When we inspect this form we find the following: The 1 multiplied by the 2 (r) gives 2, which is the first number of the middle row. The 4 and 2 (of the middle row) added is 6, which is the second number in the bottom row. The 6 multiplied by 2 (r) is 12, which is the second number in the middle row. This 12 and the -1 give 11. The 11 multiplied by 2 is 22. The 22 added to -16 is 6. This 6 multiplied by 2 gives 12. This 12 added to -14 is -2. When this process is followed in general, the method is called synthetic division.

Generalizing on this last example, we have the following procedure. We write down the coefficients of $f(x)$, being certain that the powers are in descending order and that zeroes are placed in for missing powers. We write the value of r to the right. We carry down the left coefficient, multiply this number by r, and place this product under the second coefficient of the top line. We add the two numbers in this second column and place the result below; then we multiply this number by r and place the result under the third coefficient of the top line. We continue until the bottom row has as many numbers as the top row. The last number in the bottom row is the remainder, the other numbers being the respective coefficients of the quotient. The first term of the quotient is of degree one less than the dividend.

Example B. By synthetic division, divide $x^5 + 2x^4 - 4x^2 + 3x - 4$ by $x + 3$.

In writing down the coefficients of $f(x)$, we must be certain to include a zero for the missing x^3 term. Also, since the divisor is $x + 3$, we must recognize that $r = -3$. The setup and synthetic division follow.

$$
\begin{array}{rrrrrr|r}
1 & 2 & 0 & -4 & 3 & -4 & -3 \\
  & -3 & 3 & -9 & 39 & -126 & \\
\hline
1 & -1 & 3 & -13 & 42 & -130 &
\end{array}
$$

Thus the quotient is $x^4 - x^3 + 3x^2 - 13x + 42$ and the remainder is -130. Notice the degree of the dividend is 5 and the degree of the quotient is 4.

Example C. By synthetic division, divide $3x^4 - 5x + 6$ by $x - 4$.

$$
\begin{array}{rrrrr|r}
3 & 0 & 0 & -5 & 6 & 4 \\
  & 12 & 48 & 192 & 748 & \\
\hline
3 & 12 & 48 & 187 & 754 &
\end{array}
$$

Thus the quotient is $3x^3 + 12x^2 + 48x + 187$ and the remainder is 754.

Example D.   By synthetic division, determine whether or not $x - 4$ is a factor of $x^4 + 2x^3 - 15x^2 - 32x - 16$.

$$
\begin{array}{rrrrr|r}
1 & 2 & -15 & -32 & -16 & \underline{4} \\
  & 4 & 24 & 36 & 16 & \\
\hline
1 & 6 & 9 & 4 & 0 &
\end{array}
$$

Since the remainder is zero, $x - 4$ is a factor. We may also conclude that $f(x) = (x - 4)(x^3 + 6x^2 + 9x + 4)$, since the bottom line gives us the coefficients in the quotient.

Example E.   By synthetic division, determine whether or not $\frac{1}{3}$ is a zero of the function $3x^3 + 2x^2 - 4x + 1$.

This problem is equivalent to dividing the function by $x - \frac{1}{3}$. If the remainder is zero, $\frac{1}{3}$ is a zero of the function.

$$
\begin{array}{rrrr|r}
3 & 2 & -4 & 1 & \underline{\tfrac{1}{3}} \\
  & 1 & 1 & -1 & \\
\hline
3 & 3 & -3 & 0 &
\end{array}
$$

Since the remainder is zero, we conclude that $\frac{1}{3}$ is a zero of the function. Also, $3x^3 + 2x^2 - 4x + 1 = (x - \frac{1}{3})(3x^2 + 3x - 3) = 3(x - \frac{1}{3})(x^2 + x - 1)$.

Exercises

In Exercises 1 through 16 perform the required divisions by synthetic division. Exercises 1 through 12 are the same as those of Section 14-1.

1. $(x^3 + 2x^2 - x - 2) \div (x - 1)$
2. $(x^3 - 3x^2 - x + 2) \div (x - 2)$
3. $(x^3 + 2x + 3) \div (x + 1)$
4. $(x^4 - 4x^3 - x^2 + x - 100) \div (x + 3)$
5. $(2x^5 - x^2 + 8x + 44) \div (x + 2)$
6. $(x^3 + 4x^2 - 25x - 98) \div (x - 5)$
7. $(x^3 + 2x^2 - 3x + 4) \div (x + 1)$
8. $(2x^3 - 4x^2 + x - 1) \div (x + 2)$
9. $(x^4 + x^3 - 2x^2 - 5x + 3) \div (x + 4)$
10. $(2x^4 - x^2 + 5x - 7) \div (x - 3)$
11. $(2x^4 - 7x^3 - x^2 + 8) \div (x - 3)$
12. $(x^4 - 5x^3 + x^2 - 2x + 6) \div (x + 4)$
13. $(x^6 + 2x^2 - 6) \div (x - 2)$
14. $(x^5 + 4x^4 - 8) \div (x + 1)$
15. $(x^7 - 128) \div (x - 2)$
16. $(x^5 + 32) \div (x + 2)$

In Exercises 17 through 20 use the factor theorem and synthetic division to determine whether or not the second expression is a factor of the first.

17. $x^3 + x^2 - x + 2$; $x + 2$
18. $x^3 + 6x^2 + 10x + 6$; $x + 3$
19. $2x^4 - x^3 + 2x^2 - 3x + 1$; $2x - 1$
20. $6x^4 + 5x^3 - x^2 + 6x - 2$; $3x - 1$

In Exercises 21 through 24 use synthetic division to determine whether or not the given numbers are zeros of the given functions.

21. $x^4 - 5x^3 - 15x^2 + 5x + 14$;   7
22. $x^4 + 7x^3 + 12x^2 + x + 4$; -4
23. $9x^3 + 9x^2 - x + 2$; $-\frac{2}{3}$
24. $2x^3 + 13x^2 + 10x - 4$; $\frac{1}{2}$

14-3 The roots of an equation

In this section we shall present certain theorems which are useful in determining the number of roots in the equation $f(x) = 0$, and the nature of some of these roots. In dealing with polynomial equations of higher degree, it is helpful to have as much of this kind of information as is readily obtainable before proceeding to solve for the roots.

The first of these theorems is so important that it is called the fundamental theorem of algebra. It states that *every polynomial equation has at least one (real or complex) root.* The proof of this theorem is of an advanced nature, and therefore we must accept its validity at this time. However, using the fundamental theorem, we can show the validity of other useful theorems.

Let us now assume that we have a polynomial equation $f(x) = 0$, and that we are looking for its roots. By the fundamental theorem, we know that it has at least one root. Assuming that we can find this root by some means (the factor theorem, for example), we shall call this root r_1. Thus

$$f(x) = (x - r_1)f_1(x),$$

where $f_1(x)$ is the polynomial quotient found by dividing $f(x)$ by $(x - r_1)$. However, since the fundamental theorem states that any polynomial equation has at least one root, this must apply to $f_1(x) = 0$ as well. Let us assume that $f_1(x) = 0$ has the root r_2. Thus $f(x) = (x - r_1)(x - r_2)f_2(x)$. Continuing this process until one of the quotients is a constant a, we have

$$f(x) = a(x - r_1)(x - r_2) \cdots (x - r_n).$$

Note that one linear factor appears each time a root is found, and that the degree of the quotient is one less each time. Thus there are n factors, if the degree of $f(x)$ is n. This leads us to two theorems. The first of these states that *each polynomial of the nth degree can be factored into n linear factors.* The second theorem states that *each polynomial equation of degree n has exactly n roots.*

Example A.   Consider the equation $f(x) = 2x^4 - 3x^3 - 12x^2 + 7x + 6 = 0$.

$$2x^4 - 3x^3 - 12x^2 + 7x + 6 = (x - 3)(2x^3 + 3x^2 - 3x - 2),$$
$$2x^3 + 3x^2 - 3x - 2 = (x + 2)(2x^2 - x - 1),$$
$$2x^2 - x - 1 = (x - 1)(2x + 1),$$
$$2x + 1 = 2(x + \tfrac{1}{2}).$$

Therefore

$$2x^4 - 3x^3 - 12x^2 + 7x + 6 = 2(x - 3)(x + 2)(x - 1)(x + \tfrac{1}{2}) = 0.$$

The degree of $f(x)$ is 4. There are 4 linear factors: $(x - 3)$, $(x + 2)$, $(x - 1)$, and $(x + \tfrac{1}{2})$. There are 4 roots of the equation: 3, -2, 1, and $-\tfrac{1}{2}$. Thus we have verified each of the theorems above for this example.

It is not necessary for each root of an equation to be different from the others. For example, the equation $(x - 1)^2 = 0$ has two roots, both of which are 1. Such roots are referred to as multiple roots.

When we solve the equation $x^2 + 1 = 0$, we get two roots, j and $-j$. In fact, if we have any equation for which the roots are complex, for every root of the form $a + bj$ ($b \neq 0$), there is also a root of the form $a - bj$. This is so because any quadratic equation can be solved by the quadratic formula. The solutions from the quadratic formula (for an equation of the form $ax^2 + bx + c = 0$) are

$$\frac{-b + \sqrt{b^2 - 4ac}}{2a} \quad \text{and} \quad \frac{-b - \sqrt{b^2 - 4ac}}{2a},$$

and the only difference between these roots is the sign before the radical. Thus we have the following theorem. *If a complex number $a + bj$ is the root of $f(x) = 0$, its conjugate $a - bj$ is also a root.*

Example B. Consider the equation $f(x) = (x - 1)^3(x^2 + x + 1) = 0$.

We observe directly (since three factors of $x - 1$ are already indicated) that there is a triple root of 1. To find the other two roots, we use the quadratic formula on the *factor* $(x^2 + x + 1)$. This is permissible, because what we are actually finding are those values of x which make $x^2 + x + 1 = 0$. For this we have

$$x = \frac{-1 \pm \sqrt{1 - 4}}{2}.$$

Thus

$$x = \frac{-1 + \sqrt{3}j}{2} \quad \text{and} \quad x = \frac{-1 - \sqrt{3}j}{2}.$$

Therefore the roots of $f(x)$ are

$$1, \quad 1, \quad 1, \quad \frac{-1 + \sqrt{3}j}{2}, \quad \frac{-1 - \sqrt{3}j}{2}.$$

One further observation can be made from Example B. Whenever enough roots are known so that the remaining factor is quadratic, it is always possible to find the remaining roots from the quadratic formula. This is true for finding real or complex roots. If there are n roots and if we find $n - 2$ of these roots, the solution may be completed by using the quadratic formula.

Example C. Solve the equation $x^4 + 3x^3 - 4x^2 - 10x - 4 = 0$, given that -1 and 2 are roots.

Using synthetic division and the root -1, we have

1	3	-4	-10	-4	$\underline{|-1}$
	-1	-2	6	4	
1	2	-6	-4	0	

Therefore we now know that

$$x^4 + 3x^3 - 4x^2 - 10x - 4 = (x + 1)(x^3 + 2x^2 - 6x - 4).$$

We now know that $x - 2$ must be a factor of $x^3 + 2x^2 - 6x - 4$, since it is a factor of the original function. Again using synthetic division and this time the root 2, we have the following:

$$
\begin{array}{rrrr|l}
1 & 2 & -6 & -4 & \underline{\;2} \\
  & 2 & 8 & 4 & \\
\hline
1 & 4 & 2 & 0 & \\
\end{array}
$$

Thus

$$x^4 + 3x^3 - 4x^2 - 10x - 4 = (x + 1)(x - 2)(x^2 + 4x + 2).$$

The roots from this last factor are now found by the quadratic formula:

$$x = \frac{-4 \pm \sqrt{16 - 8}}{2} = \frac{-4 \pm 2\sqrt{2}}{2} = -2 \pm \sqrt{2}.$$

Therefore the roots are $-1,\ 2,\ -2 + \sqrt{2},\ -2 - \sqrt{2}$.

Example D.   Solve the equation $3x^4 - 26x^3 + 63x^2 - 36x - 20 = 0$, given that 2 is a double root.

Using synthetic division, we have

$$
\begin{array}{rrrrr|l}
3 & -26 & 63 & -36 & -20 & \underline{\;2} \\
  & 6 & -40 & 46 & 20 & \\
\hline
3 & -20 & 23 & 10 & 0 & \\
\end{array}
$$

Therefore, we know that $3x^4 - 26x^3 + 63x^2 - 36x - 20 = (x - 2)(3x^3 - 20x^2 + 23x + 10)$. Also, since 2 is a double root, it must be a root of the quotient $3x^3 - 20x^2 + 23x + 10$. Using synthetic division again, we have

$$
\begin{array}{rrrr|l}
3 & -20 & 23 & 10 & \underline{\;2} \\
  & 6 & -28 & -10 & \\
\hline
3 & -14 & -5 & 0 & \\
\end{array}
$$

The quotient $3x^2 - 14x - 5$ factors into $(3x + 1)(x - 5)$. Therefore, the roots of the equation are $2,\ 2,\ -\frac{1}{3}$, and 5.

Example E.   Solve the equation $2x^4 - x^3 + 7x^2 - 4x - 4 = 0$, given that $2j$ is a root.

Since $2j$ is a root, we know that $-2j$ is also a root. Using synthetic division twice, we can then reduce the remaining factor to a quadratic function.

$$
\begin{array}{rrrrr|l}
2 & -1 & 7 & -4 & -4 & \underline{\;2j} \\
  & 4j & -8 - 2j & 4 - 2j & 4 & \\
\hline
2 & 4j - 1 & -1 - 2j & -2j & 2j & \quad \underline{\;-2j} \\
  & -4j & & 2j & 2j & \\
\hline
2 & -1 & & -1 & & \\
\end{array}
$$

The quadratic factor $2x^2 - x - 1$ factors into $(2x + 1)(x - 1)$. Therefore, the roots of the function are $2j$, $-2j$, 1, and $-\frac{1}{2}$.

Exercises

In the following exercises solve the given equations using synthetic division, given the roots indicated.

1. $x^3 + 2x^2 - x - 2 = 0$ $(r_1 = 1)$
2. $x^3 + 2x^2 + x + 2 = 0$ $(r_1 = -2)$
3. $x^3 + x^2 - 8x - 12 = 0$ $(r_1 = -2)$
4. $x^3 - 1 = 0$ $(r_1 = 1)$
5. $2x^3 + 11x^2 + 20x + 12 = 0$ $(r_1 = -\frac{3}{2})$
6. $2x^3 + 5x^2 - 11x + 4 = 0$ $(r_1 = \frac{1}{2})$
7. $3x^3 + 2x^2 + 3x + 2 = 0$ $(r_1 = j)$
8. $x^3 + 5x^2 + 9x + 5 = 0$ $(r_1 = -2 + j)$
9. $x^4 + x^3 - 2x^2 + 4x - 24 = 0$ $(r_1 = 2, r_2 = -3)$
10. $x^4 + 2x^3 - 4x^2 - 5x + 6 = 0$ $(r_1 = 1, r_2 = -2)$
11. $x^4 - 6x^2 - 8x - 3 = 0$ $(-1$ is a double root$)$
12. $4x^4 + 28x^3 + 61x^2 + 42x + 9 = 0$ $(-3$ is a double root$)$
13. $2x^5 + x^4 - 15x^3 + 5x^2 + 13x - 6 = 0$ $(r_1 = 1, r_2 = -1, r_3 = \frac{1}{2})$
14. $x^5 - 3x^4 + 4x^3 - 4x^2 + 3x - 1 = 0$ $(1$ is a triple root$)$
15. $x^6 + 2x^5 - 4x^4 - 10x^3 - 41x^2 - 72x - 36 = 0$ $(-1$ is a double root, $2j$ is a root$)$
16. $x^6 - x^5 - 2x^3 - 3x^2 - x - 2 = 0$ $(j$ is a double root$)$

14-4 Rational roots

If we form the product from the factors $(x + 2)(x - 4)(x + 3)$, we obtain $x^3 + x^2 - 14x - 24$. In forming this product, we find that the constant 24 which results is determined only by the numbers 2, 4, and 3. We note that these numbers represent the roots of the equation if the given function is set equal to zero. In fact, if we found all the integral roots of an equation, and represented the equation in the form $f(x) = (x - r_1)(x - r_2)\cdots(x - r_k)f_{k+1}(x) = 0$, where all the roots indicated are integers, the constant term of $f(x)$ must have factors of $r_1, r_2, \ldots, r_k$. This leads us to the theorem which states that *if the coefficient of the highest power of x is 1, then any integral roots are factors of the constant term of the function.*

Example A.   The equation $f(x) = x^5 - 4x^4 - 7x^3 + 14x^2 - 44x + 120 = 0$ can be written as

$$(x - 5)(x + 3)(x - 2)(x^2 + 4) = 0.$$

We now note that $5(3)(2)(4) = 120$. Thus the roots 5, -3, and 2 are numerical factors of $|120|$. The theorem states nothing in regard to the signs involved.

If the coefficient of the highest-power term of $f(x)$ is not 1, then this coefficient can be factored from every term of $f(x)$. Thus any equation of the form $f(x) = a_0x^n + a_1x^{n-1} + \cdots + a_n = 0$ can be written in the form

$$f(x) = a_0\left(x^n + \frac{a_1}{a_0}x^{n-1} + \cdots + \frac{a_n}{a_0}\right) = 0. \tag{14-4}$$

This equation, along with the theorem above, now gives us another, more inclusive, theorem. *Any rational roots of a polynomial equation $f(x) = a_0x^n + a_1x^{n-1} + \cdots + a_n = 0$ must be integral factors of a_n divided by integral factors of a_0.* The same reasoning as above, applied to the factor within parentheses of Eq. (14-4), leads us to this result.

Example B.   If $f(x) = 4x^3 - 3x^2 - 25x - 6 = 0$, any rational roots, if they exist, must be integral factors of 6 divided by integral factors of 4. The integral factors of 6 are 1, 2, 3, and 6 and the integral factors of 4 are 1, 2, and 4. Forming all possible positive and negative quotients, any rational roots that exist will be found in the following list: ± 1, $\pm\frac{1}{2}$, $\pm\frac{1}{4}$, ± 2, ± 3, $\pm\frac{3}{2}$, $\pm\frac{3}{4}$, ± 6.
The roots of this equation are -2, 3, and $-\frac{1}{4}$.

There are 16 different possible rational roots in Example B. Since we have no way of telling which of these are the actual roots, we now present a rule which will help us to find these roots. This rule is known as Descartes' rule of signs. It states that *the number of positive roots of a polynomial equation $f(x) = 0$ cannot exceed the number of changes in sign in $f(x)$ in going from one term to the next in $f(x)$. The number of negative roots cannot exceed the number of sign changes in $f(-x)$.*

We can reason this way. If $f(x)$ has all positive terms, then any positive number substituted in $f(x)$ must give a positive value for the function. This indicates that the number substituted in the function is not a root. Thus there must be at least one negative and one positive term in the function for any positive number to be a root. This is not a proof, but does indicate the type of reasoning which is used in developing the theorem.

Example C.   By Descartes' rule of signs, determine the maximum number of positive and negative roots of $3x^3 - x^2 - x + 4 = 0$.
Here $f(x) = 3x^3 - x^2 - x + 4$. The first term is positive and the second negative, which indicates a change of sign. The third term is also negative; there is no change of sign from the second to the third term. The fourth term is positive, thus giving us a second change of sign, from the third to the fourth term. Hence there are two changes in sign, and therefore no more than two positive roots of $f(x) = 0$. Then we write

$$f(-x) = 3(-x)^3 - (-x)^2 - (-x) + 4 = -3x^3 - x^2 + x + 4.$$

There is only one change of sign in $f(-x)$; therefore there is one negative root. When there is just one change of sign in $f(x)$ *there is a positive root* and when there is just one change of sign in $f(-x)$ *there is a negative root.*

Example D.   For the equation $4x^5 - x^4 - 4x^3 + x^2 - 5x - 6 = 0$, we write

$$f(x) = 4x^5 - x^4 - 4x^3 + x^2 - 5x - 6$$

and

$$f(-x) = -4x^5 - x^4 + 4x^3 + x^2 + 5x - 6.$$

Thus there are no more than three positive and two negative roots.

At this point let us summarize the information we can determine about the roots of a polynomial equation $f(x) = 0$ of degree n:

(1) There are n roots.

(2) Complex roots appear in conjugate pairs.

(3) Any rational roots must be factors of the constant term divided by factors of the coefficient of the highest-power term.

(4) The maximum number of positive roots is the number of sign changes in $f(x)$, and the maximum number of negative roots is the number of sign changes in $f(-x)$.

(5) Once we determine $n - 2$ of the roots, the remaining roots can be found by the quadratic formula.

Synthetic division is normally used to try possible roots. This is because synthetic division is relatively easy to perform, and when a root is found we have the quotient factor, which is of degree one less than the degree of the dividend. Each root we find makes the ensuing work simpler. The following examples indicate the complete method, as well as two other helpful rules.

Example E.   Determine the roots of the equation $2x^3 + x^2 + 5x - 3 = 0$.

Since $n = 3$, there are three roots. If we can find one of these roots, we can use the quadratic formula to find the other two. We have $f(x) = 2x^3 + x^2 + 5x - 3$, and therefore there is one positive root. We also have $f(-x) = -2x^3 + x^2 - 5x - 3$, and therefore there are no more than two negative roots. The *possible* rational roots are ± 1, $\pm\frac{1}{2}$, $\pm\frac{3}{2}$, ± 3. Thus, using synthetic division, we shall try these. We first try the root 1 (always a possibility if there are positive roots).

$$
\begin{array}{rrrr|r}
2 & 1 & 5 & -3 & \;1 \\
  & 2 & 3 & 8 & \\
\hline
2 & 3 & 8 & 5 &
\end{array}
$$

Thus we see that 1 is not a root, but we have gained some information, if we observe closely. If we try any positive number larger than 1, the results in the last row will be larger positive numbers than we now have. The products will be larger, and therefore the sums will also be larger. Thus there is no positive root larger than 1. This leads to the following rule: *When we are trying a root, if the bottom row contains all positive numbers, then there are no roots larger than the one tried.* This rule tells us that there is no reason to try $+\frac{3}{2}$ and $+3$ as roots. Therefore, let us now try $+\frac{1}{2}$.

$$\begin{array}{rrrr|r}
2 & 1 & 5 & -3 & \frac{1}{2} \\
& 1 & 1 & 3 & \\
\hline
2 & 2 & 6 & 0 &
\end{array}$$

Hence $+\frac{1}{2}$ is a root, and the remaining factor is $2x^2 + 2x + 6$, which itself factors to $2(x^2 + x + 3)$. By the quadratic formula we find the remaining roots.

$$x = \frac{-1 \pm \sqrt{1 - 12}}{2} = \frac{-1 \pm \sqrt{11}\,j}{2}$$

The three roots are

$$\frac{1}{2}, \qquad \frac{-1 + \sqrt{11}\,j}{2}, \qquad \text{and} \qquad \frac{-1 - \sqrt{11}\,j}{2}.$$

We note that there were actually no negative roots, because the nonpositive roots are complex. Also, in proceeding in this way, we never found it necessary to try any negative roots. It must be admitted, however, that the solutions to all problems may not be so easily determined.

Example F. Determine the roots of the equation $x^4 - 7x^3 + 12x^2 + 4x - 16 = 0$.

We write

$$f(x) = x^4 - 7x^3 + 12x^2 + 4x - 16,$$
$$f(-x) = x^4 + 7x^3 + 12x^2 - 4x - 16.$$

We see that there are four roots; there are no more than three positive roots, and there is one negative root. The possible rational roots are ± 1, ± 2, ± 4, ± 8, ± 16. Since there is only one negative root, we shall look for this one first. Trying -2, we have

$$\begin{array}{rrrrr|r}
1 & -7 & +12 & +4 & -16 & -2 \\
& -2 & +18 & -60 & +112 & \\
\hline
1 & -9 & +30 & -56 & +96 &
\end{array}$$

If we were to try any negative roots less than -2 (remember, -3 is less than -2), we would find that the numbers would still alternate from term to term in the quotient. Thus we have this rule: *If the signs alternate in the bottom row, then there are no roots less than the one tried.* So we next try -1.

$$\begin{array}{rrrrr|r}
1 & -7 & +12 & +4 & -16 & -1 \\
& -1 & 8 & -20 & 16 & \\
\hline
1 & -8 & 20 & -16 & 0 &
\end{array}$$

Thus, -1 is the negative root. Next we shall try $+1$.

$$\begin{array}{rrrr|r}
1 & -8 & 20 & -16 & 1 \\
& 1 & -7 & 13 & \\
\hline
1 & -7 & 13 & -3 &
\end{array}$$

Since $+1$ is not a root, we next try $+2$.

$$
\begin{array}{rrrr|l}
1 & -8 & 20 & -16 & \;2 \\
  & 2 & -12 & 16 & \\
\hline
1 & -6 & 8 & 0 &
\end{array}
$$

Thus $+2$ is a root. It is not necessary to find any more roots by trial and error. We use the quadratic formula on the remaining factor $x^2 - 6x + 8$, and find that the roots are 2 and 4. Thus the roots are $-1, 2, 2$, and 4. (Note that 2 is a double root.)

Exercises

In Exercises 1 through 16 solve the given equations.

1. $x^3 + 2x^2 - x - 2 = 0$
2. $x^3 + x^2 - 5x + 3 = 0$
3. $x^3 + 2x^2 - 5x - 6 = 0$
4. $x^3 + 1 = 0$
5. $2x^3 - 5x^2 - 28x + 15 = 0$
6. $2x^3 - x^2 - 3x - 1 = 0$
7. $x^4 - 11x^2 - 12x + 4 = 0$
8. $x^4 + x^3 - 2x^2 - 4x - 8 = 0$
9. $x^4 - 2x^3 - 13x^2 + 14x + 24 = 0$
10. $x^4 - x^3 + 2x^2 - 4x - 8 = 0$
11. $2x^4 - 5x^3 - 3x^2 + 4x + 2 = 0$
12. $2x^4 + 7x^3 + 9x^2 + 5x + 1 = 0$
13. $12x^4 + 44x^3 + 21x^2 - 11x - 6 = 0$
14. $9x^4 - 3x^3 + 34x^2 - 12x - 8 = 0$
15. $x^5 + x^4 - 9x^3 - 5x^2 + 16x + 12 = 0$
16. $x^6 - x^4 - 14x^2 + 24 = 0$

In Exercises 17 through 20 determine the required quantities. In Exercises 19 and 20 it is necessary to set up equations of higher degree.

17. The deflection y of a beam at a horizontal distance x from one end is given by $y = k(x^4 - 2Lx^3 + L^3x)$, where L is the length of the beam and k is a constant. For what values of x is the deflection zero?

18. Under certain conditions, the velocity of an object as a function of time is given by $v = 2t^3 - 11t^2 - 28t - 15$. For what values of t is $v = 0$?

19. A rectangular box is made from a piece of cardboard 8 in. by 12 in., by cutting a square from each corner and bending up the sides. How large is the side of the square cut out, if the volume of the box is 64 in^3?

20. A slice 2 in. thick is cut off the side of a cube, leaving 75 in^3 in the remaining volume. Find the length of the edge of the cube.

14-5 Irrational roots by linear interpolation

When a polynomial equation has more than two irrational roots, we cannot find these roots by the methods just presented. Therefore we must have some method for finding irrational roots for those equations in which we cannot reduce the given function to quadratic factors. Many methods have been developed for this purpose, but we shall discuss only one: *linear interpolation*. The basic assumption is the same as that involved in finding values which lie between listed values in tables; namely, that if two points are sufficiently close to each other, a straight line joining the points will very nearly approximate the actual curve between the two points. This method is basically a graphical one, and is illustrated in the following examples.

Example A.   Using the method of linear interpolation, find the irrational root of the equation $x^3 + 2x^2 + 8x - 2 = 0$ which lies between 0 and 1.

We know that wherever a curve crosses the x-axis, that value of x is a root. We are told that the root we want is between 0 and 1. Normally we would then expect to find the function to be either positive or negative when $x = 0$, and to have the opposite sign when $x = 1$. To check this, the remainder theorem is of use. We find that $f(0) = -2$ and $f(1) = 9$. We now *assume* that the curve between these points can be approximated by a straight line between these points. If this were exactly correct, as the magnified scale drawing in Fig. 14-1 shows, the root would lie between 0.1 and 0.2, very close to 0.2. Hence we shall try these values, using synthetic division, and rounding off to two significant digits for now.

1	2	8	-2	$\underline{\;0.1}$		1	2	8	-2	$\underline{\;0.2}$
	0.1	0.2	0.8				0.2	0.4	1.7	
1	2.1	8.2	-1.2			1	2.2	8.4	-0.3	

We note that the remainders for $x = 0.1$ and $x = 0.2$ are -1.2 and -0.3 respectively. Since the signs are the same, the root does not lie between 0.1 and 0.2. We do know, however, that it lies between 0.2 and 1. Thus we continue trying values of x nearer 1.

1	2	8	-2	$\underline{\;0.3}$
	0.3	0.7	2.6	
1	2.3	8.7	0.6	

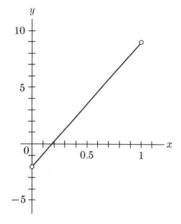

Figure 14-1

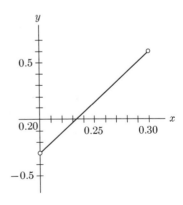

Figure 14-2

Since the sign of the remainder for $x = 0.3$ is positive, we now know that the root lies between 0.2 and 0.3. Again we make a scale drawing (Fig. 14-2) to approximate the hundredths digit. The root is apparently between 0.23 and 0.24. We shall try these values (rounding off to three significant digits).

1	2	8	−2	0.23		1	2	8	−2	0.24
	0.23	0.51	1.96				0.24	0.54	2.05	
1	2.23	8.51	−0.04			1	2.24	8.54	0.05	

Thus the root is between 0.23 and 0.24. Since the remainder is numerically smaller for $x = 0.23$, we may conclude from linear interpolation that this is the value of the root to two significant digits. The process may be continued to obtain greater accuracy if necessary.

Example B. By linear interpolation, find the root between 1 and 2 of the equation $x^4 - 5x^3 + 6x^2 - 5x + 5 = 0$.

The method followed should be clear when we observe Fig. 14-3 and the steps shown.

1	−5	6	−5	5	1		1	−5	6	−5	5	2
	1	−4	2	−3				2	−6	0	−10	
1	−4	2	−3	+2			1	−3	0	−5	−5	

1	−5	6	−5	5	1.2
	1.2	−4.6	1.7	−4.0	
1	−3.8	1.4	−3.3	+1.0	

1	−5	6	−5	5	1.3
	1.3	−4.8	1.6	−4.4	
1	−3.7	1.2	−3.4	+0.6	

1	−5	6	−5	5	1.4
	1.4	−5.0	1.4	−5.04	
1	−3.6	+1.0	−3.6	−0.04	

1	−5	6	−5	5	1.39
	1.39	−5.02	1.36	−5.06	
1	−3.61	0.98	−3.64	−0.06	

1	−5	6	−5	5	1.38
	1.38	−5.00	1.38	−4.996	
1	−3.62	1.00	−3.62	+0.004	

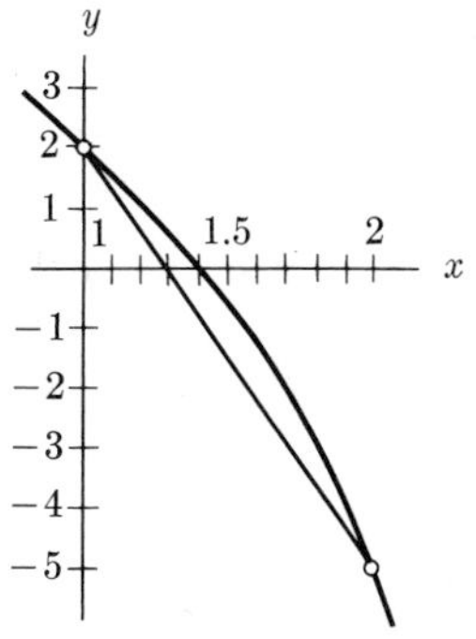

Figure 14-3

Thus $r = 1.38$ (to three significant figures).

If we must find the roots of an equation without any specific information as to the location of the roots, we first make an approximate graph. In this way we can know the integers between which the roots lie. Then linear interpolation can be used to approximate them more accurately. The following example outlines the method.

Example C.   Find the roots of the equation $2x^4 - 3x^3 - 6x^2 + 2x - 15 = 0$.

First we calculate values as shown in the following table so that we might graph the function

$$y = 2x^4 - 3x^3 - 6x^2 + 2x - 15$$

and thereby locate the roots approximately.

x	-2	-1	0	1	2	3
y	13	-18	-15	-20	-27	18

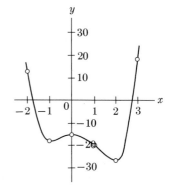

Figure 14-4

The graph is shown in Fig. 14-4. We note that the roots of the equation lie between $x = -2$ and $x = -1$, and between $x = 2$ and $x = 3$. By using linear interpolation these roots can be found more accurately. In this case, the roots are approximately $x = -1.79$ and $x = 2.79$.

Exercises

In Exercises 1 through 8 find by linear interpolation the irrational root (to two decimal places) between the indicated values of x.

1. $x^3 - 6x^2 + 10x - 4 = 0$ (0 and 1)
2. $x^3 - 3x^2 - 2x + 3 = 0$ (0 and 1)
3. $x^3 - 5x^2 + 7x - 2 = 0$ (0 and 1)
4. $x^3 - 5x^2 + 3x + 4 = 0$ (1 and 2)
5. $2x^3 + 2x^2 - 11x + 3 = 0$ (1 and 2)
6. $3x^3 + 13x^2 + 3x - 4 = 0$ (-1 and 0)
7. $x^4 - x^3 - 3x^2 - x - 4 = 0$ (2 and 3)
8. $2x^4 - x^3 + 6x^2 - 4x - 8 = 0$ (-1 and 0)

In Exercises 9 through 12 find all of the real roots of the given equations to two decimal places.

9. $x^3 - 2x^2 - 5x + 4 = 0$
10. $x^3 - 2x^2 - 2x - 7 = 0$
11. $x^4 - x^3 - 2x^2 - x - 3 = 0$
12. $x^5 - 2x^4 + 4x^3 - 7x^2 + 4 = 0$

In Exercises 13 and 14 determine the required values.

13. The ends of a 10-ft beam are supported at different levels. The deflection y of the beam is given by $y = kx^2(x^3 + 450x - 3500)$, where x is the horizontal distance from one end and k is a constant. Determine the values of x for which the deflection is zero.

14. The sides of a rectangular box are 3, 5, and 6 ft. If each side is increased by the same amount, the volume is doubled. By how much should each side be increased to accomplish this?

14-6 Miscellaneous Exercises

In Exercises 1 through 4 find the remainder of the indicated division by the remainder theorem.

1. $(2x^3 - 4x^2 - x + 4) \div (x - 1)$
2. $(x^3 - 2x^2 + 9) \div (x + 2)$
3. $(4x^3 + x + 4) \div (x + 3)$
4. $(x^4 - 5x^3 + 8x^2 + 15x - 2) \div (x - 3)$

In Exercises 5 through 8 use the factor theorem to determine whether or not the second expression is a factor of the first.

5. $x^4 + x^3 + x^2 - 2x - 3, \quad x + 1$
6. $2x^3 - 2x^2 - 3x - 2, \quad x - 2$
7. $x^4 + 4x^3 + 5x^2 + 5x - 6, \quad x + 3$
8. $9x^3 + 6x^2 + 4x + 2, \quad 3x + 1$

In Exercises 9 through 16 use synthetic division to perform the indicated divisions.

9. $(x^3 + 3x^2 + 6x + 1) \div (x - 1)$
10. $(3x^3 - 2x^2 + 7) \div (x - 3)$
11. $(2x^3 - 3x^2 - 4x + 3) \div (x + 2)$
12. $(3x^3 - 5x^2 + 7x - 6) \div (x + 4)$
13. $(x^4 - 2x^3 - 3x^2 - 4x - 8) \div (x + 1)$
14. $(x^4 - 6x^3 + x - 8) \div (x - 3)$
15. $(2x^5 - 46x^3 + x^2 - 9) \div (x - 5)$
16. $(x^6 + 63x^3 + 5x^2 - 9x - 8) \div (x + 4)$

In Exercises 17 through 20 use synthetic division to determine whether or not the given numbers are zeros of the given functions.

17. $x^3 + 8x^2 + 17x - 6; \quad -3$
18. $2x^3 + x^2 - 4x + 4; \quad -2$
19. $2x^4 - x^3 + 2x^2 + x - 1; \frac{1}{2}$
20. $6x^4 - 7x^3 + 2x^2 - 9x - 6; \quad -\frac{2}{3}$

In Exercises 21 through 24 find all of the solutions of the given equations, with the aid of synthetic division and with the roots indicated.

21. $3x^4 + 5x^3 + x^2 + x - 10 = 0 \quad (r_1 = 1, r_2 = -2)$
22. $x^4 - x^3 - 5x^2 - x - 6 = 0 \quad (r_1 = 3, r_2 = -2)$
23. $x^5 + 3x^4 - x^3 - 11x^2 - 12x - 4 = 0 \quad (-1 \text{ is a triple root})$
24. $x^4 + x^3 - 11x^2 - 9x + 18 = 0 \quad (r_1 = -3, r_2 = 1)$

In Exercises 25 through 32 solve the given equations.

25. $x^3 + x^2 - 10x + 8 = 0$
26. $x^3 - 8x^2 + 20x - 16 = 0$
27. $2x^3 - x^2 - 8x - 5 = 0$
28. $2x^3 - 3x^2 - 11x + 6 = 0$
29. $6x^3 - x^2 - 12x - 5 = 0$
30. $6x^3 + 19x^2 + 2x - 3 = 0$
31. $2x^4 + x^3 + 3x^2 + 2x - 2 = 0$
32. $2x^4 + 5x^3 - 14x^2 - 23x + 30 = 0$

In Exercises 33 through 36, find the indicated irrational root by linear interpolation. Find the value to two decimal places.

33. $x^3 - 3x^2 - x + 2 = 0$ (between 0 and 1)

34. $x^3 + 3x^2 - 6x - 2 = 0$ (between 1 and 2)

35. $3x^3 - x^2 - 8x - 2 = 0$ (between 1 and 2)

36. $x^4 + 3x^3 + 6x + 4 = 0$ (between -1 and 0)

In Exercises 37 through 40 determine the required quantities.

37. The width of a rectangular box equals the depth, and the length is 4 ft more than the width. The volume of the box is 539 ft³. What are the dimensions of the box?

38. A certain sphere floating in water sinks to a depth y which is given by the equation $y^3 - 6y^2 + 16 = 0$. Find, to one decimal place, the depth (in cm) to which the sphere sinks.

39. The area of a segment of a circle is given approximately by the equation

$$A = \frac{h^3}{2L} + \frac{2Lh}{3},$$

where L is the length of the chord and h is the altitude of the segment. Find h when $L = 3$ and $A = 4$. (Evaluate to two decimal places.)

40. Find all of the roots of the equation $6x^4 - 14x^3 + 5x^2 + 5x - 2 = 0$.

Determinants and Matrices

15

15-1 Determinants: expansion by minors

In Chapter 4 we first met the concept of a determinant and saw how it is used to solve systems of linear equations. However, at that time we limited our discussion to second- and third-order determinants. In the first two sections of this chapter we shall show methods of evaluating higher-order determinants. In the remainder of the chapter we shall develop another related concept and its use in solving systems of linear equations.

From Section 4-6, we recall that a third-order determinant is defined by the equation

$$\begin{vmatrix} a_1 & b_1 & c_1 \\ a_2 & b_2 & c_2 \\ a_3 & b_3 & c_3 \end{vmatrix} = a_1 b_2 c_3 + a_3 b_1 c_2 + a_2 b_3 c_1 - a_3 b_2 c_1 - a_1 b_3 c_2 - a_2 b_1 c_3. \quad (15\text{-}1)$$

If we rearrange the terms on the right and factor a_1, a_2, and a_3 from the terms in which they are contained, we have

$$\begin{vmatrix} a_1 & b_1 & c_1 \\ a_2 & b_2 & c_2 \\ a_3 & b_3 & c_3 \end{vmatrix} = a_1(b_2 c_3 - b_3 c_2) - a_2(b_1 c_3 - b_3 c_1) + a_3(b_1 c_2 - b_2 c_1). \quad (15\text{-}2)$$

Recalling the definition of a second-order determinant we have

$$\begin{vmatrix} a_1 & b_1 & c_1 \\ a_2 & b_2 & c_2 \\ a_3 & b_3 & c_3 \end{vmatrix} = a_1 \begin{vmatrix} b_2 & c_2 \\ b_3 & c_3 \end{vmatrix} - a_2 \begin{vmatrix} b_1 & c_1 \\ b_3 & c_3 \end{vmatrix} + a_3 \begin{vmatrix} b_1 & c_1 \\ b_2 & c_2 \end{vmatrix}. \quad (15\text{-}3)$$

In Eq. (15-3) we note that the third-order determinant is expanded with the terms of the expansion as products of the elements of the first column and specific second-order determinants. In each case the elements of the second-order determinant are those elements which are in neither the same row nor the same column as the element from the first column. These determinants are called *minors*.

In general, the minor of a given element of a determinant is the determinant which results by deleting the row and the column in which the element lies. Consider the following example.

Example A. Consider the determinant $\begin{vmatrix} 1 & 2 & 3 \\ 4 & 5 & 6 \\ 7 & 8 & 9 \end{vmatrix}$.

We find the minor of the element 1 by deleting the elements in the first row and first column because the element 1 is located in the first row and in the first column. This minor is the determinant

$$\begin{vmatrix} 5 & 6 \\ 8 & 9 \end{vmatrix}.$$

The minor for the element 2 is formed by deleting the elements in the first row and second column, for this is the location of the 2. The minor of 2 is the determinant

$$\begin{vmatrix} 4 & 6 \\ 7 & 9 \end{vmatrix}.$$

The minor for the element 6 is the determinant

$$\begin{vmatrix} 1 & 2 \\ 7 & 8 \end{vmatrix}.$$

The minor for the element 8 is the determinant

$$\begin{vmatrix} 1 & 3 \\ 4 & 6 \end{vmatrix}.$$

We now see that Eq. (15-3) expresses the expansion of a third-order determinant as the sum of the products of the elements of the first column and their minors, with the second term assigned a minus sign. Actually this is only one of several ways of expressing the expansion. However, it does lead to a general theorem regarding the expansion of a determinant of any order. The foregoing provides a basis for this theorem, although it cannot be considered as a proof. The theorem is as follows:

The value of a determinant of order n may be found by forming the n products of the elements of any column (or row) and their minors. A product is given a plus sign if the sum of the number of the column and the number of the row in which the element lies is even, and a minus sign if this sum is odd. The algebraic sum of the terms thus obtained is the value of the determinant.

The following examples illustrate the expansion of determinants by minors in accordance with the theorem above.

Example B. Evaluate $\begin{vmatrix} 1 & -3 & -2 \\ 4 & -1 & 0 \\ 4 & 3 & -5 \end{vmatrix}$ by expansion by minors.

Since we may expand by any column or row, let us select the first row. The expansion is as follows:

$$\begin{vmatrix} 1 & -3 & -2 \\ 4 & -1 & 0 \\ 4 & 3 & -5 \end{vmatrix} = +(1)\begin{vmatrix} -1 & 0 \\ 3 & -5 \end{vmatrix} - (-3)\begin{vmatrix} 4 & 0 \\ 4 & -5 \end{vmatrix} + (-2)\begin{vmatrix} 4 & -1 \\ 4 & 3 \end{vmatrix}.$$

The first term of the expansion is assigned a plus sign since the element 1 is in column 1, row 1 and $1 + 1 = 2$ (even). The second term is assigned a minus sign since the element -3 is in column 2 and row 1, and $2 + 1 = 3$ (odd). The third term is assigned a plus sign since the element -2 is in column 3 and row 1, and $3 + 1 = 4$ (even). Actually, once the first sign has been properly determined, the others are known since the signs alternate from term to term. Using the definition of a second-order determinant, we complete the evaluation.

$$\begin{vmatrix} 1 & -3 & -2 \\ 4 & -1 & 0 \\ 4 & 3 & -5 \end{vmatrix} = +(1)(5 - 0) - (-3)(-20 - 0) + (-2)[12 - (-4)]$$

$$= 1(5) + 3(-20) - 2(16) = 5 - 60 - 32 = -87.$$

Expansion of this same determinant by the third column is as follows:

$$\begin{vmatrix} 1 & -3 & -2 \\ 4 & -1 & 0 \\ 4 & 3 & -5 \end{vmatrix} = +(-2)\begin{vmatrix} 4 & -1 \\ 4 & 3 \end{vmatrix} - (0)\begin{vmatrix} 1 & -3 \\ 4 & 3 \end{vmatrix} + (-5)\begin{vmatrix} 1 & -3 \\ 4 & -1 \end{vmatrix}$$

$$= -2(12 + 4) + 0 - 5(-1 + 12)$$

$$= -2(16) - 5(11) = -32 - 55 = -87.$$

This expansion has one advantage: since one of the elements of the third column is zero, its minor does not have to be evaluated because zero times whatever the value of the determinant will give the product of zero.

Example C.   Evaluate $\begin{vmatrix} 3 & -2 & 0 & 2 \\ 1 & 0 & -1 & 4 \\ -3 & 1 & 2 & -2 \\ 2 & -1 & 0 & -1 \end{vmatrix}.$

Expanding by the third column, we have

$$\begin{vmatrix} 3 & -2 & 0 & 2 \\ 1 & 0 & -1 & 4 \\ -3 & 1 & 2 & -2 \\ 2 & -1 & 0 & -1 \end{vmatrix} = +(0)\begin{vmatrix} 1 & 0 & 4 \\ -3 & 1 & -2 \\ 2 & -1 & -1 \end{vmatrix} - (-1)\begin{vmatrix} 3 & -2 & 2 \\ -3 & 1 & -2 \\ 2 & -1 & -1 \end{vmatrix}$$

$$+(2)\begin{vmatrix} 3 & -2 & 2 \\ 1 & 0 & 4 \\ 2 & -1 & -1 \end{vmatrix} - (0)\begin{vmatrix} 3 & -2 & 2 \\ 1 & 0 & 4 \\ -3 & 1 & -2 \end{vmatrix}.$$

It is not necessary to expand the minors in the first and fourth terms, since the element in each case is zero. The minors in the second and third terms can be expanded as third-order determinants or by minors. This illustrates well that expansion by minors effectively reduces the order of the determinant to be evaluated by one. Completing the evaluation by minors, we have

$$\begin{vmatrix} 3 & -2 & 0 & 2 \\ 1 & 0 & -1 & 4 \\ -3 & 1 & 2 & -2 \\ 2 & -1 & 0 & -1 \end{vmatrix} = \begin{vmatrix} 3 & -2 & 2 \\ -3 & 1 & -2 \\ 2 & -1 & -1 \end{vmatrix} + 2\begin{vmatrix} 3 & -2 & 2 \\ 1 & 0 & 4 \\ 2 & -1 & -1 \end{vmatrix}$$

$$= \left[3\begin{vmatrix} 1 & -2 \\ -1 & -1 \end{vmatrix} - (-3)\begin{vmatrix} -2 & 2 \\ -1 & -1 \end{vmatrix} + 2\begin{vmatrix} -2 & 2 \\ 1 & -2 \end{vmatrix} \right]$$

$$+ 2\left[-(-2)\begin{vmatrix} 1 & 4 \\ 2 & -1 \end{vmatrix} + 0\begin{vmatrix} 3 & 2 \\ 2 & -1 \end{vmatrix} - (-1)\begin{vmatrix} 3 & 2 \\ 1 & 4 \end{vmatrix} \right]$$

$$= [3(-1-2) + 3(2+2) + 2(4-2)]$$
$$+ 2[2(-1-8) + (12-2)]$$

$$= [-9 + 12 + 4] + 2[-18 + 10]$$

$$= +7 + 2(-8) = -9.$$

We can use the expansion of determinants by minors to solve systems of linear equations. Cramer's rule for solving systems of equations, as stated in Section 4-6, is valid for any system of n equations in n unknowns. The following example illustrates the solution of a system of four equations in four unknowns.

Example D. Solve the following system of equations.

$$
\begin{aligned}
x + 2y + z \quad\quad &= 5 \\
2x \quad\quad + z + 2t &= 1 \\
x - y + 3z + 4t &= -6 \\
4x - y \quad\quad - 2t &= 0
\end{aligned}
$$

$$
x = \frac{\begin{vmatrix} 5 & 2 & 1 & 0 \\ 1 & 0 & 1 & 2 \\ -6 & -1 & 3 & 4 \\ 0 & -1 & 0 & -2 \end{vmatrix}}{\begin{vmatrix} 1 & 2 & 1 & 0 \\ 2 & 0 & 1 & 2 \\ 1 & -1 & 3 & 4 \\ 4 & -1 & 0 & -2 \end{vmatrix}}
$$

$$
= \frac{-(0)\begin{vmatrix} 2 & 1 & 0 \\ 0 & 1 & 2 \\ -1 & 3 & 4 \end{vmatrix} + (-1)\begin{vmatrix} 5 & 1 & 0 \\ 1 & 1 & 2 \\ -6 & 3 & 4 \end{vmatrix} - (0)\begin{vmatrix} 5 & 2 & 0 \\ 1 & 0 & 2 \\ -6 & -1 & 4 \end{vmatrix} + (-2)\begin{vmatrix} 5 & 2 & 1 \\ 1 & 0 & 1 \\ -6 & -1 & 3 \end{vmatrix}}{(1)\begin{vmatrix} 0 & 1 & 2 \\ -1 & 3 & 4 \\ -1 & 0 & -2 \end{vmatrix} - 2\begin{vmatrix} 2 & 1 & 2 \\ 1 & 3 & 4 \\ 4 & 0 & -2 \end{vmatrix} + (1)\begin{vmatrix} 2 & 0 & 2 \\ 1 & -1 & 4 \\ 4 & -1 & -2 \end{vmatrix} - (0)\begin{vmatrix} 2 & 0 & 1 \\ 1 & -1 & 3 \\ 4 & -1 & 0 \end{vmatrix}}
$$

$$
= \frac{-(-26) - 2(-14)}{1(0) - 2(-18) + 1(18)} = \frac{26 + 28}{36 + 18} = \frac{54}{54} = 1
$$

In solving for x the determinant in the numerator was evaluated by expanding by the minors of the fourth row, since it contained two zeros. The determinant in the denominator was evaluated by expanding by the minors of the first row. Now we solve for y, and we again note two zeros in the fourth row of the determinant of the numerator.

$$
y = \frac{\begin{vmatrix} 1 & 5 & 1 & 0 \\ 2 & 1 & 1 & 2 \\ 1 & -6 & 3 & 4 \\ 4 & 0 & 0 & -2 \end{vmatrix}}{54} = \frac{-4\begin{vmatrix} 5 & 1 & 0 \\ 1 & 1 & 2 \\ -6 & 3 & 4 \end{vmatrix} + (-2)\begin{vmatrix} 1 & 5 & 1 \\ 2 & 1 & 1 \\ 1 & -6 & 3 \end{vmatrix}}{54}
$$

$$
= \frac{-4(-26) - 2(-29)}{54} = \frac{104 + 58}{54} = \frac{162}{54} = 3.
$$

Substituting these values for x and y into the first equation, we can solve for z. This gives $z = -2$. Again, substituting the values for x and y into the fourth equation, we find $t = \frac{1}{2}$. Thus the required solution is $x = 1$, $y = 3$, $z = -2$, $t = \frac{1}{2}$. The solution can be checked by substituting these values into either the second or third equation.

Exercises

In Exercises 1 through 12 evaluate the given determinants by expansion by minors.

1. $\begin{vmatrix} 3 & 0 & 0 \\ -2 & 1 & 4 \\ 4 & -2 & 5 \end{vmatrix}$

2. $\begin{vmatrix} 10 & 0 & -3 \\ -2 & -4 & 1 \\ 3 & 0 & 2 \end{vmatrix}$

3. $\begin{vmatrix} -2 & -4 & 2 \\ 1 & 3 & 0 \\ -4 & 5 & 2 \end{vmatrix}$

4. $\begin{vmatrix} 5 & -1 & 2 \\ 8 & 3 & -4 \\ 0 & 2 & -6 \end{vmatrix}$

5. $\begin{vmatrix} -6 & -1 & 3 \\ 2 & -2 & -3 \\ 10 & 1 & -2 \end{vmatrix}$

6. $\begin{vmatrix} 9 & -3 & 1 \\ -1 & 2 & -1 \\ 2 & -1 & 3 \end{vmatrix}$

7. $\begin{vmatrix} 1 & 0 & 1 & 0 \\ 2 & 4 & -3 & 1 \\ 1 & 1 & 1 & 1 \\ 3 & 5 & 0 & 2 \end{vmatrix}$

8. $\begin{vmatrix} 2 & 0 & 3 & 1 \\ -1 & -1 & 4 & 0 \\ 1 & 2 & 1 & 2 \\ 3 & 3 & -2 & -1 \end{vmatrix}$

9. $\begin{vmatrix} 2 & -1 & 1 & -4 \\ 2 & 1 & 3 & -5 \\ 3 & -1 & -1 & 0 \\ 1 & 2 & 2 & 6 \end{vmatrix}$

10. $\begin{vmatrix} 3 & 6 & -2 & 4 \\ 2 & -5 & 2 & 6 \\ 5 & 3 & 4 & 0 \\ 1 & 2 & 0 & -1 \end{vmatrix}$

11. $\begin{vmatrix} 1 & 2 & 1 & 2 & 1 \\ 1 & 0 & 0 & 1 & 0 \\ 0 & 1 & 1 & 0 & 1 \\ 1 & 1 & 2 & 2 & 1 \\ 0 & 1 & 1 & 0 & 2 \end{vmatrix}$

12. $\begin{vmatrix} 3 & 1 & 1 & 1 & 2 \\ 1 & 1 & 0 & 0 & 1 \\ 1 & 1 & 2 & 2 & 3 \\ 0 & 2 & 1 & 0 & 3 \\ 1 & 1 & 0 & 1 & 0 \end{vmatrix}$

In Exercises 13 through 21 solve the given systems of equations by determinants. Evaluate the determinants by expansion by minors.

13. $2x + y + z = 6$
$x - 2y + 2z = 10$
$3x - y - z = 4$

14. $2x + y = -1$
$4x - 2y - z = 5$
$2x + 3y + 3z = -2$

15. $3x + 6y + 2z = -2$
$x + 3y - 4z = 2$
$2x - 3y - 2z = -2$

16. $x + 3y + z = 4$
$2x - 6y - 3z = 10$
$4x - 9y + 3z = 4$

17. $x + t = 0$
$3x + y + z = -1$
$2y - z + 3t = 1$
$2z - 3t = 1$

18. $2x + y + z = 4$
$2y - 2z - t = 3$
$3y - 3z + 2t = 1$
$6x - y + t = 0$

19. $x + 2y - z = 6$
    $y - 2z - 3t = -5$
    $3x - 2y + t = 2$
    $2x + y + z - t = 0$

20. $2x + 3y + z = 4$
    $x - 2y - 3z + 4t = -1$
    $3x + y + z - 5t = 3$
    $-x + 2y + z + 3t = 2$

21. In applying Kirchhoff's laws (see Exercise 13 of Section 4-5) to the given electric circuit, the following equations are found. Determine the indicated currents (see Fig. 15-1).

$$I_A + I_B + I_C + I_D = 0$$
$$2I_A - I_B = -2$$
$$3I_C - 2I_D = 0$$
$$I_B - 3I_C = 6$$

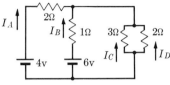

Figure 15-1

15-2 Some properties of determinants

Expansion of determinants by minors allows us to evaluate a determinant of any order. However, even for a fourth-order determinant, the amount of work necessary for the evaluation is usually excessive. There are a number of basic properties of determinants which allow us to perform the evaluation with considerably less work. We will present these properties here without proof, although each will be illustrated.

(1) *If each element below the principal diagonal of a determinant is zero, then the product of the elements of the principal diagonal is the value of the determinant.*

Example A. The value of the determinant

$$\begin{vmatrix} 2 & 1 & 5 & 8 \\ 0 & -5 & 7 & 9 \\ 0 & 0 & 4 & -6 \\ 0 & 0 & 0 & 3 \end{vmatrix}$$

equals the product $2(-5)(4)(3) = -120$. Since all of the elements below the principal diagonal are zero, there is no need to expand the determinant. It will be noted, however, that if the determinant is expanded by the first column, and successive determinants are expanded by their first columns, the same value is found. Performing the expansion we have

$$\begin{vmatrix} 2 & 1 & 5 & 8 \\ 0 & -5 & 7 & 9 \\ 0 & 0 & 4 & -6 \\ 0 & 0 & 0 & 3 \end{vmatrix}$$

$$= 2 \begin{vmatrix} -5 & 7 & 9 \\ 0 & 4 & -6 \\ 0 & 0 & 3 \end{vmatrix}$$

$$= 2(-5) \begin{vmatrix} 4 & -6 \\ 0 & 3 \end{vmatrix} = 2(-5)(4)(3)$$

$$= -120.$$

(2) *If the corresponding rows and columns of a determinant are interchanged, the value of the determinant is unchanged.*

Example B. For the determinant

$$\begin{vmatrix} 1 & 3 & -1 \\ 2 & 0 & 4 \\ -2 & 5 & -6 \end{vmatrix}$$

if we interchange the first row and first column, the second row and second column, and the third row and third column, we obtain the determinant

$$\begin{vmatrix} 1 & 2 & -2 \\ 3 & 0 & 5 \\ -1 & 4 & -6 \end{vmatrix}.$$

By expanding, we can show that the value of each is the same. We obtain very similar expansions if we expand the first by the first column, and the second by the first row. These expansions are

$$\begin{vmatrix} 1 & 3 & -1 \\ 2 & 0 & 4 \\ -2 & 5 & -6 \end{vmatrix} = (1) \begin{vmatrix} 0 & 4 \\ 5 & -6 \end{vmatrix} -2 \begin{vmatrix} 3 & -1 \\ 5 & -6 \end{vmatrix} +(-2) \begin{vmatrix} 3 & -1 \\ 0 & 4 \end{vmatrix}$$

$$= (-20) - 2(-13) - 2(12) = -18.$$

$$\begin{vmatrix} 1 & 2 & -2 \\ 3 & 0 & 5 \\ -1 & 4 & -6 \end{vmatrix} = (1) \begin{vmatrix} 0 & 5 \\ 4 & -6 \end{vmatrix} -2 \begin{vmatrix} 3 & 5 \\ -1 & -6 \end{vmatrix} +(-2) \begin{vmatrix} 3 & 0 \\ -1 & 4 \end{vmatrix}$$

$$= (-20) - 2(-13) - 2(12) = -18.$$

Therefore, we see that $\begin{vmatrix} 1 & 3 & -1 \\ 2 & 0 & 4 \\ -2 & 5 & -6 \end{vmatrix} = \begin{vmatrix} 1 & 2 & -2 \\ 3 & 0 & 5 \\ -1 & 4 & -6 \end{vmatrix}.$

(3) *If two columns (or rows) of a determinant are identical, the value of the determinant is zero.*

Example C.   The value of the determinant

$$\begin{vmatrix} 3 & 5 & 2 \\ -4 & 6 & 9 \\ -4 & 6 & 9 \end{vmatrix}$$

is zero, since the second and third rows are identical. This is easily verified by expanding by the first row.

$$\begin{vmatrix} 3 & 5 & 2 \\ -4 & 6 & 9 \\ -4 & 6 & 9 \end{vmatrix} = 3\begin{vmatrix} 6 & 9 \\ 6 & 9 \end{vmatrix} - 5\begin{vmatrix} -4 & 9 \\ -4 & 9 \end{vmatrix} + 2\begin{vmatrix} -4 & 6 \\ -4 & 6 \end{vmatrix}$$

$$= 3(0) - 5(0) + 2(0) = 0$$

(4) *If two columns (or rows) of a determinant are interchanged, the value of the determinant is changed in sign.*

Example D.   The values of the determinants

$$\begin{vmatrix} 3 & 0 & 2 \\ 1 & 1 & 5 \\ 2 & 1 & 3 \end{vmatrix} \quad \text{and} \quad \begin{vmatrix} 2 & 0 & 3 \\ 5 & 1 & 1 \\ 3 & 1 & 2 \end{vmatrix}$$

differ in sign, since the first and third columns are interchanged. We shall verify this by expanding each by the second column.

$$\begin{vmatrix} 3 & 0 & 2 \\ 1 & 1 & 5 \\ 2 & 1 & 3 \end{vmatrix} = -(0)\begin{vmatrix} 1 & 5 \\ 2 & 3 \end{vmatrix} + (1)\begin{vmatrix} 3 & 2 \\ 2 & 3 \end{vmatrix} - (1)\begin{vmatrix} 3 & 2 \\ 1 & 5 \end{vmatrix}$$

$$= 0 + (9 - 4) - (15 - 2) = 5 - 13 = -8$$

$$\begin{vmatrix} 2 & 0 & 3 \\ 5 & 1 & 1 \\ 3 & 1 & 2 \end{vmatrix} = -(0)\begin{vmatrix} 5 & 1 \\ 3 & 2 \end{vmatrix} + (1)\begin{vmatrix} 2 & 3 \\ 3 & 2 \end{vmatrix} - (1)\begin{vmatrix} 2 & 3 \\ 5 & 1 \end{vmatrix}$$

$$= 0 + (4 - 9) - (2 - 15) = -5 + 13 = 8$$

Therefore, $$\begin{vmatrix} 3 & 0 & 2 \\ 1 & 1 & 5 \\ 2 & 1 & 3 \end{vmatrix} = -\begin{vmatrix} 2 & 0 & 3 \\ 5 & 1 & 1 \\ 3 & 1 & 2 \end{vmatrix}.$$

(5) *If all the elements of a column (or row) are multiplied by the same number k, the value of the determinant is multiplied by k.*

Example E. The value of the determinant

$$\begin{vmatrix} -1 & 0 & 6 \\ 2 & 1 & -2 \\ 0 & 5 & 3 \end{vmatrix}$$

is multiplied by 3 if the elements of the second row are multiplied by 3. That is,

$$\begin{vmatrix} -1 & 0 & 6 \\ 6 & 3 & -6 \\ 0 & 5 & 3 \end{vmatrix} = 3 \begin{vmatrix} -1 & 0 & 6 \\ 2 & 1 & -2 \\ 0 & 5 & 3 \end{vmatrix}.$$

By expansion, we can show that

$$\begin{vmatrix} -1 & 0 & 6 \\ 2 & 1 & -2 \\ 0 & 5 & 3 \end{vmatrix} = 47, \quad \text{and} \quad \begin{vmatrix} -1 & 0 & 6 \\ 6 & 3 & -6 \\ 0 & 5 & 3 \end{vmatrix} = 141.$$

The validity of this property can be seen by expanding each determinant by the second row. In each case one element is three times the other corresponding element, but the minors are the same. Look at the element in the second row, first column and its minor for each determinant.

$$2 \begin{vmatrix} 0 & 6 \\ 5 & 3 \end{vmatrix} \quad \text{and} \quad 6 \begin{vmatrix} 0 & 6 \\ 5 & 3 \end{vmatrix}$$

The element, 6, in the second determinant is three times the corresponding element, 2, in the first determinant, and the minors are the same.

(6) *If all the elements of any column (or row) are multiplied by the same number k, and the resulting numbers are added to the corresponding elements of another column (or row), the value of the determinant is unchanged.*

Example F. The value of the determinant

$$\begin{vmatrix} 4 & -1 & 3 \\ 2 & 2 & 1 \\ 1 & 0 & -3 \end{vmatrix}$$

is unchanged if we multiply each element of the first row by 2, and add these numbers to the corresponding elements of the second row. This gives

$$\begin{vmatrix} 4 & -1 & 3 \\ 2+8 & 2+(-2) & 1+6 \\ 1 & 0 & -3 \end{vmatrix} = \begin{vmatrix} 4 & -1 & 3 \\ 2 & 2 & 1 \\ 1 & 0 & -3 \end{vmatrix},$$

or

$$\begin{vmatrix} 4 & -1 & 3 \\ 10 & 0 & 7 \\ 1 & 0 & -3 \end{vmatrix} = \begin{vmatrix} 4 & -1 & 3 \\ 2 & 2 & 1 \\ 1 & 0 & -3 \end{vmatrix}.$$

When each determinant is expanded, the value -37 is obtained. The great value in property 6 is that by its use zeros can be purposely placed in the resulting determinant.

With the use of the properties above, determinants of higher order can be evaluated much more readily. The technique is to obtain zeros in a given column (or row) in all positions except one. We can then expand by this column (or row), thereby reducing the order of the determinant. The following example illustrates the method.

Example G. Evaluate $\begin{vmatrix} 3 & 2 & -1 & 1 \\ -1 & 1 & 2 & 3 \\ 2 & 2 & 1 & 4 \\ 0 & -1 & -2 & 2 \end{vmatrix}.$

The evaluation is as follows. The small circled numbers above the equals signs refer to the explanations given below the setup.

$$\begin{vmatrix} 3 & 2 & -1 & 1 \\ -1 & 1 & 2 & 3 \\ 2 & 2 & 1 & 4 \\ 0 & -1 & -2 & 2 \end{vmatrix} \stackrel{①}{=} \begin{vmatrix} 0 & 5 & 5 & 10 \\ -1 & 1 & 2 & 3 \\ 2 & 2 & 1 & 4 \\ 0 & -1 & -2 & 2 \end{vmatrix} \stackrel{②}{=} \begin{vmatrix} 0 & 5 & 5 & 10 \\ -1 & 1 & 2 & 3 \\ 0 & 4 & 5 & 10 \\ 0 & -1 & -2 & 2 \end{vmatrix}$$

① Each element of the second row is multiplied by 3, and the resulting numbers are added to the corresponding elements of the first row. Here we have used property 6. In this way a zero has been placed in column 1, row 1.

② Each element of the second row is multiplied by 2, and the resulting numbers are added to the corresponding elements of the third row. Again, we have used property 6. Also, a zero has been placed in the first column, third row. We now have three zeros in the first column.

$$\overset{(3)}{=} -(-1)\begin{vmatrix} 5 & 5 & 10 \\ 4 & 5 & 10 \\ -1 & -2 & 2 \end{vmatrix} \overset{(4)}{=} 5\begin{vmatrix} 1 & 1 & 2 \\ 4 & 5 & 10 \\ -1 & -2 & 2 \end{vmatrix}$$

$$\overset{(5)}{=} 5(2)\begin{vmatrix} 1 & 1 & 1 \\ 4 & 5 & 5 \\ -1 & -2 & 1 \end{vmatrix} \overset{(6)}{=} 10\begin{vmatrix} 1 & 1 & 1 \\ 0 & 1 & 1 \\ -1 & -2 & 1 \end{vmatrix}$$

$$\overset{(7)}{=} 10\begin{vmatrix} 1 & 1 & 1 \\ 0 & 1 & 1 \\ 0 & -1 & 2 \end{vmatrix} \overset{(8)}{=} 10(1)\begin{vmatrix} 1 & 1 \\ -1 & 2 \end{vmatrix}$$

$$\overset{(9)}{=} 10(2+1) = 30.$$

③ Expand the determinant by the first column. We have now reduced the determinant to a third-order determinant.

④ Factor 5 from each element of the first row. Here we are using property 5.

⑤ Factor 2 from each element of the third column. Again we are using property 5. Also, by doing this we have reduced the size of the numbers, and the resulting numbers are somewhat easier to work with.

⑥ Each element of the first row is multiplied by -4, and the resulting numbers are added to the corresponding elements of the second row. Here we are using property 6. We have placed a zero in the first column, second row.

⑦ Each element of the first row is added to the corresponding element of the third row. Again, we have used property 6. A zero has been placed in the first column, third row. We now have two zeros in the first column.

⑧ Expand the determinant by the first column.

⑨ Expand the second order determinant.

A somewhat more systematic method is to place zeros below the principal diagonal and then use property 1. However, all such techniques are essentially equivalent.

Exercises

In Exercises 1 through 8 evaluate each of the determinants by inspection. Careful observation will allow evaluation by the use of one or more of the basic properties of this section.

1. $\begin{vmatrix} 4 & -5 & 9 \\ 0 & 3 & -8 \\ 0 & 0 & -5 \end{vmatrix}$ 2. $\begin{vmatrix} 6 & 4 & 0 \\ 0 & -2 & 3 \\ 0 & 0 & -6 \end{vmatrix}$ 3. $\begin{vmatrix} -2 & 0 & 0 \\ 15 & 4 & 0 \\ 2 & -7 & 7 \end{vmatrix}$ 4. $\begin{vmatrix} 3 & 0 & 0 \\ 0 & 10 & 0 \\ -9 & -1 & -5 \end{vmatrix}$

5. $\begin{vmatrix} -2 & 0 & -1 \\ 5 & 0 & 3 \\ 3 & 0 & -4 \end{vmatrix}$ 6. $\begin{vmatrix} -6 & -3 & 1 \\ 1 & 2 & -5 \\ 0 & 0 & 0 \end{vmatrix}$ 7. $\begin{vmatrix} 3 & -2 & 4 \\ 5 & -1 & 2 \\ 3 & -2 & 4 \end{vmatrix}$ 8. $\begin{vmatrix} -1 & -2 & -2 \\ 1 & 3 & 3 \\ -2 & 1 & 1 \end{vmatrix}$

In Exercises 9 through 16 evaluate the determinants using the properties given in this section. Do not evaluate directly more than one second-order determinant for each.

9. $\begin{vmatrix} 4 & 3 & 6 & 0 \\ 3 & 0 & 0 & 4 \\ 5 & 0 & 1 & 2 \\ 2 & 1 & 1 & 7 \end{vmatrix}$ 10. $\begin{vmatrix} -2 & 1 & 3 & 0 \\ 1 & 3 & 0 & 0 \\ 0 & 2 & -3 & -1 \\ 4 & -1 & 2 & 1 \end{vmatrix}$

11. $\begin{vmatrix} 3 & 1 & 2 & -1 \\ 2 & -1 & 3 & -1 \\ 1 & 2 & 1 & 3 \\ 1 & -2 & -3 & 2 \end{vmatrix}$ 12. $\begin{vmatrix} 6 & -3 & -6 & 3 \\ -2 & 1 & 2 & -1 \\ 18 & 7 & -1 & 5 \\ 0 & -1 & 10 & 10 \end{vmatrix}$

13. $\begin{vmatrix} 1 & 3 & -3 & 5 \\ 4 & 2 & 1 & 2 \\ 3 & 2 & -2 & 2 \\ 0 & 1 & 2 & -1 \end{vmatrix}$ 14. $\begin{vmatrix} -2 & 2 & 1 & 3 \\ 1 & 4 & 3 & 1 \\ 4 & 3 & -2 & -2 \\ 3 & -2 & 1 & 5 \end{vmatrix}$

15. $\begin{vmatrix} 1 & 2 & 0 & 1 & 0 \\ 0 & 2 & 1 & 0 & 1 \\ 1 & 0 & -1 & 1 & -1 \\ -2 & 0 & -1 & 2 & 1 \\ 1 & 0 & 2 & -1 & -2 \end{vmatrix}$ 16. $\begin{vmatrix} -1 & 3 & 5 & 0 & -5 \\ 0 & 1 & 7 & 3 & -2 \\ 5 & -2 & -1 & 0 & 3 \\ -3 & 0 & 2 & -1 & 3 \\ 6 & 2 & 1 & -4 & 2 \end{vmatrix}$

In Exercises 17 through 21, solve the given systems of equations by determinants. Evaluate the determinants by the properties of determinants given in this section.

17. $2x + y + z = 2$
    $3y - z + 2t = 4$
    $y + 2z + t = 0$
    $3x + 2z = 4$

18. $2x + y + z = 0$
    $x - y + 2t = 2$
    $2y + z + 4t = 2$
    $5x + 2z + 2t = 4$

19. $x + y + 2z = 1$
    $2x - y + t = -2$
    $x - y - z - 2t = 4$
    $2x - y + 2z - t = 0$

20. $3x + y + t = 0$
    $3z + 2t = 8$
    $6x + 2y + 2z + t = 3$
    $3x - y - z - t = 0$

21. In applying Kirchhoff's laws (see Exercise 13 of Section 4-5) to the circuit shown in Fig. 15-2, the following equations are found. Determine the indicated currents.

$$I_A + I_B + I_C + I_D + I_E = 0$$
$$-2I_A + 3I_B = 0$$
$$3I_B - 3I_C = 6$$
$$-3I_C + I_D = 0$$
$$-I_D + 2I_E = 0$$

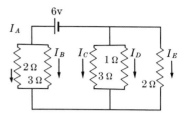

Figure 15-2

In Exercise 22 set up a system of four linear equations and solve by determinants.

22. A firm sells four types of appliances. Appliances A, B, C, and D respectively sell for \$2, \$3, \$1 and \$4 each. On a certain day it sold a total of 33 appliances, with receipts of \$91. It sold twice as many of type B as type C, and twice as many of type D as type C. How many of each were sold on this day?

15-3 Matrices: definitions and basic operations

Systems of linear equations occur in several areas of important technical and scientific applications. We indicated a few of these in Chapter 4 and in the first two sections of this chapter. Since a considerable amount of work is generally required to solve a system of equations, numerous methods have been developed for their solution.

Since the use of computers has been rapidly increasing in importance over the last several years, another mathematical concept which can be used to solve systems of equations is becoming used much more widely than in previous years. It is also used in numerous applications other than systems of equations, in such fields as business, economics, and psychology, as well as the scientific and technical areas. Since it readily adaptable to use on a computer and is applicable to numerous areas, its importance will increase for some time to come. At this point, however, we shall only be able to introduce its definitions and basic operations.

A *matrix* is an ordered rectangular array of numbers. To distinguish such an array from a determinant, we shall enclose it within parentheses. As with a determinant, the individual numbers are called *elements* of the matrix.

Example A·   Some examples of matrices are as follows:

$$\begin{pmatrix} 2 & 8 \\ 1 & 0 \end{pmatrix}, \quad \begin{pmatrix} 2 & -4 & 6 \\ -1 & 0 & 5 \end{pmatrix}, \quad \begin{pmatrix} 4 & 6 \\ 0 & -1 \\ -2 & 5 \\ 3 & 0 \end{pmatrix},$$

$$(-1 \quad 2 \quad 0 \quad 9), \qquad \begin{pmatrix} -1 & 8 & 6 & 7 & 9 \\ 2 & 6 & 0 & 4 & 3 \\ 5 & -1 & 8 & 10 & 2 \end{pmatrix}.$$

As we can see, it is not necessary for the number of columns and number of rows to be the same, although such is the case for a determinant. However, if the number of rows does equal the number of columns, the matrix is called a *square matrix*. We shall find that square matrices are of some special importance. If all the elements of a matrix are zero, the matrix is called a *zero matrix*. We shall find it convenient to designate a given matrix by a capital letter.

We must be careful to distinguish between a matrix and a determinant. A matrix is simply any *rectangular array* of numbers, whereas a determinant is a specific *value* which is associated with a *square* matrix.

Example B.   Consider the following matrices:

$$A = \begin{pmatrix} 5 & 0 & -1 \\ 1 & 2 & 6 \\ 0 & -4 & -5 \end{pmatrix}, \ B = \begin{pmatrix} 9 \\ 8 \\ 1 \\ 5 \end{pmatrix}, \ C = (-1 \quad 6 \quad 8 \quad 9), \ O = \begin{pmatrix} 0 & 0 \\ 0 & 0 \end{pmatrix}.$$

Matrix A is an example of a square matrix, matrix B is an example of a matrix with one column, matrix C is an example of a matrix with one row, and matrix O is an example of a zero matrix.

To be able to refer to specific elements of a matrix, and to give a general representation, a double-subscript notation is usually employed. That is,

$$A = \begin{pmatrix} a_{11} & a_{12} & a_{13} \\ a_{21} & a_{22} & a_{23} \\ a_{31} & a_{32} & a_{33} \end{pmatrix}.$$

We see that the first subscript refers to the row in which the element lies, and the second subscript refers to the column in which the element lies.

Two matrices are said to be equal if and only if they are identical. That is, they must have the same number of columns, the same number of rows, and the elements must respectively be equal. If these conditions are not satisfied, the matrices are not equal.

Example C. $\begin{pmatrix} a_{11} & a_{12} & a_{13} \\ a_{21} & a_{22} & a_{23} \end{pmatrix} = \begin{pmatrix} 1 & -5 & 0 \\ 4 & 6 & -3 \end{pmatrix}$

if and only if $a_{11} = 1$, $a_{12} = -5$, $a_{13} = 0$, $a_{21} = 4$, $a_{22} = 6$, and $a_{23} = -3$.

The matrices

$$\begin{pmatrix} 1 & 2 & 3 \\ -1 & -2 & -5 \end{pmatrix} \quad \text{and} \quad \begin{pmatrix} 1 & 2 & -5 \\ -1 & -2 & 3 \end{pmatrix}$$

are not equal, since the elements in the third column are reversed.

The matrices

$$\begin{pmatrix} 2 & 3 \\ -1 & 5 \end{pmatrix} \quad \text{and} \quad \begin{pmatrix} 2 & 3 \\ -1 & 5 \\ 0 & 0 \end{pmatrix}$$

are not equal, since the number of rows is different.

If two matrices have the same number of rows and the same number of columns, their sum is defined as the matrix consisting of the sums of the corresponding elements. If the number of rows or the number of columns of the two matrices is not equal, they cannot be added.

Example D.

$$\begin{pmatrix} 8 & 1 & -5 & 9 \\ 0 & -2 & 3 & 7 \end{pmatrix} + \begin{pmatrix} -3 & 4 & 6 & 0 \\ 6 & -2 & 6 & 5 \end{pmatrix}$$

$$= \begin{pmatrix} 8 + (-3) & 1 + 4 & -5 + 6 & 9 + 0 \\ 0 + 6 & -2 + (-2) & 3 + 6 & 7 + 5 \end{pmatrix}$$

$$= \begin{pmatrix} 5 & 5 & 1 & 9 \\ 6 & -4 & 9 & 12 \end{pmatrix}$$

The matrices

$$\begin{pmatrix} 3 & -5 & 8 \\ 2 & 9 & 0 \\ 4 & -2 & 3 \end{pmatrix} \quad \text{and} \quad \begin{pmatrix} 3 & -5 & 8 & 0 \\ 2 & 9 & 0 & 0 \\ 4 & -2 & 3 & 0 \end{pmatrix}$$

cannot be added since the second matrix has one more column than the first matrix. The fact that the extra column contains only zeros does not matter.

The product of a number and a matrix is defined as the matrix whose elements are obtained by multiplying each element of the given matrix by the given number. That is, kA is the matrix obtained by multiplying the elements of matrix A by k. In this way $A + A$ and $2A$ will result in the same matrix.

Example E. For the matrix

$$A = \begin{pmatrix} -5 & 7 \\ 3 & 0 \end{pmatrix},$$

we have

$$2A = \begin{pmatrix} 2(-5) & 2(7) \\ 2(3) & 2(0) \end{pmatrix} = \begin{pmatrix} -10 & 14 \\ 6 & 0 \end{pmatrix}.$$

Also,

$$5A = \begin{pmatrix} -25 & 35 \\ 15 & 0 \end{pmatrix}, \quad \text{and} \quad -A = \begin{pmatrix} 5 & -7 \\ -3 & 0 \end{pmatrix}.$$

By combining the definitions for the addition of matrices and for the multiplication of a matrix by a number, we can define the difference of matrices. That is, $A - B = A + (-B)$. Therefore, we would change the sign of each element of matrix B, and proceed as in addition.

By the definitions above we can see that the operations of addition, subtraction, and multiplication by a number on matrices are like those for real numbers. For these operations, we say that the algebra of matrices is like the algebra of real numbers. Although it is not our primary purpose to develop the algebra of matrices, we can see that the following laws hold for matrices.

$$A + B = B + A \qquad \text{(commutative law)}$$
$$A + (B + C) = (A + B) + C \qquad \text{(associative law)}$$
$$k(A + B) = kA + kB$$
$$A + 0 = A$$

Here we have let 0 represent the zero matrix. We shall find in the next section that not all laws for the operations with matrices are similar to those for real numbers.

Exercises

In Exercises 1 through 4 determine the value of the literal symbols.

1. $\begin{pmatrix} a & b \\ c & d \end{pmatrix} = \begin{pmatrix} 1 & -3 \\ 4 & 7 \end{pmatrix}$

2. $\begin{pmatrix} x & y & z \\ r & -s & -t \end{pmatrix} = \begin{pmatrix} -2 & 7 & -9 \\ 4 & -4 & 5 \end{pmatrix}$

3. $\begin{pmatrix} x \\ x + y \end{pmatrix} = \begin{pmatrix} 2 \\ 5 \end{pmatrix}$

4. $(x \quad x + y \quad x + y + z) = (5 \quad 6 \quad 8)$

In Exercises 5 through 8 find the indicated sums of matrices.

5. $\begin{pmatrix} 2 & 3 \\ -5 & 4 \end{pmatrix} + \begin{pmatrix} -1 & 7 \\ 5 & -2 \end{pmatrix}$

6. $\begin{pmatrix} 1 & 0 & 9 \\ 3 & -5 & -2 \end{pmatrix} + \begin{pmatrix} 4 & -1 & 7 \\ 2 & 0 & -3 \end{pmatrix}$

7. $\begin{pmatrix} 5 & -8 \\ -3 & 5 \\ -1 & 6 \end{pmatrix} + \begin{pmatrix} -5 & 8 \\ 4 & 1 \\ 2 & -6 \end{pmatrix}$

8. $\begin{pmatrix} 4 & 2 & -9 \\ -6 & 4 & 7 \\ -1 & 0 & 5 \end{pmatrix} + \begin{pmatrix} -4 & -9 & -2 \\ 3 & 0 & 0 \\ 5 & 10 & -1 \end{pmatrix}$

In Exercises 9 through 16 use the following matrices to determine the indicated matrices.

$$A = \begin{pmatrix} -1 & 4 & -7 & 0 \\ 2 & -6 & -1 & 2 \end{pmatrix}, \quad B = \begin{pmatrix} 1 & 5 & -6 & 3 \\ 4 & -1 & 8 & -2 \end{pmatrix}, \quad C = \begin{pmatrix} 3 & -6 & 9 \\ -4 & 1 & 2 \end{pmatrix}.$$

9. $A + B$ 10. $A - B$ 11. $A + C$ 12. $B + C$

13. $2A + B$ 14. $2B + A$ 15. $A - 2B$ 16. $3A - B$

In Exercises 17 and 18 use the given matrices to verify the indicated laws.

$$A = \begin{pmatrix} -1 & 2 & 3 & 7 \\ 0 & -3 & -1 & 4 \\ 9 & -1 & 0 & -2 \end{pmatrix}, \quad B = \begin{pmatrix} 4 & -1 & -3 & 0 \\ 5 & 0 & -1 & 1 \\ 1 & 11 & 8 & 2 \end{pmatrix}.$$

17. $A + B = B + A$ 18. $3(A + B) = 3A + 3B$

In Exercise 19 a practical situation is given to illustrate the use of matrix addition.

19. In taking inventory, a firm finds that it has in one warehouse 6 pieces of 20-ft brass pipe, 8 pieces of 30-ft brass pipe, 11 pieces of 40-ft brass pipe, 5 pieces of 20-ft steel pipe, 10 pieces of 30-ft steel pipe and 15 pieces of 40-ft steel pipe. This inventory can be represented by the matrix

$$A = \begin{pmatrix} 6 & 8 & 11 \\ 5 & 10 & 15 \end{pmatrix}.$$

In each of two other warehouses, the inventory of the same items is represented by the matrix

$$B = \begin{pmatrix} 8 & 3 & 4 \\ 6 & 10 & 5 \end{pmatrix}.$$

By matrix addition and multiplication by a constant, find the matrix which represents the total number of each item in the three warehouses.

15-4 Multiplication of matrices

The definition for the multiplication of matrices does not have an intuitive basis. However, through the solution of a system of linear equations we can, at least in part, show why multiplication is defined as it is. First, let us consider the following example.

Example A. If we solve the system of equations

$$2x + y = 1,$$
$$7x + 3y = 5,$$

we obtain the solution $x = 2$, $y = -3$. In checking this solution in each of the equations, we obtain

$$2(2) + 1(-3) = 1,$$
$$7(2) + 3(-3) = 5.$$

Let us represent the coefficients of the equations by the matrix

$$\begin{pmatrix} 2 & 1 \\ 7 & 3 \end{pmatrix},$$

and the solutions by the matrix

$$\begin{pmatrix} 2 \\ -3 \end{pmatrix}.$$

If we now multiply these matrices as

$$\begin{pmatrix} 2 & 1 \\ 7 & 3 \end{pmatrix}\begin{pmatrix} 2 \\ -3 \end{pmatrix} = \begin{pmatrix} 2(2) + 1(-3) \\ 7(2) + 3(-3) \end{pmatrix} = \begin{pmatrix} 1 \\ 5 \end{pmatrix},$$

we note that we obtain a matrix which properly represents the right-side values of the equations. (Note carefully how the products and sums in the resulting matrix are formed.)

Following reasons along the lines indicated in Example A, we shall now define the multiplication of matrices. If the number of columns in a first matrix equals the number of rows in a second matrix, the product of these matrices is formed as follows: *The element in a specified row and a specified column of the product matrix is the sum of the products formed by multiplying each element in the specified row of the first matrix by the corresponding element in the specific column of the second matrix.* The product matrix will have the same number of rows as the first matrix and the same number of columns as the second matrix. Consider the following examples.

Example B.   Find the product AB, where

$$A = \begin{pmatrix} 2 & 1 \\ -3 & 0 \\ 1 & 2 \end{pmatrix} \quad \text{and} \quad B = \begin{pmatrix} -1 & 6 & 5 & -2 \\ 3 & 0 & 1 & -4 \end{pmatrix}.$$

To find the element in the first row and first column of the product, we find the sum of the products of corresponding elements of the first row of A and first column of B. To find the element in the first row and second column of the product, we find the sum of the products of corresponding elements in the first row of A and the second column of B. We continue this process until we have found the three rows (the number of rows in A) and the four columns (the number of columns in B) of the product. The product is formed as follows.

$$\begin{pmatrix} 2 & 1 \\ -3 & 0 \\ 1 & 2 \end{pmatrix} \begin{pmatrix} -1 & 6 & 5 & -2 \\ 3 & 0 & 1 & -4 \end{pmatrix}$$

$$= \begin{pmatrix} 2(-1)+1(3) & 2(6)+1(0) & 2(5)+1(1) & 2(-2)+1(-4) \\ -3(-1)+0(3) & -3(6)+0(0) & -3(5)+0(1) & -3(-2)+0(-4) \\ 1(-1)+2(3) & 1(6)+2(0) & 1(5)+2(1) & 1(-2)+2(-4) \end{pmatrix}$$

$$= \begin{pmatrix} 1 & 12 & 11 & -8 \\ 3 & -18 & -15 & 6 \\ 5 & 6 & 7 & -10 \end{pmatrix}.$$

If we attempt to form the product BA, we find that B has four columns and A has 3 rows. Since the number of columns in B does not equal the number of rows in A, the product BA cannot be formed. In this way we see that $AB \neq BA$, which means that matrix multiplication is not commutative (except in special cases). Therefore matrix multiplication differs from the multiplication of real numbers.

Example C. Find the product

$$\begin{pmatrix} -1 & 9 & 3 & -2 \\ 2 & 0 & -7 & 1 \end{pmatrix} \begin{pmatrix} 6 & -2 \\ 1 & 0 \\ 3 & -5 \\ 3 & 9 \end{pmatrix}.$$

We can find the product because the first matrix has four columns and the second matrix has four rows. The product is found as follows.

$$\begin{pmatrix} -1 & 9 & 3 & -2 \\ 2 & 0 & -7 & 1 \end{pmatrix} \begin{pmatrix} 6 & -2 \\ 1 & 0 \\ 3 & -5 \\ 3 & 9 \end{pmatrix}$$

$$= \begin{pmatrix} -1(6)+9(1)+3(3)+(-2)(3) & -1(-2)+9(0)+3(-5)+(-2)(9) \\ 2(6)+0(1)+(-7)(3)+1(3) & 2(-2)+0(0)+(-7)(-5)+1(9) \end{pmatrix}$$

$$= \begin{pmatrix} -6+9+9-6 & 2+0-15-18 \\ 12+0-21+3 & -4+0+35+9 \end{pmatrix} = \begin{pmatrix} 6 & -31 \\ -6 & 40 \end{pmatrix}$$

There are two special matrices of particular importance in the multiplication of matrices. The first of these is the *identity matrix I*, which is a square matrix with 1's for elements on the principal diagonal, with all other elements zero. It has the property that if it is multiplied by another square matrix with the same number of rows and columns, then the second matrix equals the product matrix.

Example D.   Show that $AI = IA = A$ for the matrix

$$A = \begin{pmatrix} 2 & -3 \\ 4 & 1 \end{pmatrix}.$$

Since A has two rows and two columns, we choose I with two rows and two columns. Therefore, for this case

$$I = \begin{pmatrix} 1 & 0 \\ 0 & 1 \end{pmatrix}.$$

Forming the indicated products, we have results as follows.

$$AI = \begin{pmatrix} 2 & -3 \\ 4 & 1 \end{pmatrix}\begin{pmatrix} 1 & 0 \\ 0 & 1 \end{pmatrix} = \begin{pmatrix} 2(1) + (-3)(0) & 2(0) + (-3)(1) \\ 4(1) + 1(0) & 4(0) + 1(1) \end{pmatrix} = \begin{pmatrix} 2 & -3 \\ 4 & 1 \end{pmatrix}.$$

$$IA = \begin{pmatrix} 1 & 0 \\ 0 & 1 \end{pmatrix}\begin{pmatrix} 2 & -3 \\ 4 & 1 \end{pmatrix} = \begin{pmatrix} 1(2) + 0(4) & 1(-3) + 0(1) \\ 0(2) + 1(4) & 0(-3) + 1(1) \end{pmatrix} = \begin{pmatrix} 2 & -3 \\ 4 & 1 \end{pmatrix}.$$

Therefore, we see that $AI = IA = A$.

For a given square matrix A, its *inverse* A^{-1} is the other important special matrix. The matrix A and its inverse have the property that

$$AA^{-1} = A^{-1}A = I.$$

If the product of two matrices equals the identity matrix, the matrices are called inverses of each other. Under certain conditions the inverse of a given square matrix may not exist, although for most square matrices the inverse does exist. In the next section we shall develop the procedure for finding the inverse of a square matrix, and the section which follows shows how the inverse is used in the solution of systems of equations. At this point we shall simply show that the product of certain matrices equals the identity matrix, and that therefore these matrices are inverses of each other.

Example E.   For the given matrices A and B, show that $AB = BA = I$, and therefore that $B = A^{-1}$

$$A = \begin{pmatrix} 1 & -3 \\ -2 & 7 \end{pmatrix}, \qquad B = \begin{pmatrix} 7 & 3 \\ 2 & 1 \end{pmatrix}.$$

Forming the products AB and BA, we have the following:

$$AB = \begin{pmatrix} 1 & -3 \\ -2 & 7 \end{pmatrix}\begin{pmatrix} 7 & 3 \\ 2 & 1 \end{pmatrix} = \begin{pmatrix} 7-6 & 3-3 \\ -14+14 & -6+7 \end{pmatrix} = \begin{pmatrix} 1 & 0 \\ 0 & 1 \end{pmatrix},$$

$$BA = \begin{pmatrix} 7 & 3 \\ 2 & 1 \end{pmatrix}\begin{pmatrix} 1 & -3 \\ -2 & 7 \end{pmatrix} = \begin{pmatrix} 7-6 & -21+21 \\ 2-2 & -6+7 \end{pmatrix} = \begin{pmatrix} 1 & 0 \\ 0 & 1 \end{pmatrix}.$$

Since $AB = I$, $B = A^{-1}$.

The following example illustrates one kind of application of the multiplication of matrices.

Example F.   A particular firm produces three types of machine parts. On a given day it produces 40 of type X, 50 of type Y and 80 of type Z. Each of type X requires 4 units of material and 1 man-hour to produce; each of type Y requires 5 units of material and 2 man-hours to produce; each of type Z requires 3 units of material and 2 man-hours to produce. By representing the number of each type produced as the matrix $A = (40\ 50\ 80)$ and the material and time requirements by the matrix

$$B = \begin{pmatrix} 4 & 1 \\ 5 & 2 \\ 3 & 2 \end{pmatrix},$$

the product AB gives the total number of units of material and the total number of man-hours needed for the day's production in a one-row, two-column matrix.

$$AB = (40 \quad 50 \quad 80)\begin{pmatrix} 4 & 1 \\ 5 & 2 \\ 3 & 2 \end{pmatrix}$$

$$= (160 + 250 + 240 \quad 40 + 100 + 160) = (650 \quad 300)$$

Therefore, 650 units of material and 300 man-hours are required.

We now have seen how multiplication is defined for matrices. We see that matrix multiplication is not commutative; that is, $AB \neq BA$ in general. This is a major difference from the multiplication of real numbers. Another difference is that it is possible that $AB = 0$, even though neither A nor B is 0 (see Exercise 8, page 325). There are some similarities, however, in that $AI = A$, where we make I and the number 1 equivalent for the two types of multiplication. Also, the distributive property $A(B + C) = AB + AC$ holds for matrix multiplication. This points out some more of the properties of the algebra of matrices.

Exercises

In Exercises 1 through 12 perform the indicated matrix multiplications.

1. $(4 \ -2)\begin{pmatrix} -1 & 0 \\ 2 & 6 \end{pmatrix}$

2. $(-1 \quad 5 \ -2)\begin{pmatrix} 6 & 3 \\ 2 & -1 \\ 0 & 2 \end{pmatrix}$

3. $\begin{pmatrix} 2 & -3 \\ 5 & -1 \end{pmatrix}\begin{pmatrix} 3 & 0 & -1 \\ 7 & -5 & 8 \end{pmatrix}$

4. $\begin{pmatrix} -7 & 8 \\ 5 & 0 \end{pmatrix}\begin{pmatrix} -9 & 10 \\ 1 & 4 \end{pmatrix}$

5. $\begin{pmatrix} 2 & -3 & 1 \\ 0 & 7 & -3 \end{pmatrix}\begin{pmatrix} 9 \\ -2 \\ 5 \end{pmatrix}$

6. $\begin{pmatrix} 0 & -1 & 2 \\ 4 & 11 & 2 \end{pmatrix}\begin{pmatrix} 3 & -1 \\ 1 & 2 \\ 6 & 1 \end{pmatrix}$

7. $\begin{pmatrix} -1 & -5 \\ 4 & 0 \\ 2 & 10 \end{pmatrix}\begin{pmatrix} 2 & 0 \\ 1 & 1 \end{pmatrix}$

8. $\begin{pmatrix} 12 & -4 \\ 3 & -1 \\ 6 & -2 \end{pmatrix}\begin{pmatrix} 2 & -1 & 3 \\ 6 & -3 & 9 \end{pmatrix}$

9. $\begin{pmatrix} -1 & 7 \\ 3 & 5 \\ 10 & -1 \\ -5 & 12 \end{pmatrix}\begin{pmatrix} 2 & 1 & 0 \\ 5 & -3 & 1 \end{pmatrix}$

10. $\begin{pmatrix} 3 & -1 & 8 \\ 0 & 2 & -4 \\ -1 & 6 & 7 \end{pmatrix}\begin{pmatrix} 7 & -1 \\ 0 & 3 \\ 1 & -2 \end{pmatrix}$

11. $\begin{pmatrix} -9 & -1 & 4 \\ 6 & 9 & -1 \end{pmatrix}\begin{pmatrix} 6 & -5 \\ 4 & 1 \\ -1 & 6 \end{pmatrix}$

12. $\begin{pmatrix} 1 & 2 & -6 & 6 & 1 \\ -2 & 4 & 0 & 1 & 2 \end{pmatrix}\begin{pmatrix} 1 \\ -1 \\ 0 \\ 5 \\ 2 \end{pmatrix}$

In Exercises 13 through 16 find, if possible, AB and BA.

13. $A = (1 \ -3 \quad 8) \quad B = \begin{pmatrix} -1 \\ 5 \\ 7 \end{pmatrix}$

14. $A = \begin{pmatrix} -3 & 2 & 0 \\ 1 & -4 & 5 \end{pmatrix} \quad B = \begin{pmatrix} -2 & 0 \\ 4 & -6 \\ 5 & 1 \end{pmatrix}$

15. $A = \begin{pmatrix} -1 & 2 & 3 \\ 5 & -1 & 0 \end{pmatrix} \quad B = \begin{pmatrix} 1 \\ -5 \\ 2 \end{pmatrix}$

16. $A = \begin{pmatrix} -2 & 1 & 7 \\ 3 & -1 & 0 \\ 0 & 2 & -1 \end{pmatrix} \quad B = (4 \ -1 \quad 5)$

In Exercises 17 and 18 show that $AI = IA = A$.

17.
$$A = \begin{pmatrix} 1 & 3 & -5 \\ 2 & 0 & 1 \\ 1 & -2 & 4 \end{pmatrix}$$

18.
$$A = \begin{pmatrix} -1 & 2 & 0 \\ 4 & -3 & 1 \\ 2 & 1 & 3 \end{pmatrix}$$

In Exercises 19 through 22 determine whether or not $B = A^{-1}$.

19.
$$A = \begin{pmatrix} 5 & -2 \\ -2 & 1 \end{pmatrix} \quad B = \begin{pmatrix} 1 & 2 \\ 2 & 5 \end{pmatrix}$$

20.
$$A = \begin{pmatrix} 3 & -4 \\ 5 & -7 \end{pmatrix} \quad B = \begin{pmatrix} 7 & -4 \\ 5 & -2 \end{pmatrix}$$

21.
$$A = \begin{pmatrix} 1 & -2 & 3 \\ 2 & -5 & 7 \\ -1 & 3 & -5 \end{pmatrix} \quad B = \begin{pmatrix} 4 & -1 & 1 \\ 3 & -2 & -1 \\ 1 & -1 & -1 \end{pmatrix}$$

22.
$$A = \begin{pmatrix} 1 & -1 & 3 \\ 3 & -4 & 8 \\ -2 & 3 & -4 \end{pmatrix} \quad B = \begin{pmatrix} 8 & -5 & -4 \\ 4 & -2 & -1 \\ -1 & 1 & 1 \end{pmatrix}$$

In Exercises 23 through 26 determine by matrix multiplication whether or not A is the proper matrix of solution values.

23. $3x - 2y = -1$
$4x + y = 6$
$$A = \begin{pmatrix} 1 \\ 2 \end{pmatrix}$$

24. $4x + y = -5$
$3x + 4y = 6$
$$A = \begin{pmatrix} -2 \\ 3 \end{pmatrix}$$

25. $3x + y + 2z = 1$
$x - 3y + 4z = -3$
$2x + 2y + z = 1$
$$A = \begin{pmatrix} -1 \\ 2 \\ 1 \end{pmatrix}$$

26. $2x - y + z = 7$
$x - 3y + 2z = 6$
$3x + y - z = 8$
$$A = \begin{pmatrix} 3 \\ -2 \\ -1 \end{pmatrix}$$

In Exercise 27 an illustration of the use of matrix multiplication is given.

27. The firm referred to in Exercise 19 of Section 15-3 can determine the total number of feet of brass pipe and of steel pipe in each warehouse by multiplying the matrices of that exercise by the matrix

$$C = \begin{pmatrix} 20 \\ 30 \\ 40 \end{pmatrix}.$$

Determine the total number of feet of each type of pipe (a) in the first warehouse and (b) in all three warehouses by matrix multiplication.

15-5 Finding the inverse of a matrix

In the last section we introduced the concept of the inverse of a matrix. In this section we shall show how the inverse is found, and in the following section we shall show how this inverse is used in the solution of a system of linear equations.

We shall first show two methods of finding the inverse of a two-row, two-column (2×2) matrix. The first method is as follows:

(1) Interchange the elements on the principal diagonal.
(2) Change the signs of the off-diagonal elements.
(3) Divide each resulting element by the determinant of the given matrix.

This is illustrated in the following example.

Example A.   Find the inverse of the matrix

$$A = \begin{pmatrix} 2 & -3 \\ 4 & -7 \end{pmatrix}.$$

First we interchange the elements on the principal diagonal and change the signs of the off-diagonal elements. This gives us the matrix

$$\begin{pmatrix} -7 & 3 \\ -4 & 2 \end{pmatrix}.$$

Now we find the determinant of the original matrix, which means we evaluate

$$\begin{vmatrix} 2 & -3 \\ 4 & -7 \end{vmatrix} = -2.$$

(Note again that the matrix is the array of numbers, whereas the determinant of the matrix has a value associated with it.) We now divide each element of the second matrix by -2. This gives

$$\frac{1}{-2}\begin{pmatrix} -7 & 3 \\ -4 & 2 \end{pmatrix} = \begin{pmatrix} \dfrac{-7}{-2} & \dfrac{3}{-2} \\ \dfrac{-4}{-2} & \dfrac{2}{-2} \end{pmatrix} = \begin{pmatrix} \dfrac{7}{2} & -\dfrac{3}{2} \\ 2 & -1 \end{pmatrix}.$$

This last matrix is the inverse of matrix A. Therefore,

$$A^{-1} = \begin{pmatrix} \dfrac{7}{2} & -\dfrac{3}{2} \\ 2 & -1 \end{pmatrix}.$$

Check by multiplication gives

$$AA^{-1} = \begin{pmatrix} 2 & -3 \\ 4 & -7 \end{pmatrix}\begin{pmatrix} \dfrac{7}{2} & -\dfrac{3}{2} \\ 2 & -1 \end{pmatrix} = \begin{pmatrix} 7-6 & -3+3 \\ 14-14 & -6+7 \end{pmatrix} = \begin{pmatrix} 1 & 0 \\ 0 & 1 \end{pmatrix} = I.$$

The second method involves transforming the given matrix into the identity matrix, while at the same time transforming the identity matrix into the inverse. There are two types of steps allowable in making these transformations.

(1) Every element in any row may be multiplied by any given number other than zero.

(2) Any row may be replaced by a row whose elements are the sum of a nonzero multiple of itself and a nonzero multiple of another row.

Some reflection shows that these operations are those which are performed in solving a system of equations by addition or subtraction. The following example illustrates the method.

Example B. Find the inverse of the matrix

$$A = \begin{pmatrix} 2 & -3 \\ 4 & -7 \end{pmatrix}.$$

First we set up the given matrix along with the identity matrix in the following manner.

$$\left(\begin{array}{cc|cc} 2 & -3 & 1 & 0 \\ 4 & -7 & 0 & 1 \end{array} \right)$$

The vertical line simply shows the separation of the two matrices.

We wish to transform the left matrix into the identity matrix. Therefore, the first requirement is a 1 for element a_{11}. Therefore, we divide all elements of the first row by 2. This gives the following setup.

$$\left(\begin{array}{cc|cc} 1 & -\frac{3}{2} & \frac{1}{2} & 0 \\ 4 & -7 & 0 & 1 \end{array} \right).$$

Next we want to have a zero for element a_{21}. Therefore, we shall subtract 4 times each element of row 1 from the corresponding element in row 2, replacing the elements of row 2. This gives the following setup.

$$\left(\begin{array}{cc|cc} 1 & -\frac{3}{2} & \frac{1}{2} & 0 \\ 4 - 4(1) & -7 - 4(-\frac{3}{2}) & 0 - 4(\frac{1}{2}) & 1 - 4(0) \end{array} \right)$$

or

$$\left(\begin{array}{cc|cc} 1 & -\frac{3}{2} & \frac{1}{2} & 0 \\ 0 & -1 & -2 & 1 \end{array} \right).$$

Next, we want to have 1, not -1, for element a_{22}. Therefore, we multiply each element of row two by -1. This gives

$$\left(\begin{array}{cc|cc} 1 & -\frac{3}{2} & \frac{1}{2} & 0 \\ 0 & 1 & 2 & -1 \end{array} \right).$$

Finally, we want zero for element a_{12}. Therefore, we add $\frac{3}{2}$ times each element of row two to the corresponding elements of row one, replacing row one. This gives

$$\begin{pmatrix} 1+\frac{3}{2}(0) & -\frac{3}{2}+\frac{3}{2}(1) & \frac{1}{2}+\frac{3}{2}(2) & 0+\frac{3}{2}(-1) \\ 0 & 1 & 2 & -1 \end{pmatrix}$$

or

$$\begin{pmatrix} 1 & 0 & \frac{7}{2} & -\frac{3}{2} \\ 0 & 1 & 2 & -1 \end{pmatrix}.$$

At this point, we have transformed the given matrix into the identity matrix, and the identity matrix into the inverse. Therefore, the matrix to the right of the vertical bar in the last setup is the required inverse. Thus,

$$A^{-1} = \begin{pmatrix} \frac{7}{2} & -\frac{3}{2} \\ 2 & -1 \end{pmatrix}.$$

This is the same matrix and inverse as illustrated in Example A.

The idea to be noted most carefully in Example B is the order in which the zeros and ones were placed in transforming the given matrix to the identity matrix. We shall now give another example of finding the inverse for a 2×2 matrix, and then we shall find the inverse for a 3×3 matrix with the same method. This method is applicable for a square matrix of any number of rows or columns.

Example C. Find the inverse of the matrix $\begin{pmatrix} -3 & 6 \\ 4 & 5 \end{pmatrix}$.

$$\begin{pmatrix} -3 & 6 & 1 & 0 \\ 4 & 5 & 0 & 1 \end{pmatrix} \qquad \text{original setup}$$

$$\begin{pmatrix} 1 & -2 & -\frac{1}{3} & 0 \\ 4 & 5 & 0 & 1 \end{pmatrix} \qquad \text{row 1 divided by } -3$$

$$\begin{pmatrix} 1 & -2 & -\frac{1}{3} & 0 \\ 0 & 13 & \frac{4}{3} & 1 \end{pmatrix} \qquad -4 \text{ times row 1 added to row 2}$$

$$\begin{pmatrix} 1 & -2 & -\frac{1}{3} & 0 \\ 0 & 1 & \frac{4}{39} & \frac{1}{13} \end{pmatrix} \qquad \text{row 2 divided by 13}$$

$$\begin{pmatrix} 1 & 0 & -\frac{5}{39} & \frac{2}{13} \\ 0 & 1 & \frac{4}{39} & \frac{1}{13} \end{pmatrix} \qquad 2 \text{ times row 2 added to row 1}$$

Therefore, $A^{-1} = \begin{pmatrix} -\frac{5}{39} & \frac{2}{13} \\ \frac{4}{39} & \frac{1}{13} \end{pmatrix}$, which can be checked by multiplication.

Example D.   Find the inverse of the matrix $\begin{pmatrix} 1 & 2 & -1 \\ 3 & 5 & -1 \\ -2 & -1 & -2 \end{pmatrix}$.

$$\left(\begin{array}{ccc|ccc} 1 & 2 & -1 & 1 & 0 & 0 \\ 3 & 5 & -1 & 0 & 1 & 0 \\ -2 & -1 & -2 & 0 & 0 & 1 \end{array} \right)$$ original setup

$$\left(\begin{array}{ccc|ccc} 1 & 2 & -1 & 1 & 0 & 0 \\ 0 & -1 & 2 & -3 & 1 & 0 \\ -2 & -1 & -2 & 0 & 0 & 1 \end{array} \right)$$ -3 times row 1 added to row 2

$$\left(\begin{array}{ccc|ccc} 1 & 2 & -1 & 1 & 0 & 0 \\ 0 & -1 & 2 & -3 & 1 & 0 \\ 0 & 3 & -4 & 2 & 0 & 1 \end{array} \right)$$ 2 times row 1 added to row 3

$$\left(\begin{array}{ccc|ccc} 1 & 2 & -1 & 1 & 0 & 0 \\ 0 & 1 & -2 & 3 & -1 & 0 \\ 0 & 3 & -4 & 2 & 0 & 1 \end{array} \right)$$ row 2 multiplied by -1

$$\left(\begin{array}{ccc|ccc} 1 & 0 & 3 & -5 & 2 & 0 \\ 0 & 1 & -2 & 3 & -1 & 0 \\ 0 & 3 & -4 & 2 & 0 & 1 \end{array} \right)$$ -2 times row 2 added to row 1

$$\left(\begin{array}{ccc|ccc} 1 & 0 & 3 & -5 & 2 & 0 \\ 0 & 1 & -2 & 3 & -1 & 0 \\ 0 & 0 & 2 & -7 & 3 & 1 \end{array} \right)$$ -3 times row 2 added to row 3

$$\left(\begin{array}{ccc|ccc} 1 & 0 & 3 & -5 & 2 & 0 \\ 0 & 1 & -2 & 3 & -1 & 0 \\ 0 & 0 & 1 & -\frac{7}{2} & \frac{3}{2} & \frac{1}{2} \end{array} \right)$$ row 3 divided by 2

$$\left(\begin{array}{ccc|ccc} 1 & 0 & 3 & -5 & 2 & 0 \\ 0 & 1 & 0 & -4 & 2 & 1 \\ 0 & 0 & 1 & -\frac{7}{2} & \frac{3}{2} & \frac{1}{2} \end{array} \right)$$ 2 times row 3 added to row 2

$$\left(\begin{array}{ccc|ccc} 1 & 0 & 0 & \frac{11}{2} & -\frac{5}{2} & -\frac{3}{2} \\ 0 & 1 & 0 & -4 & 2 & 1 \\ 0 & 0 & 1 & -\frac{7}{2} & \frac{3}{2} & \frac{1}{2} \end{array} \right)$$ -3 times row 3 added to row 1

Therefore, the required inverse matrix is

$$\begin{pmatrix} \frac{11}{2} & -\frac{5}{2} & -\frac{3}{2} \\ -4 & 2 & 1 \\ -\frac{7}{2} & \frac{3}{2} & \frac{1}{2} \end{pmatrix},$$

which may be checked by multiplication.

In transforming a matrix into the identity matrix, we work on one column at a time, transforming the columns in order from left to right. It is generally wisest to make the element on the principal diagonal for the column 1 first, and then to make all the other elements in the column 0. Looking back to Example D, we see that this procedure has been systematically followed, first on column one, then on column two, and finally on column three.

Exercises

In Exercises 1 through 6 find the inverse of each of the given matrices by the method of Example A of this section.

1. $\begin{pmatrix} 2 & -5 \\ -2 & 4 \end{pmatrix}$ 2. $\begin{pmatrix} -6 & 3 \\ 3 & -2 \end{pmatrix}$ 3. $\begin{pmatrix} -1 & 5 \\ 4 & 10 \end{pmatrix}$

4. $\begin{pmatrix} 8 & -1 \\ -4 & -5 \end{pmatrix}$ 5. $\begin{pmatrix} 0 & -4 \\ 2 & 6 \end{pmatrix}$ 6. $\begin{pmatrix} 7 & -2 \\ -6 & 2 \end{pmatrix}$

In Exercises 7 through 20 find the inverse of each of the given matrices by transforming the identity matrix, as in Examples B through D.

7. $\begin{pmatrix} 1 & 2 \\ 2 & 3 \end{pmatrix}$ 8. $\begin{pmatrix} 1 & 5 \\ -1 & -4 \end{pmatrix}$ 9. $\begin{pmatrix} 2 & 4 \\ -1 & -1 \end{pmatrix}$

10. $\begin{pmatrix} -2 & 6 \\ 3 & -4 \end{pmatrix}$ 11. $\begin{pmatrix} 2 & 5 \\ -1 & 2 \end{pmatrix}$ 12. $\begin{pmatrix} -2 & 3 \\ -3 & 5 \end{pmatrix}$

13. $\begin{pmatrix} 1 & -3 & -2 \\ -2 & 7 & 3 \\ 1 & -1 & -3 \end{pmatrix}$ 14. $\begin{pmatrix} 1 & 2 & -1 \\ 3 & 7 & -5 \\ -1 & -2 & 0 \end{pmatrix}$ 15. $\begin{pmatrix} 1 & -1 & -3 \\ 0 & -1 & -2 \\ 2 & 1 & -1 \end{pmatrix}$

16. $\begin{pmatrix} 1 & 4 & 1 \\ -3 & -13 & -1 \\ 0 & -2 & 5 \end{pmatrix}$ 17. $\begin{pmatrix} 1 & 3 & 2 \\ -2 & -5 & -1 \\ 2 & 4 & 0 \end{pmatrix}$ 18. $\begin{pmatrix} 1 & 3 & 4 \\ -1 & -4 & -2 \\ 4 & 9 & 20 \end{pmatrix}$

19. $\begin{pmatrix} 2 & 4 & 0 \\ 3 & 4 & -2 \\ -1 & 1 & 2 \end{pmatrix}$
20. $\begin{pmatrix} -2 & 6 & 1 \\ 0 & 3 & -3 \\ 4 & -7 & 3 \end{pmatrix}$

15-6 Matrices and linear equations

As we stated earlier, matrices can be used to solve systems of equations. In this section we shall show how this is done.

Let us consider the system of equations

$$a_1 x + b_1 y = c_1,$$
$$a_2 x + b_2 y = c_2.$$

Recalling the definition of equality of matrices, we can write this system directly in terms of matrices as

$$\begin{pmatrix} a_1 x + b_1 y \\ a_2 x + b_2 y \end{pmatrix} = \begin{pmatrix} c_1 \\ c_2 \end{pmatrix}.$$

The left side of this equation can be written as the product of two matrices. If we let

$$A = \begin{pmatrix} a_1 & b_1 \\ a_2 & b_2 \end{pmatrix} \quad \text{and} \quad X = \begin{pmatrix} x \\ y \end{pmatrix},$$

then we have

$$AX = \begin{pmatrix} a_1 x + b_1 y \\ a_2 x + b_2 y \end{pmatrix}.$$

Therefore, the system of equations above can be written in terms of matrices as

$$AX = C,$$

where $C = \begin{pmatrix} c_1 \\ c_2 \end{pmatrix}.$

If we now multiply each side of this matrix equation by A^{-1}, we have

$$A^{-1}AX = A^{-1}C.$$

Since $A^{-1}A = I$, we have

$$IX = A^{-1}C.$$

However, $IX = X$. Therefore

$$X = A^{-1}C.$$

This last equation states that *we can solve a system of linear equations by multiplying the one-column matrix of the constants on the right by the inverse of the matrix of the coefficients.* The result is a one-column matrix whose elements are the required values. The following examples illustrate the method.

Example A. Solve by matrices the system of equations

$$2x - y = 7$$
$$5x - 3y = 18.$$

We set up the matrix of the coefficients as

$$A = \begin{pmatrix} 2 & -1 \\ 5 & -3 \end{pmatrix}.$$

By either of the methods of the previous section, we can determine the inverse of this matrix to be

$$A^{-1} = \begin{pmatrix} 3 & -1 \\ 5 & -2 \end{pmatrix}.$$

We now form the matrix product $A^{-1} C$, where $C = \begin{pmatrix} 7 \\ 18 \end{pmatrix}$. This gives

$$A^{-1}C = \begin{pmatrix} 3 & -1 \\ 5 & -2 \end{pmatrix}\begin{pmatrix} 7 \\ 18 \end{pmatrix} = \begin{pmatrix} 21 - 18 \\ 35 - 36 \end{pmatrix} = \begin{pmatrix} 3 \\ -1 \end{pmatrix}.$$

Since $X = A^{-1}C$, this means that

$$\begin{pmatrix} x \\ y \end{pmatrix} = \begin{pmatrix} 3 \\ -1 \end{pmatrix}.$$

Therefore, the required solution is $x = 3$ and $y = -1$.

Example B. Solve by matrices the system of equations

$$2x - y = 3$$
$$6x + 4y = -5.$$

Setting up matrices A and C, we have

$$A = \begin{pmatrix} 2 & -1 \\ 6 & 4 \end{pmatrix} \quad \text{and} \quad C = \begin{pmatrix} 3 \\ -5 \end{pmatrix}.$$

We now find the inverse of A to be

$$A^{-1} = \begin{pmatrix} \frac{2}{7} & \frac{1}{14} \\ -\frac{3}{7} & \frac{1}{7} \end{pmatrix}.$$

Therefore,

$$A^{-1}C = \begin{pmatrix} \frac{2}{7} & \frac{1}{14} \\ -\frac{3}{7} & \frac{1}{7} \end{pmatrix}\begin{pmatrix} 3 \\ -5 \end{pmatrix} = \begin{pmatrix} \frac{6}{7} - \frac{5}{14} \\ -\frac{9}{7} - \frac{5}{7} \end{pmatrix} = \begin{pmatrix} \frac{1}{2} \\ -2 \end{pmatrix}.$$

Therefore, the required solution is $x = \frac{1}{2}$ and $y = -2$.

Example C. Solve by matrices the system of equations

$$x + 4y - z = 4$$
$$x + 3y + z = 8$$
$$2x + 6y + z = 13.$$

Setting up matrices A and C, we have

$$A = \begin{pmatrix} 1 & 4 & -1 \\ 1 & 3 & 1 \\ 2 & 6 & 1 \end{pmatrix} \quad \text{and} \quad C = \begin{pmatrix} 4 \\ 8 \\ 13 \end{pmatrix}.$$

To give another example of finding the inverse of a 3×3 matrix, we shall briefly show the steps for finding A^{-1}.

$$\left(\begin{array}{rrr|rrr} 1 & 4 & -1 & 1 & 0 & 0 \\ 1 & 3 & 1 & 0 & 1 & 0 \\ 2 & 6 & 1 & 0 & 0 & 1 \end{array} \right), \quad \left(\begin{array}{rrr|rrr} 1 & 4 & -1 & 1 & 0 & 0 \\ 0 & -1 & 2 & -1 & 1 & 0 \\ 2 & 6 & 1 & 0 & 0 & 1 \end{array} \right),$$

$$\left(\begin{array}{rrr|rrr} 1 & 4 & -1 & 1 & 0 & 0 \\ 0 & -1 & 2 & -1 & 1 & 0 \\ 0 & -2 & 3 & -2 & 0 & 1 \end{array} \right), \quad \left(\begin{array}{rrr|rrr} 1 & 4 & -1 & 1 & 0 & 0 \\ 0 & 1 & -2 & 1 & -1 & 0 \\ 0 & -2 & 3 & -2 & 0 & 1 \end{array} \right),$$

$$\left(\begin{array}{rrr|rrr} 1 & 0 & 7 & -3 & 4 & 0 \\ 0 & 1 & -2 & 1 & -1 & 0 \\ 0 & -2 & 3 & -2 & 0 & 1 \end{array} \right), \quad \left(\begin{array}{rrr|rrr} 1 & 0 & 7 & -3 & 4 & 0 \\ 0 & 1 & -2 & 1 & -1 & 0 \\ 0 & 0 & -1 & 0 & -2 & 1 \end{array} \right),$$

$$\left(\begin{array}{rrr|rrr} 1 & 0 & 7 & -3 & 4 & 0 \\ 0 & 1 & -2 & 1 & -1 & 0 \\ 0 & 0 & 1 & 0 & 2 & -1 \end{array} \right), \quad \left(\begin{array}{rrr|rrr} 1 & 0 & 7 & -3 & 4 & 0 \\ 0 & 1 & 0 & 1 & 3 & -2 \\ 0 & 0 & 1 & 0 & 2 & -1 \end{array} \right),$$

$$\left(\begin{array}{rrr|rrr} 1 & 0 & 0 & -3 & -10 & 7 \\ 0 & 1 & 0 & 1 & 3 & -2 \\ 0 & 0 & 1 & 0 & 2 & -1 \end{array} \right). \quad \text{Thus, } A^{-1} = \begin{pmatrix} -3 & -10 & 7 \\ 1 & 3 & -2 \\ 0 & 2 & -1 \end{pmatrix}.$$

Therefore,

$$A^{-1}C = \begin{pmatrix} -3 & -10 & 7 \\ 1 & 3 & -2 \\ 0 & 2 & -1 \end{pmatrix} \begin{pmatrix} 4 \\ 8 \\ 13 \end{pmatrix} = \begin{pmatrix} -1 \\ 2 \\ 3 \end{pmatrix}.$$

This means that $x = -1$, $y = 2$, $z = 3$.

Example D.   Solve by matrices the system of equations

$$x + 2y - z = -4$$
$$3x + 5y - z = -5$$
$$-2x - y - 2z = -5.$$

Setting up matrices A and C, we have

$$A = \begin{pmatrix} 1 & 2 & -1 \\ 3 & 5 & -1 \\ -2 & -1 & -2 \end{pmatrix} \quad \text{and} \quad C = \begin{pmatrix} -4 \\ -5 \\ -5 \end{pmatrix}.$$

We now find the inverse of A to be

$$A^{-1} = \begin{pmatrix} \frac{11}{2} & -\frac{5}{2} & -\frac{3}{2} \\ -4 & 2 & 1 \\ -\frac{7}{2} & \frac{3}{2} & \frac{1}{2} \end{pmatrix}$$

(see Example D of Section 15-5). Therefore,

$$A^{-1}C = \begin{pmatrix} \frac{11}{2} & -\frac{5}{2} & -\frac{3}{2} \\ -4 & 2 & 1 \\ -\frac{7}{2} & \frac{3}{2} & \frac{1}{2} \end{pmatrix} \begin{pmatrix} -4 \\ -5 \\ -5 \end{pmatrix} = \begin{pmatrix} -2 \\ 1 \\ 4 \end{pmatrix}.$$

This means that the solution is $x = -2$, $y = 1$, $z = 4$.

After having solved systems of equations in this manner, the reader may feel that the method is much longer and more tedious than previously developed techniques. The principal problem with this method is that a great deal of numerical computation is generally required. However, methods such as this one are easily programmed for use on a computer, which can do the arithmetic work with incredible speed. Recalling that matrices are of particular importance in connection with computers, it is the method of solving them which is of primary importance.

Exercises

In Exercises 1 through 8 solve the given systems of equations by using the inverse of the coefficient matrix. The numbers in parentheses refer to exercises from Section 15-5 where the inverses may be checked.

1. $2x - 5y = -14$ (No. 1)
   $-2x + 4y = 11$

2. $-x + 5y = 4$ (No. 3)
   $4x + 10y = -4$

3. $2x + 4y = -9$ (No. 9)
   $-x - y = 2$

4. $2x + 5y = -6$ (No. 11)
   $-x + 2y = -6$

5. $x - 3y - 2z = -8$ (No. 13)
   $-2x + 7y + 3z = 19$
   $x - y - 3z = -3$

6. $x - y - 3z = -1$ (No. 15)
   $-y - 2z = -2$
   $2x + y - z = 2$

7. $x + 3y + 2z = 5$ (No. 17)
   $-2x - 5y - z = -1$
   $2x + 4y = -2$

8. $2x + 4y = -2$ (No. 19)
   $3x + 4y - 2z = -6$
   $-x + y + 2z = 5$

In Exercises 9 through 20 solve the given systems of equations by using the inverse of the coefficient matrix.

9. $2x + 7y = 16$
   $x + 4y = 9$

10. $4x - 3y = -13$
    $-3x + 2y = 9$

11. $2x - 3y = 3$
    $4x - 5y = 4$

12. $x + 2y = 3$
    $3x + 4y = 11$

13. $5x - 2y = -14$
    $3x + 4y = -11$

14. $4x - 3y = -1$
    $8x + 3y = 4$

15. $x + 2y + 2z = -4$
    $4x + 9y + 10z = -18$
    $-x + 3y + 7z = -7$

16. $x - 4y - 2z = -7$
    $-x + 5y + 5z = 18$
    $3x - 7y + 10z = 38$

17. $2x + 4y + z = 5$
    $-2x - 2y - z = -6$
    $-x + 2y + z = 0$

18. $4x + y = 2$
    $-2x - y + 3z = -18$
    $2x + y - z = 8$

19. Three forces F_1, F_2, and F_3 are acting on a certain beam. The forces (in pounds) can be found by solving the following equations.

$$F_1 + F_2 + F_3 = 30,$$
$$4F_1 + F_2 - 4F_3 = 0,$$
$$5F_2 - 3F_3 = 4.$$

Determine these forces.

20. In applying Kirchhoff's laws (see Exercise 13 of Section 4-5) to the circuit shown in Fig. 15-3, the following equations are found. Determine the indicated currents.

$$I_A + I_B + I_C = 0$$
$$2I_A - 5I_B = 6$$
$$5I_B - I_C = -3$$

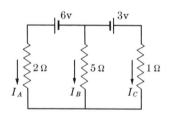

Figure 15-3

In Exercises 21 and 22, set up systems of linear equations and solve them by using matrices.

21. Type A doors cost $10 each and type B doors cost $14 each. A builder was billed $220 for a shipment of these doors. He found that had he reversed the number of each on his order, he would have been billed $212. How many of each did he actually receive?

22. Fifty shares of stock A and 30 shares of stock B cost $2600. Thirty shares of stock A and 40 shares of stock B cost $2000. What is the price per share of each stock?

15-7 Miscellaneous Exercises

In Exercises 1 through 6 evaluate the given determinants by expansion by minors.

1.
$$\begin{vmatrix} 1 & 2 & -1 \\ 4 & 1 & -3 \\ -3 & -5 & 2 \end{vmatrix}$$

2.
$$\begin{vmatrix} 3 & -1 & 2 \\ 7 & -1 & 4 \\ 2 & 1 & -3 \end{vmatrix}$$

3.
$$\begin{vmatrix} -1 & 3 & -7 \\ 0 & 5 & 4 \\ 4 & -3 & -2 \end{vmatrix}$$

4.
$$\begin{vmatrix} 6 & -5 & -7 \\ -1 & 2 & 4 \\ 2 & -3 & 1 \end{vmatrix}$$

5.
$$\begin{vmatrix} 2 & 6 & 2 & 5 \\ 2 & 0 & 4 & -1 \\ 4 & -3 & 6 & 1 \\ 3 & -1 & 0 & -2 \end{vmatrix}$$

6.
$$\begin{vmatrix} 1 & -2 & 2 & 4 \\ 0 & 1 & 2 & 3 \\ 3 & 2 & 2 & 5 \\ 2 & 1 & -2 & 0 \end{vmatrix}$$

In Exercises 7 through 12 evaluate the determinants of Exercises 1 through 6 by using the basic properties of determinants.

In Exercises 13 through 16 evaluate the given determinants by using the basic properties of determinants.

13.
$$\begin{vmatrix} 1 & 0 & -3 & -2 \\ 1 & -1 & 2 & 0 \\ -1 & 1 & 1 & 1 \\ 5 & -1 & 2 & -1 \end{vmatrix}$$

14.
$$\begin{vmatrix} 2 & 6 & -2 & 4 \\ -2 & 2 & -3 & 3 \\ 3 & 2 & 2 & -2 \\ 2 & -6 & 4 & 1 \end{vmatrix}$$

15.
$$\begin{vmatrix} 1 & -1 & 3 & 0 & 2 \\ 4 & 0 & 4 & -2 & 2 \\ 0 & 4 & 0 & -1 & -1 \\ -2 & 2 & -1 & 4 & 0 \\ 1 & -1 & 2 & 0 & 1 \end{vmatrix}$$

16.
$$\begin{vmatrix} 1 & 4 & -3 & 3 & 0 \\ 3 & 1 & -1 & 2 & 2 \\ 1 & 2 & 1 & 1 & 1 \\ -3 & -5 & -5 & 0 & -6 \\ 2 & 2 & -2 & 3 & -2 \end{vmatrix}$$

In Exercises 17 through 24 use the given matrices and perform the indicated operations.

$$A = \begin{pmatrix} 2 & -3 \\ 4 & 1 \\ -5 & 0 \\ 2 & -3 \end{pmatrix} \qquad B = \begin{pmatrix} -1 & 0 \\ 4 & -6 \\ -3 & -2 \\ 1 & -7 \end{pmatrix} \qquad C = \begin{pmatrix} 5 & -6 \\ 2 & 8 \\ 0 & -2 \end{pmatrix}$$

17. $A + B$

18. $2C$

19. $-3B$

20. $B - A$

21. $A - C$

22. $2C - B$

23. $2A - 3B$

24. $2(A - B)$

In Exercises 25 through 28 perform the indicated matrix multiplications.

25. $\begin{pmatrix} 5 & -1 \\ 3 & 2 \end{pmatrix} \begin{pmatrix} 1 \\ -8 \end{pmatrix}$

26. $\begin{pmatrix} 6 & -4 & 1 & 0 \\ 2 & 0 & -4 & 3 \end{pmatrix} \begin{pmatrix} 7 & -1 & 6 \\ 4 & 0 & 1 \\ 3 & -2 & 5 \\ 9 & 1 & 0 \end{pmatrix}$

27. $\begin{pmatrix} -1 & 7 \\ 2 & 0 \\ 4 & -1 \end{pmatrix} \begin{pmatrix} 1 & -4 & 5 \\ 5 & 1 & 0 \end{pmatrix}$

28. $\begin{pmatrix} 0 & -1 & 6 \\ 8 & 1 & 4 \\ 7 & -2 & -1 \end{pmatrix} \begin{pmatrix} 5 & -1 & 7 & 1 & 5 \\ 0 & 1 & 0 & 4 & 1 \\ 1 & -2 & 3 & 0 & 1 \end{pmatrix}$

In Exercises 29 through 36 find the inverses of the given matrices.

29. $\begin{pmatrix} 2 & -5 \\ 2 & -4 \end{pmatrix}$

30. $\begin{pmatrix} -1 & -6 \\ 2 & 10 \end{pmatrix}$

31. $\begin{pmatrix} 7 & -1 \\ 4 & 8 \end{pmatrix}$

32. $\begin{pmatrix} 5 & -1 \\ 4 & -8 \end{pmatrix}$

33. $\begin{pmatrix} 1 & 1 & -2 \\ -1 & -2 & 1 \\ 0 & 3 & 4 \end{pmatrix}$

34. $\begin{pmatrix} -1 & -1 & 2 \\ 2 & 3 & 0 \\ 1 & 4 & 1 \end{pmatrix}$

35. $\begin{pmatrix} 2 & -4 & 3 \\ 4 & -6 & 5 \\ -2 & 1 & -1 \end{pmatrix}$

36. $\begin{pmatrix} 3 & 1 & -4 \\ -3 & 1 & -2 \\ -6 & 0 & 3 \end{pmatrix}$

In Exercises 37 through 42 solve the given systems of equations using the inverse of the coefficient matrix.

37. $2x - 3y = -9$
    $4x - y = -13$

38. $5x - 7y = 62$
    $6x + 5y = -6$

39. $3x + 5y = 29$
    $4x - 7y = -57$

40. $4x - 2y = 1$
    $8x + 2y = 5$

41. $2x - 3y + 2z = 7$
    $3x + y - 3z = -6$
    $x + 4y + z = -13$

42. $2x + 2y - z = 8$
    $x + 4y + 2z = 5$
    $3x - 2y + z = 17$

In Exercises 43 through 46 solve the given systems of equations by determinants. Use the basic properties of determinants.

43. $3x - 2y + z = 6$
    $2x + 3z = 3$
    $4x - y + 5z = 6$

44. $7x + y + 2z = 3$
    $4x - 2y + 4z = -2$
    $2x + 3y - 6z = 3$

45. $2x - 3y + z - t = -8$
    $4x + 3z + 2t = -3$
    $2y - 3z - t = 12$
    $x - y - z + t = 3$

46. $3x + 2y - 2z - 2t = 0$
    $5y + 3z + 4t = 3$
    $6y - 3z + 4t = 9$
    $6x - y + 2z - 2t = -3$

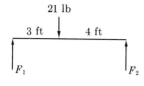

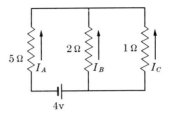

Figure 15-4   Figure 15-5

In Exercises 47 and 48 solve the given systems of equations by any appropriate method of this chapter.

47. To find the forces F_1 and F_2 shown in Figure 15-4, it is necessary to solve the following equations.

$$F_1 + F_2 = 21$$
$$3F_1 - 4F_2 = 0$$

Find F_1 and F_2.

48. To find the electric currents (in amps) indicated in Fig. 15-5, it is necessary to solve the following equations.

$$I_A + I_B + I_C = 0$$
$$5I_A - 2I_B = -4$$
$$2I_B - I_C = 0$$

Find I_A, I_B, and I_C.

In Exercises 49 and 50 set up systems of linear equations and solve by any appropriate method illustrated in this chapter.

49. By weight three alloys have the following percentages of lead, zinc, and copper.

	lead	zinc	copper
Alloy A	60%	30%	10%
Alloy B	40%	30%	30%
Alloy C	30%	70%	

How many grams of each of alloys A, B, and C must be mixed to get 100 gm of an alloy which is 44% lead, 38% zinc and 18% copper?

50. A sum of $9000 is invested, part at 6%, part at 5%, and part at 4%. The annual income from these investments is $460. The 5% investment yields $50 more than the 4% investment. How much is invested at each rate?

In Exercise 51, an application of multiplication of matrices is given.

51. Set up a matrix representing the information given in Exercise 49. A given shipment contains 500 gm of alloy A, 800 gm of alloy B, and 700 gm of alloy C. Set up a matrix for this information. By multiplying these matrices, obtain a matrix which gives the total weight of lead, zinc and copper in the shipment.

Inequalities

16

16-1 Properties of inequalities

Until now we have devoted a great deal of time to the solution of equations. Equation-solving does play an extremely important role in mathematics, but there are also times when we wish to solve inequalities. For example, we have often been faced with the problem of whether or not a given number is real or complex. We determine this from the quadratic formula, by observing the sign of the expression $b^2 - 4ac$. If this expression is positive, the resulting number is real, and if it is negative, the resulting number is complex. This is one of the important uses of inequalities. In this chapter we shall discuss some of the important properties of inequalities, methods of solving inequalities, and illustrate some of their applications.

In Chapter 1 we first came across the signs of inequality. The expression $a < b$ is read as "a is less than b," and the expression $a > b$ is read as "a is greater than b." These signs define what is known as the *sense* of the inequality. Two inequalities are said to have the same sense if the signs of inequality point in the same direction. They are said to have the opposite sense if the signs of inequality point in opposite directions. The two sides of the inequality are called *members* of the inequality.

Example A. The inequalities $x + 3 > 2$ and $x + 1 > 0$ have the same sense, as do the inequalities $3x - 1 < 4$ and $x^2 - 1 < 3$.

The inequalities $x - 4 < 0$ and $x > -4$ have the opposite sense, as do the inequalities $2x + 4 > 1$ and $3x^2 - 7 < 1$.

The solution of an inequality consists of those values of the variable for which the inequality is satisfied. Most inequalities with which we shall deal are known as *conditional inequalities*. That is, there are some values of the variable which

340

satisfy the inequality, and also there are some values which do not satisfy it. Some inequalities are satisfied for all values of the variable. These are called *absolute inequalities*. Also, a solution of an inequality may consist of only real numbers, as the terms "greater than" and "less than" have not been defined for complex numbers.

Example B. The inequality $x + 1 > 0$ is satisfied by all values of x greater than -1. Thus we would say that the solution to this inequality is $x > -1$. This illustrates the difference between the solution of an equation and the solution of an inequality. The solution to an equation normally consists of a few specific numbers, whereas the solution to an inequality normally consists of a range of values of the variable. Any and all values within this range are termed the solution of the inequality.

Example C. The inequality $x^2 + 1 > 0$ is true for all values of x, since x^2 is never negative. This is an absolute inequality. The inequality shown in Example B is a conditional inequality.

There are occasions when it is convenient to combine an inequality with an equality. For such purposes, the symbols $\leq$, read "less than or equal to," and $\geq$, read "greater than or equal to," are used.

Example D. If we wish to state that x is positive, we would write $x > 0$. However, the value zero is not included in the solution. If we wished to state that x is not negative, that is, that zero is included as a part of the solution, we can write $x \geq 0$.

We shall now present the basic operations performed on inequalities. These operations are the same as those performed on equations, but in certain cases the results take on a different form. The following are referred to as the properties of inequalities:

(1) The sense of an inequality is not changed when the same number is added to—or subtracted from—both members of the inequality. Symbolically this is stated as "if $a > b$, then $a + c > b + c$, or $a - c > b - c$."

Example E. $9 > 6$; thus $9 + 4 > 6 + 4$, or $13 > 10$. Also $9 - 12 > 6 - 12$ or $-3 > -6$.

(2) The sense of an inequality is not changed if both members are multiplied or divided by the same positive number. Symbolically this is stated as, "if $a > b$, then $ac > bc$, or $a/c > b/c$, provided that $c > 0$."

Example F. $8 < 15$; thus $8(2) < 15(2)$ or $16 < 30$. Also $\frac{8}{2} < \frac{15}{2}$ or $4 < \frac{15}{2}$.

(3) The sense of an inequality is reversed if both members are multiplied or divided by the same negative number. Symbolically this is stated as, "if $a > b$, then $ac < bc$, or $a/c < b/c$, provided that $c < 0$." Notice here that we obtain different results, depending on whether both members are multiplied by a positive or by a negative number.

Example G. $4 > -2$; thus $4(-3) < (-2)(-3)$, or $-12 < 6$. Also,

$$\frac{4}{-2} < \frac{-2}{-2}, \quad \text{or} \quad -2 < 1.$$

(4) If both members of an inequality are positive numbers and n is a positive integer, then the inequality formed by taking the nth power of each member, or the nth root of each member, is in the same sense as the given inequality. Symbolically this is stated as, "if $a > b$, then $a^n > b^n$, or $\sqrt[n]{a} > \sqrt[n]{b}$, provided that $n > 0$, $a > 0$, $b > 0$."

Example H. $16 > 9$; thus $16^2 > 9^2$ or $256 > 81$; also $\sqrt{16} > \sqrt{9}$ or $4 > 3$.

Many inequalities have more than two members. In fact, inequalities with three members are very common. For example $6 > 5 > 2$ would be an inequality with three members. All the operations stated above hold for inequalities with more than two members. Some care must be used, however, in stating inequalities with more than two members.

Example I.   The inequality $x^2 - 3x + 2 > 0$ is satisfied if x is either greater than 2 or less than 1. This would be written as $x > 2$ or $x < 1$, but it would be incorrect to state the solution as $1 > x > 2$. (If we wrote it this way, we would be saying that the same value of x is less than 1 and greater than 2. And of course no such number exists.) Any inequality must be valid for all values satisfying it. However, we would say that the inequality is not satisfied for $1 < x < 2$, which means those values of x between 1 and 2.

We shall now present two examples of other kinds of problems in which the basic properties of inequalities are used.

Example J.   If $0 < x < 1$, prove that $x^2 < x$.
From the given inequality we see that x is a positive number less than 1. Thus, if we multiply the members of the given inequality by x, we have $0 < x^2 < x$, which gives the desired result if we consider the middle and right members. Note the meaning of this inequality. The square of any positive number less than 1 is less than the number itself.

Example K.   State, by means of an inequality, the conditions that x must satisfy if a point in the xy-plane lies between the lines $x = 1$ and $x = 5$.
The x-coordinate of any point in this part of the plane is greater than 1, but at the same time less than 5. Thus the solution is $1 < x < 5$. See Fig. 16-1.

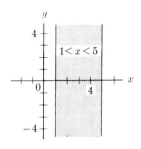

Figure 16-1

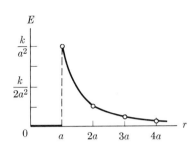

Figure 16-2

On occasion it is necessary to define a function in a different way for some values of the independent variable than for other values. Inequalities can then be used to denote the ranges over which the different definitions of the function are valid. The following example illustrates this use of inequalities, and includes a graphical representation.

Example L. The electrical intensity within a charged spherical conductor is zero. The intensity on the surface and outside of the sphere is equal to a constant divided by the square of the distance from the center of the sphere. State these relations by using inequalities, and make a graphical representation.

Let a = the radius of the sphere, r = the distance from the center of the sphere, and E = the electrical intensity.

The first statement may be written as $E = 0$ if $0 \le r < a$, since this would be read as "the electric intensity is 0 if the distance from the center is less than the radius." Negative values of r are meaningless, which is the reason for saying that r is greater than or equal to zero. The second statement may be written as $E = k/r^2$ if $a \le r$. Making a table of values for this equation, we have the following points:

E	$\dfrac{k}{a^2}$	$\dfrac{1}{4}\left(\dfrac{k}{a^2}\right)$	$\dfrac{1}{9}\left(\dfrac{k}{a^2}\right)$	$\dfrac{1}{16}\left(\dfrac{k}{a^2}\right)$
r	a	$2a$	$3a$	$4a$

The graph of E versus r is shown in Fig. 16-2.

Exercises

In Exercises 1 through 8, for the inequality $4 < 9$, state the inequality resulting when the operations given are performed on both members.

1. Add 3
2. Subtract 6
3. Multiply by 5
4. Multiply by -2
5. Divide by -1
6. Divide by 2
7. Square both
8. Take square roots

In Exercises 9 through 16 state the condition in terms of an inequality that x must satisfy to describe the location of the given point.

9. The point (x, y) lies to the right of the y-axis.
10. The point (x, y) lies to the right of the line $x = 1$.
11. The point (x, y) lies on or to the left of the y-axis.
12. The point (x, y) lies on or to the right of the line $x = -2$.
13. The point (x, y) lies outside of the region between the lines $x = -1$ and $x = 1$.
14. The point (x, y) lies in the region between the lines $x = -1$ and $x = 1$.
15. The point (x, y) lies on or to the right of the line $x = 2$ or to the left of the line $x = 6$.
16. The point (x, y) lies to the left of the line $x = -4$ or to the right of the line $x = 3$.

In Exercises 17 through 20 state the conditions in terms of inequalities that x, or y, or both, must satisfy to describe the location of the given point.

17. The point (x, y) lies in the first quadrant.
18. The point (x, y) lies in the region bounded by the lines $x = 1$, $x = 4$, $y = -3$, and $y = -1$.
19. The point (x, y) lies above the line $x = y$.
20. The point (x, y) lies within three units of the origin. [*Hint*: Use the Pythagorean theorem.]

In Exercises 21 through 24 prove the given inequalities.

21. If $x > 1$, prove that $x^2 > x$.
22. If $x > y > 0$, prove that $1/y > 1/x$.
23. If $0 < x < y$, prove that $\sqrt{xy} < y$.
24. If $x > x^2$, prove that $\sqrt{3x + 1} > x + 1$.

In Exercises 25 through 27 some applications of inequalities are shown.

25. A certain projectile is above 200 ft from 3.5 sec after it is launched until 15.3 sec after it is launched. Express this statement in terms of inequalities in terms of the time t and height h.
26. The electric potential V inside a charged spherical conductor equals a constant k divided by the radius a of the sphere. The potential on the surface of and outside the sphere equals the same constant k divided by the distance r from the center of the sphere. State these relations by the use of inequalities and make a graphical representation of V versus r.
27. A diode, an electronic device, has the property that an electric current can flow through it in only one direction. Thus, if a diode is in a circuit with an alternating-current source, the current in the circuit exists only during the half-cycle when the direction is correct for the diode. If a source of current given by $i = 0.02 \sin 120\pi t$ is connected in series with a diode, write the inequalities which are appropriate for the first four half-cycles and graph the resulting current versus the time. Assume that the diode allows a positive current to flow.

16-2 Graphical solution of inequalities

Equations can be solved by graphical and by algebraic means. This is also true of inequalities. In this section we shall take up graphical solutions, and in the following section we shall develop algebraic methods. The graphical method is shown in the following examples.

Example A.   Graphically solve the inequality $3x - 2 > 4$.

This means that we want to locate all those values of x which make the left member of this inequality greater than the right member. By subtracting 4 from each member, we have the equivalent inequality $3x - 6 > 0$.

If we find the graph of $y = 3x - 6$, all those values of x for which y is positive would satisfy the inequality $3x - 6 > 0$. Thus we graph the equation $y = 3x - 6$, and find those values of x for which y is positive. From the graph in Fig. 16-3, we see that values of $x > 2$ correspond to $y > 0$. Thus the solution to the given inequality is $x > 2$.

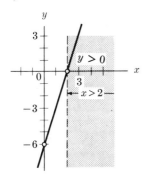

Figure 16-3

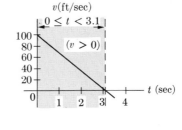

Figure 16-4

Example B.   The velocity v (in ft/sec) of a certain projectile in terms of the time t (in seconds) is given by $v = 100 - 32t$. For how long is the velocity positive? (This can be interpreted to mean "how long is the projectile moving upward?")

In terms of inequalities, we wish to know for what values of t is $v > 0$, or in other terms, solve the inequality $100 - 32t > 0$. Therefore, we graph the function $v = 100 - 32t$ as shown in Fig. 16-4. From the graph, we see that the values of t which correspond to $v > 0$ are $0 \le t < 3.1$ sec, which is the required solution. The last value is approximated from the graph.

Example C.   Graphically solve the inequality $2x^2 < x + 3$.

Finding the equivalent inequality, with 0 for a right-hand member, we have $2x^2 - x - 3 < 0$. Thus those values of x for which y is negative for the function $y = 2x^2 - x - 3$ will satisfy the inequality. So we graph the equation $y = 2x^2 - x - 3$, from the values given in the table on the next page:

x	-3	-2	-1	0	1	2	3
y	18	7	0	-3	-2	3	12

From the graph in Fig. 16-5, we can see that the inequality is satisfied for the values $-1 < x < 1.5$.

Summarizing the method for the graphical solution of an inequality, we see that we first write the inequality in an equivalent form with zero on the right. Next we set y equal to the left member and graph the resulting equation. Those values of x corresponding to the proper values of y (either above or below the x-axis) are those values which satisfy the inequality.

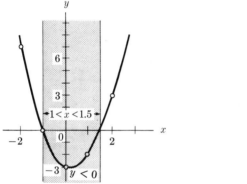

Figure 16-5

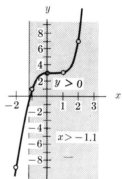

Figure 16-6

Example D.   Graphically solve the inequality $x^3 > x^2 - 3$.

Finding the equivalent inequality with 0 on the right, we have $x^3 - x^2 + 3 > 0$. By letting $y = x^3 - x^2 + 3$, we may solve the inequality by finding those values of x for which y is positive.

x	-2	-1	0	1	2
y	-9	1	3	3	7

Approximating the root of the function to be -1.1, the solution of the original inequality is $x > -1.1$ (Fig. 16-6). If greater accuracy is required, the methods of Section 14-5 may be used to find the root. This example also points out the usefulness of graphical methods, since this inequality would prove to be beyond elementary methods if an algebraic solution were required.

Exercises

In Exercises 1 through 20 solve the given inequalities graphically.

1. $2x > 4$
2. $2x - 3 < x$
3. $7x - 5 < 4x + 3$
4. $2x > 6x - 2$
5. $5x < 6x - 1$
6. $6 - x < x$

7. $x^2 > 2x$ 8. $x - 1 < x^2$ 9. $x^2 - 5x < -4$

10. $7x - 3 < -6x^2$ 11. $3x^2 - 2x - 8 > 0$ 12. $4x^2 - 2x > 5$

13. $x^3 > 1$ 14. $x^3 > x + 4$ 15. $x^4 < x^2 - 2x - 1$

16. $x^4 - 6x^3 + 7x^2 > 18 - 12x$ 17. $2^x > 0$ 18. $\log x > 1$

19. $\sin x < 0$ (limit the graph to the values $0 \leq x \leq 2\pi$)

20. $\cos 2x > 0$ (limit the graph as in exercise 19)

In Exercises 21 through 24 answer the given questions by solving appropriate inequalities graphically.

21. A salesman receives $300 monthly plus a 10% commission on sales. Therefore, his monthly income I in terms of his sales s is $I = 300 + 0.1\ s$. How much must his sales for the month be in order that his income is at least $500?

22. The basic maintenance on a certain machine is $10 per day. It also costs $2 per hour while in operation. Therefore, the total cost C to operate this machine in terms of the number of hours t that it operates in a given day is $C = 10 + 2t$. How many hours can it operate without the cost exceeding $30 for the day?

23. The electrical resistance R of a certain material depends on the temperature, according to the relation $R = 40 + 0.1T + 0.01T^2$. For what values of the temperature ($T > 0°$C) is the resistance over 42 ohms?

24. The height s of a certain object is given by $s = 140 + 60t - 16t^2$, where t is the time in seconds. For what values of t is $s > 180$ ft?

16-3 Algebraic solution of inequalities

We learned that one important step in solving inequalities by graphical means was to set up an equivalent inequality with zero as the right member. This enabled us to find the values which satisfied the inequality by simply determining the *sign* of the function which was set up. A similar procedure is useful when we solve inequalities algebraically.

A linear function is negative or positive for *all* values to the left of a particular value of x, and has the opposite sign for *all* values to the right of the same value of x. This value of x which splits the positive and negative regions of x is called the *critical value*. This critical value is found where the function is zero. Thus, to determine where a linear function is positive and where it is negative, we need to find only this critical value, and then determine the *sign* of the function to the left and to the right of this value.

Example A.   Solve the inequality $2x - 5 > 1$.

We first find the equivalent inequality with zero on the right. This is done by subtracting 1 from each member. Thus we have $2x - 6 > 0$. We now set the left member *equal* to zero to find the critical value. Thus the critical value is 3. We know that the function $2x - 6$ is of one sign for $x < 3$ and has the opposite sign for $x > 3$. Testing values in these ranges, we find that for $x > 3$, $2x - 6 > 0$. Thus the solution of the inequality is $x > 3$.

Example B.   Solve the inequality $\frac{1}{2}x - 3 \leq \frac{1}{3} - x$.

We note that this is an inequality combined with an equality. However, the solution proceeds essentially the same as with an inequality.

Multiplying by 6, we have $3x - 18 \leq 2 - 6x$. Subtracting $2 - 6x$ from each member, we have $9x - 20 \leq 0$. The critical value is $\frac{20}{9}$. If $x \leq \frac{20}{9}$, $9x - 20 \leq 0$. Thus the solution is $x \leq \frac{20}{9}$.

The analysis above is especially useful for solving inequalities involving higher-degree functions or involving fractions with x in the denominator as well as in the numerator. When the equivalent inequality with zero on the right has been found, this inequality is then factored into linear factors (and those quadratic factors which lead to complex roots). Each linear factor can change sign only at its critical value, as all possible values of x are considered. Thus the function on the left can change sign only where one of its factors changes sign. The function will have the same sign for all values of x less than the leftmost critical value. The sign of the function will also be the same within any given region between two critical values. All values to the right of the rightmost critical value will also give the function the same sign. We must find all of the critical values and then determine the sign of the function to the left of the leftmost critical value, between the critical values, and to the right of the rightmost critical value. Those intervals which give the proper sign will satisfy the given inequality.

Example C.   Solve the inequality $x^2 - 3 > 2x$.

We first find the equivalent inequality with zero on the right. Thus we have $x^2 - 2x - 3 > 0$. We then factor the left member, and have

$$(x - 3)(x + 1) > 0.$$

We find the critical value for each of the factors, for these are the only values for which the function $x^2 - 2x - 3$ is zero. The left critical value is -1, and the right critical value is 3. All values of x to the left of -1 give the same sign for the function. All values of x between -1 and 3 give the function the same sign. All values of x to the right of 3 give the same sign to the function. Thus we must determine the sign for $x < -1$, $-1 < x < 3$, and $x > 3$. For the range $x < -1$, we find that each of the factors is negative. However, the product of two negative numbers gives a positive number. Thus, if $x < -1$, then $(x - 3)(x + 1) > 0$.

For the range $-1 < x < 3$, we find that the left factor is negative, but the right factor is positive. The product of a negative and positive number gives a negative number. Thus, if $-1 < x < 3$, $(x - 3)(x + 1) < 0$. If $x > 3$, both factors are positive, making $(x - 3)(x + 1) > 0$. We tabulate the results.

If	$x < -1,$	$(x - 3)(x + 1) > 0.$
If	$-1 < x < 3,$	$(x - 3)(x + 1) < 0.$
If	$x > 3,$	$(x - 3)(x + 1) > 0.$

Thus the solution to the inequality is $x < -1$ or $x > 3$.

Example D.   Solve the inequality $x^3 - 4x^2 + x + 6 < 0$.

By methods developed in Chapter 14, we factor the function of the left and obtain $(x + 1)(x - 2)(x - 3) < 0$. The critical values are -1, 2, 3. We wish to determine the sign of the left member for the ranges $x < -1$, $-1 < x < 2$, $2 < x < 3$, and $x > 3$. This is tabulated here, with the sign of the factors in each case indicated.

Range	$(x + 1)(x - 2)(x - 3)$			Sign of $(x + 1)(x - 2)(x - 3)$
$x < -1$	$-$	$-$	$-$	$-$
$-1 < x < 2$	$+$	$-$	$-$	$+$
$2 < x < 3$	$+$	$+$	$-$	$-$
$x > 3$	$+$	$+$	$+$	$+$

Thus the solution is $x < -1$ or $2 < x < 3$.

Example E.   Solve the inequality $x^3 - x^2 + x - 1 > 0$.

This leads to $(x^2 + 1)(x - 1) > 0$. There is only one linear factor with a critical value. The factor $x^2 + 1$ is never negative. The solution is then $x > 1$.

Example F.   Solve the inequality

$$\frac{(x - 2)^2(x + 3)}{4 - x} < 0.$$

The critical values are -3, 2, and 4. Thus we have the following table.

Range	$\dfrac{(x - 2)^2(x + 3)}{4 - x}$	Sign of $\dfrac{(x - 2)^2(x + 3)}{4 - x}$
$x < -3$	$\dfrac{+ \quad -}{+}$	$-$
$-3 < x < 2$	$\dfrac{+ \quad +}{+}$	$+$
$2 < x < 4$	$\dfrac{+ \quad +}{+}$	$+$
$x > 4$	$\dfrac{+ \quad +}{-}$	$-$

The solution is $x < -3$ or $x > 4$.

Exercises

In Exercises 1 through 28 solve the given inequalities.

1. $x + 3 > 0$

2. $2x - 7 < 0$

3. $6x - 4 < 8 - x$

4. $2x - 6 < x + 4$

5. $3x - 7 \leq x + 1$

6. $7 - x \geq x - 1$

7. $\frac{1}{3}(x - 6) > 4 - x$

8. $\frac{x}{4} - 7 > \frac{x}{2} + 3$

9. $x^2 - 1 < 0$

10. $x^2 - 4x - 5 > 0$

11. $3x^2 + 5x \geq 2$

12. $2x^2 - 12 \leq -5x$

13. $6x^2 + 1 < 5x$

14. $9x^2 + 6x > -1$

15. $x^2 + 4 > 0$

16. $x^4 + 2 < 1$

17. $x^3 + x^2 - 2x > 0$

18. $x^3 - 2x^2 + x > 0$

19. $x^3 + 2x^2 - x - 2 > 0$

20. $x^4 - 2x^3 - 7x^2 + 8x + 12 < 0$

21. $\dfrac{x - 8}{3 - x} < 0$

22. $\dfrac{-5}{2x^2 + 3x - 2} < 0$

23. $\dfrac{x^2 - 6x - 7}{x + 5} > 0$

24. $\dfrac{4 - x}{3 + 2x - x^2} > 0$

25. $\dfrac{6 - x}{3 - x - 4x^2} > 0$

26. $\dfrac{(x - 2)^2(5 - x)}{(4 - x)^3} < 0$

27. $\dfrac{x^4(9 - x)(x - 5)(2 - x)}{(4 - x)^5} > 0$

28. $\dfrac{x^3(1 - x)(x - 2)(3 - x)(4 - x)}{(5 - x)^2(x - 6)^3} < 0$

In Exercises 29 through 32 determine the values of x for which the given radicals represent real numbers.

29. $\sqrt{(x - 1)(x + 2)}$

30. $\sqrt{x^2 - 3x}$

31. $\sqrt{-x - x^2}$

32. $\sqrt{\dfrac{x^3 + 6x^2 + 8x}{3 - x}}$

In Exercises 33 through 36 answer the given questions by solving the appropriate inequalities.

33. The velocity (in feet per second) of a certain object in terms of the time t (in seconds) is given by $v = 120 - 32t$. For what values of t is the object ascending ($v > 0$)?

34. The relationship between fahrenheit degrees and centigrade degrees is $F = \frac{9}{5}C + 32$. For what values of C is $F \geq 0$?

35. Determine the values of T for which the resistor of Exercise 23 of Section 16-2 has a resistance between 41 and 42 ohms.

36. The deflection y of a certain beam 9 ft long is given by $y = k(x^3 - 243x + 1458)$. For what values of x (the distance from one end of the beam) is the quantity y/k greater than 216 units?

16-4 Inequalities involving absolute values

If we wish to write the inequality $|x| > 1$ without absolute-value signs, we must note that we are considering values of x which are *numerically* larger than 1. Thus we may write this inequality in the equivalent form $x < -1$ or $x > 1$. We now note that the original inequality, with an absolute value sign, can be written in terms of two equivalent inequalities, neither involving absolute values. If we are asked to write the inequality $|x| < 1$ without the absolute-value signs, the solution would be $-1 < x < 1$.

Following reasoning similar to the above, whenever absolute values are involved in inequalities, the following two relations allow us to write equivalent inequalities without absolute values.

If $|f(x)| > n$, then $f(x) < -n$ or $f(x) > n$. $\qquad\qquad$ (16-1)

If $|f(x)| < n$, then $-n < f(x) < n$. $\qquad\qquad$ (16-2)

The use of these relations is indicated in the following examples.

Example A. Solve the inequality $|x - 3| < 2$.

Inspection of this inequality shows that we wish to find the values of x which are within 2 units of $x = 3$. Of course, such values are given by $1 < x < 5$. Let us now see how Eq. (16-2) gives us this result.

By using Eq. (16-2), we have

$$-2 < x - 3 < 2.$$

By adding 3 to all three members of this inequality, we have

$$1 < x < 5,$$

which is the desired solution.

Example B. Solve the inequality $|2x - 1| > 5$.

By using Eq. (16-1), we have

$$2x - 1 < -5 \qquad \text{or} \qquad 2x - 1 > 5.$$

Completing the solution, we have

$$2x < -4 \qquad \text{or} \qquad 2x > 6,$$
$$x < -2 \qquad \text{or} \qquad x > 3.$$

Example C. Solve the inequality $|x^2 + x - 4| > 2$.

By (16-1), we have $x^2 + x - 4 < -2$ or $x^2 + x - 4 > 2$, which means we want values of x which satisfy *either* of these inequalities. The first inequality becomes

$$x^2 + x - 2 < 0,$$
$$(x + 2)(x - 1) < 0,$$

which has the solution $-2 < x < 1$. The second inequality becomes

$$x^2 + x - 6 > 0$$
$$(x + 3)(x - 2) > 0,$$

which has the solution $x < -3$ or $x > 2$. Thus the ranges of x covered by both inequalities are $x < -3$, $-2 < x < 1$, or $x > 2$, which therefore is the solution.

Example D. Solve the inequality $|x^2 + x - 4| < 2$.

By Eq. (16-2), we have $-2 < x^2 + x - 4 < 2$, which we can write as $x^2 + x - 4 > -2$ and $x^2 + x - 4 < 2$, as long as we remember that we want values of x which satisfy *both* of these at the same time. The first inequality can be written as

$$x^2 + x - 4 > -2,$$
$$x^2 + x - 2 > 0,$$
$$(x + 2)(x - 1) > 0,$$

which has the solution $x < -2$ or $x > 1$. The second inequality is

$$x^2 + x - 4 < 2,$$
$$x^2 + x - 6 < 0,$$

or

$$(x + 3)(x - 2) < 0,$$

which has the solution $-3 < x < 2$. The values of x which satisfy both of the inequalities are those between -3 and -2 and those between 1 and 2. Thus the solution is $-3 < x < -2$ or $1 < x < 2$.

Exercises

In Exercises 1 through 16 solve the given inequalities.

1. $|x - 4| < 1$ 2. $|x + 1| < 3$ 3. $|3x - 5| > 2$
4. $|2x - 1| > 1$ 5. $|6x - 5| < 4$ 6. $|3 - x| < 2$
7. $|4x + 3| > 3$ 8. $|3x + 1| > 2$ 9. $|x + 4| < 6$
10. $|5x - 10| < 2$ 11. $|2 - 3x| > 5$ 12. $|3 - 2x| > 6$
13. $|x^2 + 3x - 1| < 3$ 14. $|x^2 - 5x - 1| < 5$
15. $|x^2 + 3x - 1| > 3$ 16. $|x^2 - 5x - 1| > 5$

In Exercises 17 through 19 use inequalities involving absolute values to solve the given problems.

17. The deflection y at a horizontal distance x from the left end of a beam is less than $\frac{1}{4}$ ft within 2 ft of a point 6 ft from the left end. State this with the use of an inequality involving absolute values.

18. A given projectile is at an altitude h between 40 and 60 ft for the time between $t = 3$ sec and $t = 5$ sec. Write this using two inequalities involving absolute values.

19. An object is oscillating at the end of a spring which is suspended from a support. The distance x of the object from the support is given by $|x - 8| < 3$. By solving this inequality, determine the distances (in inches) from the support of the extreme positions of the object.

16-5 Miscellaneous Exercises

In Exercises 1 through 20 solve the given inequalities algebraically.

1. $2x - 12 > 0$ 2. $5 - 3x < 0$ 3. $3x + 5 < 0$
4. $\frac{1}{4}x - 2 > 3x$ 5. $x^2 + 2x > 63$ 6. $6x^2 - x > 35$

7. $x^3 + 4x^2 - x > 4$

8. $2x^3 + 4 < x^2 + 8x$

9. $\dfrac{x - 8}{2x + 1} < 0$

10. $\dfrac{3x + 2}{x - 3} > 0$

11. $\dfrac{(2x - 1)(3 - x)}{x + 4} > 0$

12. $\dfrac{(3 - x)^2}{2x + 7} \leq 0$

13. $x^4 + x^2 < 0$

14. $3x^3 + 7x^2 - 20x < 0$

15. $\dfrac{1}{x} < 2$

16. $\dfrac{1}{x - 2} < \dfrac{1}{4}$

17. $|x - 2| > 3$

18. $|2x - 1| > 5$

19. $|3x + 2| < 4$

20. $|4 - 3x| < 1$

In Exercises 21 through 26 solve the given inequalities graphically.

21. $3x - 2 > x$

22. $4 - 5x < 2$

23. $x^2 + 2x + 4 > 0$

24. $3x^2 + 5 > 16x$

25. $x^3 + x + 1 < 0$

26. $\dfrac{1}{x} > 2$

In Exercises 27 and 28 determine the values of x for which the given radicals represent real numbers.

27. $\sqrt{x^2 + 4x}$

28. $\sqrt{\dfrac{x - 1}{x + 2}}$

In Exercises 29 and 30 prove the given inequalities.

29. If $y > 0$ and $x > y + 1$, prove that $x/y > (y + 1)/(x - 1)$.

30. If $x \neq y$, prove that $x^2 + y^2 > 2xy$.

In Exercises 31 through 34 solve the given problems using inequalities.

31. One leg of a right triangle is 14 in. longer than the other leg. If the hypotenuse is to be greater than 34 in., what values of the other side are permissible?

32. City A is 300 mi from city B. One car starts from A for B one hour before a second car. The first car averages 45 mi/hr and the second car averages 60 mi/hr for the trip. For what times after the first car starts is the second car ahead of the first car?

33. Two resistors have a combined resistance of 8 ohms when connected in series. What are the permissible values if they are to have a combined resistance of at least $\frac{3}{2}$ ohms when connected in parallel? (See Exercise 38 of Section 6-1.)

34. For 1 gm of ice to be melted, then heated to boiling water, and finally vaporized into steam, the relation between the temperature $T(°C)$ and the number of calories absorbed Q is given by $T = 0$ if $Q < 80$, $T = Q - 80$ if $80 < Q < 180$, and $T = 100$ if $180 < Q < 720$. Plot the graph of T (along the y-axis) versus Q (along the x-axis) if 720 calories of heat are absorbed by 1 gm of ice originally at $0°C$.

Variation

17

17-1 Ratio and proportion

In mathematics and its applications, we often come across the terms "ratio" and "proportion." In fact, in Chapter 3 when we first introduced the trigonometric functions of angles, we used ratios which had a specific meaning. In general, a *ratio* of a number a to a number b ($b \neq 0$) is the quotient a/b. Thus, a fraction is a ratio.

Any measurement made is the ratio of the measured magnitude to an accepted unit of measurement. For example, when we say that an object is five feet long, we are saying that the length of that object is five times as long as an accepted unit of length, the foot. Other examples of ratios are density (weight/volume), specific gravity (density of object/density of water), and pressure (force/area). As these examples illustrate, ratios may compare quantities of the same kind, or they may express a division of magnitudes of different quantities.

Example A. The approximate air-line distance from New York to San Francisco is 2500 mi, and the approximate air-line distance from New York to Minneapolis is 1000 mi. The ratio of these distances is

$$\frac{2500 \text{ mi}}{1000 \text{ mi}} = \frac{5}{2}.$$

Since the units in both are miles, the resulting ratio is a dimensionless number.

If a jet travels from New York to San Francisco in 4 hours, its average speed is

$$\frac{2500 \text{ mi}}{4 \text{ hr}} = 625 \text{ mi/hr}.$$

In this case we must attach the proper units to the resulting ratio.

As we noted in Example A, we must be careful to attach the proper units to the resulting ratio. Generally, the ratio of measurements of the same kind should be expressed as a dimensionless number. Consider the following example.

Example B.   The length of a certain room is 24 ft, and the width of the room is 18 ft. Therefore the ratio of the length to the width is $\frac{24}{18}$ or $\frac{4}{3}$.

If the width of the room were expressed as 6 yd, we should not express the ratio as 24 ft/6 yd = 4 ft/1 yd. It is much better and more meaningful to first change the units of one of the measurements. Changing the length from 6 yd to 18 ft, we express the ratio as $\frac{4}{3}$, as we saw above. From this ratio we can easily see that the length is $\frac{4}{3}$ as long as the width.

A statement of equality between two ratios is called a *proportion*. One way of denoting a proportion is $a:b = c:d$, which is read "*a* is to *b* as *c* is to *d*." (Another notation used for a proportion is $a:b::c:d$.) Of course, by the definition, $a/b = c/d$, which means that a proportion is an equation. Any operation applicable to an equation is also applicable to a proportion.

Example C.   On a certain map 1 in. represents 10 mi. Thus on this map we have a ratio of 1 in./10 mi. To find the distance represented by 3.5 in., we can set up the proportion

$$\frac{3.5 \text{ in.}}{x \text{ mi}} = \frac{1 \text{ in.}}{10 \text{ mi}}.$$

From this proportion we find the value of $x = 35$ mi.

Example D.   The magnitude of an electrical field E is defined as the ratio between the force F on a charge q and the magnitude of q. This can be written as $E = F/q$. If we know the force exerted on a particular charge at some point in the field, we can determine the force which would be exerted on another charge placed at the same point. For example, if we know that a force of 10^{-8} newton is exerted on a charge of 4×10^{-9} coulomb, we can then determine the force which would be exerted on a charge of 6×10^{-9} coulomb by the proportion

$$\frac{10^{-8}}{4 \times 10^{-9}} = \frac{F}{6 \times 10^{-9}},$$

or

$$F = 1.5 \times 10^{-8} \text{ newton}.$$

Exercises

In Exercises 1 through 6 express the ratios in the simplest form.

1. 18 volts to 3 volts
2. 27 ft to 18 ft
3. 48 in. to 3 ft
4. 120 seconds to 4 minutes
5. 20 qt to 25 gal
6. 4 lb to 8 oz

In Exercises 7 through 10 find the required ratios.

7. The ratio of the density of an object to the density of water is known as the *specific gravity* of the object. If the density of gold is 1200 lb/ft³ and the density of water is 62.4 lb/ft³, what is the specific gravity of gold?

8. The *atomic weight* of an element is the ratio of the weight of an atom of the element to the weight of an atom of oxygen, which is taken as 16. The ratio of the atomic weight of carbon to that of oxygen is $\frac{3}{4}$. What is the atomic weight of carbon?

9. A certain body of water exerts a force of 18,000 lb on an area of 20 in². Find the pressure (force per unit area) on this area.

10. The electric current in a given circuit is the ratio of the voltage to the resistance. What is the current (volt/ohm = ampere) for a circuit where the voltage is 24 volts and the resistance is 10 ohms?

In Exercises 11 through 20 answer the given questions by setting up and solving the appropriate proportions.

11. If 1 lb = 454 gm, what weight in grams is 20 lb?

12. If 9 ft² = 1 yd², what area in square yards is 45 ft²?

13. How many feet per second are equivalent to 45 mi/hr?

14. How many gallons per hour are equivalent to 500 quarts per minute?

15. The length of a picture is 48 in, and its width is 36 in. In a reproduction of the picture the length is 36 in. What is the width of the reproduction?

16. A car will travel 93 mi on 6 gal of gasoline. How far will it travel on 10 gal of gasoline?

17. In physics, power is defined as the time rate at which work is done. If a given motor does 6000 ft-lb of work in 20 sec, what work will it do in 4 min?

18. It is known that 98 lb of sulfuric acid are required to neutralize 80 lb of sodium hydroxide. Given 37 lb of sulfuric acid, determine the weight of sodium hydroxide which will be neutralized.

19. A board 10 ft long is cut into two pieces, the lengths of which are in the ratio 2:3. Find the lengths of the pieces.

20. A total of 322 bolts are in two containers. The ratio of the number in one container to the number in the other container is 5:9. How many are in each container?

17-2 Variation

Scientific laws are often stated in terms of ratios and proportions. For example, Charles' law can be stated as "for a perfect gas under constant pressure, the ratio of any two volumes this gas may occupy equals the ratio of the absolute temperatures." Symbolically this could be stated as $V_1/V_2 = T_1/T_2$. Thus, if the ratio of the volumes and one of the values of the temperature are known, we can easily find the other temperature.

By multiplying both sides of the proportion of Charles' law by V_2/T_1, we can change the form of the proportion to $V_1/T_1 = V_2/T_2$. This statement says that the ratio of the volume to the temperature (for constant pressure) is constant. Thus, if any pair of values of volume and temperature are known, this ratio of V_1/T_1 can be calculated. This ratio of V_1/T_1 can be called a constant k, which means that Charles' law can be written as $V/T = k$. We now have the statement that the ratio of the volume to temperature is always constant; or, as it is normally stated, "the volume is proportional to the temperature." Therefore we write $V = kT$, the clearest and most informative statement of Charles' law.

Thus, for any two quantities always in the same proportion, we say that one is proportional to (or varies directly as) the second, and in general this is written as $y = kx$, where k is the *constant of proportionality*.

Example A. The circumference of a circle is proportional to (varies directly as) the radius. Symbolically this is written as $C = kr$, where (in this case) $k = 2\pi$.

Example B. The fact that the electric resistance of a wire varies directly as (is proportional to) its length is stated as $R = kL$.

It is very common that, when two quantities are related, the product of the two quantities remains constant. In such a case $yx = k$, or $y = k/x$. This is stated as "y varies inversely as x," or "y is inversely proportional to x."

Example C. Boyle's law states that "at a given temperature, the pressure of a gas varies inversely as the volume." This we write symbolically as $P = k/V$.

For many relationships, one quantity varies as a specified power of another. The terms "varies directly" and "varies inversely" are used in the following examples with the specified power of the relation.

Example D. The statement that the volume of a sphere varies directly as the cube of its radius is written as $V = kr^3$. In this case we know that $k = 4\pi/3$.

Example E. The fact that the gravitational force of attraction between two bodies varies inversely as the square of the distance between them is written as $F = k/d^2$.

Finally, one quantity may vary as the product of other quantities, or powers of other quantities. Such variation is termed *joint variation*.

Example F. The cost of sheet metal varies jointly as the area of the sheet and the cost per unit area of the metal. This we write as $C = kAc$.

Example G. Newton's law of gravitation states that "the force of gravitation between two objects varies jointly as the product of the masses of the objects, and inversely as the square of the distance between their centers." We write this symbolically as $F = km_1m_2/d^2$.

Once we know how to express the given statement in terms of the variables and the constant of proportionality, we may compute the value of k if one set of values of the variables is known. This value of k can then be used to compute values of one variable, when given the others.

Example H. If y varies inversely as x, and $x = 15$ when $y = 4$, find the value of y when $x = 12$.

First we write $y = k/x$ to denote that y varies inversely as x. Next we substitute $x = 15$ and $y = 4$ into the equation. This leads to

$$4 = \frac{k}{15}.$$

or $k = 60$. Thus for our present discussion the constant of proportionality is 60, and this may be substituted into $y = k/x$, giving

$$y = \frac{60}{x}$$

as the equation between y and x. Now, for any given value of x, we may find the value of y. For $x = 12$, we have

$$y = \tfrac{60}{12} = 5.$$

Example I.   The distance an object falls under the influence of gravity varies directly as the square of the time of fall. If an object falls 64 ft in 2 sec, how far will it fall in 3 sec?

We first write the relation $d = kt^2$. Then we use the fact that $d = 64$ for $t = 2$. This gives $64 = 4k$. In this way we find that $k = 16$ ft/sec². We now know a general relation between d and t, which is $d = 16t^2$. Now we put in the value 3 for t, so that we can find d for this particular value for the time. This gives $d = 16(9) = 144$ ft. We also note in this problem that k will normally have a certain set of units associated with it.

Example J.   The kinetic energy of a moving object varies jointly as the mass of the object and the square of its velocity. If a 5-gm object, traveling at 10 cm/sec, has a kinetic energy of 250 ergs, find the kinetic energy of an 8-gm object traveling at 50 cm/sec.

We first write the relation $KE = kmv^2$. Then we use the known set of values to find k. We write $250 = k \cdot 5 \cdot 100$, giving

$$k = 0.5 \frac{\text{erg}}{\text{gm (cm/sec)}^2}$$

[actually 1 erg = 1 gm (cm/sec)², which means that $k = 0.5$, with no physical units.] Next we find the desired value for KE by substituting the other given values, and the value of k, in the original relation:

$$KE = 0.5 \, mv^2 = 0.5 \cdot 8 \cdot 50^2 = 10{,}000 = 10^4 \text{ ergs.}$$

Example K.   The heat developed in a resistor varies jointly as the time and the square of the current in the resistor. If the heat developed in t_0 sec with a current i_0 passing through the resistor is H_0, how much heat is developed if both the time and current are doubled?

First we set up the relation $H = kti^2$, where t is the time and i is the current. From the given information we can write $H_0 = kt_0i_0^2$. Thus $k = H_0/t_0i_0^2$, and the original equation becomes $H = H_0 t i^2 / t_0 i_0^2$. We now let $t = 2t_0$ and $i = 2i_0$, so that we can find H when the time and current are doubled. With these values we obtain

$$H = \frac{H_0 (2t_0)(2i_0)^2}{t_0 i_0^2} = \frac{8 H_0 t_0 i_0^2}{t_0 i_0^2} = 8 H_0.$$

This tells us that the heat developed is eight times as much as for the original values of i and t.

Exercises

In Exercises 1 through 4 express the given statements as equations.

1. y varies directly as z
2. s varies inversely as the square of t
3. w varies jointly as x and the cube of y
4. q varies as the square of r and inversely as the fourth power of t

In Exercises 5 through 8 give the equation relating the variables after evaluating the constant of proportionality for the given set of values.

5. r varies inversely as y, and $r = 2$ when $y = 8$.
6. y varies directly as the square root of x, and $y = 2$ when $x = 64$.
7. p is proportional to q and inversely proportional to the cube of r, and $p = 6$ when $q = 3$ and $r = 2$.
8. v is proportional to t and the square of s, and $v = 80$ when $s = 2$ and $t = 5$.

In Exercises 9 through 16 find the required value by setting up the general equation and then evaluating.

9. Find y when $x = 10$ if y varies directly as x and $y = 20$ when $x = 8$.
10. Find y when $x = 5$ if y varies directly as the square of x and $y = 6$ when $x = 8$.
11. Find s when $t = 10$ if s is inversely proportional to t and $s = 100$ when $t = 5$.
12. Find p for $q = 0.8$ if p is inversely proportional to the square of q and $p = 18$ when $q = 0.2$.
13. Find y for $x = 6$ and $z = 5$ if y varies directly as x and inversely as z and $y = 60$ when $x = 4$ and $z = 10$.
14. Find r when $n = 16$ if r varies directly as the square root of n and $r = 4$ when $n = 25$.
15. Find f when $p = 2$ and $c = 4$ if f varies jointly as p and the cube of c and $f = 8$ when $p = 4$ and $c = 0.1$.
16. Find v when $r = 2$, $s = 3$ and $t = 4$ if v varies jointly as r and s and inversely as the square of t and $v = 8$ when $r = 2$, $s = 6$ and $t = 6$.

In Exercises 17 through 30 solve the given applied problems.

17. Hooke's law states that the force needed to stretch a spring is proportional to the amount the spring is stretched. If 10 lb stretches a certain spring 4 in., how much will the spring be stretched by a force of 6 lb?

18. In modern physics we learn that the energy of a photon (a "particle" of light) is directly proportional to its frequency f. Given that the constant of proportionality is 6.6×10^{-27} erg·sec (this is known as *Planck's constant*), what is the energy of a photon whose frequency is 3×10^{15}/sec?

19. The intensity of a light source varies inversely as the square of the distance from the source. Given that the intensity is 25 units at a distance of 200 cm, find the general relation between the intensity and distance for this light source.

20. The rate of emission of radiant energy from the surface of a body is proportional to the fourth power of the absolute temperature. Given that a 25-watt (the rate of emission) lamp has an operating temperature of $2500°$K, what is the operating temperature of a similar 40-watt lamp?

21. The electric resistance of a wire varies directly as its length and inversely as its cross-sectional area. Find the relation between resistance, length, and area for a wire which has a resistance of 0.2 ohm for a length of 200 ft and cross-sectional area of 0.05 in².

22. The general gas law states that the pressure of an ideal gas varies directly as the absolute temperature, and inversely as the volume. By first finding the relation between P, T, and V, find V for $P = 4$ atm and $T = 400°$K, given that $P = 6$ atm for $V = 10$ cm³ and $T = 300°$K.

23. The frequency of vibration of a wire varies directly as the square root of the tension on the wire. Express the relation between f and T. If $f = 400$/sec when $T = 10^5$ dynes, find f when $T = 3.4 \times 10^5$ dynes.

24. The period of a pendulum is directly proportional to the square root of its length. Given that a pendulum 2 ft long has a period of $\pi/2$ sec, what is the period of a pendulum 4 ft long?

25. The distance s that an object falls due to gravity varies jointly as the acceleration due to gravity g and the square of the time t of fall. On earth $g = 32$ ft/sec² and on the moon $g = 5.5$ ft/sec². On earth an object falls 144 ft in 3 sec. How far does an object fall in 7 sec on the moon?

26. The power of an electric current varies jointly as the resistance and the square of the current. Given that the power is 10 watts when the current is 0.5 amp and the resistance is 40 ohms, find the power if the current is 2 amp and the resistance is 20 ohms.

27. Under certain conditions the velocity of an object is proportional to the logarithm of the square root of the time elapsed. Given that $v = 18$ cm/sec after 4 sec, what is the velocity after 6 sec?

28. The level of intensity of a sound wave is proportional to the logarithm of the ratio of the sound intensity to an arbitrary reference intensity, normally defined as 10^{-16} watt/cm². Assuming that the intensity level is 100 decibels (db) for $I = 10^{-6}$ watt/cm², what is the constant of proportionality?

29. When the volume of a gas changes very rapidly, an approximate relation is that the pressure varies inversely as the $\frac{3}{2}$ power of the volume. Express P as a function of V. Given that P is 3 atm when $V = 100$ cm³, find P when $V = 25$ cm³.

30. The x-component of the velocity of an object moving around a circle with constant angular velocity ω varies jointly as ω and $\sin \omega t$. Given that ω is constant at $\pi/6$ rad/sec, and the x-component of the velocity is -4π ft/sec when $t = 1$ sec, find the x-component of the velocity when $t = 9$ sec.

31. The acceleration in the x-direction of the object referred to in Exercise 30 varies jointly as cos ωt and the square of ω. Under the same conditions as stated in Exercise 30, calculate the x-component of the acceleration.

32. Under certain conditions, the logarithm to the base e of the ratio of an electric current at time t to the current at time $t = 0$ is proportional to the time. Given that the current is $1/e$ of its initial value after 0.1 sec, what is its value after 0.2 sec?

17-3 Miscellaneous Exercises

In Exercises 1 through 8 answer the given questions by setting up and solving the appropriate proportions.

1. On a certain map, 1 in. represents 16 mi. What distance on the map represents 52 mi?

2. Given that 1 meter equals 39.4 in., what length in inches is 2.45 meters?

3. Given that 1 liter equals 61 in³, how many liters is 105 in³?

4. Given that 1 cal equals 4.19 joules, how many calories equal 81.9 joules?

5. An electronic data-processing card sorter can sort 45,000 cards in 20 min. How many cards can it sort in 5 hr?

6. A given machine can produce 80 bolts in 5 min. How many bolts can it produce in an hour?

7. Assuming that 195 gm of zinc sulfide are used to produce 128 gm of sulfur dioxide, how many grams of sulfur dioxide are produced by the use of 750 gm of zinc sulfide?

8. Given that 32 lb of oxygen are required to burn 20 lb of a certain fuel gas, how much air (which can be assumed to be 21% oxygen) is required to burn 100 lb of the fuel gas?

In Exercises 9 through 12 give the equation relating the variables after evaluating the constant of proportionality for the given set of values.

9. y varies directly as the square of x, and $y = 27$ when $x = 3$.

10. f varies inversely as l, and $f = 5$ when $l = 8$.

11. v is directly proportional to x and inversely proportional to the cube of y, and $v = 10$ when $x = 5$ and $y = 4$.

12. r varies jointly as u, v and the square of w, and $r = 8$ when $u = 2$, $v = 4$ and $w = 3$.

In Exercises 13 through 25 solve the given applied problems.

13. The power of a gas engine is proportional to the area of the piston. If an engine with a piston area of 8 in² can develop 30 horsepower, what power is developed by an engine with a piston area of 6 in²?

14. Ohm's law states that the voltage across a given resistor is proportional to the current in the resistor. Given that 18 volts are across a certain resistor in which a current of 8 amp is flowing, express the general relationship between voltage and current for this resistor.

15. The surface area of a sphere varies directly as the square of its radius. The surface area of a certain sphere is 36π square units when the radius is 3 units. What is the surface area when the radius is 4 units?

16. The difference in pressure in a fluid between that at the surface and that at a point below varies jointly as the density of the fluid and the depth of the point. The density of water is 1 gm/cm³ and the density of alcohol is 0.8 gm/cm³. This difference in pressure at a point 20 cm below the surface of water is 19,600 dynes/cm². What is the difference in pressure at a point 30 cm below the surface of alcohol?

17. The velocity of a pulse traveling in a string varies directly as the square root of the tension of the string. Given that the velocity in a certain string is 450 ft/sec when the tension is 20 lb, determine the velocity if the tension were 30 lb.

18. The velocity of a jet of fluid flowing from an opening in the side of a container is proportional to the square root of the depth of the opening. If the velocity of the jet from an opening at a depth of 4 ft is 16 ft/sec, what is the velocity of a jet from an opening at a depth of 25 ft?

19. The crushing load of a pillar varies as the fourth power of its radius and inversely as the square of its length. Express L in terms of r and l for a pillar 20 ft tall and 1 ft in diameter which is crushed by a load of 20 tons.

20. The acoustical intensity of a sound wave is proportional to the square of the pressure amplitude and inversely proportional to the velocity of the wave. Given that the intensity is 474 ergs/cm²/sec for a pressure amplitude of 200 dynes/cm² and a velocity of 3.46×10^4 cm/sec, what is the intensity if the pressure amplitude is 150 dynes/cm² and the velocity is 3.20×10^4 cm/sec?

21. In any given electric circuit containing an inductance and capacitance, the resonant frequency is inversely proportional to the square root of the capacitance. If the resonant frequency in a circuit is 25 cycles/sec and the capacitance is 10^{-4} farad, what is the resonant frequency of this circuit if the capacitance is 2.5×10^{-5} farad?

22. The safe uniformly distributed load on a horizontal beam, supported at both ends, varies jointly as the width and the square of the depth and inversely as the distance between supports. Given that one beam has double the dimensions of another, how many times heavier is the safe load it can support than the first can support?

23. Kepler's third law of planetary motion states that the square of the period of any planet is proportional to the cube of the mean radius (about the sun) of that planet, with the constant of proportionality being the same for all planets. Using the fact that the period of the earth is one year and its mean radius is 93 million mi, calculate the mean radius for Venus, given that its period is $7\frac{1}{2}$ months.

24. The amount of heat per unit of time passing through a wall t feet thick is proportional to the temperature difference ΔT and the area A, and is inversely proportional to t. The constant of proportionality is called the coefficient of conductivity. Calculate the coefficient of conductivity of a 21-cm-thick concrete wall if 0.1 cal/sec pass through an area of 105 cm² when the temperature difference is 10.5 deg.

25. The percentage error in determining an electric current due to a small error in reading a galvanometer is proportional to $\tan \theta + \cot \theta$, where θ is the angular deflection of the galvanometer. Given that the percentage error is 2% when $\theta = 4°$, determine the percentage error as a function of θ.

26. Newton's law of gravitation is stated in Example G of Section 17-2. Here k is the same for any two objects. A spacecraft is traveling the 240,000 mi from the earth to the moon, whose mass is $\frac{1}{81}$ that of the earth. How far from the earth is the gravitational force of the earth on the spacecraft equal to the gravitational force of the moon on the spacecraft?

Progressions

18

18-1 Arithmetic progressions

In this chapter we are going to consider briefly the properties of certain sequences of numbers. In itself a sequence is some set of numbers arranged in some specified manner. There are two kinds of sequences of particular interest: sequences of numbers which form what are known as arithmetic progressions and sequences which form geometric progressions. Applications of these progressions can be found in many areas, including interest calculations and certain areas in physics. However, one of the principal uses comes later, in mathematics itself, where they are used to develop mathematical topics which in themselves have wide technical application.

An *arithmetic progression* (AP) is a sequence of numbers in which each number after the first can be obtained from the preceding one by adding to it a fixed number called the common difference.

Example A. The sequence 2, 5, 8, 11, 14, ... is an AP with a common difference of 3. The sequence 7, 2, -3, -8, ... is an AP with a common difference of -5.

If we know the first term of an AP, we can find any other term in the progression by successively adding the common difference enough times for the desired term to be obtained. This, however, is a very inefficient method, and we can learn more about the progression if we establish a general way of finding any particular term.

In general, if a is the first term and d the common difference, the second term is $a + d$, the third term is $a + 2d$, and so forth. If we are looking for the nth term, we note that we need only add d to the first term $n - 1$ times. Thus the nth term l of an AP is given by

$$l = a + (n - 1)d. \tag{18-1}$$

Occasionally l is referred to as the last term of an AP, but this is somewhat misleading. In reality there is no actual limit to the possible number of terms in an AP, although we may be interested only in a particular number of them. For this reason it is clearer to call l the nth term, rather than the last term. Also, this is the reason for writing three dots after the last indicated term of an AP. These dots indicate that the progression may continue.

Example B. Find the tenth term of the progression 2, 5, 8, ...
By subtracting any given term from the following term, we find that the common difference is $d = 3$. From the terms given, we know that the first term is $a = 2$. From the statement of the problem, the desired term is the tenth, or $n = 10$. Thus we may find the tenth term l by

$$l = 2 + (10 - 1)3 = 2 + 9 \cdot 3 = 29.$$

Example C. Find the number of terms in the progression for which $a = 5$, $l = -119$, and $d = -4$.
Substitution into Eq. (18-1) gives

$$-119 = 5 + (n - 1)(-4)$$

which leads to

$$-124 = -4n + 4,$$
$$4n = 128,$$
$$n = 32.$$

Example D. How many numbers between 10 and 1000 are divisible by 6?
We must first find the smallest and the largest numbers in this range which are divisible by 6. These numbers are 12 and 996. Obviously the common difference between all multiples of 6 is 6. Thus $a = 12$, $l = 996$, and $d = 6$. Therefore,

$$996 = 12 + (n - 1)6,$$
$$6n = 990,$$
$$n = 165.$$

Thus there are 165 numbers between 10 and 1000 which are divisible by 6.

Another important quantity concerning an AP is the sum s of the first n terms. We can indicate this sum by either of the two equations,

$$s = a + (a + d) + (a + 2d) + \cdots + (l - d) + l,$$

or

$$s = l + (l - d) + (l - 2d) + \cdots + (a + d) + a.$$

If we now add these equations, we have

$$2s = (a + l) + (a + l) + (a + l) + \cdots + (a + l) + (a + l).$$

There is one factor $(a + l)$ for each term, and there are n terms. Thus

$$s = \frac{n}{2}(a + l). \tag{18-2}$$

Example E.   Find the sum of the first 1000 positive integers.
  Here $a = 1$, $l = 1000$, and $n = 1000$. Thus

$$s = \tfrac{1000}{2}(1 + 1000) = 500(1001) = 500{,}500.$$

Example F.   Find the sum of the AP for which $n = 10$, $a = 4$, and $d = -5$.
We first find the nth term. We write

$$l = 4 + (10 - 1)(-5) = 4 - 45 = -41.$$

Now we can solve for s:

$$s = \tfrac{10}{2}(4 - 41) = 5(-37) = -185.$$

Example G.   Suppose that each swing of a pendulum is 3 in. shorter than the preceding swing. If the first swing is 10 ft, determine the total distance traveled by the pendulum bob in the first 5 swings.
  In this problem each of the terms of the progression represents the distance traveled in the respective swing. This means that $a = 10$. Also the given information tells us that $d = -\frac{1}{4}$. Using these values, we find that the distance traversed in the fifth swing is $l = 10 + 4(-\frac{1}{4}) = 9$. The total distance traversed is

$$s = \tfrac{5}{2}(10 + 9) = \tfrac{95}{2} \text{ ft.}$$

Exercises

In Exercises 1 through 4 write five terms of the AP with the given values.

1. $a = 4$, $d = 2$
2. $a = 6$, $d = -\frac{1}{2}$
3. Third term $= 5$, fifth term $= -3$
4. Second term $= -2$, fifth term $= 7$

In Exercises 5 through 8 find the nth term of the AP with the given values.

5. $a = -7$, $d = 4$, $n = 12$
6. $a = \frac{3}{2}$, $d = \frac{1}{6}$, $n = 50$
7. $a = b$, $d = 2b$, $n = 25$
8. $a = -c$, $d = 3c$, $n = 30$

In Exercises 9 through 12 find the indicated sum of the terms of the AP.

9. $n = 20$, $a = 4$, $l = 40$
10. $n = 8$, $a = -12$, $l = -26$
11. $n = 10$, $a = -2$, $d = -\frac{1}{2}$
12. $n = 40$, $a = 3$, $d = \frac{1}{3}$

In Exercises 13 through 22 find any of the values of a, d, l, n, or s that are missing.

13. $a = 5$, $d = 8$, $l = 45$
14. $a = -2$, $n = 60$, $l = 28$
15. $a = \frac{5}{3}$, $n = 20$, $s = \frac{40}{3}$
16. $a = 0.1$, $l = -5.9$, $s = -8.7$

17. $d = 3, n = 30, s = 1875$

18. $d = 9, l = 86, s = 455$

19. $a = 74, d = -5, l = -231$

20. $a = -\frac{9}{7}, n = 19, l = -\frac{36}{7}$

21. $a = -c, l = b/2, s = 2b - 4c$

22. $d = -2, n = 50, s = 0$

In Exercises 23 through 32 find the indicated quantities.

23. Sixth term $= 56$, tenth term $= 72$ (find a, d, s for $n = 10$).

24. Seventeenth term $= -91$, second term $= -73$ (find a, d, s for $n = 40$).

25. Find the sum of the first 100 integers.

26. Find the sum of the first 100 odd integers.

27. Find the sum of the first 200 multiples of 5.

28. Find the number of multiples of 8 between 99 and 999.

29. A man accepts a position which pays $8200 per year, and receives a raise of $450 each year. During what year of his association with the firm will his salary be $16,300?

30. A body falls 16 ft during the first second, 48 ft during the second second, 80 ft during the third second, etc. How far will it fall in the twentieth second?

31. For the object in Exercise 30, what is the total distance fallen in the first 20 sec?

32. A well-driller charges $3 for drilling the first foot of a well, and for every foot thereafter he charges 1¢ more than the preceding foot. How much does he charge for drilling a 500-ft well?

18-2 Geometric progressions

A second type of sequence is the *geometric progression*. A geometric progression (GP) is a sequence of numbers in which each number after the first can be obtained from the preceding one by multiplying it by a fixed number called the common ratio. One important application of geometric progressions is in computing interest on savings accounts. Other applications can be found in biology and physics.

Example A. The sequence 2, 4, 8, 16, . . . forms a GP with a common ratio of 2. The sequence 9, 3, 1, $\frac{1}{3}$, . . . forms a GP with a common ratio of $\frac{1}{3}$.

If we know the first term, we can then find any other desired term by multiplying by the common ratio a sufficient number of times. When we do this for a general GP, we can determine the nth term in terms of the first term a, the common ratio r, and n. Thus the second term is ra, the third term is r^2a, and so forth. In general, the expression for the nth term is

$$l = ar^{n-1}. \tag{18-3}$$

Example B. Find the eighth term of the GP 8, 4, 2, ...

Here $a = 8$, $r = \frac{1}{2}$, and $n = 8$. The eighth term is given by

$$l = 8\left(\frac{1}{2}\right)^{8-1} = \frac{8}{2^7} = \frac{1}{16}.$$

Example C. Find the tenth term of a GP when the second term is 3 and the fourth term is 9.

We can find r, if we let $a = 3$, $l = 9$, and $n = 3$ (we are at this time considering the progression made up of 3, the next number, and 9). Thus

$$9 = 3r^2, \qquad \text{or} \qquad r = \sqrt{3}.$$

We now can find a, by using just two terms (a and 3) for a progression:

$$3 = a(\sqrt{3})^{2-1} \qquad \text{or} \qquad a = \sqrt{3}.$$

We now can find the tenth term directly:

$$l = \sqrt{3}(\sqrt{3})^{10-1} = \sqrt{3}(\sqrt{3})^9 = \sqrt{3}(3^4\sqrt{3}) = 3^5 = 243.$$

We could have shortened this procedure one step by letting the second term be the first term of a new progression of 9 terms. If the first term is of no importance in itself, this is perfectly acceptable.

Example D. Under certain circumstances, 20% of a substance changes chemically each 10 min. If there are originally 100 gm of a substance, how much will remain after an hour?

Let $P =$ the portion of the substance remaining after each minute. From the statement of the problem, $r = 0.8$ (80% remains after each 10-min period), $a = 100$, and n represents the number of minutes elapsed. This means $P = 100(0.8)^{n/10}$. It is necessary to divide n by 10 because the ratio is given for a 10-min period. In order to find P when $n = 60$, we write $P = 100(0.8)^6$. Logarithms provide a quick method of determining the value of $(0.8)^6$, which is 0.262. This means that 26.2 gm are left after an hour.

A general expression for the sum of the first n terms of a geometric progression may be found by directly forming the sum, and multiplying this equation by r. By doing this, we have

$$s = a + ar + ar^2 + \cdots + ar^{n-1}$$
$$rs = ar + ar^2 + ar^3 + \cdots + ar^n.$$

If we now subtract the first of these equations from the second, we have $rs - s = ar^n - a$. All other terms cancel by subtraction. Solving this equation for s and writing both the numerator and the denominator in the final solution in the form generally used, we obtain

$$s = \frac{a(1 - r^n)}{1 - r} \qquad (r \neq 1). \tag{18-4}$$

Example E.   Find the sum of the first 7 terms of the GP $2, 1, \frac{1}{2}, \ldots$.
Here $a = 2$, $r = \frac{1}{2}$, and $n = 7$. Hence

$$s = \frac{2(1 - (\frac{1}{2})^7)}{1 - \frac{1}{2}} = \frac{2(1 - \frac{1}{128})}{\frac{1}{2}} = 4\left(\frac{127}{128}\right) = \frac{127}{32}.$$

Example F.   If \$1 is invested each year at 4% interest compounded annually, what would be the total amount after 10 yr (before the eleventh deposit is made)?
Here we are asked to sum the GP: $(1.04) + (1.04)^2 + \cdots + (1.04)^{10}$. Thus $a = 1.04$, $r = 1.04$, and $n = 10$. Therefore

$$s = \frac{1.04(1 - (1.04)^{10})}{1 - 1.04} = \frac{1.04}{-0.04}(1 - 1.479) = \frac{1.04(-0.479)}{-0.04} = \$12.45.$$

The total amount would be \$12.45 (of which \$2.45 is interest.) Logarithms were used to find $(1.04)^{10}$.

Exercises

In Exercises 1 through 4 write down the first five terms of the GP with the given values.

1. $a = 45$, $r = \frac{1}{3}$
2. $a = 9$, $r = -\frac{2}{3}$
3. $a = 2$, $r = 3$
4. $a = -3$, $r = 2$

In Exercises 5 through 8 find the nth term of the GP which has the given values.

5. $a = -27$, $r = -\frac{1}{3}$, $n = 6$
6. $a = 48$, $r = \frac{1}{2}$, $n = 9$
7. $a = 2$, $r = 10$, $n = 7$
8. $a = -2$, $r = 2$, $n = 6$

In Exercises 9 through 12 find the sum of the n terms of the GP with the given values.

9. $a = 8$, $r = 2$, $n = 5$
10. $a = 162$, $r = -\frac{1}{3}$, $n = 6$
11. $a = 192$, $l = 3$, $n = 4$
12. $a = 9$, $l = -243$, $n = 4$

In Exercises 13 through 16 find any of the values of a, r, l, n, or s that are missing.

13. $l = 27$, $n = 4$, $s = 40$
14. $a = 3$, $n = 5$, $l = 48$
15. $a = 75$, $r = \frac{1}{5}$, $l = \frac{3}{25}$
16. $r = -2$, $n = 6$, $s = 42$

In Exercises 17 through 29 find the indicated quantities.

17. Find the tenth term of a GP if the fourth term is 8 and the seventh term 16.

18. Find the sum of the first 8 terms of the geometric progression for which the fifth term is 5, the seventh term is 10, and $r > 0$.

19. What is the value of an investment of \$100 after 20 yr, if it draws interest of 4% annually?

20. A man invests \$1000 each year for 10 yr. How much is his investment worth after 10 full years, if the interest is 5% compounded annually?

21. If the population of a certain town increases 20% each year, how long will it take for the population to double?

22. If you decided to save money by putting away 1¢ on a given day, 2¢ one week later, 4¢ a week later, etc., how much would you have to put aside one year later?

23. A ball is dropped from a height of 8 ft, and on each rebound it rises $\frac{1}{2}$ of the height it last fell. What is the total distance the ball has traveled when it hits the ground for the fourth time?

24. How many direct ancestors (parents, grandparents, etc.) does a person have in the 10 generations which preceded him?

25. The American Wire Gauge standard of wire diameters is based on a geometric progression. The ratio of one diameter to the next is the 39th root of 92. If the diameter of No. 30 wire is 0.010 in., what is the diameter of the wire which is 10 sizes larger (No. 20 wire)?

26. A certain object, after being heated, cools at such a rate that its temperature decreases 10% each minute. If the object is originally heated to 100°C, what is its temperature 10 min later?

27. The half-life of tungsten 176 is 80 min. This means that half of a given amount will disintegrate in 80 min. After 160 min three-fourths will have disintegrated. How much will disintegrate in 120 min?

28. Derive a formula for s in terms of a, r, and l.

29. Write down several terms of a general GP. Then verify the statement that, if the logarithm of each term is taken, the resulting sequence is an AP.

18-3 Geometric progressions with infinitely many terms

If we consider the sum of the first n terms of the GP with terms $1, \frac{1}{2}, \frac{1}{4}, \ldots$, we find that we get the values in the following table.

n	2	3	4	5	6	7	8	9	10
s	$\frac{3}{2}$	$\frac{7}{4}$	$\frac{15}{8}$	$\frac{31}{16}$	$\frac{63}{32}$	$\frac{127}{64}$	$\frac{255}{128}$	$\frac{511}{256}$	$\frac{1023}{512}$

We see that as n gets larger, the numerator of each fraction becomes more nearly twice the denominator. In fact, we would find that if we continued to compute s as n becomes larger, s can be found as close to the value 2 as desired, although it will never actually reach the value 2. For example if $n = 100$, $s = 2 - 1.6 \times 10^{-30}$, which could be written as

$$1.9999999999999999999999999999984$$

to 32 significant figures. In the formula for the sum of n terms of a GP,

$$s = a\,\frac{1 - r^n}{1 - r},$$

the term r^n becomes exceedingly small, and if we consider n as being sufficiently large, we can see that this term is effectively zero. *If* this term were *exactly* zero, then the sum would be

$$s = 1\,\frac{1 - 0}{1 - \frac{1}{2}} = 2.$$

The only problem is that we cannot find any number large enough for n to make $(\frac{1}{2})^n$ zero. There is, however, an accepted notation for this. This notation is

$$\lim_{n \to \infty} r^n = 0, \qquad (\text{if } |r| < 1),$$

and it is read as "the limit as n approaches infinity of r to the nth power is zero."

The symbol ∞ is read as "infinity," but it must not be thought of as a number. It is simply a symbol which stands for a *process* of considering numbers which become large without bound. The number which is called the *limit* of the sums is simply the number which the sums get closer and closer to, as n is considered to approach infinity. This notation and terminology are of particular importance in the calculus.

If we consider values of r such that $|r| < 1$, and let the values of n become unbounded, we find that $\lim_{n \to \infty} r^n = 0$. The formula for the sum of a geometric progression with infinitely many terms then becomes

$$s = \frac{a}{1 - r}. \tag{18-5}$$

(If $r \geq 1$, s is unbounded in value.)

Example A. Find the sum of the geometric progression for which $a = 4$, $r = \frac{1}{8}$, and for which n increases without bound.

$$s = \frac{4}{1 - \frac{1}{8}} = \frac{4}{1} \cdot \frac{8}{7} = \frac{32}{7}$$

Example B. Find the fraction which has as its decimal form $0.44444444\ldots.$

This decimal form can be thought of as being

$$0.4 + 0.04 + 0.004 + 0.0004 + \cdots,$$

which means that it can also be thought of as the sum of a GP with infinitely many terms, where $a = 0.4$ and $r = 0.1$. With these considerations, we have

$$s = \frac{0.4}{1 - 0.1} = \frac{0.4}{0.9} = \frac{4}{9}.$$

Thus the fraction $\frac{4}{9}$ and the decimal $0.4444\ldots$ represent the same number.

Example C. Find the fraction which has as its decimal form $0.121212\ldots.$

This decimal form can be considered as being

$$0.12 + 0.0012 + 0.000012 + \cdots,$$

which means that we have a GP with infinitely many terms, and that $a = 0.12$ and $r = 0.01$. Thus

$$s = \frac{0.12}{1 - 0.01} = \frac{0.12}{0.99} = \frac{4}{33}.$$

Therefore the decimal $0.121212\ldots$ and the fraction $\frac{4}{33}$ represent the same number.

The decimals in Examples B and C are called *repeating decimals*, because the numbers in the decimal form appear over and over again in a particular order. These two examples verify the theorem that any repeating decimal represents a rational number. However, all repeating decimals do not necessarily start repeating immediately. If numbers never do repeat, the decimal represents an irrational number. For example, there is no repeating decimal which represents π or $\sqrt{2}$.

Example D.   Find the fraction which has as its decimal form the repeating decimal $0.50345345345\ldots$.

We first separate the decimal into the beginning, nonrepeating part, and the infinite repeating decimal which follows. Thus we have $0.50 + 0.00345345345\ldots$. This means that we are to add $\frac{50}{100}$ to the fraction which represents the sum of the terms of the GP $0.00345 + 0.00000345 + \cdots$. For this GP, $a = 0.00345$ and $r = 0.001$. We find the sum of this GP to be

$$s = \frac{0.00345}{1 - 0.001} = \frac{0.00345}{0.999} = \frac{115}{33300} = \frac{23}{6660}.$$

Therefore

$$0.50345345\ldots = \frac{5}{10} + \frac{23}{6660} = \frac{5(666) + 23}{6660} = \frac{3353}{6660}.$$

Example E.   Each swing of a certain pendulum bob is 95% as long as the preceding swing. How far does the bob travel in coming to rest if the first swing is 40 in. long?

We are to find the sum of a geometric progression with infinitely many terms, for which $a = 40$ and $r = 95\% = \frac{19}{20}$. Substituting these values into Eq. (18-5), we obtain

$$s = \frac{40}{1 - \frac{19}{20}} = \frac{40}{\frac{1}{20}} = (40)(20) = 800 \text{ in.}$$

Therefore, the pendulum bob travels 800 in. (about 67 ft) in coming to rest.

Exercises

In Exercises 1 through 10 find the sum of the given infinite geometric progressions.

1. $4, 2, 1, \frac{1}{2}, \ldots$

2. $6, -2, \frac{2}{3}, \ldots$

3. $5, 1, 0.2, 0.04, \ldots$

4. $2, \sqrt{2}, 1, \ldots$

5. $20, -1, 0.05, \ldots$

6. $9, 8.1, 7.29, \ldots$

7. $1, \frac{7}{8}, \frac{49}{64}, \ldots$

8. $6, -4, \frac{8}{3}, \ldots$

9. $1, 0.0001, 0.00000001, \ldots$

10. $1 + \sqrt{2}, -1, \sqrt{2} - 1, \ldots$

In Exercises 11 through 20 find the fractions equal to the given decimals.

11. $0.33333\ldots$

12. $0.55555\ldots$

13. $0.181818\ldots$

14. $0.272727\ldots$

15. $0.273273273\ldots$

16. $0.792792792\ldots$

17. 0.366666...

18. 0.66424242...

19. 0.100841841841...

20. 0.184561845618456...

In Exercises 21 and 22 solve the given problems by use of the sum of a geometric progression with infinitely many terms.

21. If the ball in Exercise 23 of Section 18-2 is allowed to bounce indefinitely, what is the total distance it will travel?

22. An object suspended on a spring is oscillating up and down. If the first oscillation is 10 in. and each oscillation thereafter is nine-tenths of the preceding one, find the total distance the object travels.

18-4 Miscellaneous Exercises

In Exercises 1 through 8 find the indicated term of each progression.

1. $1, 6, 11, \ldots$ (17th)

2. $1, -3, -7, \ldots$ (21st)

3. $\frac{1}{2}, 0.1, 0.02, \ldots$ (9th)

4. $0.025, 0.01, 0.004, \ldots$ (7th)

5. $8, \frac{7}{2}, -1, \ldots$ (16th)

6. $-1, -\frac{5}{3}, -\frac{7}{3}, \ldots$ (25th)

7. $\frac{3}{4}, \frac{1}{2}, \frac{1}{3}, \ldots$ (7th)

8. $\frac{2}{3}, 1, \frac{3}{2}, \ldots$ (7th)

In Exercises 9 through 16 find the indicated quantities for the appropriate progressions.

9. $a = 17, d = -2, n = 9, s = ?$

10. $d = \frac{4}{3}, a = -3, l = 17, n = ?$

11. $a = 18, r = \frac{1}{2}, n = 6, s = ?$

12. $l = \frac{49}{8}, r = -\frac{2}{7}, s = \frac{17199}{288}, a = ?$

13. $a = -1, l = 32, n = 12, s = ?$ (AP)

14. $a = 1, l = 64, s = 325, n = ?$ (AP)

15. $a = 1, n = 7, l = 64, s = ?$

16. $a = \frac{1}{3}, n = 7, l = 48, s = ?$

In Exercises 17 through 22 find the fractions equal to the given decimals.

17. 0.77777...

18. 0.484848...

19. 0.123123123...

20. 0.0727272...

21. 0.166666...

22. 0.25399399399...

In Exercises 23 through 31 solve the given problems by use of an appropriate progression.

23. Find the sum of the first 1000 positive even integers.

24. How many numbers divisible by 4 lie between 23 and 121?

25. Fifteen layers of logs are so piled that there are 20 logs in the bottom layer, and each layer contains one log less than the layer below it. How many logs are in the pile?

26. A contractor employed in the construction of a building was penalized for taking more time than the contract allowed. He forfeited $150 for the first day late, $225 for the second day, $300 for the third day, and so forth. If he forfeited a total of $6750, how many additional days did he require to complete the building?

27. What is the value after 20 years of an investment of $2500, if it draws interest at 5% annually?

28. A tank contains 100 gal of a given chemical. Thirty gallons are drawn off and replaced with water. Then 30 gal of the resulting solution are drawn off and replaced with water. If this operation is performed a total of 5 times, how much of the original chemical remains?

29. A ball, starting from rest, rolls down a uniform incline so that it covers 10 in. during the first second, 30 in. during the second second, 50 in. during the third second, and so on. How long will it take to cover $333\frac{1}{3}$ ft?

30. The successive distances traveled by a pendulum bob are 90 in., 60 in., 40 in., ... Find the total distance the bob travels before it comes to rest.

31. The terms a, $a + 12$, $a + 24$ form an AP, and the terms a, $a + 24$, $a + 12$ form a GP. Find these progressions.

Additional Topics in Trigonometry

19

19-1 Fundamental trigonometric identities

The definitions of the trigonometric functions were first introduced in Section 3-2, and were again summarized in Section 7-1. If we take a close look at these definitions, we find that there are many relationships among the various functions. For example, the definition of the sine of an angle is $\sin \theta = y/r$, and the definition of the cosecant of an angle is $\csc \theta = r/y$. But we know that $1/(r/y) = y/r$, which means that $\sin \theta = 1/\csc \theta$. In writing this down we made no reference to any particular angle, and since the definitions hold for *any* angle, this relation between the $\sin \theta$ and $\csc \theta$ also holds for any angle. A relation such as this, which holds for any value of the variable, is called an *identity*. Of course, specific values where division by zero would be indicated are excluded.

Several important identities exist among the six trigonometric functions, and we shall develop these identities in this section. We shall also show how we can use the basic identities to verify other identities among the functions.

By the definitions, we have

$$\sin \theta \csc \theta = \frac{y}{r} \cdot \frac{r}{y} = 1, \qquad \text{or} \qquad \sin \theta = \frac{1}{\csc \theta} \text{ or } \csc \theta = \frac{1}{\sin \theta};$$

$$\cos \theta \sec \theta = \frac{x}{r} \cdot \frac{r}{x} = 1, \qquad \text{or} \qquad \cos \theta = \frac{1}{\sec \theta} \text{ or } \sec \theta = \frac{1}{\cos \theta};$$

$$\tan \theta \cot \theta = \frac{y}{x} \cdot \frac{x}{y} = 1, \qquad \text{or} \qquad \tan \theta = \frac{1}{\cot \theta} \text{ or } \cot \theta = \frac{1}{\tan \theta};$$

$$\text{\textasteriskcentered} \quad \frac{\sin \theta}{\cos \theta} = \frac{y/r}{x/r} = \frac{y}{x} = \tan \theta; \quad \text{\textasteriskcentered} \quad \frac{\cos \theta}{\sin \theta} = \frac{x/r}{y/r} = \frac{x}{y} = \cot \theta.$$

Also, by the definitions and the Pythagorean theorem in the form of $x^2 + y^2 = r^2$, we arrive at the following identities:

By dividing the Pythagorean relation through by r^2, we have

$$\left(\frac{x}{r}\right)^2 + \left(\frac{y}{r}\right)^2 = 1, \qquad \text{which leads us to } \cos^2 \theta + \sin^2 \theta = 1.$$

By dividing the Pythagorean relation by x^2, we have

$$1 + \left(\frac{y}{x}\right)^2 = \left(\frac{r}{x}\right)^2, \qquad \text{which leads us to } 1 + \tan^2 \theta = \sec^2 \theta.$$

By dividing the Pythagorean relation by y^2, we have

$$\left(\frac{x}{y}\right)^2 + 1 = \left(\frac{r}{y}\right)^2, \qquad \text{which leads us to } \cot^2 \theta + 1 = \csc^2 \theta.$$

The term $\cos^2 \theta$ is the common way of writing $(\cos \theta)^2$, and thus it means to square the value of the cosine of the angle. Obviously the same holds true for the other functions.

Summarizing these results, we have the following important identities among the trigonometric functions:

$$\sin \theta = \frac{1}{\csc \theta}, \qquad (19\text{-}1) \qquad\qquad \cos \theta = \frac{1}{\sec \theta}, \qquad (19\text{-}2)$$

$$\tan \theta = \frac{1}{\cot \theta}, \qquad (19\text{-}3) \qquad\qquad \tan \theta = \frac{\sin \theta}{\cos \theta}, \qquad (19\text{-}4)$$

$$\cot \theta = \frac{\cos \theta}{\sin \theta}, \qquad (19\text{-}5) \qquad\qquad \sin^2 \theta + \cos^2 \theta = 1, \qquad (19\text{-}6)$$

$$1 + \tan^2 \theta = \sec^2 \theta, \qquad (19\text{-}7) \qquad\qquad 1 + \cot^2 \theta = \csc^2 \theta. \qquad (19\text{-}8)$$

In using these identities, θ may stand for any angle or number or expression representing them.

Example A. $\quad \sin (x + 1) = \dfrac{1}{\csc (x + 1)}; \qquad \tan 157^\circ = \dfrac{\sin 157^\circ}{\cos 157^\circ};$

$$1 + \tan^2 \left(\frac{\pi}{6}\right) = \sec^2 \left(\frac{\pi}{6}\right).$$

Example B. We shall verify three of the identities for particular values of θ.

From Table 3, we find that $\cos 52^\circ = 0.6157$ and $\sec 52^\circ = 1.624$. Using Eq. (19-2), and dividing, we find that

$$\cos 52^\circ = \frac{1}{\sec 52^\circ} = \frac{1}{1.624} = 0.6157,$$

and this value checks.

Using Table 3, we find that sin 157° = 0.3907 and cos 157° = −0.9205. Using Eq. (19-4), and dividing, we find that

$$\tan 157° = \frac{\sin 157°}{\cos 157°} = \frac{0.3907}{-0.9205} = -0.4245.$$

Checking with Table 3, we see that this value checks.

From Section 3-3, we recall that

$$\sin 45° = \frac{1}{\sqrt{2}} = \frac{\sqrt{2}}{2}, \quad \text{and} \quad \cos 45° = \frac{\sqrt{2}}{2}.$$

Using Eq. (19-6), we have

$$\sin^2 45° + \cos^2 45° = \left(\frac{\sqrt{2}}{2}\right)^2 + \left(\frac{\sqrt{2}}{2}\right)^2 = \frac{1}{2} + \frac{1}{2} = 1.$$

We see that this identity checks for these values.

A great many identities exist among the trigonometric functions. A number of these are found in applications, where certain problems rely on a change of form for solution. This is especially true in calculus.

We are going to use the basic identities and a few additional ones given in later sections to prove the validity of these other identities. One of the reasons for doing this is for you to become familiar with the basic identities. *The ability to prove such identities depends to a large extent on being* **very** *familiar with the basic identities*, so that you can recognize them in somewhat different forms. If you do not learn these basic identities and learn them well, you will have difficulty in following the examples and doing the exercises. The more readily you recognize these forms, the more easily you will be able to prove such identities.

In proving identities, we should look for combinations which appear in, or are very similar to, those in the basic identities. Consider the following examples.

Example C.   If a certain identity contained the expression $\sin^4 x - \cos^4 x$, we should note quickly that this may be factored into $(\sin^2 x - \cos^2 x)(\sin^2 x + \cos^2 x)$, and that $\sin^2 x + \cos^2 x$ may be replaced by 1. In this way, this expression is simplified for use in proving the identity. Thus, $\sin^4 x - \cos^4 x = \sin^2 x - \cos^2 x$.

Example C also illustrates another important point. To prove identities, basic algebraic operations must be performed. Unless these operations are performed carefully and correctly, an improper algebraic step may make the proof appear impossible.

Example D.   Either of the expressions $\tan^2 x$ or $\sec^2 x$ should bring to mind the possibility of using the squared relation Eq. (19-7).

$$\frac{\sec^2 y}{\cot y} - \tan^3 y = \frac{\sec^2 y}{1/\tan y} - \tan^3 y = \sec^2 y \tan y - \tan^3 y$$

$$= \tan y \, (\sec^2 y - \tan^2 y) = \tan y \, (1) = \tan y$$

Here we have used Eq. (19-7) in the form $\sec^2 y - \tan^2 y = 1$.

Example E.   The combination $1 - \sin x$ also suggests $1 - \sin^2 x$, since multiplying $(1 - \sin x)$ by $(1 + \sin x)$ gives $1 - \sin^2 x$, which can then be replaced by $\cos^2 x$.

$$\frac{(1 - \sin x)}{\sin x \cot x} = \frac{(1 - \sin x)(1 + \sin x)}{\sin x \cot x(1 + \sin x)}$$

$$= \frac{1 - \sin^2 x}{\sin x(\cos x/\sin x)(1 + \sin x)} = \frac{\cos^2 x}{\cos x(1 + \sin x)}$$

$$= \frac{\cos x}{1 + \sin x} \, .$$

In problems involving proving identities we are given both sides, and we must show by changing one side or the other that the two expressions are equal. Although this restriction is not entirely necessary, we shall restrict the method of proof to changing only one side into the same form as the other side. In this way, we know precisely what form we are to change to, and therefore by looking ahead to what changes may be made, we are better able to make the proper changes.

There is no set procedure which can be stated for working with identities. The most important factors are to be able to *recognize the proper forms*, to be able to *see what effect any change may have* before we actually perform it, and then *perform it correctly*. Normally it is more profitable to change the more complicated side of an identity to the same form as the less complicated side. If the two sides are of approximately the same complexity, a close look at each side usually suggests steps which will lead to the solution.

Example F.   Prove the identity $\dfrac{\cos x \csc x}{\cot^2 x} = \tan x$.

First, we note that the left-hand side has several factors and the right-hand side has only one. Therefore, let us transform the left-hand side. Next, we note that we want $\tan x$ as the final result. We know that $\cot x = 1/\tan x$. Thus

$$\frac{\cos x \csc x}{\cot^2 x} = \frac{\cos x \csc x}{1/\tan^2 x} = \cos x \csc x \tan^2 x.$$

At this point, we have two factors of $\tan x$ on the left. Since we want only one, let us factor out one. Therefore,

$$\cos x \csc x \tan^2 x = \tan x \, (\cos x \csc x \tan x).$$

Now, replacing $\tan x$ within the parentheses by $\sin x/\cos x$, we have

$$\tan x(\cos x \csc x \tan x) = \frac{\tan x(\cos x \csc x \sin x)}{\cos x}$$

Now we may cancel $\cos x$. Also, $\csc x \sin x = 1$ from Eq. (19-1). Finally,

$$\frac{\tan x(\cos x \csc x \sin x)}{\cos x} = \tan x \left(\frac{\cos x}{\cos x}\right)(\csc x \sin x)$$

$$= \tan x\,(1)\,(1) = \tan x.$$

Since we have transformed the left-hand side into $\tan x$, we have proven the identity. Of course, it is not necessary to rewrite expressions as we did in this example. This was done here only to include the explanations between steps.

Example G. Prove the identity $\sec^2 x + \csc^2 x = \sec^2 x \csc^2 x$.

Here we note the presence of $\sec^2 x$ and $\csc^2 x$ on each side. This suggests the possible use of the square relationships. By replacing the $\sec^2 x$ on the right-hand side by $1 + \tan^2 x$, we can create $\csc^2 x$ plus another term. The left-hand side is the $\csc^2 x$ plus another term, so this procedure should help. Thus

$$\sec^2 x + \csc^2 x = \sec^2 x \csc^2 x$$
$$= (1 + \tan^2 x)(\csc^2 x)$$
$$= \csc^2 x + \tan^2 x \csc^2 x.$$

Now we note that $\tan x = \sin x/\cos x$ and $\csc x = 1/\sin x$. Thus

$$\sec^2 x + \csc^2 x = \csc^2 x + \left(\frac{\sin^2 x}{\cos^2 x}\right)\left(\frac{1}{\sin^2 x}\right)$$

$$= \csc^2 x + \frac{1}{\cos^2 x}.$$

But $\sec x = 1/\cos x$, and therefore $\sec^2 x + \csc^2 x = \csc^2 x + \sec^2 x$, which therefore proves the identity. We could have used many other variations of this procedure, and they would have been perfectly valid.

Example H. Prove the identity $\dfrac{\csc x}{\tan x + \cot x} = \cos x$.

Here we shall simplify the left-hand side until we have the expression which appears on the right-hand side.

$$\frac{\csc x}{\tan x + \cot x} = \frac{\csc x}{\tan x + \dfrac{1}{\tan x}} = \frac{\csc x}{\dfrac{\tan^2 x + 1}{\tan x}}$$

$$= \frac{\csc x \tan x}{\tan^2 x + 1} = \frac{\csc x \tan x}{\sec^2 x}$$

$$= \frac{\dfrac{1}{\sin x} \cdot \dfrac{\sin x}{\cos x}}{\dfrac{1}{\cos^2 x}} = \frac{1}{\sin x} \cdot \frac{\sin x}{\cos x} \cdot \frac{\cos^2 x}{1}$$

$$= \cos x.$$

Therefore, we have $\cos x = \cos x$, which proves the identity.

Exercises

In Exercises 1 through 4 verify the indicated basic identities for the given angles.

1. Verify Eq. (19-3) for $\theta = 56°$

2. Verify Eq. (19-5) for $\theta = 80°$

3. Verify Eq. (19-6) for $\theta = \dfrac{2\pi}{3}$

4. Verify Eq. (19-8) for $\theta = \dfrac{7\pi}{6}$

In Exercises 5 through 34 prove the given identities.

5. $\tan x \csc x = \sec x$

6. $\sin \theta \cot \theta = \cos \theta$

7. $\sin x \tan x + \cos x = \sec x$

8. $\sec x \csc x - \cot x = \tan x$

9. $\csc^2 x \, (1 - \cos^2 x) = 1$

10. $\cos^2 x \, (1 + \tan^2 x) = 1$

11. $\sin x \, (\csc x - \sin x) = \cos^2 x$

12. $\sin x \cos x \tan x = 1 - \cos^2 x$

13. $\tan x + \cot x = \sec x \csc x$

14. $\tan x + \cot x = \tan x \csc^2 x$

15. $\cos^2 x - \sin^2 x = 1 - 2 \sin^2 x$

16. $\tan^2 y \sec^2 y - \tan^4 y = \tan^2 y$

17. $\dfrac{\sin x}{1 - \cos x} = \csc x + \cot x$

18. $\dfrac{1 + \cos x}{\sin x} = \dfrac{\sin x}{1 - \cos x}$

19. $\dfrac{\sec x + \csc x}{1 + \tan x} = \csc x$

20. $\dfrac{\cot x + 1}{\cot x} = 1 + \tan x$

21. $\dfrac{\cot 2y}{\sec 2y - \tan 2y} - \dfrac{\cos 2y}{\sec 2y + \tan 2y} = \sin 2y + \csc 2y$

22. $\dfrac{1}{2} \sin 5y \left(\dfrac{\sin 5y}{1 - \cos 5y} + \dfrac{1 - \cos 5y}{\sin 5y} \right) = 1$

23. $\tan^2 x \cos^2 x + \cot^2 x \sin^2 x = 1$

24. $\cos^3 x \csc^3 x \tan^3 x = \csc^2 x - \cot^2 x$

25. $4 \sin x + \tan x = \dfrac{4 + \sec x}{\csc x}$

26. $\dfrac{1 + \tan x}{\sin x} - \sec x = \csc x$

27. $\sec x + \tan x + \cot x = \dfrac{1 + \sin x}{\cos x \sin x}$

28. $\sec x \, (\sec x - \cos x) + \dfrac{\cos x - \sin x}{\cos x} + \tan x = \sec^2 x$

29. $2 \sin^4 x - 3 \sin^2 x + 1 = \cos^2 x \, (1 - 2 \sin^2 x)$

30. $\dfrac{\sin^4 x - \cos^4 x}{1 - \cot^4 x} = \sin^4 x$

31. $1 + \sin^2 x + \sin^4 x + \cdots = \sec^2 x$

32. $1 - \tan^2 x + \tan^4 x - \cdots = \cos^2 x$

33. In determining the rate of radiation by an accelerated electric charge, it is necessary to show that $\sin^3 \theta = \sin \theta - \cos^2 \theta \sin \theta$. Show that this is valid, by transforming the left-hand side.

34. In determining the path of least time between two points under certain circumstances, it is necessary to show that

$$\sqrt{\frac{1 + \cos \theta}{1 - \cos \theta}} \sin \theta = (1 + \cos \theta).$$

Show this by transforming the left-hand side.

19-2 Sine and cosine of the sum and difference of two angles

There are other important relations among the trigonometric functions. The most important and useful relations are those which involve twice an angle and half an angle. To obtain these relations, we shall first derive the expressions for the sine and cosine of the sum and difference of two angles. These expressions will lead directly to the desired relations of double and half angles.

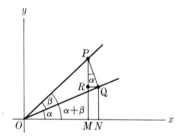

Figure 19-1

In Fig. 19-1, the angle α is in standard position, and the angle β has as its initial side the terminal side of α. Thus the angle of interest, $\alpha + \beta$, is in standard position. From a point P, on the terminal side of $\alpha + \beta$, perpendiculars are dropped to the x-axis and to the terminal side of α, at the points M and Q respectively. Then perpendiculars are dropped from Q to the x-axis and to the line MP at points N and R respectively. By this construction, $\angle RPQ$ is equal to $\angle \alpha$. (The $\angle RQO = \angle \alpha$ by alternate interior angles; $\angle RQO + \angle RQP = 90°$ by construction; $\angle RQP + \angle RPQ = 90°$ by the sum of the angles of a triangle being $180°$. Thus $\angle \alpha = \angle RPQ$.) By definition,

$$\sin (\alpha + \beta) = \frac{MP}{OP} = \frac{MR + RP}{OP} = \frac{NQ}{OP} + \frac{RP}{OP}.$$

These last two fractions do not define any function of either α or β, and therefore we multiply the first fraction (numerator and denominator) by OQ, and the second fraction by QP. When we do this and rearrange the fractions, we have functions of α and β:

$$\sin (\alpha + \beta) = \frac{NQ}{OP} + \frac{RP}{OP} = \frac{NQ}{OQ} \cdot \frac{OQ}{OP} + \frac{RP}{QP} \cdot \frac{QP}{OP}$$

$$= \sin \alpha \cos \beta + \cos \alpha \sin \beta.$$

Using the same figure, we can also obtain the expression for $\cos(\alpha + \beta)$. Thus we have the relations

$$\sin(\alpha + \beta) = \sin\alpha\cos\beta + \cos\alpha\sin\beta \qquad (19\text{-}9)$$

and

$$\cos(\alpha + \beta) = \cos\alpha\cos\beta - \sin\alpha\sin\beta. \qquad (19\text{-}10)$$

Example A.   Find $\sin 75°$ from $\sin 75° = \sin(45° + 30°)$.

$$\sin 75° = \sin(45° + 30°) = \sin 45°\cos 30° + \sin 30°\cos 45°$$

$$= \frac{\sqrt{2}}{2} \cdot \frac{\sqrt{3}}{2} + \frac{1}{2} \cdot \frac{\sqrt{2}}{2} = \frac{\sqrt{6}}{4} + \frac{\sqrt{2}}{4} = \frac{\sqrt{6} + \sqrt{2}}{4}$$

$$= 0.9659.$$

Example B.   Verify that $\sin 90° = 1$, by finding $\sin(60° + 30°)$.

$$\sin 90° = \sin(60° + 30°) = \sin 60°\cos 30° + \sin 30°\cos 60°$$

$$= \frac{\sqrt{3}}{2} \cdot \frac{\sqrt{3}}{2} + \frac{1}{2} \cdot \frac{1}{2} = \frac{3}{4} + \frac{1}{4} = 1.$$

[It should be obvious from this example that $\sin(\alpha + \beta)$ is *not* equal to $\sin\alpha + \sin\beta$, something which many students assume before they are familiar with the formulas and ideas of this section. If we used such a formula, we would get $\sin 90° = \sqrt{3}/2 + \frac{1}{2} = 1.366$ for the combination $(60° + 30°)$. This is not possible, since the values of the sine never exceed 1 in value. Also, if we used the combination $(45° + 45°)$, we would get 1.414, a different value for the same function.]

From Eqs. (19-9) and (19-10), we can easily find expressions for $\sin(\alpha - \beta)$ and $\cos(\alpha - \beta)$. This is done by finding $\sin(\alpha + (-\beta))$ and $\cos(\alpha + (-\beta))$. Thus we have

$$\sin(\alpha - \beta) = \sin(\alpha + (-\beta)) = \sin\alpha\cos(-\beta) + \cos\alpha\sin(-\beta).$$

Since $\cos(-\beta) = \cos\beta$ and $\sin(-\beta) = -\sin\beta$ (see Exercise 39 of Section 7-2), we have

$$\sin(\alpha - \beta) = \sin\alpha\cos\beta - \cos\alpha\sin\beta. \qquad (19\text{-}11)$$

In the same manner we find that

$$\cos(\alpha - \beta) = \cos\alpha\cos\beta + \sin\alpha\sin\beta. \qquad (19\text{-}12)$$

Example C.   Find $\cos 15°$ from $\cos(45° - 30°)$.

$$\cos 15° = \cos (45° - 30°) = \cos 45° \cos 30° + \sin 45° \sin 30°$$

$$= \frac{\sqrt{2}}{2} \cdot \frac{\sqrt{3}}{2} + \frac{\sqrt{2}}{2} \cdot \frac{1}{2} = \frac{\sqrt{6} + \sqrt{2}}{4} = 0.9659.$$

We get the same results as in Example A, which should be the case since $\sin 75° = \cos 15°$. (See Section 3-2.)

By using Eqs. (19-9) and (19-10), we can find expressions for $\tan (\alpha + \beta)$, $\cot (\alpha + \beta)$, $\sec (\alpha + \beta)$ and $\csc (\alpha + \beta)$. These expressions are less applicable than those for the sine and cosine, and therefore we shall not derive them here, although the expression for $\tan (\alpha + \beta)$ is found in the exercises at the end of this section. By using Eqs. (19-11) and (19-12), we can find similar expressions for the functions of $(\alpha - \beta)$.

Certain trigonometric identities can also be worked out by using the formulas derived in this section. The following examples illustrate the use of these formulas in identities.

Example D.   Show that $\dfrac{\sin (\alpha - \beta)}{\sin \alpha \sin \beta} = \cot \beta - \cot \alpha.$

By using Eq. (19-11), we have

$$\frac{\sin (\alpha - \beta)}{\sin \alpha \sin \beta} = \frac{\sin \alpha \cos \beta - \cos \alpha \sin \beta}{\sin \alpha \sin \beta} = \frac{\sin \alpha \cos \beta}{\sin \alpha \sin \beta} - \frac{\cos \alpha \sin \beta}{\sin \alpha \sin \beta}$$

$$= \frac{\cos \beta}{\sin \beta} - \frac{\cos \alpha}{\sin \alpha} = \cot \beta - \cot \alpha.$$

Example E.   Show that

$$\sin \left(\frac{\pi}{4} + x\right) \cos \left(\frac{\pi}{4} + x\right) = \frac{1}{2} (\cos^2 x - \sin^2 x).$$

$$\sin \left(\frac{\pi}{4} + x\right) \cos \left(\frac{\pi}{4} + x\right)$$

$$= \left(\sin \frac{\pi}{4} \cos x + \cos \frac{\pi}{4} \sin x\right)\left(\cos \frac{\pi}{4} \cos x - \sin \frac{\pi}{4} \sin x\right)$$

$$= \sin \frac{\pi}{4} \cos \frac{\pi}{4} \cos^2 x - \sin^2 \frac{\pi}{4} \sin x \cos x + \cos^2 \frac{\pi}{4} \sin x \cos x$$

$$- \sin^2 x \sin \frac{\pi}{4} \cos \frac{\pi}{4}$$

$$= \frac{\sqrt{2}}{2} \frac{\sqrt{2}}{2} \cos^2 x - \left(\frac{\sqrt{2}}{2}\right)^2 \sin x \cos x + \left(\frac{\sqrt{2}}{2}\right)^2 \sin x \cos x - \frac{\sqrt{2}}{2} \frac{\sqrt{2}}{2} \sin^2 x$$

$$= \tfrac{1}{2} \cos^2 x - \tfrac{1}{2} \sin^2 x = \tfrac{1}{2} (\cos^2 x - \sin^2 x).$$

Example F.   Show that $\sin (x + y) \cos y - \cos (x + y) \sin y = \sin x$.

If we let $x + y = z$, we note that the left-hand side of the above expression becomes $\sin z \cos y - \cos z \sin y$, which is the proper form for $\sin (z - y)$. By replacing z with $x + y$, we obtain $\sin (x + y - y)$, which is $\sin x$. Therefore the above expression has been shown to be true. We again see that proper recognition of a basic form leads to the solution.

Exercises

In Exercises 1 through 4 determine the values of the given functions as indicated.

1. Find $\sin 105°$ by using $105° = 60° + 45°$.
2. Find $\cos 75°$ by using $75° = 30° + 45°$.
3. Find $\cos 15°$ by using $15° = 60° - 45°$.
4. Find $\sin 15°$ by using $15° = 45° - 30°$.

In Exercises 5 and 6 evaluate the indicated functions with the following given information: $\sin \alpha = \frac{4}{5}$ (in first quadrant), and $\cos \beta = -\frac{12}{13}$ (in second quadrant).

5. $\sin (\alpha + \beta)$ 6. $\cos (\beta - \alpha)$

In Exercises 7 through 10 reduce each of the given expressions to a single term. Expansion of any term is not necessary; proper recognition of the form of the expression leads to the proper result.

7. $\sin x \cos 2x + \sin 2x \cos x$ 8. $\sin 3x \cos x - \sin x \cos 3x$
9. $\cos (x + y) \cos y + \sin (x + y) \sin y$ 10. $\cos (2x - y) \cos y - \sin (2x - y) \sin y$

In Exercises 11 through 20 prove the given identities.

11. $\sin (270° - x) = -\cos x$ 12. $\sin (90° + x) = \cos x$

13. $\cos \left(\dfrac{\pi}{2} - x \right) = \sin x$ 14. $\cos \left(\dfrac{3\pi}{2} + x \right) = \sin x$

15. $\sin \left(\dfrac{\pi}{4} + x \right) = \dfrac{\sin x + \cos x}{\sqrt{2}}$ 16. $\cos \left(\dfrac{\pi}{3} + x \right) = \dfrac{\cos x - \sqrt{3} \sin x}{2}$

17. $\sin (x + y) \sin (x - y) = \sin^2 x - \sin^2 y$
18. $\cos (x + y) \cos (x - y) = \cos^2 x - \sin^2 y$
19. $\cos (\alpha + \beta) + \cos (\alpha - \beta) = 2 \cos \alpha \cos \beta$
20. $\cos (x - y) + \sin (x + y) = (\cos x + \sin x)(\cos y + \sin y)$

In Exercises 21 through 24 additional trigonometric identities are shown. Derive in the indicated manner. Equations (19-13), (19-14), and (19-15) are known as the product · formulas.

21. By dividing Eq. (19-9) by Eq. (19-10), show that $\tan (\alpha + \beta) = \dfrac{\tan \alpha + \tan \beta}{1 - \tan \alpha \tan \beta}$.

  [*Hint:* Divide numerator and denominator by $\cos \alpha \cos \beta$.]

22. By adding Eqs. (19-9) and (19-11), derive the equation

$$\sin \alpha \cos \beta = \tfrac{1}{2} [\sin (\alpha + \beta) + \sin (\alpha - \beta)]. \tag{19-13}$$

23. By adding Eqs. (19-10) and (19-12), derive the equation

$$\cos \alpha \cos \beta = \tfrac{1}{2} [\cos (\alpha + \beta) + \cos (\alpha - \beta)]. \tag{19-14}$$

24. By subtracting Eq. (19-10) from Eq. (19-12), derive

$$\sin \alpha \sin \beta = \tfrac{1}{2} [\cos (\alpha - \beta) - \cos (\alpha + \beta)]. \tag{19-15}$$

In Exercises 25 through 28 additional trigonometric identities are shown. Derive them by letting $\alpha + \beta = x$ and $\alpha - \beta = y$, which leads to $\alpha = \tfrac{1}{2}(x + y)$ and $\beta = \tfrac{1}{2}(x - y)$. The resulting equations are known as the factor formulas.

25. Use Eq. (19-13) and the substitutions above to derive the equation

$$\sin x + \sin y = 2 \sin \tfrac{1}{2}(x + y) \cos \tfrac{1}{2}(x - y). \tag{19-16}$$

26. Use Eqs. (19-9) and (19-11) and the substitutions above to derive the equation

$$\sin x - \sin y = 2 \sin \tfrac{1}{2}(x - y) \cos \tfrac{1}{2}(x + y). \tag{19-17}$$

27. Use Eq. (19-14) and the substitutions above to derive the equation

$$\cos x + \cos y = 2 \cos \tfrac{1}{2}(x + y) \cos \tfrac{1}{2}(x - y). \tag{19-18}$$

28. Use Eq. (19-15) and the substitutions above to derive the equation

$$\cos x - \cos y = -2 \sin \tfrac{1}{2}(x + y) \sin \tfrac{1}{2}(x - y). \tag{19-19}$$

In Exercises 29 and 30 use the equations of this section to solve the given problems.

29. The displacements y_1 and y_2 of two waves traveling through the same medium are given by $y_1 = A \sin 2\pi(t/T - x/\lambda)$ and $y_2 = A \sin 2\pi(t/T + x/\lambda)$. Find an expression for the displacement $y_1 + y_2$ of the combination of the waves.

30. In the analysis of the angles of incidence i and reflection r of a light ray subject to certain conditions, the following expression is found:

$$E_2 \left(\frac{\tan r}{\tan i} + 1 \right) = E_1 \left(\frac{\tan r}{\tan i} - 1 \right).$$

Show that an equivalent expression is

$$E_2 = E_1 \frac{\sin (r - i)}{\sin (r + i)}.$$

19-3 Double-angle formulas

If we let $\beta = \alpha$ in Eqs. (19-9) and (19-10), we can derive the important double-angle formulas. Thus, by making this substitution in Eq. (19-9), we have

$$\sin (\alpha + \alpha) = \sin (2\alpha) = \sin \alpha \cos \alpha + \cos \alpha \sin \alpha = 2 \sin \alpha \cos \alpha.$$

Using the same substitution in Eq. (19-10), we have

$$\cos (\alpha + \alpha) = \cos \alpha \cos \alpha - \sin \alpha \sin \alpha = \cos^2 \alpha - \sin^2 \alpha.$$

By using the basic identity (19-6), other forms of this last equation may be derived. Thus, summarizing these formulas, we have

$$\sin 2\alpha = 2 \sin \alpha \cos \alpha, \qquad\qquad (19\text{-}20)$$
$$\cos 2\alpha = \cos^2 \alpha - \sin^2 \alpha, \qquad\qquad (19\text{-}21)$$
$$= 2 \cos^2 \alpha - 1, \qquad\qquad (19\text{-}22)$$
$$= 1 - 2 \sin^2 \alpha. \qquad\qquad (19\text{-}23)$$

We should note carefully that these equations give expressions for the sine and cosine of twice an angle in terms of functions of the angle. They can be used any time we have expressed one angle as twice another. These double-angle formulas are widely used in applications of trigonometry, especially in the calculus. They should be known and recognized quickly in any of the various forms.

Example A.   If $\alpha = 30°$, we have $\cos 2\,(30°) = \cos 60° = \cos^2 30° - \sin^2 30°$.

If $\alpha = 3x$, we have $\sin 2\,(3x) = \sin 6x = 2 \sin 3x \cos 3x$.

If $2\alpha = x$, we may write $\alpha = x/2$, which means that

$$\sin 2 \left(\frac{x}{2}\right) = \sin x = 2 \sin \frac{x}{2} \cos \frac{x}{2}.$$

Example B.   Using the double-angle formulas, simplify the expression

$$\cos^2 2x - \sin^2 2x.$$

By using Eq. (19-21) and letting $\alpha = 2x$, we have

$$\cos^2 2x - \sin^2 2x = \cos 2(2x) = \cos 4x.$$

Example C.   Verify the values of $\sin 90°$ and $\cos 90°$ by use of the functions of 45°.

$$\sin 90° = \sin 2\,(45°) = 2 \sin 45° \cos 45° = 2 \left(\frac{\sqrt{2}}{2}\right)\left(\frac{\sqrt{2}}{2}\right) = 1;$$

$$\cos 90° = \cos 2\,(45°) = \cos^2 45° - \sin^2 45° = \left(\frac{\sqrt{2}}{2}\right)^2 - \left(\frac{\sqrt{2}}{2}\right)^2 = 0.$$

Example D.   Given that $\cos \alpha = \frac{3}{5}$ (in the fourth quadrant), find $\sin 2\alpha$.

Knowing that $\cos \alpha = \frac{3}{5}$ for an angle in the fourth quadrant, we then determine that the

$$\sin \alpha = -\tfrac{4}{5}$$

(see Fig. 19-2). Thus

$$\sin 2\alpha = 2(-\tfrac{4}{5})(\tfrac{3}{5}) = -\tfrac{24}{25}.$$

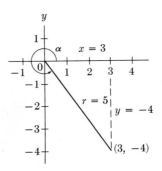

Figure 19-2

Example E.   Prove the identity $\dfrac{2}{1 + \cos 2x} = \sec^2 x.$

$$\frac{2}{1 + \cos 2x} = \frac{2}{1 + (2 \cos^2 x - 1)} = \frac{2}{2 \cos^2 x} = \sec^2 x.$$

Example F.   Show that $\dfrac{\sin 3x}{\sin x} + \dfrac{\cos 3x}{\cos x} = 4 \cos 2x.$

The first step is to combine the two fractions on the left, so that we can see if any usable forms will emerge:

$$\frac{\sin 3x \cos x + \cos 3x \sin x}{\sin x \cos x} \overset{?}{=} 4 \cos 2x.$$

We now note that the numerator is of the form $\sin (A + x)$, where $A = 3x$. Also, the denominator is $\frac{1}{2} \sin 2x$. Making these substitutions, we have

$$\frac{\sin (3x + x)}{\frac{1}{2} \sin 2x} = \frac{2 \sin 4x}{\sin 2x} \overset{?}{=} 4 \cos 2x.$$

By expanding $\sin 4x$ into $2 \sin 2x \cos 2x$, we obtain

$$\frac{2 (2 \sin 2x \cos 2x)}{\sin 2x} = 4 \cos 2x.$$

Therefore the expression is shown to be valid.

Exercises

In Exercises 1 through 4 determine the values of the indicated functions in the given manner.

1. Find $\sin 60°$ by using the functions of $30°$.
2. Find $\sin 120°$ by using the functions of $60°$.
3. Find $\cos 120°$ by using the functions of $60°$.
4. Find $\cos 60°$ by using the functions of $30°$.

In Exercises 5 through 8 evaluate the indicated functions with the given information.

5. Find $\sin 2x$ if $\cos x = \frac{4}{5}$ (in first quadrant).
6. Find $\cos 2x$ if $\sin x = -\frac{12}{13}$ (in third quadrant).
7. Find $\cos 2x$ if $\tan x = \frac{1}{2}$ (in third quadrant).
8. Find $\sin 4x$ if $\sin x = \frac{3}{5}$ (in first quadrant) $[4x = 2(2x)]$.

In Exercises 9 through 12 reduce the given expressions to a single term. Expansion of any term is not necessary; proper recognition of the form of the expression leads to the proper result.

9. $4 \sin 4x \cos 4x$
10. $4 \sin^2 x \cos^2 x$
11. $1 - 2 \sin^2 4x$
12. $\sin^2 4x - \cos^2 4x$

In Exercises 13 through 20 prove the given identities.

13. $\cos^2 \alpha - \sin^2 \alpha = 2 \cos^2 \alpha - 1$

14. $\cos^2 \alpha - \sin^2 \alpha = 1 - 2 \sin^2 \alpha$

15. $\cos^4 x - \sin^4 x = \cos 2x$

16. $(\sin x + \cos x)^2 = 1 + \sin 2x$

17. $2 \csc 2x \tan x = \sec^2 x$

18. $2 \sin x + \sin 2x = \dfrac{2 \sin^3 x}{1 - \cos x}$

19. $\dfrac{\sin 3x}{\sin x} - \dfrac{\cos 3x}{\cos x} = 2$

20. $\dfrac{\sin 3x}{\sin x} + \dfrac{\cos 3x}{\cos x} = 4 \cos 2x$

In Exercises 21 and 22 prove the given identities by letting $3x = 2x + x$.

21. $\sin 3x = 3 \cos^2 x \sin x - \sin^3 x$

22. $\cos 3x = \cos^3 x - 3 \sin^2 x \cos x$

In Exercises 23 through 26 solve the given problems.

23. In Exercise 21 of Section 19-2, let $\beta = \alpha$, and show that

$$\tan 2\alpha = \frac{2 \tan \alpha}{1 - \tan^2 \alpha}.$$

24. Given that $x = \cos 2\theta$ and $y = \sin \theta$, find the relation between x and y by eliminating θ.

25. The equation for the displacement of a certain object at the end of a spring is $y = A \sin 2t + B \cos 2t$. Show that this equation may be written as

$$y = C \sin (2t + \alpha),$$

where $C = \sqrt{A^2 + B^2}$ and $\tan \alpha = B/A$. [*Hint*: Let $A/C = \cos \alpha$ and $B/C = \sin \alpha$.]

26. In finding the horizontal range R of a projectile, the equation $R = vt \cos \alpha$ is used, where α is the angle between the line of fire and the horizontal, v is the initial velocity of the projectile, and t is the time of flight. It can be shown that $t = (2v \sin \alpha)/g$, where g is the acceleration due to gravity. Show that $R = (v^2 \sin 2\alpha)/g$.

19-4 Half-angle formulas

If we let $\theta = \alpha/2$ in the identity $\cos 2\theta = 1 - 2 \sin^2 \theta$ and then solve for $\sin (\alpha/2)$, we obtain

$$\sin \frac{\alpha}{2} = \pm \sqrt{\frac{1 - \cos \alpha}{2}}. \qquad (19\text{-}24)$$

Also, with the same substitution in the identity $\cos 2\theta = 2 \cos^2 \theta - 1$, which is then solved for $\cos (\alpha/2)$, we have

$$\cos \frac{\alpha}{2} = \pm \sqrt{\frac{1 + \cos \alpha}{2}}. \qquad (19\text{-}25)$$

In each of Eqs. (19-24) and (19-25), the sign chosen depends on the quadrant in which $\alpha/2$ lies.

We can use these half-angle formulas to find values of the functions of angles which are half of those of which the functions are known. The examples given on the following page illustrate how these identities are used in evaluations and in identities.

Example A.   We can find sin 15° by using the relation

$$\sin 15° = \sqrt{\frac{1 - \cos 30°}{2}} = \sqrt{\frac{1 - 0.8660}{2}} = 0.2588.$$

Here the plus sign is used, since 15° is in the first quadrant.

Example B.   We can find the cos 165° by use of the relation

$$\cos 165° = -\sqrt{\frac{1 + \cos 330°}{2}} = -\sqrt{\frac{1 + 0.8660}{2}} = -0.9659.$$

Here the minus sign is used, since 165° is in the second quadrant, and the cosine of a second-quadrant angle is negative.

Example C.   Simplify the expression $\sqrt{18 - 18 \cos 4x}$.
  First we factor the 18 from each of the terms under the radical, and note that $18 = 9(2)$ and 9 is a perfect square. This leads to

$$\sqrt{18 - 18 \cos 4x} = \sqrt{9(2)(1 - \cos 4x)} = 3\sqrt{2(1 - \cos 4x)}.$$

This last expression is very similar to that for sin $(\alpha/2)$, except that no 2 appears in the denominator. Therefore, multiplying the numerator and the denominator under the radical by 2 leads to the solution.

$$3\sqrt{2(1 - \cos 4x)} = 3\sqrt{\frac{4(1 - \cos 4x)}{2}} = 6\sqrt{\frac{1 - \cos 4x}{2}}$$

$$= 6 \sin \frac{4x}{2} = 6 \sin 2x.$$

Example D.   Prove the identity

$$\sec \frac{\alpha}{2} + \csc \frac{\alpha}{2} = \frac{2[\sin (\alpha/2) + \cos (\alpha/2)]}{\sin \alpha}.$$

$$\frac{2[\sin (\alpha/2) + \cos (\alpha/2)]}{2 \sin (\alpha/2) \cos (\alpha/2)} = \frac{1}{\cos (\alpha/2)} + \frac{1}{\sin (\alpha/2)} = \sec \frac{\alpha}{2} + \csc \frac{\alpha}{2}.$$

Example E.   We can find relations for the other functions of $\alpha/2$ by expressing these functions in terms of sin $(\alpha/2)$ and cos $(\alpha/2)$. For example:

$$\sec \frac{\alpha}{2} = \frac{1}{\cos (\alpha/2)} = \pm \frac{1}{\sqrt{(1 + \cos \alpha)/2}} = \pm \sqrt{\frac{2}{1 + \cos \alpha}}.$$

Example F.   Show that $2 \cos^2 (x/2) - \cos x = 1$.
  The first step is to substitute for cos $(x/2)$, which will result in each term containing x on the left being in terms of x, and no $x/2$ terms will exist. This

might allow us to combine terms. So we perform this operation, and we have

$$2\left(\frac{1 + \cos x}{2}\right) - \cos x = 1.$$

Combining terms, we can complete the proof:

$$1 + \cos x - \cos x = 1.$$

Exercises

In Exercises 1 through 4 use the half-angle formulas to evaluate the given functions.

1. $\cos 15°$ 2. $\sin 22.5°$ 3. $\sin 75°$ 4. $\cos 112.5°$

In Exercises 5 through 8 use the half-angle formulas to simplify the given expressions.

5. $\sqrt{\dfrac{1 - \cos 6\alpha}{2}}$

6. $\sqrt{\dfrac{4 + 4 \cos 8\beta}{2}}$

7. $\sqrt{8 + 8 \cos 4x}$

8. $\sqrt{2 - 2 \cos 16x}$

In Exercises 9 and 10 evaluate the indicated functions with the information given.

9. Find the value of $\sin (\alpha/2)$, if $\cos \alpha = \frac{12}{13}$ (in first quadrant).
10. Find the value of $\cos (\alpha/2)$, if $\sin \alpha = -\frac{4}{5}$ (in third quadrant).

In Exercises 11 and 12 derive the required expressions.

11. Derive an expression for $\csc (\alpha/2)$ in terms of $\cos \alpha$.
12. Derive an expression for $\cot (\alpha/2)$ in terms of $\sin \alpha$ and $\cos \alpha$.

In Exercises 13 through 16 prove the given identitites.

13. $\sin \dfrac{\alpha}{2} = \dfrac{1 - \cos \alpha}{2 \sin (\alpha/2)}$

14. $2 \cos \dfrac{x}{2} = (1 + \cos x) \sec \dfrac{x}{2}$

15. $\tan \dfrac{\alpha}{2} = \pm\sqrt{\dfrac{1 - \cos \alpha}{1 + \cos \alpha}}$

16. $\tan \dfrac{\alpha}{2} = \dfrac{\sin \alpha}{1 + \cos \alpha}$

In Exercises 17 and 18 use the half-angle formulas to solve the given problems.

17. In the kinetic theory of gases, the expression

$$\sqrt{(1 - \cos \alpha)^2 + \sin^2 \alpha \cos^2 \beta + \sin^2 \alpha \sin^2 \beta}$$

is found. Show that this expression equals $2 \sin \dfrac{\alpha}{2}$.

18. The index of refraction n, the angle of a prism A, and the minimum angle of refraction ϕ are related by

$$n = \frac{\sin [(A + \phi)/2]}{\sin A/2}.$$

Show that an equivalent expression is

$$n = \sqrt{\frac{1 + \cos \phi}{2}} + \left(\cot \frac{A}{2}\right)\sqrt{\frac{1 - \cos \phi}{2}}.$$

19-5 Trigonometric equations

One of the most important uses of the trigonometric identities is in the solution of equations involving the trigonometric functions. When an equation is written in terms of more than one function, the identities provide a way of transforming many of them to equations or factors involving only one function of the same angle. If we can accomplish this we can employ algebraic methods from then on to complete the solution. No general methods exist for the solution of such equations, but the following examples illustrate methods which prove to be useful.

Example A.   Solve the equation $2 \cos \theta - 1 = 0$ for all values of θ such that $0 \leq \theta < 2\pi$.

Solving the equation for $\cos \theta$, we obtain $\cos \theta = \frac{1}{2}$. The problem asks for all values of θ between 0 and 2π that satisfy the equation. We know that the cosine of angles in the first and fourth quadrants is positive. Also we know that $\cos (\pi/3) = \frac{1}{2}$. Therefore $\theta = \pi/3$ and $\theta = 5\pi/3$.

Example B.   Solve the equation $2 \cos^2 x - \sin x - 1 = 0$ $(0 \leq x < 2\pi)$.

By use of the identity $\sin^2 x + \cos^2 x = 1$, this equation may be put in terms of $\sin x$ only. Thus we have $2(1 - \sin^2 x) - \sin x - 1 = 0$.

$$-2 \sin^2 x - \sin x + 1 = 0,$$
$$2 \sin^2 x + \sin x - 1 = 0$$

or

$$(2 \sin x - 1)(\sin x + 1) = 0.$$

Just as in solving algebraic equations, we can set each factor equal to zero to find valid solutions. Thus $\sin x = \frac{1}{2}$ and $\sin x = -1$. For the range between 0 and 2π, the value $\sin x = \frac{1}{2}$ gives values of x as $\pi/6$ and $5\pi/6$, and $\sin x = -1$ gives the value $x = 3\pi/2$. Thus the complete solution is $x = \pi/6$, $x = 5\pi/6$, and $x = 3\pi/2$.

Example C.   Solve the equation $\sin 2x + \sin x = 0$ $(0 \leq x < 2\pi)$.

By using the double-angle formula for $\sin 2x$, we can write the equation in the form

$$2 \sin x \cos x + \sin x = 0, \quad \text{or} \quad \sin x (2 \cos x + 1) = 0.$$

The first factor gives $x = 0$ or $x = \pi$. The second factor, for which $\cos x = -\frac{1}{2}$, gives $x = 2\pi/3$ and $x = 4\pi/3$. Thus the complete solution is $x = 0$, $x = 2\pi/3$, $x = \pi$, and $x = 4\pi/3$.

Example D.   Solve the equation $\cos (x/2) = 1 + \cos x$ $(0 \leq x < 2\pi)$.

By using the half-angle formula for $\cos x/2$ and then squaring both sides of the resulting equation, this equation can be solved.

$$\pm \sqrt{\frac{1 + \cos x}{2}} = 1 + \cos x;$$

$$\frac{1 + \cos x}{2} = 1 + 2 \cos x + \cos^2 x.$$

Simplifying this last equation, we have

$$2 \cos^2 x + 3 \cos x + 1 = 0$$
$$(2 \cos x + 1)(\cos x + 1) = 0.$$

The values of the cosine which come from these factors are $\cos x = -\frac{1}{2}$ and $\cos x = -1$. Thus the values of x which satisfy the last equation are $x = 2\pi/3$, $x = 4\pi/3$, and $x = \pi$. However, when we solved this equation, we squared both sides of it. In doing this we may have introduced extraneous solutions (see Section 13-3). Thus we must check each solution in the original equation to see if it is valid. Hence

$$\cos \frac{\pi}{3} \overset{?}{=} 1 + \cos \frac{2\pi}{3} \quad \text{or} \quad \tfrac{1}{2} \overset{?}{=} 1 + (-\tfrac{1}{2}) \quad \text{or} \quad \tfrac{1}{2} = \tfrac{1}{2};$$

$$\cos \frac{2\pi}{3} \overset{?}{=} 1 + \cos \frac{4\pi}{3} \quad \text{or} \quad -\tfrac{1}{2} \overset{?}{=} 1 + (-\tfrac{1}{2}) \quad \text{or} \quad -\tfrac{1}{2} \neq \tfrac{1}{2}.$$

$$\cos \frac{\pi}{2} \overset{?}{=} 1 + \cos \pi \quad \text{or} \quad 0 \overset{?}{=} 1 - 1 \quad \text{or} \quad 0 = 0.$$

Thus the apparent solution $x = 4\pi/3$ is not a solution of the original equation. The correct solutions are $x = 2\pi/3$ and $x = \pi$.

Example E. Solve the equation $\tan 3\theta - \cot 3\theta = 0 \ (0 \le \theta < 2\pi.)$

$$\tan 3\theta - \frac{1}{\tan 3\theta} = 0 \quad \text{or} \quad \tan^2 3\theta = 1 \quad \text{or} \quad \tan 3\theta = \pm 1.$$

Thus

$$3\theta = \frac{\pi}{4}, \frac{3\pi}{4}, \frac{5\pi}{4}, \frac{7\pi}{4}, \frac{9\pi}{4}, \frac{11\pi}{4}, \frac{13\pi}{4}, \frac{15\pi}{4}, \frac{17\pi}{4}, \frac{19\pi}{4}, \frac{21\pi}{4}, \frac{23\pi}{4}.$$

Here we must include values of angles which when divided by 3 give angles between 0 and 2π. Thus values of 3θ from 0 to 6π are necessary. The solutions are

$$\theta = \frac{\pi}{12}, \frac{\pi}{4}, \frac{5\pi}{12}, \frac{7\pi}{12}, \frac{3\pi}{4}, \frac{11\pi}{12}, \frac{13\pi}{12}, \frac{5\pi}{4}, \frac{17\pi}{12}, \frac{19\pi}{12}, \frac{7\pi}{4}, \frac{23\pi}{12}.$$

It is noted that these values satisfy the original equation. Since we multiplied through by $\tan 3\theta$ in the solution, any value of θ which leads to $\tan 3\theta = 0$ would not be valid, since this would indicate division by zero in the original equation.

Example F.   Solve the equation $\cos 3x \cos x + \sin 3x \sin x = 1 \; (0 \leq x < 2\pi)$.
   The left side of this equation is of the form $\cos (A - x)$, where $A = 3x$.
Therefore

$$\cos 3x \cos x + \sin 3x \sin x = \cos (3x - x) = \cos 2x.$$

The original equation becomes

$$\cos 2x = 1.$$

This equation is satisfied if $2x = 0$ and $2x = 2\pi$. The solutions are $x = 0$ and $x = \pi$. Only through recognition of the proper trigonometric form can we readily solve this equation.

Exercises

In Exercises 1 through 26 solve the given trigonometric equations for values of x so that $0 \leq x < 2\pi$.

1. $\sin x - 1 = 0$
2. $2 \sin x + 1 = 0$
3. $\tan x + 1 = 0$
4. $2 \cos x + 1 = 0$
5. $4 \sin^2 x - 3 = 0$
6. $3 \tan^2 x - 1 = 0$
7. $2 \sin^2 x - \sin x = 0$
8. $3 \cos x - 4 \cos^2 x = 0$
9. $\sin 4x - \cos 2x = 0$
10. $\sin 4x - \sin 2x = 0$
11. $\sin 2x \sin x + \cos x = 0$
12. $\cos 2x + \sin^2 x = 0$
13. $2 \sin x - \tan x = 0$
14. $\sin x - \sin \dfrac{x}{2} = 0$
15. $2 \cos^2 x - 2 \cos 2x - 1 = 0$
16. $2 \cos^2 2x + 1 = 3 \cos 2x$
17. $\sin^2 x - 2 \sin x - 1 = 0$
18. $\tan^2 x - 5 \tan x + 6 = 0$
19. $4 \tan x - \sec^2 x = 0$
20. $\tan^2 x - 2 \sec^2 x + 4 = 0$
21. $\sin 2x \cos x - \cos 2x \sin x = 0$
22. $\cos 3x \cos x - \sin 3x \sin x = 0$
23. $\sin 2x + \cos 2x = 0$
24. $2 \sin 4x + \csc 4x = 3$
25. $\tan x + 3 \cot x = 4$
26. $\sin x \sin \frac{1}{2}x = 1 - \cos x$

In Exercises 27 and 28 solve the indicated equations.

27. The angular displacement θ of a certain pendulum in terms of the time t is given by $\theta = e^{-0.1t}(\cos 2t + 3 \sin 2t)$. What is the smallest value of t for which the displacement is zero?

28. The vertical displacement y of an object at the end of a spring, which itself is being moved up and down, is given by $y = 2 \cos 4t + \sin 2t$. Find the smallest value of t (in seconds) for which $y = 0$.

In Exercises 29 through 31 solve the given equations graphically.

29. $\sin 2x = x$

30. $\cos 2x = 4 - x^2$

31. In the study of light diffraction, the equation $\tan \theta = \theta$ is found. Solve this equation for $0 \leq \theta < 2\pi$.

19-6 Introduction to the inverse trigonometric functions

When we studied logarithms, we found that we often wished to change a given expression from exponential to logarithmic form, or from logarithmic to exponential form. Each of these forms has its advantages for particular purposes. We found that the exponential function $y = b^x$ can also be written in logarithmic form with x as a function of y, or $x = \log_b y$. We then represented both of these functions as y in terms of x, saying that the letter used for the dependent and independent variables did not matter, when we wished to express a functional relationship. Since y is normally the dependent variable, we wrote the logarithmic function as $y = \log_b x$.

These two functions, the exponential function $y = b^x$ and the logarithmic function $y = \log_b x$, are called *inverse functions*. This means that if we solve for the independent variable in terms of the dependent variable in one, we will arrive at the functional relationship expressed by the other. It also means that, for every value of x, there is only one corresponding value of y.

Just as we are able to solve $y = b^x$ for the exponent by writing it in logarithmic form, there are times when it is necessary to solve for the independent variable (the *angle*) in trigonometric functions. Therefore we define the *inverse sine of x* by the relation

$$y = \arcsin x \text{ (the notation } y = \sin^{-1} x \text{ is also used).} \qquad (19\text{-}26)$$

Similar relations exist for the other inverse trigonometric relations. In Eq. (19-26), x is the value of the sine of the angle y, and therefore the most meaningful way of reading it is "y is the angle whose sine is x."

Example A. $y = \arccos x$ would be read as "y is the angle whose cosine is x."

The equation $y = \arctan 2x$ would be read as "y is the angle whose tangent is $2x$."

It is important to emphasize that $y = \arcsin x$ and $x = \sin y$ express the same relationship between x and y. The advantage of having both forms is that a trigonometric relation may be expressed in terms of a function of an angle or in terms of the angle itself.

If we consider closely the equation $y = \arcsin x$ and possible values of x, we note that there are an unlimited number of possible values of y for a given value of x. Consider the following example.

Example B. For $y = \arcsin x$, if $x = \frac{1}{2}$, we have $y = \arcsin \frac{1}{2}$. This means that we are to find an angle whose sine is $\frac{1}{2}$. We know that $\sin (\pi/6) = \frac{1}{2}$. Therefore, $y = \pi/6$.

However, we also know that $\sin (5\pi/6) = \frac{1}{2}$. Therefore, $y = 5\pi/6$ is also a proper value. If we consider negative angles, such as $-7\pi/6$, or angles generated by additional rotations, such as $13\pi/6$, we conclude that there are an unlimited number of possible values for y.

To have a properly defined *function* in mathematics, there must be only one value of the dependent variable for a given value of the independent variable. A *relation*, on the other hand, may have more than one such value. Therefore, we see that $y = \arcsin x$ is not really a function, although it is properly a relation. It is necessary to restrict the values of y in order to define the *inverse trigonometric functions*, and this is done in the following section. It is the purpose of this section to introduce the necessary notation and to develop an understanding of the basic concept. The following examples further illustrate the meaning of the notation.

Example C.   If $y = \arccos 0$, y is the angle whose cosine is zero. The smallest positive angle for which this is true is $\pi/2$. Therefore, $y = \pi/2$ is an acceptable value.

If $y = \arctan 1$, an acceptable value for y is $\pi/4$. This is the same as saying $\tan \pi/4 = 1$.

Example D.   Given that $y = \sec 2x$, solve for x.

We first express the inverse relation as $2x = \operatorname{arcsec} y$. Then we solve for x by dividing through by 2. Thus we have $x = \frac{1}{2} \operatorname{arcsec} y$. Note that we first wrote the inverse relation by writing the expression for the angle, which in this case was $2x$. Just as $\sec 2x$ and $2 \sec x$ are different relations, so are the arcsec $2x$ and $2 \operatorname{arcsec} x$.

Example E.   Given that $4y = \operatorname{arccot} 2x$, solve for x.

Writing this as the cotangent of $4y$ (since the given expression means "$4y$ is the angle whose cotangent is $2x$"), we have

$$2x = \cot 4y \qquad \text{or} \qquad x = \tfrac{1}{2} \cot 4y.$$

Example F.   Given that $\pi - y = \operatorname{arccsc} \tfrac{1}{3}x$, solve for x.

$$\tfrac{1}{3}x = \csc (\pi - y) \qquad \text{or} \qquad x = 3 \csc y,$$

[since $\csc (\pi - y) = \csc y$].

Exercises

In Exercises 1 through 6 write down the meaning of each of the given equations. See Example A.

1. $y = \arctan x$ 2. $y = \operatorname{arcsec} x$ 3. $y = \operatorname{arccot} 3x$
4. $y = \operatorname{arccsc} 4x$ 5. $y = 2 \arcsin x$ 6. $y = 3 \arctan x$

In Exercises 7 through 16 find the smallest positive angle (in terms of π) for each of the given expressions.

7. $\arccos \tfrac{1}{2}$ 8. $\arcsin 1$ 9. $\operatorname{arcsec} (-\sqrt{2})$

10. $\arccos \dfrac{\sqrt{2}}{2}$ 11. $\arctan (-1)$ 12. $\operatorname{arccsc} (-1)$

13. $\arctan \sqrt{3}$

14. $\text{arcsec } 2$

15. $\text{arccot } (-\sqrt{3})$

16. $\arcsin \left(-\dfrac{\sqrt{3}}{2}\right)$

In Exercises 17 through 24 solve the given equations for x.

17. $y = \sin 3x$

18. $y = \cos (x - \pi)$

19. $y = \arctan \left(\dfrac{x}{4}\right)$

20. $y = 2 \arcsin \left(\dfrac{x}{6}\right)$

21. $y = 1 + \sec 3x$

22. $4y = 5 - \csc 8x$

23. $1 - y = \arccos (1 - x)$

24. $2y = \text{arccot } 3x - 5$

In Exercises 25 through 28 determine the required quadrants.

25. In which quadrants is $\arcsin x$ if $0 < x < 1$?
26. In which quadrants is $\arctan x$ if $0 < x < 1$?
27. In which quadrants is $\arccos x$ if $-1 < x < 0$?
28. In which quadrants is $\arcsin x$ if $-1 < x < 0$?

In Exercises 29 through 32 solve the given problems with the use of the inverse trigonometric relations.

29. A body is moving along a straight line in such a way that its acceleration is directed toward a fixed point, and is proportional to its distance from that point. Its position is given by $x = A \cos t \sqrt{k/m}$. Solve for k.

30. Under certain conditions the magnetic potential V at a distance r from a circuit with a current I is given by

$$V = \frac{kI \cos \theta}{r^2},$$

where k is a constant and θ is the angle between the radius vector r and the direction perpendicular to the plane of the circuit. Solve for θ.

31. The magnitude of a certain ray of polarized light is given by $E = E_0 \cos \theta \sin \theta$. Solve for θ.

32. The equation for the displacement of a certain object oscillating at the end of a spring is given by $y = A \sin 2t + B \cos 2t$. Solve for t. [*Hint*: See Exercise 25 of Section 19-3.]

19-7 The inverse trigonometric functions

We noted in the preceding section that we could find many values of y if we assumed some value for x in the relation $y = \arcsin x$. As these relations were defined, any one of the various possibilities would be considered correct. This, however, does not meet a basic requirement for a function, and it also leads to ambiguity. In order to define *inverse trigonometric functions* properly, so that this ambiguity does not exist, there must be only a single value of y for any given value of x. Therefore, the following values are defined for the given functions.

$$-\frac{\pi}{2} \le \text{Arcsin } x \le \frac{\pi}{2}, \qquad 0 \le \text{Arccos } x \le \pi, \qquad -\frac{\pi}{2} < \text{Arctan } x < \frac{\pi}{2},$$

$$\text{(19-27)}$$

$$0 < \text{Arccot } x < \pi, \qquad 0 \le \text{Arcsec } x \le \pi, \qquad -\frac{\pi}{2} \le \text{Arccsc } x \le \frac{\pi}{2}.$$

This means that when we are looking for a value of y to correspond to a given value for x, we must use a value of y as defined in Eqs. (19-27). The capital letter designates the use of the inverse trigonometric *function*.

Example A. $\text{Arcsin}\left(\dfrac{1}{2}\right) = \dfrac{\pi}{6}.$

This is the only value of the function which lies within the defined range. The value $5\pi/6$ is not correct, since it lies outside the defined range of values.

Example B. $\text{Arccos}\left(-\dfrac{1}{2}\right) = \dfrac{2\pi}{3}.$

Other values such as $4\pi/3$ and $-2\pi/3$ are not correct, since they are not within the defined range of values for the function Arccos x.

Example C. $\text{Arctan }(-1) = -\dfrac{\pi}{4}.$

This is the only value within the defined range for the function Arctan x. We must remember that when x is negative for Arcsin x and Arctan x, the value of y is a fourth-quadrant angle, expressed as a *negative angle*. This is a direct result of the definition.

Example D. $\text{Arcsin}\left(-\dfrac{\sqrt{3}}{2}\right) = -\pi/3, \qquad \text{Arccos }(-1) = \pi,$

$\qquad\qquad \text{Arctan } 0 = 0, \qquad\qquad\qquad \text{Arcsin }(-0.1564) = -\pi/20,$

$\qquad\qquad \text{Arccos }(-0.8090) = 4\pi/5, \qquad \text{Arctan }(\sqrt{3}) = \pi/3.$

One might logically ask why these values are chosen when there are so many different possibilities. The values are so chosen that, if x is positive, the resulting answer gives an angle in the first quadrant. We must, however, account for the possibility that x might be negative. We could not choose second-quadrant angles for the Arcsin x. Since the sine of second-quadrant angles is also positive, this then would lead to ambiguity. The sine is negative for fourth-quadrant angles, and to have a continuous range of values of x we express the fourth-quadrant angles in the form of negative angles. This range is also chosen for the Arctan x, for similar reasons. However, the Arccos x cannot be chosen in this way, since the cosine of fourth-quadrant angles is also positive. Thus, again to keep a continuous range of values for Arccos x, the second-quadrant angles are chosen for negative values of x.

As for the values for the other functions, we chose values such that if x is positive, the result is also an angle in the first quadrant. As for negative values of x, it rarely makes any difference, since either positive values of x arise, or we can use one of the other functions. Our definitions, however, are those which are generally used.

The graphs of the inverse trigonometric relations can be used to show the fact that many values of y correspond to a given value of x. We can also show the choice of the ranges used in defining the inverse trigonometric functions, and that it is a specific section of the curve.

Since $y = \text{arcsin } x$ and $x = \sin y$ are equivalent equations, we can obtain the graph of the inverse sine by sketching the sine curve *along the y-axis*. In Figures (19-3), (19-4) and (19-5), the graphs of the inverse trigonometric relations are shown, with the darker portions indicating the graphs of the inverse trigonometric functions. The graphs of the other inverse relations are found in the same way.

Figure 19-3

Figure 19-4

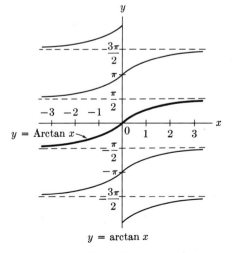

$y = \text{arctan } x$

Figure 19-5

If we know the value of x for one of the inverse functions, we can find the trigonometric functions of the angle. If general relations are desired, a representative triangle is very useful. The following examples illustrate these methods.

Example E.   Find cos (Arcsin 0.5). [Remember again: the inverse functions are *angles*.]

We know Arcsin 0.5 is a first-quadrant angle, since 0.5 is positive. Thus we find Arcsin $0.5 = \pi/6$. The problem now becomes one of finding cos $(\pi/6)$. This is, of course, $\sqrt{3}/2$ or 0.8660.

Example F. $\sin$ (Arccot 1) $= \sin \dfrac{\pi}{4} = \dfrac{\sqrt{2}}{2} = 0.7071,$

$$\tan\,[\text{Arccos}\,(-1)] = \tan \pi = 0$$

Example G.   Find sin (Arctan x).

We know that Arctan x is another way of stating "the angle whose tangent is x." Thus let us draw a right triangle (as in Fig. 19-6) and label one of the acute angles θ, the side opposite θ as x, and the side adjacent to θ as 1. In this way we see that, by definition, tan $\theta = x/1$, or $\theta = $ Arctan x, which means θ is the desired angle. By the Pythagorean theorem, the hypotenuse of this triangle is $\sqrt{x^2 + 1}$. Now we find that the sin θ, which is the same as sin (Arctan x), is $x/\sqrt{x^2 + 1}$, from the definition of the sine. Thus sin (Arctan x) $= x/\sqrt{x^2 + 1}$.

Figure 19-6

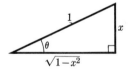

Figure 19-7

Example H.   Find cos (2 Arcsin x).

From Fig. 19-7, we see that $\theta = $ Arcsin x. From the double-angle formulas, we have cos $2\theta = 1 - 2 \sin^2 \theta$. Thus, since sin $\theta = x$, we have

$$\cos\,(2\,\text{Arcsin}\,x) = 1 - 2x^2.$$

Exercises

In Exercises 1 through 24 evaluate the given expressions.

1. Arccos $\left(\frac{1}{2}\right)$
2. Arcsin (1)
3. Arcsin 0

4. Arccos 0
5. Arctan $(-\sqrt{3})$
6. Arcsin $\left(-\frac{1}{2}\right)$

7. Arcsec 2
8. Arccot $\sqrt{3}$
9. Arctan $\left(\dfrac{\sqrt{3}}{3}\right)$

10. Arctan 1

11. Arcsin $\left(-\dfrac{\sqrt{2}}{2}\right)$

12. Arccos $\left(-\dfrac{\sqrt{3}}{2}\right)$

13. Arccsc $\sqrt{2}$

14. Arccot 1

15. Arctan (-3.732)

16. Arccos (-0.5878)

17. $\sin(\text{Arctan}\ \sqrt{3})$

18. $\tan\left(\text{Arcsin}\ \dfrac{\sqrt{2}}{2}\right)$

19. $\cos[\text{Arctan}\ (-1)]$

20. $\sec[\text{Arccos}\ (-\tfrac{1}{2})]$

21. $\tan[\text{Arccos}\ (-0.6561)]$

22. $\cot[\text{Arcsin}\ (-0.3827)]$

23. $\cos(2\ \text{Arcsin}\ 1)$

24. $\sin(2\ \text{Arctan}\ 2)$

In Exercises 25 through 32 find an algebraic expression for each of the expressions given.

25. $\tan(\text{Arcsin}\ x)$

26. $\sin(\text{Arccos}\ x)$

27. $\cos(\text{Arcsec}\ x)$

28. $\cot(\text{Arccot}\ x)$

29. $\sec(\text{Arccsc}\ 3x)$

30. $\tan(\text{Arcsin}\ 2x)$

31. $\sin(2\ \text{Arcsin}\ x)$

32. $\cos(2\ \text{Arctan}\ x)$

In Exercises 33 and 34 solve the problems.

33. Show that

Arcsin $\tfrac{3}{5}$ + Arcsin $\tfrac{5}{13}$ = Arcsin $\tfrac{56}{65}$.

[*Hint:* Use the relation for

$\sin(\alpha + \beta)$.]

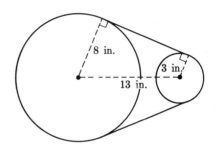

34. Show that the length of the pulley belt indicated in Fig. 19-8 is given by the expression

$L = 24 + 11\pi + 10\ \text{Arcsin}\ (\tfrac{5}{13})$.

Figure 19-8

19-8 Miscellaneous Exercises

In Exercises 1 through 6 determine the values of the indicated functions in the given manner.

1. Find $\sin 120°$ by using $120° = 90° + 30°$.
2. Find $\cos 30°$ by using $30° = 90° - 60°$.
3. Find $\cos 180°$ by using $180° = 2(90°)$.
4. Find $\sin 180°$ by using $180° = 2(90°)$.
5. Find $\sin 45°$ by using $45° = \tfrac{1}{2}(90°)$.
6. Find $\cos 45°$ by using $45° = \tfrac{1}{2}(90°)$.

In Exercises 7 through 12 reduce each of the given expressions to a single term. Expansion of any term is not necessary; proper recognition of the form of the expression leads to the proper result.

7. $\sin 2x \cos 3x + \cos 2x \sin 3x$

8. $\cos 7x \cos 3x + \sin 7x \sin 3x$

9. $8 \sin 6x \cos 6x$

10. $\cos^2 2x - \sin^2 2x$

11. $\sqrt{2 + 2 \cos 2x}$

12. $\sqrt{32 - 32 \cos 4x}$

In Exercises 13 through 20 evaluate the given expressions.

13. Arcsin (-1)

14. Arcsec $\sqrt{2}$

15. Arccos (0.9659)

16. Arctan (-0.6249)

17. $\tan [\text{Arcsin} (-\tfrac{1}{2})]$

18. $\cos [\text{Arctan} (-\sqrt{3})]$

19. Arcsin $(\tan \pi)$

20. Arccos $\left[\tan \left(-\dfrac{\pi}{4} \right) \right]$

In Exercises 21 through 40 prove the given identities.

21. $\dfrac{1}{\sin \theta} - \sin \theta = \cot \theta \cos \theta$

22. $\sin \theta \sec \theta \csc \theta \cos \theta = 1$

23. $\cos \theta \cot \theta + \sin \theta = \csc \theta$

24. $\dfrac{\sin x \cot x + \cos x}{\cot x} = 2 \sin x$

25. $\dfrac{\sec^4 x - 1}{\tan^2 x} = 2 + \tan^2 x$

26. $\cos^2 y - \sin^2 y = \dfrac{1 - \tan^2 y}{1 + \tan^2 y}$

27. $2 \csc 2x \cot x = 1 + \cot^2 x$

28. $\cos^8 x - \sin^8 x = (\cos^4 x + \sin^4 x) \cos 2x$

29. $\sin \dfrac{\theta}{2} \cos \dfrac{\theta}{2} = \dfrac{\sin \theta}{2}$

30. $\sin \dfrac{x}{2} = \dfrac{\sec x - 1}{2 \sec x \sin (x/2)}$

31. $\sec x + \tan x = \dfrac{\cos x}{1 - \sin x}$

32. $\dfrac{\cos \theta - \sin \theta}{\cos \theta + \sin \theta} = \dfrac{\cot \theta - 1}{\cot \theta + 1}$

33. $\cos (x - y) \cos y - \sin (x - y) \sin y = \cos x$

34. $\sin 3y \cos 2y - \cos 3y \sin 2y = \sin y$

35. $\sin 4x (\cos^2 2x - \sin^2 2x) = \dfrac{\sin 8x}{2}$

36. $\csc 2x + \cot 2x = \cot x$

37. $\dfrac{\sin x}{\csc x - \cot x} = 1 + \cos x$

38. $\cos x - \sin \dfrac{x}{2} = \left(1 - 2 \sin \dfrac{x}{2} \right)\left(1 + \sin \dfrac{x}{2} \right)$

39. $\dfrac{\sin (x + y) + \sin (x - y)}{\cos (x + y) + \cos (x - y)} = \tan x$

40. $\sec \dfrac{x}{2} + \csc \dfrac{x}{2} = \dfrac{2[\sin (x/2) + \cos (x/2)]}{\sin x}$

In Exercises 41 through 44 solve for x.

41. $y = 2 \cos 2x$

42. $y - 2 = 2 \tan (x - \pi/2)$

43. $y = (\pi/4) - 3 \arcsin 5x$

44. $2y = \text{arcsec} \, 4x - 2$

In Exercises 45 through 50 solve the given equations for x such that $0 \le x < 2\pi$.

45. $4 \cos^2 x - 3 = 0$

46. $\cos 2x = \sin x$

47. $\sin^2 x - \cos^2 x + 1 = 0$

48. $\cos 3x \cos x + \sin 3x \sin x = 0$

49. $\sin^2 (x/2) - \cos x + 1 = 0$

50. $\sin x + \cos x = 1$

In Exercises 51 and 52 find an algebraic expression for each of the expressions.

51. $\sin (2 \text{ Arccos } x)$

52. $\cos (\pi - \text{Arctan } x)$

In Exercises 53 through 62 use the formulas and methods of this chapter to solve the given problems.

53. In determining the motion of an object, the expression $\cos \alpha \sin (\omega t + \phi) - \sin \alpha \cos (\omega t + \phi)$ is found. Simplify this expression.

54. In surveying, when determining an azimuth (a measure used for reference purposes), it might be necessary to simplify the expression

$$\frac{1}{2 \cos \alpha \cos \beta} - \tan \alpha \tan \beta.$$

Perform this operation by expressing it in the simplest possible form when $\alpha = \beta$.

55. An object is under the influence of a central force (an example of one type of central force is the attraction of the sun for the earth). The y-coordinate of its path is given by $y = 20 \sin \frac{1}{3}t$. Solve for t.

56. Under certain conditions, the current in an electric circuit is given by

$$i = I_m [\sin (\omega t + \alpha) \cos \phi + \cos (\omega t + \alpha) \sin \phi].$$

Solve for t.

57. In the theory dealing with the reflection of light, the expression

$$\frac{\cos (\phi + \alpha)}{\cos (\phi - \alpha)}$$

is found. Express this in terms of functions of α if $\phi = 2\alpha$.

58. In developing an expression for the power in an alternating-current circuit, the expression $\sin \omega t \sin (\omega t + \phi)$ is found. Show that this expression can be written as $\frac{1}{2} [\cos \phi - \cos (2\omega t + \phi)]$.

59. In the theory dealing with the motion of fluid in cylinders, the expression

$$4 \sin^2 \alpha \cos^2 \alpha + (\cos^2 \alpha - \sin^2 \alpha)^2$$

is found. Simplify this expression.

60. In the theory of interference of light, the expression $1 - 2r^2 \cos \beta + r^4$ is found. Show that this expression can be written as $(1 - r^2)^2 + 4r^2 \sin^2 (\beta/2)$.

61. In the theory of diffraction of light, an equation found is

$$y = R \sin 2\pi \left(\frac{t}{T} - \frac{a}{\lambda}\right) \cos \alpha - R \cos 2\pi \left(\frac{t}{T} - \frac{a}{\lambda}\right) \sin \alpha.$$

Show that

$$y = R \sin 2\pi \left(\frac{t}{T} - \frac{a}{\lambda} - \frac{\alpha}{2\pi}\right).$$

62. The electric current as a function of the time for a particular circuit is given by $i = 8e^{-20t}(\sqrt{3} \cos 10t - \sin 10t)$. Find the time in seconds when the current is first zero.

Plane Analytic Geometry

20

20-1 Basic definitions

We first introduced the graph of a function in Chapter 2, and since that time we have made extensive use of graphs for representing functions. We have used graphs to represent the trigonometric functions, the exponential and logarithmic functions, and the inverse trigonometric functions. We have also seen how graphs may be used in solving equations and systems of equations. In this chapter we shall consider certain basic principles relating to the graphs of functions. We shall also show how certain graphs can be constructed by recognizing the form of the equation.

It is necessary when studying many of the concepts of the calculus to have the ability to recognize certain curves and their basic characteristics. Also, curves have many technical applications, many of which are illustrated or indicated in the examples and exercises in this chapter.

The underlying principle of analytic geometry is the relationship of geometry to algebra. A great deal can be learned about a geometric figure if we can find the function which represents its graph. Also, by analyzing certain characteristics of a function, we can obtain useful information as to the nature of its graph. In this section we shall develop certain basic concepts which will be needed for future use in establishing the proper relationships between an equation and a curve.

The first of these concepts involves the distance between any two points in the coordinate plane. If these two points lie on a line parallel to one of the axes, for instance the x-axis, the absolute value of the distance between them is the difference of the abscissas of these points. The abscissa of any point represents the distance from the y-axis to that point, and this distance may be either positive or negative, depending upon the location of the point. Thus the distance between the points is the difference of these distances from the y-axis. Also, if two points are on a line parallel to the y-axis, the distance between them is the difference between the ordinates of the points (see Fig. 20-1).

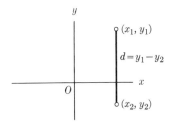

Figure 20-1

Example A.   The distance between $(2, -3)$ and $(2, 6)$ is 9 units. The line joining these points is parallel to the y-axis, and thus we need to find the difference between the y-coordinates. In a similar manner the distance between $(-1, 5)$ and $(-4, 5)$ is 3 units.

If two points are on a line which is not parallel to either of the axes (Fig. 20-2), we must use the Pythagorean theorem to find the distance between them. By making a right triangle with the line segment joining the two points as the hypotenuse, and line segments parallel to the axes as the legs, we have the formula which gives the distance between any two points in the plane. This formula, called the *distance formula*, is

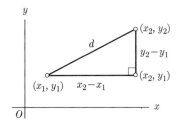

Figure 20-2

$$d = \sqrt{(x_2 - x_1)^2 + (y_2 - y_1)^2}. \tag{20-1}$$

Example B.   The distance between $(3, -1)$ and $(-2, -5)$ is given by

$$d = \sqrt{[(-2) - 3]^2 + [(-5) - (-1)]^2}$$
$$= \sqrt{(-5)^2 + (-4)^2} = \sqrt{25 + 16} = \sqrt{41}.$$

It makes no difference which point is chosen as (x_1, y_1) and which is chosen as (x_2, y_2), since the difference in the x-coordinates (and y-coordinates) is squared. We also obtain $\sqrt{41}$ if we set up the distance as

$$d = \sqrt{[3 - (-2)]^2 + [(-1) - (-5)]^2}.$$

Another important quantity which is defined for a line is its *slope*. The slope gives a measure of the direction of a line, and is defined as the vertical distance from one point to another on the same straight line, divided by the horizontal distance from the first point to the second. Thus, using the letter m to represent slope, we have

$$m = \frac{y_2 - y_1}{x_2 - x_1}. \tag{20-2}$$

Example C.   The slope of the line joining $(3, -5)$ and $(-2, -6)$ is

$$m = \frac{-6 - (-5)}{-2 - 3} = \frac{-6 + 5}{-5} = \frac{1}{5}.$$

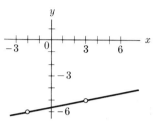

See Fig. 20-3. Again we may interpret either of the points as (x_1, y_1) and the other as (x_2, y_2). We can also obtain the slope of this same line from

$$m = \frac{-5 - (-6)}{3 - (-2)} = \frac{1}{5}.$$

Figure 20-3

The larger the numerical value of the slope of a line, the more nearly vertical is the line. Also, a line rising to the right has a positive slope, and a line falling to the right has a negative slope.

Example D.   The line through the two points in Example C has a positive slope, which is numerically small. From Fig. 20-3 it can be seen that the line rises slightly to the right.

The line joining $(3, 8)$ and $(4, -6)$ has a slope of -14. This line falls sharply to the right (see Fig. 20-4).

From the definition of slope, we may conclude that the slope of a line parallel to the y-axis cannot be defined (the x-coordinates of any two points on the line would be the same, which would then necessitate division by zero). This, however, does not prove to be of any trouble.

If a given line is extended indefinitely in either direction, it must cross the x-axis at some point unless it is parallel to the x-axis. The angle measured from the x-axis in a positive direction to the line is called the *inclination* of the line (see Fig. 20-5). The inclination of a line parallel to the x-axis is defined to be zero. An alternative definition of slope, in terms of the inclination, is

$$m = \tan \alpha, \qquad 0 \le \alpha < 180°, \tag{20-3}$$

where α is the inclination. This can be seen from the fact that the slope can be defined in terms of any two points on the line. Thus, if we choose as one of these points that point where the line crosses the x-axis and any other point, we see from the definition of the tangent of an angle that Eq. (20-3) is in agreement with Eq. (20-2).

Example E.   The slope of a line with an inclination of $45°$ is $\tan 45° = 1$. The slope of a line having an inclination of $120°$ is $\tan 120° = -\sqrt{3}$ (see Fig. 20-6).

Any two parallel lines crossing the x-axis will have the same inclination. Therefore, the slopes of parallel lines are equal. This can be stated as

$$m_1 = m_2, \qquad \text{for} \parallel \text{lines.} \tag{20-4}$$

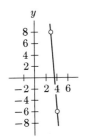

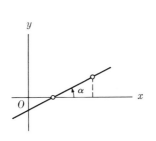

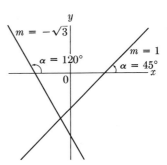

Figure 20-4   Figure 20-5   Figure 20-6

If two lines are perpendicular, this means that there must be 90° between their inclinations (Fig. 20-7). The relation between their inclinations is

$$\alpha_2 = \alpha_1 + 90°,$$

which can be written as

$$90° - \alpha_2 = -\alpha_1.$$

Taking the tangent of each of the angles in this last relation, we have

$$\tan (90° - \alpha_2) = \tan (-\alpha_1)$$

or

$$\cot \alpha_2 = -\tan \alpha_1,$$

since a function of the complement of an angle is equal to the cofunction of that angle (see Section 3-4), and since $\tan (-\alpha) = -\tan \alpha$ (see Exercise 37 of Section 7-2). But $\cot \alpha = 1/\tan \alpha$, which means $1/\tan \alpha_2 = -\tan \alpha_1$. Using the inclination definition of slope, we may write, as the relation between slopes of perpendicular lines,

$$m_2 = -\frac{1}{m_1} \quad \text{or} \quad m_1 m_2 = -1, \quad \text{for} \perp \text{lines.} \quad (20\text{-}5)$$

Example. F. Lines with slopes of 2 and $-\frac{1}{2}$ would be perpendicular. Lines joining $(3, -5)$ and $(2, -7)$, and $(4, -6)$ and $(2, -5)$ are such lines (see Fig. 20-8).

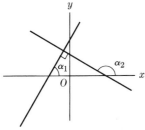

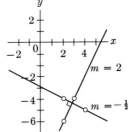

Figure 20-7   Figure 20-8

Using the formulas for distance and slope, we can show certain basic geometric relations. The following examples illustrate the use of the formulas, and thus show the use of algebra in solving problems which are basically geometric. This illustrates the methods of analytic geometry.

Example G. Show that line segments joining $A(-5, 3)$, $B(6, 0)$, and $C(5, 5)$ form a right triangle (see Fig. 20-9).

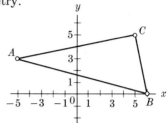

Figure 20-9

If these points are vertices of a right triangle, the slopes of two of the sides must be negative reciprocals. This would show perpendicularity. Thus we find the slopes of the three lines to be

$$m_{AB} = \frac{3-0}{-5-6} = -\frac{3}{11}, \quad m_{AC} = \frac{3-5}{-5-5} = \frac{1}{5}, \quad m_{BC} = \frac{0-5}{6-5} = -5.$$

We see that the slopes of AC and BC are negative reciprocals, which means that $AC \perp BC$. From this we can conclude that the triangle is a right triangle.

Example H. Find the area of the triangle in Example G.

Since the right angle is at C, the legs of the triangle are AC and BC. The area is one-half the product of the lengths of the legs of a right triangle. Therefore the area of the triangle is

$$\text{Area} = \tfrac{1}{2}\sqrt{(-5-5)^2 + (3-5)^2}\sqrt{(6-5)^2 + (0-5)^2}$$

$$= \tfrac{1}{2}\sqrt{104}\sqrt{26} = \tfrac{1}{2}\sqrt{(8\cdot13)(2\cdot13)}$$

$$= 26.$$

Exercises

In Exercises 1 through 8 find the distances between the given pairs of points.

1. $(3, 8)$ and $(-1, -2)$
2. $(-1, 3)$ and $(-8, -4)$
3. $(4, -5)$ and $(4, -8)$
4. $(-3, 7)$ and $(2, 10)$
5. $(-1, 0)$ and $(5, -7)$
6. $(15, -1)$ and $(-11, 1)$
7. $(-4, -3)$ and $(3, -3)$
8. $(-2, 5)$ and $(-2, -2)$

In Exercises 9 through 16 find the slopes of the lines through the points in Exercises 1 through 8.

In Exercises 17 and 18 find the slopes of the lines with the given inclinations.

17. $150°$
18. $135°$

In Exercises 19 and 20 find the inclinations of the lines with the given slopes.

19. 0.3640
20. -1.428

In Exercises 21 through 24 determine whether the lines through the two pairs of points are parallel or perpendicular.

21. $(6, -1)$ and $(4, 3)$, and $(-5, 2)$ and $(-7, 6)$
22. $(-3, 9)$ and $(4, 4)$, and $(9, -1)$ and $(4, -8)$
23. $(-1, -4)$ and $(2, 3)$, and $(-5, 2)$ and $(-19, 8)$
24. $(-1, -2)$ and $(3, 6)$, and $(2, -6)$ and $(5, 0)$

In Exercises 25 and 26 determine the value of k.

25. The points $(6, -1)$, $(3, k)$, and $(-3, -7)$ are all on the same line.
26. The points in Exercise 25 are the vertices of a right triangle, with the right angle at $(3, k)$.

In Exercises 27 through 30 show that the given points are vertices of the indicated geometric figures.

27. Show that the points $(2, 3)$, $(4, 9)$, and $(-2, 7)$ are the vertices of an isosceles triangle.
28. Show that $(-1, 3)$, $(3, 5)$, and $(5, 1)$ are the vertices of a right triangle.
29. Show that $(3, 2)$, $(7, 3)$, $(-1, -3)$, and $(3, -2)$ are the vertices of a parallelogram.
30. Show that $(-5, 6)$, $(0, 8)$, $(-3, 1)$, and $(2, 3)$ are the vertices of a square.

In Exercises 31 and 32 find the indicated areas.

31. Find the area of the triangle of Exercise 28.
32. Find the area of the square of Exercise 30.

20-2 The straight line

Using the definition of slope, we can derive the equation which always represents a straight line. This is another basic method of analytic geometry. That is, equations of a particular form can be shown to represent a particular type of curve. When we recognize the form of the equation, we know the kind of curve it represents. This can be of great assistance in sketching the graph.

A straight line can be defined as a "curve" with constant slope. By this we mean that for any two different points chosen on a given line, if the slope is calculated, the same value is always found. Thus, if we consider one point (x_1, y_1) on a line to be fixed (Fig. 20-10), and another point $P(x, y)$ which can *represent* any other point on the line, we have

$$m = \frac{y - y_1}{x - x_1},$$

which can be written as

$$y - y_1 = m(x - x_1). \qquad (20\text{-}6)$$

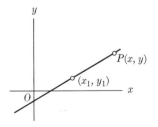

Figure 20-10

Equation (20-6) is known as the *point-slope form* of the equation of a straight line. It is useful when we know the slope of a line and some point through which the line passes. Direct substitution can then give us the equation of the line. Such information is often available about a given line.

Example A. Find the equation of the line which passes through $(-4, 1)$ with a slope of -2.

By using Eq. (20-6), we find that

$$y - 1 = (-2)(x + 4),$$

which can be simplified to

$$y + 2x + 7 = 0.$$

This line is shown in Fig. 20-11.

Example B. Find the equation of the line through $(2, -1)$ and $(6, 2)$.

We first find the slope of the line through these points:

$$m = \frac{2 + 1}{6 - 2} = \frac{3}{4}.$$

Then, by using either of the two known points and Eq. (20-6), we can find the equation of the line:

$$y + 1 = \tfrac{3}{4}(x - 2)$$

or

$$4y + 4 = 3x - 6$$

or

$$4y - 3x + 10 = 0.$$

This line is shown in Fig. 20-12.

Equation (20-6) can be used for any line except one parallel to the y-axis. Such a line has an undefined slope. However, it does have the property that all points have the same x-coordinate, regardless of the y-coordinate. We represent a line parallel to the y-axis as

$$x = a. \tag{20-7}$$

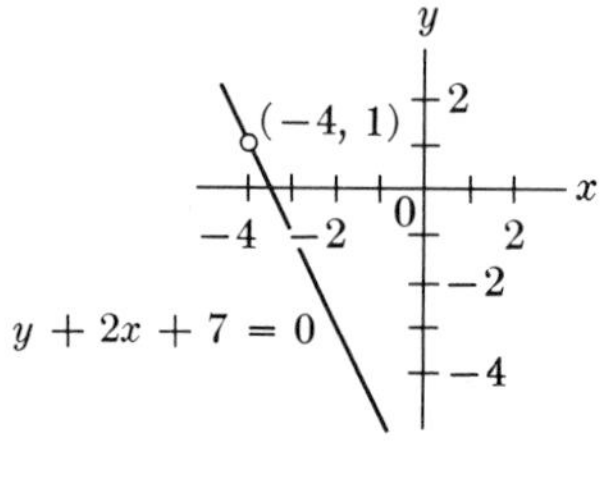

Figure 20-11

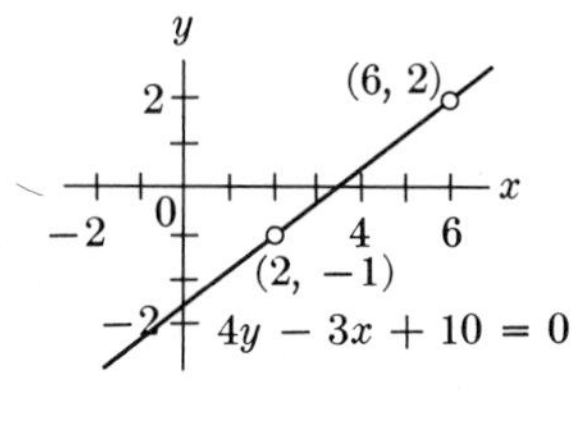

Figure 20-12

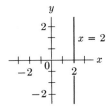

Figure 20-13

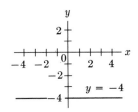

Figure 20-14

A line parallel to the x-axis has a slope of 0. From Eq. (20-6), we can find its equation to be $y = y_1$. To keep the same form as Eq. (20-7), we normally write this as

$$y = b. \tag{20-8}$$

Example C.   The line $x = 2$ is a line parallel to the y-axis and two units to the right of it. This line is shown in Fig. 20-13.

Example D.   The line $y = -4$ is a line parallel to the x-axis and 4 units below it. This line is shown in Fig. 20-14.

If we choose the special point $(0, b)$, which is the y-intercept of the line, as the point to use in Eq. (20-6), we have

$$y - b = m(x - 0)$$

or

$$y = mx + b. \tag{20-9}$$

Equation (20-9) is known as the *slope-intercept* form of the equation of a straight line. Its usefulness lies in the fact that once we find the equation of a line and then write it in slope-intercept form, we know that the slope of the line is the coefficient of the x-term and that it crosses the y-axis with the coordinate indicated by the constant term.

Example E.   Find the slope of the $2y + 4x - 5 = 0$.
  We write this equation in slope-intercept form:

$$2y = -4x + 5 \quad \text{or} \quad y = -2x + \tfrac{5}{2}.$$

Thus the coefficient of x in this form is -2, which means that the slope is -2.

From Eqs. (20-6) and (20-9), and from the examples of this section, we see that the equation of the straight line has certain characteristics: we have a term in y, a term in x, and a constant term if we simplify as much as possible. This form is represented by the equation

$$Ax + By + C = 0, \tag{20-10}$$

which is known as the *general form* of the equation of the straight line. We have seen this form before in Chapter 4. Now we have shown why it represents a straight line.

Example F.   What are the intercepts of the line $3x - 4y - 12 = 0$?

We know that the intercepts of a curve are those points where it crosses each of the axes. At the point where any curve crosses the x-axis, the y-coordinate must be 0. Thus, by letting $y = 0$ in the equation above, we solve for x, and obtain $x = 4$. Hence one intercept is $(4, 0)$. By letting $x = 0$, we find the other intercept as $(0, -3)$.

In many physical situations a linear relationship exists between variables. A few examples of situations where such relationships exist are between (1) the amount a spring stretches and the force applied, (2) the change in electrical resistance and the change in temperature, (3) the force applied to an object and the resulting acceleration, and (4) the pressure at a certain point within a liquid and the depth of the point. The following example illustrates the use of a straight line in dealing with an applied problem.

Example G.   Under the condition of constant acceleration, the velocity of an object varies linearly with the time. If after 1 sec a certain object has a velocity of 40 ft/sec, and 3 sec later it has a velocity of 55 ft/sec, find the equation relating the velocity and time, and graph this equation. From the graph determine the initial velocity (the velocity when $t = 0$) and the velocity after 6 sec.

If we treat the velocity v as the dependent variable, and the time t as the independent variable, the slope of the straight line is

$$m = \frac{v_2 - v_1}{t_2 - t_1}.$$

Using the information given in the problem, we have

$$m = \frac{55 - 40}{4 - 1} = 5.$$

Then, using the point-slope form of the equation of a straight line, we have $v - 40 = 5(t - 1)$, or $v = 5t + 35$, which is the required equation (see Fig. 20-15). For purposes of graphing the line, the values given are sufficient. Of course, there is no need to include negative values of t, since these have no physical meaning. From the graph we see that the line crosses the v-axis at 35. This means that the initial velocity is 35 ft/sec. Also, when $t = 6$ we see that $v = 65$ ft/sec.

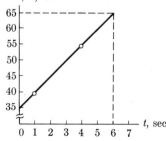

Figure 20-15

Exercises

In Exercises 1 through 16 find the equation of each of the lines with the given properties.

1. Passes through $(-3, 8)$ with a slope of 4
2. Passes through $(-2, -1)$ with a slope of -2
3. Passes through $(-2, -5)$ and $(4, 2)$
4. Passes through $(-3, -5)$ and $(-2, 3)$
5. Passes through $(1, 3)$ and has an inclination of $45°$
6. Has a y-intercept of -2 and an inclination of $120°$
7. Passes through $(6, -3)$ and is parallel to the x-axis
8. Passes through $(-4, -2)$ and is perpendicular to the x-axis
9. Is parallel to the y-axis and is 3 units to the left of it
10. Is parallel to the x-axis and is 5 units below it
11. Has an x-intercept of 4 and a y-intercept of -6
12. Has an x-intercept of -3 and a slope of 2
13. Is perpendicular to a line with a slope of 3 and passes through $(1, -2)$
14. Is perpendicular to a line with a slope of -4 and has a y-intercept of 3
15. Is perpendicular to the line joining $(4, 2)$ and $(3, -5)$ and passes through $(4, 2)$
16. Is parallel to the line $2y - 6x - 5 = 0$, and passes through $(-4, -5)$

In Exercises 17 and 18 draw the lines with the given equations.

17. $4x - y = 7$
18. $2x - 3y - 6 = 0$

In Exercises 19 through 22 reduce the equations to slope-intercept form and determine the slope and y-intercept.

19. $3x - 2y - 1 = 0$
20. $4x + 2y - 5 = 0$
21. $5x - 2y + 5 = 0$
22. $6x - 3y - 4 = 0$

In Exercises 23 and 24 determine the value of k.

23. What must be the value of k if the lines $4x - ky = 6$ and $6x + 3y + 2 = 0$ are to be parallel?
24. What must k equal in Exercise 23, if the given lines are to be perpendicular?

In Exercises 25 and 26 show that the given lines are perpendicular.

25. $6x - 3y - 2 = 0$ and $x + 2y - 4 = 0$
26. $4x - y + 2 = 0$ and $2x + 8y - 1 = 0$

In Exercises 27 and 28 find the equations of the indicated lines.

27. Find the equation of the line with a slope of -3 which also passes through the intersection of the lines $5x - y = 6$ and $x + y = 12$.
28. Find the equation of the line which passes through the point of intersection of $2x + y - 3 = 0$ and $x - y - 3 = 0$ and through the point $(4, -3)$.

In Exercises 29 through 37 some applications and methods involving straight lines are shown.

29. Within certain limits, the amount which a spring stretches varies linearly with the amount of force applied. If a spring whose natural length is 15 in. stretches 2 in. when 3 lb of force are applied, find the equation relating the length of the spring and the applied force.

30. The electric resistance of a certain resistor increases by 0.005 ohm for every increase of 1°C. Given that its resistance is 2.000 ohms at 0°C, find the equation relating the resistance and temperature. From the equation find the resistance when the temperature is 50°C.

31. The amount of heat required to raise the temperature of water varies linearly with the increase in temperature. However, a certain quantity of heat is required to change ice (at 0°C) into water without a change in temperature. An experiment is performed with 10 gm of ice at 0°C. It is found that it requires 1000 cal to change it into water at 20°C. Another 300 cal is required to warm the water to 50°C. How many calories were required to melt the ice at 0°C into water at 0°C?

32. The pressure at a point below the surface of a body of water varies linearly with the depth of the water. If the pressure at a depth of 1000 cm is 1.99×10^6 dynes/cm² and the pressure at a depth of 3000 cm is 3.95×10^6 dynes/cm², what is the pressure at the surface? (This is the atmospheric pressure of the air above the water.)

33. Sometimes it is desirable to treat a nonlinear function as a linear function. For example, if $y = 2 + 3x^2$, this can be plotted as a straight line by plotting y versus x^2. A table of values for this graph is

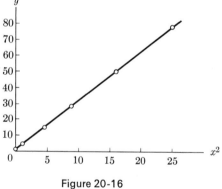

x	0	1	2	3	4	5
x^2	0	1	4	9	16	25
y	2	5	14	29	50	77

and the graph appears in Fig. 20-16. Using this method, sketch the function $C = 10/E$ as a linear function. That is, plot C versus $1/E$. This is the equation between the voltage across a capacitor and the capacitance, assuming the charge on the capacitor is constant.

Figure 20-16

34. Another method of treating a nonlinear function as a linear one is to use logarithms. In Section 12-8 we noted that curves plotted on logarithmic and semilogarithmic paper often come out as straight lines. Since distances corresponding to log y and log x are plotted automatically if the graph is logarithmic in the respective directions, many nonlinear functions are linear when plotted on this paper. A function of the form $y = ax^n$ is straight when plotted on logarithmic paper, since log $y = \log a + n \log x$ is in the form of a straight line. The variables are log y and log x; the slope can be found from $(\log y - \log a)/\log x = n$, and the intercept is a. (To get the slope from the graph, it is necessary to measure vertical and horizontal distances between two points. The log y intercept is found where log $x = 0$, and this occurs when $x = 1$.) Plot $y = 3x^4$ on logarithmic paper to verify this analysis.

35. A function of the form $y = a(b^x)$ is a straight line on semilogarithmic paper, since $\log y = \log a + x \log b$ is in the form of a straight line. The variables are $\log y$ and x, the slope is $\log b$, and the intercept is a. [To get the slope from the graph, we must calculate $(\log y - \log a)/x$ for some set of values x and y. The intercept is read directly off the graph where $x = 0$.] Plot $y = 3(2^x)$ on semilogarithmic paper to verify this analysis.

36. If experimental data is plotted on logarithmic paper and the points lie on a straight line, it is possible to determine the function (see Exercise 34). The following data comes from an experiment to determine the functional relation between the tension in a string and the velocity of a wave in the string. From the graph on logarithmic paper, determine v as a function of T.

v (cm/sec)	1600	3200	4530	5540	6400
T (10^4 dynes)	1.00	4.00	8.00	12.0	16.0

37. If experimental data are plotted on semilogarithmic paper, and the points lie on a straight line, it is possible to determine the function (see Exercise 35). The following data come from an experiment designed to determine the relationship between the voltage across an inductor and the time, after the switch is opened. Determine v as a function of t.

v (volts)	40	15	5.6	2.2	0.8
t (10^{-2} sec)	0	2	4	6	8

20-3 The circle

We have found that we can obtain a general equation which represents a straight line by considering a fixed point on the line and then a general point $P(x, y)$ which can represent any other point on the same line. Mathematically we can state this as "the line is the *locus* of a point $P(x, y)$ which *moves* along the line." That is, the point $P(x, y)$ can be considered as a variable point which moves along the line.

In this way we can define a number of important curves. The *circle* is defined as the locus of a point $P(x, y)$ which moves so that it is always equidistant from a fixed point. This fixed distance we call the radius, and the fixed point is called the center of the circle. Thus, using this definition, calling the fixed point (h, k) and the radius r, we have

$$\sqrt{(x - h)^2 + (y - k)^2} = r$$

or, by squaring both sides, we have

$$(x - h)^2 + (y - k)^2 = r^2. \quad (20\text{-}11)$$

Equation (20-11) is called the *standard equation* of a circle with center at (h, k) and radius r (Fig. 20-17).

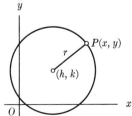

Figure 20-17

Example A. The equation $(x - 1)^2 + (y + 2)^2 = 16$ represents a circle with center at $(1, -2)$ and a radius of 4. We determine these values by considering the equation to be in the form of Eq. (20-11) as $(x - 1)^2 + (y - (-2))^2 = 4^2$. Note carefully the way in which we find the y-coordinate of the center. This circle is shown in Fig. 20-18.

If the center of the circle is at the origin, which means that the coordinates of the center are $(0, 0)$, the equation of the circle becomes

$$x^2 + y^2 = r^2. \tag{20-12}$$

A circle of this type clearly exhibits an important property of the graphs of many equations. It is *symmetrical* to the x-axis and also to the y-axis. Symmetry to the x-axis can be thought of as meaning that the lower half of the curve is a reflection of the upper half, and conversely. It can be shown that *if $-y$ can replace y in an equation without changing the equation, the graph of the equation will be symmetrical to the x-axis.* Symmetry to the y-axis has a similar meaning, so *if $-x$ can replace x in the equation without changing the equation, the graph is symmetrical to the y-axis.*

Example B. The equation of the circle with its center at the origin and with a radius of 6 is $x^2 + y^2 = 36$.

The symmetry of this circle can be shown analytically by the substitutions mentioned above. If we replace x by $-x$, we obtain $(-x)^2 + y^2 = 36$. Since $(-x)^2 = x^2$, the equation can be written as $x^2 + y^2 = 36$. Since this substitution did not change the equation, the graph is symmetrical to the y-axis.

Replacing y by $-y$, we obtain $x^2 + (-y)^2 = 36$, which is the same as $x^2 + y^2 = 36$. This means that the curve is symmetrical to the x-axis. The circle is shown in Fig. 20-19.

Example C. Find the equation of the circle with center at $(2, 1)$ and which passes through $(4, 8)$.

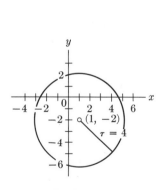

Figure 20-18

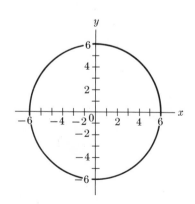

Figure 20-19

In Eq. (20-11), we can determine the equation if we can find h, k, and r for this circle. From the given information, $h = 2$ and $k = 1$. To find r, we use the fact that *all points on the circle must satisfy the equation of the circle*. The point (4, 8) must satisfy Eq. (20-11), with $h = 2$ and $k = 1$. Thus $(4 - 2)^2 + (8 - 1)^2 = r^2$. From this relation we find $r^2 = 53$. The equation of the circle is

$$(x - 2)^2 + (y - 1)^2 = 53.$$

This circle is shown in Fig. 20-20.

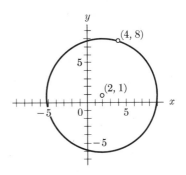

Figure 20-20

If we multiply out each of the terms in Eq. (20-11), we may combine the resulting terms to obtain

$$x^2 - 2hx + h^2 + y^2 - 2ky + k^2 = r^2,$$
$$x^2 + y^2 - 2hx - 2ky + (h^2 + k^2 - r^2) = 0. \qquad (20\text{-}13)$$

Since each of h, k, and r is constant for any given circle, the coefficients of x and y and the term within parentheses in Eq. (20-13) are constants. Equation (20-13) can then be written as

$$x^2 + y^2 + Dx + Ey + F = 0. \qquad (20\text{-}14)$$

Equation (20-14) is called the *general equation* of the circle. It tells us that any equation which can be written in that form will represent a circle.

Example D. Find the center and radius of the circle

$$x^2 + y^2 - 6x + 8y - 24 = 0.$$

We can find this information if we can write the given equation in standard form. To do so, we must complete the square in the x-terms and also in the y-terms. This is done by first writing the equation in the form

$$(x^2 - 6x \quad) + (y^2 + 8y \quad) = 24.$$

To complete the square of the x-terms, we take half of 6, which is 3, square it, and add the result, 9, to each side of the equation. In the same way, we complete the square of the y-terms by adding 16 to each side of the equation, which gives

$$(x^2 - 6x + 9) + (y^2 + 8y + 16)$$
$$= 24 + 9 + 16,$$
$$(x - 3)^2 + (y + 4)^2 = 49.$$

Thus the center is (3, −4), and the radius is 7 (see Fig. 20-21).

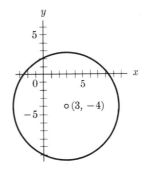

Figure 20-21

Example E.   The equation $3x^2 + 3y^2 + 6x - 20 = 0$ can be seen to represent a circle by writing it in general form. This is done by dividing through by 3. In this way we have

$$x^2 + y^2 + 2x - \tfrac{20}{3} = 0.$$

To determine the center and radius for this circle, we write the equation in standard form and then complete the necessary squares. This leads to

$$(x^2 + 2x + 1) + y^2 = \tfrac{20}{3} + 1,$$
$$(x + 1)^2 + y^2 = \tfrac{23}{3}.$$

Thus the center is $(-1, 0)$; the radius is $\sqrt{23/3} = 2.77$ (see Fig. 20-22).

We can also see that this circle is symmetric to the x-axis, but it is not symmetric to the y-axis. If we replace y by $-y$, the equation does not change, but if we replace x by $-x$, the $6x$ term in the original equation becomes negative, and equation *does* change.

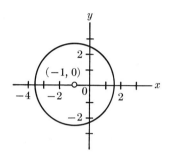

Figure 20-22

Exercises

In Exercises 1 through 4 determine the center and radius of each circle.

1. $(x - 2)^2 + (y - 1)^2 = 25$ 2. $(x - 3)^2 + (y + 4)^2 = 49$
3. $(x + 1)^2 + y^2 = 4$ 4. $x^2 + (y + 6)^2 = 64$

In Exercises 5 through 16 find the equation of each of the circles from the given information.

5. Center at $(0, 0)$, radius 3   6. Center at $(0, 0)$, radius 1
7. Center at $(2, 2)$, radius 4   8. Center at $(0, 2)$, radius 2
9. Center at $(-2, 5)$, radius $\sqrt{5}$ 10. Center at $(-3, -5)$, radius 8
11. Center at $(2, 1)$, passes through $(4, -1)$
12. Center at $(-1, 4)$, passes through $(-2, 3)$
13. Center at $(-3, 5)$, tangent to the x-axis
14. Tangent to both axes, radius 4, and in the second quadrant
15. Center on the line $5x = 2y$, radius 5, tangent to the x-axis
16. The points $(3, 8)$ and $(-3, 0)$ are the ends of a diameter

In Exercises 17 through 24 determine the center and radius of each circle. Sketch each circle.

17. $x^2 + y^2 - 25 = 0$ 18. $x^2 + y^2 - 9 = 0$
19. $x^2 + y^2 - 2x - 8 = 0$ 20. $x^2 + y^2 - 4x - 6y - 12 = 0$
21. $x^2 + y^2 + 8x - 10y - 8 = 0$ 22. $x^2 + y^2 + 8x + 6y = 0$
23. $2x^2 + 2y^2 - 4x - 8y - 1 = 0$ 24. $3x^2 + 3y^2 - 12x + 4 = 0$

In Exercises 25 through 31 find the indicated quantities.

25. Determine where the circle $x^2 - 6x + y^2 - 7 = 0$ crosses the x-axis.

26. Find the points of intersection of the circle $x^2 + y^2 - x - 3y = 0$ and the line $y = x - 1$.

27. Find the locus of a point $P(x, y)$ which moves so that its distance from $(2, 4)$ is twice its distance from $(0, 0)$. Describe the locus.

28. Find the equation of the locus of a point $P(x, y)$ which moves so that the line joining it and $(2, 0)$ is always perpendicular to the line joining it and $(-2, 0)$. Describe the locus.

29. If an electrically charged particle enters a magnetic field of flux density B with a velocity v at right angles to the field, the path of the particle is a circle. The radius of the path is given by $R = mv/Bq$, where m is the mass of the particle and q is its charge. If a proton ($m = 1.67 \times 10^{-27}$ kg, $q = 1.60 \times 10^{-19}$ coul) enters a magnetic field of flux density 1.5 webers/m^2 with a velocity of 10^8 m/sec, find the equation of the path of the proton. (The fact that a charged particle travels in a circular path in a magnetic field is an important basis for the construction of a cyclotron.)

30. For a constant (magnitude) impedance and capacitive reactance, sketch the graph of resistance versus inductive reactance (see Section 11-7).

31. A cylindrical oil tank, 4 ft in diameter, is on its side. A circular hole, with center 18 in. below the center of the end of the tank, has been drilled in the end of the tank. If the radius of the hole is 3 in., what is the equation of the circle of the end of the tank and the equation of the circle of the hole? Use the center of the end of the tank as the origin.

20-4 The parabola

Another important curve is the parabola. We have come across this curve several times in the past. In this section we shall find the form of the equation of the parabola and see that this is a familiar form.

The parabola is defined as the locus of a point $P(x, y)$ which moves so that it is always equidistant from a given line and a given point. The given line is called the *directrix*, and the given point is called the *focus*. The line through the focus which is perpendicular to the directrix is called the *axis* of the parabola. The point midway between the directrix and focus is the *vertex* of the parabola. Using the definition, we shall find the equation of the parabola for which the focus is the point $(p, 0)$ and the directrix is the line $x = -p$. By choosing the focus and directrix in this manner, we shall be able to find a general representation of the equation of a parabola with its vertex at the origin.

According to the definition of the parabola, the distance from a point $P(x, y)$ on the parabola to the focus $(p, 0)$ must equal the distance from $P(x, y)$ to the directrix $x = -p$. The distance from P to the focus can be found by use of the distance formula. The distance from P to the directrix is the perpendicular distance, and this can be found as the distance between two points on a line parallel to the x-axis. These distances are indicated in Fig. 20-23. Thus we have

$$\sqrt{(x-p)^2 + (y-0)^2} = x + p.$$

Squaring both sides of this equation, we have

$$(x-p)^2 + y^2 = (x+p)^2$$

or

$$x^2 - 2px + p^2 + y^2 = x^2 + 2px + p^2.$$

Simplifying, we obtain

$$y^2 = 4px. \qquad (20\text{-}15)$$

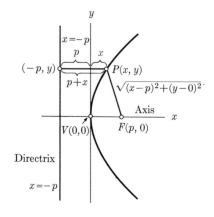

Figure 20-23

Equation (20-15) is called the *standard form* of the equation of a parabola with its axis along the x-axis and the vertex at the origin. Its symmetry to the x-axis can be proven since $(-y)^2 = 4px$ is the same as $y^2 = 4px$.

Example A.   Find the coordinates of the focus, the equation of the directrix, and sketch the graph of the parabola $y^2 = 12x$.

From the form of the equation, we know that the vertex is at the origin (Fig. 20-24). The coefficient of 12 tells us that the focus is (3, 0), since $p = \frac{12}{4}$ [note that the coefficient of x in Eq. (20-15) is $4p$]. Also, this means that the directrix is the line $x = -3$.

Example B.   If the focus is to the left of the origin, with the directrix an equal distance to the right, the coefficient of the x-term will be negative. This tells us that the parabola opens to the left, rather than to the right, as is the case when the focus is to the right of the origin. For example, the parabola $y^2 = -8x$ has its vertex at the origin, its focus at $(-2, 0)$, and the line $x = 2$ as its directrix. This is consistent with Eq. (20-15), in that $4p = -8$, or $p = -2$. The parabola opens to the left as shown in Fig. 20-25.

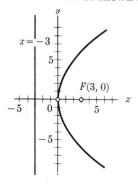

Figure 20-24

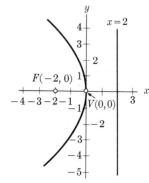

Figure 20-25

If we chose the focus as the point $(0, p)$ and the directrix as the line $y = -p$, we would find that the resulting equation is

$$x^2 = 4py. \tag{20-16}$$

This is the standard form of the equation of a parabola with the y-axis as its axis and the vertex at the origin. Its symmetry to the y-axis can be proven since $(-x)^2 = 4py$ is the same as $x^2 = 4py$. We note that the difference between this equation and Eq. (20-15) is that x is squared and y appears to the first power in Eq. (20-16), rather than the reverse, as in Eq. (20-15).

Example C.   The parabola $x^2 = 4y$ has its vertex at the origin, focus at the point $(0, 1)$ and its directrix the line $y = -1$. The graph is shown in Fig. 20-26, and we see that in this case that the parabola opens up.

Example D.   The parabola $x^2 = -6y$ has its vertex at the origin, its focus at the point $(0, -\frac{3}{2})$, and its directrix the line $y = \frac{3}{2}$. This parabola opens down, as Fig. 20-27 shows.

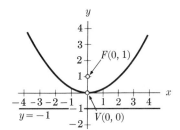

Figure 20-26

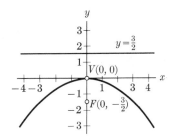

Figure 20-27

Equations (20-15) and (20-16) give us the general form of the equation of a parabola with its vertex at the origin and its focus on one of the coordinate axes. The following example illustrates the use of the definition of the parabola to find the equation of a parabola which has its vertex at a point other than at the origin.

Example E.   Using the definition of the parabola, determine the equation of the parabola with its focus at $(2, 3)$ and its directrix the line $y = -1$ (see Fig. 20-28).

Choosing a general point $P(x, y)$ on the parabola, and equating the distances from this point to $(2, 3)$ and to the line $y = -1$, we have

$$\sqrt{(x - 2)^2 + (y - 3)^2} = y + 1.$$

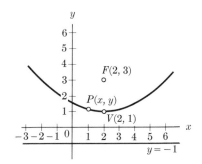

Figure 20-28

Squaring both sides of this equation and simplifying, we have

$$(x - 2)^2 + (y - 3)^2 = (y + 1)^2,$$
$$x^2 - 4x + 4 + y^2 - 6y + 9 = y^2 + 2y + 1,$$

or

$$8y = 12 - 4x + x^2.$$

When we see it in this form, we note that this type of equation has appeared numerous times previously in earlier chapters. The x-term and the constant (12 in this case) are characteristic of a parabola which does not have its vertex at the origin if the directrix is parallel to the x-axis.

Thus we can conclude that a parabola is characterized by the presence of the square of either (but not both) x or y, and a first-power term in the other. In this way we can recognize a parabola by inspecting the equation.

Exercises

In Exercises 1 through 12 determine the coordinates of the focus and the equation of the directrix of each of the given parabolas. Sketch each curve.

1. $y^2 = 4x$	2. $y^2 = 16x$	3. $y^2 = -4x$	4. $y^2 = -16x$
5. $x^2 = 8y$	6. $x^2 = 10y$	7. $x^2 = -4y$	8. $x^2 = -12y$
9. $y^2 = 2x$	10. $x^2 = 14y$	11. $y = x^2$	12. $x = 3y^2$

In Exercises 13 through 20 find the equations of the parabolas satisfying the given conditions.

13. Focus $(3, 0)$, directrix $x = -3$ 14. Focus $(-2, 0)$, directrix $x = 2$
15. Focus $(0, 4)$, vertex $(0, 0)$ 16. Focus $(-3, 0)$, vertex $(0, 0)$
17. Vertex $(0, 0)$, directrix $y = -1$ 18. Vertex $(0, 0)$, directrix $y = \frac{1}{2}$
19. Vertex at $(0, 0)$, axis along the y-axis, passes through $(-1, 8)$
20. Vertex at $(0, 0)$, axis along the x-axis, passes through $(2, -1)$

In Exercises 21 through 24 use the definition of the parabola to find the equations of the parabolas satisfying the given conditions. Sketch each curve.

21. Focus $(6, 1)$, directrix $x = 0$ 22. Focus $(1, -4)$, directrix $x = 2$
23. Focus $(1, 1)$, vertex $(1, 3)$ 24. Vertex $(-2, -4)$, directrix $x = 3$

In Exercises 25 through 30 find the indicated quantities.

25. In calculus it can be shown that a light ray emanating from the focus of a parabola will be reflected off parallel to the axis of the parabola. Suppose that a light ray from the focus of the parabola $y^2 = 8x$ strikes the parabola at the point $(2, 4)$. What is the equation of the reflected light ray?

26. The rate of development of heat H (measured in watts) in a resistor R (resistance measured in ohms) of an electric circuit is given by $H = Ri^2$, where i is the current (measured in amperes) in the resistor. Sketch the graph of H versus i, if $R = 6$ ohms.

27. The period T (measured in seconds) of the oscillation for resonance in an electric circuit is given by $T = 2\pi\sqrt{LC}$, where L is the inductance (in henrys) and C is

the capacitance (in farads). Sketch the graph of the period versus capacitance for a constant inductance of 1 henry. Assume values of C from 10^{-6} farad to 250×10^{-6} farad, for this is a common range of values.

28. The vertical position of a projectile is given by the equation $y = 120t - 16t^2$, and its horizontal position is given by $x = 60t$. By eliminating t between the equations, show that the path of the projectile is a parabola. Sketch the path of this parabola for the length of time it would need to strike the ground, assuming level terrain.

29. Under certain conditions, a cable which hangs between two supports can be closely approximated as being parabolic. Assuming that this cable hangs in the shape of a parabola, find its equation if a point 10 ft horizontally from its lowest point is 1 ft above its lowest point. Choose the lowest point as the origin of the coordinate system.

30. Under certain circumstances, the maximum power P in an electric circuit varies as the square of the voltage of the source E_0 and inversely as the internal resistance R_i of the source. If 10 watts is the maximum power for a source of 2 volts and internal resistance of 0.1 ohm, sketch the graph of P versus E_0, if R_i remains constant.

20-5 The ellipse

The next important curve we shall discuss is the ellipse. The ellipse is defined as the locus of a point $P(x, y)$ which moves so that the sum of its distances from two fixed points is constant. These two fixed points are called the *foci* of the ellipse. Letting this fixed sum equal $2a$ and the foci be the points $(c, 0)$ and $(-c, 0)$, we have (see Fig. 20-29) from the definition of the ellipse

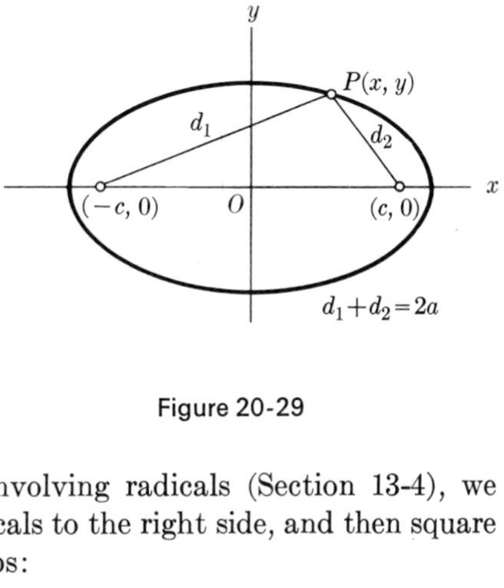

$$\sqrt{(x-c)^2 + y^2} + \sqrt{(x+c)^2 + y^2} = 2a.$$

Figure 20-29

From the section on solving equations involving radicals (Section 13-4), we find that we should remove one of the radicals to the right side, and then square each side. Thus we have the following steps:

$$\sqrt{(x+c)^2 + y^2} = 2a - \sqrt{(x-c)^2 + y^2},$$

$$(x+c)^2 + y^2 = 4a^2 - 4a\sqrt{(x-c)^2 + y^2} + (\sqrt{(x-c)^2 + y^2})^2,$$

$$x^2 + 2cx + c^2 + y^2 = 4a^2 - 4a\sqrt{(x-c)^2 + y^2} + x^2 - 2cx + c^2 + y^2,$$

$$4a\sqrt{(x-c)^2 + y^2} = 4a^2 - 4cx,$$

$$a\sqrt{(x-c)^2 + y^2} = a^2 - cx,$$

$$a^2(x^2 - 2cx + c^2 + y^2) = a^4 - 2a^2cx + c^2x^2,$$

$$(a^2 - c^2)x^2 + a^2y^2 = a^2(a^2 - c^2).$$

At this point we define (and the usefulness of this definition will be shown presently) $a^2 - c^2 = b^2$. This substitution gives us

$$b^2x^2 + a^2y^2 = a^2b^2.$$

Dividing through by a^2b^2, we have

$$\frac{x^2}{a^2} + \frac{y^2}{b^2} = 1. \tag{20-17}$$

If we let $y = 0$, we find that the x-intercepts are $(-a, 0)$ and $(a, 0)$. We see that the distance $2a$, originally chosen as the sum of the distances in the derivation of Eq. (20-17), is the distance between the x-intercepts. These two points are known as the *vertices* of the ellipse, and the line between them is known as the *major axis* of the ellipse. Thus, a is called the *semi-major axis*.

If we now let $x = 0$, we find the y-intercepts to be $(0, -b)$ and $(0, b)$. The line joining these two intercepts is called the *minor axis* of the ellipse (Fig. 20-30) which means b is called the semi-minor axis. The point $(0, b)$ is on the ellipse, and is also equidistant from $(-c, 0)$ and $(c, 0)$. Since the sum of the distances from these points to $(0, b)$ equals $2a$, the distance from $(c, 0)$ to $(0, b)$ must be a. Thus we have a right triangle formed by line segments of lengths a, b, and c, with a as the hypotenuse. From this we have the relation

$$a^2 = b^2 + c^2 \tag{20-18}$$

between the distances a, b, and c. This equation also shows us why b was defined as it was in the derivation.

Equation (20-17) is called the *standard equation* of the ellipse with its major axis along the x-axis and its center at the origin.

If we choose points on the y-axis as the foci, the standard equation of the ellipse, with its center at the origin and its major axis along the y-axis, is

$$\frac{y^2}{a^2} + \frac{x^2}{b^2} = 1. \tag{20-19}$$

In this case the vertices are $(0, a)$ and $(0, -a)$, and the foci are $(0, c)$ and $(0, -c)$.

The symmetry of the ellipses given by Eqs. (20-17) and (20-19) to each of the axes can be proven since each of x and y can be replaced by its negative in these equations without changing the equations.

Example A.   The ellipse

$$\frac{x^2}{25} + \frac{y^2}{9} = 1$$

has vertices at $(5, 0)$ and $(-5, 0)$. Its minor axis extends from $(0, 3)$ to $(0, -3)$, as we see in Fig. 20-31. This information is directly obtainable from this form of the equation, since the 25 tells us that $a^2 = 25$, or $a = 5$. In the same way we have $b = 3$. Since we know both a^2 and b^2, we can find c^2 from the relation $c^2 = a^2 - b^2$. Thus $c^2 = 16$, or $c = 4$. This in turn tells us that the foci of this ellipse are at $(4, 0)$ and $(-4, 0)$.

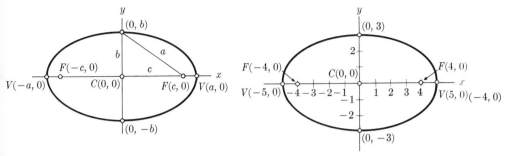

Figure 20-30   Figure 20-31

Example B.   The ellipse

$$\frac{x^2}{4} + \frac{y^2}{9} = 1$$

has vertices at $(0, 3)$ and $(0, -3)$. The minor axis extends from $(2, 0)$ to $(-2, 0)$. This we can find directly from the equation, since $a^2 = 9$ and $b^2 = 4$. One might ask how we chose $a^2 = 9$ in this example and $a^2 = 25$ in the preceding example. Since $a^2 = b^2 + c^2$, a is always larger than b. Thus we can tell which axis (x or y) the major axis is along by seeing which number (in the denominator) is larger, when the equation is written in standard form. The larger one stands for a^2. In this example, the foci are $(0, \sqrt{5})$ and $(0, -\sqrt{5})$ (see Fig. 20-32).

Example C.   Find the coordinates of the vertices, the ends of the minor axis, and the foci of the ellipse $4x^2 + 16y^2 = 64$.

This equation must be put in standard form first, which we do by dividing through by 64. When this is done, we obtain

$$\frac{x^2}{16} + \frac{y^2}{4} = 1.$$

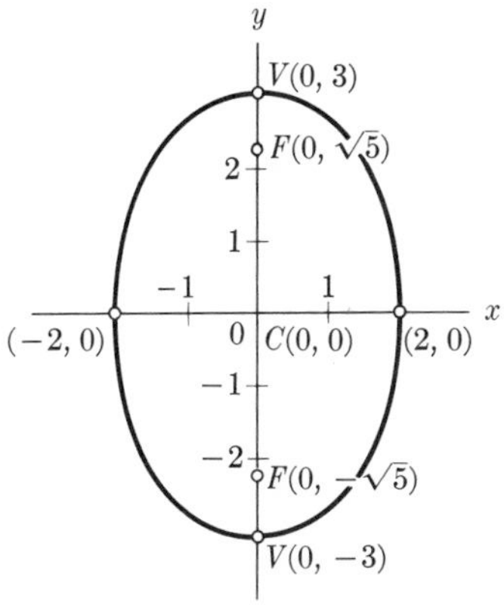

Figure 20-32

Thus $a = 4$, $b = 2$, and $c = 2\sqrt{3}$. The vertices are at $(4, 0)$ and $(-4, 0)$. The ends of the minor axis are $(0, 2)$ and $(0, -2)$ and the foci are $(2\sqrt{3}, 0)$ and $(-2\sqrt{3}, 0)$ (see Fig. 20-33).

Example D.   Find the equation of the ellipse for which the center is at the origin, the major axis is along the y-axis, the minor axis is 6 units long, and there are 8 units between foci.

Directly we know that $2b = 6$, or $b = 3$. Also $2c = 8$, or $c = 4$. Thus we find that $a = 5$. Since the major axis is along the y-axis, we have the equation

$$\frac{y^2}{25} + \frac{x^2}{9} = 1.$$

This ellipse is shown in Fig. 20-34.

Equations (20-17) and (20-19) give us the standard form of the equation of an ellipse with its center at the origin and its foci on one of the coordinate axes. The following example illustrates the use of the definition of the ellipse to find the equation of an ellipse with its center at a point other than the origin.

Example E.   Using the definition, find the equation of the ellipse with foci at $(1, 3)$ and $(9, 3)$, with a major axis of 10.

Using the same method as in the derivation of Eq. (20-17), we have the following steps. (Remember, the sum of distances in the definition equals the length of the major axis.)

$$\sqrt{(x - 1)^2 + (y - 3)^2} + \sqrt{(x - 9)^2 + (y - 3)^2} = 10$$

$$\sqrt{(x - 1)^2 + (y - 3)^2} = 10 - \sqrt{(x - 9)^2 + (y - 3)^2}$$

$$(x - 1)^2 + (y - 3)^2 = 100 - 20\sqrt{(x-9)^2+(y-3)^2}$$

$$+ (\sqrt{(x - 9)^2 + (y - 3)^2})^2$$

$$x^2 - 2x + 1 + y^2 - 6y + 9 = 100 - 20\sqrt{(x-9)^2+(y-3)^2}$$

$$+ x^2 - 18x + 81 + y^2 - 6y + 9$$

$$20\sqrt{(x - 9)^2 + (y - 3)^2} = 180 - 16x$$

$$5\sqrt{(x - 9)^2 + (y - 3)^2} = 45 - 4x$$

$$25(x^2 - 18x + 81 + y^2 - 6y + 9) = 2025 - 360x + 16x^2$$

$$25x^2 - 450x + 2250 + 25y^2 - 150y = 2025 - 360x + 16x^2$$

$$9x^2 - 90x + 25y^2 - 150y + 225 = 0$$

The additional x- and y-terms are characteristic of the equation of an ellipse whose center is not at the origin (see Fig. 20-35).

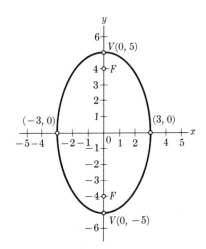

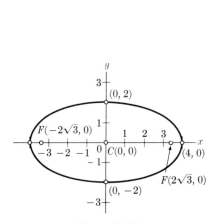

Figure 20-33

Figure 20-34

We can conclude that the equation of an ellipse is characterized by the presence of both an x^2- and a y^2-term, having different coefficients (in value but not in sign). The difference between the equation of an ellipse and that of a circle is that the coefficients of the squared terms in the equation of the circle are the same, whereas those of the ellipse differ.

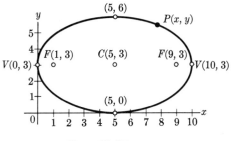

Figure 20-35

Exercises

In Exercises 1 through 12 find the coordinates of the vertices and foci of the given ellipses. Sketch each curve.

1. $\dfrac{x^2}{4} + \dfrac{y^2}{1} = 1$

2. $\dfrac{x^2}{100} + \dfrac{y^2}{64} = 1$

3. $\dfrac{x^2}{25} + \dfrac{y^2}{36} = 1$

4. $\dfrac{x^2}{49} + \dfrac{y^2}{81} = 1$

5. $4x^2 + 9y^2 = 36$

6. $x^2 + 36y^2 = 144$

7. $49x^2 + 4y^2 = 196$

8. $25x^2 + y^2 = 25$

9. $8x^2 + y^2 = 16$

10. $2x^2 + 3y^2 = 6$

11. $4x^2 + 25y^2 = 25$

12. $9x^2 + 4y^2 = 9$

In Exercises 13 through 20 find the equations of the ellipses satisfying the given conditions. The center of each is at the origin.

13. Vertex $(15, 0)$, focus $(9, 0)$

14. Minor axis 8, vertex $(0, -5)$

15. Focus $(0, 2)$, major axis 6

16. Semi-minor axis 2, focus $(3, 0)$

17. Vertex $(8, 0)$, passes through $(2, 3)$

18. Focus $(0, 2)$, passes through $(-1, \sqrt{3})$
19. Passes through $(2, 2)$ and $(1, 4)$
20. Passes through $(-2, 2)$ and $(1, \sqrt{6})$

In Exercises 21 and 22 find the equations of the ellipses with the given properties by use of the definition of an ellipse.

21. Foci at $(-2, 1)$ and $(4, 1)$, a major axis of 10
22. Vertices at $(1, 5)$ and $(1, -1)$, foci at $(1, 4)$ and $(1, 0)$

In Exercises 23 through 26 solve the given problems.

23. The arch of a bridge across a stream is in the form of half an ellipse above the water level. If the span of the arch at water level is 100 ft and the maximum height of the arch above water level is 30 ft, what is the equation of the arch? Choose the origin of the coordinate system at the most convenient point.

24. An elliptical gear (Fig. 20-36) which rotates about its center is kept continually in mesh with a circular gear which is free to move horizontally. If the equation of the ellipse of the gear (with the origin of the coordinate system at its center) in its present position is $3x^2 + 7y^2 = 20$, how far does the center of the circular gear move going from one extreme position to the other? (Assume the units are inches.)

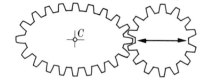

Figure 20-36

25. An artificial satellite of the earth has a minimum altitude of 500 mi and a maximum altitude of 2000 mi. If the path of the satellite about the earth is an ellipse with the center of the earth at one focus, what is the equation of its path? (Assume the radius of the earth is 4000 mi.)

26. An electric current is caused to flow in a loop of wire rotating in a magnetic field. In a study of this phenomenon, a piece of wire is cut into two pieces, one of which is bent into a circle and the other into a square. If the sum of areas of the circle and square is always π units, find the relation between the radius r of the circle and the side x of the square. Sketch the graph of r versus x.

20-6 The hyperbola

The final curve we shall discuss in detail is the hyperbola. The hyperbola is defined as the locus of a point $P(x, y)$ which moves so that the difference of the distances from two fixed points is a constant. These fixed points are the *foci* of the hyperbola. Assuming that the foci of the hyperbola are the points $(c, 0)$ and $(-c, 0)$ (see Fig. 20-37) and the constant difference is $2a$, we have

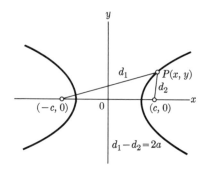

Figure 20-37

$$\sqrt{(x+c)^2 + y^2} - \sqrt{(x-c)^2 + y^2} = 2a.$$

Following the same procedure as in the preceding section, we find the equation of this hyperbola to be

$$\frac{x^2}{a^2} - \frac{y^2}{b^2} = 1. \tag{20-20}$$

When we derive this equation, we have a definition of the relation between a, b, and c which is different from that for the ellipse. This relation is

$$c^2 = a^2 + b^2. \tag{20-21}$$

An analysis of Eq. (20-20) will reveal the significance of a and b. First, by letting $y = 0$, we find that the x-intercepts are $(a, 0)$ and $(-a, 0)$, just as they are for the ellipse. These points are called the *vertices* of the hyperbola. By letting $x = 0$, we find that we have imaginary solutions for y, which means that there are no points on the curve which correspond to a value of $x = 0$.

To find the significance of b, we shall solve Eq. (20-20) for y in a particular form. First we have

$$\frac{y^2}{b^2} = \frac{x^2}{a^2} - 1$$

$$= \frac{x^2}{a^2} - \frac{a^2 x^2}{a^2 x^2}$$

$$= \frac{x^2}{a^2}\left(1 - \frac{a^2}{x^2}\right).$$

Multiplying through by b^2 and then taking the square root of each side, we have

$$y^2 = \frac{b^2 x^2}{a^2}\left(1 - \frac{a^2}{x^2}\right),$$

$$y = \pm\frac{bx}{a}\sqrt{(1 - a^2/x^2)}. \tag{20-22}$$

We note that, if large values of x are assumed in Eq. (20-22), the quantity under the radical becomes approximately 1. In fact, the larger x becomes, the nearer 1 this expression becomes, since the x^2 in the denominator of a^2/x^2 makes this term nearly zero. Thus, for large values of x, Eq. (20-22) is approximately

$$y = \pm bx/a. \tag{20-23}$$

Equation (20-23) can be seen to represent the equations for two straight lines, each of which passes through the origin. One has a slope of b/a and the other a slope of $-b/a$. These lines are called the *asymptotes* of the hyperbola. An asymptote is a line which a curve *approaches* as one of the variables *approaches* some particular value. The tangent curve also has asymptotes, as we can see in Fig. 9-17. We can designate this limiting procedure with notation introduced in Chapter 18, by saying that

$$y \to bx/a \quad \text{as} \quad x \to \infty.$$

Since straight lines are easily sketched, the easiest way to sketch a hyperbola is to draw its asymptotes and then to draw the hyperbola so that it comes closer and closer to these lines as x becomes larger numerically. To draw in the asymptotes, the usual procedure is to first draw a small rectangle, $2a$ by $2b$, with the origin in the center. Then straight lines are drawn through opposite vertices. These lines are the asymptotes (see Fig. 20-38). Thus we see that the significance of the value of b lies in the slope of the asymptotes of the hyperbola.

Equation (20-20) is called the *standard equation* of the hyperbola with its center at the origin. It has a *transverse axis* of length $2a$ along the x-axis and a *conjugate axis* of length $2b$ along the y-axis. This means that a represents the length of the semi-transverse axis, and b represents the length of the semi-conjugate axis. The relation between a, b, and c is given in Eq. (20-21).

If the transverse axis is along the y-axis and the conjugate axis is along the x-axis, the equation of a hyperbola with its center at the origin is

$$\frac{y^2}{a^2} - \frac{x^2}{b^2} = 1. \tag{20-24}$$

The symmetry of the hyperbolas given by Eqs. (20-20) and (20-24) to each of the axes can be proven since each of x and y can be replaced by its negative in these equations without changing the equations.

Example A.   The hyperbola

$$\frac{x^2}{16} - \frac{y^2}{9} = 1$$

has vertices at $(4, 0)$ and $(-4, 0)$. Its transverse axis extends from one vertex to the other. Its conjugate axis extends from $(0, 3)$ to $(0, -3)$. Since $c^2 = a^2 + b^2$, we find that $c = 5$, which means that the foci are the points $(5, 0)$ and $(-5, 0)$. Drawing in the rectangle and then the asymptotes (Fig. 20-39), we draw the hyperbola from each vertex toward the asymptotes. Thus the curve is sketched.

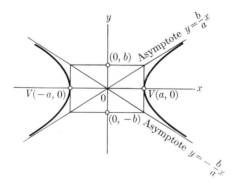

Figure 20-38

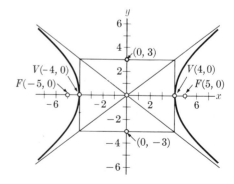

Figure 30-39

Example B. The hyperbola

$$\frac{y^2}{4} - \frac{x^2}{16} = 1$$

has vertices at $(0, 2)$ and $(0, -2)$. Its conjugate axis extends from $(4, 0)$ to $(-4, 0)$. The foci are $(0, 2\sqrt{5})$ and $(0, -2\sqrt{5})$. Since, with 1 on the right side of the equation, the y^2-term is the positive term, this hyperbola is in the form of Eq. (20-24). [Example A illustrates a hyperbola of the type of Eq. (20-20), since the x^2-term is the positive term.] Since $2a$ extends along the y-axis, we see that the equations of the asymptotes are $y = \pm(a/b)x$. This is not a contradiction of Eq. (20-23), but an extension of it for the case of a hyperbola with its transverse axis along the y-axis. The ratio a/b simply expresses the slope of the asymptote (see Fig. 20-40).

Example C. Find the coordinates of the vertices and foci of the hyperbola $4x^2 - 9y^2 = 36$.

First, by dividing through by 36, we can put this equation in standard form. Thus we have

$$\frac{x^2}{9} - \frac{y^2}{4} = 1.$$

The transverse axis is along the x-axis with vertices at $(3, 0)$ and $(-3, 0)$, since $c^2 = a^2 + b^2$ and $c = \sqrt{13}$. This means that the foci are at $(\sqrt{13}, 0)$ and $(-\sqrt{13}, 0)$ (see Fig. 20-41).

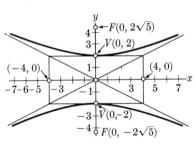

Figure 20-40

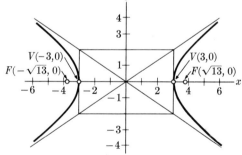

Figure 20-41

Example D. Find the equation of the hyperbola with its center at the origin, a vertex at $(3, 0)$, and which passes through $(5, \frac{4}{3})$.

When we know that the hyperbola has its center at the origin and a vertex at $(3, 0)$, we know that the standard form of its equation is given by Eq. (20-20). This also tells us that $a = 3$. By using the fact that the coordinates of the point $(5, \frac{4}{3})$ must satisfy the equation, we are able to find the value of b^2. Substituting, we have

$$\frac{25}{9} - \frac{(16/9)}{b^2} = 1,$$

from which we find $b^2 = 1$. Therefore the equation of the hyperbola is

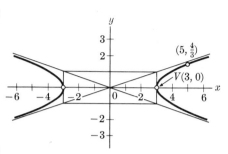

$$\frac{x^2}{9} - \frac{y^2}{1} = 1$$

or

$$x^2 - 9y^2 = 9.$$

This hyperbola is shown in Fig. 20-42.

Figure 20-42

Equations (20-20) and (20-24) give us the standard form of the equation of the hyperbola with its center at the origin and its foci on one of the coordinate axes. There is one other important equation form which represents a hyperbola, and that is

$$xy = c. \tag{20-25}$$

The asymptotes of this hyperbola are the coordinate axes, and the foci are on the line $y = x$, or on the line $y = -x$, if c is negative. The following example illustrates this type of hyperbola.

Example E. Plot the graph of the equation $xy = 4$.

We find the values in the following table, and then plot the appropriate points. Here it is permissible to use a limited number of points, since we know that the equation represents a hyperbola (Fig. 20-43). Thus, using $y = 4/x$, we obtain the values in the table.

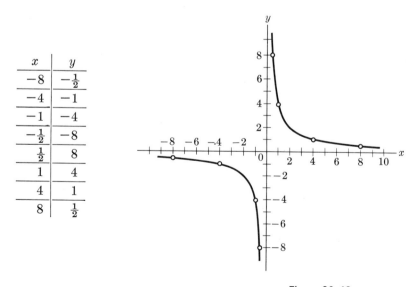

x	y
-8	$-\frac{1}{2}$
-4	-1
-1	-4
$-\frac{1}{2}$	-8
$\frac{1}{2}$	8
1	4
4	1
8	$\frac{1}{2}$

Figure 20-43

We conclude that the equation of a hyperbola is characterized by the presence of both an x^2- and a y^2-term, having different signs, or by the presence of an xy-term with no squared terms.

Exercises

In Exercises 1 through 12 find the coordinates of the vertices and the foci of the given hyperbolas. Sketch each curve.

1. $\dfrac{x^2}{25} - \dfrac{y^2}{144} = 1$ 2. $\dfrac{x^2}{16} - \dfrac{y^2}{4} = 1$ 3. $\dfrac{y^2}{9} - \dfrac{x^2}{1} = 1$

4. $\dfrac{y^2}{2} - \dfrac{x^2}{2} = 1$ 5. $2x^2 - y^2 = 4$ 6. $3x^2 - y^2 = 9$

7. $2y^2 - 5x^2 = 10$ 8. $3y^2 - 2x^2 = 6$ 9. $4x^2 - y^2 + 4 = 0$

10. $9x^2 - y^2 - 9 = 0$ 11. $4x^2 - 9y^2 = 16$ 12. $y^2 - 9x^2 = 25$

In Exercises 13 through 18 find the equations of the hyperbolas satisfying the given conditions. The center of each is at the origin.

13. Vertex $(3, 0)$, focus $(5, 0)$
14. Vertex $(0, 1)$, focus $(0, \sqrt{3})$
15. Conjugate axis $= 12$, vertex $(0, 10)$
16. Focus $(8, 0)$, transverse axis $= 4$
17. Passes through $(2, 3)$, focus $(2, 0)$
18. Passes through $(1, 2)$ and $(2, 2\sqrt{2})$

In Exercises 19 and 20 sketch the graphs of the hyperbolas given.

19. $xy = 2$
20. $xy = -4$

In Exercises 21 and 22 find the equations of the hyperbolas with the given properties by use of the definition of the hyperbola.

21. Foci at $(1, 2)$ and $(11, 2)$, with a transverse axis of 8
22. Center at $(1, -1)$, focus at $(1, 4)$, vertex at $(1, 2)$

In Exercises 23 through 27 solve the given problems.

23. Sketch the graph of impedance versus resistance if the reactance $X_L - X_C$ of a given electric circuit is constant at 60 ohms (see Section 11-7).
24. One statement of Boyle's law is that the product of the pressure and volume, for constant temperature, remains a constant for a perfect gas. If one set of values for a perfect gas under the condition of constant temperature is that the pressure is 3 atm for a volume of 8 liters, sketch a graph of pressure versus volume.
25. The relationship between the frequency f, wavelength λ, and the velocity v of a wave is given by $v = f\lambda$. The velocity of light is a constant, being 3×10^{10} cm/sec. The visible spectrum ranges in wavelength from about 4×10^{-5} cm (violet) to about 7×10^{-5} cm (red). Sketch a graph of frequency f (in cycles/sec) as a function of wavelength for the visible spectrum.

26. The wavelength of gamma rays varies from about 10^{-8} cm to about 10^{-13} cm, but they have the same velocity as light. On logarithmic paper, plot the graph of frequency versus wavelength for gamma rays. What type of curve results when this type of hyperbola is plotted on logarithmic paper?

27. An electronic instrument located at point P records the sounds of a rifle shot and the impact of the bullet striking the target at the same instant. Show that P lies on a branch of a hyperbola.

20-7 Translation of axes

Until now, the equations considered for the parabola, the ellipse, and the hyperbola have been restricted to the particular cases in which the vertex of the parabola is at the origin and the center of the ellipse or hyperbola is at the origin. In this section we shall consider the equations of these curves for the cases in which the axis of the curve is parallel to one of the coordinate axes. This is done by *translation of axes*.

We choose a point (h, k) in the xy-coordinate plane and let this point be the origin of another coordinate system, the $x'y'$-coordinate system. The x'-axis is parallel to the x-axis and the y'-axis is parallel to the y-axis. Every point in the plane now has two sets of coordinates associated with it, (x, y) and (x', y'). From Fig. 20-44 we see that

$$x = x' + h \quad \text{and} \quad y = y' + k. \quad (20\text{-}26)$$

Equations (20-26) can also be written in the form

$$x' = x - h \quad \text{and} \quad y' = y - k. \quad (20\text{-}27)$$

The following examples illustrate the use of Eqs. (20-27) in the analysis of equations of the parabola, ellipse, and hyperbola.

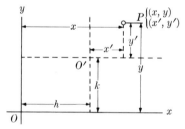

Figure 20-44

Example A.   Describe the locus of the equation

$$\frac{(x-3)^2}{25} + \frac{(y+2)^2}{9} = 1.$$

In this equation, given that $h = 3$ and $k = -2$, we have $x' = x - 3$ and $y' = y + 2$. In terms of x' and y', the equation is

$$\frac{(x')^2}{25} + \frac{(y')^2}{9} = 1.$$

We recognize this equation as that of an ellipse (see Fig. 20-45) with a semi-major axis of 5 and a semi-minor axis of 3. The center of the ellipse is at $(3, -2)$ since this was the choice of h and k to make the equation fit a standard form.

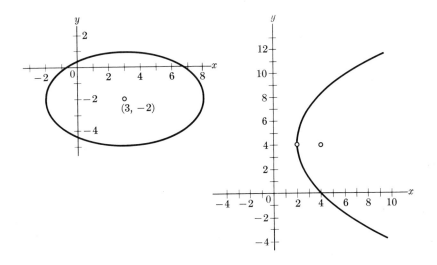

Figure 20-45   Figure 20-46

Example B.   Find the equation of the parabola with vertex at (2, 4) and focus at (4, 4).

If we let the origin of the $x'y'$-coordinate system be the point (2, 4), the point (4, 4) would be the point (2, 0) in the $x'y'$-system. This means that $p = 2$ and $4p = 8$ (Fig. 20-46). In the $x'y'$-system, the equation is

$$(y')^2 = 8(x').$$

Since (2, 4) is the origin of the $x'y'$-system, this means that $h = 2$ and $k = 4$. Using Eq. (20-27), we have

$$(y - 4)^2 = 8(x - 2)$$

as the equation of the parabola in the xy-coordinate system. If this equation is multiplied out, and like terms are combined, we obtain

$$y^2 - 8x - 8y + 32 = 0.$$

Example C.   Find the center of the hyperbola $2x^2 - y^2 - 4x - 4y - 4 = 0$.

To analyze this curve, we first complete the square in the x-terms and in the y-terms. This will allow us to recognize properly the choice of h and k.

$$2x^2 - 4x - y^2 - 4y = 4,$$
$$2(x^2 - 2x \qquad) - (y^2 + 4y \qquad) = 4,$$
$$2(x^2 - 2x + 1) - (y^2 + 4y + 4) = 4 + 2 - 4,$$
$$2(x - 1)^2 - (y + 2)^2 = 2,$$
$$\frac{(x - 1)^2}{1} - \frac{(y + 2)^2}{2} = 1.$$

Thus, if we let $h = 1$ and $k = -2$, the equation in the $x'y'$-system becomes

$$\frac{(x')^2}{1} - \frac{(y')^2}{2} = 1.$$

This means that the center is at $(1, -2)$, since this point corresponds to the origin of the $x'y'$-coordinate system (see Fig. 20-47).

Example D. Glass beakers are to be made with a height of 3 in. Express the surface area of the beakers in terms of the radius of the base. Sketch the graph of area versus radius.

The total surface area of a beaker is the sum of the area of the base and the lateral surface area of the side. In general, this surface area S in terms of the radius r of the base and the height h of the side is

$$S = \pi r^2 + 2\pi r h.$$

Since h is constant at 3 in., we have

$$S = \pi r^2 + 6\pi r,$$

which is the desired relationship.

For purposes of sketching the graph of S and r, we now complete the square of the r terms:

$$S = \pi(r^2 + 6r),$$
$$S + 9\pi = \pi(r + 6r + 9),$$
$$S + 9\pi = \pi(r + 3)^2.$$

We note that this equation represents a parabola with vertex at $(-3, -9\pi)$ for its coordinates (r, S). Since $4p = \pi$, $p = \pi/4$ and the focus of this parabola is at $(-3, -35\pi/4)$. Only positive values for S and r have meaning, and therefore the part of the graph for negative r is shown as a dashed curve (see Fig. 20-48).

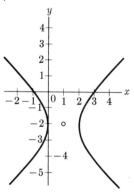

Figure 20-47

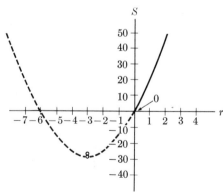

Figure 20-48

Exercises

In Exercises 1 through 6 describe the locus of each of the given equations. Identify the type of curve and its center (vertex if it is a parabola). Sketch each curve.

1. $(y - 2)^2 = 4(x + 1)$

2. $\dfrac{(x + 4)^2}{4} + \dfrac{(y - 1)^2}{1} = 1$

3. $\dfrac{(x - 1)^2}{4} - \dfrac{(y - 2)^2}{9} = 1$

4. $(y + 5)^2 = -8(x - 2)$

5. $\dfrac{(x + 1)^2}{1} + \dfrac{y^2}{9} = 1$

6. $\dfrac{(y - 4)^2}{16} - \dfrac{(x + 2)^2}{4} = 1$

In Exercises 7 through 12 find the equation of each of the curves described by the given information.

7. Parabola: vertex $(-1, 3)$, $p = 4$, axis parallel to x-axis
8. Parabola: vertex $(2, -1)$, directrix $y = 3$
9. Ellipse: center $(-2, 2)$, focus $(-5, 2)$, vertex $(-7, 2)$
10. Ellipse: center $(0, 3)$, focus $(12, 3)$, major axis 26 units
11. Hyperbola: vertices $(2, 1)$ and $(-4, 1)$, focus $(-6, 1)$
12. Hyperbola: center $(1, -4)$, focus $(1, 1)$, transverse axis 8 units

In Exercises 13 through 18 determine the center (or vertex if the curve is a parabola) of the given curves. Identify and sketch each curve.

13. $x^2 + 2x - 4y - 3 = 0$
14. $y^2 - 2x - 2y - 9 = 0$
15. $4x^2 + 9y^2 + 24x = 0$
16. $2x^2 + 9y^2 + 8x - 72y + 134 = 0$
17. $9x^2 - y^2 + 8y - 7 = 0$
18. $5x^2 - 4y^2 + 20x + 8y = 4$

In Exercises 19 and 20 find the required equations.

19. Find the equation of the hyperbola with asymptotes $x - y = -1$ and $x + y = -3$, and vertex $(3, -1)$.

20. Verify each of the following equations as being the standard form as indicated. Parabola, vertex at (h, k), axis parallel to the x-axis:

$$(y - k)^2 = 4p(x - h).$$

Parabola, vertex at (h, k), axis parallel to the y-axis:

$$(x - h)^2 = 4p(y - k).$$

Ellipse, center at (h, k), major axis parallel to the x-axis:

$$\frac{(x - h)^2}{a^2} + \frac{(y - k)^2}{b^2} = 1.$$

Ellipse, center at (h, k), major axis parallel to the y-axis:

$$\frac{(y - k)^2}{a^2} + \frac{(x - h)^2}{b^2} = 1.$$

Hyperbola, center at (h, k), transverse axis parallel to the x-axis:

$$\frac{(x - h)^2}{a^2} - \frac{(y - k)^2}{b^2} = 1.$$

Hyperbola, center at (h, k), transverse axis parallel to the y-axis:

$$\frac{(y - k)^2}{a^2} - \frac{(x - h)^2}{b^2} = 1.$$

In Exercises 21 and 22 solve the given problems.

21. The power supplied to a circuit by a battery with a voltage E and an internal resistance r is given by $P = EI - rI^2$, where P is the power (in watts) and I is the current (in amps). Sketch the graph of P versus I for a 6-volt battery with an internal resistance of 0.3 ohms.

22. A rectangular tract of land is to have a perimeter of 800 ft. Express the area in terms of its width and sketch the graph.

20-8 The second-degree equation

The equations of the circle, parabola, ellipse, and hyperbola have certain properties in common. In this section we shall briefly discuss some of these properties.

Each of these curves can be represented by a second-degree equation of the form

$$Ax^2 + Bxy + Cy^2 + Dx + Ey + F = 0. \tag{20-28}$$

[This equation is the same as Eq. (13-1).] The coefficients of the second-degree terms determine the type of curve which results. From the previous sections of this chapter, we have the following results.

Equation (20-28) represents the indicated curve for the given conditions for A, B, and C.

(1) If $A = C$, $B = 0$, a circle.
(2) If $A \neq C$ (but they have the same sign), $B = 0$, an ellipse.
(3) If A and C have different signs, $B = 0$, a hyperbola.
(4) If $A = 0$, $C = 0$, $B \neq 0$, a hyperbola.
(5) If either $A = 0$ or $C = 0$ (but not both), $B = 0$, a parabola.

(Special cases, such as a single point or no real locus, can also result.)

Another conclusion about Eq. (20-28) is that, if either $D \neq 0$ or $E \neq 0$ (or both), the center (or vertex of a parabola) of the curve is not at the origin. If $B \neq 0$, the axis of the curve has been rotated. We have considered only one such case (the hyperbola $xy = c$) in this chapter.

Example A. The equation $3x^2 = 6x - y^2 + 3$ represents an ellipse. Before we analyze the equation, we should put it in the form of Eq. (20-28). For the given equation, this form is

$$3x^2 + y^2 - 6x - 3 = 0.$$

Here we see that $B = 0$ and $A \neq C$. Therefore it is an ellipse. The $-6x$ term indicates that the center of the ellipse is not at the origin.

Example B.   The equation $2(x + 3)^2 = y^2 + 2x^2$ represents a parabola. Putting it in the form of Eq. (20-28), we have

$$2(x^2 + 6x + 9) = y^2 + 2x^2,$$
$$2x^2 + 12x + 18 = y^2 + 2x^2,$$
$$y^2 - 12x - 18 = 0.$$

We now note that $A = 0$, $B = 0$, and $C \neq 0$. This indicates that the equation represents a parabola. Here, the -18 term indicates that the vertex is not at the origin.

In Chapter 13, when these curves were first introduced, they were referred to as *conic sections*. If a plane is passed through a cone, the intersection of the plane and the cone results in one of these curves, the curve formed depends on the angle of the plane with respect to the axis of the cone. This is indicated in Fig. 20-49.

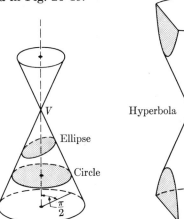
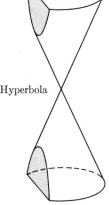
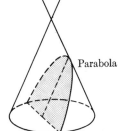

Figure 20-49

Exercises

In Exercises 1 through 16 identify each of the equations as representing either a circle, parabola, ellipse, or hyperbola.

1. $2x^2 + 2y^2 - 3y - 1 = 0$
2. $x^2 - 2y^2 - 3x - 1 = 0$
3. $2x^2 - x - y = 1$
4. $2x^2 + 4y^2 - y - 2x = 4$
5. $x^2 = y^2 - 1$
6. $3x^2 = 2y - 4y^2$
7. $x^2 = y - y^2$
8. $y = 3 - 6x^2$
9. $x(y + 3x) = x^2 + xy - y^2 + 1$
10. $x(2 - x) = y^2$
11. $2xy + x - 3y = 6$
12. $(y + 1)^2 = x^2 + y^2 - 1$
13. $2x(x - y) = y(3 - y - 2x)$
14. $2x^2 = x(x - 1) + 4y^2$
15. $y(3 - 2y) = 2(x^2 - y^2)$
16. $4x(x - 1) = 2x^2 - 2y^2 + 3$

In Exercises 17 and 18 set up the necessary equation and then determine the type of graph it represents.

17. For a given alternating current circuit the resistance and capacitive reactance are constant. What type of curve is represented by the equation relating impedance and inductive reactance?

18. The legs of a right triangle are x and y and the hypotenuse is 12. What type of curve is represented by the equation relating x and y?

20-9 Polar coordinates

Thus far we have graphed all curves in one coordinate system. This system, the rectangular coordinate system, is probably the most useful and widely applicable system. However, for certain types of curves, other coordinate systems prove to be better adapted. These coordinate systems are widely used, especially when certain applications of higher mathematics are involved. We shall discuss one of these systems here.

Instead of designating a point by its x- and y-coordinates, we can specify its location by its radius vector and the angle which the radius vector makes with the x-axis. Thus the r and θ that are used in the definitions of the trigonometric functions can also be used as the coordinates of points in the plane. The important aspect of choosing coordinates is that, for each set of values, there must be only one point which corresponds to this set. We can see that this condition is satisfied by the use of r and θ as coordinates. In polar coordinates the origin is called the *pole*, and the positive x-axis is called the *polar axis* (see Fig. 20-50).

Example A. If $r = 2$ and $\theta = \pi/6$, we have the point as indicated in Fig. 20-51. The coordinates (r, θ) of this point are written as $(2, \pi/6)$ when polar coordinates are used. This point corresponds to $(\sqrt{3}, 1)$ in rectangular coordinates.

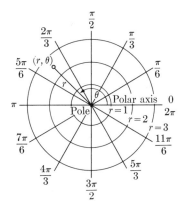

Figure 20-50

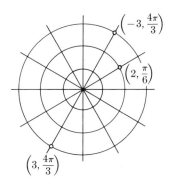

Figure 20-51

One difference between rectangular coordinates and polar coordinates is that, for each point in the plane, there are limitless possibilities for the polar coordinates of that point. For example, the point $(2, \pi/6)$ can also be represented by $(2, 13\pi/6)$ since the angles $\pi/6$ and $13\pi/6$ are coterminal. We also remove one restriction on r that we imposed in the definitions of the trigonometric functions. That is, r is allowed to take on positive and negative values. If r is considered negative, then the point is found on the opposite side of the pole from that on which it is positive.

Example B. The coordinates $(3, 4\pi/3)$ and $(3, -2\pi/3)$ represent the same point. However, the point $(-3, 4\pi/3)$ is on the opposite side of the pole, three units from the pole. Another possible set of coordinates for $(-3, 4\pi/3)$ is $(3, \pi/3)$ (see Fig. 20-51).

The relationships between the polar coordinates of a point and the rectangular coordinates of the same point come directly from the definitions of the trigonometric functions. Those most commonly used are

$$x = r \cos \theta, \qquad y = r \sin \theta \qquad (20\text{-}29)$$

and

$$\tan \theta = \frac{y}{x}, \qquad r = \sqrt{x^2 + y^2}. \qquad (20\text{-}30)$$

Equations (20-29) are used when a relation in x and y is transformed into r and θ, and they are often used for the reverse process along with the second of Eqs. (20-30). Equations (20-30) are normally used for changing values of particular sets of coordinates.

Example C. Using Eq. (20-29), we can transform the polar coordinates of $(4, \pi/4)$ into the rectangular coordinates $(2\sqrt{2}, 2\sqrt{2})$, since

$$x = 4 \cos (\pi/4) = 4(\sqrt{2}/2) = 2\sqrt{2}$$

and

$$y = 4 \sin (\pi/4) = 4(\sqrt{2}/2) = 2\sqrt{2}.$$

Example D. If the rectangular coordinates of a point are $(3, -5)$, we can find the polar coordinates of the same point by $\tan \theta = -\frac{5}{3}$. This means that $\theta = 5.25$ (or -1.03), since we know that the terminal site of θ is in the fourth quadrant. Also, $r = \sqrt{9 + 25} = \sqrt{34} = 5.83$. Therefore, the point $(3, -5)$ in rectangular coordinates is the point $(5.83, 5.25)$ in polar coordinates.

Example E. Find the polar equation of the circle $x^2 + y^2 = 2x$.
   Since $r^2 = x^2 + y^2$ and $x = r \cos \theta$, we have $r^2 = 2r \cos \theta$, or $r = 2 \cos \theta$. This is the polar equation; that is, the equation of the curve expressed in the variables r and θ.

Example F. Find the rectangular equation of the "rose" $r = 4 \sin 2\theta$.
   Using the relation $2 \sin \theta \cos \theta = \sin 2\theta$, we have $r = 8 \sin \theta \cos \theta$. Then, using Eqs. (20-29) and (20-30), we have

$$\sqrt{x^2 + y^2} = 8 \left(\frac{y}{r}\right)\left(\frac{x}{r}\right) = \frac{8xy}{r^2} = \frac{8xy}{x^2 + y^2}.$$

Squaring both sides, we obtain

$$x^2 + y^2 = \frac{64x^2y^2}{(x^2 + y^2)^2} \quad \text{or} \quad (x^2 + y^2)^3 = 64x^2y^2.$$

From this example we can see that plotting the graph from the rectangular equation would be complicated.

Exercises

In Exercises 1 through 10 plot the given points on polar coordinate paper.

1. $(3, \pi/6)$ 2. $(2, \pi)$ 3. $(4, 7\pi/6)$ 4. $(5, -\pi/3)$ 5. $(\frac{5}{2}, -8\pi/3)$
6. $(-5, \pi/4)$ 7. $(3, -5\pi)$ 8. $(4, 2\pi/5)$ 9. $(-4, -5\pi/3)$ 10. $(-1, -1)$

In Exercises 11 through 14 find a set of polar coordinates for each of the given points expressed in rectangular coordinates.

11. $(\sqrt{3}, 1)$ 12. $(-1, -1)$ 13. $(-\sqrt{3}/2, -\frac{1}{2})$ 14. $(-5, 4)$

In Exercises 15 through 18 find the rectangular coordinates corresponding to the points for which the polar coordinates are given.

15. $(8, 4\pi/3)$ 16. $(-4, -\pi)$ 17. $(3, -\pi/8)$ 18. $(-1, -1)$

In Exercises 19 through 24 find the polar equation of each of the given rectangular equations.

19. $x = 3$ 20. $y = 2$ 21. $x^2 + y^2 = a^2$

22. $x^2 - y^2 = a^2$ 23. $x^2 + 4y^2 = 4$ 24. $y = x^2$

In Exercises 25 through 28 find the rectangular equation of each of the given polar equations.

25. $r = \sin \theta$ 26. $r \cos \theta = 4$ 27. $r = 2(1 + \cos \theta)$ 28. $r^2 = 16 \cos 2\theta$

In Exercises 29 through 33 find the required equations.

29. If we refer back to Eqs. (7-10) and (7-11), we see that the length along the arc of a circle and the area within a circular sector vary with two variables. These variables are those which we refer to as the polar coordinates. Express the arc length s and the area A in terms of rectangular coordinates. (How must we express θ?)

30. Under certain conditions, the x- and y-components of a magnetic field B are given by the equations

$$B_x = \frac{-ky}{x^2 + y^2} \quad \text{and} \quad B_y = \frac{kx}{x^2 + y^2}.$$

Write these equations in terms of polar coordinates.

31. Express the equation of the cable (see Exercise 29 of Section 20-4) in polar coordinates.

32. The x- and y-coordinates of the position of a certain moving object as functions of time are given by $x = 2t$ and $y = \sqrt{8t^2 + 1}$. Find the polar equation of the path of the object.

33. The polar equation of the path of an artificial satellite of the earth is

$$r = \frac{4800}{1 + 0.14 \cos \theta},$$

where r is measured in miles. Find the rectangular equation of the path of this satellite. The path is an ellipse, with the earth at one of the foci.

20-10 Curves in polar coordinates

The basic method for finding a curve in polar coordinates is the same as in rectangular coordinates. We assume values of θ and then find the corresponding values of r. These points are plotted and joined, thus forming the curve which represents the function. The following examples illustrate the method.

Example A.   The graph of the polar equation $r = 3$ is a circle of radius 3, with center at the pole. This is the case since $r = 3$, regardless of the value of θ. It is not really necessary to find specific points for this circle. See Fig. 20-52 on the next page.

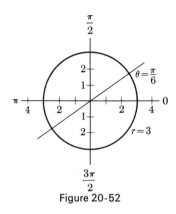

Figure 20-52

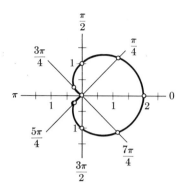

Figure 20-53

The graph of $\theta = \pi/6$ is a straight line through the pole. It represents all points for which $\theta = \pi/6$, regardless of the value of r, positive or negative. See Fig. 20-52.

Example B. Plot the graph of $r = 1 + \cos \theta$.

We find the following table of values of r corresponding to the assumed values of θ.

θ	0	$\dfrac{\pi}{4}$	$\dfrac{\pi}{2}$	$\dfrac{3\pi}{4}$	π	$\dfrac{5\pi}{4}$	$\dfrac{3\pi}{2}$	$\dfrac{7\pi}{4}$	2π
r	2	1.7	1	0.3	0	0.3	1	1.7	2

We now see that the points on the curve start repeating, and it is unnecessary to find additional points. This curve is called a *cardioid* and is shown in Fig. 20-53.

Example C. Plot the graph of $r = 1 - 2 \sin \theta$.

θ	0	$\dfrac{\pi}{4}$	$\dfrac{\pi}{2}$	$\dfrac{3\pi}{4}$	π	$\dfrac{5\pi}{4}$	$\dfrac{3\pi}{2}$	$\dfrac{7\pi}{4}$	2π
r	1	-0.4	-1	-0.4	1	2.4	3	2.4	1

Particular care should be taken in plotting the points for which r is negative. This curve is known as a *limaçon* and is shown in Fig. 20-54.

Example D. Plot the graph of $r = 2 \cos 2\theta$.

θ	0	$\dfrac{\pi}{12}$	$\dfrac{\pi}{6}$	$\dfrac{\pi}{4}$	$\dfrac{\pi}{3}$	$\dfrac{5\pi}{12}$	$\dfrac{\pi}{2}$	$\dfrac{7\pi}{12}$	$\dfrac{2\pi}{3}$	$\dfrac{3\pi}{4}$	$\dfrac{5\pi}{6}$	$\dfrac{11\pi}{2}$	π
r	2	1.7	1	0	-1	-1.7	-2	-1.7	-1	0	1	1.7	2

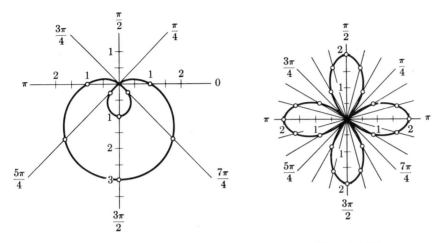

Figure 20-54   Figure 20-55

For the values of θ from π to 2π, the values of r repeat. We have a four-leaf *rose* (Fig. 20-55).

Example E. Plot the graph of $r^2 = 9 \cos 2\theta$.

θ	0	$\dfrac{\pi}{8}$	$\dfrac{\pi}{4}$	$\cdots$	$\dfrac{3\pi}{4}$	$\dfrac{7\pi}{8}$	π
r	± 3	± 2.5	0		0	± 2.5	± 3

There are no values of r corresponding to values of θ in the range $\pi/4 < \theta < 3\pi/4$, since twice these angles are in the second and third quadrants, and the cosine is negative for such angles. The value of r^2 cannot be negative. Also, the values of r repeat for $\theta > \pi$. The figure is called a *lemniscate* (Fig. 20-56).

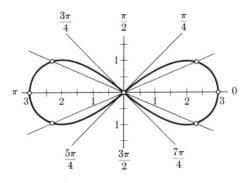

Figure 20-56

Exercises

In Exercises 1 through 22 plot the given curves in polar coordinates.

1. $r = 4$ 2. $r = 2$ 3. $\theta = \dfrac{3\pi}{4}$ 4. $\theta = \dfrac{5\pi}{3}$

5. $r = 4 \sec \theta$ 6. $r = 4 \csc \theta$ 7. $r = 2 \sin \theta$ 8. $r = 3 \cos \theta$

9. $r = 1 - \cos \theta$ (cardioid)   10. $r = \sin \theta - 1$ (cardioid)

11. $r = 2 - \cos \theta$ (limaçon)   12. $r = 2 + 3 \sin \theta$ (limaçon)

13. $r = 4 \sin 2\theta$ (rose)   14. $r = 2 \sin 3\theta$ (rose)

15. $r^2 = 4 \sin 2\theta$ (lemniscate)   16. $r^2 = 2 \sin \theta$

17. $r = -4 \sin 4\theta$ (rose)   18. $r = 10^\theta$ (spiral)

19. $r = \dfrac{1}{2 - \cos \theta}$ (ellipse)   20. $r = \dfrac{1}{1 - \cos \theta}$ (parabola)

21. $r = 3 - \sin 3\theta$ 22. $r = 4 \tan \theta$

In Exercises 23 through 26 sketch the indicated graphs.

23. The charged particle (see Exercise 29 of Section 20-3) is originally traveling along the line $\theta = \pi$ toward the pole. When it reaches the pole it enters the magnetic field. Its path is described by the equation $r = 2a \sin \theta$, where a is the radius of the circle. Sketch the graph of this path.

24. A cam is shaped such that the equation of the edge of the upper "half" is given by $r = 2 + \cos \theta$, and the equation of the edge of the lower "half" by $r = 3/(2 - \cos \theta)$. Plot the curve which represents the shape of the cam.

25. A satellite at a height proper to make one revolution per day around the earth will have for an excellent approximation of its projection on the earth of its path the curve

$$r^2 = R^2 \cos 2 \left(\theta + \frac{\pi}{2} \right),$$

where R is the radius of the earth. Sketch the path of the projection.

26. Sketch the graph of the rectangular equation

$$4(x^6 + 3x^4y^2 + 3x^2y^4 + y^6 - x^4 - 2x^2y^2 - y^4) + y^2 = 0.$$

[*Hint*: The equation can be written as

$$4(x^2 + y^2)^3 - 4(x^2 + y^2)^2 + y^2 = 0.$$

Transform to polar coordinates, and then sketch the curve.]

20-11 Miscellaneous Exercises

In Exercises 1 through 12 find the equation of the indicated curve subject to the given conditions. Sketch each curve.

1. Straight line: passes through $(1, -7)$ with a slope of 4
2. Straight line: passes through $(-1, 5)$ and $(-2, -3)$

3. Straight line: perpendicular to $3x - 2y + 8 = 0$ and has a y-intercept of -1

4. Straight line: parallel to $2x - 5y + 1 = 0$ and has a x-intercept of 2

5. Circle: center at $(1, -2)$, passes through $(4, -3)$

6. Circle: tangent to the line $x = 3$, center at $(5, 1)$

7. Parabola: focus $(3, 0)$, vertex $(0, 0)$

8. Parabola: directrix $y = -5$, vertex $(0, 0)$

9. Ellipse: vertex $(10, 0)$, focus $(8, 0)$, center $(0, 0)$

10. Ellipse: center $(0, 0)$, passes through $(0, 3)$ and $(2, 1)$

11. Hyperbola: vertex $(0, 13)$, center $(0, 0)$, conjugate axis of 24

12. Hyperbola: foci $(0, 10)$ and $(0, -10)$, vertex $(0, 8)$

In Exercises 13 through 24 find the indicated quantities for each of the given equations. Sketch each curve.

13. $x^2 + y^2 + 6x - 7 = 0$, center and radius

14. $x^2 + y^2 - 4x + 2y - 20 = 0$, center and radius

15. $x^2 = -20y$, focus and directrix

16. $y^2 = 24x$, focus and directrix

17. $16x^2 + y^2 = 16$, vertices and foci

18. $2y^2 - 9x^2 = 18$, vertices and foci

19. $2x^2 - 5y^2 = 8$, vertices and foci

20. $2x^2 + 25y^2 = 50$, vertices and foci

21. $x^2 - 8x - 4y - 16 = 0$, vertex and focus

22. $y^2 - 4x + 4y + 24 = 0$, vertex and directrix

23. $4x^2 + y^2 - 16x + 2y + 13 = 0$, center

24. $x^2 - 2y^2 + 4x + 4y + 6 = 0$, center

In Exercises 25 through 30 plot the given curves in polar coordinates.

25. $r = 4 (1 + \sin \theta)$

26. $r = 1 + 2 \cos \theta$

27. $r = \cot \theta$

28. $r = \dfrac{1}{2 (\sin \theta - 1)}$

29. $r = 2 \sin \left(\dfrac{\theta}{2}\right)$

30. $r = \theta$

In Exercises 31 and 32 find the polar equation of each of the given rectangular equations.

31. $y = 2x$

32. $x^2 + y^2 = 7 - 6y$

In Exercises 33 and 34 find the rectangular equation of each of the given polar equations.

33. $r = 2 \sin 2\theta$

34. $r = \dfrac{2}{1 - \sin \theta}$

In Exercises 35 through 57 solve the given problems.

35. Find the points of intersection of the ellipses $25x^2 + 4y^2 = 100$ and $4x^2 + 9y^2 = 36$.

36. Find the points of intersection of the hyperbola $y^2 - x^2 = 1$ and the ellipse $x^2 + 25y^2 = 25$.

37. In two ways show that the line segments joining $(-3, 11)$, $(2, -1)$ and $(14, 4)$ form a right triangle.

38. Show that the altitudes of the triangle with vertices $(2, -4)$, $(3, -1)$, and $(-2, 5)$ meet at a single point.

39. By means of the definition of a parabola, find the equation of the parabola with focus at $(3, 1)$ and directrix the line $y = -3$. Find the same equation by the method of translation of axes.

40. Repeat the instructions of Exercise 39 for the parabola with focus at $(0, 2)$ and directrix the line $y = 4$.

41. In a certain electric circuit, two resistors R_1 and R_2 act as a voltage divider. The relation between them is $\alpha = R_1/(R_1 + R_2)$, where α is a constant less than 1. Sketch the curve of R_1 versus R_2 (both in ohms), if $\alpha = \frac{1}{2}$.

42. Let C and F denote corresponding centrigrade and fahrenheit temperature readings. If the equation relating the two is linear, determine this equation given that $C = 0$ when $F = 32$ and $C = 100$ when $F = 212$.

43. The arch of a small bridge across a stream is parabolic. If, at water level, the span of the arch is 80 ft, and the maximum height of the span above water level is 20 ft, what is the equation of the arch? Choose the most convenient point for the origin of the coordinate system.

44. If a source of light is placed at the focus of a parabolic reflector, the reflected rays are parallel. Where is the focus of a parabolic reflector which is 8 in. across and 6 in. deep?

45. Sketch the curve of the total surface area of a right circular cylinder as a function of its radius, if the height is always 10 units.

46. At very low temperatures certain metals have an electric resistance of zero. This phenomenon is called superconductivity. A magnetic field also effects the superconductivity. A certain level of magnetic field, the threshold field, is related to the temperature T by

$$\frac{H_T}{H_0} = 1 - \left(\frac{T}{T_0}\right)^2,$$

where H_0 and T_0 are specifically defined values of magnetic field and temperature. Sketch H_T/H_0 versus T/T_0.

47. Under certain conditions the work W done on a wire by increasing the tension from T_1 to T_2 is given by $W = k(T_2{}^2 - T_1{}^2)$, where k is a constant depending on the properties of the wire. If the work is constant for various sets of initial and final tensions, sketch a graph of T_2 versus T_1.

48. A machine-part designer wishes to make a model for an elliptical cam by placing two pins in his design board, putting a loop of string over the pins and marking off the outline by keeping the string taut. (Note that he is using the definition of the ellipse.) If the cam is to measure 10 in. by 6 in., how long should the loop of string be and how far apart should the pins be?

49. The vertical position of a projectile is given by the equation $y = 120t - 16t^2$, and its horizontal position is given by $x = 60t$. By eliminating t, determine the path of the projectile. Sketch this path for the length of time it would need to strike the ground, assuming level terrain.

50. In order to study the relationship between velocity and pressure of a stream of water, a pipe is constructed such that its cross section is a hyperbola. If the pipe is 10 ft long, 1 ft in diameter at the narrow point (middle) and 2 ft in diameter at the ends, what is the equation of the cross-section of the pipe? (In physics it is shown that where the velocity of a fluid is greatest, the pressure is the least.)

51. The inside of the top of an arch is a semi-ellipse with a major axis (width) of 26 ft and a minor axis of 10 ft. The arch is 7 ft thick at all points. Is the outside of the arch a portion of an ellipse? (*Hint*: Check the equation of the outer "ellipse" 1 ft to the right of center.)

52. The earth moves about the sun in an elliptical path. If the closest the earth gets to the sun is 90.5 million miles, and the farthest it gets from the sun is 93.5 million miles, find the equation of the path of the earth. The sun is at one focus of the ellipse. Assume the major axis to be along the x-axis and the center of the ellipse is at the origin.

53. Soon after reaching the vicinity of the moon, Apollo 11 (the first spacecraft to land a man on the moon) went into an elliptical lunar orbit. The closest the craft was to the moon in this orbit was 70 mi, and the farthest it was from the moon was 190 mi. What was the equation of the path if the moon was at one of the foci of the ellipse? Assume the major axis to be along the x-axis and the center of the ellipse is at the origin. The radius of the moon is 1080 mi.

54. A 60-ft rope passes over a pulley 10 ft above the ground and an object on the ground is attached at one end. A man holds the other end at a level of 4 ft above the ground. If the man walks away from the pulley, express the height of the object above the ground in terms of the distance the man is from directly below the object. Sketch the graph of distance versus height.

55. Express the equation of the artificial satellite (see Exercise 25 of Section 20-5) in polar coordinates.

56. Under certain circumstances, the path that an electron follows when passing through a magnetic field is closely approximated by the parabola $x^2 = ky$, where k is a constant. Express this equation in polar coordinates.

57. Under a force which varies inversely as the square of the distance from an attracting object (such as the force the sun exerts on the earth), it can be shown that the equation that an object follows is given in general by

$$\frac{1}{r} = a + b \cos \theta,$$

where a and b are constant for a particular path. By transforming this equation to rectangular coordinates, show that this equation represents one of the conic sections, the particular section depending on the values of a and b. It is through this kind of analysis that we know that the paths of the planets and comets are conic sections.

Introduction to Statistics and Empirical Curve Fitting

21

21-1 Probability

Much of that which we "know" is probable knowledge. In building any field of knowledge, we accept certain basic concepts as being true, without having complete proof. That situation exists in mathematics as in all other fields of knowledge. For example, in mathematics the concepts of a point, of a line, of the whole being greater than any of its parts, and similar *axioms* or undefinable quantities are used as the basis for later conclusions. Those concepts accepted without proof in mathematics are normally those which cannot be conceived to be wrong (although there have been systems of mathematics in which certain axioms are not valid). Definitions are based on those properties which exhibit consistency within a given set of axioms. In other fields, it is possible to make only a limited number of observations and to base predictions of future happenings on these results. This is well documented in the study of physics, for example. Throughout the history of physics, certain concepts believed true at one time have been shown to be wrong at a later date. However, in the course of developing a new theory in any field, we learn a great deal more about the phenomena.

This chapter will deal with determining information based on either what should be expected or past experience. Thus we shall show some of the ways of dealing with limited information.

In the study of probability, a numerical value is given to the likelihood of some particular event actually happening. In determining such a value, we assume that all events are equally likely to occur, unless we have special knowledge to the contrary.

Example A. Consider the toss of a coin; we assume that the coin will land either heads or tails, and that either of these possibilities is equally likely.

Example B. If a study were made of the percentages of usable and defective parts produced by a particular machine, it would normally be expected that the machine would not turn out as many defective as usable parts. Thus, by studying a random group of parts, we can count the number of defective parts produced. This number would then form a basis of the probable percentage of defective parts which the machine would produce.

Probability, as used in this chapter, is defined as follows: If an event can turn out in any one of n equally likely ways, and s of these would be successful, then the probability of the event occuring successfully is

$$P = \frac{s}{n}. \tag{21-1}$$

If the number of equally likely ways an event may turn out cannot be determined from theoretical considerations and N trials are made, of which S are successful, the probability of success is given by

$$P = \frac{S}{N}. \tag{21-2}$$

If the events are equally likely, as expressed in Eq. (21-1), the probability is called an *a priori* probability, meaning that this is what should happen. If the probability is based on past experience, as expressed in Eq. (21-2), the probability is termed *empirical.*

Example C. When a card is drawn from a bridge deck, the probability that this card is a diamond is $\frac{1}{4}$, since there are 13 diamonds out of 52 cards. This means that $n = 52$ and $s = 13$. (This assumes, of course, that the card is drawn purely at random.) In the same way, the probability of drawing an ace is $\frac{1}{13}$, since there are 4 aces in the 52 cards. Here $n = 52$ and $s = 4$.

Example D. If a particular machine produced 20 defective parts from a lot of 1000, the empirical probability of a defective part being produced is $\frac{1}{50}$. In this case $N = 1000$ and $S = 20$. If should be pointed out here that the larger the number inspected and counted, the more accurate is the empirical probability. Again, however, the number sampled must not be so large that it is impractical.

We can see from the definitions and examples that the value of a particular probability can extend from 0 (impossible) to 1 (the sure thing). A probability of $\frac{1}{2}$ expresses equal likelihood of success or failure.

There are cases in which it is more practical to compute the probability of the failure of an event, in order to calculate the probability of its success. This is based on the fact that the probability of failure is

$$F = 1 - \frac{s}{n}.$$

Thus the probability of success, in terms of the probability of failure, is

$$P = 1 - F. \tag{21-3}$$

Example E.   A bag contains 3 red balls, 4 white balls, and 7 black balls. What is the probability of drawing a red or a black ball?

This can be computed directly, or it can be computed by determining that the probability of drawing a white ball is $\frac{4}{14}$ or $\frac{2}{7}$. This would be the probability of failure. This means that the probability of success is $\frac{5}{7}$.

One misconception is often encountered when we are talking about probability. In dealing with the probability that a single event will occur, we should remember that the occurrence of this event in the past does not alter the probability of the event occurring in the future.

Example F.   If a coin is tossed 7 times and it comes up tails each time, the probability that it will come up heads on the next toss is still $\frac{1}{2}$. On any given toss, the probability is $\frac{1}{2}$. If we wished to find the probability of heads coming up at least once in 8 tosses we would find it to be $\frac{255}{256}$. This, however, is a different problem from that of finding the probability of heads on a particular toss of the coin.

So far we have considered only the probability of success of a single event. The following examples illustrate how the probability of success of a combination of events is found.

Example G.   What is the probability of a coin turning up heads in each of two successive tosses?

We can use the definition of probability to determine this result. On the first toss there are two possibilities. On the second toss there are also two possibilities, which means there are, in all, four possible ways in which the coin may fall in two successive tosses. These are HH, HT, TT, TH. Only one of these is successful (heads on two successive tosses). Thus the probability is $\frac{1}{4}$. This is equivalent to multiplying the probability of success of the first toss by the probability of success of the second toss, or $(\frac{1}{2})\,(\frac{1}{2}) = \frac{1}{4}$. When we use this multiplication method it is not necessary to figure out all possibilities, a procedure which is often very lengthy, or even impossible from a practical point of view. This multiplication may be stated roughly as "there is a probability of $\frac{1}{2}$ (the second toss) of a probability of $\frac{1}{2}$ (the first toss) of success."

Example H.   Two cards are drawn from a deck of bridge cards. If the first card is not replaced before the second is drawn, what is the probability that both will be hearts?

The probability of drawing a heart on the first draw is $\frac{13}{52}$, or $\frac{1}{4}$. If this first card is a heart, there are only 12 hearts of 51 remaining cards for the second draw. Thus the probability of success on the second draw is $\frac{12}{51}$. Multiplying these results, we have the probability of success for both, or

$$P = (\tfrac{1}{4})(\tfrac{12}{51}) = \tfrac{1}{17}.$$

This means there is a 1-in-17 chance of drawing two successive hearts in this manner.

Thus the probability of success of a compound event is given in terms of the probabilities of the separate events by

$$P_{1 \text{ and } 2} = P_1 P_2. \tag{21-4}$$

Example I. In three tosses of a single die, what is the probability of tossing at least one 2?

Instead of calculating the various combinations, it is easier to calculate the probability of failure to get a 2, and subtract that from 1. This is due to the fact that the probability of failure is $\frac{5}{6}$ each time, and this must occur three times successively for failure of the compound event. Thus

$$F = (\tfrac{5}{6})(\tfrac{5}{6})(\tfrac{5}{6}) = \tfrac{125}{216} \quad \text{or} \quad P = 1 - \tfrac{125}{216} = \tfrac{91}{216}.$$

Exercises

In Exercises 1 through 8 consider a bag which contains 5 red balls, 6 white balls, and 9 black balls. What is the probability of drawing each of the following?

1. A red ball

2. A white ball

3. A white or black ball

4. A red or white ball

5. Two red balls on successive draws, if the first ball is replaced before the second draw is made

6. Two white balls on successive draws, if the first ball is replaced before the second draw is made

7. Two red balls on successive draws if the first ball is not replaced before the second draw is made

8. A red ball and then a white ball if the first ball is not replaced before the second draw is made

In Exercises 9 through 16 assume that we are tossing a single die. What is the probability of tossing the following?

9. A 4

10. A 2 or 4

11. Other than a 4

12. Other than a 2 or 4

13. Two successive 4's

14. Three successive 4's

15. At least one 4 in two successive tosses

16. At least one 4 in four successive tosses

In Exercises 17 through 22 assume that we are tossing two dice. What is the probability of tossing a total of the following?

17. 2 (We must first determine that there are 36 different ways in which the dice may fall.)

18. 3   19. 7   20. 10, 11, or 12

21. 7 on two successive tosses

22. At least one 7 in two successive tosses

In Exercises 23 through 26 use the following information. An insurance company, in compiling mortality tables, found that of 10,000 10-year olds, 5,800 lived to be 60 and 3,800 lived to be 70.

23. What is the probability of a 10-year-old living to the age of 70?

24. What is the probability of a 60-year-old living to the age of 70?

25. What is the probability of two 10-year-old people living to the age of 60?

26. What is the probability of two 60-year-old people living to the age of 70?

In Exercises 27 through 34 solve the given problems in probability.

27. What is the probability of drawing an ace on each of two successive draws from a standard bridge deck of cards, if the first card is not replaced before drawing the second card?

28. What is the probability of drawing at least one ace in two draws, if the first card is not replaced before drawing the second card?

29. For the machine in Example D, how many defective parts should we expect to find in 300 total parts?

30. A certain college, which accepts students only from the upper quarter of the high-school graduating class, finds that 12% of its students attain an average of 3.0 or better (based on a highest attainable score of 4.0). If all the graduates from a particular high school were to apply to this college, what is the probability of a particular one of them attaining an average of 3.0 or better in his classes at the college?

31. One of the first three trials in a series of complicated scientific experiments was unsuccessful due to a failure in a piece of equipment. Based on these three trials, what is the probability of success of the next two successive trials?

32. In Exercise 31, if the fourth trial is successful, what is the probability at this point of the fifth trial being successful?

33. In a random test of newly manufactured transistors, if there are two defective transistors in a particular group of 20, and two of the 20 are tested, what is the probability that at least one of those tested will be defective?

34. How many of the transistors of Exercise 33 would have to be tested in order for there to be a 50% chance of testing one of the defective ones?

21-2 Frequency distributions and measures of central tendency

When a mathematician wishes to state the relation between the area of a circle and its radius, he writes $A = \pi r^2$, and he knows that this relation is true for all circles. When an engineer wishes to find the safe load which a particular cable is able to support, he cannot so simply write an equation for the relation, because the load which a cable may support depends on the diameter of the cable, the material of which it is made, the quality of material in the particular cable, any possible defects in its manufacture, and anything else which could make this cable different from all other cables. Thus, to determine the load which a cable can support, he may test many cables of particular specifications. He will find that most of the cables can support approximately the same load, but that there is some variation, and occasionally perhaps a great variation for some reason or other. Any conclusions he may draw will, by the nature of their source, yield probable knowledge of the cable.

In this section and in the remainder of this chapter, we are going to discuss the methods of tabulating and analyzing this kind of statistical information. The first thing to be done, after the information is collected, is to tabulate it in some convenient form.

Normally the number of measurements is sufficiently large that it is not feasible to attempt to tabulate the number of occurrences for a particular value. Values are therefore within specific ranges of values, and the number of values within each range is then counted. This is then called a *frequency distribution;* that is, the association of a set of values with the number of times this set occurs.

Example A.   A certain mathematics course had 80 students enrolled in it. After all the tests and exams were recorded, the instructors determined a numerical average (based on 100) for each student. The following is a list of the numerical grades, with the number of students receiving each.

22—1, 37—1, 40—2, 44—1, 47—1, 53—1, 55—3, 56—1, 60—3, 61—1, 63—4, 65—2, 66—1, 67—5, 68—2, 70—2, 71—4, 72—3, 74—5, 75—4, 77—7, 78—4, 79—1, 81—2, 82—4, 84—1, 85—1, 86—3, 87—2, 88—1, 90—2, 92—1, 93—2, 95—1, 97—1.

We can observe from this listing that it is difficult to see just how the grades were distributed. Therefore the instructors grouped the grades into intervals, which included five possible grades in each interval. This led to the following table.

Interval	20–24	25–29	30–34	35–39	40–44	45–49	50–54	55–59
Number in Interval	1	0	0	1	3	1	1	4
Interval	60–64	65–69	70–74	75–79	80–84	85–89	90–94	94–99
Number in Interval	8	10	14	16	7	7	5	2

We can see that the distribution of grades becomes much clearer in the above table. Finally, since the school graded students only with the letters A, B, C, D, and F, the instructors then grouped the grades in intervals below 60, from 60–69, from 70–79, from 80–89, and from 90–100, and assigned the appropriate letter grade to each numerical grade within each interval. This led to the following table.

Grade	A	B	C	D	F
Number receiving this grade	7	14	30	18	11

Thus we can see the distribution according to letter grades. We can also note that, if the number of intervals were reduced much further, it would be difficult to draw any reasonable conclusions regarding the distribution of grades.

Just as graphs are useful in representing algebraic functions, so also are they a very convenient method of representing frequency distributions. There are several useful methods of graphing such distributions, among which the most important are the *histogram* and the *frequency curve*. The following examples illustrate these graphical representations.

Example B.   A histogram represents a particular set of data by use of rectangles. The width of each rectangle is the width of the interval being represented, and the height is the number of values within the interval. Also, it is common to use one number, the middle value, to represent the interval. The histograms in Figs. 21-1 and 21-2 represent the grouped data of Example A.

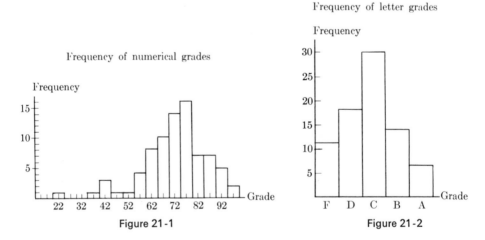

Figure 21-1   Figure 21-2

Example C.   The frequency curve represents a set of data by plotting as abscissas (*x*-values) the representative value of the interval, and as ordinates (*y*-values) the number of values in the interval (the frequency). If the resulting points are joined by straight-line segments, the figure is called a frequency polygon. If the points are joined by a smooth curve, the figure is called a fre-quency curve. Figures 21-3 and 21-4 represent a frequency polygon and a frequency curve illustrating the data of Example A.

Tables and graphical representations give a general description of data. However, it is often profitable and convenient to find representative values

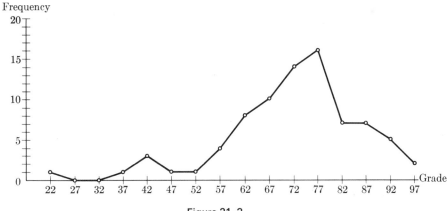

Figure 21-3

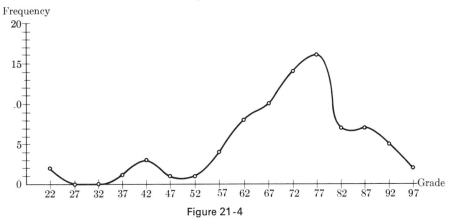

Figure 21-4

for the location of the center of distribution, and other numbers to give a measure of the deviation from this central value. In this way we can obtain an arithmetical description of the data. We shall now discuss the values commonly used to measure the location of the center of the distribution. These are referred to as "measures of central tendency."

The first of these measures of central tendency is the *median*. The median is the middle number, that number for which there are as many above it as below it in the distribution. If there is no middle number, the median is that number halfway between the two numbers nearest the middle of the distribution.

Example D.   Given the numbers 5, 2, 6, 4, 7, 4, 7, 2, 8, 9, 4, 11, 9, 1, 3, we find that when they are arranged in numerical order, the median (the middle number) is 5.

Example E.   In the distribution of grades given in Example A of this section, the median is 74. There are 80 grades in all, and if they are listed in numerical order we find that the 39th through the 43rd grade is 74. This means that the 40th and 41st grades are both 74. The number halfway between the 40th and 41st grades would be the median. The fact that both are 74 means that the median is also 74.

Another, and more widely applied, measure of central tendency is the *arithmetic mean*. The mean is calculated by finding the sum of all the values and then dividing by the number of values. This calculation can be somewhat simplified if any of the numbers appears more than once. By multiplying each number by its frequency, adding these results, and then dividing by the total number of values considered, the mean can be calculated. Letting $\bar{x}$ (usually read as "x bar") stand for the mean of the values $x_1, x_2, \ldots, x_n$, which occur $f_1, f_2, \ldots, f_n$ times, respectively, we have

$$\bar{x} = \frac{x_1 f_1 + x_2 f_2 + \cdots + x_n f_n}{f_1 + f_2 + \cdots + f_n}. \tag{21-5}$$

(This notation can be simplified by letting

$$x_1 f_1 + x_2 f_2 + \cdots + x_n f_n = \sum_{i=1}^{n} x_i f_i,$$

and

$$f_1 + f_2 + \cdots + f_n = \sum_{i=1}^{n} f_i.$$

This notation is often used to indicate a sum, where Σ is known as the *summation sign*.)

Example F. We find the mean of the numbers in Example D of this section by

$$\bar{x} = \frac{1(1) + 2(2) + 3(1) + 4(3) + 5(1) + 6(1) + 7(2) + 8(1) + 9(2) + 11(1)}{15}$$

$$= \frac{82}{15} = 5.5.$$

Example G. We find the arithmetic mean (average) of the grades in Example A by

$$\bar{x} = \frac{22(1) + (37)(1) + (40)(2) + \cdots + (67)(5) + \cdots + (97)(1)}{80}$$

$$= \frac{5733}{80} = 71.7.$$

Exercises

In Exercises 1 through 12 find the indicated numbers given the sets of numbers

A: 53, 54, 59, 57, 50, 53, 59;

B: 2, 5, 3, 8, 6, 7, 8, 3, 4, 1, 9, 7, 5, 2, 1, 7, 5;

C: 36, 15, 22, 18, 35, 27, 43, 53, 26, 25, 30;

D: 11, 14, 17, 12, 15, 22, 23, 13, 14, 12, 17, 16, 14, 13, 20, 11, 22, 17, 14, 15.

1. The median of set A
2. The median of set B
3. The median of set C
4. The median of set D
5. The mean of set A
6. The mean of set B
7. The mean of set C
8. The mean of set D
9. A frequency table with intervals 49–51, 52–54, *etc.*, for set A.
10. A frequency table with intervals 0–1, 2–3, *etc.*, for set B.
11. A frequency table with intervals 0–9, 10–19, *etc.*, for set C.
12. A frequency table with intervals 10–12, 13–15, *etc.*, for set D.

In Exercises 13 through 16 draw histograms for the data found in the given exercise.

13. Exercise 9   14. Exercise 10   15. Exercise 11   16. Exercise 12

In Exercises 17 through 20 draw a frequency curve for the data found in the given exercise.

17. Excersise 9   18. Exercise 10   19. Exercise 11   20. Exercise 12

In Exercises 21 through 28 find the indicated quantities.

21. Form a histogram for the data given in the following table, which was compiled when a particular type of cable was being tested for its breaking load.

Load interval, pounds	830–839	840–849	850–859	860–869	870–879	880–889	890–899
Number of cables breaking	4	14	48	531	85	22	2

22. Form a frequency polygon for the data given in Exercise 21.
23. A researcher, testing an electric circuit, found the following values for the current (in milliamperes) in the circuit on successive trials: 3.44, 3.46, 3.39, 3.44, 3.48, 3.40, 3.29, 3.46, 3.41, 3.37, 3.45, 3.47, 3.43, 3.38, 3.50, 3.41, 3.42, 3.47. Form a histogram for the intervals 3.25–3.29, 3.30–3.34, etc.
24. Form a histogram for the data given in Exercise 23 for the intervals 3.21–3.30, 3.31–3.40, etc.
25. Find the median of the data given in Exercise 23.
26. Find the mean of the data given in Exercise 23.
27. Take two dice and toss them 100 times, recording at each toss the sum which appears. Draw a frequency polygon of the sum and the frequency with which it occurred. Compare this with the expected frequency as based on probability.
28. From the financial section of a newspaper, record (to the nearest dollar) the closing price of the first 50 stocks listed. Form a frequency table with intervals 0–9, 10–19, and so forth. Form a histogram of these data. Finally, find the median price.

In Exercises 29 and 30 use the following information. The *mode* of a frequency distribution, another measure of central tendency, is defined as the measure with the maximum frequency, if there is one. A set of numbers may have more than one mode. Using this definition, find the mode of the numbers in the indicated sets of numbers at the beginning of this exercise set.

29. Set B 30. Set D

21-3 Standard deviation

As we mentioned in the preceding section, numbers which give a measure of the deviation from the measure of central tendency are of importance in analyzing statistical data. If there is a great deviation from the mean, this probably signifies that the data are less meaningful than if the deviation is relatively small. The measure of deviation presented in this section is called the *standard deviation*.

The standard deviation of a set of numbers is given by the equation

$$s = \sqrt{\overline{(x - \bar{x})^2}}. \tag{21-6}$$

The definition of s indicates that the following steps are to be taken in computing its value.

(1) Find the arithmetic mean $\bar{x}$ of the set of numbers.

(2) Subtract the mean from each of the numbers of the set.

(3) Square these differences.

(4) Find the arithmetic mean of these squares. (Note that a bar over any quantity signifies the mean of the set of values of that quantity.)

(5) Find the square root of this last arithmetic mean. Defined in this way, s must be a positive number, and thus indicates a deviation from the mean, regardless of whether or not individual numbers are greater or less than the mean.

Example A.   Find the standard deviation of the numbers 1, 5, 4, 2, 6, 2, 1, 1, 5, 3. The most efficient method of finding s is to make a table in which Steps (1) to (4) are indicated.

x	$x - \bar{x}$	$(x - \bar{x})^2$
1	-2	4
5	2	4
4	1	1
2	-1	1
6	3	9
2	-1	1
1	-2	4
1	-2	4
5	2	4
3	0	0
$\overline{30}$		$\overline{32}$

$$\bar{x} = \tfrac{30}{10} = 3,$$

$$\overline{(x - \bar{x})^2} = \tfrac{32}{10} = 3.2,$$

$$s = \sqrt{3.2} = 1.8.$$

We can see from this example that had there been a great many numbers, and had $\bar{x}$ been a decimal of some form, the calculations would have been much more tedious to carry out. There is one way we can reduce the amount of work somewhat: by algebraic manipulation within the radical of the definition of s.

To find the mean of the sum of two sets of numbers, x_i and y_i, we can determine the mean of the x's and the mean of the y's and add the results. That is,

$$\overline{x + y} = \bar{x} + \bar{y}. \tag{21-7}$$

This is true by the meaning of the definition of the arithmetic mean.

$$\overline{x + y} = \frac{x_1 + x_2 + \cdots + x_n + y_1 + y_2 + \cdots + y_n}{n}$$

$$= \frac{x_1 + x_2 + \cdots + x_n}{n} + \frac{y_1 + y_2 + \cdots y_n}{n} = \bar{x} + \bar{y}.$$

Also, when we find the arithmetic mean, if all the numbers contain a constant factor, this number can be factored before the mean is found. That is,

$$\overline{kx} = k\bar{x}. \tag{21-8}$$

If we multiply out the quantity under the radical in Eq. (21-6), and then apply Eq. (21-7), we obtain

$$\overline{x^2 - 2x\bar{x} + \bar{x}^2} = \overline{x^2} - \overline{2x\bar{x}} + \overline{\bar{x}^2}.$$

In this equation the number 2 and $\bar{x}$ are constants for any given problem. Thus, by using Eq. (21-8), we have

$$\overline{x^2} - \overline{2x\bar{x}} + \overline{\bar{x}^2} = \overline{x^2} - 2\bar{x}(\bar{x}) + \bar{x}^2(1) = \overline{x^2} - \bar{x}^2.$$

Substituting this last result into Eq. (21-6), we have

$$s = \sqrt{\overline{x^2} - \bar{x}^2}. \tag{21-9}$$

Equation (21-9) shows us that the standard deviation s may be found by finding the mean of the squares of the x's, subtracting the square of $\bar{x}$, and then finding the square root. This eliminates the step of subtracting $\bar{x}$ from each x, a step required by the original definition.

Example B.   By using Eq. (21-9), find s for the numbers in Example A. Again, a table is the most convenient form.

x	x^2
1	1
5	25
4	16
2	4
6	36
2	4
1	1
1	1
5	25
3	9
30	122

$$\bar{x} = \tfrac{30}{10} = 3, \qquad \bar{x}^2 = 9,$$

$$\overline{x^2} = \tfrac{122}{10} = 12.2,$$

$$\overline{x^2} - \bar{x}^2 = 12.2 - 9 = 3.2,$$

$$s = \sqrt{3.2} = 1.8.$$

Example C. In an ammeter, two resistances are connected in parallel. Most of the current passing through the meter goes through the one called the shunt. In order to determine the accuracy of the resistance of shunts being made for ammeters, a manufacturer tested a sample of 100 shunts. The resistance of each, to the nearest hundredth of an ohm, is indicated in the following table. Calculate the standard deviation of the resistances of the shunts.

R, ohms	f	fR	fR^2
0.200	1	0.200	0.0400
0.210	3	0.630	0.1323
0.220	5	1.100	0.2420
0.230	10	2.300	0.5290
0.240	17	4.080	0.9792
0.250	40	10.000	2.5000
0.260	13	3.380	0.8788
0.270	6	1.620	0.4374
0.280	3	0.840	0.2352
0.290	2	0.580	0.1682
	100	24.730	6.1421

$$\bar{R} = \frac{\Sigma fR}{\Sigma f} = \frac{24.73}{100} = 0.2473,$$

$$\bar{R}^2 = 0.06116,$$

$$\overline{R^2} = \frac{\Sigma fR^2}{\Sigma f} = \frac{6.142}{100} = 0.06142,$$

$$\overline{R^2} - \bar{R}^2 = 0.00026,$$

$$s = \sqrt{0.00026} = 0.016.$$

The arithmetic mean of the resistances is 0.247 ohm, with a mean deviation of 0.016 ohm. Note in the calculations that one extra significant digit was carried.

Example D. Find the standard deviation of the grades in Example A of Section 21-2. Use the frequency distribution as grouped in intervals 20–24, 25–29, and so forth, and then assume that each value in the interval is equal to the representative value (middle value) of the interval. (This method is not exact, but when a problem involves a large number of values, the method provides a very good approximation and eliminates a great deal of arithmetic work.)

x	f	fx	fx^2
22	1	22	484
27	0	0	0
32	0	0	0
37	1	37	1,370
42	3	126	5,290
47	1	47	2,210
52	1	52	2,700
57	4	228	13,000
62	8	496	30,800
67	10	670	44,900
72	14	1,008	72,600
77	16	1,232	94,900
82	7	574	47,100
87	7	609	53,000
92	5	460	42,300
97	2	194	18,800
	80	5,755	429,500

$$x = \frac{\sum fx}{\sum f} = \frac{5,755}{80} = 71.9,$$

$$\bar{x}^2 = 5,170,$$

$$\overline{x^2} = \frac{\sum fx^2}{80} = \frac{429,500}{80} = 5,370,$$

$$\overline{x^2} - \bar{x}^2 = 200,$$

$$s = \sqrt{200} = 14.1.$$

(Three significant figures are used so that the slide rule may be employed for calculations. Actually s is good only to two significant digits, because 200 only has two: see Appendix C.)

The significance of the standard deviation lies in the fact that, in practice, about 68% of the values are found within the limits of $\bar{x} - s$ to $\bar{x} + s$. This forms part of the basis of deriving what is known as the *normal distribution curve* (see Fig. 21-5), which is a curve giving the theoretical distribution about the arithmetic mean. In a more complete discussion of the normal distribution curve, it is shown that its theoretical equation is

$$y = \frac{1}{\sqrt{2\pi}} e^{-x^2/2}. \tag{21-10}$$

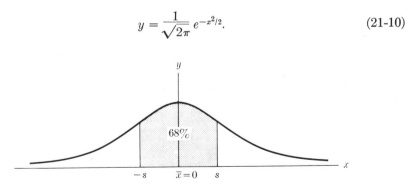

The normal distribution curve

Figure 21-5

In Example D we find that 59 of the 80 values (74%) are from 58 to 86, which is the range of $\bar{x} - s$ to $\bar{x} + s$. This means that there are more values near the mean than there are in a theoretical distribution.

Exercises

In Exercises 1 through 6 use Eq. (21-6) to find s for the indicated sets of numbers from exercises of Section 21-2.

1. Set A 2. Set B 3. Set C
4. Set D 5. Exercise 21   6. Exercise 23

In Exercises 7 through 12 use Eq. (21-9) to find s for the indicated sets of numbers from exercises of Section 21-2.

7. Set A 8. Set B 9. Set C
10. Set D 11. Exercise 21   12. Exercise 23

In Exercise 13 through 16 find the percentage of values in the range $\bar{x} - s$ to $\bar{x} + s$ for the indicated sets of numbers from the exercises of Section 21-2.

13. Set A 14. Set B 15. Set D 16. Exercise 23

21-4 Fitting a straight line to a set of points

We have considered statistical methods for dealing with one variable. We have discussed methods of tabulating, graphing, measuring the central tendency and the deviations from this value for one variable. We now shall discuss how to obtain a relationship between two variables for which a set of points is known.

In this section we shall show a method of "fitting" a straight line to a given set of points. In the following section fitting suitable nonlinear curves to given sets of points will be discussed. Some of the reasons for doing this are (1) to have a concise relationship expressed between the variables, (2) to use the equation for the purpose of predicting certain fundamental results, (3) to determine the reliability of certain sets of data, and (4) to use the data for testing theoretical concepts.

We shall assume for the examples and exercises of the remainder of this chapter that there is some relationship between the variables. Often when we are analyzing statistics for variables between which we think a relationship might exist, the points are so scattered as to give no reasonable idea regarding the possible functional relationship. We shall assume here that such combinations of variables have been discarded in the analysis.

Example A.   All the students enrolled in the mathematics course referred to in Example A of Section 21-2 took an entrance test in mathematics. To study the reliability of this test, an instructor tabulated the test scores of 10 students (selected at random), along with their course averages, and made a graph of these figures (see table below, and Fig. 21-6).

Student	Entrance test score, based on 40	Course average, based on 100
A	29	63
B	33	88
C	22	77
D	17	67
E	26	70
F	37	93
G	30	72
H	32	81
I	23	47
J	30	74

We now ask whether or not there is a functional relationship between the test scores and the course grades. Certainly no clear-cut relationship exists, but in general we see that the higher the test score, the higher the course grade. This leads to the possibility that there might be some straight line, from which none of the points would vary too significantly. If such a line could be found, then it could be the basis of predictions as to the possible success a student might have in the course, on the basis of his grade on the entrance test. Assuming that such a straight line exists, the problem is to find the equation of this line. Figure 21-7 shows two such possible lines.

There are various methods of determining the line which best fits the given points. We shall employ the one which is most widely used: the *method of least squares*. The basic principle of this method is that the sum of the squares of the deviation of all points from the best line (in accordance with this method) is the least it can be. By "deviation" we mean the difference between the y-value of the line and the y-value for the point (of original data) for a particular value of x.

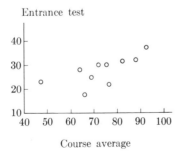

Figure 21-6

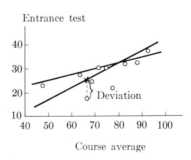

Figure 21-7

Example B.   In Fig. 21-7 the deviation of one point is indicated. The point
(67, 17) (student D of Example A) has a deviation of 8 from the indicated line
of Fig. 21-7. Thus we square the value of this deviation to obtain 64. The method
of least squares requires that the sum of all such squares be a minimum in
order to determine the line which fits best.

Therefore, in applying this method, it is necessary to use the equation of a
straight line and the coordinates of the points of the data. The deviation of
these is indicated and squared. The problem then arises as to the method of
determining the constants m and b in the equation of the line $y = mx + b$ for
which these squares are a minimum. Since we are dealing with squared quantities, the problem is one of finding the minimum of a quadratic-type function.
The following example indicates the method employed.

Example C.   For what value of x is the quadratic function

$$y = x^2 - 8x + 19 \quad \text{a minimum?}$$

By inspection we see that this equation represents a parabola. From the
properties of this type of parabola, we know that the minimum value of y will
occur at the vertex. Thus we are to find the x-coordinate of the vertex. To do
this, we complete the square of the x-terms. And so we have

$$y = (x^2 - 8x + 16) + 3 \quad \text{or} \quad y = (x - 4)^2 + 3.$$

We now see that if $x = 4$, $y = 3$. If x is anything other than 4, $y > 3$, since
$(x - 4)$ is squared and is always positive for values other than $x = 4$. Therefore the minimum value of this function is 3, and it occurs for $x = 4$.

By finding the deviations, squaring, and then applying the method above for
finding the minimum of the sum of the squares, the equation of the *least-squares
line*,

$$y = mx + b, \tag{21-10}$$

can be found by the values

$$m = \frac{\overline{xy} - \bar{x}\bar{y}}{s_x^2}, \tag{21-11}$$

and

$$b = \bar{y} - m\bar{x}. \tag{21-12}$$

In Eqs. (21-11) and (21-12), the x's and y's are those of the points in the data
and s is the standard deviation of the x-values.

Example D.   Find the least-squares line of the data of Example A.
   Here the y-values will be the entrance-test scores, and the x-values the course
averages. The results are best obtained by tabulating the necessary quantities,
as we do in the following table.

x	y	xy	x^2
63	29	1,830	3,970
88	33	2,900	7,740
77	22	1,690	5,930
67	17	1,140	4,490
70	26	1,820	4,900
93	37	3,440	8,650
72	30	2,160	5,180
81	32	2,590	6,560
47	23	1,080	2,210
74	30	2,220	5,480
732	279	20,870	55,110

$$\bar{x} = \frac{732}{10} = 73.2, \quad \bar{x}^2 = 5358,$$

$$\bar{y} = \frac{279}{10} = 27.9, \quad \bar{x}\bar{y} = 2040,$$

$$\overline{xy} = \frac{20,870}{10} = 2087, \quad \overline{x^2} = \frac{55,110}{10} = 5511,$$

$$s_x^2 = \overline{x^2} - \bar{x}^2 = 153$$

$$m = \frac{\overline{xy} - \bar{x}\bar{y}}{s_x^2} = \frac{2087 - 2040}{153}$$

$$= \frac{47}{153} = 0.307,$$

$$b = \bar{y} - m\bar{x} = 27.9 - (0.307)(73.2) = 27.9 - 22.5 = 5.4;$$

$$y = 0.307x + 5.4.$$

Thus the equation of the line is $y = 0.307x + 5.4$. This is the line indicated in Fig. 21-8.

Remark 1: For ease of computation and to keep the graph within the same limits as the original points, we can reduce all x-values by 40 and all y-values by 10. The origin of these values would be at the intersection of the light lines in Fig. 21-8.

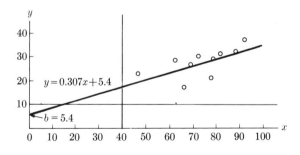

Figure 21-8

Remark 2: When we are plotting the least-squares line, we know two points on it. These are $(0, b)$ and $(\bar{x}, \bar{y})$. We can see that $(\bar{x}, \bar{y})$ satisfies the equation from the solution for b [Eq. (21-12)].

Example E. In an experiment to determine the relation between the load on a spring and the length of the spring, the following data were found.

Load (lb)	0.0	1.0	2.0	3.0	4.0	5.0
Length (in.)	10.0	11.2	12.3	13.4	14.6	15.9

Find the least-squares line for this data which expresses the length as a function of the load.

x	y	xy	x^2
0.0	10.0	0.0	0.0
1.0	11.2	11.2	1.0
2.0	12.3	24.6	4.0
3.0	13.4	40.2	9.0
4.0	14.6	58.4	16.0
5.0	15.9	79.5	25.0
15.0	77.4	213.9	55.0

$$\bar{x} = \frac{15.0}{6} = 2.50, \quad \bar{x}^2 = 6.25,$$

$$\bar{y} = \frac{77.4}{6} = 12.9, \quad \bar{x}\bar{y} = 32.25,$$

$$\overline{xy} = \frac{213.9}{6} = 35.65, \quad \overline{x^2} = \frac{55.0}{6} = 9.17,$$

$$s_x^2 = \overline{x^2} - \bar{x}^2 = 9.17 - 6.25 = 2.92,$$

$$m = \frac{35.65 - 32.25}{2.92} = 1.16, \quad b = 12.9 - (1.16)(2.50) = 10.0.$$

Therefore, the least-squares line in this case is

$$y = 1.16x + 10.0,$$

where y is the length of the spring and x is the load. In Fig. 21-9, the line shown is the least-squares line, and the points are the experimental data points.

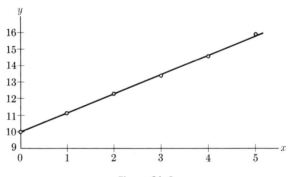

Figure 21-9

Exercises

In Exercises 1 through 8 find the equation of the least-squares line for the given data. In each case graph the line and the data points on the same graph.

1. The points in the following table:

x	4	6	8	10	12
y	1	4	5	8	9

2. The points in the following table:

x	1	2	3	4	5	6	7
y	10	17	28	37	49	56	72

3. The points in the following table:

x	20	26	30	38	48	60
y	160	145	135	120	100	90

4. The points in the following table:

x	1	3	6	5	8	10	4	7	3	8
y	15	12	10	8	9	2	11	9	11	7

5. In an electrical experiment, the following data were found for the values of current and voltage for a particular element of the circuit. Find the voltage as a function of the current.

Voltage (volts)	3.00	4.10	5.60	8.00	10.50
Current (milliamperes)	15.0	10.8	9.30	3.55	4.60

6. The velocity of a falling object was found each second by use of an electrical device as shown. Find the velocity as a function of time.

Velocity (cm/sec)	970	1950	2950	3940	4920	5890	6860
Time (sec)	1.00	2.00	3.00	4.00	5.00	6.00	7.00

7. In an experiment on the photoelectric effect, the frequency of the light being used was measured as a function of the stopping potential (the voltage just sufficient to stop the photoelectric current) with the results given below. Find the least-squares line for V as a function of f. The frequency for $V = 0$ is known as the *threshold frequency*. From the graph, determine the threshold frequency.

V (volts)	0.35	0.60	0.85	1.10	1.45	1.80
$f (\times 10^{14} \ 1/\text{sec})$	5.50	6.05	6.60	7.35	8.05	8.80

8. If a gas is cooled under conditions of constant volume, it is noted that the pressure falls nearly proportionally as the temperature. If this were to happen until there was no pressure, the theoretical temperature for this case is referred to as *absolute zero*. In an elementary experiment, the following data were found for pressure and temperature for a gas under constant volume.

P (cm of Hg)	100	107	115	121	129	137
T (°C)	0.0	20	40	50	80	100

Find the least-squares line for P as a function of T, and, from the graph, determine the value of absolute zero found in this experiment.

The linear coefficient of correlation, a measure of the relatedness of two variables, is defined by

$$r = m \frac{s_x}{s_y}.$$

Due to its definition, the values of r lie in the range $-1 \le r \le 1$. If r is near 1, the correlation is considered good. For values of r between $-\frac{1}{2}$ and $+\frac{1}{2}$, the correlation is poor. If r is near -1, the variables are said to be negatively correlated; that is, one increases while the other decreases.

In Exercises 9 through 12 compute r for the given sets of data.

9. Exercise 1   10. Exercise 2   11. Exercise 4   12. Example A

21-5 Fitting nonlinear curves to data

If the experimental points do not appear to be on a straight line, but we recognize them as being approximately on some other type of curve, the method of least squares can be extended to use on these other curves. For example, if the points are apparently on a parabola, we could use the function $y = a + bx^2$. To use the above method, we shall extend the least-squares line to

$$y = m[f(x)] + b. \tag{21-13}$$

Here, $f(x)$ must be calculated first, and then the problem can be treated as a least-squares line to find the values of m and b. Some of the functions $f(x)$ which may be considered for use are x^2, $1/x$, and 10^x.

Example A.   Find the least-squares curve $y = mx^2 + b$ for the points in the following table.

y	1	5	12	24	53	76
x	0	1	2	3	4	5

The necessary quantities are tabluated for purposes of calculation.

x	y	$f(x) = x^2$	yx^2	$(x^2)^2$
0	1	0	0	0
1	5	1	5	1
2	12	4	48	16
3	24	9	216	81
4	53	16	848	256
5	76	25	1900	625
	171	55	3017	979

$$\overline{x^2} = \frac{55}{6} = 9.17, \ \overline{x^2}^2 = 84.1,$$

$$\overline{y} = \frac{171}{6} = 28.5, \ \overline{x^2 y} = 261,$$

$$\overline{yx^2} = \frac{3017}{6} = 503, \ \overline{(x^2)^2} = \frac{979}{6} = 163.2,$$

$$s^2_{(x^2)} = 163.2 - 84.1 = 79.1,$$

$$m = \frac{503 - 261}{79.1} = \frac{242}{79.1} = 3.06, \ b = 28.5 - (3.06)(9.17) = 0.40.$$

Therefore the desired equation is $y = 3.06x^2 + 0.40$. The graph of this equation and the data points are shown in Fig. 21-10.

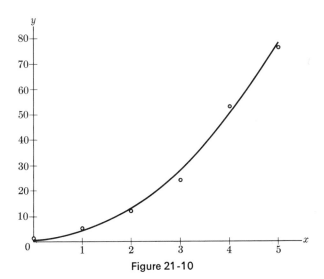

Figure 21-10

Example B. In a physics experiment designed to measure the pressure and volume of a gas at constant temperature, the following data were found. When the points were plotted, they were seen to approximate the hyperbola $y = c/x$. Find the least-squares approximation to this hyperbola $[y = m(1/x) + b]$ (see Fig. 21-11).

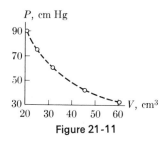

Figure 21-11

P, cm Hg	V, cm³	$x(= V)$	$y(= P)$	$f(x) = 1/x$	$y(1/x)$	$(1/x)^2$
90.0	21.0	21.0	90.0	0.0476	4.29	0.00227
74.4	25.0	25.0	74.4	0.0400	2.98	0.00160
61.0	31.8	31.8	61.0	0.0314	1.92	0.00100
45.5	41.1	41.1	45.5	0.0243	1.11	0.00059
32.0	60.1	60.1	32.0	0.0166	0.53	0.00028
			302.9	0.1599	10.83	0.00574

$$\overline{\frac{1}{x}} = 0.0320, \qquad \overline{\left(\frac{1}{x}\right)}^2 = 0.00102, \qquad \bar{y} = 60.6, \qquad \overline{\frac{1}{x}}\bar{y} = 1.94,$$

$$\overline{y\left(\frac{1}{x}\right)} = 2.17, \qquad \overline{\left(\frac{1}{x}\right)^2} = 0.00115, \qquad s_{(1/x)}^2 = 0.00115 - 0.00102$$

$$= 0.00013,$$

$$m = \frac{2.17 - 1.94}{0.00013} = 1770, \qquad b = 60.6 - 1770(0.032) = 4.0.$$

Thus the equation of the hyperbola $y = m(1/x) + b$ is $y = 1770/x + 4$. The graph of this hyperbola and the points representing the data are shown in Fig. 21-12.

Example C.   It has been found experimentally that the tensile strength of brass (a copper-zinc alloy) increases (within certain limits) with the percentage of zinc. The following table indicates the values which have been found (also see Fig. 21-13).

Tensile strength (10^5 lb/in.^{2})	0.32	0.36	0.40	0.44	0.48
Percentage of zinc	0	5	13	22	34

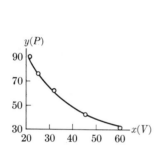

Figure 21-12

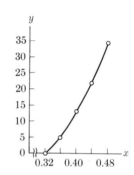

Figure 21-13

Fit a curve of the form $y = m(10^x) + b$ to the data. Let x = tensile strength ($\times 10^5$) and y = percentage of zinc.

x	y	$f(x) = 10^x$	$y(10^x)$	$(10^x)^2$
0.32	0	2.09	0.0	4.37
0.36	5	2.29	11.4	5.25
0.40	13	2.51	32.6	6.31
0.44	22	2.75	60.5	7.59
0.48	34	3.02	102.7	9.12
	74	12.66	207.2	32.64

To find $f(x) = 10^x$, we use logarithms. When $x = 0.32$, $10^{0.32}$ may be found by looking up the number for which 0.32 is the logarithm. This is due to the definition of a logarithm. Values of $(10^x)^2$ are found in the same manner. When $x = 0.32$, $(10^{0.32})^2 = (10)^{0.64}$, and the antilogarithm of 0.64 is required.

$$\overline{10^x} = 2.53,$$

$$\overline{10^x}^2 = 6.40,$$

$$\bar{y} = 14.8,$$

$$\overline{10^x\,\bar{y}} = 37.4,$$

$$\overline{y(10^x)} = 41.4,$$

$$\overline{(10^x)^2} = 6.53,$$

$$s^2_{(10^x)} = 6.53 - 6.40 = 0.13,$$

$$m = \frac{41.4 - 37.4}{0.13} = 31,$$

$$b = 14.8 - 31(2.53) = -64.$$

The equation of the curve is $y = 31(10^x) - 64$. It must be remembered that for practical purposes y must be positive. The graph of the equation is shown in Fig. 21-14, with the solid portion denoting the meaningful part of the curve. The points of the data are as also shown.

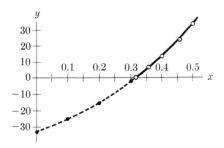

Figure 21-14

Exercises

In each of the following exercises find the indicated least-squares curve. Sketch the curve and plot the data points on the same graph.

1. For the points in the following table, find the least-squares curve $y = mx^2 + b$.

x	2	4	6	8	10
y	12	38	72	135	200

2. For the points in the following table, find the least-squares curve $y = m\sqrt{x} + b$.

x	0	4	8	12	16
y	1	9	11	14	15

3. For the points in the following table, find the least-squares curve $y = m(1/x) + b$.

x	1.10	2.45	4.04	5.86	6.90	8.54
y	9.85	4.50	2.90	1.75	1.48	1.30

4. For the points in the following table, find the least-squares curve $y = m(10^x) + b$.

x	0.00	0.200	0.500	0.950	1.325
y	6.00	6.60	8.20	14.0	26.0

5. The following data was found for the distance y that an object rolled down an inclined plane in time t. Determine the least-squares curve $y = mt^2 + b$.

y (cm)	6.0	23	55	98	148
t (sec)	1.0	2.0	3.0	4.0	5.0

6. The increase in length of a certain metallic rod was measured in relation to particular increases in temperature. If y represents the increase in length for the corresponding increase in temperature x, find the least-squares curve $y = m(x^2) + b$ for these data.

x (°C)	50.0	100	150	200	250
y (cm)	1.00	4.40	9.40	16.4	24.0

7. Use the data of Exercise 6 and determine the least-squares curve $y = m(10^z) + b$ where $z = x/1000$.

8. Measurements were made of the current in an electric circuit as a function of time. The circuit contained a resistance of 5 ohms and an inductance of 10 henries. The following data was found.

i (amps)	0.00	2.52	3.45	3.80	3.92
t (sec)	0.00	2.00	4.00	6.00	8.00

Find the least-squares curve $i = m(e^{-0.5t}) + b$ for this data. Use natural logarithms. From the equation, determine the value the current approaches as t approaches infinity.

9. The resonant frequency of an electric circuit containing a 4×10^{-6} farad capacitor was measured as a function of an inductance in the circuit. The following data were found.

f (1/sec)	490	360	250	200	170
L (henries)	1	2	4	6	9

Find the least-squares curve $f = m(1/\sqrt{L}) + b$.

10. The displacement of a pendulum bob from its equilibrium position as a function of time gave the following results.

Displacement (cm)	0.00	7.80	10.0	8.10	0.00
Time (sec)	0.00	0.90	1.60	2.20	3.15

Find the least-squares curve of the form $y = m(\sin x) + b$, expressing the displacement as y and the time as x.

21-6 Miscellaneous Exercises

In Exercises 1 through 4 assume two dice are being tossed.

1. What is the probability of tossing a number greater than 4?
2. What is the probability of tossing a 7 or an 11?
3. What is the probability of tossing a 7 and then an 11 in successive tosses?
4. What is the probability of tossing a 2, a 3, and a 4 in successive tosses?

In Exercises 5 through 8 use the following set of numbers:

$$2.3, 2.6, 4.2, 3.6, 3.5, 4.1, 4.8, 2.5, 3.0, 4.1, 3.8.$$

5. Determine the median of the set of numbers.
6. Determine the arithmetic mean of the set of numbers.
7. Determine the standard deviation of the set of numbers.
8. Construct a frequency table with intervals 2.0–2.9, 3.0–3.9 and 4.0–4.9.

In Exercises 9 through 12 use the following data:

   An important property of oil is its coefficient of viscosity, which gives a measure of how well it flows. In order to determine the viscosity of a certain motor oil, a refinery took samples from 12 different storage tanks and tested them at 130°F (a standard reference temperature). The results (in centipoise units) were 240, 280, 290, 260, 270, 260, 250, 270, 280, 260, 260, 250.

9. Determine the arithmetic mean.   10. Determine the median.
11. Determine the standard deviation.   12. Make a histogram.

In Exercises 13 through 16 use the following data.

   Two machine parts are considered satisfactorily assembled if their total thickness (to the nearest one-hundredth of an inch) is between or equal to 0.92 and 0.94 in. One hundred sample assemblies are tested, and the thicknesses, to the nearest one-hundredth of an inch, are given in the following table:

Total thickness	0.90	0.91	0.92	0.93	0.94	0.95	0.96
Number	3	9	31	38	12	5	2

13. Determine the arithmetic mean.   14. Determine the median.
15. Determine the standard deviation.   16. Make a frequency polygon.

In Exercises 17 through 20 use the following data.

   A Geiger counter records the presence of high-energy nuclear particles. Even though no apparent radioactive source is present, a certain number of particles will be recorded. These are primarily cosmic rays, which are caused by very high-energy particles from outer space. In an experiment to measure the amount of cosmic radiation, the number of counts were recorded during 200 5-sec intervals. The following table gives the number of counts, and the number of 5-sec intervals having this number of counts. Draw a frequency curve for this data.

Counts	0	1	2	3	4	5	6	7	8	9	10
Intervals	3	10	25	45	29	39	26	11	7	2	3

17. Determine the median.   18. Determine the arithmetic mean.

19. Make a histogram.   20. Make a frequency polygon.

In Exercises 21 through 24 solve the given problems in probability.

21. An integer n, where $10 < n < 20$, is chosen at random. What is the probability that n is even?

22. What is the probability of drawing both red aces from a standard bridge deck of cards in two draws, if the first card is not replaced before drawing the second card?

23. A manufacturer finds that 3% of the parts produced by a certain machine are defective. A testing machine fails to operate properly in its determination of a defective part 0.1% of the time. What is the probability of a defective part not being detected by the testing machine?

24. A certain team won 12 of its first 20 games. Using the complete past record to determine the probability of winning a next game, what is the probability of this team winning the next two games?

In Exercises 25 through 30 find the indicated least-squares curves.

25. In a certain experiment, the resistance of a certain resistor was measured as a function of the temperature. The data found were as follows:

R (ohms)	25.0	26.8	28.9	31.2	32.8	34.7
T (°C)	0	20	40	60	80	100

Find the least-squares line for this data, expressing R as a function of T. Sketch the line and data points on the same graph.

26. The solubility of sodium chloride (table salt) (in grams per 100 cm³ of water) as a function of temperature (°C) is measured as follows:

Solubility	35.7	36.0	36.6	37.3	38.4
Temperature	0	20	40	60	80

Find the least-squares straight line for these data.

27. The coefficient of friction of an object sliding down an inclined plane was measured as a function of the angle of incline of the plane. The following results were obtained.

Coefficient of friction	0.16	0.34	0.55	0.85	1.24	1.82	2.80
Angle (deg)	10	20	30	40	50	60	70

Find the least-squares curve of the form $y = m(\tan x) + b$, expressing the coefficient of friction as y and the angle as x.

28. An electrical device recorded the total distance (in cm) which an object fell at 0.1 sec intervals. Following are the data which were found.

Distance	4.90	19.5	44.0	78.1	122.0
Time	0.10	0.20	0.30	0.40	0.50

Find the least-squares curve of the form $y = mx^2 + b$, using y to represent distance and x to represent the time.

29. The period of a pendulum as a function of its length was measured, giving the following results.

Period (sec)	1.10	1.90	2.50	2.90	3.30
Length (ft)	1.00	3.00	5.00	7.00	9.00

Find the least-squares curve of the form $y = m\sqrt{x} + b$, which expresses the period as a function of the length.

30. In an elementary experiment which measured the wavelength of sound as a function of the frequency, the following results were obtained.

Wavelength (cm)	140	107	81	70	60
Frequency (1/sec)	240	320	400	480	560

Find the least-squares curve of the form $y = m(1/x) + b$ for this data, expressing wavelength as y and frequency as x.

Appendix A–Study Aids

A-1 Introduction

The primary objective of this text is to give you an understanding of mathematics so that you can use it effectively as a tool in your technology. Without understanding of the basic methods, knowledge is usually short-lived. However, if you do understand, you will find your work much more enjoyable and rewarding. This is true in any course you may take, be it in mathematics or in any other field.

Mathematics is an indispensable tool in almost all scientific fields of study. You will find it used to a greater and greater degree as you work in your chosen field. Generally, in the introductory portions of allied courses, it is enough to have a grasp of elementary concepts in algebra and geometry. However, as you develop in your field, the need for more mathematics will be apparent. This text is designed to develop these necessary tools so they will be available in your allied courses. You cannot derive the full benefit from your mathematics course unless you devote the necessary amount of time to developing a sound understanding of the subject.

It is assumed in this text that you have a background which includes geometry and some algebra. Therefore, many of the topics covered in this book may seem familiar to you, especially in the earlier chapters. However, it is likely that your background in some of these areas is not complete, either because you have not studied mathematics for a year or two or because you did not understand the topics when you first encountered them. If a topic is familiar, do not reason that there is no sense in studying it again, but take the opportunity to clarify any points on which you are not certain. In almost every topic you will probably find certain points which can use further study. If the topic is new, use your time effectively to develop an understanding of the methods involved, and do not simply memorize problems of a certain type.

There is only one good way to develop the understanding and working knowledge necessary in any course, and that is to *work with it*. Many students consider mathematics difficult. They will tell you that it is their lack of mathematical ability and the complexity of the material itself which make it difficult. Some topics in mathematics, especially in the more advanced areas, do require a certain aptitude for full comprehension. However, a large proportion of poor grades in elementary mathematics courses result from the fact that the student is not willing to put in the necessary time to develop the understanding. The student takes a quick glance through the material, tries a few exercises, is largely unsuccessful, and then decides that the material is "impossible." A detailed reading of the text, a careful following of the illustrative examples, and then solving the exercises would lead to more success and therefore would make the work much more enjoyable and rewarding. No matter what text is used or what methods are used in the course or what other variables may be introduced, if you do not put in an adequate amount of time for studying, you will not derive the proper results. More detailed suggestions for study are included in the following section.

If you consider these suggestions carefully, and follow good study habits, you should enjoy a successful learning experience in this as well as in other courses.

A-2 Suggestions for study

When you are studying the material presented in this text, the following suggestions may help you to derive full benefit from the time you devote to it.

(1) Before attempting to do the exercises, read through the material preceding them.

(2) Follow the illustrative examples carefully, being certain that you know how to proceed from step to step. You should then have a good idea of the methods involved.

(3) Work through the exercises, spending a reasonable amount of time on each problem. If you cannot solve a certain problem in a reasonable amount of time, leave it and go to the next. Return to this problem later. If you find many problems difficult, you should reread the explanatory material and the examples to determine what point or points you have not understood.

(4) When you have completed the exercises, or at least most of them, glance back through the explanatory material to be sure you understand the methods and principles.

(5) If you have gone through the first four steps and certain points still elude you, ask to have these points clarified in class. Do not be afraid to ask questions; only be sure that you have made a sincere effort on your own before you ask them.

Some study habits which are useful not only here but in all of your other subjects are the following:

(1) Put in the time required to develop the material fully, being certain that you are making effective use of your time. A good place to study helps immeasurably.

(2) Learn the *methods and principles* being presented. Memorize as little as possible, for although there are certain basic facts which are more expediently learned by memorization, these should be kept to a minimum.

(3) Keep up with the material in all of your courses. Do not let yourself get so behind in your studies that it becomes difficult to make up the time. Usually the time is never really made up. Studying only before tests is a poor way of learning, and is usually rather ineffective.

(4) When you are taking examinations, always read each question carefully before attempting the solution. Solve those you find easiest first, and do not spend too much time on any one problem. Also, use all the time available for the examination. If you finish early, use the remainder of the time to check your work.

A-3 Problem analysis

Drill-type problems require a working knowledge of the methods presented. However, they do not require, in general, much analysis before being put in proper form for solution. Stated problems, on the other hand, do require proper interpretation before they can be put in a form for solution. The remainder of this section is devoted to some suggestions for solving stated problems.

We have to put stated problems in symbolic form before we attempt to solve them. It is this step which most students find difficult. Because such problems require the student to do more than merely go through a certain routine, they demand more analysis and thus appear more "difficult." There are several reasons for the student's difficulty, some of them being: (1) unsuccessful previous attempts at solving such problems, leading the student to believe that all stated problems are "impossible"; (2) failure to read the problem carefully; (3) a poorly organized approach to the solution; and (4) improper and incomplete interpretation of the statements given. The first two of these can be overcome only with the proper attitude and care.

There are over 70 completely worked examples of stated problems (as well as many other problems which indicate a similar analysis) throughout this text, illustrating proper interpretations and approaches to these problems. Therefore, we shall not include specific examples here. However, we shall set forth the method of analysis of any stated problem. Such an analysis generally follows these steps:

(1) Read the problem carefully.
(2) Carefully identify known and unknown quantities.
(3) Draw a figure when appropriate (which is quite often the case).
(4) Write, in symbols, the relations given in the statements.
(5) Solve for the desired quantities.

If you follow this step-by-step method, and write out the solution neatly, you should find that stated problems lend themselves to solution more readily than you had previously found.

Appendix B—Measurement and Approximate Numbers

B-1 Units of measurement

The solution of most technical problems involves the use of the basic operations on numbers, where many of these numbers represent some sort of measurement or calculation. Therefore, associated with these numbers are *units of measurement*, and for the calculations to be meaningful, we must know these units. For example, if we measure the length of an object to be 12, we must know whether it is being measured in feet, yards, or some other specified unit of length.

Certain universally accepted units are used to measure fundamental quantities. Numerous other quantities are expressed in terms of the units of the fundamental quantities. Quantities which are commonly considered fundamental are (1) length, (2) time, (3) force (engineering systems of units choose force, whereas physics systems of units choose mass; either is proper, since mass and force are proportional), (4) temperature, and (5) electric charge. Other quantities are measurable in terms of these quantities.

Even though all other quantities can be expressed in terms of the fundamental ones, many have units which are given a specified name. This is done primarily for those quantities which are used very commonly, although it is not done for all such quantities. For example, in physics you will find the common unit, the volt, defined as a newton-meter/coulomb, which is in terms of (a unit of force) (a unit of length)/(a unit of electric charge). The unit for acceleration has no special name, and is left in terms of the fundamental units; for example, feet/second^2. For convenience, units are usually abbreviated. The units for acceleration would be written as ft/sec^2.

There are two basic systems of units in common use today: the *British system* and the *metric system*. In each system the fundamental units are specified, and all others are then expressed in terms of these. The British system is used in English-speaking countries for general purposes, including engineering and technical applications. The metric system is used generally in the rest of the world and for scientific work in all parts of the world. Therefore technicians and engineers need to have some knowledge of both systems.

Table B-1 lists many commonly used quantities, the symbols used to represent them, and their associated units. In the British engineering system, the fundamental unit of length is the *foot* and that of force is the *pound*. The metric system itself is broken into two systems, the cgs system and the mks system. In the cgs system the unit of length used is the centimeter and the unit of mass is the gram, and in the mks system, the unit of length is the meter and the unit of mass is the kilogram. In each of these, the unit of time is the second. (We see that cgs stands for centimeter-gram-second, and mks stands for meter-kilogram-

TABLE B–1

QUANTITIES AND THEIR ASSOCIATED UNITS

Quantity	Symbol	Unit		
		Engineering	cgs	mks
Length	s	foot, ft	centimeter, cm	meter, m
Time	t	second, sec	second, sec	second, sec
Mass	m	slug	gram, gm	kilogram, kg
Force, weight	F, w	pound, lb	dyne	newton, n
Area	A	ft^2	cm^2	m^2
Volume	V	ft^3	cm^3	m^3
Velocity	v	ft/sec	cm/sec	m/sec
Acceleration	a	ft/sec^2	cm/sec^2	m/sec^2
Density	d, ρ	lb/ft^3	gm/cm^3	kg/m^3
Energy, work	E, W	ft-lb	erg (dyne-cm)	joule (n-m)
Power	P	horsepower, hp (ft-lb/sec)	erg/sec	watt (joule/sec)
Period	T	sec	sec	sec
Frequency	f	1/sec	1/sec	1/sec
Angle	θ	radian, rad	rad	rad
Temperature	T	Fahrenheit degrees, °F	Centigrade degrees, °C	Centigrade degrees, °C
Quantity of heat		British thermal unit Btu	calorie, cal	cal
Electric charge	q	coulomb, coul	abcoul; statcoul	coulomb, coul
Electric potential	V, E	volt, v	abvolt; statvolt	volt, v
Electric current	I	ampere, amp	abamp; statamp	ampere, amp
Capacitance	C	farad, f	abfarad; statfarad	farad, f
Inductance	L	henry, h	abhenry; stathenry	henry, h
Resistance	R	ohm, Ω	abohm; statohm	ohm, Ω

second.) As for temperature, degrees *fahrenheit* (°F) are generally used with the British system, and degrees *celsius* (centigrade)(°C) are used with the metric systems. In each of these systems, the *coulomb* is the unit of electric charge.

Due to greatly varying sizes of certain quantities, the metric system employs certain prefixes to units to denote different orders of magnitude. Some of the more commonly used prefixes, with their meanings, are as follows:

mega-	million (10^6)	centi-	hundredth (10^{-2})
kilo-	thousand (10^3)	milli-	thousandth (10^{-3})
deci-	tenth (10^{-1})	micro-	millionth (10^{-6})

For example, a millimeter is a thousandth of a meter, whereas a kilogram is one thousand grams.

When we are working with numbers that represent units of measurement (referred to as *denominate numbers*), it is sometimes necessary to change from one set of units to another. A change within a given system is called a *reduction*, and a change from one system to another is called a *conversion*. Table B-2 gives some basic reduction and conversion factors.

TABLE B-2

BASIC REDUCTION AND CONVERSION FACTORS

1 in. = 2.54 cm	1 joule = 10^7 ergs
1 lb = 453.6 g	1 Btu = 778 ft-lb
1 ft^3 = 28.32 liters	1 cal = 4.18 joules
1 liter = 1.057 qt	1 Btu = 252 cal
1 n = 10^5 dynes	1 hp = 550 ft-lb/sec

To change a given number of one set of units into another set of units, *we perform algebraic operations with units in the same manner as we do with any algebraic symbol.* Consider the following example.

Example A.   If we had a number representing feet/second to be multiplied by another number representing seconds/minute, as far as the units are concerned, we have

$$\frac{ft}{sec} \times \frac{sec}{min} = \frac{ft \times \cancel{sec}}{\cancel{sec} \times min} = \frac{ft}{min}.$$

This means that the final result would be in feet/minute.

In changing a number of one set of units to another set of units, we use reduction and conversion factors and the principle illustrated in Example A. The convenient way to use the values in the tables is in the form of fractions. Since the given values are equal to each other, their quotient is 1. For example, since

1 in. = 2.54 cm,

$$\frac{1 \text{ in.}}{2.54 \text{ cm}} = 1 \quad \text{or} \quad \frac{2.54 \text{ cm}}{1 \text{ in.}} = 1,$$

since each represents the division of a certain length by itself. Multiplying a quantity by 1 does not change its value. The following examples illustrate reduction and conversion of units.

Example B.   Change 30 mi/hr to ft/sec.

$$30 \frac{\text{mi}}{\text{hr}} = \left(30 \frac{\text{mi}}{\text{hr}}\right)\left(\frac{5280 \text{ ft}}{1 \text{ mi}}\right)\left(\frac{1 \text{ hr}}{60 \text{ min}}\right)\left(\frac{1 \text{ min}}{60 \text{ sec}}\right) = \frac{(30)(5280) \text{ ft}}{(60)(60) \text{ sec}} = 44 \frac{\text{ft}}{\text{sec}}$$

Note that the only units remaining after the division are those required.

Example C.   Change 62 lb/in² to kg/m².

$$62 \frac{\text{lb}}{\text{in}^2} = \left(62 \frac{\text{lb}}{\text{in}^2}\right)\left(\frac{1 \text{ kg}}{1000 \text{ g}}\right)\left(\frac{453.6 \text{ g}}{1 \text{ lb}}\right)\left(\frac{1 \text{ in.}}{2.54 \text{ cm}}\right)\left(\frac{1 \text{ in.}}{2.54 \text{ cm}}\right)\left(\frac{100 \text{ cm}}{1 \text{ m}}\right)\left(\frac{100 \text{ cm}}{1 \text{ m}}\right)$$

$$= \frac{(62)(453.6)(100)(100)\text{kg}}{(1000)(2.54)(2.54) \text{ m}^2} = 44,000 \frac{\text{kg}}{\text{m}^2}.$$

Note that the in. × in. of the numerator equals the in² of the denominator.

Exercises

In the following exercises use the values given in Table B-1 and basic reduction factors such as those used in Example B.

1. Reduce 1 km to centimeters.
2. Reduce 1 kg to milligrams.
3. Reduce 1 ft² to square inches.
4. Reduce 1 yd³ to cubic feet.
5. Convert 5 in. to centimeters.
6. Convert 6 kg to pounds.
7. Reduce 8 gal to pints.
8. Reduce 20 kiloliters to milliliters.
9. Convert 10 quarts to liters.
10. Convert 18 cm to inches.
11. Convert 73.8 g to pounds.
12. Convert 0.36 in. to meters.
13. Convert 829 in³ to liters.
14. Convert 0.068 kiloliters to cubic feet.
15. Convert 1 hp to kg-cm/sec.
16. Convert 8 Btu to joules.
17. Reduce 25.2 cal to ergs.
18. Reduce 1 Btu/min to horsepower.
19. An Atlas rocket weighed 260,000 lb at takeoff. How many tons is this?
20. An airplane is flying at 37,000 ft. What is its altitude in miles? (Round off to hundredths.)
21. The speedometer of a European car is calibrated to km/hr. If the speedometer of such a car reads 60, how fast in mi/hr is the car traveling (round off to units)?
22. The acceleration due to gravity is about 980 cm/sec². Convert this to ft/sec² (round off to tenths).

23. The speed of sound is about 1130 ft/sec. Change this speed to mi/hr.

24. The density of water is about 62.4 lb/ft³. Convert this to kg/m³ (round off to tenths).

25. The average density of the earth is about 5.52 gm/cm³. Convert this to lb/ft³ (round off to units).

26. The moon travels about 1,500,000 miles in about 28 days in one rotation about the earth. Express its velocity in ft/sec (round off to tens).

27. At sea level, atmospheric pressure is about 14.7 lb/in². Express this pressure in g/cm² (round off to tens).

B-2 Approximate numbers and significant digits

When we perform calculations on numbers, we must consider the accuracy of these numbers, since this affects the accuracy of the results obtained. Most of the numbers involved in technical and scientific work are *approximate*, having been arrived at through some process of measurement. However, certain other numbers are *exact*, having been arrived at through some definition or counting process. We can determine whether or not a number is approximate or exact if we know how the number was determined.

Example A.   If we measure the length of a rope to be 15.3 ft, we know that the 15.3 is approximate. A more precise measuring device may cause us to determine the length as 15.28 ft. However, regardless of the method of measurement used, we shall not be able to determine this length exactly.

If a voltage shown on a voltmeter is read as 116 volts, the 116 is approximate. A more precise voltmeter may show the voltage as 115.7 volts. However, this voltage cannot be determined exactly.

Example B.   If a computer counts the cards it has processed and prints this number as 837, this 837 is exact. We know the number of cards was not 836 or 838. Since 837 was determined through a counting process, it is exact.

When we say that 60 seconds = 1 minute, the 60 is exact, since this is a definition. By this definition there are exactly 60 seconds in one minute.

When we are writing approximate numbers we often have to include some zeros so that the decimal point will be properly located. However, except for these zeros, all other digits are considered to be *significant digits*. When we make computations with approximate numbers, we must know the number of significant digits. The following example illustrates how we determine this.

Example C.   All numbers in this example are assumed to be approximate.

34.7 has three significant digits.

8900 has two significant digits. We assume that the two zeros are place holders (unless we have specific knowledge to the contrary.)

0.039 has two significant digits. The zeros are for proper location of the decimal point.

706.1 has four significant digits. The zero is not used for the location of the decimal point. It shows specifically the number of tens in the number.

5.90 has three significant digits. The zero is not necessary as a place holder, and should not be written unless it is significant.

Other approximate numbers with the proper number of significant digits are listed below.

96000	two	0.0709	three	1.070	four
30900	three	6.000	four	700.00	five
4.006	four	0.0005	one	20008	five

Note from the example above that all nonzero digits are significant. Zeros, other than those used as place holders for proper positioning of the decimal point, are also significant.

In computations involving approximate numbers, the position of the decimal point as well as the number of significant digits is important. The *precision* of a number refers directly to the decimal position of the last significant digit, whereas the *accuracy* of a number refers to the number of significant digits in the number. Consider the illustrations in the following example.

Example D. Suppose that you are measuring an electric current with two ammeters. One ammeter reads 0.031 amp and the second ammeter reads 0.0312 amp. The second reading is more precise, in that the last significant digit is the number of ten-thousandths, and the first reading is expressed only to thousandths. The second reading is also more accurate, since it has three significant digits rather than two.

A machine part is measured to be 2.5 cm long. It is coated with a film 0.025 cm thick. The thickness of the film has been measured to a greater precision, although the two measurements have the same accuracy: two significant digits.

A segment of a newly completed highway is 9270 ft long. The concrete surface is 0.8 ft thick. Of these two numbers, 9270 is more accurate, since it contains three significant digits, and 0.8 is more precise, since it is expressed to tenths.

The last significant digit of an approximate number is known not to be completely accurate. It has usually been determined by estimation or *rounding off*. However, we do know that it is at most in error by one-half of a unit in its place value.

Example E. When we measure the length of the rope referred to in Example A to be 15.3 ft, we are saying that the length is at least 15.25 ft and no longer than 15.35 ft. Any value between these two, rounded off to tenths, would be expressed as 15.3 ft.

In converting the fraction $\frac{2}{3}$ to the decimal form 0.667, we are saying that the value is between 0.6665 and 0.6675.

The principle of rounding off a number is to write the closest approximation, with the last significant digit in a specified position, or with a specified number of significant digits. We shall now formalize the process of rounding off as follows: If we want a certain number of significant digits, we examine the digit in the next place to the right. If this digit is less than 5, we accept the digit in the last place. If the next digit is 5 or greater, we increase the digit in the last place by 1, and this resulting digit becomes the final significant digit of the approximation. If necessary, we use zeros to replace other digits in order to locate the decimal point properly. Except when the next digit is a 5, and no other nonzero digits are discarded, we have the closest possible approximation with the desired number of significant digits.

Example F.   70360 rounded off to three significant digits is 70400.

70430 rounded off to three significant digits is 70400.

187.35 rounded off to four significant digits is 187.4.

71500 rounded off to two significant digits is 72000.

With the advent of high-speed electronic computers, another method of reducing numbers to a specified number of significant digits is used. This is the process of *truncation*, in which the digits beyond a certain place are discarded. For example, 3.17482 truncated to thousandths is 3.174. For our purposes in this text, when working with approximate numbers, we have used only rounding off.

Exercises

In Exercises 1 through 8 determine whether the numbers given are exact or approximate.

1. There are 24 hours in one day.
2. The velocity of light is 186,000 mi/sec.
3. The 3-stage rocket took 74.6 hours to reach the moon.
4. A man bought 5 lb of nails for $1.56.
5. The melting point of gold is 1063°C.
6. The 21 students had an average test grade of 81.6.
7. A building lot 100 ft by 200 ft cost $3200.
8. In a certain city 5% of the people have their money in a bank that pays 5% interest.

In Exercises 9 through 16 determine the number of significant digits in the given approximate numbers.

9. 37.2; 6844   10. 3600; 730   11. 107; 3004   12. 0.8735; 0.0075

13. 6.80; 6.08   14. 90050; 105040   15. 30000; 30000.0   16. 1.00; 0.01

In Exercises 17 through 24 determine which of each pair of approximate numbers is (a) more precise and (b) more accurate.

17. 3.764, 2.81   18. 0.041, 7.673   19. 30.8, 0.01   20. 70,370, 50,400

21. 0.1, 78.0   22. 7040, 37.1   23. 7000, 0.004   24. 50.060, 8.914

In Exercises 25 through 32 round off each of the given approximate numbers (a) to three significant digits, and (b) to two significant digits.

25. 4.933   26. 80.53   27. 57893   28. 30490

29. 861.29   30. 9555   31. 0.30505   32. 0.7350

B-3 Arithmetic operations with approximate numbers

When performing arithmetic operations on approximate numbers we must be careful not to express the result to a precision or accuracy which is not warranted. The following two examples illustrate how a false indication of the accuracy of a result could be obtained when using approximate numbers.

Example A.   A pipe is made in two sections. The first is measured to be 16.3 ft long and the second is measured to be 0.927 ft long. A plumber wants to know what the total length will be when the two sections are put together.

At first, it appears we might simply add the numbers as follows to obtain the necessary result.

$$
\begin{array}{r}
16.3 \ \text{ft} \\
0.927 \ \text{ft} \\
\hline
17.227 \ \text{ft}
\end{array}
$$

However, the first length is precise only to tenths, and the digit in this position was obtained by rounding off. It might have been as small as 16.25 ft or as large as 16.35 ft. If we consider only the precision of this first number, the total length might be as small as 17.177 ft or as large as 17.277 ft. These two values agree when rounded off to two significant digits (17). They vary by 0.1 when rounded off to tenths (17.2 and 17.3). When rounded to hundredths, they do not agree at all, since the third significant digit is different (17.18 and 17.28). Therefore there is no agreement at all in the digits after the third when these two numbers are rounded off to a precision beyond tenths. This may also be deemed reasonable, since the first length is not expressed beyond tenths. The second number does not further change the precision of the result, since it is expressed to thousandths. Therefore we may conclude that the result must be rounded off at least to tenths, the precision of the first number.

Example B.   We can find the area of a rectangular piece of land by multiplying the length, 207.54 ft, by the width, 81.4 ft. Performing the multiplication, we find the area to be (207.54 ft)(81.4 ft) = 16893.756 sq ft.

However, we know this length and width were found by measurement and that the least each could be is 207.535 ft and 81.35 ft. Multiplying these values, we find the least value for the area to be

$$(207.535 \text{ ft})(81.35 \text{ ft}) = 16882.97225 \text{ sq ft.}$$

The greatest possible value for the area is

$$(207.545 \text{ ft})(81.45 \text{ ft}) = 16904.54025 \text{ sq ft.}$$

We now note that the least possible and greatest possible values of the area agree when rounded off to three significant digits (16900 sq ft) and there is no agreement in digits beyond this if the two values are rounded off to a greater accuracy. Therefore we can conclude that the accuracy of the result is good to three significant digits, or certainly no more than four. We also note that the width was accurate to three significant digits, and the length to five significant digits.

The following rules are based on reasoning similar to that in Examples A and B; we go by these rules when we perform the basic arithmetic operations on approximate numbers.

(1) When approximate numbers are added or subtracted, the result is expressed with the precision of the least precise number.

(2) When approximate numbers are multiplied or divided, the result is expressed with the accuracy of the least accurate number.

(3) When the root of an approximate number is found, the result is accurate to the accuracy of the number.

(4) Before the calculation is performed, all the numbers except the least precise or least accurate should be rounded off to one place beyond that of the least precise or least accurate.

The last of these rules is designed to make the calculation as easy as possible, since carrying the additional figures is meaningless in the intermediate steps. The following examples illustrate the use of these rules.

Example C.   Add the approximate numbers 73.2, 8.0627, 93.57, 66.296.

The least precise of these numbers is 73.2. Therefore, before performing the addition, we shall round off the other numbers to hundredths. After the addition is performed, we shall round off the result to tenths. This leads to

$$
\begin{array}{r}
73.2 \\
8.06 \\
93.57 \\
66.30 \\
\hline
241.13
\end{array}
$$

Therefore the final result is 241.1.

Example D.   Divide 292.6 by 3.4.

Since the divisor is accurate only to 2 significant digits, the final result is accurate to 2 significant digits. Therefore we shall round off the dividend to three significant digits, and divide until we have three significant digits in the quotient. The result will then be rounded off to two significant digits.

$$
\begin{array}{r}
86.1 \\
34{\overline{\smash{\big)}\,2930.0}} \\
272 \\
\overline{210} \\
204 \\
\overline{60} \\
34 \\
\overline{}
\end{array}
$$

Therefore, the final result is 86.

Example E.   When we subtract 36.1 from 727.842, we have

$$
\begin{array}{r}
727.84 \\
36.1 \\
\hline
691.74.
\end{array}
$$

Therefore the result is 691.7.

When we find the product of 2.4832 and 30.5, we have

$$(2.483)(30.5) = 75.7315.$$

Therefore the final result is 75.7.

When we find the square root of 3.7, we have

$$
\begin{array}{r}
1.92 \\
\sqrt{3.7000} \\
1 \\
\hline
29\ {\big|}\ 270 \\
261 \\
\hline
382\ {\big|}\ 900 \\
764
\end{array}
$$

Therefore the final result is 1.9.

The rules stated in this section are usually sufficiently valid for the computations encountered in technical work. They are intended only as good practical rules for working with approximate numbers. It was recognized in Examples A and B that the last significant digit obtained by these rules is subject to some possible error. Therefore it is possible that the most accurate result is not obtained by their use, although this is not often the case.

If an exact number is included in a calculation, there is no limitation to the number of decimal positions it may take on. The accuracy of the result is limited only by the approximate numbers involved.

Exercises

In Exercises 1 through 4 add the given approximate numbers.

1.	3.8	2.	26	3.	0.36294	4.	56.1
	0.154		5.806		0.086		3.0645
	47.26		147.29		0.5056		127.38
					0.74		0.055

In Exercises 5 through 8 subtract the given approximate numbers.

5.	468.14	6.	1.03964	7.	57.348	8.	8.93
	36.7		0.69		26.5		6.8947

In Exercises 9 through 12 multiply the given approximate numbers.

9. $(3.64)(17.06)$ 10. $(0.025)(70.1)$

11. $(704.6)(0.38)$ 12. $(0.003040)(6079.52)$

In Exercises 13 through 16 divide the given approximate numbers.

13. $608 \div 3.9$ 14. $0.4962 \div 827$

15. $\dfrac{596000}{22}$ 16. $\dfrac{53.267}{0.3002}$

In Exercises 17 through 20 find the indicated square roots of the given approximate numbers.

17. $\sqrt{32}$ 18. $\sqrt{6.5}$ 19. $\sqrt{19.3}$ 20. $\sqrt{0.0694}$

In Exercises 21 through 24 evaluate the given expression. All numbers are approximate.

21. $3.862 + 14.7 - 8.3276$ 22. $(3.2)(0.386) + 6.842$

23. $\dfrac{8.60}{0.46} + (0.9623)(3.86)$ 24. $9.6 - 0.1962(7.30)$

In Exercises 25 through 28 perform the indicated operations. The first number given is approximate and the second number is exact.

25. $3.62 + 14$ 26. $17.382 - 2.5$

27. $(0.3142)(60)$ 28. $8.62 \div 1728$

In Exercises 29 through 38 the solution to some of the problems will require the use of reduction and conversion factors.

29. Two forces, 18.6 lb and 2.382 lb, are acting on an object. What is the sum of these forces?

30. Three sections of a bridge are measured to be 52.3 ft, 36.38 ft, and 38 ft, respectively. What is the total length of these three sections?

31. Two planes are reported to have flown at speeds of 938 mi/hr and 1400 km/hr, respectively. Which plane is faster, and by how many miles per hour?

32. The density of a certain type of iron is 7.10 g/cm³. The density of a type of tin is 448 lb/ft³. Which is greater?

33. If the temperature of water is raised from 4°C to 30°C, its density reduces by 0.420%. If the density of water at 4°C is 62.4 lb/ft³, what is its density at 30°?

34. The power (in watts) developed in an electric circuit is found by multiplying the current, in amps, by the voltage. In a certain circuit the current is 0.0125 amp and the voltage is 12.68 volts. What is the power that is developed?

35. A certain ore is 5.3% iron. How many tons of ore must be refined to obtain 45,000 lb of iron?

36. An electric data-processing card sorter sorts 32,000 cards, by count, in 10.25 min. At what rate does the sorter operate?

37. In order to find the velocity, in feet/second, of an object which has fallen a certain height, we calculate the square root of the product of 64.4 (an approximate number) and the height in feet. What is the velocity of an object which has fallen 63 meters?

38. A student reports the current in a certain experiment to be 0.02 amp at one time and later notes that it is 0.023 amp. He then states that the change in current is 0.003 amp. What is wrong with his conclusion?

Appendix C—The Slide Rule

C-1 Introduction: Reading the slide rule

The slide rule is an instrument that can be used to perform many numerical operations rapidly, if three-significant-digit accuracy is sufficient. (See Appendix B for a discussion of significant digits.) The slide rule operations discussed in this appendix are multiplication, division, squaring, finding square roots, and the finding of trigonometric functions. In Chapter 8 the use of the trigonometric scales in triangle solution is discussed. The operations of addition and subtraction cannot be done on a slide rule.

The only proper way to learn to operate a slide rule successfully is to *use it*. Ample practice is essential, particularly when first learning to use a slide rule. Once the first few basic operations are mastered, other operations are easily learned.

There are a great many types of slide rules. However, the discussions in this appendix are general enough to apply to most slide rules. Nearly all slide rules come with a manual that can be used to supplement this material, particularly to learn any variations which your slide rule may have.

In the calculations we shall discuss, the slide rule gives only three significant digits of the answer and does not indicate where the decimal point should be located. The decimal point can be located by approximating the answer. In the approximation, all that we require is a number of the proper general magnitude. The following example shows how approximations can be made, and in later sections when calculations are actually performed, the process will be illustrated further.

Example A. If we were to perform the multiplication 39.1×839 on the slide rule, we would find that the first three significant digits of the result were 328. Now by approximating the multiplication as $40 \times 800 = 32,000$, we know that the result is near 32,000. Therefore we know that the result, to three significant digits, is 32,800.

If we were to calculate the value of

$$\frac{(0.0327)(72.6)}{0.912}$$

on the slide rule, we would find that the first three significant digits of the result were 260. By approximating the value as

$$\frac{(0.03)(70)}{1} = 2.1$$

we know that the result is 2.60.

The long sliding part in the middle of the rule is called the *slide*. The vertical line on the transparent runner is called the *hairline*. Various *scales*, which are lettered, are found horizontally along the slide rule. Any marking labeled with a 1 is called an *index* of that scale (with the exceptions of the smaller 1's which appear on the C- and D-scales). See Fig. C-1.

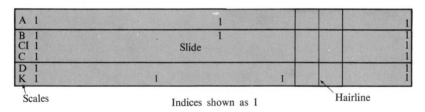

Scales   Indices shown as 1   Hairline

Figure C-1

In reading a number on a scale of a slide rule, we must keep in mind that only three (possibly four on the C- and D-scales) significant digits of any number can be determined. We shall now describe the way a number is located on the C-scale or D-scale. Since these two scales are identical, the readings are made in the same way on each. Consider the following examples.

Example B.   Locate 135.6 on the D-scale.

Since the first significant digit is 1, the position of the number 135.6 will lie between the large (primary) 1 and the primary 2 (see Fig. C-2). Since the second significant digit is 3, the position would then be further located between the small (secondary) 3 and the secondary 4. The divisions between the secondary 3 and 4 are marked but not numbered. Since there are ten divisions, the third of the significant digits, 5, locates the number between the fifth and sixth marks. The final position is found by estimating, as well as possible, six-tenths of the way between these divisions. This position would also be used for 13.56, 0.001356, or for any number with 1356 as the significant digits. It is only for numbers with a first significant digit of 1 that four-place accuracy is possible, and then only on the C- and D-scales.

Example C. Locate 347 on the D-scale.

The first significant digit, 3, locates the position as being between the primary 3 and 4 (see Fig. C-2). The second significant digit, 4, further locates the position as being between the fourth and fifth secondary division markings. Note that there are only five divisions between these secondary divisions. Thus each of these small divisions represents two units. Therefore the final position lies halfway between the third and fourth of these marks.

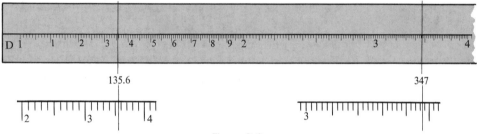

Figure C-2

Note also that there are only two divisions between the secondary marks for numbers with a first digit of 4 to 9. It is therefore necessary to estimate the third significant digit, remembering that each of the smallest divisions represents 5 units.

Numbers are located on the other scales in a similar manner. The way in which the scale is marked should be carefully noted, so that the estimation of the third digit can be properly determined.

Example D. The locations of 0.244, 45.7, and 6.73 on the A-scale are shown in Fig. C-3.

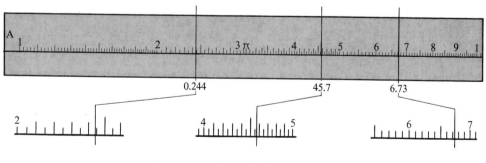

Figure C-3

Exercises

In Exercises 1 through 12 read the three (or four) significant digits indicated in Fig. C-4. The number of each arrow is the exercise number.

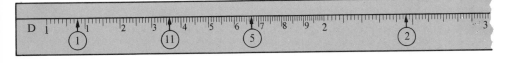

Figure C-4

In Exercises 13 through 20 locate the three (or four) significant digits on the D-scale.

13. 470   14. 325   15. 144   16. 250

17. 669   18. 946   19. 1023   20. 404

In Exercises 21 through 28 locate the three significant digits on the A-scale. Note that the left-hand side and the right-hand side of the A-scale are exactly the same. Locate the positions on each side.

21. 325   22. 892   23. 702   24. 240

25. 149   26. 458   27. 809   28. 606

In Exercises 29 through 36 find approximations of the results.

29. $(829)(0.485)$ 30. $(0.0895)(63.7)$ 31. $\dfrac{568,000}{0.0247}$

32. $\dfrac{0.0734}{60.8}$ 33. $\sqrt{73.9}$ 34. $\sqrt{846}$

35. $\dfrac{(0.934)(726)}{45.2}$ 36. $\dfrac{\sqrt{1520}}{(9.07)(448)}$

C-2 Multiplication and division

The first slide-rule operations that we shall discuss are multiplication and division. We perform each by using two scales together, one on the main portion of the slide rule and the other on the slide. Normally the two scales used are the C- and D-scales. First let us consider how numbers are multiplied on the slide rule.

The process of multiplication on the C- and D-scales is as follows:

(1) Locate the first number on the D-scale.

(2) Place the index of the C-scale directly over this position.

(3) Locate the second number on the C-scale.

(4) Place the hairline over this second number.

(5) Read the significant digits of the answer on the D-scale, under the hairline.

(6) Determine the decimal point by approximating the answer (this also provides a rough check).

Example A.   Multiply 12.0 by 41.0 (see Fig. C-5).

First we locate 12.0 on the D-scale as directly on the secondary 2, and place the left index of the C-scale directly above this position. Now we locate 41.0 on the C-scale as directly on the first secondary mark past the primary 4. We place the hairline over this position. Under the hairline, on the D-scale, we observe the significant digits 492. A quick calculation tells us that $10 \times 40 = 400$, and therefore the answer is 492.

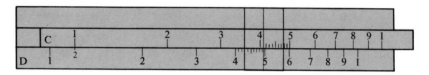

Figure C-5

About half the time it is necessary to use the right index of the C-scale in the multiplication. In such cases, if the left index is placed over the first number, the second number appears on the C-scale beyond the extent of the D-scale. In order to avoid a trial-and-error process in choosing the index to use, quickly observe the numbers being multiplied. If the product of the first significant digits is less than 10, use the left index; otherwise use the right index.

Example B.   Multiply 0.834 by 28.6.

Since the product of the first significant digits, 8 and 2, is 16, we use the right index. The setup for the multiplication is shown in Fig. C-6. The observed significant digits of the result are 239. Since $0.8 \times 30 = 24$, the result is therefore 23.9.

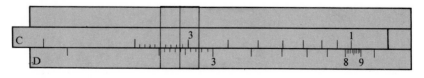

Figure C-6

Division is the reverse process of multiplication, a fact which also holds true in the use of the slide rule. When one uses the C- and D-scales for division, here are the steps to follow:

(1) Locate the numerator on the D-scale.

(2) Locate the denominator on the C-scale, and place it directly over the position of the numerator.

(3) Find the significant digits of the answer on the D-scale, directly under the index of the C-scale.

(4) Approximate the answer to determine the location of the decimal point. Whichever index of the C-scale is over the D-scale is the proper one, and there is no problem of "which index" in division.

Example C.   Divide 78.3 by 3.57 (see Fig. C-7).

First we locate 78.3 on the D-scale. Next we place the position of 3.57 on the C-scale directly above the 78.3. We find the significant digits of the answer, 219, directly under the left index of the C-scale. Approximating the answer as $80 \div 4 = 20$, we find the result to be 21.9.

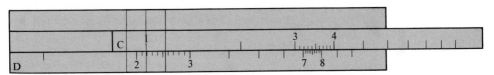

Figure C-7

Example D.   Divide 6.07 by 926 (see Fig. C-8).

First we find 6.07 on the D-scale, and place 926 on the C-scale directly above. We find the significant digits of the result, 656, under the right index of the C-scale. Approximating the answer by $\frac{6}{1000} = 0.006$, the result is 0.00656.

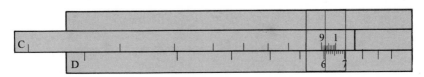

Figure C-8

Exercises

In Exercises 1 through 32 find the indicated products and quotients on a slide rule.

1. (2.00)(3.00)
2. (4.70)(0.111)
3. (562)(0.320)
4. (99.0)(3.46)
5. (0.0601)(0.1425)
6. (73.4)(0.401)
7. (0.00620)(850)
8. (506)(0.0211)
9. (9.38)(0.000360)
10. (25000)(0.706)
11. (8.37)(88.4)
12. (1060)(732)

13. $14 \div 2$ 14. $85 \div 5.0$ 15. $5.5 \div 11$ 16. $196 \div 140$

17. $760 \div 2.44$ 18. $0.243 \div 0.711$ 19. $9.34 \div 0.0240$ 20. $65.5 \div 8.21$

21. $60200 \div 0.0411$ 22. $0.00404 \div 1.17$ 23. $84.4 \div 0.0556$ 24. $2.99 \div 860$

25. $(2.68)(3.10)(502)$ 26. $(0.0360)(20.5)(13.9)$

27. $(3070)(81.0)(0.913)$ 28. $(0.0990)(1.05)(36.4)$

29. $\dfrac{(36.8)(827)}{40.5}$ 30. $\dfrac{(0.0304)(86.1)}{0.944}$ 31. $\dfrac{687}{(0.0421)(4070)}$ 32. $\dfrac{70400}{(36.9)(4.19)}$

C-3 Squares and square roots

As with multiplication and division, we use two scales together to find the squares and square roots of numbers on a slide rule. However, the scales which are generally used, the A- and D-scales, are both on the main body of the slide rule. Another pair of scales, the B- and C-scales, which are both on the slide, can also be used to find squares and square roots. (Some slide rules use the D-scale in conjunction with the Sq 1 and Sq 2 scales for this purpose. Some added accuracy is obtained in this way.) Since the A- and D-scales are on the main body of the slide rule, the slide does not enter into the process of finding squares and square roots.

The procedure for squaring a number is as follows:

(1) Locate the number to be squared on the D-scale.
(2) Place the hairline over this position.
(3) Read the significant digits of the result on the A-scale under the hairline.
(4) Approximate the answer to get the location of the decimal point.

Example A. Find the square of 28.4 (see Fig. C-9).

First locate 28.4 on the D-scale, then place the hairline over this position. The significant digits 807 are then found under the hairline on the A-scale. Approximating the answer as $30 \times 30 = 900$, we find the result to be 807.

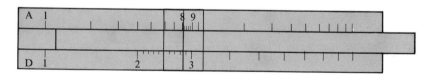

Figure C-9

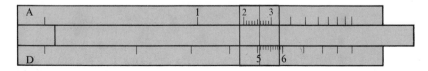

Figure C-10

Example B.   Find the square of 0.509 (see Fig. C-10).

We locate 0.509 on the D-scale, then place the hairline over this position. The significant digits 259 are found under the hairline on the A-scale. When we approximate the answer as $0.5 \times 0.5 = 0.25$, the result is 0.259.

Finding square roots is the reverse of finding squares. The number whose square root is to be found is located on the A-scale. By use of the hairline, we can find the significant digits of the result on the D-scale. Finally, an approximation gives us the position of the decimal point.

However, there are two identical parts of the A-scale. The major problem in finding square roots is in determining which side of the A-scale to use. For example, if we followed the procedure above to find $\sqrt{25}$, we would find the significant digits 158 if 25 is located on the left half of the A-scale, or we would find the significant digits 500 if 25 is located on the right half. Obviously, since $\sqrt{25} = 5$, the significant digits 500 are correct. (Further observation would tell us, however, that $\sqrt{250} = 15.8$, and therefore the significant digits 158 are not meaningless.)

There are several ways of properly choosing which side of the A-scale to use. We shall adopt a rather simple procedure, based on the basic numerical method by which square roots are found, as follows:

(1) Indicate the grouping by twos of the digits for the determination of the square root.

(2) Find the first significant digit of the square root and the location of the decimal point of the result (this replaces the need for the approximation).

(3) Use the half of the A-scale which gives the proper first significant digit.

Example C.

To find the square root of	Set up square root	First significant digit	Use side of A-scale	Approximate result
31.0	$\overset{5.}{\sqrt{31.\ 00}}$	5	Right	5
310	$\overset{1\quad.}{\sqrt{3\ 10.\ 00}}$	1	Left	10
5260000	$\overset{2\qquad\quad}{\sqrt{5\ 26\ 00\ 00.}}$	2	Left	2000
526000	$\overset{7\qquad\ }{\sqrt{52\ 60\ 00.}}$	7	Right	700
0.000472	$\overset{.\ \ 0\ \ 2}{\sqrt{0.\ 00\ 04\ 72}}$	2	Left	0.02
0.0000472	$\overset{.\ \ 0\ \ 0\ \ 6}{\sqrt{0.\ 00\ 00\ 47\ 2}}$	6	Right	0.006

Example D.   Following the procedure outlined for finding square roots, we can find the square root of each of the numbers of Example C by placing the hairline over the position of the given number on the proper side of the A-scale. Therefore we have the following results.

To find the square root of	Significant digits of result	Final result
31.0	557	5.57
310	176	17.6
5260000	229	2290
526000	725	725
0.000472	217	0.0217
0.0000472	687	0.00687

Exercises

In Exercises 1 through 16 find the squares of the given numbers on the slide rule.

1. 14.0
2. 3.10
3. 46.0
4. 0.360
5. 0.0200
6. 0.133
7. 6.71
8. 7.85
9. 9.94
10. 888
11. 66,200
12. 0.00315
13. 1550
14. 0.0401
15. 0.440
16. 7090

In Exercises 17 through 32 find the square roots of the given numbers on the slide rule.

17. 41.0
18. 410
19. 0.0136
20. 0.136
21. 572
22. 57.2
23. 0.572
24. 0.0572
25. 47500
26. 863
27. 0.0652
28. 7640
29. 22.4
30. 33600
31. 9060
32. 306

In Exercises 33 through 36 make the indicated calculations on the slide rule.

33. $38.6\sqrt{0.562}$
34. $\dfrac{\sqrt{3080}}{69.4}$
35. $\dfrac{89400}{(3.92)^2}$
36. $(472)^2\sqrt{0.0609}$

C-4 Combined operations

For problems consisting of several operations, there are several general methods which might be employed. We cannot cover all possibilities here, but a person who gets experience in using the slide rule normally develops insight as to the best procedures to use.

If a problem consists of several multiplications and divisions, the best procedure is to alternate between division and multiplication, starting with division. Thus we find the result with the fewest possible settings on the slide rule.

Example A. To calculate the value of

$$\frac{(3.10)(0.464)}{(17.5)(0.0105)},$$

the first step is to divide 3.10 by 17.5. The result of this division is under the index of the C-scale, but there is no need to record this result, since we can immediately multiply it by 0.464 by moving the hairline over the 0.464 on the C-scale. By leaving the hairline in place, we can divide this result by 0.0105 by moving the slide so that 0.0105 on the C-scale is under the hairline. The final result, 7.82, is observed under the index of the C-scale. Thus, with only two settings of the slide, it is possible to find the final result. The decimal point is determined by the approximation

$$\frac{(3)(0.5)}{(20)(0.01)} = \frac{1.5}{0.2} = 7.5.$$

For a problem consisting of several indicated multiplications and divisions, quantity to be squared, the best procedure is to find the results of the multiplications and divisions first. This result can then be squared by immediate reference to the A-scale.

Example B. When we wish to calculate the value of

$$\left[\frac{(87.5)(0.0236)}{659}\right]^2,$$

the first step is to divide 87.5 by 659. The result of this division is under the index of the C-scale, and it can be multiplied by 0.0236 by placing the hairline over 0.0236 of the C-scale. The result of the division and multiplication is under the hairline on the D-scale. However, it is the square of this result that is required. Therefore, by referring to the square on the A-scale, we obtain the result 0.00000982. We obtain the decimal point by the approximation

$$\left[\frac{(90)(0.02)}{700}\right]^2 = \left[\frac{1.8}{700}\right]^2 = \left[\frac{2}{700}\right]^2 = [0.003]^2 = 0.000009.$$

Example C. For a problem such as

$$\frac{(\sqrt{1.37})(4.46)^2}{86.2},$$

it is generally best to first replace the squares and square roots by their equivalent values. This leads to

$$\frac{(1.17)(19.9)}{86.2},$$

which is then solved by dividing 1.17 by 86.2 and then multiplying the result by 19.9. This gives the value of 0.270. The decimal point is found by the approximation

$$\frac{(1)(20)}{80} = 0.25.$$

As we mentioned in Section C-1, only continued practice will enable a person to master the operation of the slide rule. This point cannot be overemphasized, for those who find difficulty in using a slide rule generally have not put in sufficient time practicing.

Exercises

In the following exercises perform all indicated calculations on a slide rule.

1. $\dfrac{(14.0)(2.00)}{4.50}$

2. $\dfrac{(173)(562)}{780}$

3. $\dfrac{19.6}{(0.0159)(372)}$

4. $\dfrac{0.000356}{(456)(0.608)}$

5. $\dfrac{(15.0)(36.0)}{(47.0)(5.56)}$

6. $\dfrac{(4.56)(0.0676)}{(0.798)(50.5)}$

7. $\dfrac{(38.7)(5.62)(1.92)}{307}$

8. $\dfrac{(46.2)(4960)(0.106)}{(0.0309)(727)}$

9. $\left(\dfrac{47.3}{15.1}\right)^2$

10. $\left(\dfrac{0.0306}{4.37}\right)^2$

11. $\left[\dfrac{(12.9)(0.735)}{27.8}\right]^2$

12. $\left[\dfrac{(37.4)(0.436)}{96.2}\right]^2$

13. $\sqrt{\dfrac{86.4}{6.72}}$

14. $\sqrt{\dfrac{9320}{20.7}}$

15. $\sqrt{\dfrac{(67.0)(905)}{14.2}}$

16. $\sqrt{\dfrac{(863)(5.26)}{73.4}}$

17. $\dfrac{\sqrt{15.6}}{46.2}$

18. $\dfrac{\sqrt{829}}{3.63}$

19. $\dfrac{872}{\sqrt{3.72}}$

20. $\dfrac{59.1}{\sqrt{4060}}$

21. $\dfrac{(\sqrt{4.16})(0.814)^2}{36.7}$

22. $\dfrac{\sqrt{(16.4)(72.0)}}{73.5}$

23. $\dfrac{(487)(\sqrt{682})}{(31.4)(655)^2}$

24. $\dfrac{(3.65)^2(0.0526)}{\sqrt{0.00427}}$

C-5 Trigonometric scales

Values of the trigonometric ratios can be found on most slide rules to three significant digits. Generally the trigonometric scales, ST, S, and T, are read in conjunction with the C-(or D-) and CI-scales. [If a slide rule does not have an ST-scale, the S-and T-scales are used together with the B-(or A-) scale.] Although any of the six ratios can be found on most slide rules, we shall restrict our attention to finding values of the sine, cosine, and tangent of acute angles.

To find values of the sine of angles from about 0.6° to about 5.7°, one places the hairline over the angle on the ST-scale and reads the value on the C-scale (or D-scale if they are lined up.) All such values are in the range 0.01 to 0.1. To find values of the sine from about 5.7° to 90°, one places the hairline over the angle on the S-scale, and reads the value on the C-scale. All such values are in the range from 0.1 to 1.0.

Example A. The value of sin 1.60° is found by placing the hairline over 1.6 on the ST-scale and reading the answer 0.0279 on the C-scale. See setting *a* in Fig. C-11.

The value of sin 38° is found by placing the hairline over 38 on the S-scale and reading the result, 0.616, on the C-scale. See setting *b* in Fig. C-11.

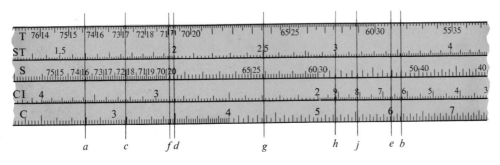

Figure C-11

To find values of the cosine we read the sine values "backward." On the S-scale we read cosine values from right to left (they are usually marked on the *left* side of the divisions of the S-scale). The S scale is used for angles from 0° to about 84.3°. The ST-scale is used for angles from about 84.3° to about 89.4°.

Example B. The value of cos 72° is found by placing the hairline over the left 72 of the S-scale and reading the result, 0.309, on the C-scale. See setting *c* in Fig. C-11.

The value of cos 88° is found by placing the hairline over 2 (since 90 − 88 = 2) of the ST-scale and reading the result, 0.0349, on the C-scale. See setting *d* in Fig. C-11.

The values of the sine and tangent are very nearly equal for small angles. For that reason values of the sine and tangent are found for such angles by use of the ST-scale. Therefore, to find values of the tangent for angles from about 0.6° to about 5.7°, we follow the same procedure as for values of the sine. To find values of the tangent for angles from about 5.7° to 45°, one places the hairline over the angle on the T-scale, and reads the value on the C-scale.

Example C. The value of tan 1.60° is the same as sin 1.60°. See setting *a* in Fig. C-11.

The value of tan 31° is found by placing the hairline over the 31 of the T-scale and reading the result, 0.601, on the C-scale. See setting e in Fig. C-11.

For angles from 45° to about 84.3° the numbers are marked on the left side of the divisions on the T-scale. To find the tangents of these angles, place the hairline over the appropriate angle (being sure to read from right to left), and read the result on the CI-scale. All such values are from 1.00 to 10.0. Also note that the CI-scale is read from right to left. For angles from about 84.3° to about 89.4° the angle is found on the ST-scale by subtracting the angle from 90°, and setting the hairline over this difference. The result is read on the CI-scale, with values ranging from 10.0 to 100.

Example D.   The value of tan 71° is found by placing the hairline over the 71 (on the left of the division) on the T-scale and reading the result, 2.90, on the CI-scale. See setting f in Fig. C-11.

The value of tan 87.5° is found by placing the hairline over the 2.5 (90 − 87.5 = 2.5) of the ST-scale and reading the result, 22.9, on the CI-scale. See setting g in Fig. C-11.

Just as with tables, if we know values of trigonometric ratios, we can determine the angles by using the slide rule. We must be careful, however, to note the decimal point of the ratio and to use the proper scales. This procedure is illustrated in the following example.

Example E.   If we know that sin α = 0.523, we set the hairline over 523 on the C-scale, and read α = 31.5° on the S-scale. If we knew that sin α = 0.0523, we would still set the hairline over 523 on the C-scale, but we would read α = 3.00° on the ST-scale. See setting h in Fig. C-11.

If we know that tan α = 1.81, we place the hairline over 181 on the CI-scale, not the C-scale. The result, α = 61.1°, is read on the T-scale, reading right to left. See setting j in Fig. C-11.

Since the trigonometric scales are read directly, it is not possible to include values for all angles. Those for which the ratios are less than 0.01 or greater than 100 are not included.

Exercises

In Exercises 1 through 16 find the indicated trigonometric ratios by using a slide rule.

1. sin 26°	2. tan 37°	3. cos 14°	4. sin 15.5°
5. sin 3.40°	6. cos 5°	7. tan 4.75°	8. cos 86.2°
9. tan 58°	10. sin 83°	11. cos 71.5°	12. tan 89.1°
13. sin 1.72°	14. tan 5.48°	15. tan 48.2°	16. cos 61.3°

In Exercises 17 through 32 find the angle α from a slide rule.

17. sin α = 0.652	18. cos α = 0.219	19. tan α = 0.492	20. sin α = 0.927

21. $\sin \alpha = 0.0873$ 22. $\tan \alpha = 0.0759$
23. $\cos \alpha = 0.0233$ 24. $\tan \alpha = 25.6$
25. $\tan \alpha = 7.82$ 26. $\sin \alpha = 0.107$
27. $\cos \alpha = 0.408$ 28. $\cos \alpha = 0.0617$
29. $\sin \alpha = 0.0996$ 30. $\tan \alpha = 2.79$
31. $\tan \alpha = 85.0$ 32. $\cos \alpha = 0.0851$

C-6 Review Exercises

In Exercises 1 through 44 perform the indicated calculations on a slide rule.

1. 3.46×4.92 2. 80.5×2.37 3. 362×51.9
4. 0.706×95.1 5. 6480×11.5 6. 0.0460×0.772

7. 89100×27.8 8. 38.9×687 9. $\dfrac{46.7}{1.39}$

10. $\dfrac{509}{26.7}$ 11. $\dfrac{6.32}{0.192}$ 12. $\dfrac{4080}{69200}$

13. $\dfrac{0.754}{0.0888}$ 14. $\dfrac{0.0901}{74.7}$ 15. $\dfrac{3.83}{5.64}$

16. $\dfrac{684}{90.9}$ 17. $(11.8)^2$ 18. $(2.73)^2$

19. $(52.7)^2$ 20. $(818)^2$ 21. $(0.715)^2$

22. $(0.0493)^2$ 23. $(3.79)^2$ 24. $(92.9)^2$

25. $\sqrt{6.85}$ 26. $\sqrt{23.6}$ 27. $\sqrt{4520}$

28. $\sqrt{0.0319}$ 29. $\sqrt{784}$ 30. $\sqrt{0.957}$

31. $\sqrt{183000}$ 32. $\sqrt{54600}$ 33. $\dfrac{(82.7)(2.40)}{36.5}$

34. $\dfrac{(491)(7.26)}{0.133}$ 35. $\dfrac{\sqrt{29.7}}{5.68}$ 36. $\dfrac{\sqrt{683}}{0.712}$

37. $\left[\dfrac{3.55}{0.0443}\right]^2$ 38. $[(6.88)(12.7)]^2$ 39. $\sqrt{(86.1)(2.36)}$

40. $\sqrt{\dfrac{7.42}{92.3}}$ 41. $\dfrac{(8.94)^2}{\sqrt{18.4}}$ 42. $\dfrac{(2.75)^2\sqrt{7.31}}{52.7}$

43. $\dfrac{(68.5)(14.9)^2}{\sqrt{524}}$ 44. $\dfrac{(81.5)(3.14)(68.1)}{(799)(0.0574)}$

In Exercises 45 through 52 find the indicated values on a slide rule.

45. $\sin 24°$ 46. $\cos 18°$ 47. $\tan 63.8°$ 48. $\sin 48.5°$
49. $\sin \alpha = 0.785$; find α 50. $\tan \alpha = 2.56$; find α
51. $\cos \alpha = 0.156$; find α 52. $\sin \alpha = 0.0852$; find α

Appendix D−Review of Geometry

D-1 Basic geometric figures and definitions

In this appendix we shall present geometric terminology and formulas that are related to the basic geometric figures. It is intended only as a brief summary of basic geometry.

Geometry deals with the properties and measurement of angles, lines, surfaces, and volumes, and the basic figures that are formed. We shall restrict our attention in this appendix to the basic figures, and concepts which are related to these figures.

Repeating the definition in Section 3-1, an *angle* is generated by rotating a half-line about its endpoint from an initial position to a terminal position. One complete rotation of a line about a point is defined to be an angle of 360 degrees, written as 360°. A *straight angle* contains 180°, and a *right angle* contains 90°. If two lines meet so that the angle between them is 90°, the lines are said to be *perpendicular*.

An angle less than 90° is an *acute angle*. An angle greater than 90°, but less than 180°, is an *obtuse angle*. *Supplementary angles* are two angles whose sum is 180°, and *complementary angles* are two angles whose sum equals 90°.

In a plane, if a line crosses two *parallel* or nonparallel lines, it is called a *transversal*. If a transversal crosses a pair of parallel lines, certain pairs of equal *angles* result. In Fig. D-1, the *corresponding angles* are equal. (That is, $\angle 1 = \angle 5$, $\angle 2 = \angle 6$, $\angle 3 = \angle 7$, $\angle 4 = \angle 8$.) Also, the *alternate interior angles* are equal ($\angle 3 = \angle 6$ and $\angle 4 = \angle 5$).

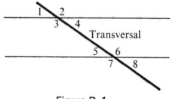

Figure D-1

Adjacent angles have a common vertex and a side common to them. For example, in Fig. D-1, ∡5 and 6 are adjacent angles. *Vertical angles* are equal angles formed "across" the point of intersection of two intersecting lines. In Fig. D-1, ∡5 and 8 are vertical angles.

When a part of the plane is bounded and closed by straight line segments, it is called a *polygon*. In general, polygons are named according to the number of sides they contain. A *triangle* has three sides, a *quadrilateral* has four sides, a *pentagon* has five sides, and so on. In a *regular* polygon, all of the sides are equal in length, and all of the interior angles are equal.

There are several important types of triangles. In an *equilateral triangle* the three sides are equal, and the three angles are also equal, each being 60°. In an *isosceles triangle* two of the sides are equal, as are the two *base angles* (the angles opposite the equal sides). In a *scalene triangle* no two sides are equal, and none of the angles is a right angle. In a *right triangle* one of the angles is a right angle. The side opposite the right angle is called the *hypotenuse*.

There are certain basic properties of triangles which we shall mention here. One very important property is that *the sum of the three angles of any triangle is 180°*. Also, the three *medians* (line segments drawn from a vertex to the *midpoint* of the opposite side) meet at a single point. This point of intersection of the medians is called the *centroid* of the triangle. It is also true that the three *angle bisectors* meet at a common point, as do the three *altitudes* (heights) which are drawn from a vertex perpendicular to the opposite side (or the extension of the opposite side).

Of particular importance is the *Pythagorean theorem*, which states that *in a right triangle, the square of the length of the hypotenuse equals the sum of the squares of the lengths of the other two sides*.

Two triangles are said to be *congruent* if corresponding angles are equal and if corresponding sides are equal. Two triangles are said to be *similar* if corresponding angles are equal. In similar triangles corresponding sides are proportional.

A *quadrilateral* is a plane figure having four sides and therefore four interior angles. A *parallelogram* is a quadrilateral with opposite sides *parallel* (extensions of the sides will not intersect). Also opposite sides and opposite angles of a parallelogram are equal. A *rectangle* is a parallelogram with intersecting sides perpendicular, which means that all four angles are right angles. It also means that opposite sides of a rectangle are equal and parallel. A *square* is a rectangle all sides of which are equal. A *trapezoid* is a quadrilateral with two of the sides parallel. These parallel sides are called the *bases* of the trapezoid. A *rhombus* is a parallelogram all four sides of which are equal.

All of the points on a *circle* are the same distance from a fixed point in the plane. This point is the *center* of the circle. The distance from the center to a point on the circle is the *radius* of the circle. The distance between two points on the circle and on a line passing through the center of the circle is the *diameter* of the circle. Thus the diameter is twice the radius.

Also associated with the circle is the *chord*, which is a line segment having its endpoints on the circle. A *tangent* is a line that touches a circle (does not pass through) at one point. A *secant* is a line that passes through two points of a circle. An *arc* is a part of the circle. When two radii form an angle at the center, the angle is called a *central angle*. An *inscribed angle* of an arc is one for which the endpoints of the arc are points on the sides of the angle, and for which the vertex is a point of the arc, although not an endpoint.

There are two important properties of a circle which we shall mention here.
(1) *A tangent to a circle is perpendicular to the radius drawn to the point of contact.*
(2) *An angle inscribed in a semicircle is a right angle.*

D-2 Basic geometric formulas

For the indicated figures, the following symbols are used: A = area, B = area of base, c = circumference, S = lateral area, V = volume.

1. *Triangle.* $A = \frac{1}{2}bh$ (Fig. D-2)
2. *Pythagorean theorem.* $c^2 = a^2 + b^2$ (Fig. D-3)
3. *Parallelogram.* $A = bh$ (Fig. D-4)
4. *Trapezoid.* $A = \frac{1}{2}(a + b)h$ (Fig. D-5)
5. *Circle.* $A = \pi r^2$, $c = 2\pi r$ (Fig. D-6)
6. *Rectangular solid.* $A = 2(lw + lh + wh)$, $V = lwh$ (Fig. D-7)
7. *Cube.* $A = 6e^2$, $V = e^3$ (Fig. D-8)
8. *Any cylinder or prism with parallel bases.* $V = Bh$ (Fig. D-9)
9. *Right circular cylinder.* $S = 2\pi rh$, $V = \pi r^2 h$ (Fig. D-10)
10. *Any cone or pyramid.* $V = \frac{1}{3}Bh$ (Fig. D-11)
11. *Right circular cone.* $S = \pi rs$, $V = \frac{1}{3}\pi r^2 h$ (Fig. D-12)
12. *Sphere.* $A = 4\pi r^2$, $V = \frac{4}{3}\pi r^3$ (Fig. D-13)

Also, the *perimeter* of a plane figure is the distance around it. For example, the perimeter p of the triangle in Fig. D-3 is $p = a + b + c$.

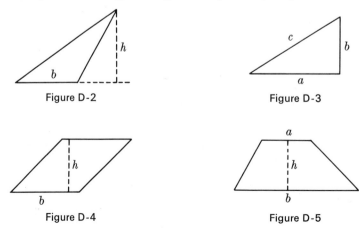

Figure D-2   Figure D-3

Figure D-4   Figure D-5

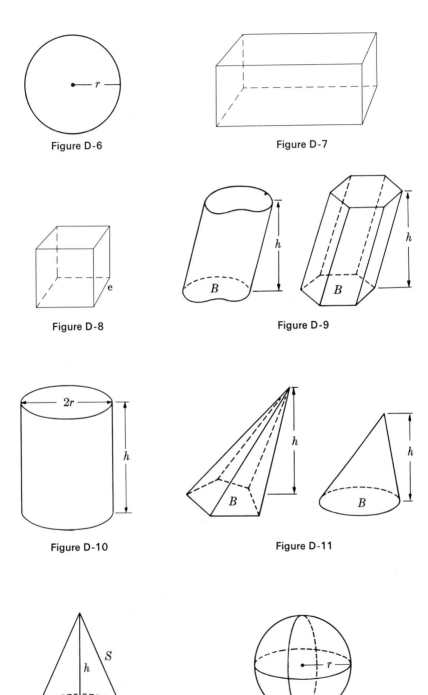

Figure D-6

Figure D-7

Figure D-8

Figure D-9

Figure D-10

Figure D-11

Figure D-12

Figure D-13

Exercises

In Exercises 1 through 4 refer to Fig. D-14, in which AOP and KOT are straight lines. $\angle TOP = 40°$, $\angle OBC = 90°$, and $\angle AOL = 55°$. Determine the indicated angles.

1. $\angle LOT$ 2. $\angle POL$ 3. $\angle KOP$ 4. $\angle KCB$

In Exercises 5 through 8 refer to Fig. D-15, where AB is a diameter, line TB is tangent to the circle at B, and $\angle ABC = 65°$. Determine the indicated angles.

5. $\angle CBT$ 6. $\angle BCT$ 7. $\angle CAB$ 8. $\angle BTC$

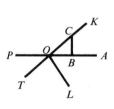

Figure D-14

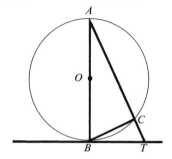

Figure D-15

In Exercises 9 through 20 use the Pythagorean theorem to solve for the unknown side of the right triangle. In each case c is the hypotenuse. If the answer is not exact, round off to three digits.

	a	b	c			a	b	c
9.	3	4	?		10.	9	12	?
11.	8	15	?		12.	24	10	?
13.	6	?	10		14.	2	?	4
15.	5	?	7		16.	3	?	9
17.	?	12	16		18.	?	10	18
19.	?	15	32		20.	?	5	36

In Exercises 21 and 22 find the required values.

21. Two triangles are similar, and the sides of the larger triangle are 3.0 in., 5.0 in., and 6.0 in., and the shortest side of the other triangle is 2.0 in. Find the remaining sides of the smaller triangle.

22. Two triangles are similar. The angles of the smaller triangle are 50°, 100°, and 30°, and the sides of the smaller triangle are 7.00 in., 9.00 in., and 4.57 in. The longest side of the larger triangle is 15.00 in. Find the other two sides and the three angles of the larger triangle.

In Exercises 23 through 32 find the perimeters (or circumferences) of the indicated figures.

23. A triangle with sides 6 ft, 8 ft, and 11 ft

24. A quadrilateral with sides 3 in., 4 in., 6 in., and 9 in.

25. An isosceles triangle whose equal sides are 3 yd long and whose third side is 4 yd long

26. An equilateral triangle whose sides are 7 ft long

27. A rectangle 5.14 in. long and 4.09 in. wide

28. A square of side 8.18 cm

29. A rhombus of side 15.6 m

30. A trapezoid whose bases are 17.8 in. and 7.4 in., and whose other sides are each 8.1 in.

31. A circle of radius 10.0 ft

32. A circle of diameter 7.06 cm

In Exercises 33 through 40 find the areas of the indicated figures.

33. A parallelogram of base 7.0 in. and height 4.0 in.

34. A rectangle of base 8.2 ft and height 2.5 ft

35. A triangle of base 6.3 yd and height 4.1 yd

36. A triangle of base 14.2 cm and height 6.83 cm

37. A trapezoid of bases 3.0 ft and 9.0 ft and height 4.0 ft

38. A trapezoid of bases 18.5 in. and 26.3 in. and height 10.5 in.

39. A circle of radius 7.00 in.

40. A semicircle of diameter 8.24 ft

In Exercises 41 through 52 evaluate the volume of the indicated figures.

41. A rectangular solid of length 9.00 ft, width 6.00 ft, and height 4.00 ft

42. A cube of edge 7.15 ft

43. Prism, square base of side 2.0 ft, altitude 5.0 ft

44. Prism, trapezoidal base (bases 4.0 in. and 6.0 in. and height 3.0 in.), altitude 6.0 in.

45. Cylinder, radius of base 7.00 in., altitude 6.00 in.

46. Cylinder, diameter of base 6.36 ft, altitude 18.0 in.

47. Pyramid, rectangular base 12.5 in. by 8.75 in., altitude 4.20 in.

48. Pyramid, equilateral triangular base of side 3.00 in., altitude 4.25 in.

49. Cone, radius of base 2.66 ft, altitude 1.22 yd

50. Cone, diameter of base 16.3 in., altitude 18.4 in.

51. Sphere, radius 5.48 ft

52. Sphere, diameter 15.7 yd

In Exercises 53 through 58 find the total surface area of the indicated figure for the given values.

53. Prism, rectangular base 4.00 in. by 8.00 in., altitude 6.00 in.

54. Prism, parallelogram base (base 16.0 in., height 4.25 in., perimeter 42.0 in.), altitude 6.45 in.

55. Cylinder, radius of base 8.58 in., altitude 1.38 ft

56. Cylinder, diameter of base 12.5 ft, altitude 4.60 ft

57. Sphere, radius 16.0 ft

58. Sphere, diameter 15.3 in.

Table 1. Powers and Roots

No.	Sq.	Sq. Root	Cube	Cube Root	No.	Sq.	Sq. Root	Cube	Cube Root
1	1	1.000	1	1.000	51	2,601	7.141	132,651	3.708
2	4	1.414	8	1.260	52	2,704	7.211	140,608	3.733
3	9	1.732	27	1.442	53	2,809	7.280	148,877	3.756
4	16	2.000	64	1.587	54	2,916	7.348	157,464	3.780
5	25	2.236	125	1.710	55	3,025	7.416	166,375	3.803
6	36	2.449	216	1.817	56	3,136	7.483	175,616	3.826
7	49	2.646	343	1.913	57	3,249	7.550	185,193	3.849
8	64	2.828	512	2.000	58	3,364	7.616	195,112	3.871
9	81	3.000	729	2.080	59	3,481	7.681	205,379	3.893
10	100	3.162	1,000	2.154	60	3,600	7.746	216,000	3.915
11	121	3.317	1,331	2.224	61	3,721	7.810	226,981	3.936
12	144	3.464	1,728	2.289	62	3,844	7.874	238,328	3.958
13	169	3.606	2,197	2.351	63	3,969	7.937	250,047	3.979
14	196	3.742	2,744	2.410	64	4,096	8.000	262,144	4.000
15	225	3.873	3,375	2.466	65	4,225	8.062	274,625	4.021
16	256	4.000	4,096	2.520	66	4,356	8.124	287,496	4.041
17	289	4.123	4,913	2.571	67	4,489	8.185	300,763	4.062
18	324	4.243	5,832	2.621	68	4,624	8.246	314,432	4.082
19	361	4.359	6,859	2.668	69	4,761	8.307	328,509	4.102
20	400	4.472	8,000	2.714	70	4,900	8.367	343,000	4.121
21	441	4.583	9,261	2.759	71	5,041	8.426	357,911	4.141
22	484	4.690	10,648	2.802	72	5,184	8.485	373,248	4.160
23	529	4.796	12,167	2.844	73	5,329	8.544	389,017	4.179
24	576	4.899	13,824	2.884	74	5,476	8.602	405,224	4.198
25	625	5.000	15,625	2.924	75	5,625	8.660	421,875	4.217
26	676	5.099	17,576	2.962	76	5,776	8.718	438,976	4.236
27	729	5.196	19,683	3.000	77	5,929	8.775	456,533	4.254
28	784	5.292	21,952	3.037	78	6,084	8.832	474,552	4.273
29	841	5.385	24,389	3.072	79	6,241	8.888	493,039	4.291
30	900	5.477	27,000	3.107	80	6,400	8.944	512,000	4.309
31	961	5.568	29,791	3.141	81	6,561	9.000	531,441	4.327
32	1,024	5.657	32,768	3.175	82	6,724	9.055	551,368	4.344
33	1,089	5.745	35,937	3.208	83	6,889	9.110	571,787	4.362
34	1,156	5.831	39,304	3.240	84	7,056	9.165	592,704	4.380
35	1,225	5.916	42,875	3.271	85	7,225	9.220	614,125	4.397
36	1,296	6.000	46,656	3.302	86	7,396	9.274	636,056	4.414
37	1,369	6.083	50,653	3.332	87	7,569	9.327	658,503	4.431
38	1,444	6.164	54,872	3.362	88	7,744	9.381	681,472	4.448
39	1,521	6.245	59,319	3.391	89	7,921	9.434	704,969	4.465
40	1,600	6.325	64,000	3.420	90	8,100	9.487	729,000	4.481
41	1,681	6.403	68,921	3.448	91	8,281	9.539	753,571	4.498
42	1,764	6.481	74,088	3.476	92	8,464	9.592	778,688	4.514
43	1,849	6.557	79,507	3.503	93	8,649	9.644	804,357	4.531
44	1,936	6.633	85,184	3.530	94	8,836	9.695	830,584	4.547
45	2,025	6.708	91,125	3.557	95	9,025	9.747	857,375	4.563
46	2,116	6.782	97,336	3.583	96	9,216	9.798	884,736	4.579
47	2,209	6.856	103,823	3.609	97	9,409	9.849	912,673	4.595
48	2,304	6.928	110,592	3.634	98	9,604	9.899	941,192	4.610
49	2,401	7.000	117,649	3.659	99	9,801	9.950	970,299	4.626
50	2,500	7.071	125,000	3.684	100	10,000	10.000	1,000,000	4.642

Table 2. Four-Place Logarithms of Numbers

N	0	1	2	3	4	5	6	7	8	9
10	0000	0043	0086	0128	0170	0212	0253	0294	0334	0374
11	0414	0453	0492	0531	0569	0607	0645	0682	0719	0755
12	0792	0828	0864	0899	0934	0969	1004	1038	1072	1106
13	1139	1173	1206	1239	1271	1303	1335	1367	1399	1430
14	1461	1492	1523	1553	1584	1614	1644	1673	1703	1732
15	1761	1790	1818	1847	1875	1903	1931	1959	1987	2014
16	2041	2068	2095	2122	2148	2175	2201	2227	2253	2279
17	2304	2330	2355	2380	2405	2430	2455	2480	2504	2529
18	2553	2577	2601	2625	2648	2672	2695	2718	2742	2765
19	2788	2810	2833	2856	2878	2900	2923	2945	2967	2989
20	3010	3032	3054	3075	3096	3118	3139	3160	3181	3201
21	3222	3243	3263	3284	3304	3324	3345	3365	3385	3404
22	3424	3444	3464	3483	3502	3522	3541	3560	3579	3598
23	3617	3636	3655	3674	3692	3711	3729	3747	3766	3784
24	3802	3820	3838	3856	3874	3892	3909	3927	3945	3962
25	3979	3997	4014	4031	4048	4065	4082	4099	4116	4133
26	4150	4166	4183	4200	4216	4232	4249	4265	4281	4298
27	4314	4330	4346	4362	4378	4393	4409	4425	4440	4456
28	4472	4487	4502	4518	4533	4548	4564	4579	4594	4609
29	4624	4639	4654	4669	4683	4698	4713	4728	4742	4757
30	4771	4786	4800	4814	4829	4843	4857	4871	4886	4900
31	4914	4928	4942	4955	4969	4983	4997	5011	5024	5038
32	5051	5065	5079	5092	5105	5119	5132	5145	5159	5172
33	5185	5198	5211	5224	5237	5250	5263	5276	5289	5302
34	5315	5328	5340	5353	5366	5378	5391	5403	5416	5428
35	5441	5453	5465	5478	5490	5502	5514	5527	5539	5551
36	5563	5575	5587	5599	5611	5623	5635	5647	5658	5670
37	5682	5694	5705	5717	5729	5740	5752	5763	5775	5786
38	5798	5809	5821	5832	5843	5855	5866	5877	5888	5899
39	5911	5922	5933	5944	5955	5966	5977	5988	5999	6010
40	6021	6031	6042	6053	6064	6075	6085	6096	6107	6117
41	6128	6138	6149	6160	6170	6180	6191	6201	6212	6222
42	6232	6243	6253	6263	6274	6284	6294	6304	6314	6325
43	6335	6345	6355	6365	6375	6385	6395	6405	6415	6425
44	6435	6444	6454	6464	6474	6484	6493	6503	6513	6522
45	6532	6542	6551	6561	6571	6580	6590	6599	6609	6618
46	6628	6637	6646	6656	6665	6675	6684	6693	6702	6712
47	6721	6730	6739	6749	6758	6767	6776	6785	6794	6803
48	6812	6821	6830	6839	6848	6857	6866	6875	6884	6893
49	6902	6911	6920	6928	6937	6946	6955	6964	6972	6981
50	6990	6998	7007	7016	7024	7033	7042	7050	7059	7067
51	7076	7084	7093	7101	7110	7118	7126	7135	7143	7152
52	7160	7168	7177	7185	7193	7202	7210	7218	7226	7235
53	7243	7251	7259	7267	7275	7284	7292	7300	7308	7316
54	7324	7332	7340	7348	7356	7364	7372	7380	7388	7396

Table 2. Continued

N	0	1	2	3	4	5	6	7	8	9
55	7404	7412	7419	7427	7435	7443	7451	7459	7466	7474
56	7482	7490	7497	7505	7513	7520	7528	7536	7543	7551
57	7559	7566	7574	7582	7589	7597	7604	7612	7619	7627
58	7634	7642	7649	7657	7664	7672	7679	7686	7694	7701
59	7709	7716	7723	7731	7738	7745	7752	7760	7767	7774
60	7782	7789	7796	7803	7810	7818	7825	7832	7839	7846
61	7853	7860	7868	7875	7882	7889	7896	7903	7910	7917
62	7924	7931	7938	7945	7952	7959	7966	7973	7980	7987
63	7993	8000	8007	8014	8021	8028	8035	8041	8048	8055
64	8062	8069	8075	8082	8089	8096	8102	8109	8116	8122
65	8129	8136	8142	8149	8156	8162	8169	8176	8182	8189
66	8195	8202	8209	8215	8222	8228	8235	8241	8248	8254
67	8261	8267	8274	8280	8287	8293	8299	8306	8312	8319
68	8325	8331	8338	8344	8351	8357	8363	8370	8376	8382
69	8388	8395	8401	8407	8414	8420	8426	8432	8439	8445
70	8451	8457	8463	8470	8476	8482	8488	8494	8500	8506
71	8513	8519	8525	8531	8537	8543	8549	8555	8561	8567
72	8573	8579	8585	8591	8597	8603	8609	8615	8621	8627
73	8633	8639	8645	8651	8657	8663	8669	8675	8681	8686
74	8692	8698	8704	8710	8716	8722	8727	8733	8739	8745
75	8751	8756	8762	8768	8774	8779	8785	8791	8797	8802
76	8808	8814	8820	8825	8831	8837	8842	8848	8854	8859
77	8865	8871	8876	8882	8887	8893	8899	8904	8910	8915
78	8921	8927	8932	8938	8943	8949	8954	8960	8965	8971
79	8976	8982	8987	8993	8998	9004	9009	9015	9020	9025
80	9031	9036	9042	9047	9053	9058	9063	9069	9074	9079
81	9085	9090	9096	9101	9106	9112	9117	9122	9128	9133
82	9138	9143	9149	9154	9159	9165	9170	9175	9180	9186
83	9191	9196	9201	9206	9212	9217	9222	9227	9232	9238
84	9243	9248	9253	9258	9263	9269	9274	9279	9284	9289
85	9294	9299	9304	9309	9315	9320	9325	9330	9335	9340
86	9345	9350	9355	9360	9365	9370	9375	9380	9385	9390
87	9395	9400	9405	9410	9415	9420	9425	9430	9435	9440
88	9445	9450	9455	9460	9465	9469	9474	9479	9484	9489
89	9494	9499	9504	9509	9513	9518	9523	9528	9533	9538
90	9542	9547	9552	9557	9562	9566	9571	9576	9581	9586
91	9590	9595	9600	9605	9609	9614	9619	9624	9628	9633
92	9638	9643	9647	9652	9657	9661	9666	9671	9675	9680
93	9685	9689	9694	9699	9703	9708	9713	9717	9722	9727
94	9731	9736	9741	9745	9750	9754	9759	9763	9768	9773
95	9777	9782	9786	9791	9795	9800	9805	9809	9814	9818
96	9823	9827	9832	9836	9841	9845	9850	9854	9859	9863
97	9868	9872	9877	9881	9886	9890	9894	9899	9903	9908
98	9912	9917	9921	9926	9930	9934	9939	9943	9948	9952
99	9956	9961	9965	9969	9974	9978	9983	9987	9991	9996

Table 3. Four-Place Values of Functions and Radians

Degrees	Radians	Sin θ	Cos θ	Tan θ	Cot θ	Sec θ	Csc θ		
0° 00′	.0000	.0000	1.0000	.0000	—	1.000	—	1.5708	90° 00′
10	.0029	.0029	1.0000	.0029	343.8	1.000	343.8	1.5679	50
20	.0058	.0058	1.0000	.0058	171.9	1.000	171.9	1.5650	40
30	.0087	.0087	1.0000	.0087	114.6	1.000	114.6	1.5621	30
40	.0116	.0116	.9999	.0116	85.94	1.000	85.95	1.5592	20
50	.0145	.0145	.9999	.0145	68.75	1.000	68.76	1.5563	10
1° 00′	.0175	.0175	.9998	.0175	57.29	1.000	57.30	1.5533	89° 00′
10	.0204	.0204	.9998	.0204	49.10	1.000	49.11	1.5504	50
20	.0233	.0233	.9997	.0233	42.96	1.000	42.98	1.5475	40
30	.0262	.0262	.9997	.0262	38.19	1.000	38.20	1.5446	30
40	.0291	.0291	.9996	.0291	34.37	1.000	34.38	1.5417	20
50	.0320	.0320	.9995	.0320	31.24	1.001	31.26	1.5388	10
2° 00′	.0349	.0349	.9994	.0349	28.64	1.001	28.65	1.5359	88° 00′
10	.0378	.0378	.9993	.0378	26.43	1.001	26.45	1.5330	50
20	.0407	.0407	.9992	.0407	24.54	1.001	24.56	1.5301	40
30	.0436	.0436	.9990	.0437	22.90	1.001	22.93	1.5272	30
40	.0465	.0465	.9989	.0466	21.47	1.001	21.49	1.5243	20
50	.0495	.0494	.9988	.0495	20.21	1.001	20.23	1.5213	10
3° 00′	.0524	.0523	.9986	.0524	19.08	1.001	19.11	1.5184	87° 00′
10	.0553	.0552	.9985	.0553	18.07	1.002	18.10	1.5155	50
20	.0582	.0581	.9983	.0582	17.17	1.002	17.20	1.5126	40
30	.0611	.0610	.9981	.0612	16.35	1.002	16.38	1.5097	30
40	.0640	.0640	.9980	.0641	15.60	1.002	15.64	1.5068	20
50	.0669	.0669	.9978	.0670	14.92	1.002	14.96	1.5039	10
4° 00′	.0698	.0698	.9976	.0699	14.30	1.002	14.34	1.5010	86° 00′
10	.0727	.0727	.9974	.0729	13.73	1.003	13.76	1.4981	50
20	.0756	.0756	.9971	.0758	13.20	1.003	13.23	1.4952	40
30	.0785	.0785	.9969	.0787	12.71	1.003	12.75	1.4923	30
40	.0814	.0814	.9967	.0816	12.25	1.003	12.29	1.4893	20
50	.0844	.0843	.9964	.0846	11.83	1.004	11.87	1.4864	10
5° 00′	.0873	.0872	.9962	.0875	11.43	1.004	11.47	1.4835	85° 00′
10	.0902	.0901	.9959	.0904	11.06	1.004	11.10	1.4806	50
20	.0931	.0929	.9957	.0934	10.71	1.004	10.76	1.4777	40
30	.0960	.0958	.9954	.0963	10.39	1.005	10.43	1.4748	30
40	.0989	.0987	.9951	.0992	10.08	1.005	10.13	1.4719	20
50	.1018	.1016	.9948	.1022	9.788	1.005	9.839	1.4690	10
6° 00′	.1047	.1045	.9945	.1051	9.514	1.006	9.567	1.4661	84° 00′
		Cos θ	Sin θ	Cot θ	Tan θ	Csc θ	Sec θ	Radians	Degrees

Table 3. Continued

Degrees	Radians	Sin θ	Cos θ	Tan θ	Cot θ	Sec θ	Csc θ		
6° 00′	.1047	.1045	.9945	.1051	9.514	1.006	9.567	1.4661	84° 00′
10	.1076	.1074	.9942	.1080	9.255	1.006	9.309	1.4632	50
20	.1105	.1103	.9939	.1110	9.010	1.006	9.065	1.4603	40
30	.1134	.1132	.9936	.1139	8.777	1.006	8.834	1.4573	30
40	.1164	.1161	.9932	.1169	8.556	1.007	8.614	1.4544	20
50	.1193	.1190	.9929	.1198	8.345	1.007	8.405	1.4515	10
7° 00′	.1222	.1219	.9925	.1228	8.144	1.008	8.206	1.4486	83° 00′
10	.1251	.1248	.9922	.1257	7.953	1.008	8.016	1.4457	50
20	.1280	.1276	.9918	.1287	7.770	1.008	7.834	1.4428	40
30	.1309	.1305	.9914	.1317	7.596	1.009	7.661	1.4399	30
40	.1338	.1334	.9911	.1346	7.429	1.009	7.496	1.4370	20
50	.1367	.1363	.9907	.1376	7.269	1.009	7.337	1.4341	10
8° 00′	.1396	.1392	.9903	.1405	7.115	1.010	7.185	1.4312	82° 00′
10	.1425	.1421	.9899	.1435	6.968	1.010	7.040	1.4283	50
20	.1454	.1449	.9894	.1465	6.827	1.011	6.900	1.4254	40
30	.1484	.1478	.9890	.1495	6.691	1.011	6.765	1.4224	30
40	.1513	.1507	.9886	.1524	6.561	1.012	6.636	1.4195	20
50	.1542	.1536	.9881	.1554	6.435	1.012	6.512	1.4166	10
9° 00′	.1571	.1564	.9877	.1584	6.314	1.012	6.392	1.4137	81° 00′
10	.1600	.1593	.9872	.1614	6.197	1.013	6.277	1.4108	50
20	.1629	.1622	.9868	.1644	6.084	1.013	6.166	1.4079	40
30	.1658	.1650	.9863	.1673	5.976	1.014	6.059	1.4050	30
40	.1687	.1679	.9858	.1703	5.871	1.014	5.955	1.4021	20
50	.1716	.1708	.9853	.1733	5.769	1.015	6.855	1.3992	10
10° 00′	.1745	.1736	.9848	.1763	5.671	1.015	5.759	1.3963	80° 00′
10	.1774	.1765	.9843	.1793	5.576	1.016	5.665	1.3934	50
20	.1804	.1794	.9838	.1823	5.485	1.016	5.575	1.3904	40
30	.1833	.1822	.9833	.1853	5.396	1.017	5.487	1.3875	30
40	.1862	.1851	.9827	.1883	5.309	1.018	5.403	1.3846	20
50	.1891	.1880	.9822	.1914	5.226	1.018	5.320	1.3817	10
11° 00′	.1920	.1908	.9816	.1944	5.145	1.019	5.241	1.3788	79° 00′
10	.1949	.1937	.9811	.1974	5.066	1.019	5.164	1.3759	50
20	.1978	.1965	.9805	.2004	4.989	1.020	5.089	1.3730	40
30	.2007	.1994	.9799	.2035	4.915	1.020	5.016	1.3701	30
40	.2036	.2022	.9793	.2065	4.843	1.021	4.945	1.3672	20
50	.2065	.2051	.9787	.2095	4.773	1.022	4.876	1.3643	10
12° 00′	.2094	.2079	.9781	.2126	4.705	1.022	4.810	1.3614	78° 00′
		Cos θ	Sin θ	Cot θ	Tan θ	Csc θ	Sec θ	Radians	Degrees

Table 3. Continued

Degrees	Radians	Sin θ	Cos θ	Tan θ	Cot θ	Sec θ	Csc θ		
12° 00′	.2094	.2079	.9781	.2126	4.705	1.022	4.810	1.3614	78° 00′
10	.2123	.2108	.9775	.2156	4.638	1.023	4.745	1.3584	50
20	.2153	.2136	.9769	.2186	4.574	1.024	4.682	1.3555	40
30	.2182	.2164	.9763	.2217	4.511	1.024	4.620	1.3526	30
40	.2211	.2193	.9757	.2247	4.449	1.025	4.560	1.3497	20
50	.2240	.2221	.9750	.2278	4.390	1.026	4.502	1 3468	10
13° 00′	.2269	.2250	.9744	.2309	4.331	1.026	4.445	1.3439	77° 00′
10	.2298	.2278	.9737	.2339	4.275	1.027	4.390	1.3410	50
20	.2327	.2306	.9730	.2370	4.219	1.028	4.336	1.3381	40
30	.2356	.2334	.9724	.2401	4.165	1.028	4.284	1.3352	30
40	.2385	.2363	.9717	.2432	4.113	1.029	4.232	1.3323	20
50	.2414	.2391	.9710	.2462	4.061	1.030	4.182	1.3294	10
14° 00′	.2443	.2419	.9703	.2493	4.011	1.031	4.134	1.3265	76° 00′
10	.2473	.2447	.9696	.2524	3.962	1.031	4.086	1.3235	50
20	.2502	.2476	.9689	.2555	3.914	1.032	4.039	1.3206	40
30	.2531	.2504	.9681	.2586	3.867	1.033	3.994	1.3177	30
40	.2560	.2532	.9674	.2617	3.821	1.034	3.950	1.3148	20
50	.2589	.2560	.9667	.2648	3.776	1.034	3.906	1.3119	10
15° 00′	.2618	.2588	.9659	.2679	3.732	1.035	3.864	1.3090	75° 00′
10	.2647	.2616	.9652	.2711	3.689	1.036	3.822	1.3061	50
20	.2676	.2644	.9644	.2742	3.647	1.037	3.782	1.3032	40
30	.2705	.2672	.9636	.2773	3.606	1.038	3.742	1.3003	30
40	.2734	.2700	.9628	.2805	3.566	1.039	3.703	1.3974	20
50	.2763	.2728	.9621	.2836	3.526	1.039	3.665	1.3945	10
16° 00′	.2793	.2756	.9613	.2867	3.487	1.040	3.628	1.2915	74° 00′
10	.2822	.2784	.9605	.2899	3.450	1.041	3.592	1.2886	50
20	.2851	.2812	.9596	.2931	3.412	1.042	3.556	1.2857	40
30	.2880	.2840	.9588	.2962	3.376	1.043	3.521	1.2828	30
40	.2909	.2868	.9580	.2994	3.340	1.044	3.487	1.2799	20
50	.2938	.2896	.9572	.3026	3.305	1.045	3.453	1.2770	10
17° 00′	.2967	.2924	.9563	.3057	3.271	1.046	3.420	1.2741	73° 00′
10	.2996	.2952	.9555	.3089	3.237	1.047	3.388	1.2712	50
20	.3025	.2979	.9546	.3121	3.204	1.048	3.356	1.2683	40
30	.3054	.3007	.9537	.3153	3.172	1.049	3.326	1.2654	30
40	.3083	.3035	.9528	.3185	3.140	1.049	3.295	1.2625	20
50	.3113	.3062	.9520	.3217	3.108	1.050	3.265	1.2595	10
18° 00′	.3142	.3090	.9511	.3249	3.078	1.051	3.236	1.2566	72° 00′
		Cos θ	Sin θ	Cot θ	Tan θ	Csc θ	Sec θ	Radians	Degrees

Table 3. Continued

Degrees	Radians	Sin θ	Cos θ	Tan θ	Cot θ	Sec θ	Csc θ		
18° 00′	.3142	.3090	.9511	.3249	3.078	1.051	3.236	1.2566	72° 00′
10	.3171	.3118	.9502	.3281	3.047	1.052	3.207	1.2537	50
20	.3200	.3145	.9492	.3314	3.018	1.053	3.179	1.2508	40
30	.3229	.3173	.9483	.3346	2.989	1.054	3.152	1.2479	30
40	.3258	.3201	.9474	.3378	2.960	1.056	3.124	1.2450	20
50	.3287	.3228	.9465	.3411	2.932	1.057	3.098	1.2421	10
19° 00′	.3316	.3256	.9455	.3443	2.904	1.058	3.072	1.2392	71° 00′
10	.3345	.3283	.9446	.3476	2.877	1.059	3.046	1.2363	50
20	.3374	.3311	.9436	.3508	2.850	1.060	3.021	1.2334	40
30	.3403	.3338	.9426	.3541	2.824	1.061	2.996	1.2305	30
40	.3432	.3365	.9417	.3574	2.798	1.062	2.971	1.2275	20
50	.3462	.3393	.9407	.3607	2.773	1.063	2.947	1.2246	10
20° 00′	.3491	.3420	.9397	.3640	2.747	1.064	2.924	1.2217	70° 00′
10	.3520	.3448	.9387	.3673	2.723	1.065	2.901	1.2188	50
20	.3549	.3475	.9377	.3706	2.699	1.066	2.878	1.2159	40
30	.3578	.3502	.9367	.3739	2.675	1.068	2.855	1.2130	30
40	.3607	.3529	.9356	.3772	2.651	1.069	2.833	1.2101	20
50	.3636	.3557	.9346	.3805	2.628	1.070	2.812	1.2072	10
21° 00′	.3665	.3584	.9336	.3839	2.605	1.071	2.790	1.2043	69° 00′
10	.3694	.3611	.9325	.3872	2.583	1.072	2.769	1.2014	50
20	.3723	.3638	.9315	.3906	2.560	1.074	2.749	1.1985	40
30	.3752	.3665	.9304	.3939	2.539	1.075	2.729	1.1956	30
40	.3782	.3692	.9293	.3973	2.517	1.076	2.709	1.1926	20
50	.3811	.3719	.9283	.4006	2.496	1.077	2.689	1.1897	10
22° 00′	.3840	.3746	.9272	.4040	2.475	1.079	2.669	1.1868	68° 00′
10	.3869	.3773	.9261	.4074	2.455	1.080	2.650	1.1839	50
20	.3898	.3800	.9250	.4108	2.434	1.081	2.632	1.1810	40
30	.3927	.3827	.9239	.4142	2.414	1.082	2.613	1.1781	30
40	.3956	.3854	.9228	.4176	2.394	1.084	2.595	1.1752	20
50	.3985	.3881	.9216	.4210	2.375	1.085	2.577	1.1723	10
23° 00′	.4014	.3907	.9205	.4245	2.356	1.086	2.559	1.1694	67° 00′
10	.4043	.3934	.9194	.4279	2.337	1.088	2.542	1.1665	50
20	.4072	.3961	.9182	.4314	2.318	1.089	2.525	1.1636	40
30	.4102	.3987	.9171	.4348	2.300	1.090	2.508	1.1606	30
40	.4131	.4014	.9159	.4383	2.282	1.092	2.491	1.1577	20
50	.4160	.4041	.9147	.4417	2.264	1.093	2.475	1.1548	10
24° 00′	.4189	.4067	.9135	.4452	2.246	1.095	2.459	1.1519	66° 00′
		Cos θ	Sin θ	Cot θ	Tan θ	Csc θ	Sec θ	Radians	Degrees

Table 3. Continued

Degrees	Radians	Sin θ	Cos θ	Tan θ	Cot θ	Sec θ	Csc θ		
24° 00′	.4189	.4067	.9135	.4452	2.246	1.095	2.459	1.1519	66° 00′
10	.4218	.4094	.9124	.4487	2.229	1.096	2.443	1.1490	50
20	.4247	.4120	.9112	.4522	2.211	1.097	2.427	1.1461	40
30	.4276	.4147	.9100	.4557	2.194	1.099	2.411	1.1432	30
40	.4305	.4173	.9088	.4592	2.177	1.100	2.396	1.1403	20
50	.4334	.4200	.9075	.4628	2.161	1.102	2.381	1.1374	10
25° 00′	.4363	.4226	.9063	.4663	2.145	1.103	2.366	1.1345	65° 00′
10	.4392	.4253	.9051	.4699	2.128	1.105	2.352	1.1316	50
20	.4422	.4279	.9038	.4734	2.112	1.106	2.337	1.1286	40
30	.4451	.4305	.9026	.4770	2.097	1.108	2.323	1.1257	30
40	.4480	.4331	.9013	.4806	2.081	1.109	2.309	1.1228	20
50	.4509	.4358	.9001	.4841	2.066	1.111	2.295	1.1199	10
26° 00′	.4538	.4384	.8988	.4877	2.050	1.113	2.281	1.1170	64° 00′
10	.4567	.4410	.8975	.4913	2.035	1.114	2.268	1.1141	50
20	.4596	.4436	.8962	.4950	2.020	1.116	2.254	1.1112	40
30	.4625	.4462	.8949	.4986	2.006	1.117	2.241	1.1083	30
40	.4654	.4488	.8936	.5022	1.991	1.119	2.228	1.1054	20
50	.4683	.4514	.8923	.5059	1.977	1.121	2.215	1.1025	10
27° 00′	.4712	.4540	.8910	.5095	1.963	1.122	2.203	1.0996	63° 00′
10	.4741	.4566	.8897	.5132	1.949	1.124	2.190	1.0966	50
20	.4771	.4592	.8884	.5169	1.935	1.126	2.178	1.0937	40
30	.4800	.4617	.8870	.5206	1.921	1.127	2.166	1.0908	30
40	.4829	.4643	.8857	.5243	1.907	1.129	2.154	1.0879	20
50	.4858	.4669	.8843	.5280	1.894	1.131	2.142	1.0850	10
28° 00′	.4887	.4695	.8829	.5317	1.881	1.133	2.130	1.0821	62° 00′
10	.4916	.4720	.8816	.5354	1.868	1.134	2.118	1.0792	50
20	.4945	.4746	.8802	.5392	1.855	1.136	2.107	1.0763	40
30	.4974	.4772	.8788	.5430	1.842	1.138	2.096	1.0734	30
40	.5003	.4797	.8774	.5467	1.829	1.140	2.085	1.0705	20
50	.5032	.4823	.8760	.5505	1.816	1.142	2.074	1.0676	10
29° 00′	.5061	.4848	.8746	.5543	1.804	1.143	2.063	1.0647	61° 00′
10	.5091	.4874	.8732	.5581	1.792	1.145	2.052	1.0617	50
20	.5120	.4899	.8718	.5619	1.780	1.147	2.041	1.0588	40
30	.5149	.4924	.8704	.5658	1.767	1.149	2.031	1.0559	30
40	.5178	.4950	.8689	.5696	1.756	1.151	2.020	1.0530	20
50	.5207	.4975	.8675	.5735	1.744	1.153	2.010	1.0501	10
30° 00′	.5236	.5000	.8660	.5774	1.732	1.155	2.000	1.0472	60° 00′
		Cos θ	Sin θ	Cot θ	Tan θ	Csc θ	Sec θ	Radians	Degrees

Table 3. Continued

Degrees	Radians	Sin θ	Cos θ	Tan θ	Cot θ	Sec θ	Csc θ		
30° 00′	.5236	.5000	.8660	.5774	1.732	1.155	2.000	1.0472	60° 00′
10	.5265	.5025	.8646	.5812	1.720	1.157	1.990	1.0443	50
20	.5294	.5050	.8631	.5851	1.709	1.159	1.980	1.0414	40
30	.5323	.5075	.8616	.5890	1.698	1.161	1.970	1.0385	30
40	.5352	.5100	.8601	.5930	1.686	1.163	1.961	1.0356	20
50	.5381	.5125	.8587	.5969	1.675	1.165	1.951	1.0327	10
31° 00′	.5411	.5150	.8572	.6009	1.664	1.167	1.942	1.0297	59° 00′
10	.5440	.5175	.8557	.6048	1.653	1.169	1.932	1.0268	50
20	.5469	.5200	.8542	.6088	1.643	1.171	1.923	1.0239	40
30	.5498	.5225	.8526	.6128	1.632	1.173	1.914	1.0210	30
40	.5527	.5250	.8511	.6168	1.621	1.175	1.905	1.0181	20
50	.5556	.5275	.8496	.6208	1.611	1.177	1.896	1.0152	10
32° 00′	.5585	.5299	.8480	.6249	1.600	1.179	1.887	1.0123	58° 00′
10	.5614	.5324	.8465	.6289	1.590	1.181	1.878	1.0094	50
20	.5643	.5348	.8450	.6330	1.580	1.184	1.870	1.0065	40
30	.5672	.5373	.8434	.6371	1.570	1.186	1.861	1.0036	30
40	.5701	.5398	.8418	.6412	1.560	1.188	1.853	1.0007	20
50	.5730	.5422	.8403	.6453	1.550	1.190	1.844	.9977	10
33° 00′	.5760	.5446	.8387	.6494	1.540	1.192	1.836	.9948	57° 00′
10	.5789	.5471	.8371	.6536	1.530	1.195	1.828	.9919	50
20	.5818	.5495	.8355	.6577	1.520	1.197	1.820	.9890	40
30	.5847	.5519	.8339	.6619	1.511	1.199	1.812	.9861	30
40	.5876	.5544	.8323	.6661	1.501	1.202	1.804	.9832	20
50	.5905	.5568	.8307	.6703	1.492	1.204	1.796	.9803	10
34° 00′	.5934	.5592	.8290	.6745	1.483	1.206	1.788	.9774	56° 00′
10	.5963	.5616	.8274	.6787	1.473	1.209	1.781	.9745	50
20	.5992	.5640	.8258	.6830	1.464	1.211	1.773	.9716	40
30	.6021	.5664	.8241	.6873	1.455	1.213	1.766	.9687	30
40	.6050	.5688	.8225	.6916	1.446	1.216	1.758	.9657	20
50	.6080	.5712	.8208	.6959	1.437	1.218	1.751	.9628	10
35° 00′	.6109	.5736	.8192	.7002	1.428	1.221	1.743	.9599	55° 00′
10	.6138	.5760	.8175	.7046	1.419	1.223	1.736	.9570	50
20	.6167	.5783	.8158	.7089	1.411	1.226	1.729	.9541	40
30	.6196	.5807	.8141	.7133	1.402	1.228	1.722	.9512	30
40	.6225	.5831	.8124	.7177	1.393	1.231	1.715	.9483	20
50	.6254	.5854	.8107	.7221	1.385	1.233	1.708	.9454	10
36° 00′	.6283	.5878	.8900	.7265	1.376	1.236	1.701	.9425	54° 00′
		Cos θ	Sin θ	Cot θ	Tan θ	Csc θ	Sec θ	Radians	Degrees

Table 3. Continued

Degrees	Radians	Sin θ	Cos θ	Tan θ	Cot θ	Sec θ	Csc θ		
36° 00′	.6283	.5878	.8090	.7265	1.376	1.236	1.701	.9425	54° 00′
10	.6312	.5901	.8073	.7310	1.368	1.239	1.695	.9396	50
20	.6341	.5925	.8056	.7355	1.360	1.241	1.688	.9367	40
30	.6370	.5948	.8039	.7400	1.351	1.244	1.681	.9338	30
40	.6400	.5972	.8021	.7445	1.343	1.247	1.675	.9308	20
50	.6429	.5995	.8004	.7490	1.335	1.249	1.668	.9279	10
37° 00′	.6458	.6018	.7986	.7536	1.327	1.252	1.662	.9250	53° 00′
10	.6487	.6041	.7969	.7581	1.319	1.255	1.655	.9221	50
20	.6516	.6065	.7951	.7627	1.311	1.258	1.649	.9192	40
30	.6545	.6088	.7934	.7673	1.303	1.260	1.643	.9163	30
40	.6574	.6111	.7916	.7720	1.295	1.263	1.636	.9134	20
50	.6603	.6134	.7898	.7766	1.288	1.266	1.630	.9105	10
38° 00′	.6632	.6157	.7880	.7813	1.280	1.269	1.624	.9076	52° 00′
10	.6661	.6180	.7862	.7860	1.272	1.272	1.618	.9047	50
20	.6690	.6202	.7844	.7907	1.265	1.275	1.612	.9018	40
30	.6720	.6225	.7826	.7954	1.257	1.278	1.606	.8988	30
40	.6749	.6248	.7808	.8002	1.250	1.281	1.601	.8959	20
50	.6778	.6271	.7790	.8050	1.242	1.284	1.595	.8930	10
39° 00′	.6807	.6293	.7771	.8098	1.235	1.287	1.589	.8901	51° 00′
10	.6836	.6316	.7753	.8146	1.228	1.290	1.583	.8872	50
20	.6865	.6338	.7735	.8195	1.220	1.293	1.578	.8843	40
30	.6894	.6361	.7716	.8243	1.213	1.296	1.572	.8814	30
40	.6923	.6383	.7698	.8292	1.206	1.299	1.567	.8785	20
50	.6952	.6406	.7679	.8342	1.199	1.302	1.561	.8756	10
40° 00′	.6981	.6428	.7660	.8391	1.192	1.305	1.556	.8727	50° 00′
10	.7010	.6450	.7642	.8441	1.185	1.309	1.550	.8698	50
20	.7039	.6472	.7623	.8491	1.178	1.312	1.545	.8668	40
30	.7069	.6494	.7604	.8541	1.171	1.315	1.540	.8639	30
40	.7098	.6517	.7585	.8591	1.164	1.318	1.535	.8610	20
50	.7127	.6539	.7566	.8642	1.157	1.322	1.529	.8581	10
41° 00′	.7156	.6561	.7547	.8693	1.150	1.325	1.524	.8552	49° 00′
10	.7185	.6583	.7528	.8744	1.144	1.328	1.519	.8523	50
20	.7214	.6604	.7509	.8796	1.137	1.332	1.514	.8494	40
30	.7243	.6626	.7490	.8847	1.130	1.335	1.509	.8465	30
40	.7272	.6648	.7470	.8899	1.124	1.339	1.504	.8436	20
50	.7301	.6670	.7451	.8952	1.117	1.342	1.499	.8407	10
42° 00′	.7330	.6691	.7431	.9004	1.111	1.346	1.494	.8378	48° 00′
		Cos θ	Sin θ	Cot θ	Tan θ	Csc θ	Sec θ	Radians	Degrees

Table 3. Continued

Degrees	Radians	Sin θ	Cos θ	Tan θ	Cot θ	Sec θ	Csc θ		
42° 00′	.7330	.6691	.7431	.9004	1.111	1.346	1.494	.8378	48° 00′
10	.7359	.6713	.7412	.9057	1.104	1.349	1.490	.8348	50
20	.7389	.6734	.7392	.9110	1.098	1.353	1.485	.8319	40
30	.7418	.6756	.7373	.9163	1.091	1.356	1.480	.8290	30
40	.7447	.6777	.7353	.9217	1.085	1.360	1.476	.8261	20
50	.7476	.6799	.7333	.9271	1.079	1.364	1.471	.8232	10
43° 00′	.7505	.6820	.7314	.9325	1.072	1.367	1.466	.8203	47° 00′
10	.7534	.6841	.7294	.9380	1.066	1.371	1.462	.8174	50
20	.7563	.6862	.7274	.9435	1.060	1.375	1.457	.8145	40
30	.7592	.6884	.7254	.9490	1.054	1.379	1.453	.8116	30
40	.7621	.6905	.7234	.9545	1.048	1.382	1.448	.8087	20
50	.7650	.6926	.7214	.9601	1.042	1.386	1.444	.8058	10
44° 00′	.7679	.6947	.7193	.9657	1.036	1.390	1.440	.8029	46° 00′
10	.7709	.6967	.7173	.9713	1.030	1.394	1.435	.7999	50
20	.7738	.6988	.7153	.9770	1.024	1.398	1.431	.7970	40
30	.7767	.7009	.7133	.9827	1.018	1.402	1.427	.7941	30
40	.7796	.7030	.7112	.9884	1.012	1.406	1.423	.7912	20
50	.7825	.7050	.7092	.9942	1.006	1.410	1.418	.7883	10
45° 00′	.7854	.7071	.7071	1.000	1.000	1.414	1.414	.7854	45° 00′
		Cos θ	Sin θ	Cot θ	Tan θ	Csc θ	Sec θ	Radians	Degrees

Table 4. Four-Place Logarithms of Trigonometric Functions
Angle θ in Degrees
Attach—10 to logarithms obtained from this table

Angle θ	log sin θ	log csc θ	log tan θ	log cot θ	log sec θ	log cos θ	
0° 00'	No value	No value	No value	No value	10.0000	10.0000	90° 00'
10	7.4637	12.5363	7.4637	12.5363	10.0000	10.0000	50
20	7.7648	12.2352	7.7648	12.2352	10.0000	10.0000	40
30	7.9408	12.0592	7.9409	12.0591	10.0000	10.0000	30
40	8.0658	11.9342	8.0658	11.9342	10.0000	10.0000	20
50	8.1627	11.8373	8.1627	11.8373	10.0000	10.0000	10
1° 00	8.2419	11.7581	8.2419	11.7581	10.0001	9.9999	89° 00'
10	8.3088	11.6912	8.3089	11.6911	10.0001	9.9999	50
20	8.3668	11.6332	8.3669	11.6331	10.0001	9.9999	40
30	8.4179	11.5821	8.4181	11.5819	10.0001	9.9999	30
40	8.4637	11.5363	8.4638	11.5362	10.0002	9.9998	20
50	8.5050	11.4950	8.5053	11.4947	10.0002	9.9998	10
2° 00'	8.5428	11.4572	8.5431	11.4569	10.0003	9.9997	88° 00'
10	8.5776	11.4224	8.5779	11.4221	10.0003	9.9997	50
20	8.6097	11.3903	8.6101	11.3899	10.0004	9.9996	40
30	8.6397	11.3603	8.6401	11.3599	10.0004	9.9996	30
40	8.6677	11.3323	8.6682	11.3318	10.0005	9.9995	20
50	8.6940	11.3060	8.6945	11.3055	10.0005	9.9995	10
3° 00'	8.7188	11.2812	8.7194	11.2806	10.0006	9.9994	87° 00'
10	8.7423	11.2577	8.7429	11.2571	10.0007	9.9993	50
20	8.7645	11.2355	8.7652	11.2348	10.0007	9.9993	40
30	8.7857	11.2143	8.7865	11.2135	10.0008	9.9992	30
40	8.8059	11.1941	8.8067	11.1933	10.0009	9.9991	20
50	8.8251	11.1749	8.8261	11.1739	10.0010	9.9990	10
4° 00'	8.8463	11.1564	8.8446	11.1554	10.0011	9.9989	86° 00'
10	8.8613	11.1387	8.8624	11.1376	10.0011	9.9989	50
20	8.8783	11.1217	8.8795	11.1205	10.0012	9.9988	40
30	8.8946	11.1054	8.8960	11.1040	10.0013	9.9987	30
40	8.9104	11.0896	8.9118	11.0882	10.0014	9.9986	20
50	8.9256	11.0744	8.9272	11.0728	10.0015	9.9985	10
5° 00'	8.9403	11.0597	8.9420	11.0580	10.0017	9.9983	85° 00'
10	8.9545	11.0455	8.9563	11.0437	10.0018	9.9982	50
20	8.9682	11.0318	8.9701	11.0299	10.0019	9.9981	40
30	8.9816	11.0184	8.9836	11.0164	10.0020	9.9980	30
40	8 9945	11.0055	8.9966	11.0034	10.0021	9.9979	20
50	9.0070	10.9930	9.0093	10.9907	10.0023	9.9977	10
6° 00'	9.0192	10.9808	9.0216	10.9784	10.0024	9.9976	84° 00'
	log cos θ	log sec θ	log cot θ	log tan θ	log csc θ	log sin θ	Angle θ

Table 4. Continued
Attach—10 to logarithms obtained from this table

Angle θ	log sin θ	log csc θ	log tan θ	log cot θ	log sec θ	log cos θ	
6° 00′	9.0192	10.9808	9.0216	10.9784	10.0024	9.9976	84° 00′
10	9.0311	10.9689	9.0336	10.9664	10.0025	9.9975	50
20	9.0426	10.9574	9.0453	10.9547	10.0027	9.9973	40
30	9.0539	10.9461	9.0567	10.9433	10.0028	9.9972	30
40	9.0648	10.9352	9.0678	10.9322	10.0029	9.9971	20
50	9.0755	10.9245	9.0786	10.9214	10.0031	9.9969	10
7° 00′	9.0859	10.9141	9.0891	10.9109	10.0032	9.9968	83° 00′
10	9.0961	10.9039	9.0995	10.9005	10.0034	9.9966	50
20	9.1060	10.8940	9.1096	10.8904	10.0036	9.9964	40
30	9.1157	10.8843	9.1194	10.8806	10.0037	9.9963	30
40	9.1252	10.8748	9.1291	10.8709	10.0039	9.9961	20
50	9.1345	10.8655	9.1385	10.8615	10.0041	9.9959	10
8° 00′	9.1436	10.8564	9.1478	10.8522	10.0042	9.9958	82° 00′
10	9.1525	10.8475	9.1569	10.8431	10.0044	9.9956	50
20	9.1612	10.8388	9.1658	10.8342	10.0046	9.9954	40
30	9.1697	10.8303	9.1745	10.8255	10.0048	9.9952	30
40	9.1781	10.8219	9.1831	10.8169	10.0050	9.9950	20
50	9.1863	10.8137	9.1915	10.8085	10.0052	9.9948	10
9° 00′	9.1943	10.8057	9.1997	10.8003	10.0054	9.9946	81° 00′
10	9.2022	10.7978	9.2078	10.7922	10.0056	9.9944	50
20	9.2100	10.7900	9.2158	10.7842	10.0058	9.9942	40
30	9.2176	10.7824	9.2236	10.7764	10.0060	9.9940	30
40	9.2251	10.7749	9.2313	10.7687	10.0062	9.9938	20
50	9.2324	10.7676	9.2389	10.7611	10.0064	9.9936	10
10° 00′	9.2397	10.7603	9.2463	10.7537	10.0066	9.9934	80° 00′
10	9.2468	10.7532	9.2536	10.7464	10.0069	9.9931	50
20	9.2538	10.7462	9.2609	10.7391	10.0071	9.9929	40
30	9.2606	10.7394	9.2680	10.7320	10.0073	9.9927	30
40	9.2674	10.7326	9.2750	10.7250	10.0076	9.9924	20
50	9.2740	10.7260	9.2819	10.7181	10.0078	9.9922	10
11° 00′	9.2806	10.7194	9.2887	10.7113	10.0081	9.9919	79° 00′
10	9.2870	10.7130	9.2953	10.7047	10.0083	9.9917	50
20	9.2934	10.7066	9.3020	10.6980	10.0086	9.9914	40
30	9.2997	10.7003	9.3085	10.6915	10.0088	9.9912	30
40	9.3058	10.6942	9.3149	10.6851	10.0091	9.9909	20
50	9.3119	10.6881	9.3212	10.6788	10.0093	9.9907	10
12° 00′	9.3179	10.6821	9.3275	10.6725	10.0096	9.9904	78° 00′
	log cos θ	log sec θ	log cot θ	log tan θ	log csc θ	log sin θ	Angle θ

Table 4. Continued

Attach—10 to logarithms obtained from this table

Angle θ	log sin θ	log csc θ	log tan θ	log cot θ	log sec θ	log cos θ	
12° 00′	9.3179	10.6821	9.3275	10.6725	10.0096	9.9904	78° 00′
10	9.3238	10.6762	9.3336	10.6664	10.0099	9.9901	50
20	9.3296	10.6704	9.3397	10.6603	10.0101	9.9899	40
30	9.3353	10.6647	9.3458	10.6542	10.0104	9.9896	30
40	9.3410	10.6590	9.3517	10.6483	10.0107	9.9893	20
50	9.3466	10.6534	9.3576	10.6424	10.0110	9.9890	10
13° 00′	9.3521	10.6479	9.3634	10.6366	10.0113	9.9887	77° 00′
10	9.3575	10.6425	9.3691	10.6309	10.0116	9.9884	50
20	9.3629	10.6371	9.3748	10.6252	10.0119	9.9881	40
30	9.3682	10.6318	9.3804	10.6196	10.0122	9.9878	30
40	9.3734	10.6266	9.3859	10.6141	10.0125	9.9875	20
50	9.3786	10.6214	9.3914	10.6086	10.0128	9.9872	10
14° 00′	9.3837	10.6163	9.3968	10.6032	10.0131	9.9869	76° 00′
10	9.3887	10.6113	9.4021	10.5979	10.0134	9.9866	50
20	9.3937	10.6063	9.4074	10.5926	10.0137	9.9863	40
30	9.3986	10.6014	9.4127	10.5873	10.0141	9.9859	30
40	9.4035	10.5965	9.4178	10.5822	10.0144	9.9856	20
50	9.4083	10.5917	9.4230	10.5770	10.0147	9.9853	10
15° 00′	9.4130	10.5870	9.4281	10.5719	10.0151	9.9849	75° 00′
10	9.4177	10.5823	9.4331	10.5669	10.0154	9.9846	50
20	9.4223	10.5777	9.4381	10.5619	10.0157	9.9843	40
30	9.4269	10.5731	9.4430	10.5570	10.0161	9.9839	30
40	9.4314	10.5686	9.4479	10.5521	10.0164	9.9836	20
50	9.4359	10.5641	9.4527	10.5473	10.0168	9.9832	10
16° 00′	9.4403	10.5597	9.4575	10.5425	10.0172	9.9828	74° 00′
10	9.4447	10.5553	9.4622	10.5378	10.0175	9.9825	50
20	9.4491	10.5509	9.4669	10.5331	10.1079	9.9821	40
30	9.4533	10.5467	9.4716	10.5284	10.0183	9.9817	30
40	9.4576	10.5424	9.4762	10.5238	10.0186	9.9814	20
50	9.4618	10.5382	9.4808	10.5192	10.0190	9.9810	10
17° 00′	9.4659	10.5341	9.4853	10.5147	10.0194	9.9806	73° 00′
10	9.4700	10.5300	9.4898	10.5102	10.0198	9.9802	50
20	9.4741	10.5259	9.4943	10.5057	10.0202	9.9798	40
30	9.4781	10.5219	9.4987	10.5013	10.0206	9.9794	30
40	9.4821	10.5179	9.5031	10.4969	10.0210	9.9790	20
50	9.4861	10.5139	9.5075	10.4925	10.0214	9.9786	10
18° 00′	9.4900	10.5100	9.5118	10.4882	10.0218	9.9782	72° 00′
	log cos θ	log sec θ	log cot θ	log tan θ	log csc θ	log sin θ	Angle θ

Table 4. Continued
Attach—10 to logarithms obtained from this table

Angle θ	log sin θ	log csc θ	log tan θ	log cot θ	log sec θ	log cos θ	
18° 00′	9.4900	10.5100	9.5118	10.4882	10.0218	9.9782	72° 00′
10	9 4939	10.5061	9.5161	10.4839	10.0222	9.9778	50
20	9.4977	10.5023	9.5203	10.4797	10.0226	9.9774	40
30	9.5015	10.4985	9.5245	10.4755	10.0230	9.9770	30
40	9.5052	10.4948	9.5287	10.4713	10.0235	9.9765	20
50	9.5090	10.4910	9.5329	10.4671	10.0239	9.9761	10
19° 00′	9.5126	10.4874	9.5370	10.4630	10.0243	9.9757	71° 00′
10	9.5163	10.4837	9.5411	10.4589	10.0248	9.9752	50
20	9.5199	10.4801	9.5451	10.4549	10.0252	9.9748	40
30	9.5235	10.4765	9.5491	10.4509	10.0257	9.9743	30
40	9.5270	10.4730	9.5531	10.4469	10.0261	9.9739	20
50	9.5306	10.4694	9.5571	10.4429	10.0266	9.9734	10
20° 00′	9.5341	10.4659	9.5611	10.4389	10.0270	9.9730	70° 00′
10	9.5375	10.4625	9.5650	10 4350	10.0275	9.9725	50
20	9.5409	10.4591	9.5689	10.4311	10.0279	9.9721	40
30	9.5443	10.4557	9.5727	10.4273	10.0284	9.9716	30
40	9.5477	10.4523	9.5766	10.4234	10.0289	9.9711	20
50	9.5510	10.4490	9.5804	10.4196	10.0294	9.9706	10
21° 00′	9.5543	10.4457	9.5842	10.4158	10.0298	9.9702	69° 00′
10	9.5576	10.4424	9.5879	10.4121	10.0303	9.9797	50
20	9.5609	10.4391	9.5917	10.4083	10.0308	9.9692	40
30	9.5641	10.4359	9.5954	10.4046	10.0313	9.9687	30
40	9.5673	10.4327	9.5991	10.4009	10.0318	9.9682	20
50	9.5704	10.4296	9.6028	10.3972	10.0323	9.9677	10
22° 00′	9.5736	10.4264	9.6064	10.3936	10.0328	9.9672	68° 00′
10	9.5767	10.4233	9.6100	10.3900	10.0333	9.9667	50
20	9.5798	10.4202	9.6136	10.3864	10.0339	9.9661	40
30	9.5828	10.4172	9.6172	10.3828	10.0344	9.9656	30
40	9.5859	10.4141	9.6208	10.3792	10.0349	9.9651	20
50	9.5889	10.4111	9.6243	10.3757	10.0354	9.9646	10
23° 00′	9.5919	10.4081	9.6279	10.3721	10.0360	9.9640	67° 00′
10	9.5948	10.4052	9.6314	10.3686	10.0365	9.9635	50
20	9.5978	10.4022	9.6348	10.3652	10.0371	9.9629	40
30	9.6007	10.3993	9.6383	10.3617	10.0376	9.9624	30
40	9.6036	10.3964	9.6417	10.3583	10.0382	9.9618	20
50	9.6065	10.3935	9.6452	10.3548	10.0387	9.9613	10
24° 00′	9.6093	10.3907	9.6486	10.3514	10.0393	9.9607	66° 00′
	log cos θ	log sec θ	log cot θ	log tan θ	log csc θ	log sin θ	Angle θ

Table 4. Continued
Attach—10 to logarithms obtained from this table

Angle θ	log sin θ	log csc θ	log tan θ	log cot θ	log sec θ	log cos θ	
24° 00′	9.6093	10.3907	9.6486	10.3514	10.0393	9.9607	66° 00′
10	9.6121	10.3879	9.6520	10.3480	10.0398	9.9602	50
20	9.6149	10.3851	9.6553	10.3447	10.0404	9.9596	40
30	9.6177	10.3823	9.6587	10.3413	10.0410	9.9590	30
40	9.6205	10.3795	9.6620	10.3380	10.0416	9.9584	20
50	9.6232	10.3768	9.6654	10.3346	10.0421	9.9579	10
25° 00′	9.6259	10.3741	9.6687	10.3313	10.0427	9.9573	65° 00′
10	9 6286	10.3714	9.6720	10.3280	10.0433	9.9567	50
20	9.6313	10.3687	9.6752	10.3248	10.0439	9.9561	40
30	9.6340	10.3660	9.6785	10.3215	10.0445	9.9555	30
40	9.6366	10.3634	9.6817	10.3183	10.0451	9.9549	20
50	9.6392	10.3608	9.6850	10.3150	10.0457	9.9543	10
26° 00′	9.6418	10.3582	9.6882	10.3118	10.0463	9.9537	64° 00′
10	9.6444	10.3556	9.6914	10.3086	10.0470	9.9530	50
20	9.6470	10.3530	9.6946	10.3054	10.0476	9.9524	40
30	9.6495	10.3505	9.6977	10.3023	10.0482	9.9518	30
40	9.6521	10.3479	9.7009	10.2991	10.0488	9.9512	20
50	9.6546	10.3454	9.7040	10.2960	10.0495	9.9505	10
27° 00′	9.6570	10.3430	9.7072	10.2928	10.0501	9.9499	63° 00′
10	9.6595	10.3405	9.7103	10.2897	10.0508	9.9492	50
20	9.6620	10.3380	9.7134	10.2866	10.0514	9.9486	40
30	9.6644	10.3356	9.7165	10.2835	10.0521	9.9479	30
40	9.6668	10.3332	9.7196	10.2804	10.0527	9.9473	20
50	9.6692	10.3308	9.7226	10.2774	10.0534	9.9466	10
28° 00′	9.6716	10.3284	9.7257	10.2743	10.0541	9.9459	62° 00′
10	9.6740	10.3260	9.7287	10.2713	10.0547	9.9453	50
20	9.6763	10.3237	9.7317	10.2683	10.0554	9.9446	40
30	9.6787	10.3213	9.7348	10.2652	10.0561	9.9439	30
40	9.6810	10.3190	9.7378	10.2622	10.0568	9.9432	20
50	9.6833	10.3167	9.7408	10.2592	10.0575	9.9425	10
29° 00	9.6856	10.3144	9.7438	10.2562	10.0582	9.9418	61° 00′
10	9.6878	10.3122	9.7467	10.2533	10.0589	9.9411	50
20	9.6901	10.3099	9.7497	10.2503	10.0596	9.9404	40
30	9.6923	10.3077	9.7526	10.2474	10.0603	9.9397	30
40	9.6946	10.3054	9.7556	10.2444	10.0610	9.9390	20
50	9.6968	10.3032	9.7585	10.2415	10.0617	9.9383	10
30° 00′	9.6990	10.3010	9.7614	10.2386	10.0625	9.9375	60° 00′
	log cos θ	log sec θ	log cot θ	log tan θ	log csc θ	log sin θ	Angle θ

Table 4. Continued
   Attach—10 to logarithms obtained from this table

Angle θ	log sin θ	log csc θ	log tan θ	log cot θ	log sec θ	log cos θ	
30° 00'	9.6990	10.3010	9.7614	10.2386	10.0625	9.9375	60° 00'
10	9.7012	10.2988	9.7644	10.2356	10.0632	9.9368	50
20	9.7033	10.2967	9.7673	10.2327	10.0639	9.9361	40
30	9.7055	10.2945	9.7701	10.2299	10.0647	9.9353	30
40	9.7076	10.2924	9.7730	10.2270	10.0654	9.9346	20
50	9.7097	10.2903	9.7759	10.2241	10.0662	9.9338	10
31° 00'	9.7118	10.2882	9.7788	10.2212	10.0669	9.9331	59° 00'
10	9.7139	10.2861	9.7816	10.2184	10.0677	9.9323	50
20	9.7160	10.2840	9.7845	10.2155	10.0685	9.9315	40
30	9.7181	10.2819	9.7873	10.2127	10.0692	9.9308	30
40	9.7201	10.2799	9.7902	10.2098	10.0700	9.9300	20
50	9.7222	10.2778	9.7930	10.2070	10.0708	9.9292	10
32° 00'	9.7242	10.2758	9.7958	10.2042	10.0716	9.9284	58° 00'
10	9.7262	10.2738	9.7986	10.2014	10.0724	9.9276	50
20	9.7282	10.2718	9.8014	10.1986	10.0732	9.9268	40
30	9.7302	10.2698	9.8042	10.1958	10.0740	9.9260	30
40	9.7322	10.2678	9.8070	10.1930	10.0748	9.9252	20
50	9.7342	10.2658	9.8097	10.1903	10.0756	9.9244	10
33° 00'	9.7361	10.2639	9.8125	10.1875	10.0764	9.9236	57° 00'
10	9.7380	10.2620	9.8153	10.1847	10.0772	9.9228	50
20	9.7400	10.2600	9.1880	10.1820	10.0781	9.9219	40
30	9.7419	10.2581	9.8208	10.1792	10.0789	9.9211	30
40	9.7438	10.2562	9.8235	10.1765	10.0797	9.9203	20
50	9.7457	10.2543	9.8263	10.1737	10.0806	9.9194	10
34° 00'	9.7476	10.2524	9.8290	10.1710	10.0814	9.9186	56° 00'
10	9.7494	10.2506	9.8317	10.1683	10.0823	9.9177	50
20	9.7513	10.2487	9.8344	10.1656	10.0831	9.9169	40
30	9.7531	10.2469	9.8371	10.1629	10.0840	9.9160	30
40	9.7550	10.2450	9.8398	10.1602	10.0849	9.9151	20
50	9.7568	10.2432	9.8425	10.1575	10.0858	9.9142	10
35° 00'	9.7586	10.2414	9.8452	10.1548	10.0866	9.9134	55° 00'
10	9.7604	10.2396	9.8479	10.1521	10.0875	9.9125	50
20	9.7622	10.2378	9.8506	10.1494	10.0884	9.9116	40
30	9.7640	10.2360	9.8533	10.1467	10.0893	9.9107	30
40	9.7657	10.2343	9.8559	10.1441	10.0902	9.9098	20
50	9.7675	10.2325	9.8586	10.1414	10.0911	9.9089	10
36° 00'	9.7692	10.2308	9.8613	10.1387	10.0920	9.9080	54° 00'
	log cos θ	log sec θ	log cot θ	log tan θ	log csc θ	log sin θ	Angle θ

Table 4. Continued

Attach—10 to logarithms obtained from this table

Angle θ	log sin θ	log csc θ	log tan θ	log cot θ	log sec θ	log cos θ	
36° 00′	9.7692	10.2308	9.8613	10.1387	10.0920	9.9080	54° 00′
10	9.7710	10.2290	9.8639	10.1361	10.0930	9.9070	50
20	9.7727	10.2273	9.8666	10.1334	10.0939	9.9061	40
30	9.7744	10.2256	9.8692	10.1308	10.0948	9.9052	30
40	9.7761	10.2239	9.8718	10.1282	10.0958	9.9042	20
50	9.7778	10.2222	9.8745	10.1255	10.0967	9.9033	10
37° 00′	9.7795	10.2205	9.8771	10.1229	10.0977	9.9023	53° 00′
10	9.7811	10.2189	9.8797	10.1203	10.0986	9.9014	50
20	9.7828	10.2172	9.8824	10.1176	10.0996	9.9004	40
30	9.7844	10.2156	9 8850	10.1150	10.1005	9.8995	30
40	9.7861	10.2139	9.8876	10.1124	10.1015	9.8985	20
50	9.7877	10.2123	9.8902	10.1098	10.1025	9.8975	10
38° 00′	9.7893	10.2107	9.8928	10.1072	10.1035	9.8965	52° 00′
10	9.7910	10.2090	9.8954	10.1046	10.1045	9.8955	50
20	9.7926	10.2074	9.8980	10.1020	10.1055	9.8945	40
30	9.7941	10.2059	9.9006	10.0994	10.1065	9.8935	30
40	9.7957	10.2043	9.9032	10.0968	10.1075	9.8925	20
50	9.7973	10.2027	9.9058	10.0942	10.1085	9.8915	10
39° 00′	9.7989	10.2011	9.9084	10.0916	10.1095	9.8905	51° 00′
10	9.8004	10.1996	9.9110	10.0890	10.1105	9.8895	50
20	9.8020	10.1980	9.9135	10.0865	10.1116	9.8884	40
30	9.8035	10.1965	9.9161	10.0839	10.1126	9.8874	30
40	9.8050	10.1950	9.9187	10.0813	10.1136	9.8864	20
50	9.8066	10.1934	9.9212	10.0788	10.1147	9.8853	10
40° 00′	9.8081	10.1919	9.9238	10.0762	10.1157	9.8843	50° 00′
10	9.8096	10.1904	9.9264	10.0736	10.1168	9.8832	50
20	9.8111	10.1889	9.9289	10.0711	10.1179	9.8821	40
30	9.8125	10.1875	9.9315	10.0685	10.1190	9.8810	30
40	9.8140	10.1860	9.9341	10.0659	10.1200	9.8800	20
50	9.8155	10.1845	9.9366	10.0634	10.1211	9.8789	10
41° 00′	9.8169	10.1831	9.9392	10.0608	10.1222	9.8778	49° 00′
10	9.8184	10.1816	9.9417	10.0583	10.1233	9.8767	50
20	9.8198	10.1802	9.9443	10.0557	10.1244	9.8756	40
30	9.8213	10.1787	9.9468	10.0532	10.1255	9.8745	30
40	9.8227	10.1773	9.9494	10.0506	10.1267	9.8733	20
50	9.8241	10.1759	9.9519	10.0481	10.1278	9.8722	10
42° 00′	9.8255	10.1745	9.9544	10.0456	10.1289	9.8711	48° 00′
	log cos θ	log sec θ	log cot θ	log tan θ	log csc θ	log sin θ	Angle θ

Table 4. Continued
Attach −10 to logarithms obtained from this table

Angle θ	log sin θ	log csc θ	log tan θ	log cot θ	log sec θ	log cos θ	
42° 00′	9.8255	10.1745	9.9544	10.0456	10.1289	9.8711	48° 00′
10	9.8269	10.1731	9.9570	10.0430	10.1301	9.8699	50
20	9.8283	10.1717	9.9595	10.0405	10.1312	9.8688	40
30	9.8297	10.1703	9.9621	10.0379	10.1324	9.8676	30
40	9.8311	10.1689	9.9646	10.0354	10.1335	9.8665	20
50	9.8324	10.1676	9.9671	10.0329	10.1347	9.8653	10
43° 00′	9.8338	10.1662	9.9697	10.0303	10.1359	9.8641	47° 00′
10	9.8351	10.1649	9.9722	10.0278	10.1371	9.8629	50
20	9.8365	10.1635	9.9747	10.0253	10.1382	9.8618	40
30	9.8378	10.1622	9.9772	10.0228	10.1394	9.8606	30
40	9.8391	10.1609	9.9798	10.0202	10.1406	9.8594	20
50	9.8405	10.1595	9.9823	10.0177	10.1418	9.8582	10
44° 00′	9.8418	10.1582	9.9848	10.0152	10.1431	9.8569	46° 00′
10	9.8431	10.1569	9.9874	10.0126	10.1443	9.8557	50
20	9.8444	10.1556	9.9899	10.0101	10.1455	9.8545	40
30	9.8457	10.1543	9.9924	10.0076	10.1468	9.8532	30
40	9.8469	10.1531	9.9949	10.0051	10.1480	9.8520	20
50	9.8482	10.1518	9.9975	10.0025	10.1493	9.8507	10
45° 00′	9.8495	10.1505	10.0000	10.0000	10.1505	9.8495	45° 00′
	log cos θ	log sec θ	log cot θ	log tan θ	log csc θ	log sin θ	Angle θ

J

Answers to Odd-numbered Exercises

Section 1-1

1. integer, rational, real; irrational, real   3. imaginary; irrational, real
5. $3, \frac{7}{2}$ 7. $\frac{6}{7}, \sqrt{3}$ 9. $6 < 8$ 11. $\pi > -1$ 13. $-\sqrt{2} > -9$
15. $\frac{1}{3}, -\frac{1}{2}$ 17. $-\pi/5, 1/x$
19.   21.

23. $-18, -|-3|, -1, \sqrt{5}, \pi, |-8|, 9$ 25. (a) to right of origin
     (b) to left of -4 27. P, V variables; c constant
29. For $s < 3, I > 8$

Sections 1-2 and 1-3

1. 11   3. -11 5. 9   7. -3 9. -24 11. 35   13. -3
15. -1 17. 9   19. undefined   21. 0   23. -9 25. commutative law
    of multiplication   27. distributive law   29. associative law of addition
31. positive   33. $2(6 + 4)$; distributive law

Section 1-4

1. x^7 3. $2b^6$ 5. m^2 7. $1/n^4$ 9. $8n^3$ 11. a^8 13. $-t^{14}$
15. $8/b^3$ 17. $64x^{12}$ 19. $64g^2s^6$ 21. $5a/n$ 23. a^5/y 25. 5   27. 5
29. 2   31. 5   33. $3\sqrt{2}$ 35. $2\sqrt{3}$ 37. $14\sqrt{2}$ 39. 63
41. $-wLx^3/12EI$ 43. No; true for $a \geq 0$

Section 1-5

1. $8x$ 3. $a + c - e$ 5. $-4 + 5x - 2v$ 7. $x + 3xy$ 9. $5a - 5$
11. $2 - 5a$ 13. $7r - 2s$ 15. $-50 + 19c$ 17. $9 - t^2$ 19. $21 - 3a$
21. $2a\sqrt{xy} + 1$ 23. $6 + 4c$ 25. $22 - 4x^2$ 27. $R + 1$ 29. $12x - 2x^2$

Section 1-6

1. a^3x 3. $-a^2c^3x^3$ 5. $-8a^3x^5$ 7. $2a^4x$ 9. $a^2x + a^2y$
11. $5m^3n + 15m^2n$ 13. $3x^2 - 3xy + 6x$ 15. $a^2b^2c^5 - ab^3c^5 - a^2b^3c^4$

531

17. $acx^4 + acx^3y^3$ 19. $x^2 + 2x - 15$ 21. $2x^2 + 9x - 5$ 23. $x^3 + 2x^2 - 8x$
25. $x^3 - 2x^2 - x + 2$ 27. $x^5 - x^4 - 6x^3 + 4x^2 + 8x$ 29. $2x^3 + 6x^2 - 8x$
31. $4x^2 - 20x + 25$ 33. $x^2y^2z^2 - 4xyz + 4$ 35. $-x^3 + 2x^2 + 5x - 6$
37. $6x^4 + 21x^3 + 12x^2 - 12x$ 39. $252T_f - 6250$ 41. $wl^4 - 2wl^2x^2 + wx^4$
43. $n^2k - 2njkK + j^2kK^2 - k + 2n^2 - 4njK + 2j^2K^2 - 2$

Section 1-7

1. $-4x^2y$ 3. $16t^4/5r^2$ 5. $4x^2$ 7. $a^2 + 4y$ 9. $\frac{1}{5}an - a - 2n$

11. $\dfrac{2L}{R} - R$ 13. $\dfrac{2ab}{3} - \dfrac{b}{3}$ 15. $x^2 + a$ 17. $x - 1$

19. $4x^2 - x - 1,\ R = -3$ 21. $3x + 2,\ R = 4$ 23. $x^2 + 7x + 10$

25. $x - y$ 27. $V^2 - \dfrac{aV}{RT} + \dfrac{ab}{RT}$ 29. $\dfrac{1}{R_1} + \dfrac{1}{R_2} + \dfrac{1}{R_3}$

Section 1-8

1. 3   3. -3 5. $-\frac{7}{2}$ 7. $\frac{10}{3}$ 9. 0   11. $6/a$ 13. $2a$ 15. $-\frac{7}{5}$

17. $2bc + 3c$ 19. $\frac{4}{3} + b$ 21. E/I 23. $\dfrac{v_0 - v}{t}$ 25. $\dfrac{M}{Afj}$ 27. $\dfrac{l - a + d}{d}$

29. $\dfrac{5F - 160}{9}$ 31. $\dfrac{Rgm_0 + 2E_p}{2}$ 33. \$5200, \$2600   35. 6.5 ft

37. 6 hr after second car leaves

Section 1-9

1. -10 3. -20 5. -2 7. -4 9. $-x^6$ 11. $6m^2/nt^2$ 13. $9 - xy$
15. $2x^2 + 9x - 5$ 17. $7a - 6b$ 19. $hk - 3h^2k^4$ 21. $13xy - 10z$

23. $-9p^2 + 3pq + 18p^2q$ 25. $\dfrac{6q}{p} - 2 + \dfrac{3q^4}{p^3}$ 27. $-3x^2y + 24xy^2 - 48y^3$

29. $15r - 3s - 3t$ 31. $y^2 + 5y - 1,\ R = 4$ 33. $-\frac{7}{3}$ 35. 3   37. $-b/3$

39. ϕ/B 41. $\dfrac{4\epsilon_0 n^2h^2E_k}{e^4}$ 43. $\dfrac{D_p(N + 2)}{N}$ 45. $\dfrac{Y_{n+1}(R_D + 1) - X_0}{R_D}$

47. $\dfrac{2s - n^2d + nd}{2n}$ 49. 450 lb to carbon dioxide, 50 lb to carbon monoxide

51. 2 hp, 4 hp, 6 hp

Section 2-1

1. $A = s^2$ 3. $c = \pi d$ 5. $A = 5l$ 7. $p = 4\sqrt{A}$ 9. $I = 8t$
11. 3, -1, 9   13. -18, 70, -20 15. 0, $2a^3$ 17. 7, $-6a - a^2 - 2a^3$
19. $12s^2 - 2s + 6,\ 3s^2 - 7s + 10$ 21. Square the value of the independent variable and add 2.   23. Cube the value of the independent variable and subtract this value from 6 times the value of the independent variable.
25. $y \neq 1$ 27. $z \neq 1,\ z \neq -2$ 29. $\frac{273}{35}$ 31. $\frac{1}{16}p^2 + (60 - p)^2/4\pi$
33. $0.006T^2 + 2.8T + 0.012hT + 2.8h + 0.006h^2$

Section 2-2

1. (2, 1),   3.   5. Isosceles triangle   7. On same line
   (−1, 2),
   (−2, −3)

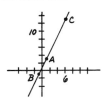

9. $\frac{9}{2}$

11. On a line parallel to the x-axis, three units below   13. 0   15. To right of
   y-axis   17. Second quadrant, above a line one unit above the x-axis

Section 2-3

1.

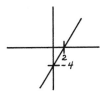

3.

5.

7.

9.

11.

13.

15.

17.

19.

21.

23.

25.

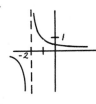

27.

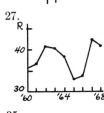

29.

31.

33.

35.

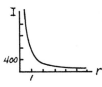

37. steepness varies for (a), (b), (c).

Section 2-4

1. 2   3. $-\frac{9}{4}$ 5. 3.5   7. 0.5   9. 0.0, -1.0 11. No (real) zeros
13. 0.7   15. 2.5   17. 1.8, -2.8 19. 5.6, -1.6 21. 0.0, 2.0, -2.0
23. 0.0, 1.3   25. After 1.9 sec   27. 1.8 ft from end

Section 2-5

1. $V = 8\pi r^2$ 3. $F = \frac{9}{5}C + 32$ 5. 16, -47 7. $u - 21u^3$ 9. $6hx + 3h^2 - 2h$
11.   13.   15.   17.   19.

21. -0.5 23. 0.0, 4.0   25. 1.0, -1.5 27. -2.4, 0.0, 2.4   29. 0.0
31. 0.4   33. 0.2, 5.8   35. 1.3   37. -0.7, 0.7   39. On a line in first
    quadrant, one unit to right of y-axis   41. 19
43.   45.   47.   49.

  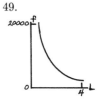

Sections 3-1 and 3-2

1.   3.   5. $-315°$ 7. $-289°30'$

9. $15.2°$ 11. $86.05°$

13. $47°30'$ 15. $5°37'$

17. $\sin\theta = \frac{3}{5}$, $\cos\theta = \frac{4}{5}$, $\tan\theta = \frac{3}{4}$, $\cot\theta = \frac{4}{3}$, $\sec\theta = \frac{5}{4}$, $\csc\theta = \frac{5}{3}$
19. $\sin\theta = \frac{8}{17}$, $\cos\theta = \frac{15}{17}$, $\tan\theta = \frac{8}{15}$, $\cot\theta = \frac{15}{8}$, $\sec\theta = \frac{17}{15}$, $\csc\theta = \frac{17}{8}$
21. $\sin\theta = \sqrt{15}/4$, $\cos\theta = \frac{1}{4}$, $\tan\theta = \sqrt{15}$, $\cot\theta = 1/\sqrt{15}$, $\sec\theta = 4$, $\csc\theta = 4/\sqrt{15}$
23. $\sin\theta = 5/\sqrt{29}$, $\cos\theta = 2/\sqrt{29}$, $\tan\theta = \frac{5}{2}$, $\cot\theta = \frac{2}{5}$, $\sec\theta = \sqrt{29}/2$,
    $\csc\theta = \sqrt{29}/5$ 25. $1/\sqrt{2}$, $\sqrt{2}$ 27. $\sqrt{5}/2$, $2/\sqrt{5}$ 29. $\sqrt{51}/7$, $\frac{10}{7}$
31. $\sin\theta = \frac{4}{5}$, $\tan\theta = \frac{4}{3}$ 33. $\sec\theta$, $\tan\theta$

Section 3-3

1. $\sin 40° = 0.64$, $\cos 40° = 0.77$, $\tan 40° = 0.84$, $\cot 40° = 1.19$, $\sec 40° = 1.30$,
   $\csc 40° = 1.56$ 3. $\sin 15° = 0.26$, $\cos 15° = 0.97$, $\tan 15° = 0.27$,
   $\cot 15° = 3.73$, $\sec 15° = 1.04$, $\csc 15° = 3.86$ 5. 0.3256   7. 2.356
9. 0.9250   11. 0.8339   13. 1.029   15. 0.8930   17. 0.6596   19. 0.3068
21. 0.9663   23. 4.720   25. 5°30'   27. 72°10'   29. 33°11'   31. 39°7'
33. 45°13'   35. 79°17'   37. 162 ft/sec   39. 67.8 volts

Section 3-4

1.

3. $A = 52.2°, B = 37.8°, c = 71.8$

5. $A = 53°, b = 0.668, c = 1.11$

7. $A = 52.4°, B = 37.6°, b = 7.70$

9. $A = 81°, a = 0.481, c = 0.487$ 11. $a = 7.70, B = 47.5°, c = 11.4$
13. $a = 334, A = 75.8°, b = 84.6$ 15. $a = c \sin A, b = c \cos A, B = 90° - A$
17. $A = 90° - B, b = a \tan B, c = a/\cos B$ 19. 384 ft   21. 503 ft
23. 471 ft   25. 5.10 mi   27. 27.9 ohms   29. 8.24 cm   31. 103.5°
33. 1080 mi

Section 3-5

1. $377°, -343°; 143°, -577°$ 3. $31.9°; 174.75°$ 5. $17°30'; 65°24'$
7. $\sin \theta = \frac{7}{25}$, $\cos \theta = \frac{24}{25}$, $\tan \theta = \frac{7}{24}$, $\cot \theta = \frac{24}{7}$, $\sec \theta = \frac{25}{24}$, $\csc \theta = \frac{25}{7}$
9. $\sin \theta = 1/\sqrt{2}$, $\cos \theta = 1/\sqrt{2}$, $\tan \theta = 1$, $\cot \theta = 1$, $\sec \theta = \sqrt{2}$, $\csc \theta = \sqrt{2}$
11. $\cos \theta = \frac{12}{13}$, $\cot \theta = \frac{12}{5}$ 13. $\cos \theta = 1/\sqrt{5}$, $\csc \theta = \frac{1}{2}\sqrt{5}$ 15. 0.9511
17. 1.829   19. 6.498   21. 0.5609   23. 32°10'   25. 62°10'   27. 41°27'
29. 60°4'   31. $a = 1.99, B = 73°, c = 6.80$ 33. $A = 22°, b = 2660, c = 2870$
35. $A = 6.44°, B = 83.56°, b = 9.40$ 37. 6.12×10^{-5} cm   39. 1.58 mi
41. 4820 ft   43. 47.2 ft   45. 25°   47. 367 ft   49. 67.0 ft

Section 4-1

1. Yes, No   3. Yes, Yes   5. $-1, -16$ 7. $-\frac{9}{5}, -\frac{16}{5}$ 9. Yes   11. No
13. No   15. Yes   17. Yes

Section 4-2

1. $(3.0, 0.0)$ 3. $(3.0, 0.0)$ 5. $(2.2, -0.3)$ 7. $(-0.9, -2.3)$
9. Dependent   11. $(0.0, 3.0)$ 13. $(-14.0, -5.0)$ 15. $(4.0, 7.5)$
17. $(-3.6, -1.4)$ 19. $(0.9, 0.6)$ 21. Inconsistent   23. $(-1.2, -3.6)$
25. 9.0 mi, 3.0 mi   27. $I = 0.9$ amp, $E = 3.6$ volts

Section 4-3

1. $(1, -2)$ 3. $(7, 3)$ 5. $(-1, -4)$ 7. $(\frac{1}{2}, 2)$ 9. $(-\frac{1}{3}, 4)$
11. $(\frac{9}{22}, -\frac{16}{11})$ 13. $(3, 1)$ 15. $(-1, -2)$ 17. $(1, 2)$ 19. Inconsistent
21. $(-\frac{14}{5}, -\frac{16}{5})$ 23. $(\frac{69}{29}, \frac{13}{29})$ 25. $(\frac{1}{2}, -4)$ 27. $(-\frac{2}{3}, 0)$
29. Dependent   31. $i_1 = 1.5$ amps, $i_2 = 0.5$ amp   33. 7.5 ft from one end
35. 2800 cards/min, 1900 cards/min   37. 105 cm³ and 75 cm³

Section 4-4

1. -10 3. 29   5. 32   7. 93   9. 83   11. 96   13. $(3, 1)$
15. $(-1, -2)$ 17. $(1, 2)$ 19. Inconsistent   21. $(-\frac{14}{5}, -\frac{16}{5})$

23. $\left(\frac{69}{29}, \frac{13}{29}\right)$ 25. $\left(\frac{1}{2}, -4\right)$ 27. $\left(-\frac{2}{3}, 0\right)$ 29. Dependent
31. $s_0 = 15$ ft, $v = 10$ ft/sec   33. 58, 31   35. \$600, \$7400
37. $R = \frac{1}{600} T + \frac{11}{30}$

Section 4-5

1. $x = 2, y = -1, z = 1$ 3. $x = 4, y = -3, z = 3$ 5. $x = \frac{1}{2}, y = \frac{2}{3}, z = \frac{1}{6}$
7. $x = \frac{2}{3}, y = -\frac{1}{3}, z = 1$ 9. $x = \frac{4}{15}, y = -\frac{3}{5}, z = \frac{1}{3}$
11. $r = 0, s = 0, t = 0, u = -1$ 13. $-\frac{3}{22}$ amp, $-\frac{39}{110}$ amp, $\frac{27}{55}$ amp
15. 16 parts/hr, 20 parts/hr, 28 parts/hr   17. 50% alloy B, 50% alloy C

Section 4-6

1. 122   3. 651   5. -439 7. 202   9. $x = -1, y = 2, z = 0$
11. $x = 2, y = -1, z = 1$ 13. $x = 4, y = -3, z = 3$
15. $x = \frac{1}{2}, y = \frac{2}{3}, z = \frac{1}{6}$ 17. $x = \frac{2}{3}, y = -\frac{1}{3}, z = 1$
19. $x = \frac{4}{15}, y = -\frac{3}{5}, z = \frac{1}{3}$ 21. $-\frac{3}{22}$ amp, $-\frac{39}{110}$ amp, $\frac{27}{55}$ amp
23. \$12,000, \$7000, \$1000

Section 4-7

1. -17 3. -35 5. $(2.0, 0.0)$ 7. $(2.2, 2.7)$ 9. $(1.5, 0.3)$ 11. $(1, 2)$
13. $\left(\frac{1}{2}, -2\right)$ 15. $\left(-\frac{1}{3}, \frac{7}{4}\right)$ 17. $\left(\frac{11}{19}, -\frac{26}{19}\right)$ 19. $\left(-\frac{6}{19}, \frac{36}{19}\right)$ 21. $(1, 2)$
23. $\left(\frac{1}{2}, -2\right)$ 25. $\left(-\frac{1}{3}, \frac{7}{4}\right)$ 27. $\left(\frac{11}{19}, -\frac{26}{19}\right)$ 29. $\left(-\frac{6}{19}, \frac{36}{19}\right)$ 31. -115
33. 220   35. $x = 2, y = -1, z = 1$ 37. $x = \frac{2}{3}, y = -\frac{1}{2}, z = 0$
39. $r = 3, s = -1, t = \frac{3}{2}$ 41. $x = 2, y = -1, z = 1$
43. $x = \frac{2}{3}, y = -\frac{1}{2}, z = 0$ 45. $r = 3, s = -1, t = \frac{3}{2}$ 47. $x = \frac{8}{3}, y = -8$
49. $x = 1, y = 3$ 51. -6 53. $R_1 = 5$ ohms, $R_2 = 2$ ohms
55. $a = 10, b = 12, c = 15$ 57. 450 mi/hr, 50 mi/hr   59. 11 ft
61. 79% nickel, 16% iron, 5% molybdenum

Section 5-1

1. $40x - 40y$ 3. $2x^3 - 8x^2$ 5. $y^2 - 36$ 7. $9v^2 - 4$ 9. $25f^2 + 40f + 16$
11. $4x^2 + 28x + 49$ 13. $x^2 - 4xy + 4y^2$ 15. $36s^2 - 12st + t^2$
17. $x^2 + 6x + 5$ 19. $c^2 + 9c + 18$ 21. $6x^2 + 13x - 5$ 23. $20x^2 - 21x - 5$
25. $6ax^2 + 24abx + 24ab^2$ 27. $16a^3 - 48a^2 + 36a$
29. $x^2 + y^2 + 2xy + 2x + 2y + 1$ 31. $x^2 + y^2 + 2xy - 6x - 6y + 9$
33. $125 - 75t + 15t^2 - t^3$ 35. $8x^3 + 60x^2t + 150xt^2 + 125t^3$
37. $x^3 + 8$ 39. $64 - 27x^3$ 41. $Ri_1^2 + 2Ri_1i_2 + Ri_2^2$
43. $192 - 16t - 16t^2$

Section 5-2

1. $6(x + y)$ 3. $3x(x - 3)$ 5. $3ab(b - 2 + 4b^2)$ 7. $(a - b)(x + y)$
9. $(2 + x)(2 - x)$ 11. $(9s + 5t)(9s - 5t)$ 13. $(x + 1)^2$ 15. $(2m + 5)^2$
17. $(x - 2)^2$ 19. $(2x - 3)^2$ 21. $(x + 1)(x + 4)$ 23. $(s - 7)(s + 6)$
25. $(3x + 1)(x - 2)$ 27. Prime   29. $(3t - 4)(3t - 1)$ 31. $(8b - 1)(b + 4)$
33. $2(x + 2)(x - 2)$ 35. $2(2x - 1)(x + 4)$ 37. $(x^2 + 4)(x + 2)(x - 2)$
39. $2(x^2 + 2y^2)(x^2 - 2y^2)$ 41. $(x + 1)^3$ 43. $(2x + 1)(4x^2 - 2x + 1)$
45. $(3 + b)(x - y)$ 47. $(a - b)(a + x)$ 49. $i(R_1 + R_2 + r)$
51. $16(t - 4)(t + 2)$ 53. $(x - 2L)(x - L)$ 55. $p(a - b)^2(1 - p)$

Section 5-3

1. $\frac{14}{21}$　　3. $\dfrac{2ax^2}{2xy}$　　5. $\dfrac{ax^2 - ay^2}{x^2 - xy - 2y^2}$　　7. $\frac{7}{11}$　　9. $\dfrac{2xy}{4y^2}$　　11. $\dfrac{x-5}{2x-1}$

13. $\frac{1}{4}$　　15. $\frac{3}{4}x$　　17. $\dfrac{1}{5a}$　　19. $\dfrac{3a-2b}{2a-b}$　　21. $\dfrac{x-4}{x+4}$　　23. $\dfrac{2x-1}{x+8}$

25. $(x^2 + 4)(x - 2)$　　27. $\dfrac{x^2 y^2 (y + x)}{y - x}$　　29. $\dfrac{x+3}{x-3}$　　31. $-\frac{1}{2}$

33. $\dfrac{(x+5)(x-3)}{(5-x)(x+3)}$　　35. $\dfrac{x^2 + xy + y^2}{x + y}$　　37. $\dfrac{(x+1)^2}{x^2 - x + 1}$　　39. (a)

Section 5-4

1. $\frac{3}{28}$　　3. $6xy$　　5. $\frac{7}{18}$　　7. $\dfrac{xy^2}{bz^2}$　　9. $4t$　　1. $3(u+v)$　　13. $\dfrac{10}{3(a+4)}$

15. $\dfrac{x-3}{x(x+3)}$　　17. $\dfrac{3x}{5a}$　　19. $\dfrac{(x+1)(x-1)(x-4)}{4(x+2)}$　　21. $\dfrac{x^2}{a+x}$　　23. $\frac{15}{4}$

25. $\dfrac{7x^4}{3a^4}$　　27. $\frac{1}{2}(x+y)$　　29. $(x+y)(3p+7q)$　　31. $\dfrac{(T+100)(T-400)}{2(T-40)}$

Section 5-5

1. $\frac{9}{5}$　　3. $8/x$　　5. $\frac{5}{4}$　　7. $\dfrac{ax-b}{x^2}$　　9. $\dfrac{14-a^2}{10a}$

11. $\dfrac{-x^2 + 4x + xy + y - 2}{xy}$　　13. $\dfrac{5-3x}{2x(x+1)}$　　15. $\dfrac{-3}{4(s-3)}$　　17. $\dfrac{x+6}{x^2-9}$

19. $\dfrac{x+27}{(x-5)(x+5)(x-6)}$　　21. $\dfrac{9x^2 + x - 2}{(3x-1)(x-4)}$　　23. $\dfrac{13t^2 + 27t}{(t-3)(t+2)(t+3)^2}$

25. $\dfrac{x+1}{x-1}$　　27. $-\dfrac{(x+1)(x^3 + x^2 - 3x - 1)}{x^2(x+2)}$　　29. $\dfrac{h}{(x+1)(x+h+1)}$

31. $\dfrac{y^2 - rx + r^2}{r^2}$　　33. $\dfrac{3\pi l^3 - 12cl^2 + \pi c^3}{3\pi l^3}$　　35. $\dfrac{b(y^2 - x^2)}{(x^2 + y^2)^2}$

Section 5-6

1. 4　　3. -3　　5. $\frac{7}{2}$　　7. -9　　9. $-\frac{6}{5}$　　11. -2　　13. $\frac{3}{4}$　　15. 6

17. No solution　　19. $\frac{2}{3}$　　21. $\dfrac{3b}{1-2b}$　　23. $\dfrac{(2b-1)(b+6)}{2(b-1)}$

25. $\dfrac{2EI - 2IV_0 - p^2 - ImV^2}{IV^2}$　　27. $\dfrac{rR - rR_2 + RR_2}{R_2 - R}$　　29. 3.6 min

31. 60 yd, 36 yd

Section 5-7

1. $12ax + 15a^2$　　3. $4a^2 - 49b^2$　　5. $4a^2 + 4a + 1$　　7. $b^2 + 3b - 28$

9. $2x^2 - 13x - 45$　　11. $16c^2 + 6cd - d^2$　　13. $a^2(x^2 + 1)$

15. $(x+12)(x-12)$　　17. $(3t-1)^2$　　19. $(x+8)(x-7)$

21. $(2x-9)(x+4)$　　23. $(5b-1)(2b+5)$　　25. $4(x+4)(x-4)$

27. $(x-1)^3$　　29. $(a-3)(b^2+1)$　　31. $16x^2/9a^2$　　33. $\dfrac{3x+1}{2x-1}$

35. $\dfrac{16}{5x(x-y)}$ 37. $\dfrac{6}{5-x}$ 39. $\dfrac{1}{x-1}$ 41. $\dfrac{5y+6}{2xy}$ 43. $\dfrac{-2(a+3)}{a(a+2)}$

45. $\dfrac{x^3+6x^2-2x+2}{x(x-1)(x+3)}$ 47. 2   49. $\dfrac{7}{2c+4}$ 51. $-\dfrac{(a-1)^2}{2a}$ 53. 6

55. $\dfrac{1-t}{(t+1)^3}$ 57. $\dfrac{120T^4+20w^2x^2T^2-3w^4x^4}{120T^4}$ 59. $\dfrac{\mu R}{r+R+\mu R}$

61. $\dfrac{fp}{p-f}$ 63. $\dfrac{wL^3-240EI}{4L}$ 65. $\frac{48}{7}$ days

Section 6-1

1. $a=1, b=-8, c=5$ 3. $a=1, b=-2, c=-4$ 5. Not quadratic
7. $a=1, b=-1, c=0$ 9. $2, -2$ 11. $3, 4$ 13. $0, -2$ 15. $\frac{3}{2}, -\frac{3}{2}$
17. $\frac{1}{3}, 4$ 19. -4 (double root)   21. $\frac{2}{3}, \frac{3}{2}$ 23. $\frac{1}{2}, -\frac{3}{2}$ 25. $2, -1$
27. $2b, -2b$ 29. $0, \frac{5}{2}$ 31. $0, -2$ 33. $b-a, -b-a$ 35. 10 sec
37. $-3, -5$ 39. 12 mm, 8 mm

Section 6-2

1. $2, -4$ 3. $-1, -2$ 5. $2 \pm \sqrt{2}$ 7. $\frac{1}{2}, -3$ 9. $\frac{1}{4}(1 \pm \sqrt{17})$

11. $-b \pm \sqrt{b^2-c}$

Section 6-3

1. $2, -4$ 3. $-1, -2$ 5. $2 \pm \sqrt{2}$ 7. $\frac{1}{2}, -3$ 9. $\frac{1}{4}(1 \pm \sqrt{17})$

11. $\frac{1}{4}(7 \pm \sqrt{17})$ 13. $\frac{1}{2}(-5 \pm \sqrt{-5})$ 15. $\frac{1}{6}(1 \pm \sqrt{109})$ 17. $\frac{3}{2}, -\frac{3}{2}$

19. $\frac{3}{4}, -\frac{5}{8}$ 21. $-c \pm \sqrt{c^2+1}$ 23. $\dfrac{b+1 \pm \sqrt{-3b^2+2b+4b^2a+1}}{2b^2}$

25. 0.382 atm   27. 0.915 in.   29. 3.06 mm   31. 8 in.

Section 6-4

1. $1, -4$ 3. $2, 8$ 5. $\frac{1}{3}, -4$ 7. $\frac{1}{2}, \frac{5}{3}$ 9. $0, \frac{25}{6}$ 11. $1, -4$
13. $2, 8$ 15. $\frac{1}{3}, -4$ 17. $\frac{1}{2}, \frac{5}{3}$ 19. $0, \frac{25}{6}$ 21. $-2 \pm 2\sqrt{2}$

23. $\frac{1}{3}(-4 \pm \sqrt{10})$ 25. $\frac{5}{4}, -1$ 27. $\frac{1}{4}(-3 \pm \sqrt{-47})$ 29. $\dfrac{-1 \pm \sqrt{-1}}{a}$

31. $6, -5$ 33. $\frac{1}{4}(1 \pm \sqrt{33})$ 35. $3 \pm \sqrt{11}$ 37. 0 (3 is not a solution)

39. $-5 \pm 5\sqrt{-79}$ 41. $\dfrac{-v \pm \sqrt{v^2+2as}}{a}$ 43. 8, 12 volts   45. 0.106 in.

Section 7-1

1. $+, -, -$ 3. $+, +, -$ 5. $+, +, +$ 7. $+, -, +$
9. $\sin\theta = 1/\sqrt{5}, \cos\theta = 2/\sqrt{5}, \tan\theta = \frac{1}{2}, \cot\theta = 2, \sec\theta = \frac{1}{2}\sqrt{5}, \csc\theta = \sqrt{5}$
11. $\sin\theta = -3/\sqrt{13}, \cos\theta = -2/\sqrt{13}, \tan\theta = \frac{3}{2}, \cot\theta = \frac{2}{3}, \sec\theta = -\frac{1}{2}\sqrt{13}, \csc\theta =$
   $-\frac{1}{3}\sqrt{13}$ 13. $\sin\theta = \frac{12}{13}, \cos\theta = -\frac{5}{13}, \tan\theta = -\frac{12}{5}, \cot\theta = -\frac{5}{12}$,
   $\sec\theta = -\frac{13}{5}, \csc\theta = \frac{13}{12}$ 15. $\sin\theta = -2/\sqrt{29}, \cos\theta = 5/\sqrt{29}$,
   $\tan\theta = -\frac{2}{5}, \cot\theta = -\frac{5}{2}, \sec\theta = \frac{1}{5}\sqrt{29}, \csc\theta = -\frac{1}{2}\sqrt{29}$ 17. II   19. II

Section 7-2

1. $\sin 20°$; $-\cos 40°$ 3. $-\tan 75°$; $-\csc 58°$ 5. $-\sin 57°$; $-\cot 6°$
7. $\cos 40°$; $-\tan 40°$ 9. -0.2588 11. -0.2756 13. -1.036
15. -2.366 17. -0.6036 19. -1.838 21. $28°, 208°$ 23. $238°, 302°$
25. $252°19', 287°41'$ 27. $125°33', 305°33'$ 29. -0.7002 31. -0.7771
33. $<$ 35. $=$ 37. 72.7 lb   39. $\cos(-\theta) = x/r$; $\tan(-\theta) = -y/x$;
   $\cot(-\theta) = x/-y$; $\sec(-\theta) = r/x$; $\csc(-\theta) = r/-y$.

Section 7-3

1. $\pi/12, 5\pi/6$ 3. $5\pi/12, 11\pi/6$ 5. $7\pi/6, 3\pi/2$ 7. $72°, 270°$
9. $10°, 315°$ 11. $170°, 300°$ 13. 0.401 15. 4.40 17. 5.82
19. $43.0°$ 21. $172°$ 23. $140°$ 25. 0.7071 27. 3.732 29. -1.732
31. -0.1219 33. $0.314, 2.83$ 35. $2.93, 6.07$ 37. $0.831, 5.45$
39. $2.44, 3.84$ 41. $\tan 4.49 = 4.49$ 43. 1.50 cm/sec

Section 7-4

1. 10.5 in.   3. 52.4 in²   5. 12 rad   7. 2.88 in²   9. 0.262 ft
11. 129 mi   13. 5660 in.   15. 75.4 rad/sec   17. 3700 mi/hr
19. 5200 ft/min   21. 2.60×10^{-6} rad/sec, 0.623 mi/sec   23. 65.9 in²

Section 7-5

1. $2\pi/9$; $17\pi/20$ 3. $4\pi/15$; $9\pi/8$ 5. $252°$; $130°$ 7. $12°$; $330°$ 9. $32.1°$
11. $206.3°$ 13. 1.745 15. 0.358 17. $-\cos 48°$; $\tan 14°$
19. $-\sin 71°$; $\sec 15°$ 21. -0.4226 23. 4.230 25. -0.5878 27. 1.195
29. $17°, 163°$ 31. $70°45', 289°15'$ 33. $0.576, 5.70$ 35. $4.18, 5.24$
37. -120 volts   39. 0.393 ft   41. 188 in./sec   43. 18 in.   45. 19%

Section 8-1

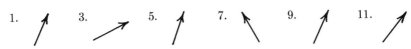

1.   3.   5.   7.   9.   11.

13. $3.22, 7.98$ 15. $-62.9, 44.0$ 17. $2.14, -8.78$ 19. $0.540, 0.841$
21. $10.0, 58.8°$ 23. $2.74, 111°$ 25. $2130, 107.7°$ 27. $1.42, 299.3°$
29. $29.2, 10.6°$ 31. $47.1, 101°$ 33. $27.2, 32.7°$ 35. $50.2, 50.3°$
37. $230, 125°$

Section 8-2

1. 81.5 lb, $56.5°$ from 45 lb force   3. 510 mi, $28.1°$ S of W
5. $v_H = 80.3$ ft/sec, $v_V = 89.2$ ft/sec   7. 31.6 lb, $71.6°$ 9. 340 ft/sec,
   $25°$ from direction of plane   11. Yes   13. 94.0 lb   15. 420 ft/sec at
   $17.7°$ from horizontal   17. 6.95 rad/sec²   19. 4.06 amp/m, $11.6°$ with
   magnet

Section 8-3

1. $b = 38.1$, $C = 66°$, $c = 46.1$ 3. $a = 2790$, $b = 2590$, $C = 109°$
5. $B = 12°$, $C = 150°$, $c = 7.44$ 7. $A = 126°$, $a = 0.0772$, $c = 0.0050$

9. $A = 99.4°$, $b = 55.0$, $c = 24.4$ 11. $A = 68.1°$, $a = 552$, $c = 538$

13. $A_1 = 61.5°$, $C_1 = 70.4°$, $c_1 = 5.61$; $A_2 = 118.5°$, $C_2 = 13.4°$, $c_2 = 1.38$

15. No solution   17. 10.6 ft, 7.83 ft   19. 25,200 ft

Section 8-4

1. $A = 50.2°$, $B = 75.8°$, $c = 6.31$ 3. $A = 70.9°$, $B = 11.1°$, $c = 4750$

5. $A = 34.6°$, $B = 40.5°$, $C = 104.9°$ 7. $A = 18.0°$, $B = 22.0°$, $C = 140°$

9. $A = 6.0°$, $B = 16.0°$, $c = 1150$ 11. $A = 82.3°$, $b = 21.6$, $C = 11.4°$

13. $A = 39.0°$, $B = 36.4°$, $b = 97.4$ 15. $A = 46.9°$, $B = 61.8°$, $C = 71.3°$

17. 1140 ft   19. 83°   21. 8.88 mi/hr at 13.4° with bank   23. 42.4°

Section 8-5

1. $A_x = 57.4$, $A_y = 30.5$ 3. $A_x = -0.754$, $A_y = -0.528$ 5. 956, 8.6°

7. 26.1, 146°   9. 99.2, 359.3°   11. $b = 18.1$, $C = 64°$, $c = 17.5$

13. $A = 21.2°$, $b = 34.8$, $c = 51.5$ 15. $a = 52.0$, $A = 40°$, $C = 30°$

17. $A_1 = 54.8°$, $a_1 = 12.7$, $B_1 = 68.6°$; $A_2 = 12.0°$, $a_2 = 3.24$, $B_2 = 111.4°$

19. $A = 32.3°$, $b = 267$, $C = 17.7°$ 21. $A = 148.7°$, $B = 9.3°$, $c = 5.67$

23. $A = 36.8°$, $B = 25.0°$, $C = 118.2°$ 25. $A = 20.6°$, $B = 35.5°$, $C = 123.9°$

27. 20 sec   29. 27.0 ft/sec, 34° with ground   31. 268 mi/hr, 465 mi/hr

33. 770 ft   35. 174 ft   37. 310 lb, 330.5°

Section 9-1

1. $0, -0.7, -1, -0.7, 0, 0.7, 1, 0.7, 0, -0.7, -1, -0.7, 0, 0.7, 1, 0.7, 0$

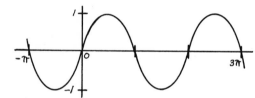

3.

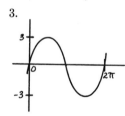

5.

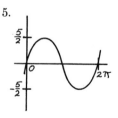

7.

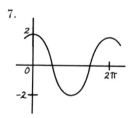

9.

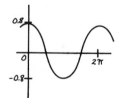

11.

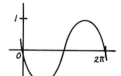

13.

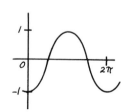

15. 0, 0.84, 0.91, 0.14, −0.76, −0.96, −0.28, 0.66

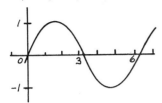

17. 1, 0.54, −0.42, −0.99, −0.65, 0.27, 0.96, 0.74

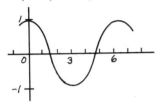

Section 9-2

1. $\pi/3$ 3. $\pi/4$ 5. $\pi/6$ 7. $\pi/8$ 9. 1   11. $\frac{1}{2}$ 13. 6π 15. 3π
17. 3   19. $2/\pi$

21.

23.

25.

27.

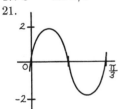

29.

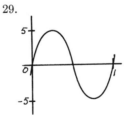

31.

33.

35.

37.

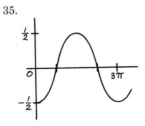

39.

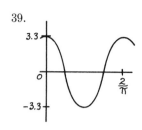

41.

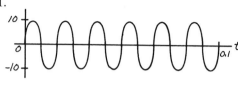

Section 9-3

1. $1, 2\pi, \dfrac{\pi}{6}(R)$

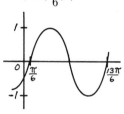

3. $1, 2\pi, \dfrac{\pi}{6}(L)$

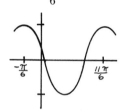

5. $2, \pi, \dfrac{\pi}{4}(L)$

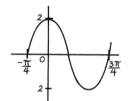

7. $1, \pi, \dfrac{\pi}{2}(R)$

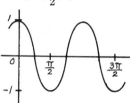

9. $\dfrac{1}{2}, 4\pi, \dfrac{\pi}{2}(R)$

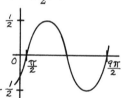

11. $3, 6\pi, \pi(L)$

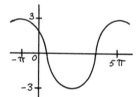

13. $1, 2, \tfrac{1}{8}(L)$

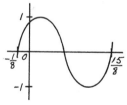

15. $\dfrac{3}{4}, \dfrac{1}{2}, \dfrac{1}{20}(R)$

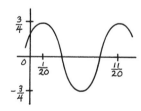

17. $0.6, 1, \dfrac{1}{2\pi}(R)$

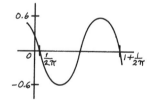

19. $4, \dfrac{2}{3}, \dfrac{2}{3\pi}(L)$

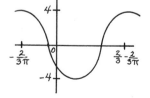

21. $1, \dfrac{2}{\pi}, \dfrac{1}{\pi}(R)$

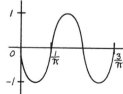

23.

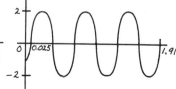

Section 9-4

1. undef., -1.7, -1, -0.58, 0, 0.58,
   1, 1.7, undef., -1.7, -1, -0.58, 0

3. undef., 2, 1.4, 1.2, 1, 1.2, 1.4, 2,
   undef., -2, -1.4, -1.2, -1

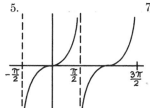

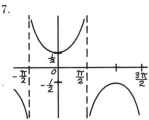

5.

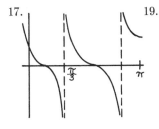

7.

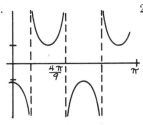

9.

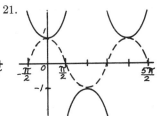

11.

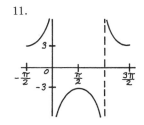

13.

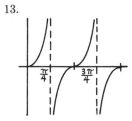

15.

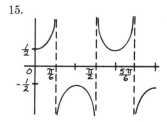

17.

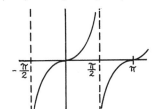

19.

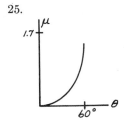

21.

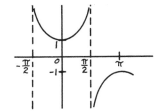

23.

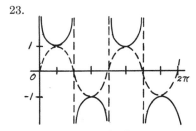

25.

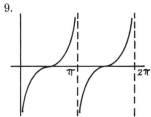

Section 9-5

1.
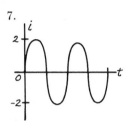

3.
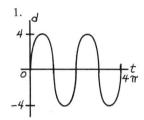

5.
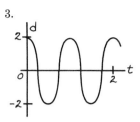

7.
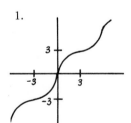

9.
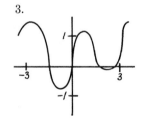

11.
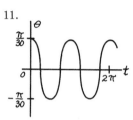

13.
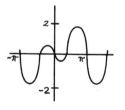

Section 9-6

1.

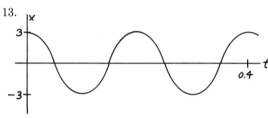

3.
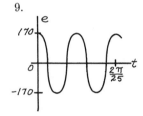

5.
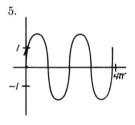

7.
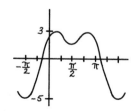

9.
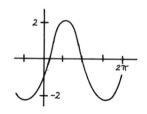

11.
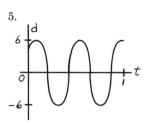

13.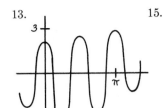

15.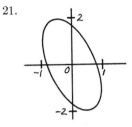

17.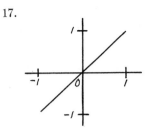

19.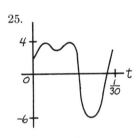

21.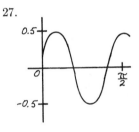

23.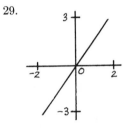

25.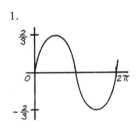

27.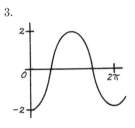

29.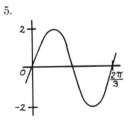

Section 9-7

1.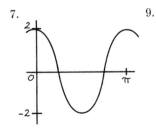

3.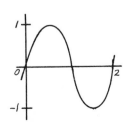

5.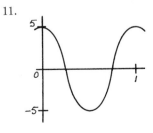

7.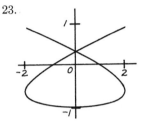

9.

11.

13.

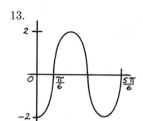

15.

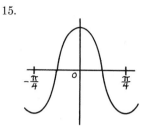

17.

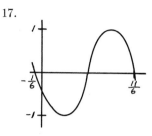

19.

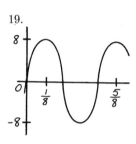

21.

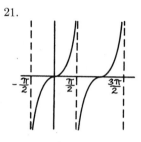

23.

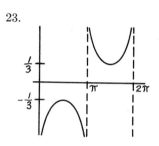

25.

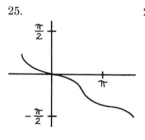

27.

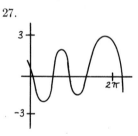

29.

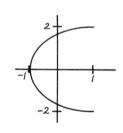

31.

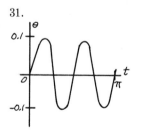

33.

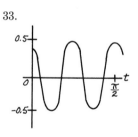

35.

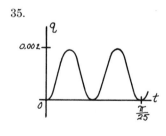

37.

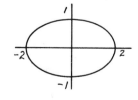

39.

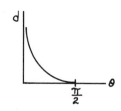

Section 10-1

1. 1   3. $2/a^2$ 5. $3/c^2$ 7. $1/(a+b)$ 9. 1   11. b^2 13. a^6b^4

15. a/x^2 17. $x^3/64a^3$ 19. $x^2y^6/16$ 21. $1/81x^8$ 23. $20/t^{13}$ 25. $b^3/3^34^5a$

27. $\dfrac{x^8 - y^2}{x^4 y^2}$ 29. $\dfrac{ab}{a+b}$ 31. $-x/y$ 33. $\dfrac{a^2 - ax + x^2}{ax}$ 35. $\dfrac{2x}{(x-1)(x+1)}$

37. $\dfrac{rR}{r+R}$ 39. $\dfrac{r_1 r_2}{(\mu - 1)(r_2 - r_1)}$

Section 10-2

1. 45,000   3. 0.00201   5. 3.23   7. 18.6   9. 4×10^4 11. 8.7×10^{-3}

13. 6.89×10^0 15. 6.3×10^{-2} 17. 2.04×10^8 19. 4.85×10^9

21. 9.76×10^6 23. 3.66×10^5 25. 2.25×10^4 lb/in^2 27. 0.00061 atm

29. 4500 ohms   31. 1.1×10^{-5} ft   33. 0.00000000000000000000000167 gm

35. 6.04×10^{-2} ohm

Section 10-3

1. 5   3. 3   5. 16   7. 10^{25} 9. $\frac{1}{2}$ 11. $\frac{1}{16}$ 13. 25   15. 1024

17. $-\frac{1}{2}$ 19. $\frac{39}{1000}$ 21. $a^{7/6}$ 23. $1/y^{9/10}$ 25. $s^{23/12}$ 27. $2ab^2$

29. $27/64t^3$ 31. $b^{11/10}/2a^{1/12}$ 33. $\frac{2}{3}x^{1/6}y^{11/12}$

35. $\dfrac{x}{(x+2)^{1/2}}$ 37. $\dfrac{a^2+1}{a^4}$ 39. $\dfrac{a+1}{a^{1/2}}$ 41. 56%

Section 10-4

1. $2\sqrt{6}$ 3. $3\sqrt{5}$ 5. $x\sqrt{5}$ 7. $3ac^2\sqrt{2ab}$ 9. $2\sqrt[3]{2}$ 11. $2\sqrt[5]{3}$

13. $2\sqrt[3]{a^2}$ 15. $2st\sqrt[4]{4r^3t}$ 17. 2   19. $ab\sqrt[3]{b^2}$ 21. $\sqrt{6}/2$ 23. $\sqrt{ab}/b$

25. $\sqrt[3]{6}/2$ 27. $2\sqrt{5}$ 29. 200   31. 2000   33. $\sqrt{2a}$ 35. $\sqrt{2}/2$

37. $\sqrt[3]{2}$ 39. $\sqrt[8]{2}$ 41. $\sqrt{6}/6$ 43. $a+b$ 45. $\sqrt{b(a^2+b)}/ab$

47. $\pi\sqrt{6}/4$ sec   49. $\sqrt[3]{4MN^2\rho^2}/2N\rho$

Section 10-5

1. $7\sqrt{3}$ 3. $-2\sqrt{2}$ 5. $13\sqrt[3]{3}$ 7. $-4\sqrt{5}$ 9. $23\sqrt{3} - 6\sqrt{2}$

11. $\sqrt[4]{2}$ 13. $7\sqrt{15}/3$ 15. 0   17. $(a - 2b^2)\sqrt{ab}$ 19. $(3 - 2a)\sqrt{10}$

21. $(2b - a)\sqrt[3]{3a^2b}$ 23. $\dfrac{(a^2 - c^3)\sqrt{ac}}{a^2c^3}$ 25. $\dfrac{(a - 2b)\sqrt[3]{ab^2}}{ab}$

27. $\dfrac{2b\sqrt{a^2 - b^2}}{b^2 - a^2}$ 29. $\sqrt{a^3 - a} - \dfrac{\sqrt{a^2 - 1}}{a(a+1)}$

Section 10-6

1. $2\sqrt{3}$ 3. 2   5. 50   7. $\frac{1}{3}\sqrt{30}$ 9. $\sqrt{6} - \sqrt{15}$ 11. $8 - 12\sqrt{3}$

13. -1 15. $48 + 9\sqrt{15}$ 17. $a\sqrt{b} + \sqrt{ac}$ 19. $2a - 3b + 2\sqrt{2ab}$

21. $\sqrt{6} - \sqrt{10} - 2$ 23. 1   25. $\sqrt[6]{72}$ 27. $\sqrt[12]{a^3b^7c^4}$ 29. $(2/a) - 1 - a$

31. $4x^2 + x - 2y - 4x\sqrt{x - 2y}$ (valid for $x \geq 2y$)   33. c/a

Section 10-7

1. $\sqrt{7}$ 3. $\frac{1}{2}\sqrt{14}$ 5. $\frac{1}{6}\sqrt[3]{9x^2}$ 7. $\frac{1}{2}\sqrt[6]{4a^3}$ 9. $\dfrac{a\sqrt{2} - b\sqrt{a}}{a}$

11. $\frac{1}{4}(\sqrt{7} - \sqrt{3})$ 13. $\frac{1}{3}(\sqrt{35} + \sqrt{14})$ 15. $-\frac{3}{8}(\sqrt{5} + 3)$

17. $\frac{1}{11}(\sqrt{7} + 3\sqrt{2} - 6 - \sqrt{14})$ 19. $\frac{1}{13}(4 - \sqrt{3})$ 21. $\dfrac{8(3\sqrt{a} + 2\sqrt{b})}{9a - 4b}$

23. $-\dfrac{\sqrt{x^2 - y^2} + \sqrt{x^2 + xy}}{y}$ 25. 1.49   27. 1.41   29. $\dfrac{Vx\sqrt[3]{xd^2}}{d^2}$

Section 10-8

1. 49,300   3. 0.91   5. 9.5×10^4 7. 6.67×10^{-4} 9. $6a^3n^3$ 11. $2/a^2$

13. 375   15. $64a^2b^5$ 17. $\dfrac{2y}{x + y}$ 19. $4a(a^2 + 4)^{1/2}$ 21. $\dfrac{-2(x + 1)}{(x - 1)^3}$

23. $2\sqrt{17}$ 25. $3ab^2\sqrt{a}$ 27. $mn^2\sqrt[4]{8m^2n}$ 29. $\sqrt{2}$ 31. $\dfrac{5\sqrt{2s}}{2s}$

33. $14\sqrt{2}$ 35. $3ax\sqrt{2x}$ 37. $10 - \sqrt{55}$ 39. $33 - 7\sqrt{21}$

41. $-\dfrac{8 + \sqrt{6}}{29}$ 43. $\dfrac{13 - 2\sqrt{35}}{29}$ 45. $\dfrac{\sqrt{a^2b^2 + a}}{a}$ 47. $\dfrac{15 - 2\sqrt{15}}{4}$

49. 2.5×10^4 mi/hr   51. 176,000,000,000 coul/kg   53. 2×10^{-7} in.

55. 0.22 cal/kg·°C   57. $\dfrac{e^{i\alpha t}}{e^{i\omega t}}$ 59. $3750\sqrt{166.2} = 48{,}400$ cm/sec

61. $\dfrac{\sqrt{LC_1C_2(C_1 + C_2)}}{2\pi LC_1C_2}$

Section 11-1

1. $9j$ 3. $-2j$ 5. $2\sqrt{2}j$ 7. $\frac{1}{2}\sqrt{7}j$ 9. $-j$ 11. 1   13. 0
15. $-2j$ 17. $2 + 3j$ 19. $-2 + 3j$ 21. $3\sqrt{2} - 2\sqrt{2}j$ 23. -1
25. $6 + 7j$ 27. $-2j$ 29. $x = 2, y = -2$ 31. $x = 10, y = -6$
33. $x = 0, y = -1$ 35. $x = -2, y = 3$ 37. It is a real number.

Section 11-2

1. $5 - 8j$ 3. $-9 + 6j$ 5. $7 - 5j$ 7. $-5j$ 9. -1 11. $7 + 49j$
13. $-8 - 20j$ 15. $22 + 3j$ 17. $-42 - 6j$ 19. $-18\sqrt{2}j$ 21. $3\sqrt{3}j$
23. $-28j$ 25. $-40 - 42j$ 27. $-2 - 2j$ 29. $\frac{1}{29}(-30 + 12j)$
31. $\frac{1}{37}(12 + 2j)$ 33. $-j$ 35. $\frac{1}{11}(-13 + 8\sqrt{2}j)$ 37. $\frac{1}{5}(-1 + 3j)$
39. $(a + bj) + (a - bj) = 2a$ 41. $(a + bj) - (a - bj) = 2bj$

Section 11-3

1. $8 + j$ **3.** $-3j$ **5.** $-1 + 4j$ **7.** $-2 + 3j$

9. $7 + j$ **11.** $-13 + j$ **13.**    **15.**

Section 11-4

1. $10(\cos 36.9° + j \sin 36.9°)$

3. $5(\cos 306.9° + j \sin 306.9°)$

5. $3.61(\cos 123.7° + j \sin 123.7°)$

7. $5.39(\cos 201.8° + j \sin 201.8°)$

9. $2(\cos 60° + j \sin 60°)$

11. $3(\cos 180° + j \sin 180°)$

13. $2.94 + 4.05j$

15. $-1.39 + 0.80j$

17. $9.66 - 2.59j$

19. -6

21. $-3.76 - 1.37j$

23. $-0.500 - 0.866j$

Section 11-5

1. $3e^{1.05j}$ 3. $4.5e^{4.92j}$ 5. $5.00e^{5.35j}$ 7. $3.61e^{2.55j}$ 9. $5.39e^{0.381j}$
11. $7.81e^{3.84j}$ 13. $3(\cos 28.6° + j \sin 28.6°); 2.63 + 1.44j$
15. $4(\cos 106° + j \sin 106°); -1.10 + 3.85j$
17. $3.2(\cos 310° + j \sin 310°); 2.06 - 2.45j$
19. $0.1(\cos 137° + j \sin 137°); -0.073 + 0.068j$ 21. $0.55e^{0.415j}; 0.55$ amp

Section 11-6

1. $8(\cos 80° + j \sin 80°)$ 3. $3(\cos 250° + j \sin 250°)$
5. $2(\cos 35° + j \sin 35°)$ 7. $2.4(\cos 110° + j \sin 110°)$
9. $8(\cos 105° + j \sin 105°)$ 11. $256(\cos 0° + j \sin 0°)$
13. $65(\cos 345.7° + j \sin 345.7°) = 63 - 16j$
15. $0.385(\cos 120.5° + j \sin 120.5°) = \frac{1}{169}(-33 + 56j)$
17. $625(\cos 212.4° + j \sin 212.4°) = -527 - 336j$
19. $2(\cos 30° + j \sin 30°), 2(\cos 210° + j \sin 210°)$
21. $-0.384 + 1.67j, -1.25 - 1.17j, 1.63 - 0.50j$ 23. $1, -1, j, -j$
25. $j, -\frac{1}{2}(\sqrt{3} + j), \frac{1}{2}(\sqrt{3} - j)$

Section 11-7

1. 30 volts   3. (a) 18.0 ohms (b) $-56.3°$ (c) 54.0 volts   5. (a) 3.0 ohms
(b) $-90°$ 7. (a) 11.7 ohms (b) $-59.0°$ 9. 44.4 volts   11. 2000 ohms,
3000 ohms   13. 4120 ohms; voltage leads by 14.0°   15. 2×10^{-4} farad
17. 9.41 watts

Section 11-8

1. $10 - j$ 3. $6 + 2j$ 5. $9 + 2j$ 7. $-12 + 66j$ 9. $\frac{1}{53}(16 + 50j)$
11. $x = -\frac{2}{3}, y = -2$ 13. $3 + 11j$ 15. $4 + 8j$

17. $1.41(\cos 315° + j \sin 315°) = 1.41 e^{5.50j}$
19. $7.28(\cos 254.1° + j \sin 254.1°) = 7.28 e^{4.43j}$ 21. $-1.41 - 1.41j$
23. $-2.72 + 4.19j$ 25. $1.94 + 0.49j$ 27. $-1.63 + 4.73j$
29. $15(\cos 84° + j \sin 84°)$ 31. $8(\cos 59° + j \sin 59°)$
33. $2^{10}(\cos 160° + j \sin 160°)$ 35. $32(\cos 270° + j \sin 270°) = -32j$
37. $\frac{625}{2}(\cos 270° + j \sin 270°) = -\frac{625}{2}j$ 39. $1.00 + 1.73j, -2, 1.00 - 1.73j$
41. $\cos 67.5° + j \sin 67.5°, \cos 157.5° + j \sin 157.5°,$
$\cos 247.5° + j \sin 247.5°, \cos 337.5° + j \sin 337.5°$
43. 12.5 ohms, $-53.1°$ 45. 10.2 ohms, current leads by 8.7°   47. 36.1 volts

Section 12-1

1. $\log_3 27 = 3$ 3. $\log_4 256 = 4$ 5. $\log_4 \left(\frac{1}{16}\right) = -2$ 7. $\log_2 \left(\frac{1}{64}\right) = -6$
9. $\log_8 2 = \frac{1}{3}$ 11. $\log_{1/4} \left(\frac{1}{16}\right) = 2$ 13. $81 = 3^4$ 15. $9 = 9^1$
17. $5 = 25^{1/2}$ 19. $3 = 243^{1/5}$ 21. $0.01 = 10^{-2}$ 23. $16 = (0.5)^{-4}$
25. 2   27. -2 29. 343   31. $\frac{1}{4}$ 33. 9   35. $\frac{1}{64}$ 37. 0.2
39. -3 41. $t = -(L/R) \log_e (E/E_m)$

Section 12-2

1.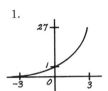

3.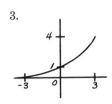

5.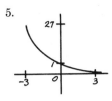

7.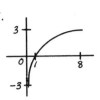

9.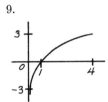

11.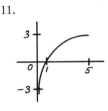

13.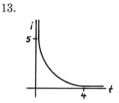

Section 12-3

1. $\log_5 x + \log_5 y$ 3. $\log_3 r - \log_3 s$ 5. $3 \log_2 a$ 7. $2 + \log_3 2$
9. $-1 - \log_2 3$ 11. $\frac{1}{2}(1 + \log_3 2)$ 13. $4 + 3 \log_2 3$ 15. $3 + \log_{10} 3$
17. $\log_b ac$ 19. $\log_5 3$ 21. $\log_b (x^{3/2})$ 23. $\log_e (4n^3)$ 25. $y = 2x$
27. $y = 49/x^3$ 29. 0.602 31. -0.301 33. $S = \log_e (T^c/P^{nR})$

Section 12-4

1. 2.7536   3. 8.8062 − 10   5. 6.9657   7. 6.0682 − 10
9. 0.0224   11. 9.3773 − 10   13. 8.8652   15. 8.6512 − 10
17. 27400   19. 0.0496   21. 2000   23. 0.724   25. 89.02
27. 4.065×10^{-4} 29. 1.427   31. 0.005788   33. 9.0607   35. 8.8751 − 10

Section 12-5

1. 64.58   3. 0.03742   5. 98.74   7. 1.757   9. 308.8
11. 0.6046   13. 1.323   15. 25.33   17. 3.740   19. 0.003190
21. 1011   23. 1.46×10^9 25. 1.544   27. 3.324×10^4 cm/sec   29. 0.2319 ft

Section 12-6

1. 9.5767 − 10   3. 0.2107   5. 9.7916 − 10   7. 0.1834
9. 9.8982 − 10   11. 9.2766 − 10   13. 28°10′   15. 50°16′
17. 48°56′   19. 1°40′ or 1°50′   21. $a = 85.35$, $b = 11.87$, $B = 7°55′$
23. $b = 9506$, $C = 42°10′$, $c = 6703$ 25. $a = 12.22$, $C = 68°8′$, $c = 12.31$
27. $A = 37°58′$, $B = 52°2′$, $c = 485.3$ 29. 21.85 lb, 52.24 lb
31. 19.97 lb   33. −32°3′

Section 12-7

1. 3.258   3. 6.447   5. 0.4447   7. 3.822   9. −0.6912
11. −2.957   13. 1.921   15. 6.427   17. 1.602   19. 0.3053
21. 257 yr   23. −0.2

Section 12-8

1.   3.   5.   7.

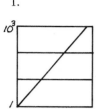 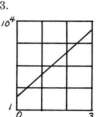 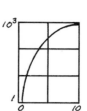 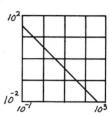

9.   11.   13.   15.

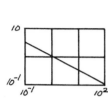 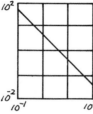 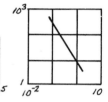

Section 12-9

1. 10,000   3. $\frac{1}{5}$ 5. 6   7. $\frac{5}{3}$ 9. 6   11. 100   13. $2 + \log_2 7$
15. $1 + \frac{1}{2}\log_4 3$ 17. $y = 4/x$ 19. $y = 8/x$ 21. 9.422   23. 122.8
25. 1.180×10^{15} 27. 2.037   29. 4.771   31. 29.28
33. $b = 99.73$, $C = 67°50'$, $c = 100.2$ 35. 2.181   37. 0.7277
39. $P = 10^{(a+bT)/T}$ 41. 52.84%   43. 477.1 ft   45. -2.506 volts

Section 13-1

1. $(1.8, 3.6)$, $(-1.8, -3.6)$ 3. $(0.0, -2.0)$, $(2.7, -0.7)$ 5. $(1.5, 0.2)$
7. $(1.1, 2.8)$, $(-1.1, 2.8)$, $(2.4, -1.8)$, $(-2.4, -1.8)$ 9. No solution
11. $(-2.8, -1.0)$, $(-2.8, 1.0)$, $(2.8, -1.0)$, $(2.8, 1.0)$
13. $(0.7, 0.7)$, $(-0.7, -0.7)$ 15. $(0.0, 0.0)$, $(0.9, 0.8)$ 17. $(1.0, 0.0)$
19. 360 yd, 210 yd

Section 13-2

1. $(0, 1)$, $(1, 2)$ 3. $(-\frac{19}{5}, \frac{17}{5})$, $(5, -1)$ 5. $(1.26, 0.52)$, $(0.45, -1.09)$
7. $(\frac{2}{3}, \frac{9}{2})$, $(-3, -1)$ 9. $(1, 2)$, $(-1, 2)$
11. $(1, 0)$, $(-1, 0)$, $(\frac{1}{2}\sqrt{6}, \frac{1}{2})$, $(-\frac{1}{2}\sqrt{6}, \frac{1}{2})$
13. $(\sqrt{19}, \sqrt{6})$, $(\sqrt{19}, -\sqrt{6})$, $(-\sqrt{19}, \sqrt{6})$, $(-\sqrt{19}, -\sqrt{6})$
15. $(\sqrt{22}/11, \sqrt{770}/11)$, $(\sqrt{22}/11, -\sqrt{770}/11)$, $(-\sqrt{22}/11, \sqrt{770}/11)$,
    $(-\sqrt{22}/11, -\sqrt{770}/11)$ 17. $(-5, -2)$, $(-5, 2)$, $(5, -2)$, $(5, 2)$
19. 0, 1.25 sec   21. 8, 13   23. 8 in., 12 in.

Section 13-3

1. $-3, -2, 2, 3$ 3. $-\frac{1}{2}, \frac{1}{4}$ 5. $1, 9$ 7. $1, -2$ 9. $-27, 125$ 11. 5
13. $-2, -1, 3, 4$ 15. 18 17. 24 ft by 32 ft

Section 13-4

1. 12 3. 2 5. $2, 3$ 7. 32 9. 16 11. $7, -1$ 13. 0 15. 5

17. 6 19. 258 21. $(v_0{}^2 - v^2)/2g$ 23. 9 in. by 12 in.

Section 13-5

1. 4 3. 0.8614 5. 0.285 7. 0.203 9. 4.11 11. 14.15 13. 4
15. 4 17. -0.162 19. 1.42 21. 0.00203 sec   23. 10^5 25. 3.35

Section 13-6

1. $(-0.9, 3.5), (0.8, 2.6)$ 3. $(2.0, 0.0), (1.6, -0.6)$ 5. $(0.8, 1.6), (-0.8, 1.6)$
7. $(0, 0), (2, 16)$ 9. $(7, 5), (7, -5), (-7, 5), (-7, -5)$
11. $(-2, 2), (\frac{2}{3}, \frac{10}{9})$ 13. $-4, -2, 2, 4$ 15. $\frac{1}{3}, -\frac{1}{7}$ 17. 11 19. 8
21. $\frac{9}{16}$ 23. 4.30 25. 2 27. $x = 16, y = 15$ 29. 4.67 gm-mole/liter
31. 492 ft

Section 14-1

1. 0 3. 0 5. -40 7. 8 9. 183 11. -28 13. Yes   15. Yes
17. No   19. No   21. No   23. Yes

Section 14-2

1. $x^2 + 3x + 2, R = 0$ 3. $x^2 - x + 3, R = 0$
5. $2x^4 - 4x^3 + 8x^2 - 17x + 42, R = -40$ 7. $x^2 + x - 4, R = 8$
9. $x^3 - 3x^2 + 10x - 45, R = 183$ 11. $2x^3 - x^2 - 4x - 12, R = -28$
13. $x^5 + 2x^4 + 4x^3 + 8x^2 + 18x + 36, R = 66$
15. $x^6 + 2x^5 + 4x^4 + 8x^3 + 16x^2 + 32x + 64, R = 0$ 17. Yes   19. Yes
21. Yes   23. No

Section 14-3

[*Note*: Unknown roots listed.]
1. $-1, -2$ 3. $-2, 3$ 5. $-2, -2$ 7. $-j, -\frac{2}{3}$ 9. $2j, -2j$
11. $3, -1$ 13. $2, -3$ 15. $-2j, 3, -3$

Section 14-4

1. $1, -1, -2$ 3. $2, -1, -3$ 5. $\frac{1}{2}, 5, -3$ 7. $-2, -2, 2 \pm \sqrt{3}$
9. $2, 4, -1, -3$ 11. $1, -\frac{1}{2}, 1 \pm \sqrt{3}$ 13. $\frac{1}{2}, -\frac{2}{3}, -3, -\frac{1}{2}$
15. $2, 2, -1, -1, -3$ 17. $0, L$ 19. 2 in. or 1.17 in.

Section 14-5

1. 0.59 3. 0.38 5. 1.72 7. 2.56 9. 0.68 11. $2.30, -1.30$
13. 7.01 ft

Section 14-6

1. 1   3. -107 5. Yes   7. No   9. $x^2 + 4x + 10, R = 11$
11. $2x^2 - 7x + 10, R = -17$ 13. $x^3 - 3x^2 - 4, R = -4$
15. $2x^4 + 10x^3 + 4x^2 + 21x + 105, R = 516$ 17. No   19. Yes
21. (Unlisted roots) $\frac{1}{3}(-1 \pm \sqrt{14}\,j)$ 23. (Unlisted roots), $2, -2$
25. $1, 2, -4$ 27. $-1, -1, \frac{5}{2}$ 29. $\frac{5}{3}, -\frac{1}{2}, -1$ 31. $\frac{1}{2}, -1, \sqrt{2}\,j, -\sqrt{2}\,j$
33. 0.75   35. 1.91   37. 7 ft, 7 ft, 11 ft   39. 1.64

Section 15-1

1. 39   3. 30   5. 50   7. -6 9. -86 11. -2
13. $x = 2, y = -1, z = 3$ 15. $x = -1, y = \frac{1}{3}, z = -\frac{1}{2}$
17. $x = -1, y = 0, z = 2, t = 1$ 19. $x = 1, y = 2, z = -1, t = 3$
21. $\frac{2}{7}$ amp, $\frac{18}{7}$ amp, $-\frac{8}{7}$ amp, $-\frac{12}{7}$ amp

Section 15-2

1. -60 3. -56 5. 0   7. 0   9. -13 11. -118 13. -72
15. 0   17. $x = 2, y = -1, z = -1, t = 3$ 19. $x = 1, y = 2, z = -1, t = -2$
21. $\frac{33}{16}$ amps, $\frac{11}{8}$ amps, $-\frac{5}{8}$ amp, $-\frac{15}{8}$ amps, $-\frac{15}{16}$ amp

Section 15-3

1. $a = 1, b = -3, c = 4, d = 7$ 3. $x = 2, y = 3$ 5. $\begin{pmatrix} 1 & 10 \\ 0 & 2 \end{pmatrix}$

7. $\begin{pmatrix} 0 & 0 \\ 1 & 6 \\ 1 & 0 \end{pmatrix}$ 9. $\begin{pmatrix} 0 & 9 & -13 & 3 \\ 8 & -7 & 7 & 0 \end{pmatrix}$ 11. Cannot be added

13. $\begin{pmatrix} -1 & 13 & -20 & 3 \\ 8 & -13 & 6 & 2 \end{pmatrix}$ 15. $\begin{pmatrix} -3 & -6 & 5 & -6 \\ -6 & -4 & -17 & 6 \end{pmatrix}$

17. $A + B = B + A = \begin{pmatrix} 3 & 1 & 0 & 7 \\ 5 & -3 & -2 & 5 \\ 10 & 10 & 8 & 0 \end{pmatrix}$ 19. $A + 2B = \begin{pmatrix} 22 & 14 & 19 \\ 17 & 30 & 25 \end{pmatrix}$

Section 15-4

1. $(-8 \quad -12)$ 3. $\begin{pmatrix} -15 & 15 & -26 \\ 8 & 5 & -13 \end{pmatrix}$ 5. $\begin{pmatrix} 29 \\ -29 \end{pmatrix}$ 7. $\begin{pmatrix} -7 & -5 \\ 8 & 0 \\ 14 & 10 \end{pmatrix}$

9. $\begin{pmatrix} 33 & -22 & 7 \\ 31 & -12 & 5 \\ 15 & 13 & -1 \\ 50 & -41 & 12 \end{pmatrix}$ 11. $\begin{pmatrix} -62 & 68 \\ 73 & -27 \end{pmatrix}$

13. $AB = (40)$, $BA = \begin{pmatrix} -1 & 3 & -8 \\ 5 & -15 & 40 \\ 7 & -21 & 56 \end{pmatrix}$ 15. $AB = \begin{pmatrix} -5 \\ 10 \end{pmatrix}$, BA not defined

17. $AI = IA = A$ 19. $B = A^{-1}$ 21. $B = A^{-1}$ 23. Yes   25. No

27. 800 ft of brass pipe, 1000 ft of steel pipe; 1620 ft of brass pipe, 2240 ft of steel pipe

Section 15-5

1. $\begin{pmatrix} -2 & -\frac{5}{2} \\ -1 & -1 \end{pmatrix}$ 3. $\begin{pmatrix} -\frac{1}{3} & \frac{1}{6} \\ \frac{2}{15} & \frac{1}{30} \end{pmatrix}$ 5. $\begin{pmatrix} \frac{3}{4} & \frac{1}{2} \\ -\frac{1}{4} & 0 \end{pmatrix}$ 7. $\begin{pmatrix} -3 & 2 \\ 2 & -1 \end{pmatrix}$

9. $\begin{pmatrix} -\frac{1}{2} & -2 \\ \frac{1}{2} & 1 \end{pmatrix}$ 11. $\begin{pmatrix} \frac{2}{9} & -\frac{5}{9} \\ \frac{1}{9} & \frac{2}{9} \end{pmatrix}$ 13. $\begin{pmatrix} -18 & -7 & 5 \\ -3 & -1 & 1 \\ -5 & -2 & 1 \end{pmatrix}$

15. $\begin{pmatrix} 3 & -4 & -1 \\ -4 & 5 & 2 \\ 2 & -3 & -1 \end{pmatrix}$ 17. $\begin{pmatrix} 2 & 4 & \frac{7}{2} \\ -1 & -2 & -\frac{3}{2} \\ 1 & 1 & \frac{1}{2} \end{pmatrix}$ 19. $\begin{pmatrix} \frac{5}{2} & -2 & -2 \\ -1 & 1 & 1 \\ \frac{7}{4} & -\frac{3}{2} & -1 \end{pmatrix}$

Section 15-6

1. $x = \frac{1}{2}, y = 3$ 3. $x = \frac{1}{2}, y = -\frac{5}{2}$ 5. $x = -4, y = 2, z = -1$
7. $x = -1, y = 0, z = 3$ 9. $x = 1, y = 2$ 11. $x = -\frac{3}{2}, y = -2$
13. $x = -3, y = -\frac{1}{2}$ 15. $x = 2, y = -4, z = 1$ 17. $x = 2, y = -\frac{1}{2}, z = 3$
19. 10 lb, 8 lb, 12 lb   21. 8 of type A, 10 of type B

Section 15-7

1. 6   3. 186   5. -438 7. 6   9. 186   11. -438 13. -9

15. -44 17. $\begin{pmatrix} 1 & -3 \\ 8 & -5 \\ -8 & -2 \\ 3 & -10 \end{pmatrix}$ 19. $\begin{pmatrix} 3 & 0 \\ -12 & 18 \\ 9 & 6 \\ -3 & 21 \end{pmatrix}$

21. Cannot be subtracted   23. $\begin{pmatrix} 7 & -6 \\ -4 & 20 \\ -1 & 6 \\ 1 & 15 \end{pmatrix}$ 25. $\begin{pmatrix} 13 \\ -13 \end{pmatrix}$

27. $\begin{pmatrix} 34 & 11 & -5 \\ 2 & -8 & 10 \\ -1 & -17 & 20 \end{pmatrix}$ 29. $\begin{pmatrix} -2 & \frac{5}{2} \\ -1 & 1 \end{pmatrix}$ 31. $\begin{pmatrix} \frac{2}{15} & \frac{1}{60} \\ -\frac{1}{15} & \frac{7}{60} \end{pmatrix}$

33. $\begin{pmatrix} 11 & 10 & 3 \\ -4 & -4 & -1 \\ 3 & 3 & 1 \end{pmatrix}$ 35. $\begin{pmatrix} \frac{1}{2} & -\frac{1}{2} & -1 \\ -3 & 2 & 1 \\ -4 & 3 & 2 \end{pmatrix}$ 37. $x = -3, y = 1$

39. $x = -2, y = 7$ 41. $x = -1, y = -3, z = 0$ 43. $x = 3, y = 1, z = -1$
45. $x = 1, y = 2, z = -3, t = 1$ 47. $F_1 = 12$ lb, $F_2 = 9$ lb

49. 30 gm, 50 gm, 20 gm   51. $\begin{pmatrix} 830 \\ 880 \\ 290 \end{pmatrix}$

Section 16-1

1. $7 < 12$ 3. $20 < 45$ 5. $-4 > -9$ 7. $16 < 81$ 9. $x > 0$
11. $x \le 0$ 13. $x < -1, x > 1$ 15. $2 \le x < 6$ 17. $x > 0, y > 0$
19. $y > x$ 21. Multiply both members by x 23. Multiply by y and take
square roots   25. $3.5 < t < 15.3, h > 200$
27. $i = 0.02 \sin 120\pi t$ if $0 \le t \le \frac{1}{120}, \frac{1}{60} \le t \le \frac{1}{40}$;
$i = 0$ if $\frac{1}{120} < t < \frac{1}{60}, \frac{1}{40} < t < \frac{1}{30}$

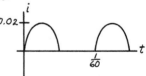

Section 16-2

[*Note*: Solid portion of curves gives desired values of x.]

1.
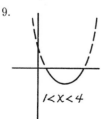

3.
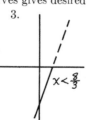

5.
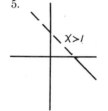

7.
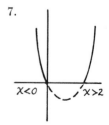

9.
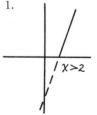

11.
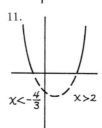

13.
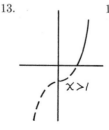

15.
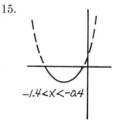

17.   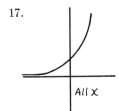 All X

19.   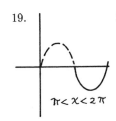 $\pi < x < 2\pi$

21.   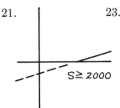 $S \geq 2000$

23.   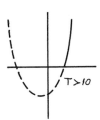 $T > 10$

Section 16-3

1. $x > -3$ 3. $x < \frac{12}{7}$ 5. $x \leq 4$ 7. $x > \frac{9}{2}$ 9. $-1 < x < 1$
11. $x \leq -2, x \geq \frac{1}{3}$ 13. $\frac{1}{3} < x < \frac{1}{2}$ 15. All x 17. $-2 < x < 0, x > 1$
19. $-2 < x < -1, x > 1$ 21. $x < 3, x > 8$ 23. $-5 < x < -1, x > 7$
25. $-1 < x < \frac{3}{4}, x > 6$ 27. $2 < x < 4, 5 < x < 9$ 29. $x \leq -2, x \geq 1$
31. $-1 \leq x \leq 0$ 33. $t < \frac{15}{4}$ sec   35. $-20°C < T < -16.2°C,$
    $6.2°C < T < 10°C$

Section 16-4

1. $3 < x < 5$ 3. $x < 1, x > \frac{7}{3}$ 5. $\frac{1}{6} < x < \frac{3}{2}$ 7. $x < -\frac{3}{2}, x > 0$
9. $-10 < x < 2$ 11. $x < -1, x > \frac{7}{3}$ 13. $-4 < x < -2, -1 < x < 1$
15. $x < -4, -2 < x < -1, x > 1$ 17. $y < \frac{1}{4}$ ft if $|x - 6| < 2$ ft
19. 5 in., 11 in.

Section 16-5

1. $x > 6$ 3. $x < -\frac{5}{3}$ 5. $x < -9, x > 7$ 7. $-4 < x < -1, x > 1$
9. $-\frac{1}{2} < x < 8$ 11. $x < -4, \frac{1}{2} < x < 3$ 13. No values   15. $x < 0, x > \frac{1}{2}$
17. $x < -1, x > 5$ 19. $-2 < x < \frac{2}{3}$
21.   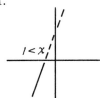 $1 < x$

23.   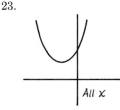 All X

25.   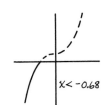 $x < -0.68$

27. $x \leq -4, x \geq 0$ 29. Divide both members by y; then use $x - 1 > y$
31. $x > 16$ in.   33. $0 < R_1 < 2$ ohms, $6 < R_2 < 8$ ohms

Section 17-1

1. 6   3. $\frac{4}{3}$ 5. $\frac{1}{5}$ 7. 19.2   9. 900 lb/in²   11. 9080 gm
13. 66 ft/sec   15. 27 in.   17. 72,000 ft-lb   19. 4 ft, 6 ft

Section 17-2

1. $y = kz$ 3. $w = kxy^3$ 5. $r = 16/y$ 7. $p = 16q/r^3$ 9. 25   11. 50
13. 180   15. 2.56×10^5 17. 2.4 in.   19. $I = 10^6/r^2$ 21. $R = (5 \times 10^{-5}l)/A$

23. $f = k\sqrt{T}$, 737 per sec   25. 135 ft   27. 23.3 cm/sec
29. $P = k/V^{3/2}$, 24 atm   31. 0 ft/sec²

Section 17-3

1. $3\frac{1}{4}$ in.   3. 1.72 liters   5. 675,000   7. 492 gm   9. $y = 3x^2$
11. $v = 128x/y^3$ 13. 22.5 hp   15. 64π sq units   17. 551 ft/sec
19. $(1.28 \times 10^5 \, r^4)/l^2$ 21. 50 cycles/sec   23. 68,000,000 mi
25. $E = 0.1392 (\tan \theta + \cot \theta)$

Section 18-1

1. 4, 6, 8, 10, 12   3. 13, 9, 5, 1, -3 5. 37   7. $49b$ 9. 440   11. $-\frac{85}{2}$
13. $n = 6, s = 150$ 15. $d = -\frac{2}{19}, l = -\frac{1}{3}$ 17. $a = 19, l = 106$
19. $n = 62, s = -4867$ 21. $n = 8, d = (b + 2c)/14$
23. $a = 36, d = 4, s = 540$ 25. 5050   27. 100,500   29. 19th   31. 6400 ft

Section 18-2

1. 45, 15, 5, $\frac{5}{3}, \frac{5}{9}$ 3. 2, 6, 18, 54, 162   5. $\frac{1}{9}$ 7. 2×10^6 9. 248
11. 255   13. $a = 1, r = 3$ 15. $n = 5, s = \frac{2343}{25}$ 17. 32   19. $219
21. 4.8 yr   23. 22 ft   25. 0.032 in.   27. 64.6%   29. Resulting
sequence is $\log a, \log a + \log r, \log a + 2 \log r, \ldots$

Section 18-3

1. 8   3. $\frac{25}{4}$ 5. $\frac{400}{21}$ 7. 8   9. $\frac{10000}{9999}$ 11. $\frac{1}{3}$ 13. $\frac{2}{11}$
15. $\frac{91}{333}$ 17. $\frac{11}{30}$ 19. $\frac{100741}{999000}$ 21. 24 ft

Section 18-4

1. 81   3. 1.28×10^{-6} 5. $-\frac{119}{2}$ 7. $\frac{16}{243}$ 9. 81   11. $\frac{567}{16}$
13. 186   15. $\frac{455}{2}$ (AP), 127 (GP) or 43 (GP)   17. $\frac{7}{9}$ 19. $\frac{41}{333}$ 21. $\frac{1}{6}$
23. 1,001,000   25. 195   27. $6633   29. 20 sec   31. $-16, -4, 8, \ldots$ (AP);
$-16, 8, -4, \ldots$ (GP)

Section 19-1

[*Note*: "Answers" to trigonometric identities are intermediate steps of suggested reductions of the left member.]

1. $1.483 = 1/0.6745$ 3. $(\frac{1}{2}\sqrt{3})^2 + (-\frac{1}{2})^2 = \frac{3}{4} + \frac{1}{4} = 1$

5. $\dfrac{\sin x}{\cos x} \cdot \csc x = \dfrac{1}{\cos x}$ 7. $\sin x \left(\dfrac{\sin x}{\cos x}\right) + \cos x = \dfrac{\sin^2 x + \cos^2 x}{\cos x} = \dfrac{1}{\cos x}$

9. $\csc^2 x (\sin^2 x)$ 11. $1 - \sin^2 x$

13. $\dfrac{\sin x}{\cos x} + \dfrac{\cos x}{\sin x} = \dfrac{\sin^2 x + \cos^2 x}{\cos x \sin x} = \dfrac{1}{\cos x \sin x}$ 15. $(1 - \sin^2 x) - \sin^2 x|$

17. $\dfrac{\sin x (1 + \cos x)}{1 - \cos^2 x} = \dfrac{1 + \cos x}{\sin x}$

19. $\dfrac{(1/\cos x) + (1/\sin x)}{1 + (\sin x/\cos x)} = \dfrac{(\sin x + \cos x)/\cos x \sin x}{(\cos x + \sin x)/\cos x} = \dfrac{\cos x}{\cos x \sin x}$

21. $\dfrac{\cot 2y (\sec 2y + \tan 2y) - \cos 2y (\sec 2y - \tan 2y)}{\sec^2 2y - \tan^2 2y}$

$\qquad = \dfrac{\cot 2y \sec 2y + 1 - 1 + \cos 2y \tan 2y}{1}$

23. $\dfrac{\sin^2 x}{\cos^2 x}\cos^2 x + \dfrac{\cos^2 x}{\sin^2 x}\sin^2 x = \sin^2 x + \cos^2 x$

25. $4 \sin x + \dfrac{\sin x}{\cos x} = \sin x \left(4 + \dfrac{1}{\cos x}\right)$

27. $\dfrac{1}{\cos x} + \dfrac{\sin x}{\cos x} + \dfrac{\cos x}{\sin x} = \dfrac{\sin x + \cos^2 x + \sin^2 x}{\sin x \cos x}$

29. $(2 \sin^2 x - 1)(\sin^2 x - 1)$

31. Infinite GP: $\dfrac{1}{1 - \sin^2 x} = \dfrac{1}{\cos^2 x}$

33. $\sin \theta \,(\sin^2 \theta) = \sin \theta \,(1 - \cos^2 \theta)$

Section 19-2

1. $\sin 105° = \sin 60° \cos 45° + \cos 60° \sin 45° = \dfrac{\sqrt{3}}{2} \cdot \dfrac{\sqrt{2}}{2} + \dfrac{1}{2} \cdot \dfrac{\sqrt{2}}{2} = 0.9659$

3. $\cos 15° = \cos (60° - 45°) = \cos 60° \cos 45° + \sin 60° \sin 45°$
$= (\tfrac{1}{2})(\tfrac{1}{2}\sqrt{2}) + (\tfrac{1}{2}\sqrt{3})(\tfrac{1}{2}\sqrt{2}) = \tfrac{1}{4}\sqrt{2} + \tfrac{1}{4}\sqrt{6} = \tfrac{1}{4}(\sqrt{2} + \sqrt{6}) = 0.9659$

5. $-\tfrac{33}{65}$ 7. $\sin 3x$ 9. $\cos x$

11. $\sin (270° - x) = \sin 270° \cos x - \cos 270° \sin x = (-1) \cos x - 0(\sin x)$

13. $\cos (\tfrac{1}{2}\pi - x) = \cos \tfrac{1}{2}\pi \cos x + \sin \tfrac{1}{2}\pi \sin x = 0 \,(\cos x) + 1 \,(\sin x)$

15. $\sin \left(\dfrac{\pi}{4} + x\right) = \sin \dfrac{\pi}{4} \cos x + \cos \dfrac{\pi}{4} \sin x = \tfrac{1}{2}\sqrt{2} \cos x + \tfrac{1}{2}\sqrt{2} \sin x$

17. $(\sin x \cos y + \cos x \sin y)(\sin x \cos y - \cos x \sin y)$
$= \sin^2 x \cos^2 y - \cos^2 x \sin^2 y = \sin^2 x \,(1 - \sin^2 y) - (1 - \sin^2 x)\sin^2 y$

19. $(\cos \alpha \cos \beta - \sin \alpha \sin \beta) + (\cos \alpha \cos \beta + \sin \alpha \sin \beta)$

21. 23. 25. 27. Use indicated method.   29. $2A \sin \dfrac{2\pi t}{T} \cos \dfrac{2\pi x}{\lambda}$

Section 19-3

1. $\sin 60° = \sin 2 \,(30°) = 2 \sin 30° \cos 30° = 2 \,(\tfrac{1}{2})(\tfrac{1}{2}\sqrt{3}) = \tfrac{1}{2}\sqrt{3}$

3. $\cos 120° = \cos 2 \,(60°) = \cos^2 60° - \sin^2 60° = (\tfrac{1}{2})^2 - (\tfrac{1}{2}\sqrt{3})^2 = -\tfrac{1}{2}$

5. $\tfrac{24}{25}$ 7. $\tfrac{3}{5}$ 9. $2 \sin 8x$ 11. $\cos 8x$ 13. $\cos^2 \alpha - (1 - \cos^2 \alpha)$

15. $(\cos^2 x - \sin^2 x)(\cos^2 x + \sin^2 x) = (\cos^2 x - \sin^2 x) \,(1)$

17. $\dfrac{2 \tan x}{\sin 2x} = \dfrac{2(\sin x/\cos x)}{2 \sin x \cos x} = \dfrac{1}{\cos^2 x}$ 19. $\dfrac{\sin 3x \cos x - \cos 3x \sin x}{\sin x \cos x} = \dfrac{\sin 2x}{\tfrac{1}{2}\sin 2x}$

21. $\sin (2x + x) = \sin 2x \cos x + \cos 2x \sin x$
$= (2 \sin x \cos x) \,(\cos x) + (\cos^2 x - \sin^2 x) \sin x$

23. Use indicated method.

25. $\cos \alpha = \dfrac{A}{C}, \ \sin \alpha = \dfrac{B}{C}:$

$A \sin 2t + B \cos 2t = C \left(\dfrac{A}{C} \sin 2t + \dfrac{B}{C} \cos 2t\right)$

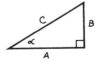

$= C \,(\cos \alpha \sin 2t + \sin \alpha \cos 2t)$

Section 19-4

1. $\cos 15° = \cos \tfrac{1}{2}(30°) = \sqrt{(1 + \cos 30°)/2} = \sqrt{1.8660/2} = 0.9659$

3. $\sin 75° = \sin \tfrac{1}{2}(150°) = \sqrt{(1 - \cos 150°)/2} = \sqrt{1.8660/2} = 0.9659$

5. $\sin 3\alpha$ 7. $4\cos 2x$ 9. $\sqrt{26}/26$ 11. $\pm\sqrt{2/(1-\cos\alpha)}$

13. $\dfrac{1-\cos\alpha}{2\sin(\alpha/2)} = \dfrac{1-\cos\alpha}{2\sqrt{(1-\cos\alpha)/2}} = \sqrt{\dfrac{1-\cos\alpha}{2}}$ 15. $\tan\dfrac{\alpha}{2} = \dfrac{\sin(\alpha/2)}{\cos(\alpha/2)}$

17. $\sqrt{1 - 2\cos\alpha + \cos^2\alpha + \sin^2\alpha\,(\cos^2\beta + \sin^2\beta)} = \sqrt{2 - 2\cos\alpha}$

Section 19-5

1. $\pi/2$ 3. $3\pi/4,\ 7\pi/4$ 5. $\pi/3,\ 2\pi/3,\ 4\pi/3,\ 5\pi/3$ 7. $0,\ \pi/6,\ 5\pi/6,\ \pi$

9. $\pi/12,\ \pi/4,\ 5\pi/12,\ 3\pi/4,\ 13\pi/12,\ 5\pi/4,\ 17\pi/12,\ 7\pi/4$ 11. $\pi/2,\ 3\pi/2$

13. $0,\ \pi/3,\ \pi,\ 5\pi/3$ 15. $\pi/4,\ 3\pi/4,\ 5\pi/4,\ 7\pi/4$ 17. 3.57, 5.85

19. 0.26, 1.31, 3.40, 4.45   21. $0,\ \pi$ 23. $3\pi/8,\ 7\pi/8,\ 11\pi/8,\ 15\pi/8$

25. 0.79, 1.25, 3.93, 4.39   27. 1.41 units of time   29. $-0.95,\ 0.00,\ 0.95$

31. 0, 4.49.

Section 19-6

1. y is the angle whose tangent is x 3. y is the angle whose cotangent is $3x$.

5. y is twice the angle whose sine is x.   7. $\pi/3$ 9. $3\pi/4$ 11. $3\pi/4$

13. $\pi/3$ 15. $5\pi/6$ 17. $x = \frac{1}{3}\arcsin y$ 19. $x = 4\tan y$

21. $x = \frac{1}{3}\operatorname{arcsec}(y-1)$ 23. $x = 1 - \cos(1-y)$ 25. I, II   27. II, III

29. $k = m\,[\arccos(x/A)]^2/t^2$ 31. $\theta = \frac{1}{2}\arcsin(2E/E_0)$

Section 19-7

1. $\pi/3$ 3. 0 5. $-\pi/3$ 7. $\pi/3$ 9. $\pi/6$ 11. $-\pi/4$ 13. $\pi/4$

15. -1.309 17. $\sqrt{3}/2$ 19. $\sqrt{2}/2$ 21. -1.150 23. -1

25. $x/\sqrt{1-x^2}$ 27. $1/x$ 29. $3x/\sqrt{9x^2-1}$ 31. $2x\sqrt{1-x^2}$

33. $\sin[\text{Arcsin}\,\frac{3}{5} + \text{Arcsin}\,\frac{5}{13}] = \frac{3}{5}\cdot\frac{12}{13} + \frac{4}{5}\cdot\frac{5}{13} = \frac{56}{65}$

Section 19-8

1. $\sin(90° + 30°) = \sin 90° \cos 30° + \cos 90° \sin 30° = (1)(\frac{1}{2}\sqrt{3}) + (0)(\frac{1}{2}) = \frac{1}{2}\sqrt{3}$

3. $\cos 2\,(90°) = \cos^2 90° - \sin^2 90° = 0 - 1 = -1$

5. $\sin\frac{1}{2}\,(90°) = \sqrt{\frac{1}{2}(1 - \cos 90°)} = \sqrt{\frac{1}{2}(1-0)} = \frac{1}{2}\sqrt{2}$ 7. $\sin 5x$

9. $4\sin 12x$ 11. $2\cos x$ 13. $-\pi/2$ 15. 0.2618

17. $-\sqrt{3}/3$ 19. 0 21. $\dfrac{1-\sin^2\theta}{\sin\theta} = \dfrac{\cos^2\theta}{\sin\theta}$

23. $\cos\theta\left(\dfrac{\cos\theta}{\sin\theta}\right) + \sin\theta = \dfrac{\cos^2\theta + \sin^2\theta}{\sin\theta}$ 25. $\dfrac{(\sec^2 x - 1)(\sec^2 x + 1)}{\tan^2 x} = \sec^2 x + 1$

27. $2\left(\dfrac{1}{\sin 2x}\right)\left(\dfrac{\cos x}{\sin x}\right) = 2\left(\dfrac{1}{2\sin x\cos x}\right)\left(\dfrac{\cos x}{\sin x}\right) = \dfrac{1}{\sin^2 x}$ 29. $\dfrac{1}{2}\left(2\sin\dfrac{\theta}{2}\cos\dfrac{\theta}{2}\right)$

31. $\dfrac{1}{\cos x} + \dfrac{\sin x}{\cos x} = \dfrac{(1+\sin x)(1-\sin x)}{\cos x\,(1-\sin x)} = \dfrac{1-\sin^2 x}{\cos x\,(1-\sin x)}$

33. $\cos[(x-y)+y]$ 35. $\sin 4x\,(\cos 4x)$

37. $\dfrac{\sin x}{(1/\sin x) - (\cos x/\sin x)} = \dfrac{\sin^2 x}{1 - \cos x} = \dfrac{1 - \cos^2 x}{1 - \cos x}$

39. $\dfrac{\sin x \cos y + \cos x \sin y + \sin x \cos y - \sin x \cos y}{\cos x \cos y - \sin x \sin y + \cos x \cos y + \sin x \sin y} = \dfrac{2 \sin x \cos y}{2 \cos x \cos y}$

41. $x = \frac{1}{2} \arccos (y/2)$ 43. $x = \frac{1}{5} \sin \frac{1}{3} (\frac{1}{4}\pi - y)$ 45. $\pi/6, 5\pi/6, 7\pi/6, 11\pi/6$

47. $0, \pi$ 49. 0 51. $2x\sqrt{1 - x^2}$ 53. $\sin (\omega t + \phi - \alpha)$

55. $t = 3 \arcsin (y/20)$ 57. $\cos^2 \alpha - 3 \sin^2 \alpha$ 59. 1 61. Factor out R and use Eq. (19-11).

Section 20-1

1. $2\sqrt{29}$ 3. 3 5. $\sqrt{85}$ 7. 7 9. $\frac{5}{2}$ 11. undefined   13. $-\frac{7}{6}$

15. 0 17. $-\frac{1}{3}\sqrt{3}$ 19. $20°$ 21. parallel   23. perpendicular   25. -3

27. two sides equal $2\sqrt{10}$ 29. $m_1 = \frac{1}{4}, m_2 = \frac{5}{4}$ 31. 10

Section 20-2

1. $4x - y + 20 = 0$ 3. $7x - 6y - 16 = 0$ 5. $x - y + 2 = 0$

7. $y = -3$ 9. $x = -3$ 11. $3x - 2y - 12 = 0$ 13. $x + 3y + 5 = 0$

15. $x + 7y - 18 = 0$

17.

19. $y = \frac{3}{2}x - \frac{1}{2}; m = \frac{3}{2}, b = -\frac{1}{2}$

21. $y = \frac{5}{2}x + \frac{5}{2}; m = \frac{5}{2}, b = \frac{5}{2}$

23. -2

25. $m_1 = 2, m_2 = -\frac{1}{2}$

27. $3x + y - 18 = 0$ 29. $L = \frac{2}{3}F + 15$ 31. 800 cal

33.   35. $m = 0.3010$ 37. $v = 40(0.643)^t$

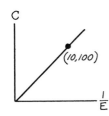

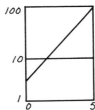

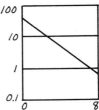

Section 20-3

1. $(2, 1), r = 5$ 3. $(-1, 0), r = 2$ 5. $x^2 + y^2 = 9$

7. $x^2 + y^2 - 4x - 4y - 8 = 0$ 9. $x^2 + y^2 + 4x - 10y + 24 = 0$

11. $x^2 + y^2 - 4x - 2y - 3 = 0$ 13. $x^2 + y^2 + 6x - 10y + 9 = 0$

15. $x^2 + y^2 - 4x - 10y + 4 = 0; x^2 + y^2 + 4x + 10y + 4 = 0$

17. $(0,0)$
    $r = 5$

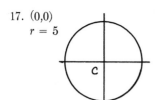

19. $(1, 0)$
    $r = 3$

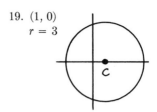

21. $(-4, 5)$
    $r = 7$

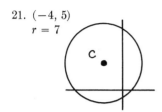

23. $(1, 2)$
    $r = \frac{1}{2}\sqrt{22}$

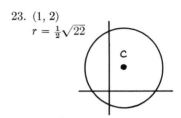

25. $(7, 0), (-1, 0)$ 27. $3x^2 + 3y^2 + 4x + 8y - 20 = 0$, circle
29. $x^2 + y^2 = 0.48$ (assume center of circle at center of coordinate system)
31. $x^2 + y^2 = 576$, $x^2 + y^2 + 36y + 315 = 0$ (in inches)

Section 20-4

1. $F(1, 0), x = -1$

3. $F(-1, 0), x = 1$

5. $F(0, 2), y = -2$

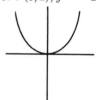

7. $F(0, -1), y = 1$

9. $F(\frac{1}{2}, 0), x = -\frac{1}{2}$

11. $F(0, \frac{1}{4}), y = -\frac{1}{4}$

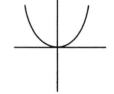

13. $y^2 = 12x$ 15. $x^2 = 16y$ 17. $x^2 = 4y$ 19. $x^2 = \frac{1}{8}y$ 25. $y = 4$
21. $y^2 - 2y - 12x + 37 = 0$ 23. $x^2 - 2x + 8y - 23 = 0$

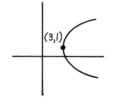

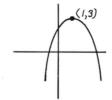

27.

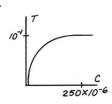

29. $x^2 = 100y$

Section 20-5

1. $V(2, 0)$, $V(-2, 0)$
   $F(\sqrt{3}, 0)$, $F(-\sqrt{3}, 0)$

3. $V(0, 6)$, $V(0, -6)$
   $F(0, \sqrt{11})$, $F(0, -\sqrt{11})$

5. $V(3, 0)$, $V(-3, 0)$
   $F(\sqrt{5}, 0)$,
   $F(-\sqrt{5}, 0)$

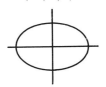

7. $V(0, 7)$, $V(0, -7)$
   $F(0, \sqrt{45}$, $F(0, -\sqrt{45})$

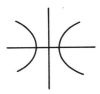

9. $V(0, 4)$, $V(0, -4)$
   $F(0, \sqrt{14})$,
   $F(0, -\sqrt{14})$

11. $V(\frac{5}{2}, 0)$, $V(-\frac{5}{2}, 0)$
    $F(\sqrt{21}/2, 0)$,
    $F(-\sqrt{21}/2, 0)$

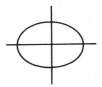

13. $144x^2 + 225y^2 = 32400$ 15. $9x^2 + 5y^2 = 45$ 17. $3x^2 + 20y^2 = 192$
19. $4x^2 + y^2 = 20$ 21. $16x^2 + 25y^2 - 32x - 50y - 359 = 0$
23. $9x^2 + 25y^2 = 22500$ 25. $2.70x^2 + 2.76y^2 = 7.45 \times 10^7$

Section 20-6

1. $V(5, 0)$, $V(-5, 0)$
   $F(13, 0)$, $F(-13, 0)$

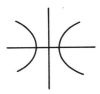

3. $V(0, 3)$, $V(0, -3)$
   $F(0, \sqrt{10})$, $F(0, -\sqrt{10})$

5. $V(\sqrt{2}, 0)$, $V(-\sqrt{2}, 0)$
   $F(\sqrt{6}, 0)$, $F(-\sqrt{6}, 0)$

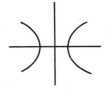

7. $V(0, \sqrt{5})$,
$V(0, -\sqrt{5})$
$F(0, \sqrt{7})$,
$F(0, -\sqrt{7})$

9. $V(0, 2)$,
$V(0, -2)$
$F(0, \sqrt{5})$,
$F(0, -\sqrt{5})$

11. $V(2, 0)$,
$V(-2, 0)$
$F(\frac{2}{3}\sqrt{13}, 0)$,
$F(-\frac{2}{3}\sqrt{13}, 0)$

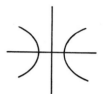

13. $16x^2 - 9y^2 = 144$
19.

15. $9y^2 - 25x^2 = 900$
21. $9x^2 - 16y^2 - 108x + 64y + 116 = 0$
23.

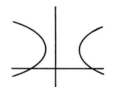

17. $3x^2 - y^2 = 3$

25.

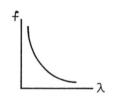

Section 20-7

1. Parabola, $(-1, 2)$

3. Hyperbola, $(1, 2)$

5. Ellipse, $(-1, 0)$

7. $y^2 - 6y - 16x - 7 = 0$ 9. $16x^2 + 25y^2 + 64x - 100y - 236 = 0$
11. $16x^2 - 9y^2 + 32x + 18y - 137 = 0$ 13. Parabola, $(-1, -1)$
15. Ellipse, $(-3, 0)$

17. Hyperbola, (0, 4)

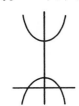

19. $x^2 - y^2 + 4x - 2y - 22 = 0$

21.

Section 20-8

1. Circle   3. Parabola   5. Hyperbola   7. Circle   9. Ellipse
11. Hyperbola   13. Ellipse   15. Parabola   17. Hyperbola

Section 20-9

1.

3.   5.   7.   9.

11. $(2, \pi/6)$ 13. $(1, 7\pi/6)$ 15. $(-4, -4\sqrt{3})$ 17. $(2.77, -1.15)$
19. $r = 3 \sec \theta$ 21. $r = a$ 23. $r^2 = 4/(1 + 3\sin^2 \theta)$ 25. $x^2 + y^2 - y = 0$
27. $x^4 + y^4 - 4x^3 + 2x^2y^2 - 4xy^2 - 4y^2 = 0$
29. $s = \sqrt{x^2 + y^2} \arctan(y/x)$, $A = \frac{1}{2}(x^2 + y^2) \arctan(y/x)$
31. $r = 100 \tan \theta \sec \theta$ 33. $0.98x^2 + y^2 + 1340x - 2.3 \times 10^7 = 0$

Section 20-10

1.   3.   5.   7.

   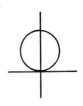

9.   11.   13.   15.

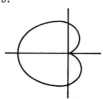 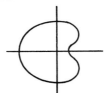  

17.

19.

21.

23.

25.

Section 20-11

1. $4x-y-11=0$ 3. $2x+3y+3=0$ 5. $x^2+y^2-2x+4y-5=0$ 7. $y^2=12x$

 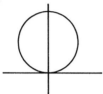 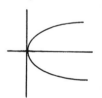

9. $9x^2 + 25y^2 = 900$ 11. $144y^2 - 169x^2 = 24336$ 13. $(-3, 0), r = 4$

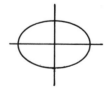 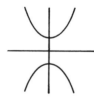 

15. $(0, -5), y = 5$ 17. $V(0, 4), V(0, -4)$ 19. $V(2,0), V(-2, 0)$
$\quad\quad F(0, \sqrt{15}), F(0, -\sqrt{15})$ $F(\frac{2}{5}\sqrt{35}, 0), F(-\frac{2}{5}\sqrt{35}, 0)$

  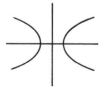

21. $V(4, -8), F(4, -7)$ 23. $(2, -1)$ 25.

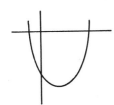   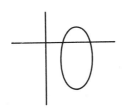   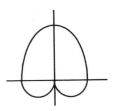

27.   29.   31. $\theta = \text{Arctan } 2 = 1.11$

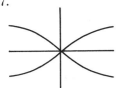   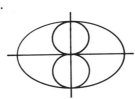

33. $(x^2 + y^2)^3 = 16x^2y^2$

35. $(1.90, 1.55), (1.90, -1.55),$
$(-1.90, 1.55),$
$(-1.90, -1.55)$

37. $m_1 = -\frac{12}{5}, m_2 = \frac{5}{12}; d_1{}^2 = 169, d_2{}^2 = 169, d_3{}^2 = 338$ 39. $x^2 - 6x - 8y + 1 = 0$

41.   43. $x^2 = -80y$ 45.   47.

   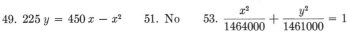

49. $225\,y = 450\,x - x^2$ 51. No   53. $\dfrac{x^2}{1464000} + \dfrac{y^2}{1461000} = 1$

55. $r^2 = \dfrac{7.45 \times 10^7}{2.70 + 0.06 \sin^2 \theta}$

57. $(a^2 - b^2)\,x^2 + a^2y^2 - 2bx - 1 = 0;$
$a = b$, parabola; $a^2 > b^2$, ellipse;
$a^2 < b^2$, hyperbola

Section 21-1

1. $\frac{1}{4}$ 3. $\frac{3}{4}$ 5. $\frac{1}{16}$ 7. $\frac{1}{19}$ 9. $\frac{1}{6}$ 11. $\frac{5}{6}$ 13. $\frac{1}{36}$ 15. $\frac{11}{36}$
17. $\frac{1}{36}$ 19. $\frac{1}{6}$ 21. $\frac{1}{36}$ 23. 0.38   25. 0.336   27. $\frac{1}{221}$ 29. 6
31. $\frac{4}{9}$ 33. 0.195

Section 21-2

1. 54   3. 27   5. 55   7. 30   9.

49–51	52–54	55–57	58–60
1	3	1	2

11.

0–9	10–19	20–29	30–39	40–49	50–59
0	2	4	3	1	1

13.

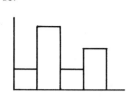

15.

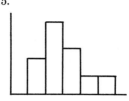

17.

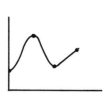

19.

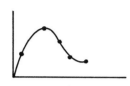

21.

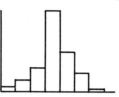

23.

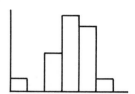

25. 3.435 amps   29. 5 and 7

Section 21-3

1. 3.2   3. 10.6   5. 5   7. 3.2   9. 10.6   11. 5   13. 57%   15. 70%

Section 21-4

1. $y = (1.0)x - 2.6$

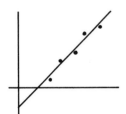

3. $y = -1.77x + 190$

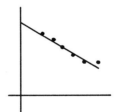

5. $V = -0.7i + 12.3$

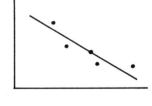

7. $V = 0.41 \times 10^{-14} f - 1.90$
$f_0 = 4.6 \times 10^{14}$ 1/sec
9. 0.985
11. -0.90

Section 21-5

1. $y = 1.96x^2 + 5.2$

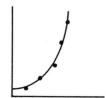

3. $y = 10.9/x$

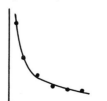

5. $y = 5.95t^2 + 0.55$

7. $y = 33.7(10^x) - 37.1$

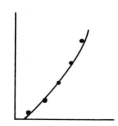

9. $f = \dfrac{480}{\sqrt{L}} + 10$

Section 21-6

1. $\frac{5}{6}$ 3. $\frac{1}{108}$ 5. 3.6   7. 0.8   9. 264 cp   11. 14 cp
13. 0.927 in.   15. 0.012 in.   17. 4   19.

21. $\frac{4}{9}$ 23. 3×10^{-5}
25. $R = 0.0985\, T + 25.0$

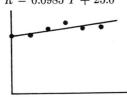

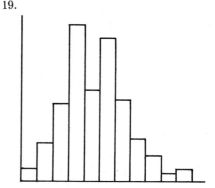

27. $y = 1.04 \tan x - 0.02$
29. $y = 1.10\sqrt{x} + 0.01$

Section B-1

1. 10^5 cm   3. 144 in²   5. 12.7 cm   7. 64 pints   9. 9.46 l
11. 0.163 lb   13. 13.59 l 15. 7603 kg-cm/sec   17. 1.05×10^9 ergs
19. 130 tons   21. 37 mi/hr   23. 770 mi/hr   25. 345 lb/ft³   27. 1030 gm/cm²

Section B-2

1. 24 is exact   3. 3 is exact, 74.6 is approx.   5. 1063 is approx.
7. 100 and 200 are approx., 3200 is exact   9. 3, 4   11. 3, 4   13. 3, 3
15. 1, 6   17. (a) 3.764, (b) 3.764   19. (a) 0.01 (b) 30.8   21. (a) same
(b) 78.0   23. (a) 0.004 (b) same   25. (a) 4.93 (b) 4.9   27. (a) 57900
(b) 58000   29. (a) 861 (b) 860   31. (a) 0.305 (b) 0.31

Section B-3

1. 51.2   3. 1.70   5. 431.4   7. 30.9   9. 62.1   11. 270   13. 160
15. 27,000   17. 5.7   19. 4.39   21. 10.2   23. 22   25. 17.62
27. 18.85   29. 21.0 lb   31. First plane, 70 mi/hr
33. 62.1 lb/ft³   35. 850,000 lb   37. 115 ft/sec

Section C-1

1. 1080   3. 442   5. 1670   7. 524   9. 388   11. 1360

13, 15,
17, 19:

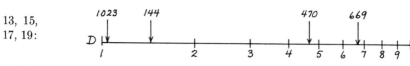

21, 23, 25, 27:

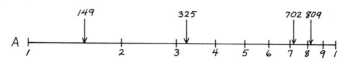

29. 400   31. 30,000,000   33. 8 (or 9)   35. 15

Section C-2

1. 6.00   3. 180   5. 0.00856   7. 5.27   9. 0.00338   11. 740   13. 7
15. 0.50   17. 311   19. 389   21. 1,465,000   23. 1518   25. 4170
27. 227,000   29. 751   31. 4.01

Section C-3

1. 196   3. 2120   5. 0.000400   7. 45.0   9. 98.8   11. 4,380,000,000
13. 2,400,000   15. 0.194   17. 6.40   19. 0.117   21. 23.9   23. 0.756
25. 218   27. 0.255   29. 4.73   31. 95.2   33. 29.0   35. 5820

Section C-4

1. 6.22   3. 3.31   5. 2.07   7. 1.36   9. 9.81   11. 0.116   13. 3.59
15. 65.3   17. 0.0855   19. 452   21. 0.0369   23. 0.000944

Section C-5

1. 0.438   3. 0.970   5. 0.0593   7. 0.0831   9. 1.60   11. 0.317
13. 0.0300   15. 1.12   17. 40.7°   19. 26.2°   21. 5.00°   23. 88.66°
25. 82.7°   27. 65.9°   29. 5.72°   31. 89.3°

Section C-6

1. 17.0   3. 18,800   5. 74,500   7. 2,480,000   9. 33.6   11. 32.9
13. 8.49   15. 0.679   17. 139   19. 2780   21. 0.511   23. 14.4
25. 2.62   27. 67.2   29. 28.0   31. 428   33. 5.44   35. 0.960
37. 6420   39. 14.2   41. 18.6   43. 664   45. 0.407   47. 2.03
49. 51.7°   51. 81.02°

Section D-2

1. 85°   3. 140°   5. 25°   7. 25°   9. 5   11. 17   13. 8   15. 4.90
17. 10.6   19. 28.3   21. 3.3 in., 4.0 in.   23. 25 ft   25. 10 yd
27. 18.46 in.   29. 62.4 m   31. 62.8 ft   33. 28 in²   35. 13 yd²
37. 24 ft²   39. 154 in²   41. 216 ft³   43. 20 ft³   45. 924 in³
47. 153 in³   49. 27.1 ft³   51. 689 ft³   53. 208 in²   55. 1350 in²
57. 3220 ft²

Index